ART LAW

"A work of sparkling clarity and sensible organization . . . Lerner and Bresler definitely lay to rest the contention of the expert and the uninitiated that 'there ain't no such animal' as art law."
— *The Los Angeles Daily Journal*

"This book has much to offer serious participants in the Canadian market as well as the U.S. and overseas markets."
— *Fine Arts & Auction Review*

"The text avoids 'legalese,' often spelling out the issues in a straightforward, point-by-point manner."
— *Ceramics Monthly*

"Each chapter is clear and cohesive. Ms. Bresler has stamped the 'Auctions' chapter with her own inimitable style of presentation—concise and to the point. Materials on tax and estate planning are superb."
— *The ABA Forum on the Entertainment and Sports Industries*

"With sections on what to expect in artist/dealer relationships, estate planning and taxes, everything you need is here, plus clarifications on confusing 'legalese.'"
— *The Artist's Magazine*

"A comprehensive, extremely readable guide."
— *Interior Design*

"This impressive volume provides practical guidance to investors, collectors, dealers, artists, appraisers, and museum directors, as well as to practicing lawyers and estate planners involved in the art world . . . essential reading for all those concerned with advising those who collect art, create art, or deal in art."
— *Estate Planning*

"An excellent reference source for anyone wanting to find the basic statutory law or seminal cases in a particular area of law."
— Herbert E. Nass, *Sculpture Review*

"This splendid book . . . could be quite valuable to a manager involved in art protection, transportation, sale, and storage."
— Robert D. McCrie, *Security Letter*

"This *Farmer's Almanac* for the field . . . helps lead the inexperienced through the gulches and ravines of art law. Those willing to read and digest (not skim) this book will find just about everything covered. An excellent citation of authorities and a good index complete this compact and carefully prepared volume."
— *Stained Glass Quarterly*

"One of the most complete reference books on the 'business' of art . . . a valuable resource in classifying art works in ways that may benefit estate planning, tax liability or charitable gifts."
— Steve Shipp, *World Fine Art*

"This book deserves a permanent place on the desk of anyone involved in the art world . . . has a good chance of turning into the standard reference for the art community."
— *Maryland Lawyers for the Arts*

"**Art Law** is a must for anyone who ventures into the art world in any guise, whether as artist, collector, curator, dealer, investor or appraiser, for buyers as well as sellers, for attorneys, of course, and for underwriters and trust officers."
— Louis Zara, *The Appraisers Association of America*

"This hefty, very practical volume . . . written by noted specialists in art law . . . distills—in plain English—the latest information from legal disciplines as varied as first amendment law, tax law, and torts."
— *ARTnewsletter*

"Sure to be a valuable tool for anyone involved in the business of art."
— *Antiques & Fine Art*

"[T]reats with thoroughness and clarity a broad spectrum of legal issues affecting art and the business of art."

— Carmina M. Diaz, *Law Library Journal*

"For real estate people who have taken up art as a sideline, this valuable guide contains answers to questions about transactions between artists and dealers, auctions, tax and estate planning, artists' rights, gallery relationships, and acquisitions and dispositions of fine art."

— *The Mortgage and Real Estate Executives Report*

"A good resource book for businesses with art collections."

— *Business Committee for the Arts, Inc.*

"This volume should be of interest to attorneys as well as collectors, dealers, appraisers, insurance agents, artists, museum and corporate curators, trust officers and accountants."

— *Journal of the American Society of CLU & ChFC*

"I have long hoped to find a concise, readable book that could provide the art world with guidance and solutions to the plethora of legal issues relating to the creation of art and to the art market. **Art Law** succeeds remarkably well in presenting an in-depth, up-to-the-minute treatment of a broad variety of legal issues affecting art and the business of art. Ralph and Judith are among the most knowledgeable people in the field and I strongly urge everyone who creates, appraises, buys, sells, invests in, or advises on art to take advantage of the authors' practical experience and avoid future problems by obtaining a copy of this book. It is a most welcome addition to the art world."

— Jeffrey Deitch, *Deitch Projects*

"For the attorney practicing in or around the field of art law, this is an excellent resource . . . a thought-provoking and useful addition to the practicing attorney's library."

— *Entertainment and Sports Lawyer*

ART LAW

The Guide for Collectors,
Investors, Dealers, and Artists

Third Edition

Volume 1

RALPH E. LERNER

JUDITH BRESLER

Practising Law Institute
New York City

#7793

This work is designed to provide practical and useful information on the subject matter covered. However, it is sold with the understanding that neither the publisher nor the author is engaged in rendering legal, accounting or other professional services. If legal advice or other expert assistance is required, the services of a competent professional should be sought.

Cover Art:

Man Ray, "Main Ray" (1935)
© 2005 Man Ray Trust / Artists Rights Society (ARS), NY / ADAGP, Paris

Pablo Picasso, "Woman with Raised Arms" (1936)
© 2005 Estate of Pablo Picasso / Artists Rights Society (ARS), New York

Practising Law Institute, New York 10019
© 1989, 1992 by Practising Law Institute
© 1998, 2005 by Practising Law Institute,
Ralph E. Lerner, and Judith Bresler
All rights reserved.
Printed in the United States of America

Library of Congress Control Number: 2005907862
ISBN: 1402406509

To our own works of art—
Alexandra Lee and Elinor Drue

And of course . . .
To Picasso

Forewords

The creation of a work of art is an activity that is quintessentially human. It is an effort that both reflects and enhances our experience. A great work of art represents, at its core, one of the highest forms of human expression.

These very special objects present unique challenges when they become objects of commerce. Even the most basic questions can elicit complex answers. When we sell a work of art, what exactly are we selling? Are we selling only the object or are we selling the image that is embodied in the object? When we sell conceptual art, what exactly is it that the buyer is purchasing? How does one assure that what is being sold is authentic—and how does one account for changes in scholarship or attribution?

Current issues in the art market have challenged even the most basic questions of title—who owns a work of art, who has the right to sell it, and who has the right to profit from its sale. The ever-increasing focus on issues of cultural property (property as diverse as the relics of ancient societies and the spiritual objects of Native American tribes) and the restitution of art that belonged to victims of World War II illustrate how the iconic and historical nature of art can have an impact on rights of ownership and transfer. Similarly, the development of the *droit de suite* and similar taxes that seek to compensate the artist or the artist's estate when a work of art is sold underscore the dual nature of a work of art as both a physical object and an act of expression.

Forewords appear in alphabetical order by author.

These issues are not resolved in a vacuum. The answers develop within the framework of the rule of law. The development of law is itself another quintessentially human endeavor—one which, as societies develop, remains always a work in progress.

Ralph Lerner and Judith Bresler have written an invaluable text that comprehensively surveys the waterfront of art law: *Art Law: The Guide for Collectors, Investors, Dealers, and Artists*. The volumes are scholarly and substantive, but also extremely practical in their approach. This third edition addresses with clarity the most current developments in the laws affecting the art market and provides welcome guidance to lawyers, artists, dealers, museums, collectors, auction houses—indeed, to anyone who is interested in art. I am privileged to assist in introducing it.

EDWARD J. DOLMAN

Chief Executive Officer
Christie's International plc

Anyone involved in the art world learns very quickly that there is a surprisingly close relationship between art and the law. I first became aware of how important this relationship is as a graduate student, when I was invited as a doctoral candidate in art history to take a course in the law school to provide, I suspect, comic relief for a group of hyper-charged lawyers to be. The class turned out to be an extremely engaging and interesting course that brought into focus the difference between the way lawyers and art historians are trained to think, as well as the many ways that the law affects almost every transaction involving a work of art. The lessons I learned in the protected comfort of the classroom have proven to be essential in the less-protected world of the museum. Questions of artists' rights, authenticity, estate planning, commissions, fair market value, among others, are ever-present in today's art world; and whether as a museum director, artist, dealer, auctioneer, purchaser, or, of course, lawyer, it is impossible to avoid dealing with these matters.

But how can one develop a body of law for something as ineffable as art? What are the governing issues that define the way we adjudicate issues pertaining to objects whose very definition defies the kind of concrete clarity demanded by law? The answer to these and many other questions can be found in Ralph Lerner and Judith Bresler's lucid and detailed compendium *Art Law: The Guide for Collectors, Investors, Dealers, and Artists.* Lerner and Bresler are among the foremost authorities in America on art and law, and their highly informative book is both a vast source of invaluable information and a very thoughtful analysis of how various laws and their interpretation affect works of art.

First published in 1989 and subsequently reissued in 1998, it has been seven years since the second edition of *Art Law* appeared. During this time there has been an explosion of interest in laws affecting art, from those that impact the buying and selling of art to those that deal with issues of authenticity and copyright. This interest has been fueled by a burgeoning art world that has seen a whole new generation of artists, dealers, and collectors emerge over the last decade. Since the late 1990s, several factors have contributed to make almost any transaction involving works of art more complicated than before, including the spiraling cost of art and everything related to it, such as insurance in the wake of the tragic events of September 11, 2001, and the continuing debates over restitution and the appropriate means of dealing with looted or stolen art. These issues, combined with the general tendency in our society to submit virtually everything to the scrutiny of the law, mean that anyone interested in art must be well informed in ways that were unimaginable even ten years ago.

The third edition of *Art Law* is an invaluable tool for the professional as well as the layman and addresses virtually every aspect of the law that touches on art.

GLENN D. LOWRY

Director
The Museum of Modern Art

People ask me all the time the rather benign question "How's the art market?" Unfortunately there is not a very good answer to that question, as there is no one monolithic art market. Instead there are dozens of art markets, each with its own regional or aesthetic prejudices, market bulls and bears, and old-time collectors who vie with new participants (not always welcome by the old guard!) in assembling their own version of treasures.

Buying or selling works of art can look on the surface relatively straightforward, but appearances can be deceptive. The art market and the art world are, in fact, extremely complex. Sotheby's operates in over thirty-five countries, and in each location the import and export laws, the cultural patrimony issues, the tax laws, and estate laws are hugely variable, evolving every day, and even occasionally open to interpretation. We maintain a staff of over fifteen lawyers who track and anticipate evolving laws in virtually every jurisdiction around the world.

It remains a challenge to find people to trust in the art world, where most objects are unique and opinions of value, authenticity, rarity, and provenance require considerable judgment. But this is where Ralph Lerner and Judith Bresler's revised and expanded book, *Art Law: The Guide for Collectors, Investors, Dealers, and Artists (Third Edition)*, is of enormous value. As I recall, it was an American president who coined the phrase "Trust, but verify." This treatise provides both very successfully. If you need help understanding your options in managing collections, or in buying, selling, or donating works of art, I encourage you to consult this extraordinary three-volume definitive text. We use it regularly.

If you were to buy the same painting in Mexico or France or New York, you may have very different obligations to shoulder as the new owner. What is required for you to export the painting? Can you resell it? Do you have tax obligations as a purchaser? What recourse do you have if the painting is not authentic? These seemingly simple questions could trigger civil and, at times, even criminal liability if you are not well advised in the process.

So however you touch the art world, make sure you deal with people you trust, and also verify their advice. Ralph and Judith are among the most respected and consulted counsel in the world when it comes to works of art. This three-volume set crystallizes their collective wisdom. If you can't carry Ralph and Judith around with you as you collect, carry Ralph and Judith's book with you as the next best thing. I know you will find that it's worth a fortune!

WILLIAM F. RUPRECHT

Chief Executive Officer
Sotheby's Holdings, Inc.

About the Authors

RALPH E. LERNER is the preeminent attorney practicing full time in the field of art law. He is a partner at Sidley Austin Brown & Wood and the coauthor of the award-winning treatise *Art Law: The Guide for Collectors, Investors, Dealers, and Artists* (First, Second, and Third Edition), acclaimed as the "industry bible" by *Forbes* magazine. He has served as Chairman of the Art Law Committee of the Association of the Bar of the City of New York, Chairman of the Fine Arts Committee of the New York State Bar Association, and Chairman of the Visual Arts Division of the American Bar Association Forum on Entertainment and Sports Law. He is currently on the Board of the New York Volunteer Lawyers for the Arts and is a Fellow of the American College of Trusts and Estates Counsel. Lerner is a nationally acclaimed speaker and writer on the topic of tax planning for collectors and artists. He has extensive experience in dealing with the Internal Revenue Service in the broadest possible manner and numbers among his clients many of the foremost artists, collectors, and art dealers in America. He is married to Judith Bresler and lives in Scarsdale, New York.

JUDITH BRESLER, a prominent lecturer and an attorney specializing in art law with the New York firm of Cowan, DeBaets, Abrahams & Sheppard, is coauthor of the award-winning treatise *Art Law: The Guide for Collectors, Investors, Dealers, and Artists* (First, Second, and Third Edition), acclaimed as the "industry bible" by *Forbes* magazine. She has taught art law as a member of the adjunct faculties of both New York Law School and the University of Pennsylvania Law

School. She has served on the Board of Trustees of New York Law School and the Philadelphia Volunteer Lawyers for the Arts. She has served as Chair of the Art Law Committee and Chair of the Entertainment, Art and Sports Law Section (EASL) of the New York State Bar Association. She is currently Co-Chair of the Alternative Dispute Resolution Committee of EASL and on the Roster of Neutrals of the New York State Supreme Court, Commercial Division. Bresler publishes extensively on all aspects of the art market and is a two-time winner of the Otto L. Walter Distinguished Writing Award—most recently for her article "Begged, Borrowed or Stolen: Whose Art Is It Anyway? An Alternative Solution of Fine Art Licensing." She is married to Ralph E. Lerner and lives in Scarsdale, New York.

Preface

Like Lewis Carroll's landscape in *Through the Looking Glass*, where one must run at top speed to remain in the same place, the ever-changing panorama of art law makes critical an up-to-the-minute summary of legal developments in the art world. Hence, the third edition of *Art Law: The Guide for Collectors, Investors, Dealers, and Artists.*

Why a book on art law? Over the past forty years, art has become the darling of big business—both of legitimate commerce and of crime. For 2004, worldwide sales for Sotheby's and Christie's auction houses alone totaled in excess of $5 billion. Worldwide trade in stolen and smuggled art and antiquities—which in recent years has exceeded $7 billion per year—is considered, other than drug trafficking, the most lucrative criminal activity in existence.

Whatever is prized in the marketplace mandates regulation, and art is no exception. Over the past thirty-five to forty years, state legislation has emerged governing the consignment of artworks to art dealers; the purchase and sale of art through private treaty and through public auction; the purchase and sale of fine prints and sculpture multiples; the recovery of stolen art under special statutes of limitations; the purchase and installation of public art; the deaccessioning of artworks by museums; and the content of artwork through obscenity, privacy, publicity and antigraffiti statutes. Federal legislation has kept pace. The creation, content, and use of art are governed by the laws of copyright, trademark, and moral rights--the last being unique to works of visual art; aspects of collecting art, inheriting art, and donating art are governed by the Internal

Revenue Code. The proliferation of digital technologies over the past dozen years or so has given rise to the enactment of federal legislation as well as case law governing the creation, content, display, and distribution of online art. To all of this, add case law governing First Amendment considerations such as art as a vehicle for defamation, and special treaties governing art in international trade. The result is a jungle of law that demands, if not a machete, an accessible guide through the thicket.

In 1970, very little had been written on the topic of art law. At that time, Ralph E. Lerner published an article entitled "Estate Planning for the Art Collector" in Prentice-Hall's *Successful Estate Planning Ideas*. This was followed, in 1974, by the first art law seminar run by the Practising Law Institute, which was chaired by Ralph E. Lerner. Subsequently, a number of texts have pioneered in the field. These include Feldman & Weil, *Art Works: Law, Policy, Practice*, revised as Feldman, Weil & Biederman, *Art Law: Rights and Liabilities of Creators and Collectors*; Duffy, *Art Law: Representing Artists, Dealers and Collectors*; DuBoff, *The Deskbook of Art Law*; Merryman & Elsen, *Law Ethics and the Visual Arts*; and Crawford, *Legal Guide for the Visual Artist*. These informative publications have stimulated interest in art law, and we gratefully acknowledge the frames of reference and assistance provided by their authors.

We felt, however, that there still did not exist a guide that would illuminate the law in an accessible way to enable investors, collectors, dealers, artists, appraisers, critics, scholars, practicing lawyers, in fact anyone with any interest in the art world, to understand and proceed with the business of art. We presented such a guide with the publication of our first edition in October 1989. With the continued growth in the art market and the corresponding complexity of art transactions, we issued in October 1998 a revised two-volume second edition. Seven years later, packed with new information in keeping with evolving law, and revised practical forms, our third edition (now three volumes) is ready.

For his encouragement and support, we are deeply grateful to William C. Cubberley of the Practising Law Institute, who envisioned this book and kept after us to ensure completion of the third edition. We also wish to thank our dedicated PLI editor, Keith Voelker, for his eagle eye and pointed questions, along with the rest of the wonderful PLI staff, and especially Paul Matsumoto and Todd Warner, for their ongoing support and their patience with us throughout the process of producing this book.

We are most appreciative of the creative efforts of Robert Antler, who designs the covers and jackets of our books, thereby endowing our contents with artful appearance.

We are extremely grateful for the valuable efforts of our research assistants. In particular, we thank Justin Lubatkin, a former law student of Judith Bresler, and Stacy Rotner for their many hours of devoted labor on this third edition. We also thank Donyale Y.H. Reavis, Sivan Rhodes, Jacqueline D. Ewenstein, Suzanne L. Schairer, Natalie Solomon, Matt Harris, Debra Meyerberg, Dana Parisi, and Gail Busby.

We also wish to acknowledge the kind contributions of Richard A. Altman, John Cahill, Karen Carolan, Alan Christenfeld, Scott A. Cohen, Sharon Cott, Louise Anne Comeau, Jeffrey Deitch, Raymond J. Dowd, Gilbert Edelson, Michael A. Einhorn, Milton Esterow, Sharon Flescher, Heather Gray, Jeffrey Haber, Barbara Hoffman, Joshua Kaufman, Larry Kaye, John Koegel, Maria Papageorge Kouroupas, Jo Laird, Stephen S. Lash, Constance Lowenthal, Eric N. Macey, Cynthia Mann, Robert A. Martin, John Merryman, Rena Moulopoulos, Jonathan Olsoff, Linda Pinkerton, Judith Prowda, Gerald Rosenberg, Stanley Rothenberg, Richard A. Rothman, Michael Salzman, Eileen Schwab, Daniel Shapiro, Carla J. Shapreau, John Silberman, Howard Spiegler, Thad Stauber, Peter Stern, Carol J. Steinberg, Stephen K. Urice, Daniel Weiner, Warren P. Weitman, John J. Weltman, Victor Wiener, Joan Young, Roger Zissu, and the Copyright Office of the Library of Congress.

We are most appreciative of the support received from New York Law School. In particular we would like to thank Richard A. Matasar, Dean of New York Law School, and Jethro K. Lieberman, Associate Dean for Academic Affairs, for their encouragement, which was tangibly expressed in making available to Judith Bresler for the purpose of this text unlimited usage of research software. In this connection we would also like to thank Professor Joyce Saltalamachia, Director of the Law School Library, as well as Camille Broussard, Professor of Legal Research and Associate Librarian for Readers Services, the latter of whom patiently instructed Judith Bresler in Lexis research. Last but certainly not least, we are appreciative of the ongoing support received from Beth Simone Novek, Associate Professor and Director of the Institute for Information Law and Policy at New York Law School.

A special thanks goes to Internet maven and New York Law School Adjunct Professor Peter Johnson for his review, insight, and comments on chapter 17 (Art Law Online).

This book would not have been possible without the generous support and extraordinary efforts of many people at Sidley Austin Brown & Wood in New York. This includes Ralph Lerner's secretary, Roz Vogelbaum, and the word processing department, with special thanks to Joe Chasen, who was always available at the eleventh hour to keep the computers up and running. We are particularly indebted to Gene Philley, word-processing whiz, who did the bulk of the typing of this manuscript. We also wish to thank Mary Anne Stewart, who helped with the typing; the Sidley Austin Brown & Wood library staff; the proofreaders; the Sidley Austin Brown & Wood administrators, including John C. Feldkamp and Maureen A. McGovern; and our family and many other friends who offered patience, support, love, and understanding over the years it took to complete this book.

Table of Chapters

VOLUME 1

VOLUME 2

VOLUME 3

Table of Contents

VOLUME 1

PART ONE   ARTISTS AND DEALERS

Chapter 1   Artist–Dealer Relations

PART TWO   ARTWORK TRANSACTIONS

Chapter 2   Private Sales

Chapter 3   Theft, Forgery, Authenticity, and Statutes of Limitations

Chapter 4   Auctions

Chapter 5   Prints and Sculpture Multiples

Chapter 6   Commissioned Works

Chapter 7   Expert Opinions and Liabilities

VOLUME 2

Chapter 8   International Trade

PART THREE   ARTISTS' RIGHTS

Chapter 9   First Amendment Rights

Chapter 10   Copyrights

Chapter 11   Moral Rights

Chapter 12 Resale Rights

PART FOUR   COLLECTORS

Chapter 13   The Collection As Investment Property

VOLUME 3

PART FIVE   TAXES AND ESTATE PLANNING

Chapter 14   Tax and Estate Planning for Collectors

Chapter 15   Tax and Estate Planning for Artists

PART SIX   MUSEUMS AND MULTIMEDIA

Chapter 16   Museums

Chapter 17   Art Law Online

Introduction

With the advent of the new millennium, art market activities capture, more than ever, the fascination of the mass media while art captures the wallet of the public. On the evening of May 5, 2004, a 1905 painting by Picasso entitled *Boy with a Pipe* sold at Sotheby's for $104.2 million, shattering a fourteen-year record for an auctioned painting. The previous record was set by Van Gogh's 1890 *Portrait of Dr. Gachet*, sold to a Japanese billionaire for $82.5 million in May 1990 at Christie's. Total combined worldwide sales for the two auction houses alone in 2004 was well over $5 billion. Global sales within the art market that same year approached $30 billion. Small wonder that the public is captivated.

The press is captivated too. Gyrations in the art market are reported as faithfully as a seismograph records earthquakes, and when a scandal comes to light, such as the lawsuits a few years ago involving Sotheby's and Christie's in a price-fixing scheme, headlines and photographs—not only of the principals but of their *attorneys*—abound. Such is the romance of the art business.

Moreover, major and regional auction houses alike are increasingly luring first-timers onto the auction premises by staging a variety of lower-priced multi-category sales—including houseware, inexpensive furniture, and memorabilia as well as art—to gently initiate newcomers to the auction process. Today, more than 75% of lots sold by the major auction houses are bought for $5,000 or less. And with the proliferation during the past decade of online auction houses offering merchandise in thousands of categories—from spare tires, to antique jewelry, to used Beanie Babies, to paintings—virtually anyone can be a bidder.

And most of us are. In view of the massive array of legislation that has been enacted over the last forty years regulating art transactions, any buyer or seller of an artwork should have a working familiarity with what is known as "art law." Art law encompasses all the legal ramifications of the creation, purchase, sale, transfer, or exhibition of a work of art. Much like entertainment law, art traverses a variety of legal disciplines, such as First Amendment law, copyright law, commercial law, tax law, contract law, and torts.

This book addresses art law from six broad perspectives:

- The artist/dealer relationship
- The commercial aspects of buying and selling artwork either through a dealer or at auction
- Artists' rights, including First Amendment rights, intellectual property rights, and resale rights
- The financial aspects—including tax consequences—of being a collector, an investor, or a dealer in artwork
- Tax and estate planning issues for collectors and artists
- Museum law, as well as the legal concerns of museums and other sectors of the art world arising from digital technologies

DEALERS

When an artist delivers works of art to a dealer for sale, the legal relationship is ordinarily one of consignment. In such a case, the dealer becomes the artist's agent and the law of agency, with the attendant fiduciary duties, applies. Much of the time, the artist-dealer relationship is not memorialized in writing. This can adversely affect the dealer as where, in *O'Keeffe v. Bry*, the failure of Doris Bry, longtime agent of artist Georgia O'Keeffe, to formalize the relationship in writing caused her to sustain considerable financial loss as well as the loss of O'Keeffe as a client. Lack of a formal contract can also harm the artist by presenting issues of proof as to the parties' accord on various aspects of the agreement, such as the degree of artistic control retained by the artist in an exhibition of the artist's works. A well-written agreement, on the other hand, protects both parties. It can assure the artist, for example, that the artworks will be sold at prices acceptable to the artist with proper and timely distribution of the sale proceeds; it can protect the dealer who invests time and money in the promotion of an artist against sudden desertion by the latter.

Chapter 1 of this treatise enumerates issues that should be addressed in the agreement memorializing the relationship between artist and dealer, discusses the impact of the Uniform Commercial Code (U.C.C.) and specific state statutes on the artist-dealer relationship, provides an analysis of insurance coverage for artists by art dealers and discusses recently decided cases on this topic, and provides models of artist-dealer representation agreements at the close of the chapter.

ARTWORK TRANSACTIONS

After art leaves the artist's studio, it enters the stream of commerce known as the art market.

Chapter 2 addresses in depth the spectrum of issues associated with the sale of art through dealers or among individual collectors. Such issues include chain-of-title questions; compliance with particular provisions of the U.C.C., including express and implied warranties, and disclaimers of warranties; mutual mistake; in-depth treatment of the concept of entrustment in art deals; a thorough analysis of the revised U.C.C. Article 9 as it applies to art transactions; and various state statutes. Some of these issues are illustrated by the 2002 case of *Holm v. Malmberg*, a multiparty dispute involving ownership of a painting by the French artist Yves Klein. A New York federal district court, in consonance with a majority view, held that where an art seller delivers a work of art not fully paid for to the buyer, title passes to the buyer, even where the invoice states that title does not pass until payment is fully made. New and expanded forms covering consignments, dealer-to-dealer sales, and dealer-to-collector sales are found at the close of the chapter.

Worldwide trade in stolen, smuggled, and looted art is reportedly in excess of $7 billion a year. Still unsolved as of 2004 is the biggest art theft in the United States—the March 18, 1990, burglary at the Isabella Stewart Gardner Museum in Boston. The $200 million in art, including masterworks by Rembrandt and Vermeer, are worth substantially more today. Chapter 3 addresses not only stolen art but also forged art, questioning whether the counterfeiter has a legitimate role in the art world. The focus of chapter 3, however, is on the application of the statute of limitations to issues of theft, conversion, and misattribution of artworks. Theories of accrual for causes of action in conversion (to recover money damages) and in replevin (to recover the artwork) such as the demand-refusal rule, formerly followed in New York, the discovery rule, subscribed to by numerous states, and the laches approach, currently used in New York, are given in-depth treatment.

Recent art sales making headlines include the $104.2 million paid for Pablo Picasso's *Boy with a Pipe* in May 2004 and the record-setting Victor and Sally Ganz Collection, which fetched $206.5 million in November 1997. Both purchases—events that excited the art-buying public—took place at auction. Chapter 4 explores the intricacies of the auction process, including a clarification of limitations to the auctioneer's fiduciary duty to the seller, a discussion of the auctioneer's responsibility to buyers, a new and in-depth discussion of antitrust and other forbidden auction practices, and an analysis of revised auction consignment agreements. Up-to-date model forms from both Sotheby's and Christie's are found at the end of the chapter.

Chapter 5 is devoted to fine art multiples and the issues involved in creating, selling, and buying fine prints or sculpture multiples. The chapter includes a summary of some of the major printmaking processes, such as the woodcut, etching, engraving, and mezzotint. Also included is a brief glossary of print terminology. Fine art multiples invite commercial abuse because of the lack of uniform, industry-wide controls in the production process and the lack of art-market consensus as to what constitutes an original. In recent years, the vast number of fake Salvador Dalí prints has made sensational headlines.

An increasing number of state and federal agencies have devoted public funds to the purchase and installation of works of art. These public commissions are discussed in chapter 6, which also addresses the problems encountered by Richard Serra in the installation and ultimate removal of his sculpture *Tilted Arc* from the Federal Plaza in New York City. Private commissions—commissions by individuals and private entities—for the creation of an artwork are also addressed, and forms for both public and private commissions are included at the close of the chapter.

When an art expert renders an opinion about an artwork's value or authenticity, such an expert may be on perilous terrain. Theories of disparagement, defamation, negligence, negligent misrepresentation, and fraud have transformed many a collector into a lawsuit plaintiff. Chapter 7 highlights the differences between product disparagement and defamation as theories of tort liability. It also clarifies the distinctions between negligence and negligent misrepresentation—particularly in terms of accessibility as a cause of action. This latter distinction is well illustrated by the 2001 *Ravenna* case, in which the plaintiff, once the owner of a painting appraised by Christie's at a value of $10,000 to $15,000, was unable to recover damages from Christie's in negligent misrepresentation when the latter subsequently reexamined and sold the same painting (now owned by another) for more than $5 million. This chapter also has a discussion on antitrust claims and authentication as well as a detailed treatment of online appraisals, including whether such appraisals comply with the guidelines for appraisers set forth in the Uniform Standards of Professional Appraisal Practice. Additionally, this chapter explores methods by which an art expert can limit her exposure when rendering an opinion about a work of art.

Chapter 8 addresses the international dimension to art transactions. It focuses on the preservation of cultural property and its illicit removal from a country. Poorer nations are often looted of their cultural heritage by black marketers who smuggle art and artifacts abroad for sale to collectors living in rich nations. To preserve cultural patrimony, most nations enact laws designed to limit the export of certain categories of cultural property. While the United States, with a number of exceptions mandated by treaty, does not ordinarily enforce the export laws of other nations, the patrimony laws of certain foreign nations have blurred the distinction (as understood in the United States) between theft and illegal export. Detailed analyses of the implications of the *Steinhardt* case and the *Schultz* case as each relates to the National Stolen Property Act illuminate how U.S. policy has evolved, since its accession to UNESCO, regarding the repatriation of art and cultural property. This chapter also includes in-depth treatment of the *Schiele* lawsuits as well as other recent case law involving Holocaust claims litigation. Among the appendixes found at the close of the chapter are revised international sales agreements including escrow arrangements and a listing of websites for locating stolen art.

ARTISTS' RIGHTS

Some rights of the artist apply with particular force to the artist's person, such as First Amendment rights addressed in chapter 9. One ongoing issue is whether the creation, exhibition, placement, and sale of a work of art is protected speech. The distinctions among pure speech, symbolic speech such as art, and conduct are discussed in the context of differing standards of permitted expression in traditional public forums, designated open public forums, and nonpublic forums. Chapter 9 addresses visual social commentary, visual satire, art as a threat, visual defamation, use of the American and state flags as vehicles of protest, and public art. There is detailed treatment of the issue of controversial art exhibited in museums, including the case of the Brooklyn Museum's *Sensation* exhibit and the case of the Cuban Museum in Miami. There is substantial discussion of trademark issues involving art, including trademark infringement (and treatment of the Tiger Woods case), trademark dilution (and discussion of the Food Chain Barbie case), and false endorsement under the Lanham Act. Limitations on freedom of expression, including obscenity, the right of privacy, and the right of publicity, are also explored in depth.

Chapter 10 offers a brief primer on copyright law as it applies to the visual artist, including an extensive treatment of the originality requirement, with a discussion of the *Bridgeman* and *Skyy Spirits* cases. Material principles of the U.S. Copyright Acts of both 1976, as amended, and 1909 are discussed, including extensive treatment of works made for hire and utilitarian objects. International perspectives are explored in a description of the international copyright conventions and relevant trade treaties to which the United States has acceded in recent years and the impact of such international agreements on U.S. copyright law. Also addressed are some of the economic forces impelling such accession by the United States. Copyright infringement is explored in some depth, as is the evolution of the matrix of factors comprising fair use. This chapter also includes a discussion of appropriation art and its ethos, questions the suitability of the fair use defense as it relates to appropriation art, and presents an original proposal for fine art licensing, along with a model licensing contract.

Chapter 11, addressing an artist's moral rights, includes a description of such rights—the right of disclosure, the right of withdrawal, the right of attribution, and the right of integrity (only the last two are recognized in the United States)—and a brief international survey of where such rights are recognized. This chapter also addresses the origins of moral rights and traces the history of moral rights recognition in the United States both before and after the enactment of the Visual Artists Rights Act (VARA) of 1990. VARA amended the copyright law to grant visual artists the moral rights of attribution and integrity. All cases decided to date under VARA are examined, with some discussion on what constitutes "recognized stature."

Chapter 12 focuses on the resale rights of the artist, raising the issue of whether an artist is entitled to a royalty on each resale of the artist's artwork. There is a discussion of the California resale royalties statute as well as an analysis of the possible impact on the art market of the 2001 European Union Directive to member nations to adopt and harmonize *droit de suite* legislation by January 2010.

COLLECTORS

As the price of art continues to rise and interest rates and the stock market remain low, the question of an individual's status as a collector, an investor, or a dealer becomes increasingly important. For a collector, expenses incurred in maintaining possession of collection will, most likely, not be tax-deductible. Expenses incurred as an investor or a dealer will be tax-deductible. Chapter 13 discusses the current state of the law in drawing the lines between a collector, an investor, and a dealer and sets forth the applicable rules for each category. This chapter also examines the availability of the tax-free exchange rules of section 1031 of the Internal Revenue Code as they apply to an investor in art and explains the nuances of the sales and use tax as it applies to the buyer of art.

TAX PLANNING AND ESTATE PLANNING

Tax and estate planning for collectors (chapter 14) and artists (chapter 15) is a crucial topic that has not received the attention it demands. Chapters 14 and 15 discuss the tax and estate planning aspects of charitable contributions, the drafting of wills, the transfer of works of art from generation to generation, pitfalls to avoid, and other relevant legal matters affecting collectors and artists. The Internal Revenue Code is marked by frequent amendments and new rulings: These chapters include a description of those provisions, including a discussion of the most recent tax legislation and estate planning innovations such as charitable remainder trusts, charitable lead trusts, private operating foundations, and the IRS advance ruling procedure for art valuations as prescribed by Revenue Procedure 96-15. Chapter 14 covers fractional gifts to museums— giving the collector the ability to obtain an income tax deduction yet keep possession of the art—and contains detailed forms and analysis of the topic. Recent decisions affecting valuation in artists' estates and the application of the blockage discount are examined, including *Estate of Georgia O'Keeffe* and *Estate of Andy Warhol*. Valuation issues for collectors are treated to an in-depth analysis.

MUSEUMS AND MULTIMEDIA

Chapter 16 discusses the legal structures of museums and presents an overview of legal issues faced by a museum in the conduct of its business, including the accessioning and deaccessioning of artworks, the handling of incoming and outgoing loans, the treatment of indefinite loans, the rendering of appraisals and authentications, the receipt of charitable donations, and the conduct of income-producing activities and their effect, if any, on the museum's tax status.

Chapter 17, which addresses digital art, includes a discussion of legal issues and the evolving law pertinent to art and digital technologies. There is an overview of copyright law as it relates to digital derivative works, with treatment of the *Greenberg, Tasini,* and *Faulkner* cases, and as it relates to the distribution and public display of digital copyrighted works. This chapter includes a discussion of the Digital Millennium Copyright Act, treatment of contributory infringement, vicarious infringement, a discussion of peer-to-peer networks, including a presentation of the *Napster* and *Grokster* cases and mention of the *Kelly* case in terms of inline linking and framing. Trademark issues are addressed, as well as First Amendment issues, including defamation law, the Communications Decency Act, rights of privacy and publicity, the Child Online Protection Act, and the Child Pornography Prevention Act. There is a section on buying and selling art online, including discussion on cyberspace jurisdiction and online art auction sales and fraud.

PART ONE

Artists and Dealers

1

Artist–Dealer Relations

In this first decade of the new millennium, the artist-dealer relationship continues to evolve. Once built on a chat and a handshake, the relationship is beginning to be memorialized in writing. One factor contributing to the trend of a somewhat more formalized relationship between the artist and dealer is financial issues, faced by artist and dealer alike, that emerged in the recession of the early 1990s like rocks at ebb tide. In the face of that recession, some artists were quick to abandon ongoing relationships with dealers, lured by the promise of more effective representation elsewhere; with the closing of certain galleries, some artists are seeking payment for artworks sold by the galleries months or years earlier.[1] Another factor that may subtly be contributing to a more formalized relationship between the artist and dealer is a lingering undermining of trust among buyers and sellers of art that arose in the aftermath of the highly publicized civil and criminal antitrust actions involving the auction houses of Sotheby's and Christie's (discussed in chapter 4). Be that as it may, the emerging practice of committing the artist-dealer relationship to writing will, happily, help avert the misfortunes that have previously befallen each party and that are discussed later in this chapter.

But first, what is an art dealer? An art dealer is anyone who buys, sells, and trades in works of art and who, unlike a commercial gallery owner, may or may not have exhibition space open to the public. The term "dealer" embraces a spectrum of commercial entities ranging from an individual proprietor trading in a small stock and perhaps operating from home to a person or a corporation having a commercial gallery with exhibition space regularly open to the public. If a dealer has a gallery, it may be the common single commercial gallery, a gallery with numerous branches, or part of a conglomerate. No governmental licensing procedure, permit application, or registration system has been established for dealers. As noted, not all dealers are galleries, but a great many are; therefore, this chapter, except where specifically indicated to the contrary, uses the terms "dealer" and "gallery" interchangeably.

The dealer's role as seller is covered at length in chapter 2, and the technical definition for tax purposes of who is a dealer, as opposed to an investor or a collector, is dealt with in chapter 13. This chapter addresses the transactions between dealer and artist and the resultant rights and obligations of each party.

On rare occasions, such as where a dealer secures a commission to be executed by an artist, each aspect of the artist-dealer relationship must be negotiated and embodied in an agreement unique to the particular circumstances. However, the legal relationship between artist and dealer usually takes one of two basic forms: outright sale or, more frequently, consignment.

OUTRIGHT SALE

Generally

A dealer may buy works from the artist outright for purposes of re-sale. Unless a portion of the purchase price remains to be paid or un-less the artist has reserved rights through the use of a contract of sale, the relationship between artist and dealer ends at the time of sale. Al-though traditionally quite common in Europe, outright purchase is rare in the United States. Many dealers do not have sufficient capital to buy works outright; even when they do have the capital, dealers are usually reluctant to use large amounts of their capital while as-suming the risk of being unable to resell a purchased work at a rea-sonable profit.

The Outright Sale Contract

On those rare occasions where an outright sale between artist and dealer takes place, it should be evidenced by a written document. The dealer may require the artist to make written warranties with re-spect to the creation and the ownership of the work. Moreover, the dealer should insist on a written document if any of the reproduction rights or any other portion of the copyright is to be licensed, sold, or otherwise transferred. Under the Copyright Act of 1976, unlike the rule at common law,[2] transfer of ownership of an object embodying the copyright does not imply transfer of the copyright itself.[3] In oth-er words, if an artist sells a painting, the copyright in the work is not transferred. If the buyer wishes to own the copyright in the work, he must obtain a specific written transfer of the copyright.[4]

The artist, too, should insist on a written contract for an outright sale. Aside from the memorialization of the sales price and the keep-ing of good records for tax purposes, any other rights that the artist is able to retain in the artwork beyond its sale to the dealer, such as the right to collect royalties on any subsequent sale of the work or the right to borrow back the work for various exhibitions, are rights that should be retained through the use of a written contract. It is the dealer, not the artist, who has privity of contract with the next purchaser,[5] and it is the dealer to whom the artist must look for recourse if agreements reached at the time of the original sale are not fulfilled. A written sales contract can require the gallery to include rights that inure to the benefit of the artist in any subsequent resale contract.

CONSIGNMENT

Generally

Under the usual arrangement in the United States, the dealer accepts works from the artist on consignment. That arrangement permits the dealer, usually operating a gallery, to increase activity without tying up large amounts of capital.

In a consignment, an artist transfers artwork to a dealer for purposes of sale, display, and exhibition. Title to the artwork ordinarily remains with the artist until the dealer effects a sale. On accepting works from an artist on consignment, the dealer becomes the artist's agent and the law of agency applies.[6] That is, in the hands of the dealer, the artwork becomes trust property and the proceeds of sale become trust funds. A fiduciary duty is imposed on the dealer with respect to each work of art consigned,[7] and that fiduciary duty continues until the completion of the delivery of the sales proceeds to the artist.[8]

Fiduciary Duties

When a dealer accepts an artist's work on consignment and thereby becomes the artist's agent, the dealer is also considered to be a fiduciary.[9] As a fiduciary, the dealer is bound to the artist by an array of obligations:

- To care for and manage the consigned property prudently[10]
- To deal fairly and honestly with the artist[11]

- To account periodically to the artist as to dispositions of the property[12]
- To disclose to the artist all information relevant to the subject matter of the agency[13]

What about the dealer who wishes to handle the works of two artists from the same school? If the artists are in competition, the dealer arguably should not handle them both in view of the general rule that an agent should not act for two or more competing principals.[14] Although common industry practices fly in the face of that general rule, the prudent dealer should require the artist to acknowledge in writing that the dealer handles works by other artists who may occupy a competitive position.

In addition, as a fiduciary, a dealer should not buy work outright from the artist unless the dealer has disclosed all the circumstances relating to the purchase and the artist fully consents.[15] An example of a breach of fiduciary duty is the dealer who purchases a work of art outright from the artist for, say, $50,000, without divulging to the artist that the dealer had made an agreement to resell the work to a third party for $250,000.

A dealer who breaches any fiduciary duties is liable to the artist for damages resulting from the breach.[16] If fraud or criminal intent can be proved under applicable criminal statutes, a dealer may be criminally liable for the wrongful conduct. In New York, for example, misappropriation by the dealer of either the artwork itself or the proceeds from a sale may subject the dealer to liability on a theory of larceny.[17]

Examples of an art dealer's breach of fiduciary duties abound in the case of *Lazarevic v. Sindin Galleries*.[18] Plaintiff Milo Lazarevic, a sculptor, consigned a stone piece entitled *From Time to Time* to the defendant, Sindin Galleries. At the time of the consignment in 1983, Sindin allegedly represented that it had a client likely to purchase the sculpture, that it would insure the sculpture for the replacement value of not less than $60,000, and that it would assume responsibility for the work until it was either sold or returned to plaintiff's studio in New York. According to the plaintiff, Sindin never sold the sculpture but instead rented it for exhibition without plaintiff's knowledge or permission and without accounting to the plaintiff for the rental proceeds. In 1995, the plaintiff allegedly learned that the sculpture had been damaged while on display at a hotel in Westchester County, New York. At that time, Sindin assured the plaintiff that he would be paid for his loss by Sindin's insurer.

When, by 1996, the plaintiff had received no payment either from Sindin or Sindin's insurer, he brought suit in the New York State Supreme Court, alleging breach of contract and fiduciary obligations, violations of various provisions of New York's Arts and Cultural Affairs Law, fraudulent misrepresentation, unjust enrichment, conversion, and deceptive business practices in violation of New York's General Business Law. Sindin moved to dismiss the complaint in its entirety.

Although it dismissed one claim (for deceptive business practices), the court denied Sindin's motion to dismiss the others. As to the plaintiff's claim of breach of contract and breach of fiduciary obligations, the court noted that the plaintiff had submitted a copy of his August 25, 1983, letter to Sindin, memorializing their consignment agreement and expressly stating that "[y]ou and I shall divide equally the proceeds from any sale of the sculpture," thereby establishing the existence of a contract. Moreover, as the court stated, under section 11.03 of the New York Arts and Cultural Affairs Law, when the plaintiff delivered his sculpture to Sindin for purpose of exhibition or sale, a relationship of "trust" between the two parties was created.

As to the claim based on a violation of section 12.01 *et seq.* of the New York Arts and Cultural Affairs Law, the court found that contrary to Sindin's contention, the plaintiff did not rely solely on a bare legal conclusion that a consignor-consignee relationship was created within the meaning of this statute. Instead, plaintiff specifically alleged that he was an artist who in 1983 consigned to Sindin a sculpture he had created and that Sindin agreed to use its best efforts to sell it for him.

With respect to fraudulent misrepresentation, the court found that the claim was facially sufficient and pleaded with sufficient particularity: That is, the sculptor alleged that in 1983 Sindin falsely represented to him that it had a likely buyer for his sculpture and that this representation induced him to enter into the consignment arrangement with Sindin rather than with his usual dealer, OK Harris, and that Sindin never had a ready buyer for the sculpture. Moreover, the plaintiff alleged that Sindin knew the representation was false when it was made. Accordingly, each of the elements of fraud—misrepresentation of material fact, falsity, scienter, deception, and injury—was set forth.

Likewise, the court found that the plaintiff's claim of unjust enrichment was sufficient. As the court noted, the elements of claim for unjust enrichment against a fiduciary are

(1) a confidential or fiduciary relationship;

(2) a promise;

(3) a transfer in reliance on the promise; and

(4) unjust enrichment.

Here, unjust enrichment was based on the money and other benefits Sindin allegedly received for the unauthorized renting and display of the plaintiff's work and without accounting to him of those funds.

Conversion, the final claim that the court permitted to stand, was based on the allegations that the plaintiff made repeated demands that Sindin return his sculpture and that Sindin failed to do so. Moreover, as the court noted,[19] although the plaintiff conceded that Sindin was not in possession of the sculpture at the time suit was brought, the gallery still may be liable for its conversion.

Exclusivity

Under section 2-306 of the Uniform Commercial Code (U.C.C.), a dealer who has the exclusive right to handle an artist's works is obligated to use best efforts to promote sales. Correspondingly, the artist must use best efforts to supply works that he agreed to consign. The parties, however, may alter those obligations by contract.[20]

Borrowing from the analogous field of real estate brokerage, the dealer may have (1) an exclusive agency or (2) an exclusive power to sell.[21] If the dealer is merely the exclusive agent, the artist can sell works directly without incurring any liability to the exclusive dealer.[22] On the other hand, if the dealer has an exclusive power to sell, the artist must pay the dealer a commission even if the artist effects a sale without involving the dealer.[23] Many dealers erroneously believe that a mere exclusive agency entitles them to a commission on any direct sale by the artist. Although that belief is contrary to the legal principles that apply, many artists, dependent on a dealer to promote the artist's reputation and sales, prefer to pay the dealer a commission even when, strictly speaking, there is no legal obligation to do so, rather than risk alienating the dealer.

The situation is similar with barter arrangements. Many dealers with some form of exclusivity vis-à-vis an artist's work feel entitled to compensation after the artist exchanges artwork for, say, a sailboat, medical services, the use of a summer house, or even the work of another artist. Whether a barter transaction violates a dealer's exclusivity depends on the intention of the artist and the dealer. In any event, it is clearly difficult if not impossible for a dealer with an exclusive power to sell to monitor the barter transactions of an artist. It is equally clear that barter transactions, when engaged in by the artist to any great extent, may actually divert a significant portion of the artist's salable production from the dealer.

Contractual Rights

As earlier noted, artists and dealers are, wisely, beginning to memorialize their relationships in writing. Although an oral agreement may indeed be as meaningful to the parties as a written agreement, varying state laws limit the scope of oral agreements enforceable in a court of law. In New York and California, for example, an oral contract, to be enforceable, must be able to be performed within one year,[24] a period significantly shorter than the usual artist-dealer relationship. Therefore, although both parties historically recoiled from a written contract believing it to be an insult to the unique, personal qualities of their relationship, economic realities, highlighted by some notorious cases, present a poignant lesson that artist and dealer are beginning to absorb.

Necessity of a Written Contract: The Dealer's Lesson

O'Keeffe v. Bry[25]

This case illustrates the nature of loss that a dealer may suffer in the absence of a written contract. For many years, Georgia O'Keeffe employed Doris Bry as a commissioned sales agent authorized to sell not only the full array of O'Keeffe's art but also the photographic works of Alfred Stieglitz, O'Keeffe's late husband. At some point, O'Keeffe and Bry had a falling-out that ended the agency arrangement and gave rise to the suit by O'Keeffe for the return of artworks and photographs and an accounting from Bry of any money due on sales. Once the artworks were transferred to a safe place, Bry filed various counterclaims, including several for breach of contract. In one counterclaim, Bry alleged that for the duration of O'Keeffe's life, in return for Bry's agreeing to act as exclusive agent, market-maker, publicist, and in-house curator for O'Keeffe's art, O'Keeffe agreed to make Bry her exclusive agent and market-maker. In another counterclaim, Bry alleged that in return for the above-stated services to O'Keeffe during O'Keeffe's life and to her estate O'Keeffe had agreed to name Bry the executor of the O'Keeffe estate and to empower Bry to act as sales agent after O'Keeffe's death. O'Keeffe sought dismissal of those counterclaims, alleging that they were barred by the statute of frauds. Bry argued that the process of discovery might yield documents containing writings satisfying the statute of frauds requirement.

Discovery unearthed a number of O'Keeffe's wills and trusts, as well as a document known as the Harvard agreement, which provided that O'Keeffe would leave a gift of her artworks to Harvard University. The document also stated that O'Keeffe expected Bry to supervise the disposition of all or most of O'Keeffe's paintings at the time of her death and that to the extent that Bry did not do so Harvard was responsible for disposing of them; furthermore, O'Keeffe wished, but did not direct, that Harvard employ Bry for the sale of the paintings.

The United States district court reviewed those documents, determined that New York law applied, and then examined Bry's first counterclaim—that O'Keeffe promised her a lifetime exclusive agency—in light of the relevant provision of New York's statute of frauds,[26] which requires a writing when an agreement, like the Harvard agreement, cannot be fully performed before the conclusion of a lifetime (in this instance, O'Keeffe's). The court found no written evidence in the Harvard document or anywhere else of a grant of a lifetime exclusive agency to Bry by O'Keeffe. The court found the Harvard agreement language to be merely precatory, not language to constitute a binding commitment. Moreover, the court found that the Harvard agreement was concerned not with Bry's lifetime agency but, rather, with the distribution of O'Keeffe's artworks after her death.

Bry had also argued that under New York case law a confluence of memoranda[27]—that is, the Harvard agreement and other documents, when pieced together—satisfied the statute of frauds. The court, however, held that a confluence of memoranda may satisfy the statute of frauds only when at least one document already exists establishing the underlying contractual commitment. The court further reasoned that additional memoranda could be looked to only to supply essential terms of an alleged agreement and only when the additional memoranda specifically referred to the transaction covered by the core document.[28] Since the court found no core document evidencing a lifetime exclusive agency, Bry's counterclaim was dismissed.

Another of Bry's counterclaims—that in return for her professional services to O'Keeffe during O'Keeffe's life and to her estate after O'Keeffe's death O'Keeffe promised to name Bry executor and to empower Bry to act as a sales agent after O'Keeffe's death—was based on alleged oral promises, which were found to be unenforceable.[29] Bry's promises to render professional services during O'Keeffe's lifetime and, thereafter, to O'Keeffe's estate came within the statute of frauds, since her performance could not be completed during O'Keeffe's lifetime. O'Keeffe's alleged promises were promises to make a testamentary disposition and, as such, were governed by section

13-2.1 of the New York Estates, Powers, and Trusts Law (EPTL). Because the promises were not evidenced in the Harvard agreement, O'Keeffe's will, or any other document, they were held to be unenforceable, and that counterclaim was dismissed.[30]

The lesson is clear. Bry would have been able to protect herself if there had been a written contract along the lines of the model agreements included at the end of this chapter (Appendixes 1-1, 1-2, and 1-3).

Estate of Jean-Michel Basquiat[31]

In a more recent case, Vrej Baghoomian's art gallery promoted and sold the artworks of Jean-Michel Basquiat during the artist's lifetime. Baghoomian alleged that in June 1988, two months before the artist died, Basquiat orally agreed to give Baghoomian "the exclusive right to buy all of his artwork including ninety-odd large canvases and works of art on paper completed by him individually, or [in collaboration] with the late Andy Warhol" and that Basquiat "further agreed to a rate of compensation as 50% of the sale price realized on each of such [works] when sold."[32]

Baghoomian further asserted that on August 13, 1988, the day after Jean-Michel Basquiat died, his father, who thereafter became the administrator of his son's estate, orally agreed to adhere to the alleged June agreement and that the agreement was subsequently confirmed in telephone conversations with the administrator's attorney. Baghoomian claimed that in reliance on those assurances he spent time and money promoting the artist's work. The administrator subsequently contracted with the Robert Miller Gallery to handle his son's work.

Baghoomian thereupon brought a $40 million lawsuit against the Robert Miller Gallery and the estate of Jean-Michel Basquiat, claiming, among other allegations, that he had the exclusive right to represent the estate.

In dismissing Baghoomian's lawsuit, the New York County Surrogate's Court determined, among other findings, that the alleged oral agreement of June 1988 between Basquiat and Baghoomian was a consignment agreement that terminated when the artist died. The court also rejected Baghoomian's assertion that the June 1988 agreement was binding because it was ratified in his August 1988 telephone conversation with Basquiat's father, the prospective administrator of the estate. In rejecting that last assertion, the court noted:

> Under EPTL 11-1.3 "an executor named in a will has no power to dispose of any part of the estate of the testator before letters testamentary or preliminary letters testamentary are granted except to pay reasonable funeral expenses. . . ." It is undisputed [here] that the claimed ratification occurred before letters of administration were granted. Before such letters issue, a prospective administrator does not have even the color of authority possessed by a nominated executor.[33]

Finally, the court stated that Baghoomian's reliance on alleged informal telephone conversations he claimed to have had with the administrator's attorney was unreasonable: "An attorney with general authority cannot bind his clients to a waiver or surrender of a substantial right."[34]

Still another instance where the dealer would have done well to memorialize in writing his understanding with the artist is illustrated in *Koeniges v. Woodward*.[35] Here, the plaintiff, Koeniges, was a photographer who took numerous exclusive photographs of the noted artist Willem de Kooning from 1966 through 1980. In April 1996, plaintiff initiated a series of meetings with defendant art dealers John and Kristine Woodward, who operated what came to be known as the Woodward Gallery. After the defendants researched the value of the de Kooning photographs, the parties agreed that the Woodward Gallery would sell them as a limited edition consisting of ten sets of sixteen photographs in each set for a total of 160 photographs. The retail price for each set was $75,000, and the parties agreed to split the sales proceeds on a fifty-fifty basis. They also agreed on numerous details relating to the sale, including the retail price of individual photographs, the amount of discount permitted, the selection and cost of frames, the selection of the photographs to be exhibited, and the timing of promotion of the sale. The defendants invested time, energy, and money in preparing the exhibition, including the framing of the photographs, and in marketing and promoting the photographs, including hosting the exhibit's opening night.

In September of 1996, the exhibition of the de Kooning photographs opened at the gallery. Four hundred people attended, security officers and staff were hired, and champagne and appetizers were served. Plaintiff, while pleased with the exhibition and the opening-night party, at no time signed the proposed contract drafted by the defendants or a proposed revised contract. The draft contracts contained, in addition to the terms relating to the exhibition, a clause giving the defendants an exclusive one-year period commencing at the end of the exhibition to sell plaintiff's photographs.

During the first few weeks in October, with none of the photographs having been sold, plaintiff visited the gallery and made some colorful comments about the unsigned draft contracts. He continued to refuse to sign, also rejecting a still later draft contract revised to address his concerns with respect to the gallery's commissions from publication rights and down payments during the one-year exclusive. When defendant Kristine Woodward then told plaintiff she had nothing more to say to him and he should leave the premises, plaintiff threatened to remove the photographs and to call the police. It was Kristine Woodward, however, who called the police, advising them that a burglary was in progress. The police advised the plaintiff that his complaint was civil in nature and that it should be resolved in court. The plaintiff shortly thereafter sent written demand for the return of the photographs, the defendants refused, and the plaintiff brought suit.

On the parties' respective breach of contract claims, the New York City Civil Court held that there was a meeting of the minds only as to the exhibition period—not as to the one-year exclusive period. Moreover, even assuming the parties agreed to the exclusive one-year period, the court found that the oral agreement was unenforceable under the statute of frauds.

Necessity of a Written Contract: The Artist's Lesson

Sonnabend Gallery v. Halley[36]

In 1986, Peter Halley, a young New York artist of note, entered into an oral agreement to be represented by the Sonnabend Gallery, a New York gallery representing well-known contemporary artists. The understanding was that Sonnabend, as the representative of Halley, would share all proceeds of sales equally with Halley, that Sonnabend would pay Halley monthly advances of $12,000 against future expected sales, and that there would be regular exhibitions and sales of Halley's work. The oral agreement included no indication that the term of representation was for any particular duration.

Halley's first showing at Sonnabend, in October 1987, was highly successful. It served to enhance Halley's reputation, thereby creating greater demand for his work. Sonnabend increased the amount of the advances payable to Halley. In June 1991, Halley allegedly agreed to provide eleven paintings (among them at least one diptych) to be sold at $75,000 each ($150,000 for the diptych) at a Sonnabend show to be held in March 1992. At Halley's request, the exhibition was rescheduled twice; in the end, it was to occur in May 1992.

In February 1992, three months before the exhibition was scheduled to take place, Halley terminated his relationship with the Sonnabend Gallery by letter, noting that he felt he and the gallery had reached "a philosophical impasse" and that he wanted "to be represented by a gallery that takes a more activist stance toward the artists it represents."[37] He then indicated that he had recently engaged in serious talks with the Gagosian Gallery and had decided to join it. In the letter Halley also acknowledged his financial debt to Sonnabend—$162,500 in stipends and production expenses for a new project—and offered to settle his debt before moving to Gagosian. Halley asserted that in his relationship with Sonnabend, written contracts had been discouraged and that they had no formal agreement that constituted a contract that could be breached. He also asserted that he and Sonnabend never reached an enforceable agreement on the details regarding the May 1992 exhibition and that Sonnabend was not his exclusive agent.

In May 1992, Gagosian advertised in the *New York Times* that it was holding a solo exhibition of Halley's new work from May 16 to June 27, 1992. Sonnabend immediately sought an emergency injunction in an attempt to stop the exhibition, claiming irreparable harm in terms of economics and reputation. Sonnabend alleged that it had already presold the paintings to be exhibited, although the gallery had no written evidence to that effect. Sonnabend alleged that it had built Halley's career and had helped to establish Halley's reputation and that Halley's "breach of contract"[38] would cost Sonnabend more than half a million dollars. Sonnabend also accused the Gagosian Gallery of tortious interference with Sonnabend's advantageous business relations by enticing Halley with a "onetime $2 million cash bonus and other extraordinary benefits,"[39] a charge that both Halley and Gagosian refuted. The New York State Supreme Court denied the injunction, noting, among other points, that

> it is interesting that in large measure, the argument . . . is not a legal one, but rather one that is addressed to its embarrassment in the art world over the loss of an artist of the caliber of . . . Halley. . . .[40]

After the injunction was denied, Halley and Gagosian sought unsuccessfully to have the case dismissed: Sonnabend was to be allowed to go to trial. In the end, the case was settled in the spring of 1993. As a condition of the settlement, Halley was required to pay certain undisclosed sums of money to Sonnabend.

Limitations on Written Contracts

The previous section stresses the importance of a written contract to memorialize the artist-dealer relationship. But a mere writing will not always suffice to keep the parties out of court. As the cases discussed below indicate, a written contract may be unclear or incomplete and require interpretation by the courts; or it may be clear enough yet modified or overridden by a statute.

Particularly significant is the need to draft the contract, whether for consignment or outright sale, with an eye to averting any dire consequences. For example, a contract should be specific in defining its intent; otherwise, it runs the risk of being recharacterized by the courts. In one instance, a contract between an artist's widow and a dealer provided that the widow "sell" her late husband's work to the dealer, and the dealer contracted to use his best efforts to sell the work and pay the widow one half of the sale proceeds. The Surrogate's Court found that the contract had elements of both a sale and a consignment, and, therefore, the court considered extrinsic evidence with respect to the parties' intent. The appellate division upheld the Surrogate's Court's conclusion that the agreement was properly treated as one of consignment.[41]

In a later example of court interpretation of an artist–dealer relationship evidenced by writing, *Naber v. Steinitz*,[42] the artist Bernd Naber sought injunctive relief to prevent the defendants—Prisunic Gallery, Inc., and its owners—from disposing, dismantling, or removing either from New York State or from the gallery premises certain pieces of his artwork. In addition, he sought a court order directing the gallery to turn that artwork over to him.

The dispute between the parties involved the interpretation of an agreement they entered into on March 22, 1991, in connection with the gallery's 1991 exhibition of Naber's artwork. The agreement provides the following in its entirety:

(1) Prisunic Gallery will spend the amount of $27,300 to produce the artwork of Bernd Naber for the show, in exchange of 2 paintings (6 feet × 7 feet) of, at this time, a value of $12,000 each.

(2) As well as, 10 percent of the value of any sculpture produced during this show, for a period of 5 years, completed or not by the time of the opening of this show.[43]

In the beginning of April, in anticipation of an April 18, 1991, exhibition, Naber commenced production of a huge sculpture to be created from cement, steel mesh wire, and metal rods. Its expected length was 150 feet, and its height was to increase steadily from 0 to

11 feet, creating a spiral configuration. It soon became clear that the agreed sum of $27,300 was insufficient to produce the sculpture. The gallery consented to pay an additional $15,000 so that the work could be completed in time for the opening of the exhibition. On April 18, the sculpture was not yet completed, and the exhibition was postponed until April 30.

By April 30, 1991, the sculpture was still incomplete, and the gallery had expended $50,000 more than the initially agreed-on sum for labor and materials. Consequently, the parties agreed that the sculpture would be exhibited as a work in progress. In addition, fifty other Naber artworks in the gallery's possession, including twenty-four that were produced before the March 1991 agreement, were to be exhibited at the show.

By September 4, 1991, the sculpture remained unfinished, and the gallery's costs had reached approximately $100,000. At that time, without Naber's permission, the gallery began dismantling the sculpture, as another show was scheduled for September 19. On September 8, Naber requested the return of his artwork from the gallery. The gallery refused to comply, and Naber brought suit.

In the course of the legal argument, the gallery contended that the March 1991 agreement the parties entered into was "a unique consignment arrangement that constituted a joint venture"[44] and that the terms of the March agreement implied that the parties intended such an arrangement. (A joint venture has been defined as a special combination of two or more parties in which, in a specific undertaking, a profit is jointly sought without any actual partnership or corporate designation.)[45]

The court, however, noted that even if it is assumed that it was a joint venture, the gallery's intention to sell the artwork over Naber's objections would amount to a breach of the joint control and management that a joint venture generally mandates.

The gallery also argued that Naber breached the March agreement when he failed to stay within the budget and to complete the big sculpture on time. The court, however, found the arguments with respect to the big sculpture moot, since it was not referred to in Naber's request for injunctive relief. The court, citing the New York

Arts and Cultural Affairs Law, held that Naber "demonstrated that a consignment agreement existed between the parties" and that Naber, as consignor, "has both title and right to possession superior to that of a consignee." Accordingly, the court held, Naber "sufficiently established that a preliminary injunction is warranted as to all fifty pieces of artwork."[46]

However, as to Naber's request for the return of all fifty pieces of his work, the court found that compliance with such a request would not be equitable before the case was adjudicated on the merits. Accordingly, the court ruled that the defendants return to Naber the twenty-four pieces of artwork created before the March 1991 agreement.[47]

Another example of court intervention in a memorialized artist-dealer relationship that generated a considerable amount of publicity involved the famous caricaturist Al Hirschfeld.[48]

Hirschfeld entered into a written agreement in 1974 with the art dealer Margo Feiden and the Margo Feiden Galleries ("Feiden") whereby Hirschfeld consigned to Feiden all his original works of art and where upon Feiden's sale of each of his works Hirschfeld received a mutually agreed-upon payment. The agreement gave Feiden exclusive reproduction rights to Hirschfeld's art as well as *an exclusive right to sell* Hirschfeld's work.[49] As noted earlier, if a dealer has an exclusive right to sell, the artist—in this case Hirschfeld—must pay the dealer a commission even if the artist effects a sale without involving the dealer. Moreover, the agreement between Hirschfeld and Feiden provided that all sales of drawings for which arrangements were made with the prospective buyer before Hirschfeld created the work would be made through Feiden.

The agreement further assured Hirschfeld a minimum payment of $10,000 each year and provided for automatic renewal on a yearly basis if he received payments of at least $12,000 during the preceding twelve-month period. Contrary to industry custom, the agreement did not include a clause providing for periodic review of prices (and moneys receivable by the artist) in light of the artist's enhanced reputation and ability to command higher sale prices. Moreover, the agreement provided Feiden with the option of terminating the agreement unilaterally. Hirschfeld had no such option.

Among other points favorable to the dealer and contrary to standard industry practice, the agreement also permitted Feiden to purchase any number, without limitation, of Hirschfeld's works for her own account and did not require her to arrange a specified minimum number of shows of Hirschfeld's work during the term. In addition, there was no provision that prevented Feiden from assigning her rights or responsibilities with respect to Hirschfeld. In view of the personal relationship between an artist and dealer, the latter ordinarily would not transfer its rights or responsibilities as set forth in the agreement—at least without the artist's prior written consent.

Despite all this, the arrangement between Hirschfeld and Feiden was apparently viable for both parties for more than two decades. Then in the late 1990s, it began to sour.

Hirschfeld, by then in his late nineties, alleged that since 1997 Feiden had been violating her responsibilities as consignee by

(1) refusing to follow Hirschfeld's instructions regarding the disposition of his art, including returning it when requested to do so;

(2) refusing to provide him with copies of documentation and records concerning his works; and

(3) wrongfully preventing the exhibition of his work for her personal reasons.

As examples of the last, Hirschfeld claimed that Feiden attempted to thwart a 1997 retrospective exhibition of his work in New York and, in a subsequent instance, blocked a Hirschfeld retrospective at the Academy of Motion Picture Arts and Sciences in Hollywood, out of her personal animosity toward an individual involved in the exhibition.

In January 2000, Hirschfeld contacted Feiden with a view to amending the 1974 agreement. The following month, Feiden rejected Hirschfeld's demands. In May, Hirschfeld formally terminated his relationship with Feiden, and the following day he brought suit against her in the New York State Supreme Court. In his complaint,

Hirschfeld sued for recovery of his consigned property; sought injunctive relief barring Feiden from disposing of his consigned work without his consent; sought an accounting; and sued for damages for conversion, breach of fiduciary duty, breach of contract, interference with prospective economic relations, and intentional infliction of emotional distress.

The court issued a temporary restraining order, barring Feiden from disposing of any of Hirschfeld's art other than in the ordinary course of business, and barring Feiden from appropriating such art for herself. In July 2000 the state court, granting Hirschfeld's motions, issued a threefold preliminary injunction against Feiden during the pendency of the action: She was restrained from disposing of any of Hirschfeld's consigned art; she was directed to provide a complete inventory of all of Hirschfeld's consigned art in her possession; and she was directed to provide Hirschfeld with a full accounting of the sale or other disposition of his work from January 1997 to the present. In the same action, Feiden unsuccessfully cross-moved for a preliminary injunction restraining Hirschfeld from accepting commissions other than from or through Feiden; refusing to complete accepted assignments arranged by Feiden prior to May 15, 2000; denying Feiden access to original drawings Hirschfeld intended to sell; and selling original drawings other than through Feiden.

In an action to secure injunctive relief, the moving party must establish—as did Hirschfeld here—three elements: irreparable harm, likelihood of success on the merits, and a balance of equities in the moving party's favor.

As to irreparable harm: Hirschfeld sought the return of his art that was in Feiden's possession. In finding that Hirschfeld established irreparable harm, the court recognized that money damages would not themselves be an adequate remedy for the loss of unique artwork. The court rejected Feiden's argument that she would be forced to go out of business should Hirschfeld's preliminary injunction be granted.

Regarding likelihood of success on the merits: In finding that Hirschfeld established this element, the court noted that section 12.01 of the New York Arts and Cultural Affairs Law provides that whenever an artist delivers a work of fine art to an art merchant for the purpose of a sale, a consignor-consignee relationship is established; the consignee is deemed to be the consignor's agent; and the art consigned is deemed to be trust property for the consignor's benefit. The court further noted that as Hirschfeld's agent, Feiden was bound to act in accordance with his reasonable instructions concerning his work and was held to the utmost good faith in her dealings with him. The court then found that Hirschfeld submitted evidence alleging that in two separate instances Feiden sought to block exhibitions of his works—suggesting that Feiden did not act in his best interests. In looking to "the plain language of the statute," the court rejected Feiden's argument that the New York Arts and Cultural Affairs Law does not supersede a valid agreement between artist and dealer. In any event, as the court observed, the evidence submitted may cause the agreement to be found unconscionable and thereby unenforceable.

As to the balance of equities: In finding that the equities favored Hirschfeld, the court again noted that New York's consignment statute provides that works of art delivered to an art merchant for purposes of sale are trust property for the benefit of the artist.

Ultimately, the case did not reach trial. Rather, the parties reached a settlement in October 2000 by entering into an agreement superseding the 1974 contract. While the terms of the settlement agreement are confidential, it has been disclosed that the agreement returned control of the exhibition of Hirschfeld's art to the artist.

The impact of a consignment statute is demonstrated by *Wesselmann v. International Images, Inc.*,[50] a case of first impression involving the interpretation of section 12.01 of the New York Arts and Cultural Affairs Law. The complaint, which initially named Tom Wesselmann Studios, Inc., as the sole plaintiff, was amended to add Tom Wesselmann and his wife individually because it was not clear who was the owner of the art in dispute. Wesselmann is a world-renowned artist who marketed his limited-edition prints through his publisher, defendant International Images, Inc. The prints were produced from silk-screen masters or lithographic plates. It was undisputed that Wesselmann conceived the images for all the prints.

A disagreement arose between Wesselmann and International Images, and Wesselmann demanded the return of the prints in International Images' possession. Wesselmann alleged that International Images took possession of the prints as trustee pursuant to section 12.01 of the New York Arts and Cultural Affairs Law. The New York State Supreme Court was called on to decide (1) whether a publisher and seller of multiples and prints conceived by an artist is an art merchant under the New York statute and (2) whether the artist who conceives the image, delivers it to a printer chosen by the publisher, approves the final prints, and signs them has delivered a "print of his creation" to an art merchant.

International Images claimed the New York statute did not apply because it was not an art merchant (it claimed that since it published the prints, it was not an art merchant but the creator); it did not sell the art (it said the art was sold through retail dealers); Wesselmann did not deliver the prints (International Images said it produced the art at the printer's plant, so there was nothing for Wesselmann to deliver); the prints were not Wesselmann's own creation, since a corporation cannot be an artist; and multiples are not classified as fine art.

The court, in issuing a temporary restraining order, found that International Images was an art merchant, since the New York statute applies to a person who has a particular skill or who employs an agent with a particular skill. The court further found that even though the prints were produced by International Images, they are treated as consigned by Wesselmann, since the consignor-consignee relationship arises whenever the artist "delivers or causes to be delivered" a print of his own creation. The court noted that the New York statute uses the terms "print" and "multiple" interchangeably and that multiples are, therefore, fine art. It also held that "an artist can be a corporation pursuant to Sections 11.01.1 and 13 of the Arts and Cultural Affairs Law."

In a related case involving the same parties, the court subsequently held that the unsold artwork and the proceeds from sold artwork were part of a trust and directed International Images to turn over all unsold artwork to Wesselmann.[51] Affirming the lower court, the Appellate Division, First Department, held that the fact that the parties' written agreement entitled International Images to be reimbursed for printing and other related costs did not alter the trust relationship and did not create a security interest in the artwork in favor of International Images.[52]

Like any other commercial agreement, the artist-dealer contract may be subject to attack as being "unconscionable" under the U.C.C.[53] and may also be vulnerable to challenge as a breach of fiduciary obligations.[54] In New York, where artist-dealer consignment relationships are governed by statute,[55] any clause of a contract in which the consignor (the artist) waives any provision of the artist-dealer consignment statute is void, except for the provision that treats sale proceeds of fine art as trust funds for the benefit of the artist. That provision alone under particular circumstances and within limits may be waived.[56] Even broader nonwaiver provisions vis-à-vis the consignor currently exist in the counterpart artist-dealer statutes of a number of other states.[57] In California,[58] for example, the consignor-artist may not, in a contract, waive any provision of the artist-dealer consignment statute.

The Artist-Dealer Agreement: A Checklist

As noted earlier, the legal relationship of artist to dealer is generally either that of seller to buyer or, far more commonly, that of consignor to consignee. In the case of the latter, we reiterate that the relationship should be memorialized in writing. An artist-dealer agreement should be distinguished from a consignment contract. An artist-dealer agreement defines the parameters of the dealer's representation of the artist and addresses all salient aspects of the relationship, such as territory, duration, exclusivity, payment, dealer's commissions, copyright, shipping, title, and termination. A consignment contract to be used with the artist-dealer agreement need only be a one-page form: It should refer to the artist-dealer agreement and should specify the works consigned, the agreed-on selling price, and the duration of the consignment. The consignment contract should be filled out and signed by both parties each and every time the artist consigns artwork to the dealer. Included at the close of this chapter are models of both the artist–dealer agreement (Appendixes 1-1 and 1-3) and the consignment contract (Appendix 1-2). Some artist–dealer agreement forms and consignment contract forms, such as those developed by various volunteer lawyer organizations throughout the country and the form developed by Artists Equity Association, Inc., are geared to reflect the interests of the artist. Other forms, such as those prepared and used by the major galleries, reflect the interests of the dealer.

The following checklist of issues that most frequently arise between artist and gallery is by no means exhaustive, nor do all these issues arise in every negotiation. Many of the issues are of mutual concern, some speak mainly to the artist, and others address largely the gallery. Negotiation, compromise, and an insightful view as to where problems may arise play pivotal roles in the successful conclusion of an agreement between artist and dealer.

1. *Contracting Parties.* An agency relationship to deal in an artist's work normally terminates on the artist's death.[59] If the gallery is to have any right to deal in the artist's work after his death, that right should be clearly set forth in the artist–dealer agreement with a clause that makes the agreement binding on the artist's heirs, executors, and assigns. The applicable state law should then be checked to ensure that the covenant is enforceable. As of this writing, no case in art law in any state deals specifically with this issue, but analogous cases in New York consider guaranty agreements and leases that contain similar clauses. Such cases indicate that when an agency is coupled with an interest, the agency relationship does not terminate on the death of the principal; rather, the decedent's estate replaces the principal in the agency relationship.[60] Like a guaranty or lease, an artist–dealer agreement addresses the dealer's continual efforts to benefit the artist; until the dealer is successful in selling the artist's work, the dealer does not benefit. Therefore, in New York at least, it is prudent to assume that inclusion in an agreement of language binding an artist's heirs, executors, and assigns will effectively bind them.

If the artist creates works of art through a corporation, a specific provision as to when the agency relationship terminates must be included, since the artist's corporation does not automatically terminate on the death of the artist. In addition, the legal entity of the gallery should be specified.

2. *Limited (Exclusive) Agency.* The artist-dealer agreement should contain a provision that establishes the principal-agent relationship between the artist and the gallery, with the artist being the principal and the gallery being the agent. Such a provision calls forth the fiduciary responsibility of the gallery to the artist within the context of their relationship; the gallery has a legal obligation to act only in the artist's interest and to forgo all personal advantage aside from the agreed compensation for its services as agent.

The agreement should address the manner and the extent of exclusivity, if any, that the gallery has in dealing in the artist's work. If the gallery has no exclusivity, the agreement should address what priority, if any, vis-à-vis other parties the gallery has in making selections from the artist's work.

If the gallery does have exclusivity, the issue must be addressed territorially; perhaps the gallery's exclusive right is limited to a particular geographic area. The exclusivity must also be addressed in terms of the type of work consigned. On occasion, an artist may wish to appoint one gallery as the agent for sculpture, another gallery as the agent for drawings or paintings, and still a third gallery as the agent for graphics. The exclusivity must also be addressed in terms of its nature. Does the gallery have merely an exclusive agency, or does it have an exclusive power to sell? (See pages 9–10.) Whichever is the case, the personal relationship between artist and dealer makes it advisable to anticipate and address in the agreement these further issues:

- The extent of the artist's studio sales, if any, that are permitted

- Whether the gallery should be paid a commission on the artist's studio sales and, if so, whether the commission should be at a lower rate, since the work was not subject to the gallery's effort and overhead expense

- Whether studio sales not exceeding a specified maximum amount should be exempt from gallery commissions

- Whether sales of particular types of works or sales to family and friends should be exempt from gallery commissions or, at least, subject to a lower than usual gallery commission

- The extent of barter transactions, if any, that the artist is permitted and whether barter transactions shall be exempt from gallery commissions or subject to full or lower than usual gallery commissions

- The extent, if any, of charitable and other gifts that the artist is permitted to make and whether those transactions shall be exempt from or subject to full or lower than usual gallery commissions

- Whether the gallery is entitled to a full or lower than usual commission or no commission at all if a gallery customer or a party unrelated to the gallery directly commissions the artist to create a work

Moreover, regardless of whether a gallery has any exclusivity to deal in an artist's work, the agreement may address the question of whether the gallery should receive a courtesy credit on loans of the artist's work.

3. *Duration.* The length of the term of consignment should be specified. The term may end on a date certain, or it may be contingent on, for example, the number or dollar value of the sales made by the gallery or on the artist's productivity. If there are any options to extend the term, those options should be included in the agreement.

The artist should give serious consideration to the duration of his initial term of consignment. A new artist may find it detrimental to be tied too long to a single gallery. However, the gallery needs the association with the artist to be lengthy enough to provide it with the proper incentive to promote the artist's works and to benefit from the artist's increased (it is hoped) reputation over the years. Most galleries want to retain the artist at least through two exhibitions of his work.

4. *Scope and Description of Work.* The works consigned should be described as specifically as possible. That includes listing the media of all the works and addressing the issue of availability of the artist's past and future work for sale by the gallery. The gallery may wish to in-

clude a provision that continuation of the contract or, say, regular monthly payments to the artist must be conditioned on the artist's creating and providing the gallery with a reasonable number of new works throughout the term of the agreement.

5. *Territory of Consignment.* Just as the territory of exclusivity should be delineated, the territory of representation should be specified. For example, an artist may engage a gallery in New York to represent his works throughout the eastern section of the United States and may simultaneously engage a gallery in Los Angeles to represent such works throughout the western section of the United States.

6. *Selling Prices.* The agreement should make provision for the initial setting of prices, which are generally jointly established by the artist and the gallery. In addition, the agreement should provide for a periodic review of prices in light of changes in the artist's reputation and the condition of the art market. Also to be considered is the matter of discounts. It is customary for galleries to give discounts to certain classes of purchasers, such as museums, architects, interior decorators, and, at times, other artists, certain collectors, and other galleries. Discounts to such purchasers are beneficial to both the artist and the gallery, as they encourage the sale of the artist's work to buyers in a position to promote the work's exposure. The agreement should specifically identify those classes of purchasers entitled to a discount and the percentage of discount those purchasers shall receive. Alternatively, the agreement may specify the maximum amount of any discount the gallery may give without consulting the artist, or the agreement may require the gallery to consult the artist before any discount is given. A discount of 10% to 20% is customary, but the gallery may request authority in the contract to grant still larger discounts to certain preferred buyers.

A gallery may also seek the right to make outright purchases from the artist at a discount. In that case, the artist should seek to keep the discount at a minimum or to limit the number of outright purchases permitted the gallery during the term of the agreement; after all, the artist stands to gain little from any increase in value in the works sold outright to the gallery and stands to lose much if the gallery, as seller, is positioned as a direct competitor. The artist also wants to keep the gallery from selecting what may be the artist's best work to inventory against a time when that work has increased in value.

The agreement should also make provision for negotiation of the price of works, if any, commissioned directly by the gallery or by a customer of the gallery. And the agreement may address the issue of the right, if any, of the gallery to rent a work of art in lieu of or in addition to the right to sell it. As a practical matter, in a consignment arrangement the right to rent a work does not exist unless it is specifically provided for, since the dealer is under a fiduciary duty to sell the works of art.

7. *Gallery Commission.* This is one of the key provisions of the agreement, as it sets forth how much of the purchase price is retained by the gallery and how much goes to the artist. Gallery commissions can range from 25% to 60%, with commissions averaging between 33% and 50%. The agreement should specify the percentage of the gallery commission and can even provide that the commission is subject to periodic review by both parties. Generally, the best-known galleries obtain the highest commissions. However, an artist with a well-established reputation whose works have a known market and command high prices can usually negotiate a more favorable—that is, lower—commission rate. In any event, when endeavoring to arrive at a fair commission, an artist should consider, among other factors, how aggressively a gallery will promote his work.

8. *Computation of Gallery Commission: Net Price Method.* Under this arrangement, the artist, with respect to each work, designates the price that must be paid net to the artist, and the gallery retains any sales proceeds in excess of that figure. Provision should be made for an accelerated review of the net prices set by the artist in the event of a rapidly changing market. Moreover, here, as in the method described below, the effect of discounts and returns must be considered in describing the manner of computing commissions.

9. *Computation of Gallery Commission: Percentage of Sales Price.* Under this more common method of computation, the gallery, with respect to each sale of the artist's work, receives a commission in an

amount equal to an agreed-on percentage of the sale proceeds. If the production of the works has been of significant expense to the artist, as in the cases of sculpture involving costly materials and foundry work and of graphics involving printer's expenses, the commission is generally computed solely on the amounts in excess of the artist's direct costs. Under that arrangement, the artist supplies the gallery with a statement of direct costs for each work of art before a price is set and the work is placed on sale.

10. *Payments to Artist.* An artist is customarily paid by the gallery on either a monthly or a quarterly basis. The agreement should specify the interval and the time within which payments must be made, as well as the amount of the payments and the currency in which the payments will be made. Special provision may be made for the timing of payments when an installment sale to a customer is involved.

The artist may wish to be paid an advance on commissions on entering into the agreement. If so, that arrangement should be included in the agreement, along with the amount of the advance. The agreement should then address the following issues: the effect of money due the artist from sales on the amounts to be advanced; when, if at all, the advance is repayable to the gallery if a sufficient number of works are not sold; whether the advance is repayable by the artist with future work and, if so, how and when the work is selected and the process of its valuation for purposes of repayment.

If the artist intends to use a royalty reservation agreement—that is, an agreement in which the artist retains certain residual rights to the artwork sold—he should require the gallery to obtain the purchaser's execution of such an agreement. (See discussion of resale rights in chapter 12.) Also, when such a royalty reservation agreement is used, the artist-dealer agreement should provide that the gallery furnish the artist with the names and addresses of the purchasers of the works so that the artist can monitor subsequent resales. That provision may disturb the gallery, however, since it could place the artist in the role of direct competitor. Nevertheless, that information should always be given in California, under whose laws artists, in certain cases, receive royalty payments on the resale of their works.[61]

A related question arising from the use of the royalty agreement or from the existence of royalty legislation that should be addressed by both parties is whether the gallery is contractually entitled to receive any portion of any royalty payments accruing to the artist from subsequent sales of the artwork. From the artist's standpoint and regardless of whether he uses a royalty reservation agreement, it is always a good idea to require the gallery to furnish the name, address, and telephone number of each purchaser. Doing so enables the artist to verify with the purchaser the price paid for a work of art, enables the artist to keep a mailing list of purchasers in case his relationship with the gallery terminates, and helps shield the artist from incurring liability for a dealer's possibly fraudulent actions, as exemplified by *Goldman v. Barnett*,[62] discussed on pages 614–617.

11. *Crating and Shipping.* The agreement should designate which party assumes the costs for crating and shipping the artist's work between the gallery and the artist's studio or storage facility. On some occasions the parties share the costs. Some factors to consider in determining responsibility for the costs are the location of the studio or storage facility in relation to the gallery, whether the works must be crated and shipped from other locations, and the scale of the works to be crated and shipped. For example, the shipping of a Henry Moore or David Smith sculpture can be a major expense because of the sculpture's size and weight.[63]

12. *Storage.* If the works require storage during the time of the consignment, the party responsible for paying the storage fees should be designated, as should the location of the storage facility. Moreover, the parties should agree on the extent of access to the facility allowed to the artist.

13. *Insurance.* No law expressly requires an art gallery to maintain insurance. Because insurance is a major expense, some galleries do without it. However, in the agreement the artist should require that his gallery maintain insurance. Generally, galleries that do so insure consigned works at between 40% and 70% of the sales price. Although the artist should, ideally, be named on the policy as the beneficiary in case of a claim, that is not always possible, since the blanket insurance policy maintained by the gallery may cover artwork con-

signed by a constantly changing list of numerous artists. When work is consigned by an artist to a gallery, the work is still owned by the artist. Therefore, the consignment agreement should specify who is entitled to the insurance proceeds. The gallery may insure the work for only a percentage of the sales price because it owes the artist only a percentage of the sales price (fair market value) of the work. The artist-dealer agreement should set forth the amount of coverage by the gallery and should make clear that both the artist and the gallery agree as to the amount payable to the artist in the case of a loss. (See page 44.)

The artist may also want the agreement to specify where the works are insured. For example, are the works insured while in transit to and from the gallery's place of business, and are they insured while on loan to locations outside the gallery's place of business? The artist should attempt to have the gallery insure the works from the moment they leave the artist's studio to the moment they are sold or returned to the studio. To make sure that the policy is not unilaterally canceled or revised by the gallery, the artist should request both a certificate of insurance setting forth the policy's terms and conditions and written notification of any change of terms. In addition, the artist should secure his own coverage for those situations in which the works are not covered by the gallery's policy.

14. *Framing.* If applicable, the contract may address the following matters: which of the parties shall bear the initial burden of framing expense with, perhaps, a cap on such expenditure; the amount of artwork to be framed; the specifications of the framing; the effect of the framing expense on works sold; and the ownership at the end of the agreement term of the frames of unsold works.

15. *Promotion.* The parties may want the agreement to specify the degree of marketing activity and promotion expected of the gallery in connection with exhibitions of the artist's work. That activity includes the production and preparation of catalogs, photographs of the artist and his work, biographical material, and other advertising and promotional matter.

The agreement may clarify the number and the type of promotional items, such as catalogs and photographs, to be produced for each exhibition and may specify which party shall assume the expenses of production. Ownership and control of each promotional item must also be made clear. In addition, the gallery may want the right to use and publish the name, the likeness, and the biography of the artist for promotional purposes. The artist may want the right to review all such material.

16. *Artistic Control.* The artist may want the agreement to indicate the degree of control, if any, held by the artist in connection with the inclusion of his consigned work in gallery group exhibitions and in other exhibitions. That control is important, as it permits the artist to withdraw works from an exhibition that is not appropriate for displaying his work. In addition, the artist may want to require the gallery to consult with the artist before hanging any exhibition. Further, if the artist is concerned that the work may fall into inappropriate or ill-meaning hands, the artist may want a contractual grant of a veto over purchasers of his work.

17. *Gallery Exhibitions.* The agreement should clearly indicate the number of solo and group exhibitions (perhaps pending the artist's consent) that the gallery is required to hold. As to each exhibition, the parties may wish to address the issues of the date, duration, space allocated to the artist's work, and selection of works to be shown. The contract may also deal with the following matters as needed:

- Control over installation
- Expenses of partitions and pedestals
- Scope and expense of opening-night events
- The artist's availability for those opening events
- Benefit exhibitions and the artist's availability
- Scope and expense of announcements of exhibitions and other mailings
- Disposition of the proceeds from the sale of exhibition catalogs

18. *Sales Tax.* The parties should designate who is responsible for the collection and the payment of any applicable sales tax. The artist

should require the gallery to collect and pay the taxes and to indemnify the artist against any liability for the taxes.

19. *Damage to or Loss or Deterioration of Consigned Works.* Some states impose absolute liability on the gallery in the event of damage to or loss of artworks consigned by artists. Moreover, some state courts view the artist as incurring a lost-opportunity cost, entitling the artist not only to the amount that he would have received had the work been sold but also to the entire fair market value of the work (even though insurance proceeds covered only a portion of the consignment value), as well as future losses from potential appreciation of the work. (See discussion of this issue on pages 44–47.) In the absence of such state legislation (or where such state legislation permits the dealer to contract away absolute liability), the artist-dealer agreement should state who is responsible for any loss, deterioration, or damage to the consigned works and when that responsibility begins. The agreement may further address, in the event of damage or deterioration, the selection of the restorer, the expense of outside restoration, compensation for any restoration performed by the artist, the artist's right to inspect the restoration, and the financial treatment of total and of partial losses.

20. *Reproduction Rights.* The agreement may address copyright notice. Although copyright notice requirements for works publicly distributed on or after March 1, 1989, are permissive, rather than mandatory, we strongly recommend the continued affixation of a copyright notice to created works to defeat an infringer's defense of innocent infringement asserted in mitigation of actual or statutory damages. (See discussion of copyright in chapter 10.) The copyright notice may be placed on the back of a painting or may be placed on other works in such a manner that it does not interfere aesthetically with the appearance or the appreciation of the work itself. Alternatively or in addition, the agreement may, as appropriate, require the gallery to affix a copyright notice on any reproduction or image of the consigned work, such as a promotional brochure prepared by the gallery.

The agreement may also address the following issues: who has control over the right to reproduce the image of the consigned work before sale; what reproduction rights, if any, will be retained by the rights holder after the transfer or the sale of the artwork; and what portion, if any, of the copyright will be transferred on the sale or the transfer of the artwork itself.

21. *Loans and Displays.* The artist may wish to require the dealer to impose certain exhibition obligations on the purchaser, such as making the artwork available for display in museum shows. The artist may require the dealer to limit the purchaser in the number of times a piece of art can be loaned and the duration of each loan. In addition, the artist may wish to exercise some censorship over the occasions on which the work is exhibited. As a practical matter, however, such rights are of limited application and may have a negative effect on the fair market value of the work.

22. *Warranties of and Indemnification by the Artist.* The gallery may want the artist to warrant that the works are original creations and that they do not impinge on any personal or property rights of third parties. Clearly, a gallery does not want to be involved in litigation brought by a third party because of an alleged invasion of privacy or copyright infringement resulting from the exhibition or the sale of a work. Because of the gallery's potentially great liability to a purchaser in the event that the gallery is not in a position to convey good title to a purchaser, the gallery may want the artist to warrant that he has good and unencumbered title to the consigned works. The gallery may also want to be indemnified and held harmless by the artist for breach by the artist of any warranties made.

23. *Warranties of and Indemnification by the Dealer.* In the wake of *Goldman v. Barnett* (see pages 614–617), the artist may want the dealer to warrant that with respect to their relationship the dealer will act solely within the scope of his agency and, specifically, will make no false representations to third parties as to the value of any of the artist's work and will furnish no appraisals to third parties likely to mislead such parties as to the value of any of the artist's work. The artist may also want to be indemnified and held harmless by the dealer for breach by the dealer of any warranties made.

24. *Artist's Right of Accounting.* It is in the artist's interest for the agreement to designate the frequency with which he will be entitled

to a full accounting of money paid and money due from the gallery. The agreement should specify the degree of completeness required in the accounting and, in addition, should afford the artist or the artist's designated representative the right to inspect all gallery books and records relating to the sale of the artist's works.

In addition, the artist may require the gallery to deliver a complete statement of inventory at regular periodic intervals, including all or some of the following information: (1) an enumeration of the particular artworks sold and the dates, amounts, and terms of each sale (that is, whether cash, barter, exchange, credit, or partial payment) and (2) a listing of all unsold artworks, their locations, and whether, if in the possession of the gallery, those works are currently being displayed and, if so, for what length of time.

25. *Billing and Terms of Sale.* If sales on an installment basis seem likely, the agreement may address the following issues: allocation of payments between the artist and the gallery, allocation of interest payments between the artist and the gallery, qualified installment sales for tax purposes, and the gallery's responsibility to file a financing statement under the U.C.C. (See chapter 2.)

With respect to any purchases, installment or not, the agreement may name the party responsible for determining the creditworthiness of any potential purchaser and which party shall bear the risk of loss if the purchaser defaults.

For those occasions where a buyer may purchase artwork from a gallery using, as currency, works by other artists accepted by the gallery, the contract may address the issues of the valuation of those works, the procedure whereby exchanges (trading up) can occur, and returns.

The agreement may provide for duplicate statements to be sent to the artist and the gallery with respect to framing, packing, shipping, and other charges.

26. *Status of Consigned Artworks and Sales Proceeds.* The agreement may confirm that ownership of the works is vested in the artist, pending sale. With respect to each work of the artist, the gallery should grant to the artist a security interest that shall vest until the sale is completed, whereupon the proceeds (minus the gallery's com-

mission) are held in trust for the artist. The gallery should authorize the artist to file a Form UCC-1 (the signature of the gallery is not required) evidencing the security interest, *and* the gallery should agree to notify its general bank creditor of the artist's security interest. In those states where artist-dealer consignment statutes have either not been adopted or have been adopted but drafted with limited skill[64] (see discussion on pages 40–43), consigned works may be subject to claims of the dealer's creditors and, therefore, perfection of the artist's security interest is essential. The agreement may also highlight the fiduciary nature of the relationship between the artist and the dealer and designate the proceeds from the sale of the consigned work as trust funds for the benefit of the artist. Further, where an artist-dealer consignment statute is in effect, the agreement may address any waiver by the artist of his rights to the extent permitted by that statute.

The gallery may wish to reserve the right to purchase the consigned works for the minimum designated sales price or, in the case of a "net-price" arrangement, for the net price. If so, that right should be specifically provided for in the agreement.[65] Even if the artist grants such a right to the gallery, the artist-dealer consignment law in a number of states, including New York[66] and California,[67] requires the dealer to fully disclose relevant information concerning the purchase to the artist, and the artist's waiver, where permitted,[68] and consent should be obtained at the time of the gallery's purchase.

A gallery may wish to reserve a lien on the consigned works for any amount—such as advances, storage charges, or freight costs—for which the artist may be contractually responsible.[69]

27. *Artist's Retention of Works.* The artist may reserve the right to retain such works as the artist shall determine.

28. *Arbitration.* If a reasonable arbitration arrangement can be agreed to by the parties, the gallery and the artist may wish to include an arbitration provision in the agreement in the event of future disputes. The American Arbitration Association now has art experts on whom it can draw if so required.

29. *Assignment.* Because the relationship between artist and gallery is often very personal, the artist may want the agreement to pro-

vide that the gallery may not transfer its responsibilities or rights under the agreement to a third party, at least not without the artist's prior written consent.

30. *Termination.* The agreement should have a clause citing the circumstances under which the agreement can be terminated. The clause should refer to any other termination provisions in the agreement, and the circumstances may include death, disablement, involuntary bankruptcy, and dissolution. If one party wishes to be released from the agreement before the normal termination date, language could be used permitting each party to terminate the agreement on, for example, sixty days' written notice to the other party, thus allowing for an orderly termination of the relationship on fairly short notice.

In addition, the agreement may provide, in the event of termination, for the gallery within a certain time to conclude its sale of the artist's works, settle the artist's account, transfer to the artist the balance of the money due, return all the artist's works currently in the gallery's possession, and allow the artist access to all photographs, transparencies, catalogs, and other materials relating to the artist or the artwork.

State Statutes on Consignment

To date, thirty-one states have enacted legislation governing the consignment of artwork for exhibition or sale.[70] The passage of those laws was fueled by concern about the inadequacy of civil and criminal law remedies for misappropriation of sale proceeds or consigned property and about certain abusive practices.

For example, some dealers attempt to undermine the principal-agent relationship between artist and dealer and the fiduciary obligations inherent in that relationship by means of disguised purchase agreements and contractual waivers. Under those circumstances, the relationship on its face resembles that of debtor and creditor, and often the artist's only remedy is a civil action for contractual amounts due if the dealer refuses to pay the artist. If the artist is reluctant to sue, the dishonest dealer may be in a position to wrongfully retain artwork or the artist's share of the sale proceeds.

That sort of victimization of the artist in New York City during the early 1960s gave rise to the passage of artist-dealer consignment legislation in New York in 1966. By clarifying the fiduciary nature of the consignment arrangement in the artist-dealer relationship, the New York statute laid the foundation for the application of criminal sanctions for misappropriation of the artist-consignor's property. In the ensuing years, thirty other states enacted art consignment legislation, many using New York's statute as a model.

Consignment Statutes in General

At the core of most artist-dealer consignment statutes is the delineation of the fiduciary nature of the relationship. Most of the statutes are based on the following premises: Unless a work has been delivered to a dealer pursuant to an outright sale or the artist has received full compensation for the work, it is a delivery on consignment; and on delivery of a consigned work, the dealer is the agent of the artist, the work delivered is trust property, and the sale proceeds are trust funds held for the benefit of the artist. Since many artists do not bother with a written consignment agreement, the statutes serve to protect the artist. A few statutes—Michigan's and Connecticut's, for example—extend to the nonartist consignor the benefits of the same fiduciary relationship with the dealer as is enjoyed by the artist delivering to the dealer a work of his own.

Consignment Statutes and the U.C.C.

An area of significant conflict between state consignment statutes and the U.C.C. involves the rights of the gallery's creditors as opposed to the rights of the artist-consignor. In the absence of a state consignment statute, a consigned artwork or the proceeds from its sale may be subject to the claims of creditors of the consignee-gallery. That is because the law ordinarily governing that issue is now section 9-102(a)(20) of the U.C.C., which provides that consigned goods are subject to the claims of creditors of the consignee, even when title is reserved, unless the consignor files a financing statement perfecting the consignor's security interest. If no financing statement is filed by the consignor, a creditor of the consignee gallery is protected, but only if the gallery is not generally known by its creditors to be substantially engaged in selling goods of others.

Prior to July 1, 2001, consignments were governed by section 2-326(3) of the U.C.C. and were subject to the claims of the consignee's creditors, unless the transaction was evidenced by a sign giving notice of consignment status; the consignee was generally known by its creditors as selling consigned goods; or the consignor filed a financing statement against the consignee. (See discussion in chapter 2, beginning on page 151, where these provisions are discussed in detail.)

A major purpose of the state artist-dealer consignment statutes is to provide a safe harbor for the artist against the claims of a dealer's creditors. The purpose of such a statute is undermined if artwork consigned by the artist to the gallery is subject to the claims of the creditors of the consignee-gallery in the event that the gallery files for bankruptcy. Some state statutes, such as that of New York,[71] do adequately grant automatic protection to the artist-consignor against the claims of a dealer-consignee's creditors. The New York statute, in explicitly exempting the artist-dealer relationship from the effect of former section 2-326(3) and current section 9-102(a)(20) of the U.C.C., intended to give artists a statutory claim on their consigned works of art that is superior to any other claim.[72] Since the consignment is outside the provisions of the U.C.C., the relationship between the artist and the gallery is more in the nature of a true consignment—that is, an agency and bailment. Therefore, the gallery has no ownership or interest in the consigned works of art that can allow a trustee in bankruptcy to claim title to the consigned artwork.[73]

In one of the latest legal pronouncements on artist-dealer relationships, a New York court held in *Zucker v. Hirschl & Adler Galleries*[74] that the New York Arts and Cultural Affairs Law not only provides a safe harbor for an artist's consigned works as against a dealer's creditors but also bars a gallery from using an artist's paintings it has accepted to sell on consignment as a security interest.

The defendants, Hirschl Galleries, Inc., and Adler Modern Inc., had periodically given advances to plaintiff-artist Joseph Zucker totaling $129,000. The gallery used Zucker's 50% share of the profits generated by the sales of his work to repay itself for the advances, but $36,322 of the advance payments were still outstanding when the artist terminated his representation by the gallery. The plaintiff sought recovery for several works of art delivered to the gallery on consignment, but the gallery refused to return them, asserting a security interest in the works against the artist's debts to the gallery.

In its defense, the gallery contended that the relevant statutory provision, the New York Arts and Cultural Affairs Law, section 12.01, should have read as follows:

> no such trust property or trust funds shall be subject or subordinate to any claims, liens or security interest of any kind or nature whatsoever *of the consignee's creditors*,[75]

adding the italicized words to the actual language of the law. The gallery based its revision on the assertion that the law was intended to "address the very specific problem created by seizure of innocent artists' consigned works by creditors of the art dealers"[76] and that it was not the legislature's intention to create special protection for artists who default on debts. The judge rejected the gallery's contention, finding that the statute was clear and unambiguous in its plain meaning, allowing for no contrary reading based on the legislative history. The judge directed the gallery to return the artworks to Zucker.[77]

A number of other state statutes provide the artist-consignor with far less effective or extensive protection than does the New York statute. For example, Florida[78] and Connecticut[79] require the artist to comply with legal procedures similar to those specified in the U.C.C. That compliance requirement seems to obviate a basic purpose of a state artist consignment statute: "to secure the rights of the artist to his work without requiring the artist to comply with legal procedures as formal as those specified in the UCC."[80]

In Florida,[81] for example, a local artist consigned sixteen works to a local dealer, who displayed the works at a local restaurant, promising the restaurant owner a percentage of the proceeds of any works sold. Subsequently, the dealer borrowed money from the restaurant owner and used the sixteen works of art as collateral; the transaction gave rise to a security interest in the artworks in favor of the restaurant owner. Sometime later, the art dealer disappeared, and the works were discovered at the restaurant. The artist demanded their return and was refused. He sued for recovery and lost.

As it happened, Florida had an artwork consignment statute that explicitly favored the artist's interests over the claims of the art dealer's creditors, the U.C.C. notwithstanding. But the consignment law was not operational; it required for effectiveness either that a label be affixed to the artwork indicating that the work is being sold subject to a consignment contract or that a notice be given by the consignee's place of business that such artwork is being sold subject to a consignment contract. Neither precondition had been met, so the restaurant owner, not the artist, had first claim on the artwork.

A number of other state statutes require the consignment agreement between the artist and the dealer to be in writing before protection is accorded the artist.[82] Still other statutes lack any language expressly exempting former section 2-326(3) or current section 9-102(a)(20) of the U.C.C. or related Code provisions.[83] Since case law supports section 1-104 of the U.C.C., which provides that the Code will prevail over subsequent conflicting legislation, courts will attempt to harmonize the Code and state consignment statutes that lack *specific* exemption language. If a court is unable to do so, it will find that the Code governs.[84] Therefore, unless a state consignment statute contains language specifically exempting the applicable provisions of the U.C.C. or the Code itself, an artist-consignor is well advised to do what an artist-consignor should do in those states that have no artist-dealer consignment legislation: Comply with the filing provisions of article 9 of the U.C.C.[85] and give written notification of the filing to any prior secured parties of the consignee-gallery.[86] The consignment contract forms at the end of this chapter (Appendixes 1-1 and 1-3) both reserve a security interest.

Risk of Loss or Damage

The U.C.C. may also come into play with respect to the issue of which party, the artist or the dealer, bears the risk of loss for works damaged or stolen while in the dealer's possession. Under the general rule of liability established in section 2-327(2)(b) of the U.C.C., the return of the goods is at the buyer's (the dealer's) risk. The statutes of California[87] and Illinois,[88] as well as the statutes of several other states,[89] are consistent with that section of the U.C.C.—that is, a burden is placed on the dealer either through negligence or strict liability. Artists have brought successful suit against dealers under such state consignment statutes. A California dealer, for example, was required to pay the plaintiff-artist the fair market value of nine of the plaintiff's paintings that had been destroyed by a fire in the dealer's gallery, even though the written consignment agreement between the parties divided the sales proceeds on a sixty-forty basis.[90] In another example, an artist's widow in Illinois successfully sued a local gallery for the fair market value of 385 artworks that were destroyed in a gallery fire. She was also able to sue for conversion of insurance proceeds.[91] Other state statutes, however, such as that of New York,[92] are silent on the matter.

When a statute is silent about liability for loss or damage, it is questionable which of the two parties, the consignor or the dealer, bears the risk of loss of or damage to the consigned work—that is, whether the U.C.C. or the usual laws of principal and agency govern. If the usual laws govern, the risk of loss is borne by the consignor unless the dealer was grossly negligent.[93] Every artist consigning a work of art to a dealer should require the dealer to have insurance covering any loss in an amount at least equal to the amount due the artist if the work of art had been sold.

Some recent New York cases, all from the Appellate Division, First Department, shed additional light on the measure of damages where an artist's works are damaged or destroyed. In *Swain v. 383 West Broadway Corp.*,[94] an artist whose paintings were destroyed when a steam pipe burst in a storage area of a building, sued the building for negligence. In a jury trial in the New York State Supreme Court, a judgment was entered awarding the artist damages in the amount of $462,268—what the court directed to be the full fair market value of the works of art destroyed. On appeal, the Appellate Division remanded the case for a new trial solely on the issue of damages. The appellate court felt that since art galleries charge artists commissions ranging from 25% to 50% of the selling price, the award went beyond making the artist whole and amounted to a windfall for the artist. The case was settled before the New York Court of Appeals was heard on this issue.

The Appellate Division took a different approach in *Indemnity Insurance Co. of North America v. Art Students League*.[95] In that case, the owner of a painting received the full fair market value of the stolen work, defeating the argument that the gallery, where the artwork was consigned, was entitled to its contractual share of the value of the work. The court held that the gallery had only a conditional interest in the painting that was contingent on the sale of the painting. Since there was no sale, the gallery was not entitled to a share of the fair market value. This holding directly contradicts the holding in *Swain*.

Swain was again contradicted in *Wool v. Ayres*.[96] In *Wool*, approximately 160 artworks (mostly on paper) were destroyed in a fire attributed to defendant's negligence. Plaintiff, the artist, was awarded the sum of $996,950. On appeal, defendant argued that the *Swain* rule should be applied and that the judgment should be reduced as a matter of law by the selling commissions that would have been paid to galleries if the works of art had been sold. The court refused to apply *Swain* and ruled that the artist was entitled to the full value of the destroyed works of art. The court held:

> Nor should the award have been reduced by commissions that would have been paid to galleries had the lost artwork been sold, since, according to the proof, the lost artwork was part of plaintiff's private collection and, as such, was not for sale (see, *Indemnity Insurance Company of North America v. Art Student's League*, 225 A.D.2d 398, 640 N.Y.S.2d 8 (N.Y.A.D. 1 Dept., March 19, 1996)).[97]

Further undermining *Swain* is *Nares v. M&W Waterproofing*.[98] Nares was a professional artist who maintained a studio in a building on West 26th Street in New York City. M&W Waterproofing was performing certain maintenance work on the exterior of that building when a spark caused a fire in the studio, setting off the sprinkler system and causing extensive damage to the artist's works. The destruction of the artwork was allegedly due to the negligence of the maintenance company. Nares had an exclusive arrangement with his gallery whereby it received a percentage of the sales price of every artwork of the artist that was sold. The owner of the building argued, based on *Swain*, that at most it should be responsible for the value of the artwork less the commissions that would otherwise be payable to the gallery. The New York State Supreme Court, in deciding a motion before trial to remove the Kasmin Gallery from the case, held that

> [t]he usual measure of damages for the complete destruction or the loss of personal property, where such property has a market value, is its reasonable market value immediately before destruction, less its salvage value. *Aurnou v. Craig*, 184 A.D.2d 1048 (4th Dep't 1992). Here, the court will not apply *Swain* in this case. Based on testimony by Nares, Gallery had only a conditional interest in the artwork and would earn a commission only if the sale of artwork was consummated. This did not occur. A commission agreed upon for the sale of artwork is not binding if the item is destroyed as compared to being sold. See, *Indemnity Insurance Company of North America*, supra.
>
> Nares is entitled to the full market value of his destroyed artwork and Gallery is not a necessary party to this action.[99]

At trial, the jury awarded the artist the full market value of the artworks. The Appellate Division agreed, noting "potential sales commissions are not deductible from the award, and the artist's retention of these works in his studio, unmarketed, as a private collection or legacy for his children, did not diminish their value."[100]

We believe that the correct view is that the measure of damages is the full fair market value of the artwork without any reduction for commissions, since the artist has lost his ability to sell the artworks in the future, whether through a dealer or otherwise, and the artist has suffered a substantial loss to his *oeuvre* as a result of the destruction of a body of work. There should be no reduction for commissions since no sale has taken place.

As to whether the dealer or the prospective buyer bears the risk of loss of a work of art when the sale is on approval, section 2-327(1) of the U.C.C. allocates the risk to the dealer (the seller) until the buyer accepts the artwork.[101]

Reclamation by the Artist

If a dealer sells a consigned work to a bona fide purchaser but fails to pay the artist, the artist-consignor cannot reclaim the work, even if the artist has filed a financing statement. That is because sections 9-315 and 9-320 of the U.C.C. provide that a buyer of consumer goods takes possession free of a security interest even though perfected if the secured party (the artist) authorized the dealer to sell the goods. State consignment statutes do not change that result.[102]

The Artist's Waiver

A question frequently arises as to whether the artist is permitted, in states having consignment statutes, to waive statutory rights by contract. Although a number of states, including California,[103] permit no waiver of rights by the artist, other states do permit limited waivers by the artist. New York's legislation, for example, permits a limited written waiver of that portion of the statute that provides that sales proceeds are trust funds for the benefit of the artist,[104] excluding from the waiver the first $2,500 of proceeds received in any twelve-month period, starting with the date of the waiver. Therefore, in New York a dealer may use a waiver to share the proceeds of installment purchases with the artist, rather than pass along all first payments to the artist and wait for the dealer's share.

COOPERATIVE GALLERIES

Unlike the typical dealer-operated gallery, cooperative galleries are run by artists, usually as joint ventures for the purposes of exhibiting their works and offering them for sale. Generally, cooperative galleries are formed by artists who are experiencing difficulty in obtaining exposure for their works in local commercial galleries. Some such galleries have endeavored to function as tax-exempt entities as a way to reduce overhead costs, but, as a practical matter, tax-exempt status is unavailable if some part of the sales proceeds goes to the individual artists.[105] Moreover, tax-exempt status is usually not necessary, since the cooperative gallery rarely operates at a profit. Cooperative galleries are not always successful, since the lack of business acumen by many artists, when coupled with a creative temperament, can interfere with effective merchandising techniques. Moreover, when the best artists in the cooperative are recognized, they often resent supporting their less fortunate colleagues, and they move on, leaving the cooperative in the hands of unappreciated and unsuccessful artists. Nevertheless, the existence of many cooperative galleries today attests to the hardships that many artists experience in securing commercial representation.

Artists who form a cooperative are advised to formalize the arrangement by a written agreement to avoid future misunderstandings. Among the topics that should be covered are the following:

- Liability for rent and other expenses
- Admission of new members
- Staffing of the gallery
- Types of exhibitions
- Frequency and dates of exhibitions
- Extent of promotional activity
- Sales commissions of the gallery
- Insurance of works
- Public liability insurance

- Monthly dues or fees
- Withdrawal from the venture

Member artists should be aware that their liability to third parties is joint and several. If the artists consider the potential liability (other than liabilities that can be protected against through insurance) to be substantial, they may wish to incorporate the gallery. If the corporation is adequately capitalized and corporate formalities are observed, the members would then be shielded from personal liability for the obligations of the corporation.

THE DEALER'S POTENTIAL TORT
AND CRIMINAL LIABILITIES

The relationship between the artist and the dealer is often fraught with complexities that for the unwary dealer can readily become liabilities.

The dealer should be aware that there is an inherent conflict of interest if he also serves as an artist's business adviser, and the dealer can be held liable for negligence in rendering such advice.[106] If a dealer signs a contract with an artist who is already under contract to another dealer, the dealer may be subject to liability for inducing a breach of contract.[107] Even in the absence of an agreement between an artist and a dealer, a dealer who actively solicits an artist from another dealer may be subject to a lawsuit for interference with advantageous business relations.[108]

Furthermore, under applicable criminal statutes, a dealer can be held jointly liable with the artist for exhibiting work that is obscene,[109] that constitutes a public nuisance,[110] or that displays protected symbols or emblems.[111] And if a work invades the privacy of another person[112] or constitutes a defamation,[113] the dealer can be held civilly liable by the injured party or parties. (If works in an exhibit represent recognizable persons or contain their names, the dealer should consider obtaining releases from those persons.) In displaying a work, both the dealer and the artist may be civilly liable for a violation of moral rights[114] and civilly or criminally liable for an infringement of copyright.[115]

THE ARTIST'S WORK
AS THE SUBJECT OF A BAILMENT

On occasion, an artist may entrust the safekeeping of his art to a bailee for an indefinite period of time. In the event of the death of such a bailee, would the deceased's successor-in-interest be deemed a constructive bailee? When the artist eventually demands the return of the art, how is the artist's demand affected by the statute of limitations? These are some of the issues addressed in the New York case of *Martin v. Briggs*.[116] Here, the renowned American artist Agnes Martin, eighty-five years old at the time, sought to recover possession of more than two dozen of her paintings from defendants Gwen Luce Briggs and Jean Davis, successors-in-possession to their mother, who took sole possession of the paintings on the death of her husband, an original bailee. In 1967, Martin left New York, where, since 1958, she had lived and worked, producing a substantial body of art, most of which had been consigned to galleries for sale. Prior to her departure, Martin entered into an agreement for the storage of her unconsigned paintings with Kim Blood and, as Martin claimed, his wife, Lois Luce Blood, both being artists and acquaintances of Martin. The agreement provided that in exchange for permitting the Bloods to live in her Manhattan loft for the remainder of Agnes's lease, the Bloods would store Agnes's paintings until she demanded their return. The Bloods stored the paintings in Martin's loft for the six months they lived there, after which time they stored the paintings at their house in Sherman, Connecticut. In 1972, Martin visited the Bloods in Sherman and removed some of her paintings, which she then consigned for sale. Later that year, Kim Blood died, and Lois continued to store Martin's art—estimated to have a value of $1.4 million and representing the largest single body of her work in the possession of anyone other than the artist herself. Although Lois had ten to twenty paintings of her own work that she displayed in her house in Sherman, she never showed any of Martin's. In the fall of 1988, Lois became ill. A few months later, Briggs and her husband moved into her house to care for her. In 1990, the Sherman house was sold and Lois moved with Briggs and her husband into a rented house in Rowayton, Connecticut, where the paintings were stored in the basement and where Lois resided until her death in 1991. When Briggs and her husband moved to a subsequent house in Rowayton, Briggs placed the paintings in a storage bin in Norwalk, Connecticut, where they remained until 1995, when Briggs retrieved them and consigned them to Sotheby's. When Sotheby's contacted Martin to authenticate her works, she learned of the daughters' claim to ownership, whereupon she demanded the return of her paintings. When Briggs and Davis refused to honor her claim to her paintings, Martin brought suit.

Daughters Briggs and Davis argued that in 1988, sixteen years after the death of their father, Kim Blood, their mother made a gift to them of the paintings. The paintings, however, were not divided between Briggs and Davis but, instead, were returned to the Sherman house and placed in a storeroom. Even after her mother's death, Briggs made no effort to divide the paintings with her sister, but rather kept them in storage until the consignment to Sotheby's for sale. The daughters argued that Kim Blood was Martin's only bailee and that the statute of limitations for an action seeking the recovery of the paintings began to run in 1972, when he died. It was at that time, they argued, that the paintings were converted by Lois Blood and that Martin's right to demand their return was complete under section 206(a) of the New York Civil Practice Law and Rules.[117] Alternatively, the daughters argued that if an actual demand, as opposed to the right to make a demand, and refusal were required to start the running of the limitations period, then Martin was required to demand return of the paintings within a reasonable time after learning of the bailee's, that is, Kim Blood's, death. The daughters further asserted that the twenty-three-year delay after Kim Blood's death was unreasonable as a matter of law, and therefore laches should bar Martin's claim.

In reversing the state supreme court's dismissal of Martin's complaint on summary judgment, the appellate court noted that

> [i]nstead of reviewing the record to determine whether issues of fact exist, the court itself resolved those issues in finding that Martin's bailment was with Kim Blood alone and that defendants never agreed to or did act as bailees of the paintings. . . . In considering a summary judgment motion, evidence should be analyzed in the light most favorable to the party opposing the motion.[118]

As the court observed, Martin contended that she had entered into a bailment with both Kim and Lois Blood and that by legal implication, the bailment continued after the death of Lois. In the alternative, she argued that if the bailment was solely with Kim Blood, then Lois and, at her death, the two daughters successively acted as constructive bailees. Therefore, as the appellate court observed, an issue of fact exists as to whether the daughters and their mother before them were acting as bailees. If that were the case, Martin's claim would not accrue until the defendants refused her demand for the return of her paintings. Referring to the New York case of *Wichner v. Fortunoff*,[119] which addressed the effect of a bailee's death on a bailment, the appellate court noted that in *Wichner*, the court implicitly ruled that the death of a bailee did not foreclose the issue of a continuing bailment with the bailee's son, even though the son denied that he had ever been a bailee. Applying *Wichner* to the case at hand, the appellate court observed that the lower court, in finding that the original bailment was solely with Kim Blood and that it was terminated upon his death, ignored the legal argument that by her conduct Lois Blood became a constructive bailee after her husband's death and that, similarly, her daughters became constructive bailees after her death. As the court stated:

> A bailment does not necessarily and always . . . depend upon a contractual relation. It is the *element of lawful possession*, however created, and *duty to account for the thing* [italics ours] as the property of another that creates the bailment, regardless of whether such possession is based on contract in the ordinary sense or not.[120]

In examining the evidence, the court noted that after the death of Kim Blood, Lois never acted as though she owned the paintings: For example, she never exhibited them, along with her own paintings, in her house in Sherman, Connecticut, nor did she ever report the tax consequences of the alleged 1988 gift. Instead, her actions were consistent with that of a bailee—as were the actions of her daughters, who stored the art for four years until consigning the pieces to Sotheby's and refusing to return them to Martin.

The defendants, arguing that the death of Kim Blood terminated the bailment, claimed that Martin may not treat the bailment as a continuing one and should have sued to enforce her rights, either in contract or tort. Disagreeing, the court noted that

> [w]hile that may be the rule in a bailment for a specific term, the bailment at issue, under either side's version, was for an indefinite duration. In such a case, absent notice of termination by either of the parties, a bailor is entitled to follow the bailed party into the hands of the bailee's successors.[121]

As to the daughters' statute of limitations defense, the court found that Martin's action was timely. The court noted that in a chattel bailment of indefinite duration, the limitations period does not begin to run against a bailee lawfully in possession until the bailor demands the chattel's return and the demand is refused; that is, at the point of refusal, the conversion accrues. In the case at hand, the defendants refused in June 1995 to return Martin's paintings, and Martin commenced the action in November 1995—a mere five months later.

The daughters then asserted a laches defense: that is, that Martin's claim was time-barred because she unreasonably delayed demanding the return of the paintings, to the detriment of the defendants. The court observed that the defendants may well be able to sustain a defense of laches: Martin's only reason for not demanding the return of the paintings far sooner was forgetfulness. She did, however, contend that she had an express contract with both Bloods and did not learn of Lois's death until after Sotheby's contacted her. The court noted that Martin's delay in asserting her claim may quite possibly have prejudiced the defense of the case at hand—but that this issue could not be determined as a matter of law.

Accordingly, the appellate court reversed the dismissal of the lower court on summary judgment and granted Martin's cross motion for leave to serve an amended complaint against the defendants, such complaint to assert that the defendants were constructive bailees.

Notes to Chapter 1

1. *See* Laurie Ziegler, *The Ties That Bind: The Importance of Artist-Dealer Contracts*, NEW ART EXAMINER, Summer 1993, for an informative article on the artist-dealer relationship.

2. *See, e.g.*, Pushman v. N.Y. Graphic Soc'y, Inc., 287 N.Y. 302, 42 N.E.2d 249 (1942).

3. 17 U.S.C. § 202. See also discussion of copyright in chapter 10.

4. 17 U.S.C. § 204.

5. But note that under Goldman v. Barnett, 793 F. Supp. 28 (D. Mass. 1992), a case ultimately settled in 1992, an argument was made whereby a consigning artist could incur liability for a dealer's acts. This case is further discussed in chapter 7.

6. *See generally* RESTATEMENT (SECOND) OF AGENCY (1958).

7. *Id.* § 13; *see also* Britton v. Ferrin, 171 N.Y. 235, 63 N.E. 954 (1902).

8. RESTATEMENT, *supra* note 6, § 13.

9. *Id.*

10. *Id.* § 379.

11. *Id.* §§ 13, 379.

12. *Id.* § 382.

13. *Id.* § 381.

14. *Id.* § 394.

15. *Id.* §§ 387, 388, 390, 393.

16. *Id.* §§ 399, 407; *see also In re* Estate of Mark Rothko, 84 Misc. 2d 830, 379 N.Y.S.2d 923 (Sur. Ct. 1975), *modified and aff'd*, 56 A.D.2d 499, 392 N.Y.S.2d 870 (1st Dep't), *aff'd*, 43 N.Y.2d 305, 401 N.Y.S.2d 449 (1977), *on remand*, 95 Misc. 2d 492, 407 N.Y.S.2d 954 (Sur. Ct. 1978). The case is discussed at pages 1798–1799.

17. N.Y. PENAL LAW § 155.05.

18. Lazarevic v. Sindin Galleries, Inc., N.Y.L.J., Oct. 27, 1997 at 29.

19. *Id.* The court, in its opinion, cited the long-standing New York Court of Appeals case Brown v. Garey, 267 N.Y. 67 (1935).

20.   U.C.C. § 2-306(2). All states in the United States except for Louisiana have adopted Article 2 of the U.C.C. In addition, Article 2 has been adopted by the District of Columbia, Guam, and the Virgin Islands.

21.   *See* E. BISKIND & C. BARASCH, THE LAW OF REAL ESTATE BROKERS § 67.03 (1969 & Supp. 1983).

22.   *Id.*

23.   *Id.*

24.   *See*, respectively, N.Y. GEN. OBLIG. LAW § 5-701 and CAL. CIV. CODE § 1624 for an enumeration of those types of contracts requiring a writing. *See* Rosenfeld v. Basquiat, 78 F.3d 84 (2d Cir. 1996).

25.   O'Keeffe v. Bry, 456 F. Supp. 822 (S.D.N.Y. 1978). For another case illustrating the importance of finalizing art arrangements in written form, *see* Gordon v. Herstand & Co., 134 A.D.2d 971, 520 N.Y.S.2d 891 (1st Dep't 1987) (between an art consultant and a gallery owner).

26.   N.Y. GEN. OBLIG. LAW § 5-701(a)(1).

27.   Bry cited Crabtree v. Elizabeth Arden Sales Corp., 305 N.Y. 48, 110 N.E.2d 551 (1953), in support of her argument. Conversely, the court noted that *Crabtree*, 305 N.Y. at 55, as well as every other case cited by Bry, permitted the use of a "confluence of memoranda" so long as at least one document existed establishing the basic, underlying contractual commitment. That continues to remain the law in New York. *See* Manala v. Milford Mgmt. Corp., 559 F. Supp. 1000 (S.D.N.Y. 1983).

28.   *See O'Keeffe*, 456 F. Supp. at 829.

29.   *Id.* at 830.

30.   *Id.*

31.   *In re* Estate of Jean-Michel Basquiat, N.Y.L.J., Sept. 3, 1991, at 25 (Sur. Ct. N.Y. County 1991); *see also* ARTNEWSLETTER, Sept. 17, 1991, at 3.

32.   N.Y.L.J., *supra* note 31.

33.   *Id.*

34.   *Id.*

35.   Koeniges v. Woodard, 183 Misc. 2d 347, 702 N.Y.S.2d 781 (2000).

36.   Sonnabend Gallery, Inc. v. Halley, N.Y.L.J. July 14, 1992, at 21, col. 2 (Sup. Ct. N.Y. County 1992).

37.   *Id.*

38.   *See* Ziegler, *supra* note 1.

39.   *See Sonnabend*, N.Y.L.J. July 14, 1992, at 21.

40.   *Id.*

41.   *In re* Friedman, 91 Misc. 2d 201, 397 N.Y.S.2d 561 (Sur. Ct. 1977), *aff'd*, 64 A.D.2d 70, 407 N.Y.S.2d 999 (2d Dep't 1978).

42. Naber v. Steinitz, N.Y.L.J., Jan. 27, 1992, at 24, col. 1 (Sup. Ct. N.Y. County 1992).

43. *Id.*

44. *Id.*

45. *Id.* (citing Ackerman v. Landes, 112 A.D.2d 1081, 493 N.Y.S.2d 59 (1985)).

46. *Id.*

47. *Id.*

48. Hirschfeld v. Margo Feiden Galleries Ltd., Index No. 00/602067, settled, Sept. 29, 2000.

49. *Id.*

50. Wesselmann v. Int'l Images, Inc., 169 Misc. 2d 476, 645 N.Y.S.2d 243 (Sup. Ct. N.Y. County 1996).

51. Wesselmann v. Int'l Images, Inc., 259 A.D.2d 448, 687 N.Y.S.2d 339 (1st Dep't 1999).

52. *Id.*

53. *Friedman*, 407 N.Y.S.2d 999.

54. *See Estate of Mark Rothko*, 84 Misc. 2d 830.

55. N.Y. Arts & Cult. Aff. Law § 12.01.

56. *Id.* § 12.01(1)(b).

57. Among the states that have adopted a consignor-art dealer statute that contains a nonwaiver provision broader than that of New York are Arizona, Arkansas, California, Colorado, Connecticut, Florida, Illinois, Kentucky, Massachusetts, Ohio, and Wisconsin. Iowa's statute contains a nonwaiver provision vis-à-vis the art dealer. For citations of those and consignor-art dealer statutes from other states, see *infra* note 70.

58. Cal. Civ. Code § 1738.8.

59. *See In re* Estate of Franz Kline, N.Y.L.J., Mar. 31, 1964, at 14, cols. 6–7 (N.Y. Sur. Ct. 1964).

60. *See, e.g.*, Schnee v. Jonas Equities, Inc., 109 Misc. 2d 221, 442 N.Y.S.2d 342 (App. Div. 2d Dep't 1981); Rusch Factors v. Sheffler, 58 A.D.2d 557, 396 N.Y.S.2d 374 (2d Dep't 1977).

61. California Resale Royalties Act, Cal. Civ. Code § 986.

62. *Goldman*, 793 F. Supp. 28.

63. In Welliver v. Fed. Express Corp., 737 F. Supp. 205 (S.D.N.Y. 1990), artists responsible for crating and shipping sued common carriers for loss or damage to artworks during transport.

64. For an excellent discussion on the subject, see Mark Marcone, *The U.C.C. and Consignment: Making the Code Safe for Artists and Other "Little Fellows,"* 12 Cardozo Arts & Ent. L.J. 579 (1994).

65. *See Estate of Franz Kline*, N.Y.L.J., Mar. 31, 1964, at 14.

66. N.Y. Arts & Cult. Aff. Law § 12.01.

67. CAL. CIV. CODE § 1738.7.

68. As indicated *supra* in note 57, a number of states have enacted consignor-art dealer statutes containing broad nonwaiver provisions.

69. *See* Sidney Janis Ltd. v. de Kooning, 33 A.D.2d 555, 304 N.Y.S.2d 826 (1st Dep't 1969), *aff'd*, 26 N.Y.2d 910, 258 N.E.2d 396, 310 N.Y.S.2d 97 (1970), in which the court held that a statutory factor's lien did not give a dealer a lien on an artist's works for advances made to the artist in the absence of a contractual provision to that effect.

70. ALASKA STAT. § 45.65.200; ARIZ. REV. STAT. ANN. § 44-1772; ARK. CODE ANN. § 4-73-207; CAL. CIV. CODE § 1738.6; COLO. REV. STAT. § 6-15-102; CONN. GEN. STAT. ANN. § 42-116*l*; FLA. STAT. ANN. § 686.503; GA. CODE ANN. § 10-1-520 to -529; IDAHO CODE § 28-11-102; 815 ILL. COMP. STAT. ANN. 320/2; IOWA CODE ANN. § 556D.2 to .5; KY. REV. STAT. ANN. § 365.855 to .860; LA. REV. STAT. ANN. § 51:2151; MD. CODE ANN., COM. LAW § 11-8A-01 to -04, MASS. ANN. LAWS ch. 104a, §§ 1–6; MICH. COMP. LAWS § 442.311 to .315; MINN. STAT. ANN. § 324.01 to .10; MO. REV. STAT. § 407.900 to .910; MONT. CODE ANN. § 22-2-501 to -503; N.H. REV. STAT. ANN. § 352:3 to :12; N.J. STAT. ANN. § 12A:2-329 to -336; N.M. STAT. ANN. § 56-11-1 to -3; N.Y. ARTS & CULT. AFF. LAW § 12.01; N.C. GEN. STAT. § 25C-1 to -4, 25C-12; OHIO REV. CODE ANN. § 1339.71 to .78; OR. REV. STAT. § 359.200 to .255; 73 PA. CONS. STAT. §§ 2121–30; TENN. CODE ANN. § 47-25-1001 to -1006; TEX. OCC. CODE ANN. § 2101.001 to .003; WASH. REV. CODE § 18.110.010 to .030; § 18.110.900; WIS. STAT. ANN. § 129.01 to .08.

71. *See* N.Y. ARTS & CULT. AFF. LAW § 12.01.

72. *Id*.; see prior law N.Y. ARTS & CULT. AFF. LAW § 11.03(1)(e), now § 12.01, and Memorandum of New York State Senator Roy Goodman, N.Y. 1975 Legis. Ann. 96 (1979).

73. Ludvigh v. Am. Woolen Co., 231 U.S. 522 (1913).

74. Zucker v. Hirschl & Adler Galleries, 170 Misc. 2d 426; 648 N.Y.S. 2d 521 (Sup. Ct. 1996).

75. *Id.*

76. *Id.*

77. *Id.*

78. *See* FLA. STAT. ANN. § 686.503.

79. *See* CONN. GEN. STAT. ANN. § 42-116*l*.

80. *See* Marcone, *supra* note 64, at 590.

81. Shuttie v. Festa Rest., Inc., 566 So. 2d 554 (Fla. Dist. Ct. App. 1990).

82. *See, e.g.*, ARIZ. REV. STAT. ANN. § 44-1775; FLA. STAT. ANN. § 686.503; N.H. REV. STAT. ANN. § 352:7.

83.   *See, e.g.*, CAL. CIV. CODE § 1738.5; IDAHO CODE § 28-11-102; 815 ILL. COMP. STAT. ANN. 320/2.

84.   *See* Marcone, *supra* note 64, at 591. *See In re* White Farm Equip. Co., 63 B.R. 800 (Bankr. N.D. Ill. 1986).

85.   U.C.C. § 9-310(a); See the general discussion on secured transactions in chapter 2 at pages 161–169.

86.   U.C.C. § 9-505 permits a financing statement to be filed that uses the terms "consignor" and "consignee," rather than "secured party" and "debtor."

87.   CAL. CIV. CODE § 1738.8.

88.   815 ILL. COMP. STAT. ANN. 320/2.

89.   *See, e.g.*, the consignment statutes for the states of Alaska, Arkansas, Colorado, Connecticut, Massachusetts, Missouri, Minnesota, Montana, New Hampshire, Oregon, Tennessee, Washington, and Wisconsin, *supra* note 70.

90.   Pelletier v. Eisenberg, 177 Cal. App. 3d 558, 223 Cal. Rptr. 84 (Ct. App. 1986). *See also* Reichman v. Warehouse One, Inc., 173 A.D.2d 250, 569 N.Y.S.2d 452 (N.Y. Ct. App. 1991).

91.   Davis v. Rowe, 1992 U.S. Dist. LEXIS 6914 (N.D. Ill. 1992).

92.   *See* N.Y. ARTS & CULT. AFF. LAW § 12.01.

93.   RESTATEMENT, *supra* note 6, at ch. 13. Under the general law of bailment, which can govern certain situations, such as the loaning of artwork to museums and other institutions, the risk of loss in many cases is borne by the bailor (lender). See the summary of the *Colburn* and *Gardini* cases and the general discussion of bailment in chapter 16 at page 1873 *et seq.*

94.   Swain v. 383 W. Broadway Corp., 216 A.D.2d 38, 627 N.Y.S. 2d 393 (1st Dep't 1995).

95.   Indem. Ins. Co. of N. Am. v. Art Students League, 225 A.D.2d 389, 640 N.Y.S.2d 8 (1st Dep't 1996).

96.   Wool v. Ayres, 283 A.D.2d 299, 724 N.Y.S.2d 612 (1st Dep't 2001).

97.   *Id.*

98.   Nares v. M&W Waterproofing, 228 N.Y.L.J. 19 (col. 5), Sept. 4, 2002 (Sup. Ct. N.Y. County 2001), Index No. 12211/99.

99.   *Id.*

100.   Nares v. M&W Waterproofing, 5 A.D.3d 155, 772 N.Y.S.2d 523, 524 (1st Dep't 2004).

101.   U.C.C. § 2-326. Goods delivered primarily for use constitute a "sale on approval," whereas goods delivered primarily for resale constitute a "sale or return."

102.   See the general discussion on secured transactions in chapter 2 at pages 161–169.

103.   *See, e.g.*, the consignment statutes for the states of Arizona, Arkansas, California, Colorado, Connecticut, Ohio, Massachusetts, and Wisconsin, *supra* note 70.

104.   *See* N.Y. ARTS & CULT. AFF. LAW § 12.01.

105.   Rev. Rul. 71-395, 1971-2 C.B. 228. To support its view, the IRS cited Treas. Reg. § 1.501(c)(3)-1(d)(1)(ii). The IRS subsequently affirmed and clarified its position in Rev. Rul. 76-152, 1976-1 C.B.152.

106.   *See* W. KEETON ET AL., PROSSER AND KEETON ON THE LAW OF TORTS § 32, at 185 (5th ed. 1984).

107.   *Id.* § 129, at 979.

108.   *Id.* § 129, at 981.

109.   *See* discussion of obscenity at pages 971–990.

110.   *See* discussion of artwork and public nuisance at pages 947–948.

111.   *See* discussion of emblems and insignia at pages 945–947.

112.   *See* discussion of invasion of privacy at pages 990–1000.

113.   *See* discussion of defamation at pages 929–933.

114.   *See* chapter 11 on moral rights.

115.   *See* discussion of copyright infringement at pages 1125–1134.

116.   Martin v. Briggs, 235 A.D.2d 192, 663 N.Y.S.2d 184 (1st Dep't 1997).

117.   *Id.* at 195, 663 N.Y.S.2d at 186.

118.   *Id.* at 196, 663 N.Y.S.2d at 187.

119.   Wichner v. Fortunoff, 107 A.D.2d 585, 483 N.Y.S.2d 315 (1st Dep't 1985).

120.   *Martin*, 235 A.D.2d at 197, 663 N.Y.S.2d at 187.

121.   *Id.*, 235 A.D.2d at 197, 663 N.Y.S.2d at 188.

Appendix 1-1

Artist Consignment with Security Agreement

AGREEMENT BETWEEN ARTIST AND
_____ GALLERY, INC.

AGREEMENT made as of the _____ day of _____, 20__, between _____, residing at _____, New York, New York, (hereinafter referred to as the "Artist"), and _____ GALLERY, INC., a New York corporation, having an office at _____, New York, New York (hereinafter referred to as the "Gallery").

W I T N E S S E T H:

WHEREAS, the Artist is in the business of creating works of art and the Gallery is in the business of selling works of art; and

WHEREAS, the parties hereto wish to enter into a business relationship for the sale by the Gallery of works of art created by the Artist;

NOW, THEREFORE, in consideration of the premises and of the mutual promises and undertakings set forth below, the parties hereto agree as follows:

1. *Exclusive Agent.* The Artist hereby appoints the Gallery, and the Gallery hereby accepts such appointment, to serve as the exclusive agent and representative of the Artist with respect to works of art created by the Artist (hereinafter sometimes referred to as the "Artist's Works"). The term "Artist's

Works" includes drawings and sculptures but excludes all other artistic creations.

2. *Territory.* The representation covered by this Agreement shall be worldwide.

3. *Term.* This Agreement will commence on _____, 20___, and will continue until _____, 20___. This Agreement will automatically terminate on _____, 20___, unless the parties hereto agree in writing to extend the term of this Agreement.

4. *Sales Prices.* The sales prices of the Artist's Works (hereinafter referred to as "Sales prices") will be set by the Gallery in a written schedule and will be subject to approval by the Artist by [his or her] signing such schedule, which approval will not be unreasonably withheld. A separate Consignment Contract in the form attached hereto will be signed by the Gallery and the Artist for each Artist's Work consigned to the Gallery for sale. The Gallery agrees to immediately inform the Artist of any sale by written memorandum listing the Artist's Work sold, the price, and the name, the address, and the telephone number of the Purchaser. The Gallery may, without notice to the Artist, allow a ten percent (10%) discount from the Sales price of an Artist's Work to a purchaser. No other discount will be allowed unless the Gallery receives the written consent of the Artist.

The Gallery agrees to be responsible for and to collect and pay over any applicable sales taxes due on the sale of the Artist's Works and to indemnify and hold harmless the Artist for any such sales taxes.

5. *Commission to Gallery.* The Gallery will be entitled to receive a commission for the sale of any of the Artist's Works in an amount equal to fifty percent (50%) of the Gallery's receipts from such sale in excess of the Artist's Direct Costs for the work of art sold. The term "Direct Costs" means the Artist's direct out-of-pocket costs actually paid or incurred in creating a particular work of art, including without limitation the cost of materials, fabrication, and labor (other than that of the Artist). The Artist agrees to supply the Gallery with the amount of such Direct Costs for each work of art prior to the time that the work of art is placed on sale with the Gallery and the price thereof set by the Gallery. The commission referred to in this paragraph will be considered earned by the Gallery only when such Direct Costs have been credited to the Artist's Sales Account as described in paragraph 6 below and when the sales proceeds are actually received by the Gallery. The remaining fifty percent (50%) of the sales proceeds in excess of the Artist's Direct Costs will be credited to the Artist's Sales Account as described in paragraph 6 below.

6. *Artist's Sales Account.* The Gallery will maintain an Artist's Sales Account in order to keep a record of money amounts due the Artist from the Gallery. On the sale of any of the Artist's Works and the receipt of the sale proceeds by the Gallery, the Gallery will first credit the Artist's Sales Account with the Direct Costs of the work of art sold. The Gallery will then credit the Artist's Sales Account with fifty percent (50%) of the Gallery's receipts from such sale over such Direct Costs. The Artist, the Artist's attorney, and the Artist's accountant will have the right to inspect the Artist's Sales Account and other books and records of the Gallery relating to the sale of the Artist's Works from time to time during normal business hours upon the Artist's giving the Gallery three (3) days' written notice. The Artist, the Artist's attorney, and the Artist's accountant will maintain in strict confidence all information relating to the Gallery obtained in the course of such inspection.

7. *Payments to Artist.* The Gallery will pay to the Artist on the first day of every month any credit balance in the Artist's Sales Account.

8. *Expenses of Sales.* The Gallery will arrange for or pay for all crating and shipping expenses of the Artist's Works from the Artist's studio or storage facility to the Gallery and from the Gallery to the Artist's studio or storage facility.

The Gallery will keep the Artist's Works insured while in transit or in the Gallery's possession up to an amount not less than that required to pay the Artist the amount the Artist would be entitled to receive if the Artist's Works had been sold at the Sales prices under the terms of this Agreement.

The Gallery will pay for such insurance from the time such Artist's Works leave the Artist's studio or storage facility for delivery to the Gallery until they are returned to the Artist's studio or storage facility or until they are sold and leave the Gallery's possession.

The Gallery will pay all the Gallery's costs and expenses in connection with the sale of the Artist's Works, including without limitation all costs and expenses for all catalogs, photographs, advertising, preview, promotion, and openings, such expenditures to be within the sole discretion of the Gallery.

In order to promote sales and for the purpose of advertisement and promotion, the Gallery will have the right to use and publish the name, the likeness, and the biography of the Artist and to reproduce and distribute material incorporating photographs of the Artist's Works. The Gallery will have the right to sell and retain the proceeds from the sale of catalogs produced by it but will not sell any other items referred to in this paragraph without the prior written approval of the Artist. The Artist will cooperate with the Gallery in such advertising and promotional efforts.

The Gallery agrees that no amount expended by it under this paragraph will be deducted from the amount due the Artist pursuant to the Artist's Sales Account.

9. *Copyright.* All the Artist's Works will be copyrighted by the Artist. The Gallery agrees to inform all purchasers that the copyright to the Artist's Works is not being transferred by the Artist.

10. *Loans.* The Gallery agrees to use its best efforts to have individual Purchasers agree to lend, at the request of the Artist, any of the Artist's Works to museum shows or other exhibitions of the Artist's Works from time to time, such loans to be of short duration and to be made infrequently.

11. *Gifts and Exchanges.* The Artist may from time to time make a reasonable number of gifts of the Artist's Works to anyone of the Artist's choice. The Artist may also make a reasonable number of exchanges of the Artist's Works for services or with other artists. The Artist will promptly notify the Gallery about any such gift or exchange and provide sufficient information to permit the Gallery to keep accurate records of the Artist's Works.

12. *Shows.* During the period of this Agreement, the Gallery will arrange for at least one exhibition and show of the Artist's Works at the Gallery's office in New York City.

13. *New Works of Art.* During the term of this Agreement, the Artist will create and provide the Gallery with new Artist's Works for sale by the Gallery, it being understood, however, that the Gallery may also offer for sale any Artist's Works heretofore produced by the Artist (and the Artist will cooperate with the Gallery in this regard).

The Artist agrees to use [his or her] best efforts to create and provide the Gallery with new Artist's Works sufficient to have at least one exhibition and show of such works in the Gallery's main gallery during the term of this Agreement.

14. *Sales by Artist.* The Artist will not exhibit or sell any works of art created by the Artist, whether from the Artist's studio or otherwise, to clients, private or public, without the prior consent of the Gallery. Such sales, if allowed, will be fully commissionable to the Gallery at the time of payment for such sales unless specifically excepted in a writing signed by the Gallery.

15. *Purchase by Gallery.* The Gallery, with the written consent of the Artist, which consent will not unreasonably be withheld, may from time to time purchase for cash any of the Artist's Works for its own account at a price equal to the sum of (a) fifty percent (50%) of the Sales price in excess of the Direct Costs and (b) the Direct Costs for such Artist's Works. In the case of sales by the Artist to the Gallery under this paragraph, the Gallery will receive no commission, and the total proceeds of such purchases by the Gallery shall be credited to the Artist's Sales Account.

16. *Artist's Works Retained by Artist.* Any other provision of this Agreement to the contrary notwithstanding, the Artist will have the right to retain for [himself or herself] such of the Artist's Works as [he or she] in [his or her] sole discretion will determine.

17. *Installations.* The Artist will have the right to create installations for exhibition from time to time at the Artist's sole discretion and at the Artist's sole expense, provided, however, that the Artist has consulted with the Gallery.

18. *Termination.* This Agreement will be terminated in accordance with paragraph 3 of this Agreement or otherwise as expressly provided in this Agreement or will terminate on the death of the Artist.

Upon any event of termination, the Gallery will have thirty (30) days to sell the Artist's Works and to settle and transfer to the Artist the balance due the Artist in the Artist's Sales Account. During such thirty (30)-day period after an event of termination, the Artist agrees to make no sales of the Artist's Works either by [himself or herself] or through another dealer.

Upon any event of termination, the Gallery, at its sole expense, will within thirty (30) days return to the Artist's studio or storage facility all the Artist's Works in the possession of the Gallery.

Upon any event of termination, the Gallery will promptly deliver to the Artist all photographs, transparencies, catalogs, and other materials pertaining in any way to the Artist or the Artist's Works.

19. *Security Interest.* The Gallery hereby grants a security interest in the Artist's Works (and any proceeds thereof) to the Artist until the sale of an Artist's Work by the Gallery, whereupon the proceeds of such sale shall be held for the Artist except for the commission due the Gallery in paragraph 5 above. The Gallery authorizes the Artist to file a UCC-1 Financing Statement evidencing such security interest without the signature of the Gallery. The Gallery agrees to inform any other secured creditor of the Gallery of the existence of the Artist's security interest. The Gallery agrees to specifically

inform any purchaser of the Artist's Works of the existence of the Artist's security interest as stated herein. The Gallery agrees not to pledge or encumber any of the Artist's works in its possession. [Perfection of the security interest is essential in those states without an artist-gallery consignment statute.]

20. *Arbitration.* Any controversy or claim arising out of or relating to this Agreement or a breach thereof will be settled by arbitration in accordance with the Commercial Arbitration Rules of the American Arbitration Association, and judgment upon the award rendered by the arbitrators may be entered in any court having jurisdiction thereof.

21. *Entire Understanding.* This Agreement contains the entire understanding of the parties with respect to the subject matter hereof, it may not be changed or amended except in writing signed by the parties, and it will be construed and governed in accordance with the laws of the state of New York.

22. *Binding Effect.* This Agreement will inure to the benefit of and will be binding upon the successors, the heirs, the executors, and the administrators of the parties.

This Agreement is not assignable by the Artist or the Gallery, except that the Gallery may assign this Agreement to any other corporation controlled by _____ individually.

IN WITNESS WHEREOF, the parties have hereunto set their hands and seals as of the date first above written.

_____ GALLERY, INC.

By:

_____

President

_____

Artist

Appendix 1-2

*Consignment Contract**

[NAME AND ADDRESS OF GALLERY]

[Date]

[Artist]
[Address]
[City, State, Zip Code]

Dear [Artist]:

[Name of gallery] hereby acknowledges receipt of the following works of art created and consigned by you:

Selling Price

1.   ["Title," medium, size, date]

2.   ["Title," medium, size, date]

. . .

---

*   To be used with Artist Consignment with Security Agreement (App. 1-1).

These above-mentioned works are hereby consigned to the Gallery as of the above date for _____ [*insert period of time*] pursuant to the terms and conditions of the Consignment Agreement between us dated _____.

Sincerely,

[Name of Gallery]

By: _____
Gallery Owner/Director

Accepted and Agreed:

By: _____
Artist

Appendix 1-3

*Artist Consignment with Security Agreement
(Short Form)*

AGREEMENT BETWEEN
ARTIST
AND
_____ GALLERY, INC.

[Date]

_____ Gallery, Inc.
[Address]
[City, State, Zip Code]

You hereby acknowledge receipt of the following oil painting (hereinafter referred to as the "Painting") created by me:

Title:
Medium:
Size:
Signature:
Date:

The purchase price of the Painting less your commission of _____ percent will be delivered by you to me within ten (10) days from and after the date on which delivery shall be made by you under any sale or contract of sale.

By signing this agreement, you grant me a security interest in the Painting (and any proceeds thereof) until the sale of the Painting by you, whereupon the proceeds of such sale will be held for me and delivered (except for such commission set forth above) to me as herein provided. You authorize me to file a UCC-1 Financing Statement evidencing my security interest in the Painting without your signature. In the event of any default by you, I shall have all the rights of a secured party under the Uniform Commercial Code.

You agree to hold the Painting for sale at a price of $_____. You agree that you will not sell the Painting for a price less than $_____ without written permission from me. You agree to have the Painting covered by an all-risks insurance policy for $_____, naming me as an insured party.

You agree to specifically inform any purchaser of the Painting from you of the existence of my security interest as stated herein. I agree to sign and file a Form UCC-3 termination statement once I have approved the terms of the sale of the Painting.

Notwithstanding the foregoing, at any time prior to any sale of the Painting by you, at my written request you will deliver the Painting to me immediately upon receipt of any instruction from me.

_____
Artist

_____
Address

The foregoing is confirmed and agreed to: _____ Gallery, Inc.

By: _____
President

PART TWO

Artwork Transactions

2

Private Sales

The purchase and sale of fine art is, as a commercial transaction, in many ways unique. The artwork, for one thing, is often singular and irreplaceable. Moreover, its value, which largely depends on the artist's reputation at the time of the sale, may fluctuate extensively because an artist's reputation is largely subject to public whim. And artwork is frequently purchased on impulse by a shockingly uninformed buyer: The buyer often turns a blind eye to securing a written purchase contract (let alone to having the contract reviewed by legal counsel), neglects to have the property physically inspected or professionally appraised, fails to do a title search, and, if the work is a fine-art multiple, makes no inquiry about the technique of production.

Defects abound in artwork as frequently as in other property. Accordingly, the art buyer should observe the same precautions ordinarily used by the prudent buyer in other commercial transactions of like value. Those precautions are addressed at length throughout the three main sections of this chapter: Sales by Dealers, Sales by Collectors, and Secured Transactions.

SALES BY DEALERS

Whether the dealer is a private dealer, a single commercial gallery, or a gallery with numerous branches or franchised outlets, the dealer's art sales are governed by principles of contract and tort law, by federal and state penal statutes, and in certain jurisdictions by specific legislation regulating sales of art. The art dealer may be selling works of art consigned to it by the artist (see chapter 1), works of art it owns, or works of art consigned to it by a collector. The most important commercial statute, the Uniform Commercial Code (U.C.C.), applies to most of the issues arising from the sale of artwork, including assurance of authenticity. It is here, therefore, that the discussion begins.

Warranties

Art's unique characteristics argue against total applicability of the U.C.C. to all art transactions. The U.C.C. deals exclusively with transactions of tangible personal property, and not all art is personal property. Art can also take the form of real property, such as buildings, earthworks, and such temporary installation pieces as Christo and Jeanne-Claude's *The Gates*, consisting of 7,503 orange nylon fabric constructions that adorned New York City's Central Park in February 2005.[1] However, to keep this discussion manageable, whenever artworks are referred to in this chapter, we are referring to those traditionally regarded as personal property. Moreover, art that is tangible personal property embodies significant intangible rights that are more or less ignored by the U.C.C. Further still, many states—New York,[2] Iowa,[3] and others[4]—doubting the sufficiency of the U.C.C. alone to safeguard art buyers, have enacted legislation that in some cases overrides the U.C.C. Nevertheless, the U.C.C. governs an array of issues arising in art transactions, and our discussion of warranties, therefore, mandates a review of both U.C.C. principles and legislative and judicial expansions of protection.

Express Warranties

Under common law, the buyer of goods generally labored under the rule of caveat emptor, absolving the seller from all responsibility for the quality of the goods sold unless the quality was expressly guaranteed. As the law evolved, the courts turned a compassionate ear to the purchaser, whereupon the rule of caveat emptor was relaxed, and the doctrine of express warranty emerged. An express warranty is created without the use of particular words of guarantee as long as the buyer can reasonably understand that the seller is affirming essential qualities of the goods and the buyer relies on such affirmation in good faith.[5]

The U.C.C. codified the judicially created rule. The foundation of the express-warranty provision as codified in the U.C.C.[6] is twofold: It rests, first, on the core description of goods to be sold[7] and, second, on those statements of the seller that become "part of the basis of the bargain."[8] Express warranties may arise regardless of a seller's intention; good faith is no defense to the falsity of an assertion.[9] They may arise in documents other than a sales contract; affirmations in catalogs,[10] brochures,[11] or advertisements,[12] for example, may give rise to express warranties if the buyer knows of and relies on the affirmation. Further, an advertisement need not necessarily set forth the precise warranty asserted by the buyer as long as it conveys the essential idea underlying the claimed warranty.[13] Express warranties may arise from assertions made before, after, or during a sale.[14] Express warranties may also arise from oral representations made by the seller; the U.C.C. does not require that all material terms of an agreement be included in a written contract.[15]

Warranty by Affirmation of Fact or Promise

The U.C.C. provides that an express warranty arises on "any af-firmation of fact or promise made by the seller to the buyer which relates to the goods and becomes part of the basis of the bargain."[16] If the goods do not conform to the affirmation or promise made, the warranty is breached, and an action may be brought, regardless of the seller's good-faith or malicious intentions in making the false state-ment. If the documentation alone of a work of art has been forged, that, too, constitutes a breach of warranty[17] as the authorship of the work has been rendered questionable. In such a case, at least one commentator has suggested[18] that the seller reimburse the buyer for any diminution in value caused by the lack of certification or com-pensate the buyer for expenses reasonably incurred in resolving the question of attribution through scientific analysis or expert opinion and that punitive damages be allowed if the seller acted in bad faith.

An example of breach of express warranty is illustrated by the New York federal court case of *Tunick v. Kornfeld*,[19] a case of apparent first impression in New York and in the Second Circuit.[20] The case underscores the imperfect fit between the U.C.C. and fine art. The New York gallery of David Tunick, a preeminent dealer in the Unit-ed States in Old Master prints, purchased at auction in June 1990 from the gallery of E.W. Kornfeld, a noted Swiss dealer in nine-teenth- and twentieth-century prints, a print of a Minotaur that Ko-rnfeld represented was signed by Pablo Picasso. Tunick paid Kornfeld $1.4 million for the print.

Subsequent to the purchase, Tunick began to have doubts about the Picasso. Although Tunick originally believed that the artwork was made by Picasso in the 1930s, he came to suspect that the signa-ture was a forgery. Tunick informed Kornfeld of his suspicion, of-fered to return the print to Kornfeld, and demanded his money back. Kornfeld refused to rescind the contract but did offer to exchange the print for another print in the series of the Minotaur that also was allegedly signed by Picasso. Tunick rejected Kornfeld's offer and, some sixteen months after the purchase, filed suit against Kornfeld. Among other claims, Tunick alleged that Kornfeld breached express warranties that (1) the signature on the print was authentic and

(2) the print had been signed in 1942 and had gone directly from Picasso to a private collector, whose widow had consigned it to Kornfeld for sale at auction.

Kornfeld, seeking dismissal on summary judgment, contended that even if the signature was not authentic, his offer to exchange the print for another print in the series, also allegedly signed by Picasso, constituted an exercise of his right under New York's U.C.C. section 2-508(2) to substitute conforming goods for the allegedly nonconforming goods rejected by Tunick. Kornfeld claimed that because his offer met the standards of the U.C.C. provision, Tunick could not properly reject the offer and seek other recourse. That claim raised an issue of apparent first impression. Does section 2-508 of New York's U.C.C. apply to artwork? That is, can a nonconforming tender of a work of art be cured by an offer of a different but similar work?

The federal district court in New York determined that two prints by the same artist and from the same plates are not interchangeable. Therefore, New York's U.C.C. section 2-508 "does not, as a matter of law, obligate a buyer to accept in lieu of a nonconforming print, a substitute print from the same series of prints."[21] In making its determination that prints are not interchangeable, the court noted that

> prints, unlike petroleum or produce, are not purchased strictly for utilitarian purposes. A print is selected by a purchaser because the traits of that print please the purchaser's aesthetic sensibilities. Thus, whether prints in a series are largely similar or slightly different is of no critical importance. The real fact to be considered is that the purchaser chose a given print because *he* viewed it as uniquely beautiful, interesting, or well suited to his collection or gallery. Nothing else will satisfy that collector but that which he bought.[22]

Because, as the court concluded in denying summary judgment to Kornfeld, prints are unique due to differences in impression, quality, and condition, New York's U.C.C. section 2-508 does not apply to prints and, therefore, did not provide Kornfeld with a defense to Tunick's claim of breach of warranty. The court's reasoning regarding fine art multiples is arguably even more applicable to cases involving individual works of art.

In a postscript to *Tunick*, which had been headed for a jury trial in a New York federal district court, the parties reached an amicable settlement, whose terms are strictly confidential but, reputedly, involve a number of works of art.[23]

Warranty by Description

A warranty may also arise from the seller's description of the goods,[24] provided the description becomes part of the basis of the bargain. The U.C.C. places no limits on what may be considered a description; included are blueprints and technical specifications[25] and, for a work of art, the results of a scientific analysis or an expert examination of the stylistic evidence.[26] Therefore, assertions made by an art merchant about a work's authenticity (whether the assertion is that the work is by a specific artist, is by a specific school, or was created during a particular period of time) and statements asserting a work's provenance are deemed to give rise to express warranties.

This is well illustrated in *Weber v. Peck*.[27] Here, the plaintiff entered into a sales contract with the defendant art dealer whereby plaintiff agreed to buy a painting by Jacob van Ruisdael for $388,500 plus 5% of the proceeds from its resale at auction. In return, the defendant promised to provide original letters of authenticity from two Ruisdael experts. Additionally, the parties signed a bill of sale in which defendant warranted that "the above described painting is authentic and as described above."[28] The applicable description included a reference to the painting's provenance. The bill of sale referred to the painting as follows:

Artist: Jacob Van Ruisdael (1628–1682)

Description: Painting entitled "A wooded river landscape with a waterfall, and travelers on a bridge" signed, being an oil on canvas; stretcher size 26" × 21"

Condition: Excellent

Provenance: "see Attached exhibit A"[29]

After the parties signed the contract and bill of sale, the painting was taken to Sotheby's, which determined that it was an authentic Ruisdael and placed it in its May 1996 Important Old Masters auction.

At the closing of the sale, the defendant failed to furnish either of the promised authenticating letters.

Approximately ten days before the auction, the plaintiff discovered that Sotheby's could not verify certain aspects of the painting's provenance, and also that the painting had previously sold as "attributed to Ruisdael"—a lesser degree of certainty than an "authenticated" painting and one that usually translates into a lower sale value. Sotheby's catalog for the painting stated its authenticity but also reflected its previous sale history, and estimated its value as $300,000 to $400,000. With the realization that changes to the provenance would devalue the painting, the plaintiff, on Sotheby's advice, proceeded with the sale.

At the auction, a high bid of $300,000 was accepted, but payment was never made. Plaintiff alleged that because the painting was bid on at auction, it could not be sold in the aftermarket, nor could it be marketed for more than $300,000.

Plaintiff sued the dealer for breach of warranty of authenticity and for breach of warranty of the accuracy of the painting's provenance. On motions for summary judgment by both parties, the New York federal district court denied the motions on the breach of warranty of authenticity claim, since plaintiff's reliance on the warranty, that is, his reservation of the right to receive the authenticating letters, was in dispute. However, the court granted the plaintiff's motion with regard to the warranty of provenance claim:

> It is apparent from the plain language of the bill of sale that it warrants the painting's provenance. The bill of sale states that the seller warrants the painting as described. The applicable description includes a reference to the painting's provenance which was attached to the bill of sale.[30]

Citing section 2-607(2) of New York's U.C.C., the court also noted that plaintiff was not entitled to rescind the sale of the painting: That is, acceptance of goods with a knowledge that they are nonconforming cannot be revoked because of the nonconformity, unless the acceptance was based on the reasonable assumption that the nonconformity would be cured. Here, the court observed, the plaintiff was aware of the missing letters of authentication at the time of the closing and was aware of problems with the painting's provenance just before the auction. In the weeks following the closing, the plaintiff repeatedly—and to no avail—requested defendant to furnish the letters of authentication. Accordingly, the plaintiff could not reasonably have believed that these nonconformities would be cured just days before the auction; on the contrary, despite these nonconformities, plaintiff never indicated to the defendant a desire to rescind the sale, but rather, proceeded with the auction of the painting.

Statements of Opinion

Both warranties by description and warranties by affirmation of fact must be distinguished from a seller's expression of opinion, which does not necessarily give rise to a warranty.[31] For example, a seller's opinion concerning the aesthetics or the value of a work of art is viewed as mere "puffing,"[32] whereas the seller's opinion as to a work's authenticity or provenance may well give rise to an express warranty if the seller is an art merchant. Since art is customarily valued on the basis of expert opinion, experts—including art merchants—are deemed to bear the commercial responsibility for rendering such opinions. Thus, it has been held that when the party making the representations has superior knowledge regarding the subject of those representations and the other party's level of expertise is such that she may reasonably rely on such supposedly superior knowledge, representations may be considered as facts and not as mere opinions.[33]

Exclusion of Warranty: Examination of Goods

In the absence of suspicious circumstances, a buyer need not examine the purchased goods to affirm the accuracy of the seller's representations: It is enough that the buyer believes in and relies on those representations. If, however, a buyer elects to inspect the purchased goods, the U.C.C. does not provide an unqualified answer as to whether that inspection nullifies the U.C.C.'s express warranties. Rather, the U.C.C. indicates that various factors surrounding the transaction must be weighed.[34] A buyer with experience in the goods being sold may be able to discover defects not discernible by an inexperienced purchaser. On the other hand, when a defect is obvious, even an unsophisticated purchaser may be held to have relied on her inspection, rather than on the seller's warranty.[35]

When the buyer is aware of the falsity of the seller's representation, that representation cannot be relied on, does not become part of the basis of the bargain, and, therefore, does not give rise to an express warranty.[36] Sales of artwork consummated for prices below market value do not in themselves necessarily constitute notice sufficient to deny relief to buyers for claimed breaches of warranty.[37] If, however, a buyer and a seller have approximately the same level of sophistication about the type of goods purchased or if there is an absence of documented pedigree, those facts, when coupled with a low price, may be sufficient to present a factual determination for a jury.[38]

Exclusion of Warranty: Disclaimer

Generally, disclaimers of warranties are viewed as contradicting the warranties and are, therefore, disfavored by the courts. Where possible, disclaimer language is construed as being consistent with the express warranty;[39] where consistency is not possible, the disclaimer language is found to be inoperative.[40] Reconciliation of the warranty and the disclaimer depends on the language used. In certain jurisdictions, such as New York[41] and Michigan,[42] the enactment of state statutes has clearly delineated the circumstances under which disclaimers are given effect. Other jurisdictions must rely on case law; although disclaimers in certain instances have been upheld when found to be clear, conspicuous, and adverting to the attribute or attributes being disclaimed with sufficient particularity to apprise the buyer of the risk,[43] such judicial precedent is not unanimous. The *Weiscz* cases described below, for example, illustrate how two different courts examined the issue of a disclaimer's effects.

Weiscz v. Parke-Bernet Galleries, Inc.[44]

At a Parke-Bernet auction in 1962, the plaintiff Arthur Weiscz purchased a painting listed in the auction catalog as the work of Raoul Dufy. In 1964, plaintiff David Schwartz likewise purchased at a Parke-Bernet auction a work listed in the catalog as a painting by Raoul Dufy. Subsequent to a criminal investigation, Weiscz and Schwartz learned that their Dufys were forgeries and commenced lawsuits against Parke-Bernet. The cases were tried jointly, and the court found that at the time of the auctions Parke-Bernet also believed the paintings ascribed to Dufy in the catalogs to be his work. Parke-Bernet defended on the grounds that in both cases the sales were "as is" and subject to the various disclaimers contained in the Conditions of Sale set forth in the auction catalogs.

The court found that plaintiff Weiscz did not know of the Conditions of Sale and could not, therefore, be charged with knowledge of its contents. In contrast, the court found that plaintiff Schwartz was chargeable with knowledge of the Conditions of Sale. Consequently, the court had to determine whether the language of the disclaimer set forth in the Conditions of Sale in the Schwartz auction catalog was effective to immunize Parke-Bernet from the legal consequences flowing from the sale.

The court concluded that the disclaimer was inoperative. It found, instead, that Parke-Bernet intended and expected that its bidders at auctions would rely on the accuracy of its descriptions, that Parke-Bernet was vested in the mind of the public with an aura of expertise and reliability, that the wording and the organization of its auction catalog were designed to emphasize the genuineness of the works to be offered, and that the disclaimer was worded in a highly technical manner that the average reader would not interpret as affecting her understanding that she was buying authentic works of art.[45]

Weiscz was appealed, and in a brief per curiam opinion the appellate court reversed the judgments and dismissed the complaints of both Weiscz and Schwartz. It held that at the time of each of the plaintiffs' purchases neither the applicable statutory law nor decisional law recognized the seller's expressed opinion or judgment as giving rise to any implied warranty of authenticity of authorship and that the disclaimer in the defendant's auction-sale catalog gave

> prominent place . . . to a clear, unequivocal disclaimer of any express or implied warranty or representation of genuineness of any paintings as products of the ascribed artist.[46]

Were the U.C.C., rather than the former Uniform Sales Act, applied to the *Weiscz* transactions and were *Weiscz* appealed today, the disposition of the appellate court would probably remain unchanged. Even though under the U.C.C. the catalog description by Parke-Bernet would probably be deemed to create an express warranty, the court's reasoning as to the disclaimer's effect would still govern (provided the catalog disclaimer was found to be sufficient to inform a purchaser in the plaintiff's position as to the risk of title), since the disclaimer specifically repudiated a representation of genuineness with respect to the items sold.

Parol Evidence Rule

The effectiveness of a disclaimer also depends on the U.C.C.'s parol evidence rule, which states that terms of a writing intended as the final expression of the parties' agreement may not be contradicted by evidence of prior or contemporaneous oral agreements.[47] Therefore, under the parol evidence rule, an oral disclaimer will be disqualified, even if it is attached to a written warranty. Similarly, an oral warranty, attached to a written disclaimer, will be excluded from evidence. The rule does, however, permit parol evidence of usage of trade or the parties' course of dealing or course of performance when that evidence explains or supplements the contract terms.[48] Moreover, evidence of consistent additional terms is admissible "unless the court finds the writing to have been intended also as a complete and exclusive statement of the terms of the agreement."[49]

Implied Warranties

After the evolution in common law of express warranties, the early nineteenth century witnessed the development of two distinct implied warranties for the quality of the goods sold: (1) that of merchantability and (2) that of fitness for a particular purpose. Today there is a somewhat Procrustean fit between commercial transactions in artworks and the law of implied warranties as embodied in the U.C.C.[50] From the U.C.C. language and the examples used in the comments, the primary thrust of the warranty of merchantability seems to be directed at the sale of goods more fungible than artworks. Nevertheless, it is entirely possible to envision those warranties being used to afford redress to the consumer in a case of art forgery. Only in the future, however, will we discover the extent of the judicial application of those warranties to the unwitting purchase of forged works.

Warranty of Merchantability

The implied warranty of merchantability, as it evolved, has come to mean that goods must be capable of passing under the description specified in the agreement of sale and be reasonably fit for the ordinary uses to which such goods are put. Unless disclaimed, that warranty is implied in a contract for the sale of goods by a merchant seller.[51] The warranty's scope limits liability to a "merchant with respect to goods of that kind," and, unlike the seller in an action for fraud, in which it is generally necessary to prove that the seller knew that her representation was false, the merchant will incur liability regardless of her knowledge of the existence of any defect in the goods sold.[52] Under the U.C.C., "merchant," in part, means a person who deals in goods of the kind or otherwise by her occupation holds herself out as having knowledge or skill peculiar to the practices or goods involved in the transaction.[53]

Thus, as it relates to dealing in art, "merchant" includes a commercial art gallery, an art auctioneer, and a private art dealer[54] and excludes a collector whose occupation is not related to art and who sells items from her art collection only occasionally.[55] Reliance by the buyer on the seller's skill and judgment is not required under this warranty.[56]

Section 2-314(2) of the U.C.C. defines "merchantability" with particularity. For goods to be merchantable, they must at least:[57]

a. Pass without objection in the trade under the contract description;

b. (If fungible goods) be of fair average quality within the description;

c. Be fit for the ordinary purposes for which such goods are used;

d. Run, within the variations permitted by the agreement of even kind, quality, and quantity within each unit and among all units involved;

e. Be adequately contained, packaged, and labeled as the agreement may require; and

f. Conform to the promises or affirmations of fact made on the container or label, if any.

Note that all the requirements must be met. In addition, U.C.C. section 2-314(2) comment 6 states that subsection (2) "does not purport to exhaust the meaning of 'merchantable.'"

For works of art, the most relevant tests of merchantability are found in subsections (a), (c), and (f).

As to subsection (a), whether goods would pass without objection is determined with reference to the standards of the particular line of trade. Accordingly, merchantability of artwork is interpreted by reference to dealer recognition, categorization, and evaluation of specific artists, periods of art, and specific works relating to those artists and periods. An original, documented work of art, therefore, would pass without objection in the trade and, consequently, be merchantable. Similarly, a poorly rendered fake or an item of significant worth without adequate documentation of provenance would not pass without objection in the trade and, accordingly, would not be merchantable.[58]

A different situation is posed by the skillfully rendered fake, say a painting purportedly by J.M.W. Turner, complete with documentation, that has passed unnoticed for 150 years. Even though it passed without objection in the trade for years, discovery that it is a fake renders the work unmerchantable, and the buyer has redress under the U.C.C. The art industry has tried to minimize the possibility of that situation arising by creating a standard classification for degrees of certainty in attributions of works of art. For example, the glossary of attributions below is reproduced from a May 2005 catalog of Christie's New York.

EXPLANATION OF CATALOGUING PRACTICE

For Pictures, Drawings, Prints and Miniatures

1. PABLO PICASSO
In Christie's opinion a work by the artist.

2. Attributed to PABLO PICASSO★
In Christie's qualified opinion a work of the period of the artist which may be in whole or part the work of the artist.

3. After PABLO PICASSO★
In Christie's qualified opinion a copy of the work of the artist.

4. 'signed'
Has a signature which in Christie's qualified opinion is the signature of the artist.

5. 'bears signature'
Has a signature which in Christie's qualified opinion might be the signature of the artist.

6. 'dated'
Is so dated and in Christie's qualified opinion was executed at about that date.

7. 'bears date'
Is so dated and in Christie's qualified opinion may have been executed at about that date.

★ This term and its definition in this Explanation of Cataloguing Practice are a qualified statement as to Authorship. While the use of this term is based upon careful study and represents the opinion of experts, Christie's and the consignor assume no risk, liability and responsibility for the authenticity of authorship of any lot in this catalogue described by this.

As to subsection (c) of section 2-314(2), even if a work of art passes without objection in the trade, it is subject to another test of merchantability: its fitness "for the ordinary purposes for which such goods are used." A U.C.C. comment[59] elaborates on the latter test by explaining that merchantable goods must be "honestly resalable in the normal course of business because they are what they purport to be." The purchase of a forgery defeats the purpose of buying an original, and a forgery is certainly not "honestly resalable" as an original.

Still another test of merchantability for artwork is posed by subsection (f), whereby, to be merchantable, goods must "conform to the promises or affirmations of fact made on the container or label, if any." Paintings and sculptures are often sold with wooden or brass plaques attached to the frame or the base of the piece. Such plaques bear the title of the work and its attribution. If plaques are regarded as labels and if a work of art and its plaque are inconsistent, it could be argued that a breach of the implied warranty of merchantability occurred. Such a breach also arises from an artist's forged signature. In fact, if a signature is fraudulently added to an original painting to improve its salability, the buyer may be able to recover for any difference in value between an unsigned work and a signed original under this subsection.

Warranty of Fitness for a Particular Purpose

Goods may be merchantable and yet still be unfit for a particular purpose. The warranty of fitness for a particular purpose arises if three requirements are met:[60]

1. The seller must know of the buyer's particular purpose; an explicit statement of purpose is unnecessary if the circumstances are such that the seller should realize the purpose.

2. The seller must have actual or constructive knowledge that the buyer is relying on the seller's skill.

3. The buyer must actually rely on the seller. A seller's intention to create this warranty is immaterial,[61] and a seller's good faith is no defense in a suit for breach of warranty.

Moreover, the fact that a defect is difficult to find does not eliminate the warranty if the warranty is otherwise created. Although the usual fact situation involves a merchant-seller, on rare occasions the warranty of fitness can be applicable to nonmerchants.[62]

Exclusion of Implied Warranties: Examination of Goods

In certain circumstances, the implied warranties of merchantability and fitness may be excluded by a buyer's examination of the goods bought or by the buyer's refusal to examine them.[63] If, for example, before the purchase a buyer of artwork refuses the seller's demand that the buyer examine it, the implied warranties are excluded as to any defects that "an examination ought in the circumstances to have revealed."[64] That exclusion results because the demand constitutes notice to the buyer that the buyer is assuming the risks of any defects that the examination would reveal. If, however, a seller's offer of examination is accompanied by statements relating to the quality or the characteristics of a work of art and the buyer indicates that she is relying on those statements, rather than on any examination, the seller will probably be deemed to have given an express warranty.[65]

Whether the buyer's examination of the goods results in the exclusion of the warranties depends on the buyer's sophistication, the normal method of examining goods in the circumstances, and the obviousness of the defect.[66] If a flaw is discernible on visible inspection before purchase, the implied warranties are excluded. If, however, a defect in forged artwork can be detected only by scientific investigation or extensive research, a buyer's inspection should not ordinarily result in an exclusion of the implied warranties.[67]

Exclusion of Implied Warranties: Disclaimer

The U.C.C. permits sellers to disclaim implied warranties under circumscribed conditions.[68] The warranty of merchantability may be disclaimed either orally or in writing.[69] If written, the disclaimer must be conspicuous.[70] The disclaimer language must specifically include the word "merchantability."[71] Alternatively, the language may be general, provided it informs the buyer that no warranties are attendant to the transaction and that the buyer assumes the risk of the quality of the goods purchased. Examples of such general language are "as is," "as they stand," and "with all faults."[72] (See discussion of *Weiscz v. Parke-Bernet* at pages 84–85.)

The warranty of fitness for a particular purpose may be disclaimed only in writing,[73] and the disclaimer must be conspicuous.[74] The disclaimer language may be general, such as, "there are no warranties that extend beyond the description on the face hereof."[75] Alternatively, the disclaimer language may include such phrases as "with all faults," "as they stand," and "as is."[76]

In addition, both implied warranties may be disclaimed through a course of dealing between the parties, a course of performance by the parties, or usage of trade.[77]

With all that said, however, the courts have significantly limited the ability of the seller of artwork to disclaim implied warranties. Courts have strictly construed the warranty disclaimer language,[78] determined that the disclaimer was not sufficiently "conspicuous,"[79] and found the disclaimer to be unconscionable.[80] Moreover, legislation in a number of states[81] has significantly impeded the ability of a seller to disclaim implied warranties of merchantability or fitness with respect to consumer goods,[82] within which category artwork falls.

Implied Warranties and Privity

Privity is that connection or relationship existing between two or more contracting parties, such as the relationship between a seller and a purchaser. Traditionally, that relationship has been the basis of liability. Although the U.C.C. takes no position with respect to the seller's liability to a subpurchaser,[83] the trend as developed by case law is away from privity and toward foreseeability as a criterion for liability.[84] The presence of advertising encourages the dispensing with privity.[85] It has been asserted that in an action for the transfer of fake art the ultimate purchaser should be able to disregard lack of privity on the basis of advertisements, and that even in the absence of advertising lack of privity should not preclude recovery by the ultimate purchaser against the remote seller if it is reasonably foreseeable that breach of an implied warranty will cause that ultimate purchaser economic loss.[86]

Warranty of Title

At common law, under the doctrine of caveat emptor, the buyer bore the risk of poor title. Today the buyer is afforded substantial protection by the U.C.C., which provides that unless specifically excluded or modified a warranty of title by the seller exists in every sales contract.[87] The statutorily imposed warranty of title includes the following assertions:

1. That the title to the work or works being conveyed is good.[88]

2. That the seller has the right to transfer title.[89]

3. That the works are delivered free from any security interest or other lien or encumbrance of which the buyer at the time of contract has no knowledge.[90]

In addition, when the sellers are merchants, there is an implied warranty on the part of the seller that the goods will be delivered free "of the rightful claim of any third person by way of infringement."[91]

Exclusion of Warranty of Title: Disclaimer

Warranty of title may be excluded or modified only by specific language[92] or by circumstances that give the buyer reason to know that the seller does not claim title in herself or that she is purporting to sell only such rights in the goods as she or a third person may have.[93] Since the U.C.C.'s objective is to prevent surprise, general disclaimer language that merely negates all warranties does not nullify the warranty of title, because it does not give the buyer reason to know of any risk of title failure. Thus, language in a bill of sale to the effect that the seller "does hereby sell . . . any right, title, and interest seller may have" was not sufficient to constitute a disclaimer of the warranty of title.[94] More than mere constructive notice imported by public recordation or filing is required to give a buyer reason to know that the seller does not claim to have full title.[95] Circumstances sufficient to put the buyer on notice would include an announcement at an art auction that the seller does not claim title in the work or that the seller is purporting to sell only such title as third persons may have.[96] Other circumstances in which a buyer should be aware that a warranty of title is not present are judicial sales and foreclosure sales.[97]

If, when there is no exclusion of warranty, a buyer can establish that the goods are subject to a security interest that was not known to the buyer or that the seller had neither the right nor the power to deliver good title, the buyer can surrender the property and recover damages.[98] If the rightful property owner brings an action against the buyer to recover the property, the buyer may sue the seller and require the seller to defend the action.

Warranty of Title and Measure of Damages: Menzel v. List[99]

In 1932, the plaintiff Erna Menzel and her husband (who died in 1960) bought a painting by Marc Chagall at auction in Brussels for approximately $150. In 1940, the Germans invaded Belgium, and the Menzels fled, leaving the Chagall painting in their residence. Six years later, the Menzels returned to find that their painting had been removed and that a receipt for the painting had been left. The Germans had, in fact, removed the painting as degenerate art in 1941, and its whereabouts remained unknown until 1955, when it was purchased for $2,800 from a Parisian art gallery by Klaus Perls and his wife, Amelia, proprietors of a New York gallery. Later that same year, the Perls, who knew nothing of the painting's previous history and made no inquiries concerning it, sold it to Albert List for $4,000. In 1962, Mrs. Menzel noticed a reproduction of the Chagall in an art book, along with a statement that the painting was in Albert List's possession.

List refused to surrender the painting to Mrs. Menzel on demand, so she instituted a replevin action (a lawsuit to reclaim possession of the painting) against him, and List, in turn, sued the Perls, alleging that they were liable to him for breach of the warranty of title. Expert testimony was introduced to establish the painting's fair market value at the time of the trial. The judge charged the jury that if it found for Mrs. Menzel against List, they were to assess the

present value of the painting. The jury did find for Mrs. Menzel, requiring that List either return the painting to her or pay her its then
fair market value ($22,500). In addition, the jury found for List as
against the Perls in the amount of $22,500 plus the legal costs in-
curred by List.

List returned the painting to Menzel, and the Perls appealed on
the issue of damages. The appellate court reduced the amount
awarded to List to $4,000 (the price he paid for the painting) plus in-
terest from the date of the purchase. The court also held that Mrs.
Menzel's action was not barred by the statutes of limitation of either
New York or Belgium, since her cause of action for replevin and
conversion arose not on the taking of the painting but on List's refusal to return the painting on demand.

List and the Perls each appealed the appellate court's modification order, and the New York Court of Appeals reversed the order,
finding that the modification order would not have fully compensated List for his loss, since he would have been deprived of the benefit—that is, the appreciated value—of his bargain. In the court's
reasoning:

> Clearly, List can only be put in the same position he would have
> occupied if the contract had been kept by the Perls if he recovers
> the value of the painting at the time when, by the judgment in
> the main action, he was required to surrender the painting to
> Mrs. Menzel or pay her the present value of the painting. Had
> the warranty been fulfilled, *i.e.*, had title been as warranted by
> the Perls, List would still have possession of a painting currently
> worth $22,500 and he could have realized that price at an auc-
> tion or private sale. If List recovers only the purchase price plus
> interest, the effect is to *put* him in the same position he would
> have occupied *if the sale had never been made.* Manifestly, an in-
> jured buyer is not compensated when he recovers only so much
> as placed him in *status quo ante* since such a recovery implicitly
> denies that he had suffered any damage.[100]

Thus, in *Menzel v. List*, the plaintiff recovered her painting, List
was awarded a sum of money equal to the painting's then fair market
value, and the Perls were left to seek recourse from a foreign defen-

dant, the Parisian art dealer.[101] The court's refusal to impose mere rescission on List as a remedy indicates judicial awareness that works of art, unlike most other chattel, sometimes appreciate in value after an initial sale. More to the point was the court's relatively highhanded treatment of the Perls. In dismissing their objection to the court's measure of damages, the court noted that a seller is in a position to ascertain a work's provenance before acquiring it for resale. Furthermore, if the seller has any doubts about its provenance, the seller can secure protection on resale of the work by employing suitable disclaimers of warranties.[102] The court, however, ignored the reality that if the seller seeks the protection of such disclaimers, she may well have trouble selling the work.

Warranty of Title and Measure of Damages: The U.C.C.

Menzel was decided under the Uniform Sales Act, as enacted in New York, which predated the U.C.C. In *Menzel*, the New York Court of Appeals, in upholding the trial court's award of damages, concluded that the proper damages in breach of warranty cases involving commodities that appreciate in value should place the injured party in the position the party would have occupied had the warranty not been breached. Thus, the buyer List was awarded damages based on the then-market value of the painting. In contrast, the U.C.C. provides that the measure of damages for breach of warranty is the difference at the time and the place of acceptance between the value of the goods accepted and the value they would have had if they had been as warranted, unless special circumstances show proximate damages of a different amount.[103] The *Menzel* measure of benefit of the bargain (which requires damages, in cases involving appreciating commodities, to acknowledge the appreciation in value) was again reinforced, despite the U.C.C. provision, in a more recent case discussed below.

In *Koerner v. Davis*,[104] plaintiff Henry Koerner, a Viennese artist living in Pennsylvania, brought one of his paintings, *The Family*, to New York City in 1964 for framing. While running an errand in the city, he left the painting in a taxi and told the driver to wait. When he returned from his errand, the taxi was gone. Koerner reported the loss to the police department and to his insurer, who paid him the insured value of the painting, $1,000.

In June 1983, the painting appeared on the market for sale at the William Doyle Galleries, and it was sold that month at auction to defendant David J. Davis for $1,200. At the time of the sale, the painting's provenance was unknown. In September 1983, after a search by Davis, he learned that Koerner was the artist, and Koerner learned that Davis had his painting. Koerner demanded the return of the painting, whereupon Davis refused and, instead, placed it for sale with the Gertrude Stein gallery. In March 1984 Koerner demanded of both Davis and the Stein gallery that the painting be returned. The gallery responded by returning the work to Davis, who did not return it to Koerner, whereupon Koerner brought suit against Davis and the gallery to recover the work of art or its fair market value. In the face of the action, Davis delivered the work to an antiques dealer, who then died. The painting had disappeared once again.

In holding for the plaintiff, the court noted that since the painting was originally stolen from the plaintiff, no title to the property could be conveyed and that, moreover, both Davis and the gallery were converters: Davis when he refused Koerner's demand to return the painting in March 1984 and the gallery when it disposed of Koerner's property by returning it to Davis with full knowledge of competing claims to it. The court further noted that plaintiff's insurance proceeds did not cover the full value of the stolen property, nor did the insurance proceeds divest him of all interest in the painting; he was, therefore, a proper party plaintiff.

As to damages, the court was satisfied with the evidence that Koerner's work had appreciated in value and that his painting, *The Family*, would command a price in the 1984 market of $30,000. Accordingly, the court applied the benefit-of-the-bargain measure propounded in *Menzel* and awarded damages to the plaintiff in the amount of $30,000.

New York and other states, however, measure damages differently where the claim is based on fraud. *Nacht v. Sotheby's Holdings*[105] exemplifies this point. There, in 1981, the plaintiff purchased a painting from Sotheby's for $23,815. In 1996, following an appraisal by Sotheby's that valued the painting at $225,000, plaintiff decided to sell the painting through Sotheby's. It was thereupon discovered that the painting's authenticity was questionable, because a group overseeing the artist's *catalogue raisonné* refused to include the painting. The plaintiff's lawsuit alleged a number of causes of action, most of which were dismissed under Sotheby's five-year warranty of authenticity limitation or other principles of law. What survived was the cause alleging fraudulent inducement, whereby plaintiff claimed that Sotheby's knew or had reason to know of the painting's questionable authenticity in 1981. In allowing that claim to proceed to discovery, the court noted that the damages recoverable in a fraud case are designed to compensate the aggrieved party for what she lost due to the fraud, not to compensate her for what she might have realized in the absence of fraud. Therefore, assuming that the plaintiff successfully proved her claim, the measure of damages would be her cost, $23,815 (plus interest), and not the fair market value if the painting had been authentic, or $225,000. This should be contrasted with *Menzel*, which was based on a breach of warranty or contract.

When there is a dispute as to a contract claim, as in *Menzel*, courts apply a "benefit of the bargain" rule, seeking to place the injured party in as good a position as she would have occupied had the contract been fully performed. But in a claim for fraud, the "out-of-pocket" rule merely returns the injured party to as good a position as she would have been in had she never entered the contract. The rationale for applying the lesser measure of damages in fraud is that the wrongdoing in fraud is the inducement to the contract, not the failure to fulfill the contract.

Notice of Breach of Warranty[106]

If, after accepting delivery of a work of art, a buyer discovers that the seller has breached a warranty, the buyer must notify the seller, either orally or in writing,[107] of that breach within a reasonable time after its discovery or risk losing whatever remedy the buyer has against the seller.[108] What constitutes reasonable time of notification varies with the facts; a more stringent test may be applied to a merchant buyer than to a consumer buyer.[109]

If the buyer is sued by a third party, the buyer should notify the seller in writing of the litigation. The notice should include all relevant information pertaining to the litigation and a demand that the seller defend the action or else be bound by any determination of fact in the litigation.[110]

The Statute of Frauds

Section 2-201 of the U.C.C. provides that a contract for the sale of goods costing $500 or more is unenforceable unless documented by a writing indicating that such a contract between the parties has been made. The document must be signed by the party against whom enforcement is sought or by that party's authorized agent or broker.[111] Therefore, in *Hoffmann v. Boone*,[112] a New York federal district court granted the defendant-art dealer Mary Boone's motion to dismiss a case in which plaintiff Paul Hoffmann, a collector-client of Mary Boone, claimed Boone agreed to sell him in April 1988 a work of contemporary art, Brice Marden's *Grey #1*, for $120,000. Although both parties agreed that there was no written contract and that the statute of frauds would apply, Hoffmann contended that Boone was barred by the reliance-based doctrine of promissory estoppel from asserting the statute of frauds.

The federal district court, noting that New York's highest state court never addressed the issue of whether New York recognizes estoppel in U.C.C. cases, held that estoppel principles are applicable to U.C.C. contracts but determined that Hoffmann did not make a satisfactory showing of promissory estoppel. In New York, the elements of promissory estoppel are

(1) a clear and unambiguous promise,

(2) a reasonable and foreseeable reliance on that promise, and

(3) an unconscionable injury.

The court determined that although the particular facts in the case satisfied the first two requirements, the injuries Hoffmann suffered—traveling to New York from Florida three times to settle the contract, plans to include the painting in an exhibition of his collection at Chicago's Museum of Contemporary Art, and the painting's special characteristics, which led him to purchase that particular work—do not rise to the level in New York of "unconscionable."[113] Therefore, promissory estoppel was not established, and the case was dismissed on Mary Boone's assertion of the statute of frauds.

In the absence of other statutory provisions, one who promises to purchase a work of art costing $500 or more has to have signed a memorandum in order to be bound to consummate the purchase.[114] An agreement memorialized in a bill of sale will suffice, as suggested by *Andre Emmerich Gallery, Inc. v. Frost*,[115] in which the plaintiff-gallery sought and won a court order, based on the existence of such a bill of sale, directing the defendant, Kenneth Frost, to return a Jackson Pollock drawing to the gallery. In that case, Frost, reputedly an art collector, contacted the Andre Emmerich Gallery in September 1993, seeking to buy an artwork by Jackson Pollock. After some discussion, the executive director of the gallery, on the following day, delivered to Frost's apartment "on approval" an untitled 1984 Pollock watercolor, ink, and graphite drawing.

After several days and further discussions between the parties, they entered into an agreement for Frost to buy the drawing for $297,687.50. The agreement was memorialized in a bill of sale dated September 29, 1993. It included a schedule of installment payments, with the first payment of $100,000 due by October 4, 1993, followed by additional specific payments due on particular dates of succeeding months. On October 25, having never received the first payment, the gallery sent Frost a written demand for return of the drawing. Frost responded by fax the following day, indicating that the "painting has been delivered to insured third party. To be delivered to your gallery." Later that day, an attorney representing Frost advised the gallery that Frost intended to pay the full price of the drawing by November 3. When the gallery still was not paid by November 9, Frost's attorney attempted unsuccessfully to facilitate the return of the drawing to the gallery.

Meanwhile, the gallery discovered that despite Frost's professed intent to buy the drawing for his own collection, he had, in fact, delivered the drawing to Christie's auction house in New York City around October 1, pursuant to a court-ordered settlement in a lawsuit requiring Frost to deliver an artwork by Jackson Pollock to Christie's by August 27, 1993.

The gallery sued Frost for the return of the Pollock drawing, alleging, among other things, fraud in the inducement to enter a contract. In response, one of Frost's contentions was that the parties orally modified the contract to extend the time in which payment was due. The New York State Supreme Court ordered Frost to return the drawing to the gallery. The court found that the September 29 bill of sale was a writing sufficient to satisfy the statute of frauds; an oral modification to extend the time of payments—if such a modification existed—did not satisfy the statute of frauds and was, therefore, not valid.

Where both the buyer and the seller are merchants, a written confirmation of the sale by either party correctly stating all material terms of the agreement and received within a reasonable time by the other party, when she should know its contents, is binding against that second party unless she objects in writing to the confirmation within ten days after its receipt.[116]

A contract not yet put into writing but otherwise meeting all U.C.C. criteria for a valid contract may be enforceable if goods are to be specially manufactured, if the person against whom enforcement is sought admits the contract in court, or if the contract is for goods for which payment has been made and accepted or that have been received and accepted.[117] An interesting question is whether the commission of any artwork is one for the sale of services or for the sale of goods. In *National Historic Shrines*[118] it was held that the commission was a contract for the sale of services and, therefore, not addressed by the sale-of-goods provision of the statute of frauds. (See chapter 15 at pages 1784–1786, which discusses the sale of services versus the sale of goods from a tax perspective vis-à-vis the artist.)

Offer and Acceptance

In *Sands & Company v. Christie's*,[119] Sands, an art dealer, claimed that Christie's breached an agreement to sell him privately an Andy Warhol painting. Christie's sent Sands an email offering the Warhol at $660,000, and Sands replied by email that "your offer is accepted at $660,000 pending my firsthand confirmation that the painting is in good condition, and also is signed." Before Sands could inspect the painting, Christie's withdrew its offer since its consignor had changed his mind about selling it. The New York State Supreme Court found that Sands had added a condition to his acceptance allowing him to reject the Warhol if it was not in good condition or not signed; as a result, a contract was not formed. Sands argued, to little avail, that acceptance conditional on inspection was standard practice in the art trade. But the court correctly pointed out that trade usage cannot be used to create a contract. It is a fundamental principle of contract law that a valid acceptance must comply with the terms of the offer, and if a purported acceptance is qualified with conditions, it is equivalent to a rejection and counteroffer. The email sent by Sands did not operate as an acceptance, because acceptance was made conditional on Christie's assent to the additional term.

The Statute of Limitations

In another New York case, a federal district court determined that because of the nature of the relationship between two art dealers, a suit by one against the other over money owed from the sale of paintings was not time-barred by the applicable limitations period. In *Tasende v. Janis*,[120] the Tasende Gallery and the Sidney Janis Gallery jointly held an exhibition from November 1989 through January 1990 in an attempt to sell certain paintings. Subsequently, a dispute arose over the proceeds from paintings sold during and following the exhibition's closure. Tasende contended that it was owed money arising from

(1) the 1997 sale of a certain painting,

(2) paintings sold at the exhibition, and

(3) two purchases related to paintings not sold at the exhibition, one of which was purchased by Janis, and the other purchased jointly by Janis and Tasende.

Janis believed that the obligation to pay for these last two purchases had accrued in 1990, and was therefore barred by the six-year statute of limitations, since the complaint was not filed until 1998. Tasende, however, alleged that there had been a continuous joint venture between the two parties, which began with the November 1989 exhibition and ended with the sale of the final painting in 1997. Hence, the six-year limitations period began to run in 1997 and not in 1990. The federal district court, evidently agreeing, held that the allegations in the complaint based on the continuing joint venture were sufficient to allow the suit to move forward, and accordingly the court denied Janis's motion to dismiss.[121]

The Unconscionable Contract

The U.C.C. provides that a court may refuse to enforce any contract or any portion of a contract that it finds as a matter of law to have been unconscionable at the time it was made.[122] Unconscionability alone may not support a claim for damages; it merely gives the court the right to refuse to enforce the contract.[123] Whether a contract or any clause of a contract is unconscionable is a matter for a court to decide against the background of the contract's commercial setting, purpose, and effect.[124] Although the statute has no guidelines as to the determination of unconscionability, the thrust of the provision is to prevent oppression and unfair surprise to the contracting parties, not to disturb the allocation of risks to a party merely because the other party has superior bargaining power.[125]

An example of unconscionability is found in the case of *Vom Lehn v. Astor Art Galleries, Ltd.*[126] The plaintiff-buyers of twenty Oriental jade carvings for the sum of $67,000 brought an action against the sellers, alleging conspiracy to fraudulently induce them to buy the carvings by misrepresenting their true value and by fraudulently misrepresenting them as being Ming dynasty jade. In the course of the transaction, which included drinks at the prospective buyers' house and going out to dinner, the sellers allegedly told a tale of woe as to their personal circumstances, and the prospective buyers ultimately made a down payment of $19,000 on the merchandise and issued four postdated checks totaling $48,000 for the balance. On subsequently discovering that the carvings were not Ming dynasty jade as represented, the buyers brought suit against the sellers. The New York State Supreme Court, among other findings, noted that no conspiracy or fraud was proved, but it did find that the purchase price was unconscionable; therefore, the court would not enforce the contract requiring the buyers to pay the balance of the purchase price.[127]

In addition to unconscionability, a court can find a contract unenforceable where the language of the contract is ambiguous. In doing so, a court will look both to the reasonable and ordinary meaning of the contract's language and to the actions of the parties. In *Weil v. Murray*,[128] a New York federal district court granted summary judgment to the plaintiff, a collector, on an action for price where the defendant, a dealer, failed to show contractual ambiguity and acted in a manner consistent with ownership. The case involved a painting entitled *Aux Courses* by French impressionist Edgar Degas. After viewing the painting at Weil's Alabama residence, Murray had the painting sent to his New York gallery for a one-week consignment period to show to a prospective buyer. Within five days, Murray informed Weil that a buyer had been found, and a price of $1 million was agreed to in writing. The signed agreement defined Murray as the "buyer" and stated that the eventual buyer was an undisclosed principal client of Murray's and that the principal was also bound by the contract. Neither Murray nor anyone else ever paid Weil the $1 million. Murray retained possession of the painting for more than four months, during which time he had the painting cleaned and restored.[129]

In granting Weil's motion for summary judgment on the contract price, the court found that pursuant to section 2-709(1)(a) of the New York U.C.C.

(1)   there was a contract;

(2)   the buyer failed to pay the purchase price; and

(3)   the buyer accepted the goods.

In response to Murray's argument that the language of the contract made him neither a buyer nor an agent, but rather an intermediary, the court said that reference to a third party did not extinguish Murray's obligation as buyer or agent and that "a contract is not made ambiguous simply because the parties urge different interpretations."[130] The court also found it indisputable that Murray had accepted the goods: He had inspected the painting, had not expressed dissatisfaction, and had acted in a manner consistent with ownership by permitting the painting to be cleaned. Having established that Murray agreed to purchase the Degas, accepted it, and failed to pay the purchase price, Weil was entitled to the contract price plus incidental damages of interest from the date the payment was due.[131]

Title in Works of Art

Passage of Title

The U.C.C. emphasizes a functional approach to sales. It attempts to avoid resolving disputes through a determination of who holds title, recognizing that it is often difficult to determine at what point in the sales transaction a seller's rights in an artwork are transferred to the buyer. But because some issues continue to turn on who holds title, U.C.C. section 2-401 was drafted to treat the topic of title and when it passes. Under the U.C.C.,[132] title to goods passes from the seller to the buyer on physical delivery of the goods, irrespective of when or even whether payment has been made. U.C.C. section 2-401(2) provides that

> [u]nless otherwise explicitly agreed title passes to the buyer at the time and place at which the seller completes his performance with respect to the physical delivery of the goods.

When an art seller delivers a work of art to the buyer and sends an invoice to the buyer that states, "Title does not pass until payment in full is made," a question arises as to whether the seller has retained title or some other interest. The majority view is that title passes and that the seller is left with, at most, a security interest.[133] One of the goals of article 2 of the U.C.C. was to replace the formalism of title inquiries with a functional approach to sales disputes. U.C.C. section 2-401(1) provides: "Any retention of or reservation by the seller of the title (property) in goods shipped or delivered to the buyer is limited in effect to a reservation of a security interest." The majority of cases support the conclusion that title passes at the completion of the seller's performance—that is, when the work of art is delivered.[134]

A persistent minority view is that the parties may contract for a time when title will pass. A New York case involved title to a yacht in which the seller was deemed to maintain title despite delivery, and several courts have read the language of U.C.C. section 2-401(2) to mean that parties may contract to allow the seller to retain title to a delivered good in much the same way that a pre-U.C.C. conditional sales contract did.[135]

The case of *AB Recur Finans v. Andersson*[136] sheds some light on the issues. On November 20, 1989, Peder Bonnier, a Swedish art dealer with a gallery in New York City, sold a Cy Twombly painting to Lennart Andersson, a Swedish art dealer based in Stockholm, for $2,800,000. It was a credit sale in that the invoice provided, "Terms: $100,000.00 deposit due upon receipt of invoice—$2,700,000.00 due February 17, 1990." The invoice was silent as to when title would pass. Shortly thereafter, the Twombly painting was transferred from Bonnier's storage space at Judson Art Warehouse—a well-known art warehouse located in Long Island City, New York, where the painting had been stored—to Andersson's storage space at Judson.

To pay for the painting, Andersson borrowed $2 million from Fortune Finans AB, a Swedish finance company. Fortune retained a security interest in the painting. In addition, Fortune required that Judson execute an agreement with Andersson whereby Judson acknowledged Fortune's security interest in the Twombly and agreed not to release the painting without the prior written consent of Fortune. The letter agreement between Andersson and Judson was stated to be for the benefit of Fortune.

In early April 1990, Andersson still had not paid Bonnier for the Twombly, including the initial $100,000 deposit. On learning of Andersson's financial difficulties, Bonnier called Judson and persuaded its director, a longtime friend, to transfer the Twombly from Andersson's storage space back to Bonnier's storage space. Bonnier told Judson's director that Bonnier was still the owner of the painting because Bonnier had not been paid for it. Judson transferred the painting, despite its agreement with Andersson, which was for Fortune's benefit, not to release the Twombly without Fortune's written consent. Within a few days of reacquiring the Twombly, Bonnier resold the painting to another New York City art dealer, who immediately shipped the painting to Japan, where it was purchased by a Japanese buyer.

Fortune sued Judson for breach of contract as the third-party beneficiary of the agreement between Andersson and Judson. As its primary defense, Judson argued that because Andersson never paid for the painting, Anderson never became its owner—that is, title never passed—and, therefore, Andersson could not have conveyed a valid security interest in the Twombly to Fortune. If Fortune did not have a valid security interest in the painting, Fortune could not have suffered any damage by Judson's releasing the painting to Bonnier in violation of the agreement.

The question was thus whether Andersson had acquired rights in the Twombly. Judge Edward Greenfield concluded that Andersson had acquired title to the Twombly, since the Twombly was delivered by Bonnier (the seller) to Andersson (the buyer) when it was transferred from Bonnier's storage space to Andersson's storage space, and the invoice was silent as to the passage of title. Judge Greenfield held that "Andersson acquired title even though he owed the purchase price when there was physical delivery of the painting."[137] The court concluded that Andersson had sufficient "rights" in the Twombly to enable Fortune to acquire a valid security interest in the painting.[138]

In commenting that the invoice from Bonnier to Andersson did not specifically state any reservation of title, the judge did not address the question of whether the result would have been different if the invoice had so stated. However, in the decision on a later motion[139] in the same case dismissing Judson's claims against Bonnier for fraudulent or negligent misrepresentations, Judge Greenfield made it clear that delivery is the most crucial element in the question of the passage of title. The decision on the motion states the following:

> Judson has been held liable because it, as bailee, disregarded the acknowledged rights of others with a superior claim of right. The sale from Bonnier to Andersson was unconditional. Bonnier reserved no rights in the painting by way of security or otherwise in the bill of sale. This contrast [*sic*] with the bill of sale in evidence of Gagosian (Exhibit 33) which provides "title will pass and delivery will be made when payment is received in full." Even with an explicit reservation of a security interest, title will pass (UCC § 2-401[2]) and "if the goods are at the time of contracting already identified (as was the Twombly painting), and no documents are to be delivered, title passes at the time and place of contracting" UCC § 2-401(3)(b). Before Bonnier attempted any rescission of the sale, the rights of *bona fide* third parties had intervened. UCC § 2-705 permits a seller to stop delivery of goods in the possession of a bailee where the buyer has failed to make a payment, but not after the bailee has acknowledged to the buyer that he is holding the goods for the buyer (or his designee).[140]

Sales of art are often conducted in a casual manner, compared with normal business sales involving comparable sums of money. Because article 9's strict standards spring into action when third parties are involved, it is unwise for art sellers to deliver a work of art and hope that by reserving title on the invoice they will protect their interest in the unpaid-for work of art. An art seller should effect a security interest and perfect it by filing a UCC-1 form, ideally at the time of the delivery of the work of art, and by notifying existing creditors.

Voidable Title

It has long been settled law that one who acquires goods from a thief has no title in and to the goods and, therefore, cannot pass ownership of the goods to successive transferees.[141] Distinguishable from that situation is one with voidable title in which valid title is passed but the sale is voidable. The U.C.C. provides that a person with voidable title has the power to transfer good title to a good-faith purchaser for value.[142] The key to the concept of voidable title is this: The original transferor voluntarily relinquishes possession of the goods and intends to pass title. The original transferor may be defrauded, the check that the transferor received may have bounced, or the transferor may have intended to sell to Y, rather than to Z; nevertheless, the transferor intended to pass title. In such cases the transferor may void the sale, but the transferee can pass good title.[143]

In the case of *Morgold, Inc. v. Keeler*,[144] a title dispute over an oil-on-canvas painting by Alfred T. Bricher of the Hudson River school, was resolved in favor of the buyer. In the absence of decisional law in either California or the Ninth Circuit on issues of title to art, a federal district court in California, seeking guidance elsewhere, applied New York case law in the decision. In the California case, two art dealers bought the painting in question in 1987; each contributed one-half of its purchase price, and each acquired a one-half interest in the painting. One of the dealers sold his interest to Morgold, Inc., in 1989, and the other dealer, Andre Lopoukhine, retained his interest. In 1990, a dispute arose between Lopoukhine and Morgold about how the painting was to be sold. The dispute was resolved through an agreement, which stated that each party owned a one-half interest in the painting and which laid out a procedure for exhibiting and selling it. Later that year, Lopoukhine, who had possession of the painting, sold it to a collector in violation of his agreement with Morgold. The collector then sold it to an antiques dealer, who in turn sold it to an art dealer named Fred E. Keeler. Keeler inspected the painting and did some research into its history. Keeler's research as to the painting's provenance did not turn up any warning signs of a potential title problem.

The court held that Keeler was entitled to possession and title to the painting because

(1) under New York law the agreement between Morgold and Lopoukhine was a joint venture and Lopoukhine's breach of the joint venture agreement with Morgold did not destroy Lopoukhine's power to convey good title;

(2) Lopoukhine was the owner of a one-half interest in the painting and, thus, was not liable for conversion when he sold it; and

(3) even if Lopoukhine did not have the power to convey good title to the painting because he was in breach of the joint-venture agreement, he had voidable title that allowed him to transfer valid title to a good-faith purchaser for value, as value is defined in U.C.C. section 1-201(44).

The court's reasoning is in line with the U.C.C., which provides that a person with voidable title still has the power to transfer valid title to a good-faith purchaser for value.[145]

Not only did Lopoukhine hold voidable title but the court also found that Keeler took the necessary steps to make himself a good-faith purchaser. The court, citing *Porter v. Wertz* and *Cantor v. Anderson*,[146] discussed below, emphasized that an art dealer must take reasonable steps—that is, those that are consistent with reasonable commercial standards in the art trade—to inquire into a painting's title in order to be a good-faith purchaser for value.

Another case animating section 2-403(1) of the U.C.C. is *Holm v. Malmberg*,[147] a dispute involving the ownership of a painting. Holm and Malmberg, dealers in contemporary art, had engaged in numerous previous art transactions. As a result of those transactions, by February 2000, defendant Malmberg was in debt to plaintiff Holm for approximately $1 million, a debt Malmberg sought to cure by offering Holm a half-share in the future purchase of two works by the French artist Yves Klein (referred to as the "Pink Klein" and the "Blue Klein"). The purchase price was $2 million and Malmberg subsequently offset its debt to Holm against the purchase price. Then, in August, Holm paid Malmberg $2 million for one-half interest in several other pieces, including another by Yves Klein ("Gold Klein"). Two months later, Malmberg sold the Pink Klein and the Blue Klein.

Subsequently, defendant Magnus Lindholm, a private collector, alleged that he had owned all three Kleins since 1981, and that the plaintiff and defendant had entered into the Klein transactions without his knowledge. According to Lindholm, he had contacted Malmberg, concerned that his Klein paintings were undervalued and therefore underinsured. Malmberg responded that it knew of a museum's interest in the Kleins; Lindholm expressed interest in having his Kleins assessed by the museum. In preparation for the museum assessment, Malmberg picked up the Kleins from Lindholm's Connecticut home and put them into storage at Lebron's, a storage and shipping facility in Queens, New York. On the blank receipt of the storage facility, Lindholm wrote a brief description of the three Kleins and then the following: "All Works above by Yves Klein for temporary storage on behalf of Magnus Lindholm."[148]

The next day, the storage facility released the Gold Klein to Holm without contacting Lindholm. Shortly thereafter, Holm acquired Malmberg's one-half interest in the Gold Klein, thereby reducing Malmberg's outstanding debt to Holm. In January 2001, Lindholm learned from Christie's auction house that it was selling the Gold Klein for $3.5 million. He then contacted the storage facility and demanded return of the three Kleins. The Pink and Blue Kleins were returned in February and Lindholm was advised that the Gold Klein would be returned in two days. Holm then sued Malmberg and Lindholm, alleging, among other contentions, breach of contract and seeking a declaration that it owned the Gold Klein and half-interests in the Pink and Blue Kleins.

Holm withdrew its claim to the Pink and Blue Kleins, but it argued that it took title to the Gold Klein as a good-faith purchaser under New York's U.C.C. section 2-403(1)–(3).[149] That is, when goods have been delivered under a purchase transaction, the purchaser has the power to transfer good title to a good-faith purchaser for value even though the delivery was procured through fraud punishable as larcenous under the criminal law. In denying Lindholm's motion to dismiss, the court found that Holm's allegations—that following a solicitation by Malmberg to buy a half-share in the Gold Klein, it forwarded significant funds to Malmberg and that Lindholm shortly thereafter released the Gold Klein to the storage facility, which acted as Malmberg's agent—comprised sufficient facts to claim it bought the Gold Klein from Malmberg after Malmberg bought it from Lindholm.[150]

Void Title

In contrast to the validity of a transfer of voidable title, where a seller has no title to convey because the title is void, it has been held that the U.C.C. does not protect the good-faith purchaser. In *Kenyon v. Abel*,[151] a Wyoming State Supreme Court affirmed a lower court's holding that the nonvoluntary (accidental) transfer of a painting to the Salvation Army and its later resale constituted a conversion by the charity to which the good faith of the buyer was not a defense. The painting, a Western scene by artist Bill Gollings, valued between $8,000 and $15,000, was among the plaintiff's aunt's possessions when she died. Plaintiff, her sole heir, cleaned out her house, choosing items to retain and items to donate to the Salvation Army. By mistake the Salvation Army took a box containing the painting. It was subsequently sold to the defendant through the charity's thrift store for $25. Immediately after discovering that the painting was not included in the items he had retained, the plaintiff tracked down the defendant to request its return. Unsuccessful, plaintiff brought suit seeking possession of the painting through actions in replevin and conversion.[152]

The court agreed with the district court's finding that plaintiff's testimony that he unintentionally included the painting with items meant for the Salvation Army and immediately attempted to recover it upon finding it missing evidenced its nonvoluntary transfer. Thus the district court's award of the painting to the plaintiff could be upheld either under the law of gifts, for lack of intent to make a gift, or under the law of conversion. The painting was converted because

(1) as the heir, plaintiff had legal title to the painting;

(2) he possessed it at the time it was removed;

(3) the Salvation Army exercised dominion over it and by its sale denied plaintiff's right to enjoy its use;

(4) plaintiff's demand for return was refused; and

(5) plaintiff suffered damages through loss of the asset without compensation.

"[A] converter has no title whatsoever (*i.e.*, his title is void) and, therefore, nothing can be conveyed to a bona fide purchaser for value."[153]

The court emphasized the difference between voidable title and void title under the U.C.C. Voidable title occurs where the transferor voluntarily delivers goods to a purchaser even though the delivery was procured by fraud. Under section 2-403(1), the transferor runs the risk of the purchaser's fraud as against innocent third parties because the transferor is best able to protect against the fraud. But where the goods are wrongfully transferred, as in a theft, section 2-403(1)(d) does not create voidable title; it makes the title void. It follows, the court reasoned, that as here, where the goods cannot be defined as "delivered" for purposes of the statute because they were obtained against the will or intent of the owner, then under section 2-403(1)(d) the Salvation Army had no title to convey to the defendant. As title never passed from the plaintiff, he was entitled to possession.[154]

Entrustment

Entrustment covers various situations where one person delivers goods to another person for a particular purpose. The two most common categories of entrustment are consignments and bailments.

Consignments were formerly governed by article 2 of the U.C.C.—specifically section 2-326(3). That section was repealed effective July 1, 2001. Consignments are now governed by article 9 of the U.C.C. and are defined in section 9-102(a)(20). Consignments under article 9 of the U.C.C. are discussed in detail beginning at page 151.

Bailments are not defined in the U.C.C. Generally, a bailment is deemed to arise when one person entrusts property to another person temporarily for some purpose and, upon fulfillment of that purpose, the property is either delivered back to the first person or otherwise in accordance with her directions.[155] For example, a loan of an artwork to a museum exhibition for a specific period of time is a bailment.

Entrustments are defined generally in section 2-403(3) of the U.C.C. to involve any delivery of goods by one party to another party and any acquiescence by the entrustor in the entrustee's retention of possession. This is so regardless of any condition expressed between the parties to the delivery or acquiescence, and regardless of whether the procurement of the entrustment or the entrustee's disposition of the goods qualifies as a crime.

The concept of entrustment, codified in the U.C.C., "converts voidable title to good title and . . . expands the merchant's power to transfer title."[156] As U.C.C. section 2-403(2) provides, when goods are entrusted to a merchant who deals in goods of that kind, that merchant is empowered to transfer all rights of the entruster to a buyer in the ordinary course of business.

"The buyer in the ordinary course of business" under the U.C.C. means

> a person who in good faith and without knowledge that the sale to him is in violation of the ownership rights or security interest of a third party in the goods buys in ordinary course from a person in the business of selling goods of that kind. . . . "Buying" . . . does not include a transfer . . . in total or partial satisfaction of a money debt.[157]

In *Cantor v. Anderson*,[158] the plaintiff Edward Cantor, a private art collector, received as security for a debt a Pierre-Auguste Renoir drawing valued at approximately $160,000 from the defendant Dennis Anderson, an art dealer, after Cantor repeatedly demanded payment for debts owed to him by Anderson. A New York federal district court held that Cantor was not a buyer in the ordinary course of business; therefore, the entrustment principle did not apply. Rather, the court held that Wildenstein & Co., Inc., the art dealer that consigned the Renoir to Anderson and that intervened in the suit to seek return of its Renoir, was, in fact, entitled to recover possession of the artwork. Cantor was not the type of creditor that U.C.C. section 2-326 (Consignment Sales and Rights of Creditors) was intended to protect, since he had knowledge that Anderson was in financial trouble.

As to the requirement of good faith, what standard must a party observe to qualify as a buyer in the ordinary course of business? In the case of a merchant, the U.C.C. defines good faith as "honesty in fact and the observance of reasonable commercial standards of fair dealing in the trade."[159] Good faith cannot include indifference on the part of the merchant-buyer as to the provenance or history of ownership of the artwork purchased by the buyer.

Thus, in *Porter v. Wertz*,[160] in which an owner of a Maurice Utrillo painting sought to recover its possession from the Richard Feigen art gallery, which had sold the painting to a buyer out of the country, the court held in favor of the plaintiff-owner. In that case, plaintiff Samuel Porter, an art collector, had a number of dealings with Harold von Maker. Von Maker used the name Peter Wertz (Wertz was an acquaintance of von Maker's) and was known as Peter Wertz to Porter. In the spring of 1973, Porter permitted von Maker to take Porter's Utrillo home temporarily, pending von Maker's decision whether to buy the painting. In July 1973, Porter discovered that von Maker had purchased another of Porter's paintings with bad notes. After an investigation, Porter learned that he had been dealing not with Peter Wertz but with a man named von Maker, who had an arrest record for theft-related crimes. Although von Maker subsequently assured Porter that he would either return the Utrillo or pay $30,000, he had already disposed of the painting by using the real Peter Wertz to effect its sale to the Feigen & Co. art gallery for $20,000.

Peter Wertz was a delicatessen employee, not an art merchant, and the Feigen art gallery seemed aware of that fact. Feigen & Co. found a buyer for the Utrillo and collected a commission. The buyer in turn sold the painting, resulting in its shipment to Venezuela. On ruling in favor of Porter and against the Feigen & Co. art gallery, the court noted that Feigen & Co. was not a buyer in the ordinary course of business, since (1) the gallery did not purchase the Utrillo from an art dealer and (2) by departing from normal commercial standards in failing to inquire into the provenance of the Utrillo and the status of the party who sold it to the gallery, the gallery was not acting in good faith.[161]

In the New York federal district court decision of *Graffman v. Espel*,[162] Sture Graffman, the owner of a Picasso painting, contracted with Miguel Espel to sell it on Graffman's behalf. The contract appointed Espel as the exclusive agent to sell the painting and authorized him to sell it through intermediaries. Espel contacted his brother-in-law Michael Delecea, a sometime private art dealer, to assist him in the sale of the painting and shipped it to him in New York. Delecea then approached the Avanti Gallery in New York City and asked for its help in identifying a buyer. Avanti found buyers— identified in the court's opinion as John and Jane Doe—who purchased the painting for $875,000. The Does paid Avanti, which, after deducting its commission, transferred the balance to Delecea. Delecea paid part of the money to Espel and used the balance to pay some of Espel's personal debts. Espel and Delecea disappeared. Graffman was never paid. Without painting or payment, Graffman then sued the Avanti Gallery and the Does.

The defendants argued that Graffman authorized Delecea to sell the painting, while Graffman claimed Delecea's sale of the painting was unauthorized. If Delecea, as an intermediary agent of Espel, had authority to sell, then the Does under section 2-403(1) of the U.C.C. would as good-faith purchasers have acquired good title. But Delecea's authority to sell, said the court, was a question for the jury.[163]

The court then addressed Graffman's claims under the U.C.C. and pointed out that section 2-403 is not applicable when a person given possession of goods makes an authorized sale of them. For purposes of the decision, the court assumed that Delecea did not have authority to sell the painting to the Avanti Gallery. Even so, said the court, "when an agent has violated his or her instructions, Section

2-403 may operate to bind the principal such that the purchaser acquires good title from the principal's agent."[164] Therefore, Graffman
may be bound to Delecea's actions irrespective of whether Delecea
had the authority to sell to Avanti. As a matter of public policy, section 2-403(2) operates to protect the buyer in the ordinary course of
business over the owner by providing that an owner who entrusts an
item to a merchant who deals in goods of that kind gives the merchant the power to transfer all rights of the owner to a buyer. Under
this provision, a buyer who makes a purchase in the ordinary course
of business will prevail over the claim of an owner who entrusts such
item to the seller merchant. This entrustment provision is designed
to enhance the reliability of commercial sales by merchants who deal
in goods of the particular kind by shifting the risk of resale to one
who releases her property to the merchant. The loss is placed upon
the party who vested the merchant with the ability to transfer the
property with apparent good title.[165]

Graffman then argued that Avanti was not entitled to the protection of the entrustment provisions because the painting was never
entrusted to Delecea. Though ordinarily put to the jury, the question of whether there had been an entrustment failed for lack of evidence from Graffman to support the assertion that the painting had
never been entrusted to Delecea. Graffman had never objected to
Delecea's custody of the painting. Furthermore, the court concluded, Delecea was, for the purposes of section 1-201(9), an art dealer—
that is, a merchant who deals in works of art. The painting was therefore entrusted to Delecea, a merchant within the meaning of the
U.C.C.[166]

Graffman did not allege that Avanti Gallery bought the painting
from Delecea with knowledge the sale was in violation of his rights.
Rather, he argued that Avanti was required, in accordance with reasonable commercial standards applicable to art dealers, to inquire
into the provenance of the painting. Failure to do so was a failure to
observe reasonable commercial standards of fair dealing in the trade
and a failure to act in good faith.[167] Avanti, citing *Morgold*, argued
that art dealers are only required to make a reasonable inquiry "if
there are warnings that something is wrong with the transaction."[168]

The court, noting that summary judgment is inappropriate where industry customs are at issue, determined that whether Avanti met the reasonable commercial standards of the art industry was a question for the trier of fact. If a jury were to determine that Avanti acted in good faith, then it would be entitled to protection under the entrustment section of section 2-403. That issue never went to trial since Avanti Gallery ceased doing business. This left Graffman's claim against the Does.

Irrespective of whether Delecea was authorized to sell the painting, the Does claimed that they were innocent purchasers entitled to protection of section 2-403(1), which provides in part that a person with voidable title has power to transfer good title to a good-faith purchaser for value. Graffman alleged that for the Does to have acted in good faith they must have inquired into the painting's provenance on their own, rather than rely on the Avanti Gallery to conduct an investigation. The Does, having had substantial dealings in the past with Avanti, made no such inquiry. In distinguishing both *Porter* and *Morgold*, where the innocent purchasers were art dealers obligated to adhere to industry standards of a merchant under the U.C.C., the court held, as a matter of law, that the Does as nonmerchant collectors had no obligation to investigate the provenance of the painting. Summary judgment was granted in favor of the Does and was later affirmed by the court of appeals.[169]

Agency Distinguished from Entrustment

The result in *Graffman* can be contrasted with the New York state court decision of *Dark Bay International, Ltd. v. Acquavella Galleries*,[170] where the plaintiff Dark Bay International (DBI) sued the defendant art gallery for breach of an alleged contract whereby the gallery was to sell Pablo Picasso's *Les Deux Enfants* to DBI. The parties' dispute centered on the role of one Michel Cohen.

The gallery claimed to have sold the painting to Cohen. According to the gallery, it delivered the painting to Cohen in September 2000, with payment due no later than October 31, 2000. When Cohen could not pay, he returned the painting to the gallery on November 1, 2000. The gallery sold the painting in June 2001 to a third party.

According to DBI, however, the gallery had, through Cohen, agreed to sell the painting to DBI. John Fielding, DBI's founder, was shown the painting by Cohen in October 2000, but Fielding rejected the price that Cohen offered. Disputing the gallery's evidence that Cohen had returned the painting to the gallery in November, DBI asserted that Cohen brought the painting to Fielding again on December 13, 2000, and offered to sell it for a reduced price of $2.27 million. After that meeting, Cohen took the painting with him. Several days later, DBI agreed to the deal, and on December 28, it paid Cohen, but it never received the painting. Cohen disappeared with the money.

DBI sued the gallery for breach of contract and conversion, seeking either damages or replevin of the painting and specific performance of the sale. Both parties moved for summary judgment. The gallery argued that it never authorized Cohen to act on its behalf and had no contract to sell the painting to DBI. DBI countered that the gallery had authorized Cohen with express, implied, or apparent authority to sell the painting to it.

Though ordinarily the question of agency is one reserved for a jury, the court found no evidence to support plaintiff's claim that the gallery had control over Cohen (an essential element to an agency relationship) and reserved the question for itself. The disappearance of Cohen, the court said, prevented DBI from establishing express authority by Cohen's testimony. Authority could be implied, however, if verbal or other acts by the gallery could reasonably give the appearance of Cohen's authority as an agent. To establish the implied authority, DBI argued that the transaction between the gallery and Cohen was a consignment. In support of its argument, DBI pointed to nine previous transactions in which the gallery had consigned work to Cohen. But the court rejected this evidence, stating that "DBI cannot impute express authority to sell the painting . . . from these earlier consignments. Otherwise, an agent would be an agent forever. . . ."[171] The gallery challenged DBI's consignment theory, arguing that its invoice to Cohen evidenced a sale, not a consignment. DBI responded by citing an 1875 U.S. Supreme Court decision holding that "an invoice is not a bill of sale, nor is it evidence of a sale."[172] The court stated that the previous consignments were evidenced by consignment agreements and where, as here, there was no evidence of any such agreement or invoicing for the painting in question, DBI's theory was questionable.

The court then turned to the alleged apparent authority of Cohen to sell the painting, which required DBI to show

(1) words or acts of the gallery communicated to DBI made it reasonable to believe that Cohen possessed the authority to act for the gallery;

(2) reasonable reliance by DBI, and

(3) that DBI made reasonable inquiries as to Cohen's actual authority.

The court concluded that even if the gallery had given Cohen apparent authority, DBI could not show reasonable reliance. "In the world of art," the court explained, "a buyer must inquire into [the art's] provenance."[173] DBI made no meaningful inquiry and, unlike in *Graffman*, where the proceeds of the sale were never forwarded and the issue was whether the consignee had the authority to sub-consign, there was no consignment agreement in this case and therefore no need to look to industry customs.

Having failed to establish an agency relationship between the gallery and Cohen where Cohen had the right to sell, DBI could not prove itself the rightful owner and allege conversion.

Furthermore, the court noted, DBI's entrustment theory could not be reconciled with the sequence of events as documented. Cohen was not in possession of the painting either when Fielding agreed to its purchase or when DBI transferred payment to Cohen. The gallery therefore could not have entrusted the painting to Cohen at the time of the alleged sale. Accordingly, the gallery's motion for summary judgment was granted.

The Duty of Inquiry into Title

If an art dealer, on buying a work of art, fails to make any inquiry into the nature of the seller's authority to sell that artwork, particularly when the circumstances are somewhat out of the ordinary, the dealer is not deemed to be a buyer in the ordinary course of business and, accordingly, is no better than a converter.[174] For example, in *Howley v. Sotheby's, Inc.*[175] the defendant purchased plaintiff's lithograph from a thief who represented himself as the plaintiff's nephew and agent. The court found that the circumstances surrounding the purchase of the lithograph were such that the defendant, an art dealer, was obligated to investigate the transaction scrupulously to insure its legitimacy. Because the purchaser did not investigate the transaction, as he was obligated to do, he was liable to the plaintiff for conversion of the lithograph. A dealer should always make some inquiry into a seller's authority to sell an artwork. A purchaser of art who is not a dealer, however, is subject to somewhat less stringent requirements in satisfying good faith.[176]

Similarly, in *Taborsky v. Maroney*,[177] a federal court of appeals affirmed a district court's holding that the suspicious circumstances surrounding the purchase and sale of a Grant Wood drawing between two art merchants imposed on the buying merchant a duty to inquire as to the selling merchant's authority. Citing Wisconsin law, the court noted that a merchant dealing in goods and entrusted with the possession of goods of that kind can transfer all rights of the entruster to a buyer in the ordinary course of business.[178] The court further addressed the more stringent standard pertaining to buyers who are also merchants and noted that a merchant buyer must

(1) be honest in fact,

(2) not have knowledge that a sale would be in violation of the ownership rights of a third party, and

(3) observe reasonable commercial standards of fair dealing in the trade and be charged with the knowledge or the skill of a merchant.[179]

That higher than usual level of knowledge attributed to a merchant means that actual knowledge of certain information concerning unusual circumstances surrounding a transaction can prevent a merchant from becoming a buyer in the ordinary course of business, even though the buyer does not have knowledge that the sale is in violation of the ownership rights of a third party. If, as in *Taborsky*, a merchant-buyer fails to inquire into the propriety of the transaction when suspicious circumstances arise, the merchant-buyer has failed to conform to the reasonable commercial practices of fair dealing in the trade and, therefore, cannot qualify as a buyer in the ordinary course of business.[180]

In *United States v. Crawford Technical Services*,[181] a jewelry dealer's purchase of a 5.04-carat diamond was found not to have been made in "good faith" when he failed to inquire into the diamond's title before acquiring it. The diamond had been reported stolen to the Las Vegas police in 1994 when it was allegedly stolen from a salesman to whom it had been consigned. After investigation by the diamond's insurer, which paid the salesman's claim of more than $69,000, the theft was reported to the Gemological Institute of America (GIA).

In early July 1996, the diamond resurfaced when a woman tried to exchange it for several items of jewelry at a retail store owned by Charles Cohen. The customer produced no bill of sale or invoice documenting the diamond's value or how she had come into its possession. Cohen then swapped several items in his store for the diamond and the customer's check for $5,069. There was no other documentation of the transaction. Cohen did not cash the check for some time (it bounced when he did), nor did he do anything with the diamond until he agreed to sell it to another dealer in September 1997. Before completing the transaction, the second dealer submitted the diamond to the GIA for a grading report; because it had been reported stolen, the GIA confiscated it and alerted the FBI.

In determining whether Cohen or the insurer was the rightful owner, the court, citing *Guggenheim*,[182] stated that "a purchaser of stolen property does not have clear title, even if the purchase was made in good faith" because "a thief has no title to give."[183] The court found it "therefore incumbent upon a good faith purchaser to inquire about the validity of title before completing the transaction."[184] In determining that Cohen could not have acted in good faith and that his claim was inferior to that of the insurance company, the court focused on the fact that he had fifty years of experience, failed to ask for a bill of sale or other documentation, undervalued the ring by more than half its value, and pursued collection from the customer lackadaisically. Had Cohen at least inquired into the customer's title, it would have been apparent she had none. The court also noted that Cohen could not be prejudiced because the report of the theft to the local police and the GIA were steps "appropriate and sufficient" to defeat a defense of laches.[185]

The Merchant's Duty of Disclosure

Case law indicates that the dealer as seller must disclose information relating to possible title problems in the works it offers for sale. In *Van Rijn v. Wildenstein*,[186] a Dutch art dealer contracted with the Wildenstein dealership to buy two paintings, one by El Greco and one by Sandro Botticelli. Michael van Rijn in turn agreed to sell the two works to a Tokyo art dealership. However, the Tokyo dealership canceled its contract with van Rijn on discovering that the government of Romania had a claim of ownership in and to the El Greco work. Van Rijn brought suit against Wildenstein for breach of warranties and fraud, claiming that Wildenstein falsely and fraudulently represented the title of the two paintings as being free of all claims. The trial, in a New York federal district court, took place in October and November 1987 and resulted in a jury verdict against the defendant for $450,000 for breach of warranty of merchantability. (There was, however, no finding of fraud or breach of warranty of title.) The parties later reached a settlement, the terms of which are confidential.

California has a unique statutory provision that requires a merchant to whom property is consigned to reveal, on demand from the consignor, the name and address of the buyer and the sales price. Any person violating this requirement may be guilty of a misdemeanor.[187]

Risk of Loss

As the U.C.C. makes clear,[188] the risk of loss for goods, including artwork, that are damaged or stolen while consigned is borne by the consignee, usually an art dealer. Even so, the consignor, usually a collector, is wise to insist that the consignee maintain insurance covering artwork delivered to it for consignment so that the consignor will be paid in full in the event of any loss. When artwork is purchased from a nonmerchant seller, the risk of loss of the goods passes to the buyer on the buyer's receipt of notification necessary to enable the buyer to take the delivery.[189] However, when artwork is purchased from a merchant, the risk of loss of the goods passes to the buyer only on actual receipt of the goods.[190]

Principles of Contract and Tort Law

An aggrieved purchaser seeking recourse through the application of existing general contract and tort law principles generally finds fewer protections than those mandated by the U.C.C. A case in point is *Mennella v. Schon*[191] in which the Fifth Circuit applied the law of Louisiana (where article 2 of the U.C.C. has not been adopted) to an art sales contract in which passage of title was the issue. The plaintiff-collector Opal Mennella agreed to buy from defendant Kurt E. Schon's New Orleans art gallery in April 1988 the painting *Princess Mary* by the Flemish master Anthony Van Dyck for $350,000. She paid Schon $50,000 up front, with a balance of $300,000, according to the invoice, to be paid on June 1, 1988.

Experiencing cash-flow problems, Mennella amicably secured a few months' extension. By Christmas of 1988, when she had managed to pay only an additional $90,000, she demanded authentication of the painting, to be used to secure a loan to pay the balance of the purchase price. Schon duly complied. Concerned that the portrait might be counterfeit, Mennella repudiated the painting's value and demanded the return of the money she had already paid. Schon responded by a letter in the spring of 1989, a full year after the ostensible sale, demanding payment of the balance of the purchase price within five days and threatening that otherwise he would be forced to return the painting to the gallery's active sale stock. When Mennella failed to respond to the letter, Schon, in May 1989, notified Mennella in writing that he considered the sale canceled and that he viewed her inaction as a default. He subsequently offered to refund $95,000—the $140,000 she paid minus the $45,000 cost of the authentication—or provide her with $140,000 of store credit. Mennella rejected both offers.

In November 1989, unbeknownst to Mennella, the painting was shipped to Christie's London, where it sold for more than $1.4 million. Unaware of the London sale, Mennella in December 1989 filed suit, seeking rescission of the sale and damages. Mennella claimed that she only agreed to buy the Van Dyck on proper authentication and that the painting was a fraud. When she learned of the London sale, her attitude changed. She now alleged that the painting was hers, that the London sale constituted a conversion, and that she was entitled to those sale proceeds.

In applying Louisiana law, the Fifth Circuit determined that title to the Van Dyck passed to Mennella in April 1988, since, in credit sales, "when the parties agree as to the price and the thing, title passes instant[ly]."[192] However, the Fifth Circuit also found that by refusing to perform, Mennella had repudiated the contract, and the court deemed the contract dissolved when Schon sent Mennella notice of default on May 2, 1989. Therefore, Schon had legal title to the painting when it was sold in London and was required to refund to Mennella merely the full amount of her payments with interest from the date of the London sale.

Contractual Mistake

Mutual Mistake

Separate and apart from a warranty claim is the legal theory of mutual mistake, in which both the buyer and the seller of a work of art are mistaken as to a material aspect of that work—for example, the identity of the artist. In the event of mutual mistake, the sole form of relief ordinarily available to the aggrieved party is rescission and restitution. If a sold object is discovered to be significantly more valuable than both parties had assumed, the seller may rescind the sale.[193] Similarly, if the object is significantly less valuable than both the buyer and the seller thought, the buyer may seek recourse.[194] When a seller, ignorant of the value of an item, sells it and the item turns out to be worth much more than its purchase price, generally the seller may get no relief. Presumably conscious of her ignorance, the seller has made no operative mistake of fact that would justify any relief.[195] If in a transaction, however, a mistake is the fault of the seller or the seller knows or has reason to know of a mistake, a buyer may obtain rescission and restitution, even if the mistake was unilateral on the buyer's part.[196]

As illustrated in such cases as *Uptown Gallery, Inc. v. Doniger*[197] and *Feigen & Co. v. Weil*,[198] the theory of mutual mistake is of particular importance to an art dealer who buys from a nonmerchant an artwork that turns out not to be authentic. The rulings in those cases, which favor the merchant-buyer, make clear that under the theory of mutual mistake an art merchant may be an aggrieved party in the course of dealing with a nonmerchant and that as an aggrieved party the art merchant may secure rescission and restitution as forms of relief. The protection the theory offers the merchant-buyer assumes particular significance, since both the U.C.C. and special statutes in a number of states— including Florida,[199] Iowa,[200] New York,[201] and Michigan[202]—provide that when an art merchant sells artwork to a nonmerchant, the transaction generally presumes an express warranty that the artwork is authentic. Similar statutes in several states cover multiples.[203] Despite the rulings in *Doniger* and in *Feigen*, the applicability of the U.C.C. and such state legislation to a transaction in which a merchant-buyer purchases art from a nonmerchant-seller remains an open question.

In *Doniger*, the plaintiff Uptown Gallery was an art gallery in New York City. The defendant Marjorie Doniger, who was never in the art business, once purchased a painting through Philip Williams, the president of Uptown. Williams came to Doniger's house to hang the painting for her, and there he saw a painting that he assumed was by the French artist Bernard Buffet and that, in fact, bore the signature "Bernard Buffet." Sometime later, in March 1990, Williams persuaded Doniger, after some initial hesitancy on her part, to sell Uptown her Bernard Buffet painting. Williams returned to Doniger's house, examined the painting closely, questioned her about its provenance (she was unclear as to the painting's ownership history), and then on behalf of Uptown bought the painting for $55,000. The purchase invoice, prepared by Uptown and signed by Doniger under the phrase "agreed and accepted," described the painting as a Bernard Buffet. In addition, in all prior discussions between the parties, the painting was referred to as a Bernard Buffet, and there was evidence that both parties genuinely believed that the painting was by Bernard Buffet.

After acquiring the painting, Uptown, in the process of seeking a certificate of authenticity for the Buffet in order to close a potential sale quickly, learned that the painting was a forgery. Uptown relayed that finding to Doniger and demanded a refund of the purchase price. Doniger expressed shock at the news but refused to refund the purchase price to Uptown. In the New York State Supreme Court, Uptown subsequently sought recovery of the $55,000 purchase price plus interest and costs from Doniger on two grounds: (1) breach of an express warranty pursuant to section 2-313 of the U.C.C. and (2) mutual mistake.

In asserting breach of express warranty, Uptown alleged that Doniger, by adopting the phrase "agreed and accepted" in the invoice, warranted that the painting was a genuine Buffet and that a merchant buyer like Uptown may enforce an express warranty as freely as may a nonmerchant. Uptown, however, did not address the issue as to whether an express warranty attaches to a transaction having a nonmerchant-*seller* like Doniger as readily as to a transaction involving a merchant-seller. The New York State Supreme Court, in its decision, did not address the plaintiff's breach of warranty claim at all.

In asserting the doctrine of mutual mistake, Uptown cited the instant facts as a textbook example of a contract voidable on the basis of that doctrine. That is, that "at all times throughout the chain of events leading up to and including" the sale of the painting by Doniger to Uptown for $55,000, both parties believed the painting to be a genuine Bernard Buffet; that the mistake creates such an imbalance in the agreed exchange that the aggrieved party cannot fairly be required to carry it out; and that the mistake demonstrates the absence of the "meeting of the minds" required to create a contract.[204] Uptown noted the similarities between its case and that of *Feigen & Co. v. Weil* (see below), also a transaction involving the sale by a nonmerchant to a merchant-buyer of a work of art. In that case too, the nonmerchant-seller argued, unsuccessfully, that the merchant-buyer should bear the loss for the mistake, since the buyer acted with conscious ignorance in failing to authenticate the artwork before purchasing it. The New York State Supreme Court in *Doniger* adopted the reasoning of *Feigen*: This was not a situation in which the parties were uncertain of a material fact and, ignoring the uncertainty, contracted anyway. Rather, both parties entered into the sale transaction on the assumption that the painting was an authentic Bernard Buffet. Accordingly, the court granted the plaintiff Uptown rescission on the contract based on mutual mistake.[205]

In *Feigen & Co. v. Weil*, the defendant Frank A. Weil, a nonmerchant art collector, sold an ink drawing entitled *Le Vase d'opaline* and signed "H. Matisse '47" to Richard L. Feigen & Co., a well-known art dealer in New York City. Weil, a prominent New York businessman of outstanding integrity, received the drawing as a gift in the late 1960s from his mother, a member of the founding family of Sears Roebuck and Co. Weil's mother had owned the drawing for ten to fifteen years before giving it to her son. Weil had made inquiries of various art dealers as to its approximate value and decided he would sell it if he could receive $100,000. Weil telephoned Feigen & Co. in early April 1989 and requested that the gallery pick up the drawing. The gallery sold it to Tom Hammons on May 5, 1989, for $165,000 and remitted $100,000 to Weil on May 15, 1989. The facts indicated that both Feigen and Weil strongly believed that the drawing was by Matisse.

One year later, the purchaser, Hammons, brought the drawing to the Acquavella Galleries in New York City, which contacted the administrator of the Matisse estate about the drawing's authenticity. The administrator responded that the drawing was a forgery, and Feigen & Co. immediately informed Weil and arranged to reimburse Hammons for his purchase price of $165,000. When Weil refused to return the $100,000 that Feigen & Co. had paid him, the gallery instituted a lawsuit, alleging

(1) rescission of a consignment contract,

(2) breach of such contract,

(3) breach of express and implied warranties relating to such contract,

(4) fraud,

(5) negligent misrepresentation, or

(6) some combination of the above causes.

Feigen & Co. moved for summary judgment, seeking rescission based on mutual mistake. Although Weil acknowledged that both parties honestly assumed that the drawing was authentic, he argued that rescission should not apply because

(1) Feigen & Co. was consciously ignorant of the drawing's authenticity;

(2) it would be most equitable under the circumstances to impose the risk of loss for a contractual mistake on Feigen & Co.;

(3) Feigen & Co. acted in bad faith and should thus bear the loss; and

(4) if there was a consignment contract between the parties, Feigen & Co. breached its fiduciary duty as an agent to Weil by failing to authenticate the work before selling it.

The court, in finding for Feigen & Co., correctly stated the following:

> [W]here a mistake in contracting is both mutual and substantial,
> there is an absence of the requisite "meeting of the minds" to
> the contract and relief will be provided in the form of
> rescission. . . .[206]

The purpose of the doctrine of mutual mistake is to prevent the injustice that would arise when one party to a contract, realizing that a
mutual mistake is to its advantage, seeks enforcement of the contract.
By allowing rescission of the contract, the parties can return to the
status quo.[207]

Weil argued that Feigen & Co., in failing to authenticate the
drawing in a timely fashion, was "consciously ignorant" of its authenticity and, therefore, cannot claim mutual mistake. The court
pointed out that all the cases Weil cited arose when the parties to the
contract assumed a risk as to the facts underlying the transaction. For
example, if a person brings a stone to a jeweler, is uncertain as to its
true nature, and sells it to the jeweler for less than its true value, a
mutual mistake has not occurred because conscious ignorance is
present; the price was fixed between the parties with consciousness
of the fact that the stone may or may not be worth the price paid.[208]
But both Feigen & Co. and Weil honestly believed that the drawing
was a Matisse, and neither assumed the risk that it was a fake. Therefore, the court concluded,

> if a party does not make a conscious decision to proceed in the
> face of insufficient information, the conscious ignorance excep-
> tion to the mutual mistake doctrine does not apply.[209]

The court pointed out that there is no authority for the proposition
that in a contract between an expert and a nonexpert rescission based
on mutual mistake is unavailable to the expert.

The court did not find that Feigen & Co. had any legal duty to
authenticate the drawing. Its acceptance of the drawing as a Matisse
was based on its examination of the work, on its rational assessment
of the source and the style of the work, and on Weil's family reputation and known integrity. Feigen & Co. was not asked to go beyond

a cursory inquiry as to the drawing's authenticity, nor did it have any substantive or legal obligation to do so.

The case of *Feigen & Co. v. Weil* should be compared with *Porter v. Wertz*, discussed earlier[210] (see page 114) in which the same Feigen & Co. had purchased a Maurice Utrillo painting from Peter Wertz. Wertz was a delicatessen employee, and the gallery was aware of that fact. Wertz had obtained the painting from Samuel Porter through trickery. When Porter learned that Feigen & Co. had sold the painting, he sued to recover it. The court, in finding for Porter against Feigen & Co., noted that the gallery, by departing from normal commercial standards in failing to inquire into the provenance of the Utrillo and the status of the party who sold it, was not acting in good faith. In other words, the fact that the Utrillo was sold by a delicatessen employee should have been sufficient to cause Feigen & Co. to inquire further into the nature of the transaction.

In contrast, in *Feigen & Co. v. Weil*, neither the facts nor Weil's behavior should have caused Feigen & Co. to suspect that the drawing was not authentic. We believe the court correctly found a mutual mistake. Weil was ordered to return the $100,000 plus interest to Feigen & Co.

The result in *Feigen* should also be contrasted with *Firestone & Parson, Inc. v. Union League of Philadelphia*,[211] in which the Union League (not an art merchant) sold a painting supposedly by Albert Bierstadt to Firestone & Parson, an art merchant. As in *Feigen & Co. v. Weil*, both parties believed at the time of the sale in 1981 that the painting was authentic. Although the court found for the Union League on the basis of the fact that the Firestone & Parson's claim was time-barred by the four-year statute of limitations, it indicated that a mutual mistake had not occurred.

> Although the procedural posture of the case is such that only the statute of limitations bar can now be addressed, my ruling that plaintiffs' claims are time-barred should not be interpreted as suggesting that plaintiffs' claims would otherwise have been valid: in the arcane world of high-priced art, market value is affected by market perceptions; the market value of a painting is determined by the prevailing views of the marketplace con-

cerning its attribution. Post-sale fluctuations in generally accepted attributions do not necessarily establish that there was a
mutual mistake of fact at the time of the sale. If both parties correctly believed at that time that the painting was generally believed to be a Bierstadt, and in fact it was then generally
regarded as a Bierstadt, it seems unlikely that plaintiff could
show that there was a mutual mistake of fact.[212]

In *Feigen & Co. v. Weil* there was no allegation that it was generally believed in the art world that the Matisse drawing was authentic
(neither Feigen nor Weil had contacted the Matisse estate in Paris);
only Weil and Feigen believed it was authentic. In contrast, in *Firestone* both Firestone and Parson and the Union League admitted that
the painting had been attributed to Bierstadt and that it was generally
regarded in art circles as being a major Bierstadt work. Only later,
when the accepted scholarship about the painting changed, did the
problem arise.

Although we agree with the technical legal result in *Feigen & Co.
v. Weil*, since no suspicious circumstances imposed a duty on Feigen
& Co. to inquire further about the Matisse, we believe that Feigen &
Co. could have avoided the lawsuit if it had acted in a more prudent
manner. An art dealer, when buying from a collector, should inform
the collector, particularly when purchasing a work of art that origi-
nates in France or another country where a recognized authenticity
committee exists, that the work of art should be authenticated before
completion of the transaction. A collector who is selling to an art
dealer should ask the art dealer to perform that service without cost
to the seller before entering into a sale or consignment agreement.[213]
Further, a collector who buys a work of art from an art dealer should
always require the art dealer to furnish a certificate of authenticity
before completing the sale.

Mutual Mistake Rebutted by Authenticity

In *Greenberg Gallery v. Bauman*,[214] a group of four art dealers purchased a sculpture that was represented to them to be by Alexander
Calder. The testimony and the exhibits established that in 1959 Al-

exander Calder created and signed with the initials "AC" a black hanging mobile entitled *Rio Nero*. In 1962 Klaus Perls of the Perls Galleries sold the *Rio Nero* to Anspach. Before selling the work, Perls took an archival photograph of the mobile. In 1967, Perls reacquired the mobile from Anspach and sold it to Patricia Bauman's father, Lionel Bauman, a collector. Except for its exhibition in 1984 at a gallery in Los Angeles, the mobile hung in Mr. Bauman's home in Palm Springs, California, until his death in 1987. Patricia Bauman inherited the mobile from her father and sold it in March 1990 for $500,000 to the four art dealers. Before the sale, Patricia Bauman obtained from the Perls Galleries documentation of the 1967 sale to her father and furnished the documentation to the dealers. She also had the mobile photographed and sent the photograph to Perls Galleries for identification. Perls Galleries then confirmed the 1967 sale. Klaus Perls is recognized as one of the world's experts on the work of Alexander Calder.

In November 1990, the four art dealers, who had originally satisfied themselves that the mobile was authentic, began to have doubts. The mobile was then sent by the dealers to Perls Galleries for inspection and review by Klaus Perls. After a ten-minute inspection, Perls concluded that the mobile was not authentic. The dealers then requested that Patricia Bauman rescind the contract. After she refused, the dealers sued her for fraud, breach of express warranty, and material mistake of fact.

Notwithstanding the testimony of Klaus Perls that the mobile was not authentic, the court found otherwise on the basis of the testimony of Linda Silverman, an art expert of less imposing stature than Klaus Perls. The court found Silverman to have been more thorough than Klaus Perls, and the court gave great weight to the provenance of the mobile—that is, the fact that "the chain of ownership from the original artist to the present owner is accepted in the art world as persuasive evidence of a work's authenticity." The court concluded that despite the great weight that must be accorded the opinion of Perls and his premier credential with respect to Calder's work, the record and the circumstantial evidence surrounding the mobile created a strong presumption that it is an authentic Calder.

That case is an excellent example of why disputes as to the authenticity of a work of art should be settled between the parties if it is at all possible before going to court. Here the dealers were double losers. Not only did they lose on the issue of rescission of the contract when the court found the mobile to be authentic, but they were also left with a court-authenticated Calder mobile that in the art market was not authentic, according to Klaus Perls's assessment and reputation, and therefore not salable.

At times, courts have erroneously voided a contract on the grounds of mutual mistake, although mutual mistake in reality did not exist. One such case is *Arnold Herstand & Co. v. Gallery: Gertrude Stein, Inc.*,[215] an action between two art galleries to rescind the sale of a drawing, *Colette de Profil*, by the renowned European artist Balthazar Klossowski de Rola (also known as Balthus) that was alleged to be a fake. The New York State Supreme Court granted the plaintiff-purchaser (Herstand) rescission based on mutual mistake of fact. The decision was reversed on appeal: The appellate court found that the defendant-seller (Stein), far from participating in any supposed mistake by Herstand, effectively defended the authenticity of the drawing as the genuine work of Balthus[216] by citing a compelling provenance and the persuasive testimony of an expert, thereby presenting a triable issue with respect to the authenticity of the work itself.

Apparently, after purchasing the drawing from Stein, Herstand in turn sold it to Claude Bernard, the operator of a Parisian art gallery. Around 1990, Bernard reportedly showed the artist Balthus a photograph of the drawing he had purchased. Balthus denounced it as a fake, writing "*faux manifeste*" on the back of the photograph. On two later occasions, in September 1991 and in January 1992, Balthus, in writing, disclaimed authorship of similar photographs of that work. Bernard subsequently rescinded his purchase of the drawing from Herstand, who, in turn, sought to rescind his purchase from Stein. Stein refused to rescind the purchase, and, in the course of the ensuing legal proceedings, Andre Emmerich, a noted American art dealer, opined, on behalf of Herstand, that an artist is the definitive expert on her own work. "When a living artist repudiates a work as

a forgery or a fake, the work becomes unmerchantable and unsal-
able."[217] The lower court, in taking a broad perspective of that view,
granted rescission of the contract, finding that the artist's rejection
was the ultimate comment on the authenticity of the artwork.

The appellate court disagreed, citing *Greenberg Gallery v. Bauman*,
discussed above. There, the same Andre Emmerich, testifying on the
genuineness of a particular mobile sculpture attributed to the late Alexander Calder, asserted that an artwork's "flawless provenance" was
"the best proof of authenticity." Applying that test in the *Herstand*
case, the appellate court noted that the defendant Stein acquired the
Colette drawing in the late 1960s directly from Frederique Tison,
who was then married to Balthus, who owned a number of works by
him, and who commonly authenticated works by him, and that the
work remained continuously in Stein's possession until Stein consigned it to the plaintiff Herstand in 1988. Therefore, according to
the appellate court, the drawing's provenance argued in favor of its
authenticity. In addition, the court was open to the supposition that
an artist may well, at times, have a motive for repudiating her own
genuine work. In considering evidence that Balthus, in repudiating
the drawing, might now be acting "from personal animus against his
former wife," the court made the following comment:

> A fundamentally false assumption would appear to animate both
> the views of Mr. Emmerich and the motion court: that nothing
> can be imagined which would induce an artist to repudiate his
> own genuine work. History tells us otherwise.[218]

Accordingly, the case was remanded for further proceedings on the
issue of the drawing's authenticity.

Fraud and Misrepresentation Versus Breach of Warranty

Fraud

The tort of fraud occurs when the seller of a work of art makes
an intentional or knowing[219] misrepresentation of a material existing

fact about the artwork, either by positive conduct or by willful non-disclosure or concealment, intending the misrepresentation to be relied on, and the purchaser in fact relies on the representation to her detriment.[220] The misrepresentation must ordinarily be one of fact, not mere opinion or the seller's puffing.[221] If, however, a seller represents herself as possessing an expertise with respect to the artwork to be sold, the seller's misrepresenting opinion may be sufficient for fraud.[222] In addition, if a seller presents a matter as fact, rather than opinion, that statement may be actionable.[223]

By virtue of the tortious character of fraud, injured parties have a choice of remedies: They can, as in the case of innocent misrepresentation or mutual mistake, rescind the transaction and obtain restitution of the money paid on redelivery of the artwork to the seller, or they can elect to affirm the contract and collect damages proximately resulting from the fraud.[224]

Negligent Misrepresentation

Like fraud, negligent misrepresentation is a tort. However, unlike fraud, which generally requires intent or knowledge of the misrepresentation, negligent misrepresentation may lead to recovery even if the wrongdoer believed the false statements to be true, provided the statements were made without reasonable grounds.[225] As in a case of fraud, a party bringing suit in negligent misrepresentation can elect either to rescind the transaction and obtain restitution or to affirm the contract and collect proximate damages.[226]

Comparisons with Breach of Warranty

There are several important distinctions between fraud or negligent misrepresentation and breach of warranty. First, in a fraud or negligent misrepresentation case, the buyer must be able to prove the requisite state of mind of the seller at the time the false statement was made; such proof is not necessary in an action for breach of warranty.[227] Second, since the concepts of both warranty and mistake are contractual, the rules governing venue and the statute of limitations are those applicable to contract actions; fraud and negligent misrepresentation are governed by rules applicable to actions in tort.[228] Third, since a warranty is a term of the sales contract, the buyer cannot offer extrinsic evidence of its exclusion or modification unless the requirements of the parole evidence rule are first satisfied.[229]

Despite those salient differences, it should be noted that fraud, negligent misrepresentation, and breach of warranty are not mutually exclusive theories of liability. An aggrieved purchaser of fine art can use all three theories in a single lawsuit against an art dealer. An example is *McKie v. R.H. Love Galleries, Inc.*,[230] in which plaintiff Paul McKie, a collector, in 1983 purchased from Chicago-based R.H. Love Galleries, Inc., a William Merritt Chase oil painting for $370,000. The painting was accompanied by an authentication and appraisal report on which McKie relied, as well as on representations by the dealer that the painting had excellent potential to appreciate in value and was "wax-resin lined." When McKie determined that the statements he relied on contained material misinformation, he brought suit against the gallery on a variety of theories, including fraud, negligent misrepresentation, breach of express warranty, breach of implied warranty of merchantability, breach of warranty for a particular purpose, and breach of contract. In denying the gallery's motion to dismiss, a federal district court in Illinois held that McKie sufficiently pleaded each count in his complaint.

A more illuminating example of the coexistence of fraud and breach of warranty, both of which were held to have occurred, is found in the case of *McCloud v. Lawrence Gallery, Ltd.*[231] The defendant Lawrence Gallery, a New York art dealer specializing in twentieth-century modern art, in September 1986 solicited plaintiff Jerry McCloud, a private collector in Ohio who was interested in upgrading his collection with modern artwork having potential investment value. On October 8, 1986, believing that McCloud might be interested, the gallery purchased at a Sotheby's auction what was represented to be a drawing by Pablo Picasso. After the gallery bought the drawing, Sotheby's advised the gallery that there was a question about its authenticity and sought the opinion of the Comité Picasso, a committee of art experts and members of Picasso's family who make definitive assessments of the authenticity of works allegedly by the artist. In November 1986, the committee officially notified Sotheby's that it did not accept the drawing as authentic. Sotheby's relayed that information to Lawrence gallery that month, advising the gallery that if Sotheby's could not locate proof of the drawing's authenticity, it would rescind the sale and refund the gallery's purchase price.

Meanwhile, in mid October, the plaintiff McCloud agreed to acquire from the gallery, on an installment plan, the Picasso drawing for $16,000, as well as a small work by Pierre-Auguste Renoir for $5,000. Believing the Picasso drawing to be authentic, the gallery on December 22, 1986, issued to McCloud an unconditional guarantee of the "absolute authenticity" of the drawing. On receipt of full payment in early January 1987, the gallery delivered the artwork to McCloud in Ohio.

After McCloud received the artwork, Sotheby's advised the gallery that the Comité Picasso had reconfirmed its negative opinion of the drawing's authenticity. In a letter dated February 2, 1987, Sotheby's repeated its offer to rescind the sale to the Lawrence Gallery on the basis of the drawing's lack of authenticity. The gallery decided not to rescind the purchase. Moreover, on receipt of the letter and against Sotheby's advice, the gallery allegedly did not even disclose to McCloud the existence of the dispute regarding the drawing's legitimacy, let alone the decision of the Comité Picasso.

McCloud, apparently on his own, hired an art expert who contacted the Comité Picasso, which again, in December 1988, rejected the drawing's authenticity. In February 1989, McCloud advised the Lawrence Gallery that the Picasso was not genuine and threatened to bring suit if the transaction was not rescinded. In April 1989, in an Ohio state court, McCloud filed suit, asserting, among a variety of claims, fraud, breach of express and implied warranties under Ohio and New York law, and violation of the Racketeer Influenced and Corrupt Organizations (RICO) Act. The Ohio court entered a default judgment in September 1989, which was enforced in the New York courts in 1992.[232]

Arts and Consumer Legislation

In addition to the redress offered the injured buyer by the U.C.C. and by tort and contract law, a number of states have enacted legislation to provide further protections to the consumer. Below is a brief survey of some of that legislation.

Penal Statutes

Most applicable penal statutes throughout the United States are concerned with forgery and fraud. The relevant forgery statutes focus on written instruments, which include certificates of authenticity and other documents related to the purchase, consignment, and sale of artwork. The forgery statutes are of a general nature and require proof of criminal intent to injure or defraud,[233] as well as proof of the forged or counterfeit nature of the work.[234] In most states, the relevant forgery statutes range from mid-level to low-level felonies to misdemeanors. Depending on the nature of the forgery and the laws of the jurisdiction, penalties range from prison terms of up to twenty years[235] to payment of a small fine.[236]

In addition, a number of states have enacted what are generally known as criminal-simulation statutes.[237] Typical is New York's statute, which provides for criminal penalties for the making or the altering of any object so that "it appears to have an antiquity, rarity, source or authorship which it does not in fact possess."[238] As with forgery, the criminal-simulation statutes require proof of criminal intent to defraud or injure,[239] as well as proof of the altered or counterfeit nature of the work.[240] Violation of the statute in most states constitutes a high-level misdemeanor, although a few states have statutes predicating the level of the crime on the value of the object altered or forged.[241]

Warranties of Authenticity

To date, New York, Florida, Iowa, and Michigan have enacted art legislation[242] providing assurances as to the authenticity of art purchases beyond those found in the U.C.C. Each of the four statutes hold art-merchant-sellers responsible to nonmerchant—buyers for any statement pertinent to the authorship of a work of fine art, notwithstanding that the statement may be merely the seller's opinion. In addition, the Michigan statute provides that

> an art merchant whose warranty of authenticity of authorship was made in good faith shall not be liable for damages beyond the return of the purchase price which the art merchant receives.[243]

However, such a warranty made in bad faith may entitle the buyer to consequential damages, rather than the mere return of the purchase price.[244]

Those statutes clarify the express warranty provision of the U.C.C.[245] by (1) ensuring that the identification of a work of fine art with any authorship in a written instrument is itself part of the basis of the bargain and (2) abolishing, insofar as authorship is concerned, the distinction between fact and the seller's mere opinion.

The New York statute at section 13.01 provides in part as follows:

> Notwithstanding any provision of any other law to the contrary:
> 1. Whenever an art merchant, in selling or exchanging a work of fine art, furnishes to a buyer of such work who is not an art merchant a certificate of authenticity or any similar written instrument it:
>   (a) Shall be presumed to be part of the basis of the bargain; and
>   (b) Shall create an express warranty for the material facts stated as of the date of such sale or exchange.

Under the New York Arts and Cultural Affairs statute, a standard for determining liability for breach of warranty has evolved from the case of *Dawson v. G. Malina, Inc.*[246]—that is, whether the representations by the art merchant had a reasonable basis in fact at the time the representations were made, as shown by the testimony taken as a whole. In *Dawson*, the plaintiff purchased a number of allegedly antique Chinese jade and ceramic art objects from the defendant art gallery for a total price of $105,400; he then sought to cancel his purchase under section 13.01 of the New York Arts and Cultural Affairs statute for breach of warranty when he came to believe that the art objects were forgeries. The court, in applying the above standard, stated:

> [I]t appears that the proper standard to be applied here in determining whether defendant is liable for breach of warranty is whether the representations furnished [plaintiff] Dawson by [defendant] Malina with respect to each of these objects can be said to have had a reasonable basis in fact, at the time that these representations were made, with the question of whether there was such a reasonable basis in fact being measured by the expert testimony provided at trial. Since the plaintiff has the burden of proof on the issue of breach of warranty, the issue presented here, when reduced to its simplest terms, is whether plaintiff Dawson has established by a fair preponderance of the evidence that the representations made by defendant were without a reasonable basis in fact at the time that these representations were made.[247]

The court weighed the expert testimony with respect to each object and concluded that the plaintiff was entitled to rescind his purchase of three of the five objects at issue because in each case the defendant's representations lacked a reasonable basis in fact. In other words, the art gallery's failure to undertake sufficient investigation in substantiating the provenance of three of the art objects allowed the buyer to rescind the transaction as to those items and obtain a refund of the purchase price. With respect to the other two art objects, the court concluded that the expert testimony at trial indicated that the art gallery had a reasonable basis in fact for its representation and therefore there was no breach of warranty.

Almost twenty years after *Dawson* was decided, the 1997 case of *Pritzker v. Krishna Gallery of Asian Arts*[248] involved the purchase of two purportedly antique Indian sandstone sculptures for a total purchase price of $1,075,000. Once again, shortly after their purchase, the buyer came to believe that the art objects were fakes and wanted his money back. The *Pritzker* case shows that the New York warranty of authenticity under section 13.01 of the Arts and Cultural Affairs statute applies when a work of art is sold from an art merchant to someone who is not an art merchant. Section 11.01.2 defines an "art merchant" as a person who by her occupation holds herself out as having knowledge or skill peculiar to such works or "to whom such knowledge or skill may be attributed by his employment of an agent or other intermediary." In *Pritzker*, the defendant art gallery argued that since Pritzker had an art adviser who had specialized knowledge in the field, the knowledge of that art adviser was imputed to Pritzker, and, therefore, the warranty provision did not apply. The magistrate judge's report and recommendation, confirmed by the court,[249] adopted a narrow view by holding that the art adviser had no authority as an agent to bind Pritzker to purchase the art objects and, therefore, Pritzker was not deemed to be an art merchant.

On the question of breach of warranty, the federal district court confirmed the reasonable-basis-in-fact standards set forth in *Dawson*, discussed above, as the applicable criteria. In declining to grant summary judgment to either party, the court concluded that there were genuine issues of material fact regarding the authenticity of the sandstone sculptures. On this issue, the magistrate judge's report stated that

> [b]ased on the standards in *Dawson* and *Balog*, Plaintiff [Pritzker] may need to show that Defendant [the art gallery] failed to undertake a sufficient investigation of the authenticity of the pieces when it sold them to Pritzker and thus lacked a reasonable basis in fact from which to assert that the objects were genuine.[250]

However, Judge Blanche Manning ruled in an unpublished in limine order that what the defendant art gallery did or did not do in order to establish its belief as to the authenticity of the sculptures is irrelevant, since liability under *Dawson* is measured by expert testimony.[251] As held in *Dawson*, whether there was a "reasonable basis in fact" for the representations which were made at the time of sale is "measured by the expert testimony provided at trial."[252] The court's unpublished order did note the following:

> This court's reading of *Dawson*, however, is different from that of the Hawaii district court in *Balog*. In *Balog*, the court read *Dawson*'s standard to "h[o]ld that the defendant's failure to have undertaken sufficient investigation in substantiating the provenance of the items in question would allow for rescission of the transaction with a refund of the purchase price plus interest." *Balog*, 745 F. Supp. at 1567. Unlike the Hawaii district court in *Balog*, this court does not construe *Dawson* to require an inquiry into the actual investigation undertaken by defendant prior to making representations as to the items of sale. Indeed, *Dawson* did not make such an inquiry. *See Dawson*, 463 F. Supp. at 467–71. The court in *Dawson* inquired into whether the representation made at the time of sale was supported by a reasonable basis in fact—as measured by the expert opinion testimony. *See id.* This court finds *Dawson* persuasive and does the same.[253]

The judge's instructions to the jury followed *Dawson*. At trial, on May 7, 1997, the plaintiff Pritzker was awarded $1.7 million.[254]

Rogath v. Siebman[255]—a breach of contract, breach of warranty, and fraud case based on the sale of an alleged Francis Bacon painting accompanied by a written warranty of authenticity in the bill of sale—provides caution to any seller of a work with doubtful authenticity. The plaintiff David Rogath purchased the painting from the defendant for $570,000 and resold it three months later to Acquavella Contemporary Art, Inc. for $950,000. When Acquavella learned of the painting's doubtful authenticity, it requested the refund of the purchase price and returned the painting to the plaintiff. The plaintiff then sued the defendant and was able to recover $950,000 in damages, the amount lost in the aborted sale to Acquavella, for a breach of warranty of authenticity, without having to prove that the work was actually a fake. The warranty provision in the bill of sale stated the following in part:

> In order to induce David Rogath to make the purchase, Seller . . . make[s] the following warranties, representations and covenants to and with the Buyer.

1. . . . ; that the Seller has no knowledge of any challenge to the
Seller's title and authenticity of the Painting; . . .

The court granted partial summary judgment to the plaintiff,
finding that "the undisputed evidence before the Court leaves no
doubt that Defendant was aware of the challenges to the authenticity
of the painting." Among other things, the court considered comments and questions about the shininess of the black paint used
(Francis Bacon's other works used matte black) and the presence of
pink paint (Bacon generally did not use pink), Sotheby's refusal to
handle the sale of the painting, and the fact that Bacon's longtime
dealer, Marlborough Gallery, had expressed doubts about the painting's authenticity to the defendant. The plaintiff did not have to
prove that the painting was not authentic (a fact that is often difficult
to prove) but only had to show that the defendant knew of the
doubts about the painting's authenticity, since the defendant had
made an express warranty, as indicated above, to induce the plaintiff
to buy and the defendant had breached that warranty.

New York's Door-to-Door Sales Protection Act

Enacted to afford consumers of goods primarily for personal or
household purposes a cooling-off period from high-pressure sales
tactics when payment of the purchase price is deferred over time,
New York's Door-to-Door Sales Protection Act[256] has been applied
in at least two judicial cases to the purchase of art by a collector.
Briefly, the act is applicable when a seller personally solicits the sale
of a consumer good and the buyer makes an offer or agreement to
purchase at some place other than the seller's place of business. The
act gives the buyer up to three business days after a door-to-door sale
to cancel the offer or agreement to purchase the goods in question.[257] The act further directs that at the time of the transaction the
seller must inform the buyer, both orally and in writing, of the right
to cancel.[258] Until the seller has complied with those requirements,
the buyer may cancel the sale by notifying the seller in any manner
and by any means of her intention.[259]

In the *Vom Lehn* case[260] (see page 102), in which the New York State Supreme Court found that the purchase price for twenty jade carvings was unconscionable and, therefore, would not enforce the contract requiring the plaintiffs to pay the balance of the purchase price, the court applied the Home Solicitation Sales Act (the predecessor statute to the Door-to-Door Sales Protection Act) to enable the plaintiffs to recover their down payment on the carvings, along with reasonable legal fees. The court noted that the purchase price was to be paid in five installments, the defendants' solicited the sale at the buyers' home, and there were no prior negotiations at the defendants' shop.[261]

More recently, in *Pritzker* (see pages 140–142), the federal district court for the Northern District of Illinois was called on to interpret the act as it applied to the sale of two antique Indian sandstone sculptures for more than $1 million. The court, in deciding not to grant a motion for summary judgment for the defendant, found that there were genuine issues of material fact as to whether the sale of the sculptures was a door-to-door sale within the meaning of the act. The court noted that the *Vom Lehn* court had held that the act is not limited to door-to-door sales.[262] In *Pritzker*, the main issue to be decided at trial was whether Pritzker offered or agreed to purchase the sculptures "at a place other than the place of business of the seller." That element is necessary in order to come within the purview of the act. At trial, the jury found in favor of Pritzker.

Native American Arts

A number of states have enacted legislation addressing the representations of authenticity made in connection with Native American arts.[263] Those statutes render it a crime for a seller to place a state-registered label on fake Indian arts and crafts or otherwise to represent those items as being authentic for the purpose of reselling them. Violations of the statutes are generally classified as misdemeanors.

Magnuson-Moss Warranty Act

Supplementary to and not in restriction of existing consumer rights and remedies under federal and state laws, the Magnuson-Moss Warranty Act[264] mandates that sellers who give written warranties with respect to the sale of consumer products adhere to certain requirements:

1. If a consumer product costs more than $15, the seller must adhere to the Federal Trade Commission (FTC) rules relating to the disclosure of warranty terms.[265]

2. The seller must clearly and conspicuously designate the written warranty as either a "full warranty" or a "limited warranty."[266] A full warranty must conform to certain federal minimum standards.[267] A limited warranty need not meet those standards but must be clearly and conspicuously labeled as a limited warranty.[268] Not subject to those designation provisions are general statements of policy concerning consumer satisfaction,[269] such as "satisfaction guaranteed or your money back."

3. A seller may not make what is deemed to be a deceptive warranty under the act. A deceptive warranty includes any written warranty that (a) contains an affirmation of fact, false or fraudulent representations, or promises or descriptions that would mislead a reasonable person exercising due care; (b) fails to contain sufficient information to prevent its terms from being misleading; or (c) uses the terms "guarantee" or "warranty" when other terms limit the breadth and the scope of the protection apparently granted, so as to deceive a reasonable person.[270]

The rules and regulations under the act are promulgated by the FTC.[271] For the act to apply to a transaction, the following conditions must be fulfilled:

1. The subject of the transaction must be a consumer product.[272]

2. The seller must have issued a written warranty in connection with the subject of the sale.[273] (Nothing in the act, however, requires that such a warranty be given.)

3. The product must either be distributed in interstate commerce or affect interstate trade, traffic, transportation, or commerce.[274] Consequently, if an artwork is produced locally and sold locally, without the use of the mails, the act may not apply.

Truth-in-Lending Act

If a collector buys a work of art on credit with the price payable in more than four installments or if a finance charge is imposed, the disclosure of the credit terms in accordance with the federal Truth-in-Lending Act[275] may be required. Willful and knowing failure to comply with the act triggers criminal penalties: a fine of up to $5,000, imprisonment for up to one year, or both.[276] Civil liability may also be incurred for failure to comply with certain provisions of the act.[277]

Federal Trade Commission Act

The Federal Trade Commission Act prohibits unfair or deceptive acts or practices in commerce.[278] Accordingly, a collector who believes that a dealer is engaged in deceptive acts or practices in the sale of artwork may lodge a complaint with the FTC. As discussed in chapter 3 (see pages 251–253), the FTC has brought at least three actions[279] in which it has sought temporary, preliminary, and permanent injunctive relief, as well as rescission and restitution for injured consumers.

New York City Truth-in-Pricing Law

The New York City Truth-in-Pricing Law,[280] which dates back to 1971, has only recently been enforced against art galleries located in New York City. The New York City Department of Consumer

Affairs (DCA) has interpreted the law to require all galleries to post prices next to exhibited works and to list those prices in a public space at the art gallery or have sheets listing those prices readily available to members of the public. The new attention to art galleries resulted from the DCA's investigation of the auction industry, which led to the recently revised New York City auction rules discussed in chapter 4. In March 1988, DCA inspectors visited numerous art galleries and issued seventeen citations for failure to conspicuously display prices. Most galleries have complied with the requirement to post prices, although at least one may challenge the requirement in court.[281]

Antitrust Claims and Restrictions on Sales—Right of First Refusal

Chapter 7, pages 624–626, addresses antitrust claims and authentication—specifically, whether a committee's determination that a work of art is or is not included in the *catalogue raisonné* for an artist can amount to a Sherman Antitrust Act violation due to the alleged control over the market for the works of that artist.[282] A related restraint-of-trade issue arises from a "right of first refusal" provision in an art dealer's invoice: that is, a requirement that before the collector can freely sell the artwork to a third party, the collector must first offer the dealer the opportunity to buy it back. Is a right of first refusal enforceable by the art dealer, or does it amount to an unreasonable restraint on the alienation of property?

In *Wildenstein & Co. v. Wallis*,[283] a New York Court of Appeals case decided in 1992, Wildenstein brought an action against the Hal Wallis estate to enforce a right of first refusal. During Wallis's life, he and Wildenstein had a dispute over the ownership of a Monet painting and a Gauguin painting. As part of the formal settlement of that dispute in 1981, the paintings were returned to Wallis; the settlement agreement further provided that Wildenstein would have a right of first refusal to purchase on thirty days' notice fifteen other paintings owned by Wallis, if he ever wanted to sell them, under the same terms and conditions offered by a third-party purchaser. Wallis died in 1986. Three years later, his heirs decided to sell some of the paintings at auction at Christie's, at which point Wildenstein sued to enforce its right of first refusal.

Holding for Wildenstein, the court examined the common law rule against unreasonable restraints on the alienation of property, which invalidates unduly restrictive controls on future transactions. The court explained that the rule must be applied on a case-by-case basis, and that the analysis measures the reasonableness of the restraint by considering the price of the property and the duration and purpose of the restraint. The court also stated that the rule attempts to find a balance between society's interest in the free alienability of property and the rights of owners to direct future transactions.[284]

The court found that the right of first refusal held by Wildenstein was not unduly restrictive: It still enabled the Wallis heirs to realize the highest possible price should they decide to sell the paintings, as long as they complied with the detailed right of first refusal provisions. The court also found that the right of first refusal did not violate New York's Rule against Perpetuities.[285]

Wildenstein may not be the final word on restrictive sale provisions appearing on dealers' invoices because that case involved a formal settlement agreement negotiated between attorneys representing fully informed parties, and there was no element of coercion with respect to the right of first refusal provisions. Furthermore, the settlement agreement set forth detailed procedures for complying with those provisions. And most importantly, there was no element of control of the market by the art dealer (Wildenstein), since impressionist paintings by Monet, Gauguin, and others are sold by many art dealers and auction houses worldwide.

Different issues are presented when an art dealer is the exclusive dealer for a particular artist and tries to control the market for that artist's work by compelling buyers to agree to restrictions on resale or else be unable to purchase an artwork by that artist. This situation may be treated differently from the situation in *Wildenstein*, where a court seeks to balance society's interest in free alienability against the rights of owners or sellers of property to direct future transfers of that property.

New York State's Donnelly Act,[286] which is similar to the federal Sherman Antitrust Act, deals with price fixing, monopolization, and restraint of trade violations. The only case touching on these issues was brought by Joan Vitale against Marlborough Gallery and the Pollock-Krasner Foundation alleging antitrust violations based on market control.[287] Vitale alleged that the authentication committee controlled the market for Jackson Pollock's work by its ability to declare a work authentic or not authentic. Although Vitale's lawsuit was dismissed, there is language in the opinion which indicates that under certain circumstances such a claim would be valid.[288]

To date, there are no cases in New York dealing with the right of first refusal provisions that are now appearing on the invoices of art dealers. To determine enforceability, the courts will apply a balancing test based on all the facts and circumstances. The outcome will depend on whether the agreement is signed by both parties, the method of determining the price, the period of the restraint, whether there were coercing factors present in the sale, and whether there are multiple dealers or only one dealer for the artist's work, which goes to the degree of control of the marketplace.

SALES BY COLLECTORS

When a collector undertakes to sell a work of art, she is bound by most of the same principles and statutes that circumscribe the conduct of dealers. However, some allowances are made for the collector's relative lack of expertise concerning both art objects and the trade, resulting in a somewhat less stringent code of required behavior by the collector as seller. The most important variances—which are found in the U.C.C., in principles of common law, and in arts and consumer legislation—are set forth below.

Express Warranties

For purposes of determining the existence of an express warranty in the absence of words of guarantee or warranty, statements by a collector concerning the attributes of a work of art, including authenticity, that are not stated as fact are more likely to be considered opinion than if those statements were made by a dealer.[289]

Implied Warranty of Merchantability

Although the implied warranty of merchantability is not applicable to a sale by someone who is not a merchant with respect to the type of goods being sold,[290] the nonmerchant seller is nevertheless obligated on principles of good faith to disclose to the buyer any knowledge she has with respect to any hidden defects in the goods.[291]

Warranty of Title

As earlier indicated, a warranty of title is statutorily imposed in every sales contract unless the warranty is specifically disclaimed or modified. However, when a nonmerchant is the seller, the warranty does not include an implied representation that the goods are free of any rightful claim of patent or trademark infringement by a third person.[292]

Statute of Frauds

A contract for the sale of goods for $500 or more must be evidenced by a signed writing. An exception to that rule exists for a sale between merchants;[293] the exception is not available to a sale by a collector who is not a merchant of the goods sold.

Voidable Title

A seller with voidable title can transfer good title to a good-faith purchaser for value. However, a private collector, unlike an art dealer, cannot pass good title when the collector is entrusted with a work of art by another who does not intend to pass title.[294]

Buyer in the Ordinary Course of Business

All purchasers of art, whether dealers or not, must meet the test of being a buyer in the ordinary course of business within the meaning of the U.C.C. in order to acquire unchallenged clear title. Although a more stringent standard is required of merchants who would be buyers in the ordinary course of business, a nonmerchant, to meet the test, must buy from a merchant in good faith and without knowledge that the sale would be in violation of third-party ownership rights. "Good faith" for nonmerchant buyers means honesty in fact.[295]

Collector-Dealer Consignments

Applicability of Revised U.C.C.

A collector more often than not sells a work of art through a dealer. When that is done, a written consignment contract is necessary to adequately protect the collector. Prior to the 1999 revisions to article 9 of the Uniform Commercial Code (effective July 1, 2001),[296] it was important to know if the consignment was governed by the provisions of article 2 or article 9 of the U.C.C., or was outside both provisions and therefore governed by the common law principles of agency.

Under former section 2-326(3),[297] goods delivered on consignment were subject to the consignee's creditors unless the transaction was a "true consignment," and either the consigned goods were properly evidenced by a sign giving notice of consignment status, the consignee was generally known by its creditors as selling consigned goods, or the consignor filed a financing statement against the consignee. Former section 2-326 led to more litigation than clarification because it was difficult to establish compliance with the signage and knowledge tests or to determine under non-U.C.C. law whether transactions were "true consignments" or ones intended as security.[298]

Accordingly, consignments have been deleted from article 2 of the U.CC. and are now subject to revised article 9 or non-U.C.C. law.

Consignments are defined in section 9-102(a)(20) of the U.C.C. as follows:

> (20) "Consignment" means a transaction, regardless of its form, in which a person delivers goods to a merchant for the purpose of sale and:
>
> (A) the merchant:
>   (i) deals in goods of that kind under a name other than the name of the person making delivery;
>   (ii) is not an auctioneer; and
>   (iii) is not generally known by its creditors to be substantially engaged in selling goods of others;
>
> (B) with respect to each delivery, the aggregate value of the goods is $1,000 or more at the time of delivery;
>
> (C) the goods are not consumer goods immediately before delivery; and
>
> (D) the transaction does not create a security interest that secures an obligation.

Under article 2 of the U.C.C., a sale is referred to as either a "sale or return"[299] or a "sale on approval."[300] A sale or return occurs when a work, which may be returned even though it conforms to the contract, is delivered to a dealer primarily for resale.[301] The consignor-collector should be aware that the consigned work may be subject to the claims of the dealer's creditors, even where title is reserved by the consignor,[302] while it is in the dealer's possession, unless the consignor-collector perfects a security interest under article 9 of the U.C.C.[303] The rule is designed to protect unwary creditors of the consignee-dealer by allowing them to make claims against goods delivered to the consignee for sale.

By contrast, under the U.C.C. a sale on approval occurs when a work, which may be returned even though it conforms to the contract, is delivered to a buyer who intends it primarily for use, rather than resale.[304] In that case, such a sale does not render the work subject to the claims of the buyer's creditors until the buyer accepts it.[305] Once the work is accepted by the buyer, it can be reached by the buyer's creditors unless a security interest is perfected by filing a financing statement and notifying the buyer's existing secured creditors.

A "true consignment" that satisfies the definition of section 9-102(a)(20) of the U.C.C. (see above) is now governed by article 9 of the U.C.C. A true consignment constitutes an agency or bailment relationship between the consignor and the consignee. The consignor, as principal, retains the ownership, may recall the goods, and sets the sale price. The consignee (dealer) receives a commission and not the profits of the sale. That type of consignment is deemed to be a sale or return, as described above, subject to the claims of the consignee's creditors[306] unless the consignor perfects a security interest under article 9.[307]

It is possible for a true consignment (one that does not meet the definition of section 9-102(a)(20) of the U.C.C.) to be outside the provisions of article 9 of the U.C.C. For example, the consignment may not be to a dealer, or may not be to a dealer who deals in goods of that kind.[308] Since the consignment does not fall within the purview of article 9 of the U.C.C., it is governed by the common law principles of agency and bailment. In that case, the consignment is not subject to the claims of the consignee's creditors, since the agent has no ownership interest in the consigned property; that is, a security interest cannot attach until the debtor (here the consignee) has rights in the consigned property.[309] If the agent has no authority to subject the property to a security interest, the creditor cannot obtain a security interest in the property.

Failure to Perfect a Security Interest

The danger in not perfecting a security interest when a collector consigns a work of art to an art dealer is best illustrated in the case of *In re Morgansen's Ltd.*[310] At a shop located on Long Island, New York, Morgansen was engaged in the business of selling expensive items such as jewelry, art, collectibles, and furniture to retail customers, other dealers, and interior decorators. Morgansen also conducted auction sales of its inventory from time to time. About 70% of the items were obtained by consignment. At Morgansen's store, the consigned items were commingled with goods obtained by direct purchase. A majority of customers walking into the store, or attending the auction sales, would not know whether a particular item was consigned by a third party or had been previously purchased by Morgansen for resale on its own account. When Morgansen filed for bankruptcy in February 2003, it had on its premises many items that were consigned to it. The bankruptcy trustee proposed to auction all of the property for the benefit of Morgansen's creditors. The consignors objected, claiming that they were entitled to remove their consigned goods prior to the auction.

The court began its analysis with the standard approach of first looking at the July 1, 2001, revised version of section 9-102(a)(20) of the U.C.C. (quoted above). If the transaction did not fit under that section, the court would turn to section 2-326 of the U.C.C. And if that section also did not apply, the court would rely upon the common law of bailments and other traditional practices. The consignors wanted out of section 9-102(a)(20), since they had not perfected their security interests and consequently would not have their goods returned by the bankruptcy trustee unless the consignment was outside the U.C.C. and treated as a common law bailment or agency. In order for a transaction to fit under section 9-102(a)(20) of the U.C.C., each of the attributes of a consignment as defined in that section must be satisfied. The burden of proof with respect to each attribute falls on the party claiming to be protected by this section. Under section 9-102(a)(20)(A)(i), Morgansen was indisputably a merchant who deals in goods delivered to it for the purpose of sale, and it operated under a trade name other than the names of the "consignors."

With respect to section 9-102(a)(20)(A)(ii), the consignors who opposed the bankruptcy trustee's auction of their property represented that Morgansen was, in fact, an auctioneer by virtue of its holding of several auctions a year, especially during the summer months, at its leased premises. The court indicated that the operative question is whether a merchant who sells items of art, collectibles, and antique furniture to retail customers, interior decorators, or other dealers, and whose sales are generated from both its own inventory and consigned inventory by occasional auction is categorically within or beyond section 9-102(a)(20). Since Morgansen did sell its own goods and some of the consigned goods in nonauction transactions with retail customers, interior decorators, and other dealers, it did not exclusively act as an auctioneer. The court found that an occasional auction by the consignee was not enough to take the consignment out of section 9-102(a)(20).

The court then stated that under section 9-102(a)(20)(A)(iii), none of the objecting consignors presented any proof that Morgansen was "not generally known by its creditors to be substantially engaged in selling the goods of others." The fact that a sign on the exterior of its leased premises may have indicated that the merchant was also an auctioneer was not sufficiently probative. Morgansen had significant unsecured claims from utility companies and other third party suppliers of goods and services that may not have known exactly what kind of business was conducted on the premises. The same knowledge by a few protesting consignors did not satisfy their burden of proof as to what subjectively the creditors generally knew or should have known about the exact nature of the debtor's business activities.

The court then proceeded to section 2-326 under the amended U.C.C. The court noted that former section 2-326(3) of the U.C.C. was repealed effective July 1, 2001, and that consignments are now governed by article 9 of the U.C.C.

In finding for the bankruptcy trustee and allowing the sale of the consigned goods for the benefit of the creditors (preventing the return of the goods to the consignors), the court stated:

> Under UCC Section 2-326 as amended, goods which are consigned for sale, are property of the bankruptcy estate of the "consignee," and subject to the claims of the creditors of the entity doing the sale (Morgansen's). If a person takes goods to one who is considered a consignee (a "buyer" for resale) and

that buyer goes into bankruptcy, the buyer/debtor's trustee will take the goods as property of the debtor's estate. . . .

The consignors were under constructive notice of the provisions of the UCC that subordinated their rights to the return of any of their goods to the superseding claims of the creditors of the buyer, the debtor. This may strike the consignors as grossly unfair, but that is the balance that the State of New York reached among competing parties in interest. The law is painfully clear—anybody who delivers goods with a "right of return" to a merchant who sells them under its own name is at risk that the merchant may file for bankruptcy relief, and the trustee will liquidate the goods for the benefit of the creditors.[311]

The lesson is clear.[312] Any collector who consigns a work of art to a dealer for sale would be foolish not to comply with and require the dealer to comply with the U.C.C. filing requirements, which are, for the most part, simple and inexpensive. (See pages 163–164, dealing with perfection of a security interest.) Such compliance protects the consignor, regardless of the characterization of the consignment, if the dealer becomes insolvent or otherwise falls into difficulty with her creditors.

This lesson was again made clear in *Ganz v. Sotheby's Financial Services*.[313] The court was faced with cross motions for summary judgment in a dispute over title to a Marc Chagall painting entitled *Soleil couchant à Saint-Paul*. Ganz, the owner of the painting, had transferred possession of it to Michel Cohen, an art dealer, who had transferred possession of it to Sotheby's as collateral for a loan. Cohen defaulted on the loan, disappeared with Sotheby's money, and became a fugitive wanted on various criminal charges. With Cohen gone, the dispute was over who had title to the painting and the legal nature of each of the aforementioned transfers of the painting. (See page 117, where another case involving the same Michel Cohen is discussed.)

The court first found that Ganz had not sold the painting to Cohen. The transfer from Ganz to Cohen was not a "transaction of purchase" within the meaning of section 2-403(1) of the U.C.C., but was more in the nature of an entrustment under sections 2-403(2) and (3).[314] Ganz then argued that he should prevail because Sotheby's was not a "buyer in the ordinary course of business" under section 2-403(2) and therefore Cohen could not have transferred good title to Sotheby's.

The court did not end its inquiry there but decided that it had to examine the transfers under revised article 9 of the U.C.C. dealing with consignments.[315] Section 9-319(a) of the U.C.C. provides that

> for purposes of determining the rights of creditors of, and purchasers for value of goods from, a consignee, while the goods are in the possession of the consignee, the consignee is deemed to have rights and title to the goods identical to those the consignor had or had power to transfer.

The court noted that consignments are defined in section 9-102(a)(20) of the U.C.C. Applying the definition, the court found that Cohen was a merchant, that he dealt in art under names other than Ganz's, that he was not an auctioneer, and that Ganz's delivery of the painting to him did not create a security interest.[316] Therefore, section 9-319(a) of the U.C.C. would allow Cohen to transfer title to Sotheby's if it was shown that Cohen "was not generally known by [his] creditors to be substantially engaged in selling the goods of others."[317] The court found that Ganz had the burden of proving that Cohen was generally known by his creditors to be substantially engaged in selling the goods of others. Accordingly, the court decided that there was an issue of fact—how Cohen was generally known by his creditors—that precluded the granting of summary judgment in favor of either party. Ganz could have avoided this problem if he had simply filed a UCC-1 Financing Statement.[318]

The Consignment Contract

The following checklist of issues that most frequently arise between owner and dealer is by no means exhaustive, nor do all the issues arise in every negotiation. Many of the points are of mutual concern, some of the issues speak mainly to the owner, and others address largely the dealer. (See discussion of artist–dealer consign-ment contracts in chapter 1 at pages 26–39 and the contract forms in Appendixes 1-1, 1-2, and 1-3 at the end of chapter 1.)

1. *Exclusive Agency, Duration, Territory.* The contract should es-tablish the principal-agent relationship so that the dealer is authorized to complete the sale of the consigned work on behalf of the owner within a specified period of time and within a defined territory.

2. *Price.* The contract should be clear that the dealer is autho-rized to sell the consigned work at a specific price and whether or not such a sale is authorized if on terms other than all cash. The contract should allow no deviation from the specific price unless the owner consents in writing to such a change.

3. *Commission to the Dealer.* The amount of the commission payable to the dealer must be clearly stated. Even where the work is consigned to a dealer for a net price to the owner, the owner may want to include a provision that imposes an upper limit on the total amount of the commission—for ex-ample, no more than 10% of the selling price.

4. *Warranties by Owner.* Since under the U.C.C. the dealer will be making warranties to the buyer, the dealer will want to obtain identical warranties from the owner. Those warran-ties should include the owner's warranties of title and assur-ances that the work is free and clear of any liens or other encumbrances and that the work is authentic. An owner may not always warrant authenticity, leaving that issue up to the dealer's expertise.

5. *Expenses.* The agreement should make clear who pays for the expenses of shipping, packing, insurance, advertising, condition reports, and other related matters.

6. *Insurance.* The owner will want all-risk insurance coverage for the work from the moment it is picked up from the owner until it is returned or sold. The agreement should state the amount of the insurance and to whom the proceeds

are payable in case of a loss. For example, if the work is insured for its full selling price, including the commission to the dealer, the agreement should provide that the dealer will receive her commission, so long as the owner has been paid the full net price due the owner.

7. *Payment terms.* The agreement should make clear who receives payment from the buyer and whether the dealer receives payment when the dealer pays the owner. If payment is not made in full, the owner should require that possession of the work not be released to the buyer unless the dealer then guarantees payment to the owner or the owner consents to such a release in writing.

8. *Noncircumvention.* Often the dealer wants a provision that protects the dealer from the owner's selling the work to a buyer to whom the dealer showed the work during the consignment period.

9. *Grant of Security Interest.* When a work of art is delivered on consignment to a dealer who maintains a place of business at which she deals in goods of the kind involved, the work of art is subject to the claims of the dealer's creditors unless the owner files a UCC-1 form. Therefore, the owner must require the dealer to grant the owner a security interest in the consigned work and must require the dealer to comply with the U.C.C. filing requirements and to comply with the notice to existing secured creditors.

10. *Miscellaneous.* The contract should make clear that the laws of a particular state apply to the consignment and clarify whether or not the parties to the contract consent to the jurisdiction of the courts in that state.

Risk of Loss

Generally, where a work of art is purchased from a merchant, the risk of loss passes to the buyer on the receipt of the work by the buyer.[319] Where a work of art is purchased from a nonmerchant seller, the risk of loss passes to the buyer on notification that the buyer can take delivery of the work.[320]

Arts and Consumer Legislation

The express warranty of authenticity of authorship, as set forth by statute in Florida, New York, Iowa, and Michigan,[321] is not applicable to a collector in the sale of a work of fine art.

Immunity from Seizure of Artwork

When a collector lends a work for exhibition out of state, the collector, absent special protections, risks having the work seized and attached by her creditors or claimants in that jurisdiction, thus rendering the collector subject to the courts of that state. The parallel situation exists in the United States on a national level; in organizing loan exhibitions, museums must often conquer the reluctance of museums in foreign countries to lend their works of art to the United States, where they may be subject to judicial seizure. To cope with that predicament and to encourage the benefits to be derived from cultural exchanges, state and federal legislatures have enacted immunity statutes. (See chapter 16, on museums.)

It is useful to compare two such statutes briefly. The federal immunity statute[322] permits a grant of immunity from judicial seizure to cultural objects imported into the United States by nonprofit organizations for temporary display, provided that before the object enters the country, the United States Department of State, on application by the borrowing institution, determines that the object is of cultural significance and finds that the temporary exhibition of the object is in the national interest. The federal statute further requires that a notice to such effect be published in the *Federal Register* and indicates that if a dispute arises over the shipping cost of an otherwise protected artwork, the work may, in that limited connection, become subject to judicial seizure.

Like the federal statute, the New York statute[323] is restricted to objects entering the state for display by a museum or other nonprofit organization. The New York statute covers only works of fine art, whereas the federal statute also embraces works of cultural significance. However, the New York statute operates automatically, without the need to file an application or secure a finding that the exhibition or display is in the public interest.

SECURED TRANSACTIONS

A number of art transactions concern people who have a financial interest in a particular work of art and yet are not parties to the transaction. Examples are the artist who consigned a work to a dealer who, in turn, sold it to a purchaser; the bank that underwrites the dealer's business; and the creditor who has supplied the dealer with, for instance, framing services and has a long-standing account receivable. In addition, dealers and, to an ever-greater extent, collectors are borrowing money to purchase works of art and are pledging artworks as security for loans. Citibank in New York City has pioneered in the lending of money secured by artwork. All those situations give rise to an array of issues, such as

(1) how to secure collateral;

(2) the rights of a creditor in and to collateral, as against the rights of other creditors; and

(3) the risk assumed by a consignor that a dealer can convey to a third-party good title in artwork, leaving the consignor unpaid.

Those issues are dealt with in article 9 of the U.C.C. on secured transactions. A brief survey of the subject as it applies to dealing in art is set forth below.

Creation of the Security Interest

For a security interest there must be a secured party (the creditor) and a debtor (obligor). The secured party is a lender of money, goods, or services, and the debtor is a borrower of the money, goods, or services. The debtor is also the grantor of the security interest.[324] For a security interest to exist between a secured party and a debtor, it must attach to the collateral given as security for the loan,[325] and it is limited by the extent of the rights of the debtor in the collateral.[326] For a secured party to enjoy the maximum protection afforded by article 9, she must make sure that the security interest in the collateral (1) attaches and (2) is perfected.[327]

Attachment

Attachment of the security interest is a prerequisite to perfection (a condition that generally must occur in order for the secured party to prevail over third-party claims to the collateral and that must occur before a secured party can sue to enforce her rights under the U.C.C.).[328] There are three requirements for attachment:

- The debtor must execute a security agreement, or the collateral must be in the possession of the secured party.
- The secured party must give value.
- The debtor must have rights in the collateral.[329]

Those three prerequisites to attachment may take place in any order; the time of attachment is the time when the last of the three, whichever that may be, occurs.[330]

Collateral is grouped into three major categories:[331]

- Tangible personal property or goods
- Semi-intangibles, encompassing instruments, documents, and chattel paper
- Pure intangibles, encompassing accounts, contract rights, and general intangibles

Tangible collateral, pertinent to most secured transactions involving art, is divided into four classifications:[332]

- Consumer goods, used primarily for personal, household, or family purposes

- Equipment, a catchall term meaning goods used or bought for use primarily in business

- Farm products, meaning goods of a described type not subjected to a manufacturing process and in the possession of a debtor who is a farmer

- Inventory (meaning goods held for sale or lease or to be furnished under service contracts), raw materials, work in process, and materials used or consumed in a business

The four classes of tangibles are mutually exclusive,[333] and the proper classification of collateral hinges on its principal use or intended principal use by the debtor.[334] Thus, if a debtor owns a large sculpture for purposes of display in her home, the sculpture is classified as a consumer good, whereas, if the same debtor holds the same piece of sculpture in her gallery for sale, the sculpture is classified as an item of inventory.[335]

Perfection

As noted earlier, the security interest in the collateral must be perfected in order for the creditor to receive priority against adverse claims by third parties to the collateral. There are three basic methods of perfection:

(1) perfection by filing,

(2) perfection by taking possession, and

(3) perfection on attachment (that is, automatic perfection).[336]

The most common method of perfection is filing,[337] and a brief financing statement may be filed in the appropriate state office[338] in lieu of the actual security agreement.[339] Filing is deemed to occur at the time of presentation to the filing officer[340] and may be made before the security interest attaches and even before the security agreement is executed.[341] The financing statement is effective for five years after the date of filing and may be renewed for additional five-year periods by filing successive continuation statements.[342] Under the revision to article 9 a financing statement is only to be filed in the state office, not also in the county office as under the pre-July 2001 law.

In perfection by taking possession, an alternative to filing, the collateral or pledge may be taken either by the secured party or by an agent on the secured party's behalf.[343] Perfection here occurs when the secured party takes possession of the collateral or when the collateral is in the hands of the party's agent when the agent receives notice of the secured party's interest.[344] According to the U.C.C., the secured party must use "reasonable care in the custody and preservation of collateral" in her possession.[345]

The third method, perfection on attachment, occurs in art transactions in situations involving the purchase-money security interest. Thus, an art gallery that sells a painting on credit has a perfected security interest at the time of the sale without the necessity of filing a financing statement so long as it retains possession of the painting. That is, when the buyer executes a security agreement, the gallery gives value in the form of an extension of credit, and the buyer receives a contractual right to the goods.[346] A party other than the seller may have a purchase-money security interest, as in the case when a lender of money takes a security interest to secure the loan to a buyer to enable the debtor to buy the painting and the debtor in fact uses the money to acquire the collateral.[347]

Signature

In what may be the most dramatic change to article 9, the U.C.C. no longer requires that the debtor (obligor) sign the financing statement.[348] The secured party can file a financing statement without the debtor's signature only if authorized by the debtor to make the filing.[349] If there is a security agreement, the authorization to file the UCC-1 financing statement without a signature is automatic.[350]

Priorities

Most secured transaction litigation deals with the issue of who has first claim on the collateral: the secured party or a competing third-party claimant. In most cases involving art, the competing claimant is

(1) a lien creditor,

(2) another secured party, or

(3) a buyer from the debtor.

Secured Party Versus Lien Creditor

Generally, an unperfected security interest is subordinate to the rights of one who becomes a lien creditor before the security interest is perfected.[351] Thus, secured party *X*, who on March 1 obtains a security interest in a painting owned by a debtor-gallery and lends the gallery funds but fails to file a financing statement until March 8, is subordinate to the claims of an unsecured creditor who on March 4 obtains a judicial lien against the gallery by way of judgment and levy.

An exception occurs with purchase-money security interests[352] in which a secured party who files within ten days[353] after the debtor takes possession of the collateral prevails over one who becomes a lien creditor between the time the security interest attaches and the time of filing. Thus, an art dealer who sells a painting on March 1 to a debtor-art gallery on credit and delivers it the same day prevails over one who becomes a judicial lien holder on March 4, even though the secured party neglects to file until March 8.

Secured Party Versus Secured Party

When a debtor grants a security interest in the same collateral to two different lenders and subsequently defaults on the loans, both secured parties may assert claims to the collateral. Here are some of the general rules of priority:[354]

1. When neither security interest is perfected, the first to attach prevails.[355]

2. When one security interest is perfected and the other is not, the perfected interest prevails.[356]

3. When both security interests are perfected, one by a means other than filing, the first party to file or perfect, whichever occurs earlier, prevails.[357]

4. When both security interests are perfected by filing, the first party to file or perfect, whichever occurs earlier, prevails.[358]

5. When the collateral is other than inventory, a purchase-money security interest prevails over conflicting claims[359] if it is perfected within ten days[360] after the debtor takes possession of the collateral. Moreover, the interest holder automatically has a security interest in the proceeds of that collateral.[361] When the collateral is inventory, a purchase-money security interest prevails over conflicting claims in the same inventory and in identifiable cash proceeds received by the time of delivery of the inventory to a buyer if, before the debtor takes possession of the collateral, the purchase-money security interest is perfected and all secured parties with perfected interests in the same collateral receive written notice of that interest.[362]

Secured Party Versus Buyer

In art transactions a secured creditor may reach collateral in the hands of a buyer except for the four instances below:

1. When the creditor has authorized the sale or other disposition of the collateral "in the security agreement or otherwise,"[363] her security interest does not survive the authorized transaction.

2. When the creditor has an unperfected security interest, the buyer prevails if she gives value and receives delivery without knowledge of the security interest before it is perfected.[364]

3. When there is a buyer in the ordinary course of business, the buyer takes possession free of a perfected security interest,

even if the buyer is aware of it, unless the buyer knows that the sale violates the security agreement's terms.[365]

4. In the case of a consumer-to-consumer sale, the holder of a purchase-money security interest in consumer goods may perfect without filing, but the holder must file in order to prevail over one who buys for personal, household, or family use without knowledge of the security interest.[366]

Creditor's Rights on Default

Once a default has occurred, the secured creditor may proceed under the U.C.C. against the collateral.[367] In addition, since the options are not mutually exclusive,[368] the creditor may proceed outside the U.C.C. by bringing suit on the debt.[369] Some of the alternatives available to the secured creditor are noted in the following discussion.

When Default Occurs

Default most commonly occurs on the debtor's failure to make payments when due. In addition, default generally occurs whenever the parties have contractually so agreed. The well-drafted security agreement specifies which acts or occurrences are to be events of default.[370] Virtually all security agreements contain an acceleration clause, requiring immediate payment under prescribed conditions of the entire remainder of the loan.[371] However, such clauses in consumer agreements are nullified in states that have adopted non-U.C.C. consumer-protection legislation whereby the debtor may cure default by paying delinquent installments.

Bringing Suit on the Debt

On default, the secured creditor may bring suit outside the U.C.C. on the debt, procure a judgment, obtain a levy on the debtor's property, and receive from the sheriff, after a public auction, whatever proceeds are required to satisfy the debt. When the collateral's value is substantially less than the outstanding debt, the lien of a postjudg-ment levy reaches all the debtor's property, not just the collateral sub-ject to the security interest.[372]

Realizing on Tangible Collateral: Right to Repossession

The secured party may proceed under the U.C.C. to repossess the collateral either through self-help, if it can be accomplished without committing a breach of the peace, or through judicial action.[373] Once the collateral is repossessed, either through self-help or after the procurement of a judgment, the creditor may realize on the col-lateral by reselling or retaining it.[374]

Retention of Collateral in Satisfaction of the Debt

The secured party may, under the U.C.C.[375] and in compliance with the U.C.C.'s notice provisions, resort to strict foreclosure. The col-lateral is retained, and the debt is discharged, with the debtor neither liable for a deficiency nor entitled to any surplus if the creditor later sells the collateral.[376] Strict foreclosure is feasible only when the col-lateral's value approximates the unpaid balance of the debt, plus the anticipated costs of disposition. However, when the collateral is con-sumer goods and the debtor has paid at least 60% of the loan or cash price, the secured party must dispose of the collateral under the U.C.C.[377] within ninety days after taking possession or risk exposure in a suit for conversion or other liabilities under the U.C.C.[378]

Sale or Other Disposition of Collateral

By far the most common method of realization on tangible collateral is by its sale or other disposition.[379] The disposition, which must be in compliance with the U.C.C.'s notice provisions,[380] can occur by auction, by private sale, or by contract,[381] so long as the disposition is commercially reasonable[382] as to method, time, manner, place, and terms.[383] Proceeds from the disposition are applied, first, to the rea-sonable expenses of repossession and sale; second, to the satisfaction of the debt; and third, to the satisfaction of third-party security interests.[384] Any surplus is turned over to the debtor.[385] When the proceeds cannot cover the unpaid balance of the debt, plus expenses, the debtor is personally liable for the deficiency unless it has been otherwise agreed.[386]

Debtor's Right of Redemption

Under any circumstances, until the secured party has sold the collateral or otherwise discharged the debt, the debtor may redeem the collateral by paying all the obligations secured by the collateral, plus reasonable expenses, including attorneys' fees.[387]

Liability of the Secured Party

When there is misconduct by the secured party in repossessing and realizing on the collateral, the debtor and other creditors may avail themselves of a number of remedies. One remedy is judicial intervention; a court may enjoin, for instance, a wrongful repossession or commercially unreasonable disposition.[388] A second remedy, if an improper disposition has already occurred, is a right of recovery by the debtor or other creditors against the secured party.[389] Other remedies not mentioned in the applicable provision of the U.C.C. but recognized in a number of jurisdictions include liability in conversion, other tort liability on grounds such as trespass and invasion of privacy, and denial of the secured party's right to recover a deficiency.

Notes to Chapter 2

1.   *See, e.g.*, ARTFORUM INT'L, May 1, 2005, at 65.
2.   *E.g.*, N.Y. ARTS & CULT. AFF. LAW § 13.01.
3.   *E.g.*, IOWA CODE ANN. § 715B.2 to .4.
4.   *See* FLA. STAT. ANN. § 686.504; MICH. COMP. LAWS § 442.321 to .325.
5.   *See* Steiner v. Jarrett, 130 Cal. App. 2d Supp. 869, 280 P.2d 235 (1954); Cole v. Weber, 69 Cal. App. 394, 231 P. 353 (Dist. Ct. App. 1924).
6.   U.C.C. § 2-313.
7.   U.C.C. § 2-313 cmts. 1, 4.
8.   U.C.C. § 2-313 cmt. 8.
9.   U.C.C. § 2-313(2); Overstreet v. Norden Labs., Inc., 669 F.2d 1286 (6th Cir. 1982); Gladden v. Cadillac Motor Car Div., 83 N.J. 320, 416 A.2d 394 (1980).
10.   McKnelly v. Sperry Corp., 642 F.2d 1101 (8th Cir. 1981).
11.   Crest Container Corp. v. R.H. Bishop Co., 111 Ill. App. 3d 1068, 445 N.E.2d 19 (1982).
12.   Eddington v. Dick, 87 Misc. 2d 793, 386 N.Y.S.2d 180 (Geneva City Ct. 1976).
13.   Sylvestri v. Warner & Swasey Co., 398 F.2d 598 (2d Cir. 1968).
14.   U.C.C. § 2-313 cmt. 7.
15.   U.C.C. § 2-202; Young & Cooper, Inc. v. Vestring, 214 Kan. 311, 521 P.2d 281 (1974).
16.   U.C.C. § 2-313(1)(a).
17.   *Id. See* Alan Riding, *Art Fraud's New Trick: Add Fakes to Archive*, N.Y. Times, June 19, 1996, at C-11.
18.   *Id.*
19.   David Tunick, Inc. v. Kornfeld, 838 F. Supp. 848 (S.D.N.Y. 1993).
20.   *But cf.* Harper & Assocs. v. Printers, Inc., 46 Wash. App. 417, 730 P.2d 733 (Ct. App. 1986), *review denied*, 108 Wash. 2d 1002 (1987).
21.   *See David Tunick*, 838 F. Supp. at 851.
22.   *Id.*

23. ARTNEWSLETTER, Jan. 25, 1994, at 2.
24. U.C.C. § 2-313(1)(b).
25. U.C.C. § 2-313(1)(b) cmt. 5.
26. *Id.*
27. Weber v. Peck, 1999 WL 493383, 1999 U.S. Dist. LEXIS 10391 (S.D.N.Y. July 8, 1999).
28. *Id.*, 1999 WL 493383, at *1, 1999 U.S. Dist. LEXIS 10391, at *2.
29. *Id.*, 1999 WL 493383, at *3, 1999 U.S. Dist. LEXIS 10391, at *6.
30. *Id.*, 1999 WL 493383, at *3, 1999 U.S. Dist. LEXIS 10391, at *7.
31. U.C.C. § 2-313(2).
32. *Id.*
33. Grinnel v. Charles Pfizer & Co., 274 Cal. App. 2d 424, 79 Cal. Rptr. 369 (1969).
34. U.C.C. § 2-316 cmt. 8.
35. *Id.*
36. *See Overstreet*, 669 F.2d at 1291.
37. Cox v. DeSoto Crude Oil Purchasing Corp., 55 F. Supp. 467 (W.D. La. 1944); Morse v. Howard Park Corp., 50 Misc. 2d 834, 272 N.Y.S.2d 16 (Sup. Ct. 1966).
38. U.C.C. § 2-316 cmt. 8.
39. U.C.C. § 2-316(1).
40. *Id.*
41. N.Y. ARTS & CULT. AFF. LAW § 13.01.
42. MICH. COMP. LAWS § 442.321 to .325.
43. *See* U.C.C. § 2-316; Giusti v. Sotheby Parke Bernet, Inc., N.Y.L.J., July 16, 1982, at 5 (N.Y. Sup. Ct. 1982).
44. Weiscz v. Parke-Bernet Galleries, Inc., 67 Misc. 2d 1077, 325 N.Y.S.2d 576 (N.Y. City Civ. Ct. 1971), *rev'd*, 77 Misc. 2d 80, 351 N.Y.S.2d 911 (App. Term 1974).
45. *Id.*, 67 Misc. 2d at 1082, 325 N.Y.S.2d at 582.
46. *See Weiscz*, 77 Misc. 2d at 80, 351 N.Y.S.2d at 912.
47. U.C.C. § 2-202.
48. U.C.C. § 2-202(a).
49. U.C.C. § 2-202(b).
50. U.C.C. § 2-314 (implied warranty of merchantability); U.C.C. § 2-315 (implied warranty of fitness for a particular purpose).
51. U.C.C. § 2-314.
52. U.C.C. § 2-314(1).

53. U.C.C. § 2-104(1).
54. U.C.C. § 2-104 cmt. 2.
55. *Id.*
56. *See, e.g.,* Daniell v. Ford Motor Co., 581 F. Supp. 728 (D.N.M. 1984); Hinderer v. Ryan, 7 Wash. App. 434, 499 P.2d 252 (1972).
57. U.C.C. § 2-314(2).
58. U.C.C. § 2-314 cmt. 2.
59. U.C.C. § 2-314 cmt. 8.
60. U.C.C. § 2-315 & cmt. 1.
61. Price Bros. Co. v. Phila. Gear Corp., 649 F.2d 416 (6th Cir. 1980), *cert. denied,* 454 U.S. 1099 (1981).
62. U.C.C. § 2-315 cmt. 4.
63. U.C.C. § 2-316(3)(b).
64. *Id.*
65. U.C.C. § 2-316 cmt. 8.
66. *Id.*
67. *Id.*
68. U.C.C. § 2-316.
69. U.C.C. § 2-316(2) & cmts. 3,5.
70. U.C.C. § 2-316(2) & cmt. 3; U.C.C. § 1-201(10).
71. U.C.C. § 2-316(2) & cmt. 3.
72. U.C.C. § 2-316(3)(a) & cmt. 7.
73. U.C.C. § 2-316(2).
74. *Id.*
75. *Id.*
76. U.C.C. § 2-316(3)(a) & cmt. 7.
77. U.C.C. § 2-316(3)(c).
78. Alger v. Abele Tractor & Equip. Co., 92 A.D.2d 677, 460 N.Y.S.2d 202 (1983); FMC Fin. Corp. v. Murphree, 632 F.2d 413 (5th Cir. 1980).
79. U.C.C. §§ 2-316(2), 1-201(10). *See, e.g.,* Lupa v. Jock's, 131 Misc. 2d 536, 500 N.Y.S.2d 962 (Sup. Ct. 1986); Natale v. Martin Volkswagen, Inc., 92 Misc. 2d 1046, 402 N.Y.S.2d 156 (Sup. Ct. 1978).
80. U.C.C. § 2-302. *See, e.g.,* Industralease Automated Scientific & Equip. Corp. v. R.M.E. Enters., Inc., 58 A.D.2d 482, 396 N.Y.S.2d 427 (1977).
81. *See, e.g.,* CAL. CIV. CODE § 1791.1 *et seq.*; MD. CODE ANN., COM. LAW § 2-316; MASS. ANN. LAWS ch. 106, § 2-316; OR. REV. STAT. § 72.8050; WASH. REV. CODE § 62A.2-316.
82. Consumer goods are generally defined in the statutes as goods purchased primarily for personal, family, or household use.

83. U.C.C. § 2-318 cmt. 3.

84. *See, e.g.*, Mayes v. Harnischfeger Corp., 60 Misc. 2d 308, 302 N.Y.S.2d 658 (Sup. Ct. 1969).

85. Lonzrick v. Republic Steel Corp., 6 Ohio St. 2d 227, 218 N.E.2d 18 (1966).

86. 3 A.R. ANDERSON, UNIFORM COMMERCIAL CODE § 2-314:391 and § 2-314:416 (3d ed. rev. 2002).

87. U.C.C. § 2-312.

88. U.C.C. § 2-312(1)(a).

89. *Id.*

90. U.C.C. § 2-312(1)(b).

91. U.C.C. § 2-312(3).

92. U.C.C. § 2-312(2).

93. *Id. See also* Duesenberg & King, *Sales and Bulk Transfers*, 3 Bender's U.C.C. Serv. § 5.03 (1987).

94. Sunseri v. RKO-Stanley Warner Theatres, Inc., 248 Pa. Super. 111, 374 A.2d 1342 (1977).

95. Duesenberg & King, *supra* note 93, § 5.03. *See also, e.g.*, Simmons Mach. Co. v. M&M Brokerage, Inc., 409 So. 2d 743 (Ala. 1981).

96. U.C.C. § 2-312 cmt. 5. But note that the warranty against infringement may be excluded by agreement between the parties. *See* Duesenberg & King, *supra* note 93, § 5.04[5].

97. U.C.C. § 2-312 cmt. 5.

98. *See, e.g.*, Cady v. Pitts, 102 Idaho 86, 625 P.2d 1089 (1981); Smith v. Taylor, 44 N.C. App. 363, 261 S.E.2d 19 (1979).

99. Menzel v. List, 49 Misc. 2d 300, 267 N.Y.S.2d 804 (Sup. Ct. 1966), *modified as to damages*, 28 A.D.2d 516, 279 N.Y.S.2d 608 (1967), *rev'd as to modifications*, 24 N.Y.2d 91, 246 N.E.2d 742, 298 N.Y.S.2d 979 (1969). *See* discussion related to the statute of limitations in chapter 3 at page 264.

100. *Menzel*, 24 N.Y.2d at 97, 246 N.E.2d at 745, 298 N.Y.S.2d at 983.

101. The Perls did not pursue their cause of action against the Parisian art dealer, as he was then deceased.

102. *Menzel*, 24 N.Y.2d at 98, 246 N.E.2d at 745, 298 N.Y.S.2d at 983.

103. U.C.C. § 2-714(2).

104. Koerner v. Davis, No. 85 Civ. 0752 (S.D.N.Y. May 21, 1987).

105. Nacht v. Sotheby's Holdings, Inc., QDS 22701016 (Sup. Ct. N.Y. County 1999).

106. U.C.C. § 2-607.

107. U.C.C. § 1-201(25), (26).
108. U.C.C. § 2-607(3)(a).
109. U.C.C. § 2-609 cmt. 4.
110. U.C.C. § 2-607(5)(a).
111. *See* Jafari v. Wally Findlay Galleries, 1989 U.S. Dist. LEXIS 11299 (S.D.N.Y. Sept. 25, 1989) (denying defendant-dealer's motion to dismiss on the basis of statute of frauds where the dealer, although he did not sign a contract, did initial a handwritten memorandum on his letterhead in a manner that seemed to verify an alteration to the document). *See* Spink & Son, Ltd. v. Gen. Atl. Corp., N.Y.L.J. Jan. 23, 1996, at 26 (Sup. Ct. N.Y. County 1996), which granted defendant's motion to dismiss on the basis of the statute of frauds in New York where the defendant made an allegedly oral contract to purchase art in England but allowed the case to proceed in New York applying the substantive law of England, the location where the art was purchased and where the statute of frauds defense may not apply and where an oral contract of this type was enforceable. *See also* Tolhurst, *Governing Law In International Art Sales*, 1 ART ANTIQUITY & LAW 153 (1996). The statute of frauds issue may also arise with respect to an agreement between two parties for a finder's fee or introductory commission for the referral of business. In Mirisola v. Habsburg Feldman, S.A., 172 A.D.2d 306, 568 N.Y.S.2d 110 (1991), the court found that a written agreement or memorandum is required to enforce an agreement to pay a finder's fee for the plaintiff's successful efforts to induce prospective sellers to consign objects for sale. In Chowaiki v. Steinhardt, Index #600250/04 (N.Y. Sup. Ct., N.Y. County, Mar. 28, 2005), the court held as void in violation of the statute of frauds an alleged oral agreement to sell a Chagall painting. In this case, the court awarded legal fees to the defendants because of the frivolous nature of the plaintiff's claim.
112. Hoffman v. Boone, 708 F. Supp. 78 (S.D.N.Y. 1989).
113. *Id.* at 81.
114. *See, e.g.*, McCulley Fine Arts Gallery, Inc. v. "X" Partners, 860 S.W. 2d 473 (Tex. Ct. App. 1993).
115. Andre Emmerich Gallery, Inc. v. Frost, N.Y.L.J., Dec. 20, 1994, at 24 (Sup. Ct. N.Y. County 1994).
116. U.C.C. § 2-201(2).
117. U.C.C. § 2-201(3).
118. Nat'l Historic Shrines Found. v. Dalí, 4 U.C.C. Rep. Serv. 71 (N.Y. Sup. Ct. 1967).
119. Sands & Co. v. Christie's, Inc., Index #600268/04 (N.Y. Sup. Ct., N.Y. County, Feb. 28, 2005).
120. Tasende v. Janis, 1999 WL 179369, 1999 U.S. Dist. LEXIS 3996 (S.D.N.Y. 1999).

121.   Tasende v. Janis, 2000 WL 377512, 2000 U.S. Dist. LEXIS 4652 (S.D.N.Y. 2000).

122.   U.C.C. § 2-302. But note that this provision is omitted entirely in California.

123.   Vom Lehn v. Astor Art Galleries, Ltd., 86 Misc. 2d 1, 11, 380 N.Y.S.2d 532, 541 (Sup. Ct. 1976).

124.   *Id.*, 86 Misc. 2d at 10, 380 N.Y.S.2d at 541.

125.   *Id.*

126.   *Id.*

127.   *Id.*, 86 Misc. 2d at 13, 380 N.Y.S.2d at 543.

128.   Weil v. Murray, 161 F. Supp. 2d 250 (S.D.N.Y. 2001).

129.   *Id.* at 253–54.

130.   *Id.* at 255 (citing Seiden Assoc., Inc. v ANC Holdings, Inc., 959 F.2d 425, 428 (2d Cir. 1992)).

131.   *Id.* at 257.

132.   U.C.C. § 2-401.

133.   Thomas H. Jackson & Ellen A. Peters, *Quest for Uncertainty: A Proposal for Flexible Resolution of the Inherent Conflicts Between Article 2 and Article 9 of the Uniform Commercial Code*, 87 YALE L.J. 907, 912 (1978). *See also* THOMAS M. QUINN, QUINN'S UNIFORM COMMERCIAL CODE COMMENTARY AND LAW DIGEST § 2-401[A][2][a] (2d ed. 2002) ("The parties are free to agree on the point in space and time when title will shift from the seller to the buyer. The agreement should be explicit since, failing that, the working rules provided by the Code would apply. Section 2-401(1) provides that 'title to goods passes from the seller to the buyer in any manner and on any conditions explicitly agreed on by the parties.' This power to determine the point at which title will pass should not be confused, however, with the common practice of a seller's 'reservation of title.' This does not activate the 'agreement' rule. Section 2-401(2) provides expressly that 'any retention or reservation by the seller of the title (property) in goods shipped or delivered to the buyer is limited in effect to a reservation of a security interest.' Thus, the agreement envisioned by this rule is a formal agreement looking to the transfer of ownership at a given point other than a reservation of title in connection with financing.").

134.   *See* White-Motor Corp. v. Bronx-Westchester White Trucks, Inc., N.Y.L.J., Dec. 23, 1975, at 6, 18 U.C.C. Rep. Serv. (CBC) 382 (N.Y. Sup. Ct. 1975); Recchio v. Mfrs. & Traders Trust Co., 55 Misc. 2d 788, 286 N.Y.S.2d 390 (Sup. Ct. 1968), *rev'd on other grounds*, 28 N.Y.2d 222, 269 N.E.2d 809, 321 N.Y.S.2d 94 (1971); L.B. Smith, Inc. v. Foley, 34 F. Supp. 810 (W.D.N.Y. 1972); Bank of N.Y. v. Margiotta, 416 N.Y.S.2d 493 (Dist. Ct. 1979); *In re* Ide Jewelry Co., 75 B.R. 969, 977 (Bankr.

S.D.N.Y. 1987) ("[I]f the consignment were intended as security, [the seller's] reservation of title is limited to a security interest. . . ."); Fulater v. Palmer's Granite Garage, Inc., 110 Misc. 2d 1003, 1005, 443 N.Y.S.2d 193, 194 (1981) ("Indeed, according to [§ 2401] any reservation of title by [the seller] was limited to a security interest once the truck was delivered."); *In re* Samuels & Co., 526 F.2d 1238, 1246 (5th Cir. 1976) ("the UCC specifically limits the seller's ability to reserve title once he has voluntarily surrendered possession to the buyer"); Dixie Bonded Warehouse v. Allstate Fin. Corp., 693 F. Supp. 1162, 1164 (M.D. Ga. 1988) ("An unpaid cash seller may not defeat a secured party's interest by retention of 'title.'"); *In re* Communications Co. of Am., 84 B.R. 822, 823 (Bankr. M.D. Fla. 1988) ("[Section 2-401] clearly dictates that despite . . . the Sales Agreement ['s reservation of title in the seller], [the seller's] reservation of title only reserved a security interest in the equipment. . . .").

135.   Silver v. Sloop Silver Cloud, 259 F. Supp. 187 (S.D.N.Y. 1966). *See In re* GEC Indus., Inc., 128 B.R. 892 (Bankr. D. Del. 1991); Puamier v. Barge BT 1793, 395 F. Supp. 1019 (E.D. Va. 1974); Goodpasture, Inc. v. M/V Pollux, 688 F.2d 1003 (5th Cir. 1982), *cert. denied*, 460 U.S. 1084 (1983).

136.   AB Recur Finans v. Andersson, Index No. 9422/90 (N.Y. Sup. Ct. July 7, 1995).

137.   *Id*. at 35.

138.   *Id*. at 36.

139.   *See* Judson Art Warehouse, Inc. v. Peder Bonnier, Index No. 9422/90 (N.Y. Sup. Ct. Aug. 29, 1995).

140.   *Id*. at 5. *Compare with* Andrew Grispo Gallery, Inc. v. Maroney, 187 A.D.2d 251, 589 N.Y.S.2d 445 (1992), where the court held that the buyer of a painting had no equitable interest in that painting after it had been resold by the seller because under the parties' purchase agreement, title to the painting was to remain with the seller until the painting was paid in full. However, in this case the painting was *not* delivered so the court could find that a reservation of title on the invoice was valid. Note that under the Gagosian invoice referred to in *Judson*, the painting also was *not* delivered until payment was made in full.

141.   *See, e.g.*, Bassett v. Spofford, 45 N.Y. 387 (1871). *See also Menzel*, 49 Misc. 2d at 315, 267 N.Y.S.2d at 819. However, note that until recently in England, the "market ouvert" system permitted buyers at street markets to acquire legal ownership of all merchandise bought between sunrise and sunset, even if the goods had been stolen. This ended July 15, 1994, by act of Parliament, spurred by a fellow's unwitting purchase for £195 of portraits by Thomas Gainsborough and Sir Joshua Reynolds, which, it

turned out, had been stolen in 1990 from one of London's Inns of Court, the training ground for barristers. ARTNEWSLETTER, July 26, 1994, at 7.

142. U.C.C. § 2-403(1).

143. *See, e.g.*, Ross v. Leuci, 194 Misc. 345, 85 N.Y.S.2d 497 (City Ct. 1949); Crocker v. Crocker, 31 N.Y. 507 (1865).

144. Morgold, Inc. v. Keeler, 891 F. Supp. 1361 (N.D. Cal. 1995).

145. U.C.C. § 2-403(1).

146. *See infra* notes 158 and 160.

147. Stellan Holm, Inc. v. Malmberg Int'l Art, AB, 2002 WL 392294, 2002 U.S. Dist. LEXIS 4126 (S.D.N.Y. 2002).

148. *Id.*, 2002 WL 392294, at *2, 2002 U.S. Dist. LEXIS 4126, at *5.

149. *Id.*, 2002 WL 392294, at *4, 2002 U.S. Dist. LEXIS 4126, at *11.

150. *Id.*, 2002 WL 392294, at *4, 2002 U.S. Dist. LEXIS 4126, at *12.

151. Kenyon v. Abel, 2001 WY 135, 36 P.3d 1161 (2001).

152. *Id.*, 36 P.3d at 1163–64.

153. *Id.* at 1165 (citing Underhill Coal Mining Co. v. Hixon, 652 A.2d 343, 346 (Pa. Super. Ct. 1994)).

154. *Id.* at 1166.

155. Glenshaw Glass Co. v. Ontario Grape Growers' Mktg. Bd., 67 F.3d 470, 475 (3d Cir. 1995); BLACK'S LAW DICTIONARY (7th ed. 1999); *In re* Atl. Computer Sys., Inc., 135 B.R. 463, 466 (Bankr. S.D.N.Y. 1992); SEC v. Credit Bancorp, Ltd., 2000 U.S. Dist. LEXIS 17171, *81–*82 (S.D.N.Y. 2000).

156. 1 WHITE & SUMMERS, UNIFORM COMMERCIAL CODE 193 (4th ed. 1995).

157. U.C.C. § 1-201(9).

158. Cantor v. Anderson, 639 F. Supp. 364 (S.D.N.Y. 1986).

159. U.C.C. § 2-103(1)(b). *See Morgold*, 891 F. Supp. 1361.

160. Porter v. Wertz, 68 A.D.2d 141, 416 N.Y.S.2d 254 (1979), *aff'd*, 53 N.Y.2d 696, 421 N.E.2d 500, 439 N.Y.S.2d 105 (Ct. App. 1981). *See also* Phillips, *The Commercial Culpability Scale*, 92 YALE L.J. 228 (1982).

161. *See Porter*, 68 A.D.2d at 145, 416 N.Y.S.2d at 257.

162. Graffman v. Espel, 1998 WL 55371, 1998 U.S. Dist. LEXIS 1339 (S.D.N.Y. 1998).

163. *Id.*, 1998 WL 55371, at *2, 1998 U.S. Dist. LEXIS 1339, at *7.

164. *Id.*, 1998 WL 55371, at *3, 1998 U.S. Dist. LEXIS 1339, at *9.

165. *Id.* (citing *Porter, supra* note 160).
166. *Id.*, 1998 WL 55371, at ★4, 1998 U.S. Dist. LEXIS 1339, at ★14.
167. *Id.*, 1998 WL 55371, at ★5, 1998 U.S. Dist. LEXIS 1339, at ★15 (citing *Porter*, 68 A.D.2d at 146, 416 N.Y.S.2d at 257).
168. *Id.*, 1998 WL 55371, at ★5 and U.S. Dist. LEXIS 1339, at ★18; *see Morgold*, 891 F. Supp. 1361.
169. *Graffman*, 1998 WL 55371, at ★6, 1998 U.S. Dist. LEXIS 1339, at ★20; Graffman v. Doe, 201 F.3d 431, 1999 WL 1295351, 1999 U.S. App. LEXIS 34236 (2d Cir. Dec. 23, 1999).
170. Dark Bay Int'l, Ltd. v. Acquavella Galleries, Inc., Index No. 02-600122/02 (Sup. Ct. N.Y. County Nov. 6, 2003), *aff'd*, 12 A.D.3d 711, 784 N.Y.S.2d 514 (1st Dep't 2004), *motion to appeal denied*, 4 N.Y.3d 705, 825 N.E.2d 1093, 792 N.Y.S.2d 898 (2005). *See also* Spanierman Gallery, Profit Sharing Plan v. Merritt, 2003 WL 289704, 2003 U.S. Dist. LEXIS 1444, 49 U.C.C. Rep. Serv. 2d (CBC) 809 (S.D.N.Y. Feb. 6, 2003) (precluding summary judgment against gallery who bought painting at auction where entrusted dealer who sought appraisal of painting could support inference he was not a dealer in the relevant type of goods); Merritt v. Fagan, 2002 WL 1331839, 2002 Conn. Super. LEXIS 1772 (Conn. Super. Ct. May 17, 2002), *aff'd*, 78 Conn. App. 590, 828 A.2d 685 (Conn. App. Ct.), *cert. denied*, 266 Conn. 916, 833 A.2d 467 (2003) (holding dealer in *Spanierman* liable to plaintiff for conversion, awarding compensatory and punitive damages); *and generally* Henkel, *Sales: What Is "Entrusting" Goods to Merchant Dealer Under UCC § 2-403*, 59 A.L.R.4th 567 (1988) (discussing where entrusting is and is not found among merchant dealers).
171. *Dark Bay Int'l*, 12 A.D.3d at 212.
172. *Dark Bay Int'l*, Index No. 02-600122/02 (citing Dows v. Nat'l Exch. Bank of Milwaukee, 91 U.S. 618, 630 (1875)).
173. *Id.* at 10 (citing Solomon R. Guggenheim Found. v. Lubell, 77 N.Y.2d 311, 320 (1991)).
174. *See* Porter v. Wertz, 68 A.D.2d 141, 416 N.Y.S.2d 254 (1979), *aff'd*, 53 N.Y.2d 696, 421 N.E.2d 500, 439 N.Y.S.2d 105 (Ct. App. 1981); *see also* Taborsky v. Maroney, No. 83-2533, 745 F.2d 60 (7th Cir. 1984) (unpublished); Taborsky v. Bolen Gallery, Inc., No. 83-2560, 745 F.2d 60 (7th Cir. 1984) (unpublished), *reproduced in* 2 F. FELDMAN, S. WEIL & BIEDERMAN, ART LAW § 9.2.4 (1986). *See* Autocephalous Greek-Orthodox Church v. Goldberg, IP 89-304C (S.D. Ind. Aug. 3, 1989); Howley v. Sotheby's, Inc., N.Y.L.J. Feb. 20, 1986, at 6 (Civ. Ct., N.Y. Cty. 1986).
175. *Howley*, N.Y.L.J. Feb. 20, 1986, at 6.
176. *See Taborsky, supra* note 174. *See also* discussion on sales by collectors at page 149.

177. *Taborsky, supra* note 174.

178. *Id.*

179. *Id.*

180. *Id. See Morgold*, 891 F. Supp. 1361.

181. United States v. Crawford Tech. Servs., 2004 WL 744670, 2004 U.S. Dist. LEXIS 5824 (S.D.N.Y. Apr. 7, 2004).

182. Solomon R. Guggenheim Found. v. Lubell, 77 N.Y. 2d 311, 567 N.Y.S. 2d 623 (1991), *aff'g* 153 A.D. 2d 143, 550 N.Y.S. 2d 618 (1990); see discussion of *Guggenheim* in chapter 3.

183. *Crawford Tech. Servs.*, 2004 WL 744670, 2004 U.S. Dist. LEXIS 5824.

184. *Id.*, 2004 WL 744670, at ★5, 2004 U.S. Dist. LEXIS 5824, at ★16.

185. *Id.*, 2004 WL 744670, at ★6, 2004 U.S. Dist. LEXIS 5824, at ★19.

186. Van Rijn v. Wildenstein, 1987 WL 11551, 1987 U.S. Dist. LEXIS 3955 (S.D.N.Y. 1987).

187. CAL. PENAL CODE § 536.

188. U.C.C. § 2-327(2)(b).

189. U.C.C. § 2-503; *see also* U.C.C. § 2-509.

190. U.C.C. § 2-509(3); Conway v. Larsen Jewelers, Inc., 104 Misc. 2d 872, 429 N.Y.S.2d 378 (N.Y. City Small Cl. Ct. 1980).

191. Mennella v. Schon, 979 F.2d 357 (5th Cir. 1992), *reh'g denied*, 1993 U.S. App. LEXIS 375 (5th Cir. Jan. 4, 1993).

192. *Id.* at 361.

193. *See, e.g.*, Ohio Co. v. Rosemeir, 32 Ohio App. 2d 116, 288 N.E.2d 326 (1972).

194. *See, e.g.*, Chapman v. Cole, 12 Gray (Mass.) 141 (1858).

195. *See* 7 A. CORBIN, CORBIN ON CONTRACTS § 28.35 (2002).

196. *See* 27 S. WILLISTON, WILLISTON ON CONTRACTS § 70:67 (4th ed. 2000).

197. Uptown Gallery, Inc. v. Marjorie Weston Doniger, Index No. 17133/90 (Sup. Ct. N.Y. County, Mar. 9, 1993).

198. Richard L. Feigen & Co. v. Weil, Index No. 13935/90 (Sup. Ct. N.Y. County, Feb. 18, 1992), *aff'd*, 191 A.D.2d 278, 595 N.Y.S.2d 683 (1st Dept. 1993).

199. FLA. STAT. ANN. § 686.504.

200. IOWA CODE ANN. §§ 715B.2 to .4.

201. N.Y. ARTS & CULT. AFF. LAW § 13.01.

202. MICH. COMP. LAWS §§ 442.321 to .325.

203. CAL. CIV. CODE § 1744.7; GA. CODE ANN. § 10-1-433; HAW. REV. STAT. ANN. § 481F-5.

204. *Uptown Gallery*, Index No. 17133/90.

205. *Id.*

206. *Richard L. Feigen & Co.*, Index No. 13935/90.

207. RALPH E. LERNER & JUDITH BRESLER, ART LAW: THE GUIDE FOR COLLECTORS, INVESTORS, DEALERS, AND ARTISTS 90 (PLI 1989).

208. *Compare* Wood v. Boynton, 64 Wis. 256 (1885), *with* Sherwood v. Walker, 66 Mich. 568 (1887).

209. *Richard L. Feigen & Co.*, Index No. 13935/90.

210. Porter v. Wertz, 416 N.Y.S.2d 254 (App. Div. 1979), *aff'd*, 439 N.Y.S.2d 105 (Ct. App. 1981). *See* LERNER & BRESLER, *supra* note 207, at 79.

211. Firestone & Parson, Inc. v. Union League of Phila., 672 F. Supp. 819 (E.D. Pa.), *aff'd*, 833 F.2d 304 (3d Cir. 1987).

212. *Id.* at 822.

213. *See Uptown Gallery*, Index No. 17133/90.

214. Greenberg Gallery v. Bauman, 817 F. Supp 167 (D.D.C. 1993), *aff'd*, 36 F.3d 127 (D.C. Cir. 1994).

215. Arnold Herstand & Co. v. Gallery: Gertrude Stein, Inc., 211 A.D.2d 77, 626 N.Y.S.2d 74 (1995).

216. *Id.*

217. *Id.*

218. *Id.*

219. Aside from knowledge and belief, two states of mind that also support a suit in fraud are (1) reckless disregard for a representation's truth or falsity and (2) awareness of a lack of sufficient basis of information to make a representation. *See* W. KEETON ET AL., PROSSER AND KEETON ON THE LAW OF TORTS §§ 105, 107 (5th ed. 1984 & Supp. 1988).

220. 26 WILLISTON, WILLISTON ON CONTRACTS §§ 69:1–69:3, 69:17 (4th ed. 1999); W. KEETON ET AL., *supra* note 219, § 105.

221. W. KEETON ET AL., *supra* note 219, § 109.

222. *Id.*

223. *Id.* Here, as in the text immediately above, the seller, depending on the circumstances, may also be liable for breach of warranty.

224. *Id.* § 105.

225. *Id.* § 107.

226. *Id.* § 105.

227. *See* discussion of breach of warranties at pages 76–98.

228. R. DUFFY, ART LAW: REPRESENTING ARTISTS, DEALERS, AND COLLECTORS 16 (1977).

229. U.C.C. § 2-202. *See also* discussion of parol evidence at page 85.

230. McKie v. R.H. Love Galleries, Inc., 1990 WL 179797, 1990 U.S. Dist. LEXIS 14748 (N.D. Ill. 1990).

231. McCloud v. Lawrence Gallery, Ltd., 1991 WL 136027, 1991 U.S. Dist. LEXIS 9631 (S.D.N.Y. 1991), 1992 WL 6199, 1992 U.S. Dist. LEXIS 170 (S.D.N.Y.), aff'd, 970 F.2d 896 (2d Cir. 1992).

232. Id., 1992 WL 6199, at *3, 1992 U.S. Dist. LEXIS 170, at *9.

233. A few statutes, such as Ohio's and Pennsylvania's, permit a suit in forgery on proof of mere knowledge, rather than intent, to defraud or injure. OHIO REV. CODE ANN. § 2913.31; 18 PA. CONS. STAT. § 4101.

234. See, e.g., N.Y. PENAL LAW § 170.05. See also Note, Legal Control of the Fabrication and Marketing of Fake Paintings, 24 STAN. L. REV. 930, 940-41 (1972).

235. MONT. CODE ANN. § 45-6-325.

236. CONN. GEN. STAT. ANN. § 53a-140.

237. See, e.g., ALA. CODE § 13A-9-10; ALASKA STAT. § 11.46.530; ARIZ. REV. STAT. ANN. § 13-2004; ARK. CODE ANN. § 5-37-213; COLO. REV. STAT. ANN. § 18-5-110; CONN. GEN. STAT. ANN. § 53a-141; KY. REV. STAT. ANN. § 516.110; N.J. STAT. ANN. § 2C:21-2; OHIO REV. CODE ANN. § 2913.32; 18 PA. CONS. STAT. § 4102; TEX. PENAL CODE ANN. § 32.22; UTAH CODE § 76-6-501; VT. STAT. ANN. tit. 13, § 2023; WIS. STAT. ANN. § 943.38(3)(A). See also CAL. PENAL CODE § 536.

238. N.Y. PENAL LAW § 170.45. See also People v. Haifif, 128 Misc. 2d 713, 491 N.Y.S.2d 226 (Sup. Ct. 1985).

239. Again, some state statutes, such as Ohio's and Pennsylvania's, supra note 233, permit the bringing of suit upon mere proof of knowledge of injury or deception rather than intent.

240. See, e.g., OHIO REV. CODE ANN. § 2913.32.

241. See, e.g., UTAH CODE § 76-6-501.

242. N.Y. ARTS & CULT. AFF. LAW § 13.01; IOWA CODE ANN. § 715B.2 to .4; FLA. STAT. ANN. § 686.504; MICH. COMP. LAWS § 442.321 to .325. See also discussion of David Tunick, Inc., supra note 19.

243. MICH. COMP. LAWS § 442.324.

244. Lawson v. London Arts Group, 708 F.2d 226 (6th Cir. 1983).

245. U.C.C. § 2-313.

246. Dawson v. G. Malina, Inc., 463 F. Supp. 461 (S.D.N.Y. 1978); see also Englehard v. Duffy, N.Y.L.J., Oct. 27, 1983, at 13 (Sup. Ct. N.Y. County 1983); Balog v. Ctr. Art Gallery-Haw., Inc., 745 F. Supp. 1556, 1565 (D. Haw. 1990).

247. See Dawson, 463 F. Supp. at 467.

248. Pritzker v. Krishna Gallery of Asian Arts, 1996 WL 563442, 1996 U.S. Dist. LEXIS 14398 (N.D. Ill. 1996) (memorandum and order); 1995 U.S. Dist. LEXIS 8778 (N.D. Ill. 1995) (magistrate's report and recommendation).

249. *Id.*, 1996 WL 563442, at *3, 1996 U.S. Dist. LEXIS 14398, at *8–*9.

250. *Id.*, 1995 U.S. Dist. LEXIS 8778, at *54–*55.

251. Pritzker v. Krishna Gallery of Asian Arts, No. 93 C 4147, unpublished order (N.D. Ill. Mar. 17, 1997).

252. *See Dawson*, 463 F. Supp. at 467.

253. *Pritzker*, No. 93 C 4147, at 11.

254. Nat'l L.J., June 9, 1997, at A6, col. 2.

255. Rogath v. Siebman, 941 F. Supp. 416 (S.D.N.Y. 1996).

256. N.Y. Pers. Prop. Law § 425 *et seq.* The Door-to-Door Sales Protection Act superseded the Home Solicitation Sales Act in September 1976. *See* N.Y. Pers. Prop. Law § 425, historical and statutory notes.

257. N.Y. Pers. Prop. Law § 427(1).

258. *Id.* § 428(1), (2).

259. *Id.* § 428(2).

260. *See* Vom Lehn v. Astor Art Galleries, Ltd., 86 Misc. 2d 1, 380 N.Y.S.2d 532 (Sup. Ct. 1976).

261. *Id.*, 86 Misc. 2d at 11, 380 N.Y.S.2d at 542.

262. *Pritzker, supra* note 248, at *22.

263. *See, e.g.*, Ariz. Rev. Stat. Ann. § 44-1231.01; Colo. Rev. Stat. Ann. § 12-44.5-101 to -108; Okla. Stat. Ann. tit. 78, §§ 71–75. *See also* Native American Graves Protection and Repatriation Act, 25 U.S.C. §§ 3001–13; *Symposium: The Native American Graves Protection and Repatriation Act of 1990 and State Repatriation—Related Legislation*, 24 Ariz. St. L.J. 1 (1992).

264. 15 U.S.C. § 2301 *et seq.*

265. 15 U.S.C. § 2302(e); 16 C.F.R. § 701.

266. 15 U.S.C. § 2303(a).

267. 15 U.S.C. §§ 2303(a)(1), 2304.

268. 15 U.S.C. § 2303(a)(3).

269. 15 U.S.C. § 2303(b).

270. 15 U.S.C. § 2310(c)(2).

271. 15 U.S.C. §§ 2302, 2312(c).

272. 15 U.S.C. § 2302.

273. *Id.*

274. 15 U.S.C. § 2311.

275. 15 U.S.C. § 1601 *et seq.*

276.   15 U.S.C. § 1611.

277.   15 U.S.C. § 1640.

278.   15 U.S.C. § 45(a).

279.   FTC v. Fed. Sterling Galleries, Inc., No. 87-2072 (D. Ariz. filed Jan. 12, 1989); FTC v. Austin Galleries of Ill., Inc., No. 88 C 3845, 1988 U.S. Dist. LEXIS 12380 (N.D. Ill. Nov. 2, 1988).

280.   N.Y. CITY ADMIN. CODE tit. 20, ch. 5, subch. 2, §§ 20-707 to -711.

281.   *See* N.Y. TIMES, Mar. 3, 1988, § 1, at 25; N.Y. TIMES, Mar. 20, 1988, § 2, at 33; ARTNEWSLETTER, Sept. 6, 1988.

282.   *See* Kramer v. Pollock-Krasner Found., 890 F. Supp. 250 (S.D.N.Y. 1995); Vitale v. Marlborough Gallery, 32 U.S.P.Q.2d (BNA) 1283 (S.D.N.Y. 1994).

283.   Wildenstein & Co. v. Wallis, 79 N.Y.2d 641, 584 N.Y.S.2d 753 (1992).

284.   *Id. See also* Metro. Transp. Auth. v. Brukan Realty Corp., 67 N.Y.2d 156, 161 (1986).

285.   *Id. See* N.Y. EST. POWERS & TRUSTS LAW § 9-1.1.

286.   N.Y. GEN. BUS. LAW §§ 340–47.

287.   Vitale v. Marlborough Gallery, 32 U.S.P.Q.2d (BNA) 1283, 1994 WL 654494 (S.D.N.Y. 1994).

288.   *Id.* at *4.

289.   *See, e.g.,* Royal Bus. Machs., Inc. v. Lorraine Corp., 633 F.2d 34 (7th Cir. 1980).

290.   U.C.C. § 2-314(1) & cmt. 3.

291.   U.C.C. § 2-314 cmt. 3.

292.   U.C.C. § 2-312(3).

293.   U.C.C. § 2-201(2).

294.   U.C.C. § 2-403(2); *Cantor, supra* note 158.

295.   *Taborsky, supra* note 174.

296.   U.C.C. § 9-701.

297.   U.C.C. § 2-326 was amended effective July 1, 200,1 to repeal prior § 2-326(3) in connection with the revision of Article 9.

298.   Christenfeld & Melzer, *Entrustments and Secured Transactions,* N.Y.L.J., Oct. 2, 2003.

299.   U.C.C. § 2-326(1)(b).

300.   U.C.C. § 2-326(1)(a).

301.   U.C.C. § 2-326(1)(b).

302.   U.C.C. § 9-315(a); U.C.C. § 9-320(a); U.C.C. § 2-403(2).

303.   Note that under U.C.C. § 2-403(2) if an artwork is consigned to an art dealer who deals in goods of that kind, the art dealer can

pass good title to a good faith buyer for value even if the consignor perfected a security interest under Article 9 of the U.C.C. *See* U.C.C. § 9-319(a); U.C.C. § 9-320(a). *See also* Nathan, *Consignment the Right Way: File a UCC Financing Statement*, 106 Bus. Credit 12 (Apr. 2004).

304.   U.C.C. § 2-326(1)(a).

305.   U.C.C. § 2-326(2).

306.   *Id. See* Marcone, *The UCC and Consignment: Making the Code Safe for Artists and Other Little Fellows*, 12 Cardozo Arts & Ent. L.J. 579 (1994).

307.   U.C.C. § 9-308(a).

308.   U.C.C. § 9-102(a)(20).

309.   *Id.; see also* Allsop v. Ernst, 20 B.R. 627 (Bankr. S.D. Ohio 1982); Bischoff v. Thomasson, 400 So. 2d 359 (Ala. 1981); *In re* Mincow Bag, 29 A.D.2d 400, 288 N.Y.S.2d 364 (App. Div. 1968), *aff'd mem.*, 24 N.Y.2d 776, 300 N.Y.S.2d 115, 248 N.E.2d 26 (N.Y. 1969).

310.   *In re* Morgansen's Ltd., 302 B.R. 784, 2003 Bankr. LEXIS 1726 (Bankr. E.D.N.Y. 2003).

311.   *Id.*, 302 B.R. at 789–90, 2003 Bankr. LEXIS 1726, at ★11– ★13.

312.   Although the lesson is clear (a consignor must file a UCC-1 Financing Statement to be protected), the statutory interpretation is far from clear. The *Morgansen* case, *supra* note 310, ignores U.C.C. § 9-102(a)(20)(C) and the definition of "consumer goods" as defined in U.C.C. § 9-102(a)(23) as "goods that are used or bought for use primarily for personal, family, or household purposes." U.C.C. § 9-102(a)(20)(C) excludes from the definition of a consignment under article 9 the consignment of a consumer good immediately before delivery. The court seems to have assumed that the consigned property (jewelry, art, collectibles, and furniture with a value of $1,000 or more) was not "consumer goods immediately before delivery." What is clear is that a consignor may prevent the application of U.C.C. § 9-102(a)(20) and U.C.C. § 9-319(a) and recover her goods from the bankruptcy debtor under either one of two exceptions: (1) the consignor files a UCC-1 Financing Statement under article 9 or (2) the consignor can prove that the consignee is generally known by its creditors to be substantially engaged in selling the goods of others. *In re* Valley Media, Inc., 279 B.R. 105, 47 U.C.C. Rep. Serv. 2d (CBC) 1178 (Bankr. D. Del. 2002); *see supra* notes 286, 291.

313.   Ganz v. Sotheby's Fin. Servs., Inc., Index No. 114827/01 (N.Y. Sup. Ct., N.Y. County, Oct. 12, 2004).

314.   *Id.*

315. U.C.C. § 2-326 was amended effective July 1, 2001, to repeal prior § 2-326(3) in connection with the revision of article 9. *See supra,* note 297.

316. U.C.C. § 9-102(a)(20) defines "consignment" as follows:

> (20) "Consignment" means a transaction, regardless of its form, in which a person delivers goods to a merchant for the purpose of sale and:
>
> (A) the merchant:
>
>> (i) deals in goods of that kind under a name other than the name of the person making delivery;
>>
>> (ii) is not an auctioneer; and
>>
>> (iii) is not generally known by its creditors to be substantially engaged in selling goods of others;
>
> (B) with respect to each delivery, the aggregate value of the goods is $1,000 or more at the time of delivery;
>
> (C) the goods are not consumer goods immediately before delivery; and
>
> (D) the transaction does not create a security interest that secures an obligation.

317. U.C.C. § 9-102(a)(20)(A)(iii).

318. *Ganz,* Index No. 114827/01, *supra* note 313. Like the court in *In re* Morgansen's Ltd., *supra* note 310, the court in *Ganz* did not discuss U.C.C. § 9-102(a)(20)(C) and the definition of "consumer goods" in U.C.C. § 9-102(a)(23) as "goods that are used or bought for use primarily for personal, family or household purposes." Official Comment 4a to revised section 9-102 states: "The definition of 'consumer goods' follows former section 9-109. The classification turns on whether the debtor uses or bought the goods for use 'primarily for personal, family, or household purposes'." U.C.C. § 9-102(a)(20)(C) excludes from the definition of a consignment under article 9 the consignment of consumer goods immediately before delivery. *See discussion supra,* note 312. What is or is not a consumer good "immediately before delivery" awaits further clarification from the courts.

319. U.C.C. § 2-509(3). *See also* Conway v. Larsen Jewelers, Inc., 104 Misc. 2d 872, 429 N.Y.S.2d 378 (N.Y. City Small Cl. Ct. 1980), *supra* note 190.

320. U.C.C. §§ 2-503, 2-509(3).

321.   *See* N.Y. ARTS & CULT. AFF. LAW § 13.01; IOWA CODE ANN. § 715B.2 to .4; FLA. STAT. ANN. § 686.504; MICH. COMP. LAWS § 442.321 to .325.

322.   79 Stat. 985, codified at 22 U.S.C. § 2459. The statute is also discussed in chapter 16, *infra*.

323.   N.Y. ARTS & CULT. AFF. LAW § 12.03. *See* People v. Museum of Modern Art (*In re* Grand Jury Subpoena Duces Tecum), 93 N.Y.2d 729, 719 N.E.2d 897, 697 N.Y.S.2d 897 (1999).

324.   U.C.C. § 9-102(a)(72).

325.   U.C.C. § 9-203.

326.   11 A.R. ANDERSON, UNIFORM COMMERCIAL CODE § 9-203 (3d ed. rev. 1999).

327.   *See* H. BAILEY III & R. HAGEDORN, SECURED TRANSACTIONS IN A NUTSHELL (4th ed. 2000); C. COOPER, THE NEW ARTICLE 9— UNIFORM COMMERCIAL CODE (1999); 11 A.R. ANDERSON, UNIFORM COMMERCIAL CODE (3d ed. rev. 1999). It is beyond the scope of this book to present a detailed treatment of secured transactions. The works referred to provide excellent basic texts on the subject.

328.   *Id.*; U.C.C. § 9-203.

329.   U.C.C. § 9-203(b).

330.   *Id.*

331.   *See* U.C.C. § 9-102. Although the terms "tangible," "semi-intangible," and "pure intangible" are not mentioned in article 9, they are widely recognized.

332.   U.C.C. §§ 9-102, 9-104.

333.   U.C.C. § 9-102.

334.   *Id.*

335.   U.C.C. § 9-102.

336.   U.C.C. § 9-308(a).

337.   *Id.*

338.   *Id.*

339.   U.C.C. §§ 9-504, 9-521.

340.   U.C.C. § 9-516(a).

341.   U.C.C. §§ 9-504, 9-502.

342.   U.C.C. §§ 9-515, 9-522.

343.   U.C.C. §§ 9-306, 9-313.

344.   *Id.*

345.   U.C.C. § 9-207(a).

346.   U.C.C. §§ 9-309, 9-310.

347.   U.C.C § 9-103.

348.   U.C.C. § 9-502. *See* Official Comment 3.

349.   U.C.C. § 9-509(a)(1).
350.   U.C.C. § 9-509(b).
351   U.C.C. § 9-317.
352.   U.C.C. § 9-317.
353.   In a number of states, including New York, the secured party has a grace period of twenty days, rather than ten days, in which to file.
354.   As it is beyond the scope of this book to enumerate every rule of priority, the reader is referred to ANDERSON, *supra* note 326, for a more exhaustive listing of priorities.
355.   U.C.C. § 9-322.
356.   U.C.C. §§ 9-317, 9-322.
357.   U.C.C. § 9-322.
358.   *Id.*
359.   U.C.C. § 9-324.
360.   *See* U.C.C. § 9-317.
361.   U.C.C. § 9-324.
362.   *Id.*
363.   U.C.C. § 9-315.
364.   U.C.C. § 9-317.
365.   U.C.C. § 9-320.
366.   *Id.*
367.   U.C.C. § 9-601.
368.   *Id.*
369.   *Id.*
370.   Insolvency or bankruptcy of the debtor, loss of or damage to the collateral, death or dissolution of the debtor, and, in general, nonperformance of any of the debtor's obligations under the security agreement are among the events commonly listed. In the absence of contractual stipulation, a court may well find that an occurrence other than nonpayment is not an event of default.
371.   *Id.*
372.   ANDERSON, *supra*, note 326.
373.   U.C.C. § 9-609.
374.   ANDERSON, *supra*, note 326.
375.   U.C.C. §§ 9-620, 9-621, 9-624.
376.   *Id.*
377.   U.C.C. § 9-610, § 9-615. Unless, that is, the debtor has signed after default a statement renouncing her rights. *See* U.C.C. § 9-620.
378.   U.C.C. §§ 9-620, 9-625, 9-627.
379.   U.C.C. § 9-610, 9-615.
380.   U.C.C. § 9-610, 9-611, 9-624.

381.   *Id.*
382.   U.C.C. §§ 9-610, 9-611, 9-624, 9-507(2).
383.   *Id.*
384.   U.C.C. §§ 9-610, 9-615.
385.   U.C.C. § 9-615.
386.   *Id.*
387.   U.C.C. § 9-623, 9-624.
388.   U.C.C. § 9-625, 9-627.
389.   *Id.* Since the amount recoverable for actual loss in small ticket consumer transactions is often insufficient to discourage creditor misconduct, the consumer-debtor may choose between actual damages and a minimum recovery, for which no proof of loss is required, consisting of the "credit service charge plus 10 percent of the principal amount of the debt or the time price differential plus 10 percent of the cash price."

Appendix 2-1

Model Collector-Dealer Consignment Agreement

THIS AGREEMENT made and entered into this _____ day of _____, 20__, by and between _____ _____, New York, New York 10022, (hereinafter referred to as "Owner") and _____, (hereinafter referred to as "Dealer").

WITNESSETH

WHEREAS, Dealer is engaged in the business of the sale of works of art; and

WHEREAS, Owner is the owner of _____ (hereinafter referred to as the "Painting"); and

WHEREAS, Owner wishes to consign the Painting to Dealer for sale.

NOW THEREFORE, in consideration of the mutual promises contained herein, each party agrees as follows:

1. A. Owner hereby grants to Dealer the sole and exclusive right throughout the world, for a period of time commencing on _____ _____, 20___, and terminating on _____ _____, 20___ ("the Consignment Period") renewable monthly thereafter in writing by both parties hereto, to offer the Painting for sale at a gross sales price ("G.S.P.") which shall realize net proceeds to Owner after payment of any and all commissions to Dealer pursuant to Paragraph 6 of this Agreement, of no less than _____ Dollars (\$_____), hereinafter referred to as the Net Proceeds.

B. During the Consignment Period Dealer or its agents shall not present the image of the Painting, or the Painting itself to more than _____ prospective purchasers.

C. Owner shall during the Consignment Period refer to Dealer all inquiries regarding the Painting's purchase.

D. Dealer may retain such other dealers and entities as it deems appropriate to the effectuation of the sale of the Painting, subject to Paragraph 1B above, and provided that any payments due such dealers or entities shall be the sole responsibility of Dealer.

2. Owner represents and warrants that he is the sole and absolute owner of the Painting, has the full right to sell and transfer same, and that the Painting is free and clear of any and all liens, mortgages, security interests or other encumbrances; and further agrees to indemnify and hold Dealer, its officers, and directors harmless from any and all demands, claims, suits, judgments, or other liability (including all expenses incurred by Dealer in connection therewith) asserted by or awarded any person or entity arising by reason of Owner's ownership, possession and sale of the Painting. Title to the Painting shall pass to a buyer upon payment in full of the Net Proceeds in good funds to Owner, at which time Owner agrees to transfer ownership and title and to provide such documentation as is reasonably required upon sale.

3. Owner shall not be responsible for any costs which Dealer may incur in connection with its efforts to sell the Painting, unless otherwise approved in advance in writing by Owner, PROVIDED, HOWEVER, if Dealer sells the Painting within the initial Consignment Period, it shall be entitled to receive reimbursement from Owner for costs incurred by Dealer directly attributable to the sale of the Painting up to a maximum amount of _____ thousand Dollars ($_____). Owner will at his expense provide to Dealer two color transparencies, and at his expense will ship the Painting to Dealer at any one location Dealer may specify.

4. Dealer shall arrange and pay for insurance for the Painting against any loss or damage in the amount of the Net Proceeds. Such insurance shall be provided from the moment the Painting is shipped to Dealer and until it is returned to Owner or to the buyer upon payment in full. Before any shipment of the Painting from the address of Owner, Dealer will specifically inform its insurance company directly of the address and means of transportation of the Painting, and this information shall be taken with full confidentiality directly between the insurance company and Dealer. Dealer agrees to use its best efforts and all due care in handling the Painting.

5.   A.   Dealer shall use its best efforts to sell the Painting during the Consignment Period. In the event that Dealer receives a bona fide offer to purchase the Painting for an all cash gross sales price equal to or greater than that which shall realize the full Net Proceeds, Dealer may accept such offer without further authorization from Owner.

B.   Should Dealer receive a bona fide offer to purchase for a gross sales price which would realize less than the full Net Proceeds, or an offer to purchase on terms other than all cash, Dealer shall inform Owner of such offer, and Owner shall expeditiously inform Dealer in writing whether it accepts or rejects such an offer.

6.   A.   In the event that the Painting is sold during the Consignment Period, all proceeds from the sale of the Painting shall initially be paid to Dealer. Dealer shall be entitled to receive (___%) percent of the gross sales price as a commission in consideration of its services. Dealer shall deduct this commission and the amount as determined under Paragraph 3 above and forward the balance to Owner within seven (7) days of receipt by it of the sales proceeds. On request from the Owner, the Dealer agrees to furnish the Owner with a copy of the Dealer's invoice to the buyer without any redaction.

B.   In the event that the Painting is not sold during the Consignment Period, Dealer shall, unless otherwise agreed in writing to extend this contract, return the Painting at its expense to Owner within seven (7) days of the expiration of the Consignment Period, or deliver it to a location in New York City as specified by Owner within such seven- (7) day period.

C.   In the event that Owner or his agent(s) sell(s) the Painting within six (6) months after the termination date of the Consignment Period or its extension, to one of the individuals or entities to whom Dealer or its agent(s) have shown the Painting during the Consignment Period, Dealer shall receive its full commission as provided in Paragraph 6A above. This provision shall not apply after the expiration of such six (6) month period.

7.   A.   Dealer hereby grants to Owner a security interest in the Painting (and any proceeds thereof) until sale of the Painting by Dealer whereupon the proceeds of such sale shall be held by Dealer for Owner and delivered (except for such commission set forth above) to Owner as herein provided.

B.   Upon execution of this Agreement, Dealer authorizes Owner to file a Form UCC-1 Financing Statement without the Dealer's signature, evincing Owner's security interest in the Painting. Dealer agrees to inform (i) any other secured creditor of the Dealer and (ii) any purchaser of the

Painting, of the existence of Owner's security interest in the Painting (and the proceeds therefrom).

C. In the event of any default under this Agreement by Dealer, Owner shall have all of the rights of a secured party under the Uniform Commercial Code. Owner agrees to file Form UCC-3 terminating Owner's security interest on receipt from Dealer of the Net Proceeds.

D. Dealer agrees not to remove the Painting from the State of New York without the written consent of the Owner.

8. This Agreement represents the entire understanding of all the Parties hereto, supersedes any and all other and prior agreements between the Parties and declares all such prior agreements between the Parties null and void. The terms of this Agreement may not be modified or amended, except in writing. This Agreement and all matters relating to it shall be governed by the Uniform Commercial Code and the laws of the State of New York.

IN WITNESS WHEREOF, the Parties hereto have hereunto signed their hands and seals the day and year first above written.

_____
Owner

_____
Dealer

Appendix 2-2

Collector Consignment with Security Agreement

[DATE]

ABC Galleries, Inc.
1234 Madison Avenue
New York, NY 10000

You hereby acknowledge receipt of the following oil painting owned by me (the "Painting"):

Title:

Medium:

Size:

Signature:

Date:

The purchase price of the Painting less your commission of ____ per cent shall be delivered by you to me within ten (10) days from and after the date on which delivery shall be made by you under any sale or contract of sale. Title to, and a security interest in, the Painting (and any proceeds thereof) is reserved in me until sale of the Painting by you whereupon the proceeds of such sale shall be held for me and delivered (except for such commission set forth above) to me as herein provided. You authorize me to file a Form UCC-1 Financing Statement without your signature covering my security interest in the Painting (and any proceeds thereof).

In the event of any default by you, I shall have all of the rights of a secured party under the Uniform Commercial Code.

You agree to hold the Painting for sale at a price of $_____.

You agree that you will not sell the Painting for a price less than $_____ without permission from me.

You agree to specifically inform any other secured creditor of the existence of my security interest prior to my delivering the Painting to you and to specifically inform any purchaser of the Painting from you of the existence of my security interest as stated herein. I agree to sign and file a Form UCC-3 termination statement once I have approved the terms of the sale of the Painting.

Notwithstanding the foregoing, at any time prior to any sale of the Painting by you, at my request you will deliver the Painting to me immediately upon receipt of any instruction from me.

_____
                                                    Collector

The foregoing is confirmed and
agreed to: ABC Galleries, Inc.

By:_____

[DATE]

Appendix 2-3

Owner-to-Dealer Consignment Agreement

CONSIGNMENT AGREEMENT

THIS AGREEMENT made and entered into this _____ day of _____ 20___, by and between _____ _____, a New York corporation having an office at _____, New York, NY _____ (hereinafter referred to as "Dealer"), and _____, residing at _____ _____, (hereinafter referred to as "Owner").

W I T N E S S E T H

WHEREAS, Dealer is engaged in the business of the purchase and sale of works of art; and

WHEREAS, Owner wishes to consign the work(s) of art listed on Schedule A attached hereto (hereinafter referred to as the "Work(s)") to Dealer for sale.

NOW THEREFORE, in consideration of the mutual promises contained herein, the parties hereto agree as follows:

1. **Term and Price**.

Subject to the provisions of Paragraph 9, Owner hereby grants to Dealer the exclusive right for a period of time commencing on _____, 20___ and terminating on _____, 20___ (the "Consignment Period") to offer the Work(s) for sale to a Buyer or Buyers at a gross sales price which shall realize net proceeds (the "Net Proceeds") to Owner, after payment of any and all commissions to Dealer pursuant to Paragraph 9 of this Agreement for each Work as listed on Schedule A attached hereto.

2. **Owner's Representations and Warranties**.

A. Owner does hereby represent and warrant that:

i. Owner has full legal authority to enter into this Agreement, to make the representations and warranties contained herein, to deliver a Bill of Sale, to authorize Dealer to deliver a Bill of Sale, and to complete the transaction contemplated herein.

ii. Owner is the sole and absolute owner of each of the Work(s), has the authority to sell and transfer good and marketable title to the Work(s), and the Work(s) are now and will at the time of transfer of title be free and clear of any and all liens, claims, mortgages, security interests or other encumbrances held by any person.

iii. The Work(s) are authentic, that is, each of them was created by the artist indicated on Schedule A attached hereto, and the attribution, provenance and description of the Work(s) made in this Agreement is accurate and correct.

B. Owner does hereby agree to indemnify and hold Dealer, its officers, and directors harmless from any and all demands, claims, suits, judgments, or other liability (including all legal fees and other expenses incurred by Dealer in connection therewith) asserted by or awarded to any person or entity arising by reason of Owner's breach or alleged breach of any representation or warranty contained in this Agreement.

C. The benefits of the representations, warranties and indemnities contained in this Agreement shall survive completion of the transaction contemplated by this Agreement but shall be applicable only to, and inure to the benefit of Dealer and the buyer from Dealer and not to subsequent owners or others who have or may acquire any interest in or to the Work(s).

3. **Title**.

Title to each of the Work(s) shall pass to the buyer from Owner through Dealer upon payment in full of the Net Proceeds in good funds to Owner pursuant to this Agreement, at which time Owner specifically authorizes Dealer to effectuate the transfer of ownership and title and to provide such documentation as is reasonably required upon sale, including a Bill of Sale for each of the Work(s).

4. **Expenses**.

Owner shall not be responsible for any costs which Dealer may incur in connection with its efforts to sell the Work(s) to a buyer, including but not limited to commissions to brokers or others, unless otherwise approved in advance in writing by Owner. Unless Dealer and Owner otherwise agree, Owner will pay all costs of and be responsible for crating, packing and shipping the Work(s) from their current location, and Dealer will pay all costs of crating, packing and shipping the Work(s) back to Owner, if the Work(s) are not sold prior to the end of the Consignment Period. Unless otherwise provided in this Agreement, Dealer shall be responsible for any New York sales tax or other fees or expenses in connection with the delivery of the Work(s) in accordance with this Agreement.

5. **Insurance**.

Dealer shall arrange and pay for insurance for the Work(s) against any loss or damage in the amount of at least the Net Proceeds for each Work as listed on Schedule A attached hereto. Such insurance shall be provided from the moment the Work(s) are delivered to Dealer, and until the Work(s) are returned to Owner or title is transferred to the buyer upon payment in full. Dealer will provide Owner with a certificate of insurance evidencing insurance coverage. Dealer and Owner shall be named as loss payees as their respective interests may appear. Dealer agrees to use its best efforts and all due care in handling the Work(s).

6. **Condition Report**.

Dealer, after consulting with Owner, may arrange for the Work(s) to be inspected and a condition report prepared verifying the condition of the Work(s) for purposes of this Agreement.

7. **Sale of the Work(s)**.

A.   Dealer shall use its best efforts to sell the Work(s) during the Consignment Period to a buyer. Dealer is authorized to complete the sale of a Work or Works to a buyer or buyers in order to realize Net Proceeds to Owner as stated in Paragraph 1 of this Agreement and as listed on Schedule A attached hereto.

B.   Dealer agrees that it will inform Owner immediately after it is informed of the decision of any buyer as to whether or not the buyer will purchase a Work on the terms and conditions herein. On request of the Owner, the Dealer agrees to furnish the Owner with a copy of the Dealer's invoice to the buyer without any redaction.

8. **Payment**.

A.   If a buyer decides to purchase a Work, Dealer shall arrange for the wire transfer of the Net Proceeds to Owner within five (5) days of receipt of the funds. Upon receipt of the Net Proceeds, Dealer is authorized to issue a Bill of Sale for the Work.

B.   If a buyer decides to purchase a Work, Dealer may, within its discretion, grant the buyer ninety (90) days to make payment in full to Dealer, provided, however, the Work shall not be physically released from Dealer's possession without the specific written consent of Owner.

C.   In the event that a Work is not sold during the Consignment Period, Dealer shall, unless otherwise agreed in writing to extend this Agreement, return the Work or Works at its expense to Owner at an address in New York within three (3) days of the expiration of the Consignment Period.

9. **Commission to Dealer**.

In the event that a Work is sold during the Consignment Period, the gross sales price from the sale of the Work shall initially be paid to Dealer. Dealer shall be entitled to receive as a commission in consideration of its services the amount of the gross sales price that exceeds the Net Proceeds for each Work, provided, however, that in no event shall the commission to Dealer exceed ten percent (10%) of the gross sales price of a Work. Dealer shall retain this commission and forward the Net Proceeds for each Work to Owner in accordance with paragraph 8 of this Agreement. Dealer shall be responsible for the collection and payment of any applicable sales taxes in the State of New York. The amount of the gross sales prices shall be confidential to Owner and to Dealer.

10. **Security Interest**.

A.   Dealer grants to Owner a security interest in the Work(s) (and any proceeds thereof) until sale of the Work(s) is completed whereupon the Net Proceeds of such sale shall be held by Dealer for Owner and delivered (except for such commission set forth above) to Owner as provided in this Agreement.

B.   In the event of any default under this Agreement by Dealer, Owner shall have all of the rights of a secured party. Upon execution of this Agreement, Dealer authorizes Owner, to file UCC-1 Financing Statements without the Dealer's signature covering the Work(s) and to inform any other secured creditor of the Dealer of the existence of Owner's security interest. If a UCC-1 is filed, then Owner agrees to sign a UCC-3 Termination Statement covering the Work(s) upon completion of the sale of the Work(s) or upon the return of the Work(s) to Owner.

C.   Dealer agrees that the Work(s) will not be physically removed from the State of New York without the specific written consent of Owner.

11. **Noncircumvention**.

In the event that Owner or Owner's Agent sells a Work within one (1) year after the end of the Consignment Period to an individual or entity to whom Dealer has shown and offered the Work during the Consignment Period, then Dealer shall receive from Owner a commission equal to ten percent (10%) of the Work's gross selling price. At the end of the Consignment Period, Dealer will provide Owner with a list of individuals or entities to whom Dealer has shown and offered the Work.

12. **Miscellaneous**.

This Agreement represents the entire understanding of all the parties hereto, supersedes any and all other and prior agreements between the parties and declares all such prior agreements between the parties null and void. The terms of this Agreement may not be modified or amended, except in a writing signed by the party to be charged. This Agreement and all matters relating to it shall be governed by the laws of the State of New York. This Agreement shall inure to the benefit of, and shall be binding upon, the successors, heirs, executors and administrators of the parties hereto. Any dispute arising hereunder shall be resolved in the New York Supreme Court, New York County or in the United States District Court for the Southern District of New York, and the parties hereto consent to the personal jurisdiction of those Courts.

IN WITNESS WHEREOF, the parties hereto have executed this Agreement the day and year first above written.

DEALER

_____

President

OWNER

_____

SCHEDULE A

Net Proceeds

1.   Artist –
      Title –
      Medium –
      Date –
      Size –
      Signature –

2.   Artist –
      Title –
      Medium –
      Date –
      Size –
      Signature –

3.   Artist-
      Title –
      Medium –
      Date –
      Size –
      Signature –

Appendix 2-4

Owner-to-Dealer Consignment Agreement

CONSIGNMENT AGREEMENT

THIS AGREEMENT made and entered into this _____ day of
_____, 20____, by and between _____
_____, a New York corporation having an office at
_____, New York, NY 10128 (hereinafter referred
to as "Seller"), and _____, having an office
at _____, (hereinafter referred to as "Dealer").

W I T N E S S E T H

WHEREAS, Seller is engaged in the business of the purchase and sale of
works of art; and

WHEREAS, Dealer is engaged in the business of the purchase and sale of
works of art that are on consignment to it; and

WHEREAS, Seller wishes to consign the work(s) of art listed on Schedule
A attached hereto (hereinafter referred to as the "Work(s)") to Dealer for sale.

NOW THEREFORE, in consideration of the mutual promises contained herein, the parties hereto agree as follows:

1. <u>Term and Price</u>.

Subject to the provisions of Paragraph 9, Seller hereby grants to Dealer the exclusive right for a period of time commencing on _____, 20___ and terminating on _____, 20___ (the "Consignment Period") to offer the Work(s) for sale to a buyer or buyers at a gross sales price which shall realize net proceeds (the "Net Proceeds") to Seller, after payment of any and all commissions to Dealer pursuant to Paragraph 9 of this Agreement for each Work as listed on Schedule A attached hereto.

2. <u>Seller's Representations and Warranties</u>.

A. Seller does hereby represent and warrant that:

i. Seller has full legal authority to enter into this Agreement, to make the representations and warranties contained herein, to deliver a Bill of Sale, to authorize Dealer to deliver a Bill of Sale, and to complete the transaction contemplated herein.

ii. Seller is representing the sole and absolute owner of each of the Work(s), has the authority to sell and transfer good and marketable title to the Work(s), and the Work(s) are now and will at the time of transfer of title be free and clear of any and all liens, mortgages, security interests or other encumbrances held by any person.

iii. The Work(s) are authentic, that is, each of them was created by the artist indicated on Schedule A attached hereto, and the attribution, provenance and description of the Work(s) made in this Agreement is accurate and correct.

B. Seller does hereby agree to indemnify and hold Dealer, its officers, and directors harmless from any and all demands, claims, suits, judgments, or other liability (including all legal fees and other expenses incurred by Dealer in connection therewith) asserted by or awarded to any person or entity arising by reason of Seller's breach or alleged breach of any representation or warranty contained in this Agreement.

C. The benefits of the representations, warranties and indemnities contained in this Agreement shall survive completion of the transaction contemplated by this Agreement but shall be applicable only to, and inure to the benefit of Dealer and the buyer from Dealer and not to subsequent owners or others who have or may acquire any interest in or to the Work(s).

3.   Title.

Title to each of the Work(s) shall pass to the buyer from Seller through Dealer upon payment in full of the Net Proceeds in good funds to Seller pursuant to this Agreement, at which time Seller specifically authorizes Dealer to effectuate the transfer of ownership and title and to provide such documentation as is reasonably required upon sale, including a Bill of Sale for each of the Work(s).

4.   Expenses.

Seller shall not be responsible for any costs which Dealer may incur in connection with its efforts to sell the Work(s) to a buyer, including but not limited to commissions to brokers or others, unless otherwise approved in advance in writing by Seller. Unless Seller and Dealer otherwise agree, Dealer will pay all costs of and be responsible for crating, packing and shipping the Work(s) from their current location, and all costs of crating, packing and shipping the Work(s) back to Seller, if the Work(s) are not sold prior to the end of the Consignment Period. Unless otherwise provided in this Agreement, Dealer shall be responsible for any New York sales tax or other fees or expenses in connection with the delivery of the Work(s) in accordance with this Agreement.

5.   Insurance.

Dealer shall arrange and pay for insurance for the Work(s) against any loss or damage in the amount of at least the Net Proceeds for each Work as listed on Schedule A attached hereto. Such insurance shall be provided from the moment the Work(s) are picked up by Dealer, and until the Work(s) are returned to Seller or title is transferred to the buyer upon payment in full. Dealer will provide Seller with a certificate of insurance evidencing insurance coverage. Seller and Dealer shall be named as loss payees as their respective interests may appear. Dealer agrees to use its best efforts and all due care in handling the Work(s).

6.   Condition Report.

Dealer, after consulting with Seller, may arrange for the Work(s) to be inspected and a condition report prepared verifying the condition of the Work(s) for purposes of this Agreement.

7.   Sale of the Work(s).

A.   Dealer shall use its best efforts to sell the Work(s) during the Consignment Period to a buyer. Dealer is authorized to complete the sale of a Work or Works to a buyer or buyers in order to realize Net Proceeds to Seller as stated in Paragraph 1 of this Agreement and as listed on Schedule A attached hereto.

B.   Dealer agrees that it will inform Seller immediately after it is informed of the decision of any buyer as to whether or not the buyer will purchase a Work on the terms and conditions herein. On request of the Seller, the Dealer agrees to furnish the Seller with a copy of the Dealer's invoice to the buyer without any redaction other than the buyer's name and address.

8.   Payment.

A.   If a buyer decides to purchase a Work, Dealer shall arrange for the wire transfer of the Net Proceeds to Seller within five (5) days of receipt of the funds. Upon receipt of the Net Proceeds, Dealer is authorized to issue a Bill of Sale for the Work.

B.   If a buyer decides to purchase a Work, Dealer may, within its discretion, grant the buyer sixty (60) days to make payment in full to Dealer, provided, however, the Work shall not be physically released from Dealer's possession without the specific written consent of Seller.

C.   In the event that a Work is not sold during the Consignment Period, Dealer shall, unless otherwise agreed in writing to extend this Agreement, return the Work or Works at its expense to Seller at an address in New York within three (3) days of the expiration of the Consignment Period.

9.   Commission to Dealer.

In the event that a Work is sold during the Consignment Period, the gross sales price from the sale of the Work shall initially be paid to Dealer. Dealer shall be entitled to receive as a commission in consideration of its services the amount of the gross sales price that exceeds the Net Proceeds for each Work, provided, however, that in no event shall the commission to Dealer exceed ten percent (10%) of the gross sales price of a Work. Dealer shall retain this commission and forward the Net Proceeds for each Work to Seller in accordance with paragraph 8 of this Agreement. Dealer shall be responsible for the collection and payment of any applicable sales taxes in the State of New

York. The amount of the gross sales prices shall be confidential to Dealer and to Seller.

10. <u>Security Interest</u>.

    A.   Dealer grants to Seller a security interest in the Work(s) (and any proceeds thereof) until sale of the Work(s) is completed whereupon the Net Proceeds of such sale shall be held by Dealer for Seller and delivered (except for such commission set forth above) to Seller as provided in this Agreement.

    B.   In the event of any default under this Agreement by Dealer, Seller shall have all of the rights of a secured party. Upon execution of this Agreement, Dealer authorizes Seller, to file UCC-1 Financing Statements without the Dealer's signature covering the Work(s) and to inform any other secured creditor of the Dealer of the existence of Seller's security interest. If a UCC-1 is filed, then Seller agrees to sign a UCC-3 Termination Statement covering the Work(s) upon completion of the sale of the Work(s) or upon the return of the Work(s) to Seller.

    C.   Dealer agrees that the Work(s) will not be physically removed from the State of New York without the specific written consent of Seller.

11. <u>Miscellaneous</u>.

This Agreement represents the entire understanding of all the parties hereto, supersedes any and all other and prior agreements between the parties and declares all such prior agreements between the parties null and void. The terms of this Agreement may not be modified or amended, except in a writing signed by the party to be charged. This Agreement and all matters relating to it shall be governed by the laws of the State of New York. This Agreement shall inure to the benefit of, and shall be binding upon, the successors, heirs, executors and administrators of the parties hereto. Any dispute arising hereunder shall be resolved in the New York Supreme Court, New York County or in the United States District Court for the Southern District of New York, and the parties hereto consent to the personal jurisdiction of those Courts.

IN WITNESS WHEREOF, the parties hereto have executed this Agreement the day and year first above written.

SELLER

_____

By: _____ President

DEALER

_____

By: _____ President

SCHEDULE A

Net Proceeds

1. Artist –
   Title –
   Medium –
   Date –
   Size –
   Signature –

2. Artist –
   Title –
   Medium –
   Date –
   Size –
   Signature –

3. Artist-
   Title –
   Medium –
   Date –
   Size –
   Signature –

Appendix 2-5

Dealer-to-Collector Sales Agreement

AGREEMENT OF SALE

Dated:

Parties: _____, having an office at
_____, New York, NY _____ ("Seller"); and
_____ ("Buyer")

1. **SALE**. For the sum of $ _____ US (the "Purchase Price"), Seller hereby sells to Buyer, subject to the terms and conditions hereinafter set forth, the following described work of art (the "Work"):

Title:
Artist:
Medium:
Size:
Date:
Signature:

2. **PURCHASE PRICE**. The Purchase Price shall be paid by Buyer to Seller in full on or prior to _____ ___, 20___. All drafts, checks or other instruments given in payment of the Purchase Price shall be accepted subject to collection.

3. **SALES TAX**. Buyer agrees to pay all applicable New York sales tax due on the sale of the Work. The New York sales tax due on this sale is ___.

4.   **DELIVERY**. Delivery of the Work will be made from Seller to Buyer via common carrier. The Work will be picked up at Seller's office at _____, New York, NY _____ by _____ _____ ("Shipper") on or about _____, 20___. Shipper will pack the Work and arrange for its delivery to Buyer at _____ _____.

5.   **TITLE.** Seller and Buyer agree that the sale of the Work and the transfer of title from Seller to Buyer shall take place only after Buyer has paid the Purchase Price in full as provided in this Agreement.

6.   **INSURANCE**. Prior to the delivery of the Work as provided in paragraph 4 herein, Buyer agrees to insure the Work for at least the full Purchase Price and name Buyer and Seller as insured parties to the extent of their respective interests in the Work. Buyer agrees that the insurance coverage will be kept in effect until delivery of the Work to Buyer as provided in paragraph 4 herein and until Buyer has paid the Purchase Price in full as provided in this Agreement.

7.   **EXPENSES**. Buyer shall pay the cost of insurance, packing, shipping and delivery of the Work to an address as directed by Buyer. Buyer shall be solely responsible for any customs duties, export or import charges, or any other fees or expenses of any kind or nature in connection with the delivery of the Work to Buyer.

8.   **BILL OF SALE**. Seller agrees to deliver to Buyer a Bill of Sale in the form attached hereto evidencing the transfer of title from Seller to Buyer upon Buyer's paying the Purchase Price in full as provided in this Agreement.

9.   **REPRESENTATIONS AND WARRANTIES OF SELLER**. Seller does hereby represent and warrant that:

(a)   The authenticity of authorship of the Work is in accordance with the description contained in this Agreement, that is, it was created by _____.

(b)   Seller has all legal authority to sell the Work, to make the representations and warranties contained herein, to deliver a Bill of Sale transferring good and marketable title to the Work, and the Work is now and will at the time of transfer of title be free and clear of all liens, encumbrances, security interests or restrictions of any kind or nature.

(c)   The Work is in good condition. [optional]

(d) Except as expressly set forth herein, Seller is selling the Work "AS IS" and hereby disclaims all other representations and warranties whatsoever, express or implied, including without limitation any warranties of fitness for a particular purpose, marketability, value or condition.

Seller does hereby agree to indemnify and hold Buyer harmless from any and all demands, claims, suits, judgments, or other liability (including all reasonable expenses incurred by Buyer in connection therewith) or awarded to any person or entity arising by reason of Seller's breach of any representation or warranty contained in this Agreement.

The benefits of the representations, warranties and indemnities contained in this Agreement shall survive completion of the transaction contemplated by this Agreement and shall be applicable only to, and inure to the benefit of Buyer and not to subsequent owners or others who have or may acquire any interest in or to the Work.

10. **ENTIRE UNDERSTANDING**. This Agreement represents the entire understanding of all the parties hereto, supersedes any and all other and prior agreements between the parties and declares such prior agreements between the parties null and void. The terms of this Agreement may not be modified or amended except in writing signed by the parties hereto. This Agreement and all matters relating to it shall be governed by the Uniform Commercial Code and the laws of the State of New York. This Agreement shall inure to the benefit of, and be binding upon, the successors, heirs, executors and administrators of the parties hereto. Any dispute arising hereunder shall be resolved in the New York Supreme Court, New York County or in the United States District Court for the Southern District of New York, and the parties hereto consent to the personal jurisdiction of those Courts.

_____, Inc.

By:_____

President – _____

(Seller)

_____

(Buyer)

[Name & Address of Dealer]

<u>BILL OF SALE</u>

Dated:

Sold by: _____ (Seller)

Sold to: _____ (Buyer)

Work sold: artist –
                    title –
                    medium –
                    date –
                    size –
                    signature –

Purchase Price:

Payable: In full at or prior to transfer of title to the Work to Buyer.

The above described Work is sold subject to terms, conditions, representations and warranties of _____, Inc. contained in an Agreement dated _____.

Title to the above described Work shall pass to Buyer upon payment in full of the Purchase Price by Buyer.

Payment of $_____ Received

_____

By: _____, President

Dated:

Appendix 2-6

Dealer-to-Collector Sales Agreement with Installments

AGREEMENT OF SALE

Dated:

Parties: _____, Inc., having an office at
_____, New York, NY _____ ("Seller"); and
_____ ("Buyer")

1. **SALE**. For the sum of $____ US (the "Purchase Price"), Seller hereby sells to Buyer, subject to the terms and conditions hereinafter set forth, the following described work of art (the "Work"):

Title:
Artist:
Medium:
Size:
Date:
Signature:

2. **PURCHASE PRICE**. The Purchase Price shall be paid by Buyer to Seller in full on or prior to _____ __, 20__. All drafts, checks or other instruments given in payment of the Purchase Price shall be accepted subject to collection. The Purchase Price shall be paid in the following installments:

A. $_____ on or before _____.

B. $_____ on or before _____.

3. **SALES TAX**. Buyer agrees to pay all applicable New York sales tax due on the sale of the Work. The New York sales tax due on this sale is ___ and shall be paid in full with the first installment as set forth above.

4. **DELIVERY**. Delivery of the Work will be made from Seller to Buyer via common carrier. The Work will be picked up at Seller's office at _____, New York, NY _____ by _____ ("Shipper") on or about _____ ____, 20___. Shipper will pack the Work and arrange for its delivery to Buyer at _____ _____.

5. **TITLE.** Seller and Buyer agree that the sale of the Work and the transfer of title from Seller to Buyer shall take place only after Buyer has paid the Purchase Price in full as provided in this Agreement.

6. **INSURANCE**. Prior to the delivery of the Work as provided in paragraph 4 herein, Buyer agrees to insure the Work for at least the full Purchase Price and name Buyer and Seller as insured parties to the extent of their respective interests in the Work. Buyer agrees that the insurance coverage will be kept in effect until delivery of the Work to Buyer as provided in paragraph 4 herein and until Buyer has paid the Purchase Price in full as provided in this Agreement.

7. **EXPENSES**. Buyer shall pay the cost of insurance, packing, shipping and delivery of the Work to an address as directed by Buyer. Buyer shall be solely responsible for any customs duties, export or import charges, or any other fees or expenses of any kind or nature in connection with the delivery of the Work to Buyer.

8. **BILL OF SALE**. Seller agrees to deliver to Buyer a Bill of Sale in the form attached hereto evidencing the transfer of title from Seller to Buyer upon Buyer's paying the Purchase Price in full as provided in this Agreement.

9. **REPRESENTATIONS AND WARRANTIES OF SELLER**. Seller does hereby represent and warrant that:

(a) The authenticity of authorship of the Work is in accordance with the description contained in this Agreement, that is, it was created by _____.

(b)   Seller has all legal authority to sell the Work, to make the representations and warranties contained herein, to deliver a Bill of Sale transferring good and marketable title to the Work, and the Work is now and will at the time of transfer of title be free and clear of all liens, encumbrances, security interests or restrictions of any kind or nature.

(c)   The Work is in good condition. [optional]

(d)   Except as expressly set forth herein, Seller is selling the Work "AS IS" and hereby disclaims all other representations and warranties whatsoever, express or implied, including without limitation any warranties of fitness for a particular purpose, marketability, value or condition.

Seller does hereby agree to indemnify and hold Buyer harmless from any and all demands, claims, suits, judgments, or other liability (including all reasonable expenses incurred by Buyer in connection therewith) or awarded to any person or entity arising by reason of Seller's breach of any representation or warranty contained in this Agreement.

The benefits of the representations, warranties and indemnities contained in this Agreement shall survive completion of the transaction contemplated by this Agreement and shall be applicable only to, and inure to the benefit of Buyer and not to subsequent owners or others who have or may acquire any interest in or to the Work.

10.   **SECURITY INTEREST**. Buyer grants to Seller a security interest in the Work (and any proceeds thereof) until the Purchase Price is paid in full as provided in this Agreement. In the event of any default under this Agreement by Buyer, Seller shall have all of the rights of a secured party. Upon execution of this Agreement, Buyer authorizes Seller, to file UCC-1 Financing Statements without the Buyer's signature covering the Work and to inform any other secured creditor of the Buyer of the existence of Seller's security interest. If a UCC-1 is filed, then Seller agrees to sign a UCC-3 Termination Statement covering the Work upon Seller's receiving the Purchase Price in full as provided in this Agreement. Buyer agrees that the Work will not be physically removed from the State of New York without the specific written consent of Seller.

11.   **ENTIRE UNDERSTANDING**. This Agreement represents the entire understanding of all the parties hereto, supersedes any and all other and prior agreements between the parties and declares such prior agreements between the parties null and void. The terms of this Agreement may not be modified or amended except in writing signed by the parties hereto. This Agreement and all matters relating to it shall be governed by the Uniform

Commercial Code and the laws of the State of New York. This Agreement shall inure to the benefit of, and be binding upon, the successors, heirs, executors and administrators of the parties hereto. Any dispute arising hereunder shall be resolved in the New York Supreme Court, New York County or in the United States District Court for the Southern District of New York, and the parties hereto consent to the personal jurisdiction of those Courts.

_____, Inc.

By:_____

President – _____

(Seller)

_____

(Buyer)

[Name & Address of Dealer]

BILL OF SALE

Dated:

Sold by: _____ (Seller)

Sold to: _____ (Buyer)

Work sold: artist –
                    title –
                    medium –
                    date –
                    size –
                    signature –

Purchase Price:

Payable: In full at or prior to transfer of title to the Work to Buyer.

The above described Work is sold subject to terms, conditions, representations and warranties of _____, Inc. contained in an Agreement dated _____.

Title to the above described Work shall pass to Buyer upon payment in full of the Purchase Price by Buyer.

Payment of $_____ Received

_____, Inc.

_____

By: _____, President

Dated:

Appendix 2-7

Introduction Commission and Noncircumvention Agreement

THIS AGREEMENT made and entered into this _____ day of _____, 20___, by and between John Dealer, having an office at _____, New York, New York _____ (hereinafter "Dealer"), and Sam Seller, residing at _____, New York, New York _____ (hereinafter "Seller").

W I T N E S S E T H

WHEREAS, Dealer is an art dealer in the business of arranging the purchase and sale of works of art and is about to introduce the Seller to the potential buyer of the following work of art:

Title:
Artist:
Medium:
Size:
Signature:
Date:

(hereinafter referred to as the "Work"); and

WHEREAS, the Seller is interested in selling the Work directly to the potential buyer; and

WHEREAS, the parties hereto wish to establish a method by which the Seller can compensate the Dealer for introducing the Seller to the potential buyer and enabling the Seller to sell the Work directly to the buyer.

NOW, THEREFORE, in consideration of the mutual promises contained herein, the parties hereto mutually agree as follows:

1.   Seller hereby agrees to pay to Dealer the sum of _____ Thousand Dollars U.S. ($_____) (hereinafter "Dealer's Commission") as Dealer's Commission for introducing the buyer and the Seller. Dealer's Commission shall be paid by the Seller to Dealer by wire transfer simultaneously with the payment of the purchase price for the Work to the Seller. Payment shall be made as follows:

John Dealer
Account #9762453
Bank of New York
ABA no. 021925975

2.   The Commission shall be due and payable to the Dealer only if and when the Bill of Sale for the Work has been signed by the Seller and it is delivered to the buyer pursuant to a separate agreement and the purchase price for the Work has been paid to the Seller.

3.   Dealer agrees to furnish Seller or Seller's agent, all information in his possession pertaining to (i) the identity of the buyer and (ii) the buyer's agent, including names, addresses and telephone numbers. Seller agrees to furnish Dealer all information in his possession pertaining to the Work. All of the facts furnished by the parties to each other is hereinafter referred to as the "Information."

4.   Dealer and Seller each agree that for a period of three (3) years, they will (a) not disclose any of the Information furnished to each other by the other to any third person; (b) not use any of the Information directly or indirectly without the prior written consent and agreement of the other; (c) not contact directly or indirectly any other person with respect to the Information without the prior written consent and agreement of the other; and (d) Seller, nor anyone employed by or connected with him in any way, will not contact directly or indirectly the buyer of the Work without the prior written consent of the Dealer.

5.   Seller agrees that for a period of three (3) years neither he, nor any one employed by or connected with him in any way, will contact directly or indirectly the buyer of the Work with respect to the potential sale of any other work of art without the prior written consent of the Dealer.

6.   Dealer and the Seller each acknowledge that the Information and the name of the buyer is proprietary and unique and that a threatened breach of this

Agreement would cause irreparable harm which may not be adequately compensated by money damages, and that therefore in such event each of the parties shall be entitled to injunctive and other equitable relief, in addition to whatever other relief a court may deem proper. In the event of a dispute arising out of this Agreement, either party may demand arbitration. The right of either party to seek arbitration shall not in any way limit its rights to seek equitable relief as provided for in this paragraph. It is recognized that such relief may be necessary before any arbitration can result in an award of damages.

7.   Dealer and the Seller agree that the terms of this Agreement shall remain completely confidential and shall not be revealed to any third party other than the buyer of the Work or their respective attorneys.

8.   This Agreement represents the entire understanding of all the Parties hereto, supersedes any and all other and prior agreements between the Parties and declares all such prior agreements between the Parties null and void. The terms of this Agreement may not be modified or amended, except in a writing signed by the party to be charged. This Agreement and all matters relating to it shall be governed by the laws of the State of New York. This Agreement shall inure to the benefit of, and shall be binding upon, the assigns, successors, heirs, executors and administrators of the Parties hereto. Any dispute arising hereunder shall be resolved in the New York State Supreme Court, New York County or in the United States District Court for the Southern District of New York, and the parties hereto consent to the personal jurisdiction of those Courts, provided, however, that the parties hereto agree that they will make concerted efforts to settle any dispute between them in an amicable manner without the necessity of litigation.

IN WITNESS WHEREOF, the Parties hereto have hereunto signed their hands and seals the day and year first above written.

_____

John Dealer

_____

Sam Seller

Appendix 2-8

Dealer's Memorandum of Delivery on Approval

[NAME AND ADDRESS OF DEALER]

Date:

TO: [Name and Address
      of Collector]

ON APPROVAL
<u>MEMORANDUM</u>

[Title of Artwork] (the "Work")

Artist:
Title:
Date:
Medium
Size:

The above Work is delivered to you On Approval for a period of _____ days commencing on the date you receive delivery. We will fully insure the Work under our "all risks" fine arts policy covering the Work in transit to and from your residence and while it is on your premises. We will be responsible for all packing and shipping expense for the Work to and from your premises. You agree to care for the Work in a manner as you would treat other similar works of art and that, other than as provided herein, you will not move the Work from your premises without our written consent. Should you notify us prior to _____ ___, 200__ that you wish to purchase the Work, we will enter into a formal agreement with you confirming your agreement to purchase the

Work and title will be transferred to you after the formal agreement is signed by both of us and you have made payment pursuant to the formal agreement. If you do not purchase the Work, you agree that we may pick up the Work on _____ ____, 200__ and you will allow access to your premises for such purpose.

ANYTHING IN THIS MEMORANDUM TO THE CONTRARY NOTWITHSTANDING, YOU AGREE THAT TITLE TO THE WORK DOES NOT PASS TO YOU UNTIL THE CONDITIONS SPECIFIED IN A FORMAL WRITTEN AGREEMENT CONCERNING THE WORK ARE SATISFIED AND PAYMENT OF THE PURCHASE PRICE HAS BEEN MADE IN FULL TO US. PRIOR TO THAT DATE, YOU ARE HOLDING THE PROPERTY AS A BAILEE ON OUR BEHALF AND YOU HAVE NO OWNERSHIP RIGHTS IN THE WORK. THIS IS NOT AN AGREEMENT TO SELL AND THE RISK OF LOSS REMAINS WITH US.

[Name of Dealer]

_____
President

Date:

Appendix 2-9

Dealer-to-Collector Bill of Sale (Short Form)

<u>BILL OF SALE</u>

Dated: _____

Sold by: [Name and Address of Dealer]   (the "Seller")

Sold to: [Name and Address of Collector]   (the "Buyer")

Work Sold: Title: (the "Work")
             Artist:
             Medium:
             Size:
             Date:
             Provenance: See attached Exhibit A

Purchase Price: $_____   (the "Purchase Price")
Sales Tax: $_____ [or notation of out-of-state shipment]
Total $_____
Payment Terms: _____

   The Seller, in consideration of the Purchase Price, the receipt and sufficiency of which is hereby acknowledged, hereby irrevocably and without condition or reservation of any kind, sells, transfers and conveys to the Buyer the Work, and all right to possession and all legal and equitable ownership of the Work, to have and to hold the Work unto the Buyer, his successors and assigns, forever.

The Seller represents and warrants to the Buyer that upon delivery by the Seller to the Buyer of the Work and the Seller's receipt of the Purchase Price, good, valid and marketable title and exclusive and unrestricted right to possession of the Work, free of all Claims (as defined below), will pass from the Seller to the Buyer.

The Seller hereby represents and warrants to the Buyer as of the date hereof and as of the payment date that: (i) the Work is a genuine and authentic work of art created by _____ as described in this Bill of Sale and that to the best of the Seller's knowledge the provenance of the Work as described in Exhibit A to this Bill of Sale is accurate; (ii) the Seller has full right and legal authority to execute and deliver this Bill of Sale, and is able in accordance with this Bill of Sale to transfer the Work to the Buyer, free and clear of all claims, liens, assessments, actions, or other encumbrances of any kind held or claimed by any party (collectively, "Claims"); (iii) the Seller has no knowledge of any Claims threatened or pending, nor any knowledge of any facts or circumstances likely to give rise to any Claims; (iv) the Seller has provided the Buyer with all information available to the Seller or of which the Seller is aware concerning the authenticity, description, provenance and title of the Work; and (v) other than as noted on the condition report attached hereto, the Seller has not restored or repaired any part of the Work, nor consented thereto, and to the best of the Seller's knowledge no other party has performed any major restoration or repair. Other than as specifically represented and warranted by the Seller as set forth in this Bill of Sale, the Buyer is purchasing the Work in "as is" condition, without any representations or warranties by the Seller as to value, condition, or fitness for a particular purpose. The representations and warranties contained in this Bill of Sale and all other terms hereof, shall survive the delivery of this Bill of Sale and transfer of the Work and cannot be assigned to unrelated third party owners.

The Seller agrees to indemnify the Buyer against all demands, suits, judgments, damages, losses or other liability, including all reasonable attorney or other professional fees, resulting from any breach of any of the Seller's representations, warranties (express or implied) or other terms set forth in this Bill of Sale.

The Seller agrees to execute and deliver such additional documents and to take such other further actions from time to time after the date hereof as the Buyer may reasonably request, to assure and confirm the Buyer's rights and/or the Seller's obligations under this Bill of Sale.

The Seller agrees to deliver the Work to the Buyer by common carrier to the Buyer at _____, _____, _____ _____ after it has received payment for the Work. The Buyer agrees to timely reimburse the Seller for reasonable third party costs and expenses approved in advance by the Buyer and paid by the Seller relating to packing, transporting, shipping and insuring the Work for delivery to the Buyer pursuant to this Bill of Sale. The Seller agrees to insure the Work at its expense for the full Purchase Price until the Work is delivered to the Buyer.

[For out-of-state sales use the following.]

The Buyer shall be responsible for any State sales or use taxes in the State of _____ or such other state to which the Work is shipped arising from the Buyer's acquisition of the Work in accordance with this Bill of Sale. [Dealer must collect the sales tax for in state sales.]

The Purchase Price is inclusive of all commissions or other fees payable to any person relating to or on account of the sale of the Work.

If the Buyer at any time alleges a breach of any representation or warranty contained in this Bill of Sale and provides Seller with written notice of such alleged breach and the basis therefore, then Seller or Seller's counsel shall furnish Buyer with a copy of the Consignment Agreement (without deletion other than the Purchase Price) under which the owner of the Work consigned it to the Seller for sale.

This Bill of Sale shall be governed by and shall be construed and enforced in accordance with the laws of the State of _____, and shall inure to the benefit of, and shall be binding upon, the successors, heirs, executors and administrators of the parties hereto.

The Seller acknowledges that the provisions and subject matter of this Bill of Sale, including but not limited to the identity of the Buyer and the Work and the purchase price of the Work, are confidential and Seller agrees not to disclose any of the foregoing information to any person or entity, except as may be required by law, whether concurrent with or subsequent to the execution and delivery of this Bill of Sale.

Agreed to sell:

Seller

[Name of Dealer]

_____

By:

Agreed to buy:

Buyer

_____

[Name of Collector]

EXHIBIT A

Provenance:

Appendix 2-10

Agreement of Sale

THIS AGREEMENT OF SALE ("Agreement") is made and entered into this _____ day of _____, 200__, by and between _____ _____, having an office at _____, _____, _____ _____ (the "Seller"), and _____, residing at _____, _____, _____ _____ (the "Buyer").

WHEREAS, the Seller is engaged in the business of the purchase and sale of works of art; and

WHEREAS, the Seller is the owner of the work of art more fully described on <u>Exhibit B</u> attached hereto and incorporated herein by this reference (the "Work"); and

WHEREAS, the Seller has agreed to sell the Work to the Buyer, and the Buyer has agreed to buy the Work from the Seller, on the terms and conditions set forth in this Agreement.

NOW, THEREFORE, in consideration of the mutual promises contained in this Agreement, the parties agree as follows:

1. SALE

The Seller agrees to sell the Work to the Buyer, and the Buyer agrees to buy the Work from the Seller, subject to the terms and conditions set forth in this Agreement.

2. PURCHASE PRICE AND MANNER OF PAYMENT

The purchase price of the Work (the "Purchase Price") is _____ Dollars U.S. ($__,000,000.00) as set forth on Exhibit A attached hereto. The Purchase Price shall be paid by the Buyer to the Seller by wire transfer on _____, 200__ (the "Closing Date") to the following account:

Bank name:

ABA number:
Account number:
Account name:

3. SELLER'S REPRESENTATIONS AND WARRANTIES

A. To induce the Buyer to enter into this Agreement, and acknowledging that the Buyer is relying on each and all of the following representations and warranties, the Seller represents and warrants to the Buyer that:

i. The Seller has the authority to execute and deliver this Agreement and to perform its obligations set forth herein.

ii. The authenticity of authorship of the Work is that it was created by _____ and it is the same work of art that is described on the attached Exhibit B.

iii. The Seller without any further action, consent or authority of any other party, and without violation of any party's rights or claims, has full right, legal authority and capacity to enter into this Agreement, to make the covenants, representations and warranties contained in this Agreement, to execute and deliver the bill of sale in the form annexed as Exhibit A to this Agreement (the "Bill of Sale"), and to perform its obligations under and complete the transaction contemplated by this Agreement.

iv.   On the Closing Date, subject only to the Buyer's payment of the Purchase Price in accordance with this Agreement, the Seller will transfer to the Buyer good, valid and marketable title and exclusive and unrestricted right to possession of the Work free and clear of any and all rights or interests of others, claims, liens, mortgages, security interests, restrictions, conditions, assessments, exceptions, options, equities or other encumbrances of any kind held or claimed by any person (collectively, "Claims"). The Seller has no knowledge of any Claims threatened or pending, nor any knowledge of any facts or circumstances likely to give rise to any Claims.

v.   The Seller is the sole and absolute owner of the Work, and has full right to sell and transfer title to the Work to the Buyer.

vi.   The Seller is not aware of any challenges or disputes (past, pending or threatened) relating to the attribution, authenticity, description or provenance of the Work as set forth in Exhibit B attached hereto, and the Seller is not is aware of, nor has the Seller received or had any communication from or with any party regarding the possibility of any such challenge or dispute, and the Seller is not aware of any facts or circumstances likely to give rise to any such challenge or dispute. The Seller has provided the Buyer with all information available to the Seller or of which Seller is aware concerning the attribution, authenticity, description and provenance of the Work.

vii.   To the best of Seller's knowledge the Work was not confiscated by a foreign government or authority at any time.

viii.   The Seller has not restored, repaired or altered any part of the Work, nor consented thereto, and to the best of the Seller's knowledge no other party has performed any of the foregoing, except as expressly indicated in Exhibit C.

ix.   Other than as specifically represented and warranted in this Agreement, the Buyer shall purchase the Work in the physical condition as stated in the Condition Report as set forth in Paragraph 4, without any representations or warranties by or on behalf of the Seller of any kind whatsoever, express or implied, including without limitation, representations or warranties as to value or condition.

B.   The Seller does hereby agree to indemnify, defend and hold the Buyer free and harmless from any and all demands, claims, suits, judgments, obligations, damages, losses, or other liability, including all attorney or other professional fees and other costs, fees and expenses, suffered or incurred by, or asserted or alleged against the Buyer arising by reason of, or in connection with, the breach of, or falsity or inaccuracy of any representation or warranty contained in this Agreement.

C.   The benefits of the representations, warranties, covenants and indemnities contained in this Agreement shall survive completion of the transaction contemplated by this Agreement, including without limitation transfer of the Work to the Buyer. It shall be a condition precedent to the Buyer's obligations that the representations and warranties contained in this Agreement are true and correct on and as of the Closing Date and transfer of the Work to the Buyer.

4.   INSPECTION

The Buyer or the Buyer's agent has inspected the Work in order to verify the appearance and condition of the Work and the Buyer is satisfied with and has approved of and accepts the appearance and condition of the Work as described in the Condition Report attached hereto as Exhibit C. On the Closing Date, or within twenty-four (24) hours prior thereto, the Buyer or Buyer's agent shall have the right to again inspect the Work to verify that the Work is in substantially the same condition as described in the Condition Report. The Buyer shall have the right to cancel the purchase of the Work if the condition of the Work (as determined by the same party who prepared the Condition Report) has deteriorated so that it is not in substantially the same condition as reflected in the Condition Report.

5.   TITLE AND DELIVERY

A.   The "Closing Date" shall mean the date upon which the Buyer pays the Purchase Price to the Seller and the Seller conveys to the Buyer title to the Work in accordance with this Agreement. Subject to the terms of this Agreement, the Closing Date shall be _____, 200__.

B.   On the Closing Date, the Seller shall deliver to the Buyer the signed Bill of Sale and any original or copies of provenance documents and shall arrange for delivery of the Work by common carrier to the Buyer at _____, _____, _____ _____.

6.   EXPENSES, INSURANCE AND SALES TAX

The Seller is responsible and shall pay all costs and expenses and delivery charges for delivering the Work to the Buyer in accordance with this Agreement. Until the Closing Date, the Seller agrees to insure the Work for the Purchase Price and to name the Buyer and the Seller as insured parties as their respective interests may appear. On payment of the Purchase Price, the Buyer will insure the Work.

The Buyer agrees to pay any and all state sales or use taxes in the State of _____ or such other state to which the Work is shipped arising from the Buyer's acquisition of the Work in accordance with this Agreement. The Seller represents that it has no office in the State of _____ and is an entity with substantial assets.

7. COMMISSION

The Seller shall not be responsible for and shall not pay any commissions or fees due any person acting on behalf of the Buyer as a result of the transaction contemplated by this Agreement. The Buyer shall not be responsible for and shall not pay any commissions or fees due any dealer or agent acting on behalf of the Seller as a result of the transaction contemplated by this Agreement.

8. CONFIDENTIALITY

During the term of this Agreement and after the closing of title, neither the Buyer nor the Seller will disclose the Purchase Price, the terms of this Agreement, or the identity of the parties to any third party without the other's written consent, except insofar as necessary to carry out the terms of this Agreement, or as may be required by law. The terms of this Paragraph shall survive the closing of title or termination of this Agreement for any reason including termination prior to closing.

9. MISCELLANEOUS

A. This Agreement (including the Exhibits attached hereto) represents the entire understanding of the parties with respect to the subject matter hereof, supersedes any and all other and prior agreements between the parties with respect to the subject matter hereof and declares all such prior agreements between the parties null and void. The terms of this Agreement may not be modified or amended, except in a writing signed by the party to be charged. This Agreement and all matters relating to it shall be governed by the laws of the State of New York. This Agreement shall inure to the benefit of, and shall be binding upon, the successors, heirs, executors and administrators of the parties hereto. Any dispute arising hereunder shall be resolved in the courts of the State of _____, or the United States federal courts located in the State of _____, and the parties hereto consent to the personal jurisdiction of such courts; provided, however, that the parties hereto agree that they will make concerted efforts to settle any dispute between them in an amicable manner without the necessity of litigation. This Agreement shall not be interpreted for or against a party because such party or such party's legal counsel drafted such provision.

B. From time to time, upon request, whether on or after the Closing Date, and without further consideration, each of the parties agrees to and shall execute and deliver such further instruments and take such further actions as the requesting party may reasonably require to fulfill the purposes of this Agreement.

C. If any term, provision, covenant, or condition of this Agreement, or the application thereof to any person or circumstance, shall be held by a court of competent jurisdiction to be invalid, unenforceable, or void, the remainder of this Agreement and such term, provision, covenant, or condition as applied to other persons or circumstances shall remain in full force and effect. This Agreement may be executed in counterparts, each of which shall be deemed an original, but all of which together shall constitute one and the same instrument.

IN WITNESS WHEREOF, the parties hereto have hereunto signed their hands and seals the day and year first-above written.

Seller:

[Name of Dealer]

_____

By: _____, President

Buyer:

_____

[Name of Collector]

BILL OF SALE

Dated: _____

Sold by: [Name and Address of Dealer]   (the "Seller")

Sold to: [Name and Address of Collector]   (the "Buyer")

Work Sold: Title: (the "Work")
             Artist:
             Medium:
             Size:
             Date:
             Provenance: See attached Exhibit A

Purchase Price: $_____ U.S.
Payment Terms: In full on: _____, 20__.

The Seller, subject only to and effective upon its receipt of the above-referenced Purchase Price and in consideration thereof, hereby irrevocably and without condition or reservation of any kind sells, transfers and conveys to the Buyer the above-described Work, good, valid and marketable title thereto, and all right to possession and all legal ownership thereof, free of all Claims, to have and to hold the Work unto the Buyer, his successors and assigns, forever.

The Work is sold subject to each and all of the terms, conditions, representations and warranties contained in an Agreement of Sale dated _____ ___, 20__ between the Seller and the Buyer (the "Agreement"), and all such terms, conditions, representations and covenants of the parties thereunder are incorporated herein by this reference as if fully set forth herein in their entirety. All capitalized terms not defined in this Bill of Sale shall have the same meaning as set forth in the Agreement.

The Seller agrees to execute and deliver such additional documents and to take such other further actions from time to time after the date hereof as the Buyer may reasonably request, to assure and confirm this transaction.

If any provision of this Bill of Sale, or the application thereof to any person or circumstance, shall be held by a court of competent jurisdiction to be invalid, unenforceable, or void, the remainder of this Bill of Sale and such term, provision, covenant or condition as applied to other persons or circumstances shall remain in full force and effect.

The terms and provisions of this Bill of Sale shall be binding upon the Seller and its successors, assigns and legal representatives and shall inure to the benefit of the Buyer and his successors, assigns and legal representatives.

The benefits of the representations, warranties and indemnities contained in the Agreement and this Bill of Sale shall survive completion of the transaction contemplated by the Agreement and this Bill of Sale, including without limitation the transfer of the Work to the Buyer.

This Bill of Sale shall be governed by and shall be construed and enforced in accordance with the internal laws of the State of _____, without regard to conflict of laws principles.

[Name of Dealer]

_____

By: _____, President

<u>EXHIBIT B</u>

PROVENANCE:

EXHIBIT C

CONDITION REPORT

ADDITIONAL FORMS

See the appendixes to chapter 8 for examples of consignment/sale forms structured to cover international transactions, including cash escrow or letter of credit escrow arrangements. These forms also cover situations where there may be an undisclosed principal—either seller or buyer.

3

Theft, Forgery, Authenticity, and Statutes of Limitations

A basic principle of our legal system is that there be a temporal limit on causes of action in order to ensure, among other things, that those who have dealt with property in good faith can enjoy secure possession after a certain period of time. This principle is put into effect through the application of a statute of limitations—the period of time within which a person must assert his rights. This chapter addresses the appropriate statute of limitations as it applies in the art world to issues of theft, forgery, and authenticity. As to stolen art, for example, do—and should—transactions between innocent parties mandate a statute of limitations computed more favorably than would be applied to, say, a bad-faith possessor? As to a dealer's guarantee of authenticity of an artwork to a buyer, how long is the dealer held to that guarantee? These are some of the issues addressed in the following pages.

ART THEFT

Query: What thriving international illicit business exceeds $7 billion? Answer: The worldwide trade in stolen, smuggled, and looted art.[1] Recent sensational reported thefts include the following:

- Two paintings by Edvard Munch, *The Scream* and *Madonna*, with a combined value of over $122 million, were stolen from the Munch Museum of Oslo in August 2004.

- Pablo Picasso's *Nature Morte à la Charlotte*, valued at $15 million, was stolen from a Pompidou Center warehouse in May 2004.

- Two paintings by Vincent van Gogh, *View of the Sea at Scheveningen* and *Congregation Leaving the Reformed Church in Nuenen*, with a combined value of over $100 million, were stolen from the Van Gogh Museum of Amsterdam in December 2002.

- Claude Monet's *Paysage à Vetheuil*, valued at $4 million, and Pierre-Auguste Renoir's *Place de la Trinite*, valued at $2.7 million, were stolen from the home of a Naples man in December 2002.

- French national Stephane Breitwieser was charged and tried in 2003 for stealing sixty-nine sixteenth- and seventeenth-century works of art in Switzerland. Experts estimate that his most valuable haul was a sixteenth-century painting by Lucas Cranach the Elder, worth more than $6 million. Further, Breitwieser admitted to stealing 239 pictures and museum exhibits, some worth millions, from seven different countries over a six-year period, including works by Antoine Watteau, Pieter Bruegel, and François Boucher, the total of which has been estimated at almost $100 million.

- Still unsolved as of May 2005 is the biggest art theft in the United States—the March 18, 1990 robbery from the Isabella Stewart Gardner Museum in Boston. The stolen works, including masterworks by Rembrandt and Vermeer, were worth $200 million at the time of the theft and are worth substantially more today.[2]

Art theft is one of the fastest growing crimes in the United States and throughout the world. Spurred by the fall of Communism and the rise of organized crime in Eastern Europe, stolen art has become illegal currency for drug barons and terrorists[3] and collateral for narcotics transactions and has been used to launder criminal profits. Although the art buyer must be aware of these sobering trends and their effects on subsequently acquired title,[4] the resources currently available for both the investigation of title to artwork and the recovery of stolen art should provide some comfort.[5]

Resources for Investigation and Recovery

Among the principal organizations focusing on art theft throughout the world are the Art Loss Register (ALR), the Art Dealers Association of America (ADAA), the International Foundation for Art Research (IFAR), and the art program of the International Criminal Police Organization (Interpol).

ALR,[6] an international for-profit clearinghouse that began operations in 1991, represents a complex alliance of London insurance brokerages, such as Lloyd's of London; major auction houses, including Sotheby's, Christie's, and Phillips; and IFAR. ALR has more than 140,000 records, including many color images; each record includes the aggrieved party's name and address, the insurer, the police report number, the date and the location of the theft, the artwork's value (which must exceed $500), the artist, the date of creation, the medium, the artwork's measurements, and any inscriptions. In addition, agreements with the major auction houses permit ALR to search all auction catalogs automatically. Dealers, collectors, museums, and other interested parties can register items with ALR in either New York, London, St. Petersburg and Cologne or can search the register for a small fee. The service is free to all police authorities.

ADAA,[7] which is based in New York City, was, for over twenty-five years, the only central source of information on stolen and missing artworks. In 1987, ADAA turned its records over to IFAR. IFAR continued to operate and develop the original ADAA theft notification service until it transferred the archive to ALR, with which it is affiliated. Thus, ADAA served as an impetus for the establishment of a data bank on stolen artworks.

IFAR,[8] also based in New York City, was established in 1968 by a group of attorneys, art historians, and scientists to study and combat fraudulent art practices. Since 1975, IFAR has maintained an archive, computerized since 1983, of art thefts from domestic and foreign dealers, private collections, and museums. IFAR responds to inquiries from any interested persons. In addition, IFAR publishes and distributes its magazine, *IFAR Reports*, a number of times each year. The magazine contains a stolen art alert—compiled in cooperation with the art community, insurance companies, the police, the Federal Bureau of Investigation (FBI), and Interpol—which lists stolen art objects, and includes an index of stolen art as part of its year-end issue.

The art program of Interpol, a group of police agencies in 176 countries,[9] is primarily involved with the dissemination of information about stolen or forged art believed to have been smuggled across international borders. The United States, a member nation since 1938, transmits to ALR, IFAR, ADAA, the FBI, customs officials, and other select agencies monthly stolen–property notices received from Interpol's headquarters in France. Since 1947, Interpol has been involved in the fight against illicit trade of cultural objects. In addition, Interpol publishes and distributes to appropriate agencies in all its member nations a biannual poster of stolen objects, compiled from the monthly notices.

Since May 1979, the FBI[10] has maintained the National Stolen Art File (NSAF) in Washington, D.C., for artwork valued at $2,000 or more. Reports of art thefts are forwarded from local police departments or regional FBI offices to FBI headquarters in Washington. However, only law enforcement agencies may search the stolen art file, and the request to search must be prompted by suspected criminal activity.

FORGERIES

Diverse forces operate to encourage art forgery today:

- Demand exceeds the supply of quality authentic work, driving prices up and creating an incentive for fraud.

- American and European modern artworks can be imitated with relative ease and are currently popular. Older paintings are frequently more difficult to imitate, since the Old Masters usually primed their own canvases and ground and mixed their own pigments, resulting in more individuality of material and workmanship.

- Valuable works with provenance deranged by war have occasionally been found in unusual places.

- Purchasers often fail to seek expert assistance.

- Serious collectors who have been defrauded may perpetuate the deceit, desiring to avoid publicity lest public awareness of the deception impair their credibility as connoisseurs.

- Dealers, in an effort to protect their sources, frequently fail to provide purchasers with accurate documentation of provenance.

- Artists are tempted to make forgeries because of their difficulty in obtaining recognition.

Ancient Forgeries

People have forged art objects for many centuries. The Romans often created copies of Greek sculptures. Albrecht Dürer, the renowned German printmaker of the late fifteenth and early sixteenth centuries, was often victimized by forgeries of his prints and ended a series of his woodcuts with the curse: "Woe to you! You thieves and imitators of other people's labor and talents. Beware of laying your audacious hand on this artwork."

Modern Forgeries

We have colorful art forgers in our own time. One is David Stein, a former art dealer who can paint in the style of Pablo Picasso, Marc Chagall, Henri Matisse, Joan Miró, Georges Braque, Paul Klee, and other great artists. After producing forty-one paintings in the styles of such noted artists, forging their signatures on the paintings, and selling them, Stein was arrested in the United States in 1967 and pleaded guilty to six counts of counterfeiting artwork and grand larceny. After serving his jail sentence, he was deported to France, where he was subsequently convicted and imprisoned for selling art forgeries there. While confined in the United States, Stein was allowed to continue painting in the style of famous artists, so long as the works bore his own signature, rather than those of the artists he copied. The paintings Stein executed in prison were exhibited and sold in 1969 in London by an affiliate of the Wright Hepburn Webster Gallery of New York. In 1970, the New York gallery advertised the exhibition of almost seventy Stein paintings by placing in its window a notice that read, "Forgeries by Stein." The show drew a large number of people willing to pay high prices, and the New York Attorney General sought to enjoin the exhibition and sale on the grounds of its being a public nuisance, contending that Stein's name could easily be removed from the master look-a-likes and that the paintings would eventually flood the market as original Chagalls, Picassos, etc.[11] The court rejected that argument, holding that the paintings could not constitute a public nuisance on the mere possibility of the future commission of a crime.[12]

Modern forgeries abound. During the 1950s and 1960s, thousands of forged Maurice Utrillos flooded the market, significantly devaluing a number of genuine works not having the benefit of unblemished provenance. In 1977, thousands of forged Giorgio de Chiricos, along with materials used to manufacture sophisticated false authentications, were discovered in a forgery factory and a warehouse in Milan.

Still more recent is the prevalence of fraud in the Salvador Dalí print market, which has caused consumers in a number of states to be swindled out of millions of dollars,[13] resulting in a number of successful criminal prosecutions. In Hawaii in May 1990, for example, a federal jury in *United States v. Center Art Galleries-Hawaii, Inc.*[14] returned a guilty verdict against the gallery and its officers on numerous counts of mail and wire fraud in the sale of prints, allegedly original Dalí lithographs, that were in reality "inexpensive calendar quality photomechanical reproductions." Since the late 1970s, Center Art Galleries had sold many of the reproductions at prices ranging from $1,000 to $20,000 each. The total amount of fraud sustained by the victims has been conservatively estimated at around $50 million.[15]

In Arizona, as another example, the Federal Trade Commission (FTC) brought suit against Federal Sterling Galleries[16] for unfair and deceptive trade practices in selling artworks purportedly by Dalí, Picasso, Miró, and other modern and contemporary artists. In 1989, the federal district court in Arizona granted a permanent injunction and an order for consumer redress of $4.6 million.

In a further instance of fraud involving Dalí artwork, the FTC in 1991 brought suit in a California federal district court against Magui Publishers, Inc.,[17] a California publisher and marketer of Dalí art to retailers throughout the United States, and against its principal, Pierre Marcand. The FTC successfully applied the Federal Trade Commission Act to establish that Magui made particular misrepresentations to its retailer-purchasers; namely, that Dalí was involved in the creation or production of the works sold by Magui, that Magui's Dalí prints were produced on paper that was signed or presigned by Dalí, that the prints were more valuable than they actually were, that all the etchings were produced entirely by hand, and that the editions of certain titles were smaller than they really were. Section 5 of the FTC Act (15 U.S.C. § 45) provides that "unfair methods of competition . . . affecting commerce, and unfair or deceptive acts or practices affecting commerce, are . . . unlawful." That section has been used to combat an array of unfair trade practices in the art market—for example, the production, distribution, and sale of fake art and sales of art for investment purposes at inflated values. In *FTC v. Magui Publishers, Inc.*, the California federal district court applied the statute to nip the fakery at its source: Magui, after all, was not a re-tailer but, rather, a publisher and distributor of prints to retailers. Accordingly, the federal district court issued a permanent injunction against both Magui Publishers and its principal, Marcand, prohibiting their misrepresentations, and an order for consumer redress in the amount of $1.96 million.

In another case,[18] Kathryn Amiel, Joanne Amiel, and Sarina Amiel, owners of arguably "the largest single source of counterfeit prints in the world,"[19] were convicted in December 1993 in a federal district court in Long Island, New York, of federal conspiracy and mail-fraud charges stemming from an art counterfeit ring. Original Artworks, Ltd., a family-owned business, was a manufacturer and distributor of purportedly original lithographs by such modern and contemporary artists as Chagall, Miró, and Dalí. In January 1992, federal postal inspectors raided the Amiels' Island Park, Long Island, warehouse and seized approximately 77,000 counterfeit prints: 50,000 "original" prints of 275 titles by Dalí, 20,000 "original" prints of 175 titles by Miró, and 650 "original" prints of sixty titles by Chagall. The raid also turned up stacks of blank sheets bearing Dalí's signature. The government charged Original Artworks, Ltd. with distributing up to $100 million worth of fake prints to a network of more than 100 commercial galleries, mostly in the United States, in locations geared to tourists, rather than to sophisticated art consumers.

Another example of fraud in the Dalí print market involved the Austin Galleries, a chain of more than thirty art galleries in Chicago, Detroit, and San Francisco, owned and operated by the art dealer Donald Austin and specializing in the sale of fine prints of both modern and contemporary artists, including Dalí, Picasso, Miró, and Chagall. Austin Galleries sold most of its art as signed original limited-edition prints. In fact, most of the prints were forgeries. (For extensive discussions of what constitutes a fine print and of forgery and other abuses in the print market, see chapter 5.) Acting on complaints, the FTC brought suit in a federal district court in Illinois against Austin Galleries in May 1988.[20] In April 1990, after an investigation that yielded widespread evidence of forgery both in prior sales and in the galleries' current inventor, Austin Galleries entered into a court-approved settlement with the FTC.[21] The settlement required the galleries to surrender all its pencil-signed Mirós, Chagalls, and Picassos and forbade the making of any misrepresentations in the sale of artwork. The settlement did permit the Dalís to be sold, provided they were not represented as being authentic works of art. In addition, the settlement ordered the galleries to pay $625,000 into a consumer redress fund to be administered by the FTC and provided that if the galleries failed to pay the entire sum by January 1, 1991, or if it declared bankruptcy before that date, the amount of redress would increase to $1.5 million. As another condition of the settlement, Donald Austin signed a stipulation admitting fraud; it was to be filed only in the event that Austin went into bankruptcy or defaulted in his payments to the FTC.

Contrary to the settlement terms, Austin failed to deliver the Mirós, Chagalls, and Picassos to the FTC. Moreover, he sold nine Chagall prints to a customer for $50,000 with an option to repurchase within six months. Of the prints, which Austin represented to the customer as having a wholesale value of $70,000 and a retail value of $140,000, at least one was a fake.[22] Consequently, the United States government initiated criminal proceedings against Austin.[23] He was indicted in 1993 and was subsequently convicted on charges of mail and wire fraud for causing money he knew to have been taken by fraud to be transmitted in interstate commerce. The convictions were affirmed on appeal in 1995 by the Federal Court of Appeals for the Seventh Circuit.[24]

Dealers and collectors alike of Dalí's prints were pleased to see the publication in February 1994 of the first *catalogue raisonné* of the artist's etchings and mixed-media prints, 1924–1980, published in English and German by Prestel, the noted Munich publisher.[25] The book includes an introduction depicting thirty authentic Dalí signatures and a discussion of watermarks, indicating that "any paper bearing a post-1980 watermark is unquestionably a forgery since Dalí issued legal instructions stating that he signed neither prints nor blank pages after 1980,"[26] when he contracted a serious illness. The catalog depicts a total of 937 Dalí fine prints known to be authentic;

for each title, it lists the dates of publication, printmaking techniques, edition size, dimensions, names of printer and publisher, and the paper and watermark used. Nevertheless, as of ten years later (2004), a prudent lawyer must still exercise caution when contemplating the purchase of a Dalí fine art multiple.[27]

Widespread forgery, of course, is not and never has been limited to the print market. The exploits of other well-known forgers—such as Hans van Meegeren, Alceo Dossena, the Spanish Forger, and Elymr de Hory—highlight the ease with which a variety of artworks can be faked and the degree of success attainable by the forgers. Before the end of World War II, Hans van Meegeren, a Dutch forger of art, had masterfully faked a number of paintings by Jan Vermeer of Delft and Pieter de Hooch. Alceo Dossena, an Italian known as the king of forgers, lived from 1878 to 1937; he was able to re-create many styles and periods, ranging from ancient Greek to Renaissance. The Spanish Forger, who lived around the turn of the century, probably in Paris, created "original" medieval and Renaissance manuscripts and paintings inspired by the Masters. He worked with ancient wood or parchment and caused the finished works to be passed off as newly discovered creations of the Masters. And between 1961 and 1967, Elymr de Hory imitated an estimated $60 million worth of paintings and drawings of such contemporary artists as Pablo Picasso, André Derain, Raoul Dufy, and Amedeo Modigliani that were sold to collectors, art dealers, and museums.

In June 1994, the French police—with the cooperation of the German, Dutch, and Swiss police and Interpol—arrested two painters, Jan van den Bergen and Ellen van den Bergen, living in a village near Orléans, France, in connection with an alleged forgery racket involving more than a thousand artworks, purportedly by such modern and contemporary artists as Chagall, Matisse, Dufy, Picasso, René Magritte, Dalí, Gustav Klimt, and Miró.[28] The two painters had allegedly created and sold huge quantities of forged paintings and prints accompanied by certificates of authenticity, also forged, from various parts of France for ten years. Many of the fakes were believed to have entered the stream of commerce in various parts of Germany, France, Switzerland, Belgium, Holland, Scandinavia, Britain, and the United States. The couple were charged with forgery, fraud, and breach of copyright.[29]

That same year, 1994, witnessed the discovery of a new faker, the well-known Paris restorer Alfred Andre (1839–1919), whose fabrications have been unknowingly on display as original Renaissance works in such major museums as the National Gallery of Art, Washington, D.C. (six showy "Renaissance jewels"); the Metropolitan Museum of Art, New York (three "Renaissance" enameled gold-mounted semiprecious stone cups); and the Louvre, Paris (a "fourteenth-century Majorcan" enameled chalice).[30] Andre's descendants continue in the restoration business in Paris to the present day. Their workshops contain hundreds of plaster and wax models of jewelry and cups in the Gothic and Renaissance styles; some are casts of old originals, and others are completely new productions. Although it is not clear how the fakes entered the market (the restorer's account books and papers were thrown away), it is known that Andre worked for Frederic Spitzer, a collector-dealer who channeled fakes through his collection to the major collectors of the day, such as the Rothschilds.[31]

Another accomplished art restorer, a self-proclaimed forger of Old Masters' drawings and paintings, was the late English-born artist Eric Hebborn. Hebborn boasted that he "restored" paintings that never existed, deceiving such a personage as the late Sir Anthony Blunt, Britain's royal conservator and longtime traitor and Soviet spy. Hebborn commemorated his string of hoaxes in his autobiography, *Drawn to Trouble: Confessions of a Master Forger* (Random House, 1993), and subsequently faced, before his death in January 1996, allegations of fakery. Graham Smith, Hebborn's former partner and lover in the 1950s and 1960s, claimed that some of Hebborn's boasts, such as that he produced a Pieter Brueghel etching now in the Metropolitan Museum of Art (and flushed the original down the toilet), were sheer nonsense. Although Hebborn's confessions caused considerable consternation in the international art market, dealers whom he allegedly deceived have apparently refrained from pressing criminal charges, lest they undermine confidence in the art market.[32]

When forgeries are well done, they can confound the experts and wreak havoc at auction houses. One notorious example embodied in a 1980s lawsuit (also discussed in chapter 4) concerned the purchase of a Peter Carl Fabergé egg by an Iranian businessman living in New York.[33] In 1977, the businessman bought the egg from Christie's in Geneva for $250,000 after representations that it had belonged to the Russian imperial family. Later, he doubted its authenticity and refused to pay for it. Christie's sued and presented an expert who pronounced the egg an authentic Imperial, whereupon the purchaser ultimately paid $400,000 for it (including $150,000 in legal fees). In 1985, however, when the same purchaser consigned the egg for auction to Christie's in New York, that same expert revised his opinion and stated that although he believed the egg to be undoubtedly by Fabergé, it had been elaborately doctored. Christie's then canceled the sale. As an Imperial, the egg was worth about $1.75 million; otherwise, it was worth about $50,000. The Iranian businessman sued Christie's for $37 million.[34] Christie's, taking the position that it had acted in good faith in both instances, filed a motion to dismiss the suit on technical grounds.[35] On settlement of the case, the court file was sealed.

Even more unsettling is this extraordinary twist on the sale of a forged work of art: Accomplices of forgers were found to have doctored the archives at the Tate Gallery in London (the Tate having no knowledge that its files were tampered with) so that when a prospective buyer of a painting consulted the record, it showed that the painting is authentic. The fraud, which was exposed when a watercolor attributed to the British artist Ben Nicholson was found to have been forged, apparently involved three stages: A work of art was forged; an accomplice altered the artist's file in the Tate or elsewhere to include the new work; and a dealer offered the work for sale, indicating to the potential buyer how its provenance could be checked.[36]

Perhaps the most mind-boggling art scam of all involved Ely Sakhi, owner of a Manhattan art gallery, who was arrested in March 2004 on charges of mail and wire fraud stemming from his involvement in an international art forgery scheme. Apparently, Sakhi bought at public auction various mid-priced artworks by Chagall, Renoir, and other impressionist and post-impressionist artists. He would then acquire forgeries of those paintings, sell the forgeries in Japan, keep the originals for seven or eight years, then sell the originals in the United States. The scheme began to come apart when the identical Gaugin painting was depicted in both Sotheby's and Christie's catalogs for their respective May 2000 auctions.[37]

Forgeries of Sculpture and Antiquities

Because there is less of a market for sculpture and because sculpture is difficult and costly to fake, forged sculpture is not as common as forged paintings and fine prints. However, unauthorized posthumous castings and recastings of artworks are prevalent and pose a significant peril to the art-buying public.[38]

In response to the threats to market stability posed by an influx of forged sculpture into the streams of commerce, New York on January 1, 1991, became the first state to implement an exclusive, comprehensive law that protects buyers of sculptures produced in multiples.[39] A California statute, enacted in 1971, contains provisions addressing both print multiples and sculpture multiples.[40] As of 2004, Iowa was the only other state that had followed suit.[41] (Sculpture multiples statutes are discussed at length in chapter 5, which addresses fine-art multiples in general.) However, as useful to the consumer as those statutes are in helping to curb abusive practices, they apply solely to works of sculpture produced in more than one copy; a sculpture produced and sold as one of a kind can well be a fake and outside the reach of such statutes.

Antiquities and artifacts, too, may be faked, and the experts can be bamboozled. In one notable instance, after a six-year probe, New York's Metropolitan Museum of Art in 1967 consigned to storage a once-revered Greek statue, *Etruscan Horse*. A Metropolitan Museum expert contended that the bronze, formerly believed to be 2,400 years old, had been cast in sand, a method not developed until the fourteenth century. The very next year, a panel of art scholars found that the first expert's determination was erroneous. Further thermoluminescent study of the statue's ceramic core prompted the panel to decide that the horse was "an irrefutably genuine work of antiquity,"[42] and the museum restored the horse to its place of honor.

Fake Art As a Crime

Art has been counterfeited since time immemorial. The following are among the most common ways to simulate art:

- The copying of a specific original work of art
- The use of another artist's style to create a work otherwise original in subject matter
- The completion of a work left unfinished by the artist
- The assemblage of diverse compositional elements from original paintings to produce new compositions attributed to a specific artist (sometimes called "pastiche")

Note, however, that the production, sale, transport, ownership, or display of counterfeit art per se is not actionable under United States law. Whether such activities involving *all* counterfeit art *should* be actionable is a separate issue, discussed below. At present, only where counterfeit art is produced, sold, or otherwise presented with the intent to deceive does the arm of the law intervene. For example, where a person, with intent to defraud or injure, affixes another's signature to a work of art, the crime of forgery has occurred. Under Pennsylvania's criminal code, which is fairly typical,

> a person is guilty of forgery if, with intent to defraud or injure anyone, or with knowledge that he is facilitating a fraud or injury to be perpetrated by anyone, the actor: (1) alters any writing of another without his authority; (2) makes, completes, executes, authenticates . . . any writing so that it purports to be the act of another who did not authorize that act.[43]

The Pennsylvania code, in common with many other state criminal codes,[44] defines a writing to include "any . . . method of recording information."[45] Commentators have raised the question of whether, under the typical state criminal code, a simulated work of art without a signature qualifies as a forgery; artwork, after all, is certainly a method of recording information.[46] In any event, forgery of an artwork, whether by fraudulent affixation of another's signature to such work or by fraudulent simulation of such a work, is determined under most[47] state criminal codes to be a class A or aggravated misdemeanor. The major offense of felony is generally reserved for the forging of government instruments or other documents affecting legal relations.[48]

Compared to forgery statutes, criminal simulation statutes enacted by several states potentially provide a better weapon against counterfeit artwork in general and counterfeit cultural objects specifically, because the statutes dispense with the "writing" requirement found in forgery statutes. The New York statute, which is fairly typical, provides that

> [a] person is guilty of criminal simulation when:
> (1) With intent to defraud, he makes or alters any object in such manner that it appears to have an antiquity, rarity, source or authorship which it does not in fact possess; or
> (2) With knowledge of its true character and with intent to defraud, he utters or possesses an object so simulated.[49]

Although criminal simulation is occasionally treated as a low-grade felony,[50] it is generally codified in state codes as a class A misdemeanor.[51] Does that mean that the law in general views the counterfeiting of artwork to defraud with a less-jaundiced eye than, say, the counterfeiting of wills, deeds, or dollars? *Is* it a less important offense? What about the counterfeiting of artwork without intent to defraud? If such doings are not codified in our legislation as crimes, is not such counterfeiting nevertheless an offense to our culture? Or does such counterfeiting somehow inure to the benefit of the public?

Does the Counterfeiter Have a Legitimate Role?

The public tends to romanticize the talented art forger. Literature abounds with books and articles by and about such counterfeiters, whose skills in the mechanics of drawing, painting, sculpting, and other techniques have enabled them to confound dealers, curators, and sophisticated collectors alike. *False Impressions: The Hunt for Big-Time Art Fakes* (1996), by Thomas Hoving, former director of the Metropolitan Museum of Art, and *Three Picassos before Breakfast* (1973), by Ann-Marie Stein, wife of the convicted forger David Stein, are two examples.

Admiration for the counterfeiter can be found in our legal culture as well. In the words of New York State Supreme Court Judge Arnold L. Fein, who rejected the New York State attorney general's application to enjoin the sale of counterfeit paintings made by convicted forger David Stein,

> Stein . . . mastered the styles of such great artists as Chagall, Picasso, Matisse, Braque, Klee, Miró, Cocteau and Rouault. . . . The court is asked to [preclude] this man from earning a livelihood by utilizing his peculiar and unusual talents. . . . His work in perfecting the style of the masters may properly be ascribed to that special talent with which true artists are uniquely endowed.[52]

Leaving aside the question of whether Judge Fein actually believed that the talents required of a master forger are one and the same with the talents required of an artist, a cogent argument can be made that the artist, unlike the mere forger, possesses an original manner of expressing his perceptions. What should serve to debunk at least some of the counterfeiter's mystique is that the master forger, in addition to confounding art experts and sophisticated and often wealthy collectors, deceives far more often the ordinary, not-so-sophisticated, and not-so-wealthy purchaser, as shown by some of the cases mentioned earlier. What is significant in the forgeries-by-Stein case is that Judge Fein denied New York's attorney general's application for an injunction because Stein was selling his works as forgeries; he was not deceiving the public.

An art forgery that does deceive the public, no matter how perfect the forgery is, strikes a blow to our culture; it is historically dishonest. When Peter Paul Rubens, for example, creates a work of art such as the altarpiece *The Raising of the Cross*, the result is far more than merely the product of the technical skills of a great artist. It is, in addition, a memorial of the artist's perceptions that reflect the cultural concerns of his time. As a Flemish artist of the early 1600s and a devout Catholic who prospered in Antwerp by executing a vast volume of work for the city, the royal households, and the Church, Rubens naturally created much artwork depicting biblical scenes. Beyond being a memorial of an artist's perceptions of then-current cultural concerns, an artwork embodies an artist's unique expression of perceptions, such expression being a reflection of artistic tradition. Rubens's altarpiece, for example, acknowledges his debt to the High Renaissance art of Italy, where he studied for a number of years early in his career.[53] The muscular figures in *The Raising of the Cross*, in their power and passionate feeling, are reminiscent of the figures on the ceiling of the Sistine Chapel, and the lighting on the altarpiece shows hints of Michelangelo da Caravaggio's lighting.[54] In sum, therefore, to own that altarpiece, as to own any original work of art, is to own a piece of history. A perfect copy of *The Raising of the Cross* might be as aesthetically pleasing as the original, but it is not a piece of history, and that difference, once it becomes known, is consistently reflected in economic terms in the art market. People want to see and, if possible, own the genuine article.[55]

That being said, is there any place in our culture for counterfeit art? It can be argued effectively that most of us cannot afford to own many (if any) works of original fine art, let alone masterpieces, and yet we enjoy being able to derive some aesthetic pleasure from fine art on a basis more constant than occasional visits to museums. If copies of artworks that are presented as copies are capable of affording some aesthetic pleasure to the public, counterfeit art should be available for purchase and exhibit on that basis. That does not, of course, include any counterfeit art that implicates copyright infringement issues. (See chapter 10.) How to ensure that counterfeit art does not deceive? Obvious reproductions presented as such, in which the scale or the medium of the reproduction is distinguishable from the original, such as Edgar Degas's *Prima Ballerina* enlarged somewhat to poster size or a photomechanical reproduction of

Claude Monet's oil painting *Water Lilies, Giverny*, are examples of counterfeit art that do not deceive.[56]

Gauging Authenticity

Artwork is generally authenticated by

   (1)   documentation,

   (2)   stylistic inquiry, and

   (3)   scientific verification.

Documentation of the history of ownership and public exposure of a work of art is sometimes unavailable, inasmuch as documentation itself is, on occasion, either forged or missing entirely.

Stylistic inquiry is subjective. An expert examines the work and on the basis of his knowledge, experience, and intuition determines its authenticity. Unfortunately, the results of stylistic inquiry may vary from expert to expert, and the opinion of an expert may change over time. Moreover, experts are often reluctant to render opinions for fear of incurring tort liability.[57] Nevertheless, stylistic inquiry remains a viable test of authenticity, particularly for contemporary works, since even the most gifted copyist cannot totally repress his personality during the execution of a forgery.

In much the same way, stylistic inquiry makes it difficult for an artist to disclaim authorship of his work when intact. In the Balthus case discussed in chapter 2, that artist denied authorship of *Colette de Profil*, a drawing allegedly his, by marking on the back of it *"faux manifeste."*[58] The court in that case relied on the stylistic research *of other experts* and on the evidence of chain of title to establish the authenticity of Balthus's work, noting that the artist, far from being the final word on the authenticity of his own work, may well have motives (such as vengeance in the case of Balthus) for renouncing authorship of his own work.

Scientific verification, frequently used in conjunction with stylistic inquiry, as illustrated in the highly praised "Rembrandt–Not Rembrandt" exhibition at New York City's Metropolitan Museum of Art in 1995,[59] uses objective procedures, thereby permitting the accuracy of the results to be tested by other scientists. Because it is objective and because technological analysis is usually the only means of securing information relating to the age and the composition of a work of art, scientific verification may be the primary method of challenging authenticity and attribution. Some of the best-known scientific techniques available for the authentication of artwork are listed below:

Radiocarbon Dating. This method, which is used to test materials derived from once-living organisms, gives estimates of the time elapsed since an organism's death by measuring the quantity of a particular radiation emitted by those materials.

Thermoluminescent Analysis. Mainly applicable to ceramic ware or fired clay, this technique measures the thermoluminescence or light of the material, thereby indicating the time elapsed since the last firing of the clay. The technique is especially suitable for dating sculpture and antiquities.

X-Ray Photography. This category includes a variety of X-ray techniques: X-radiographs, which provide insights into the structure of paintings in general; X-ray diffraction, which determines the degree and the character of the internal structure of such materials as jewelry, glass, pigments, and glazes; and autoradiography, which permits the identification and examination of the pigments in a painting.

Comparative Analysis. In this procedure, the expert examines characteristic composition patterns that can be compared with a known sample, thus permitting the scientist to deduce the information sought, such as the age of the item.

Chemical Analysis. This type of study is used primarily to date fossil bones and teeth from a single area when they are preserved under comparable conditions by measuring, in particular, the accumulation in the bones of two elements, fluorine and uranium.

Infrared Imaging. Infrared photography and reflectography are used to record graphics and underdrawings executed in carbonaceous black pigments on contrasting white or gray grounds. The methods are especially useful in the study of Northern European panel paintings of the fifteenth and sixteenth centuries.[60]

ART THEFT AND THE STATUTE OF LIMITATIONS

Introduction

Trafficking in stolen art, an exceedingly lucrative criminal activity, is surely unsurpassed in international theatrical pyrotechnics, as shown by the following events of the 1990s:

- In 1990, the Federal Court of Appeals for the Seventh Circuit affirmed a lower-court decision to award title to rare and valuable Byzantine mosaics of the sixth century to the Republic of Cyprus and the Autocephalous Greek-Orthodox Church of Cyprus, rather than to an art dealer in Indiana who had paid more than $1.2 million to acquire them.[61]

- In September 1993, the Metropolitan Museum of Art, in settlement of a lawsuit, returned to the Republic of Turkey a cache of sixth century B.C. gold and silver known as the "Lydian Hoard" that had reportedly been looted from Turkey.[62]

- In November 1993, a jury in New York awarded a collection of Roman silver known as the "Sevso Treasure," valued by Sotheby's auction house at $70 million, to the Marquess of Northampton, despite claims of title on the part of Croatia, Hungary, and Lebanon.[63]

The rising incidence of art theft is likely to spiral ever higher in the aftermath of the seismic political upheavals throughout Eastern Europe and the former Soviet Union that began in 1989 and continue even today.

With the lifting of the Iron Curtain in the autumn of 1989, the nations of Eastern Europe witnessed, for the first time since early in the twentieth century, the general circulation of Western currency. The desire to acquire that currency has led to the plundering of art-laden churches, museums, universities, and other buildings to effect a quick sale of art into Western hands.[64] Those institutions in the West generally have reasonable security, but the need for comparable protection of art-rich buildings in Eastern Europe is only now becoming apparent, and the funds to finance enhanced protection are not necessarily available. In one notable instance, four paintings by Pablo Picasso were stolen at dawn on May 6, 1991, from a palace in Prague, where the Czech Republic's National Gallery exhibits its collections of nineteenth and twentieth century European art.[65] Although the palace has an alarm system, the thieves apparently broke into the building through a garden window and removed the works before the police responded. It is assumed that the paintings—valued by Interpol, the international criminal police organization, at, collectively, $30 million—were smuggled out of the country.

The advent of *perestroika* brought the disclosure in April 1991 of the existence of secret depositories housing untold art treasures throughout the republics of the then Soviet Union, a revelation that rocked the art world.[66] In the summer and the fall of 1945, Stalin's officials seized, largely from museums in the Soviet-occupied sector of Germany, approximately 2½ million artworks, including many masterpieces, and shipped them by train and cargo plane to Moscow, Leningrad, and elsewhere.[67] Those war treasures, known as trophy art or trophies of victory, include works by, among other masters, Velázquez, Titian, El Greco, Goya, Tintoretto, Brueghel, Monet, Manet, van Gogh, and Renoir. The war treasures also include such archeological trophies as the gold treasure of Troy excavated by Heinrich Schliemann. In the 1950s, the Soviet Union returned approximately 1½ million objects of the trophy art (but not the Trojan gold) to East German museums. Of the remainder, nothing was known until the 1991 disclosures. Then, in 1995, some of the trophy art remaining in Russia—masterpieces not seen by the public in more than fifty years—began to be exhibited: The Hermitage Museum in St. Petersburg (formerly Leningrad) in a show of trophy art entitled "Hidden Treasures Revealed" displayed an extraordinary collection of seventy-four works of impressionist and post-impressionist art by such artists as Renoir, Gauguin, Degas, van Gogh, and Cézanne. The Pushkin Museum of Fine Arts in Moscow at the same time held an equally remarkable exhibit entitled "Saved Twice" exhibiting sixty-three other works of trophy art by such masters as Goya and Lucas Cranach the Elder.

In a 1990 General Relations Treaty, Russia and Germany agreed to exchange cultural treasures illegally seized during World War II. But the Russians later claimed that the treaty refers only to loot stolen by soldiers and that the works taken from the German museums by Stalin's officials as partial reparation for the atrocities Germany inflicted on Russia during the war were lawful booty.[68] Russia's intensifying nationalism was evinced by the "Spoils of War" conference held in New York City in January 1995 that led to mutual recriminations between the Russian and the German representatives and by a bill in the Russian parliament that would convert all "lawfully removed" German artworks remaining on Russian soil—that is, works removed from Germany under order of the Soviet Zone commander—into state property. It seemed clear that the Russians were not inclined to hand over much additional trophy art to the Germans.[69]

Perhaps with an eye to the volatile politics of Eastern Europe and ever conscious of New York's role as a preeminent cultural center, the New York Court of Appeals (the state's highest court) published a February 1991 ruling in the case of *Guggenheim v. Lubell*[70] that interprets the relevant New York statute of limitations to favor, strongly, the rights of the original owner of a work of art. In most other states, the statute of limitations (which defines the time interval in which a plaintiff must bring a claim before it is legally barred) has been interpreted to favor a relatively prompt repose of possession in the bona fide purchaser or even the bad-faith possessor,[71] but in both New York and California, arguably the nation's two commercial capitals for art, courts have interpreted the statute to heavily favor the claimant—that is, the original owner.[72]

Objectives

The rising incidence of art theft noted above has caused a flow into legitimate channels of commerce of numerous artworks in connection with which good title cannot pass. Since, under United States law, neither a thief nor any purchaser through a thief can take good title[73] unless subject to the exception provided by a statute of limitations, the rightful owner may either reclaim the artwork at any point, primarily through an action in replevin[74] (an action to recover stolen artwork) or may seek damages for unlawful dominion and control of the artwork through an action in conversion[75] (an action to collect damages for unlawful dominion and control of artwork). Since all art-related civil actions are subject to statutes of limitation that may vary from state to state (usually three to five years from an event), plaintiffs are occasionally time-barred from obtaining recovery except in New York[76] and California,[77] where the concept of accrual, discussed below, may still render timely a suit brought fifty to seventy-five years after the theft.

The foreclosing potential of limitations doctrines has historically been counterbalanced by the doctrines' policies and objectives:

(1) the prompt filing of suit by a party, on the premise that those having valid claims will not delay in asserting them;

(2) the protection of a defendant after a substantial period of repose from having to defend a claim with evidence lost or destroyed by the passage of time; and

(3) the promotion of the free trade of goods by making sure that those who have dealt in good faith with property can enjoy secure possession and peace after a certain period of time.[78]

The historical bases of statutes of limitation, although valid, have forced the courts to choose between two theoretically innocent parties: the aggrieved original owner and the bona fide purchaser. The trend of judicial decisions in recent years has been to favor the aggrieved original owner.[79] When such an owner has been diligent in attempting to locate missing property, that is reasonable; purchasers often buy under suspicious circumstances without adequately investigating title. Moreover, a purchaser who loses to the aggrieved original owner often has recourse against the seller. However, when an original owner has not been diligent, the reasonableness of judicial decisions favoring that party, as in the *Guggenheim* case discussed later in this chapter, seems difficult to defend.

The Concept of Accrual

The typical statute of limitations provides that the time during which a cause of action may be brought, such as to recover artwork on a theory of replevin or to obtain damages on a theory of conversion, begins to run from the time the cause of action accrues.[80] Because accrual in most states has been left to judicial interpretation,[81] several theories of accrual pertinent to art theft victims have arisen over the years, only to be subsequently rejected by a majority of states for reasons of innate injustice.[82] One theory is accrual by adverse possession,[83] a method of transferring title to property without the owner's consent. To effect a transfer under that doctrine, the property holder must have had hostile, actual, open and notorious, exclusive, and continuous possession of the property for the duration of the limitations period. One major drawback of that theory from the possessor's perspective is that the existence of each of the above-stated elements of possession must be proved with clear and convincing evidence by the defendant-possessor before the limitations period can begin to run, and the character of possession of most artwork—that is, exclusive residential display—does not satisfy the requirement of "open and notorious" possession. Accordingly, the adverse possession theory can delay the possessor's right of repose (clear title and use) indefinitely, in contradiction to the objective of the statutes of limitation.

In the majority of states today, both an action to recover stolen artwork (replevin) and an action to collect damages for unlawful dominion and control of artwork (conversion) accrue—that is, the statute of limitations begins to run—when the possessor acquires the stolen property. In those states, the law makes no distinction between a bad-faith possessor, such as a thief, and a good-faith purchaser; in all cases, the clock begins to run when the possessor acquires possession. Although that concept of accrual certainly ensures relatively prompt repose of possession, perhaps the prospective repose is too prompt; given the private character of art ownership and the frequently confidential manner of its acquisition—whether through theft or through legitimate means, such as a public auction where consignor and buyer alike are often anonymous—the aggrieved original owner, burdened with the difficulty of locating the art, may be time-barred too soon from bringing suit. That interpretation of accrual, which is harsh for aggrieved original owners, may easily encourage those jurisdictions governed by that interpretation to become havens for stolen art.

California, as noted earlier, is, in contrast, highly protective of prior owners. Still the only state with legislation governing accrual of a cause of action involving stolen artwork or artifacts, California provides that an action must be brought within three years of "the discovery of the whereabouts" of the work "by the aggrieved party";[84] the claimant is not required to locate the work. That means that forty years, say, after a good-faith purchaser has acquired a work of art, the prior owner may not be time-barred from bringing suit either for damages or for the recovery of the artwork.

Other states, by case law, have distinguished between good-faith purchasers and all other possessors by taking one of three approaches:

(1) the demand–refusal rule,

(2) the laches approach, and

(3) the discovery rule.

Demand-Refusal Rule: New York's Former Approach

The demand-refusal rule was first proposed in New York in the 1960s in *Menzel v. List*,[85] the first case in the United States to rule directly on the statute of limitations issue in a claim to recover stolen art.[86] The New York court in *Menzel* viewed a demand by the aggrieved original owner and a refusal by the current possessor as a substantive element of both conversion and replevin. Accordingly, the court reasoned, a bona fide purchaser remained a bona fide purchaser of property until that party was notified by an aggrieved original owner of a superior claim to the property and the purchaser refused to return the property on the original owner's demand. Only then, on the demand for the return of the property by the aggrieved original owner and the refusal by the bona fide purchaser, does the clock in the statute of limitations begin to run. The court believed that in applying that rule to good-faith purchasers it was giving such purchasers the benefit of the doubt until notice was given to the contrary by the aggrieved original owner.[87] The paradoxical result of the demand-refusal rule as set forth in *Menzel* was that it indefinitely postponed accrual of a cause of action against a good-faith purchaser, thereby putting off the time when a good-faith purchaser could obtain good title and repose. Under the demand-refusal rule, no demand is necessary against a bad-faith possessor, so that the statute in a case of theft, say, begins to run immediately in favor of a bad-faith possessor. This can result in barring a suit against a thief or converter at a time when a suit against a good-faith purchaser could still be brought.[88]

To mitigate that potential unfairness, New York subsequently modified the demand-and-refusal requirement to hold that when demand and refusal are necessary to start a limitations period, the rightful owner's demand may not be unreasonably delayed after the possessor of the stolen property is identified.[89]

Then, in *DeWeerth v. Baldinger*,[90] summarized below, the rule was modified yet again. The demand-refusal requirement, which required the demand to be made without unreasonable delay, then included an obligation on the part of the aggrieved original owner to use due diligence to locate the stolen property. *DeWeerth*, in the light of the still later modification of the demand-refusal rule set forth in the subsequent *Guggenheim* case (also discussed below), gave rise to a tug-of-war between Gerda DeWeerth and Edith Baldinger over a Monet painting, *Champs de Ble à Vetheuil*, that lasted eight years.

DeWeerth *Summarized*

In 1922, the plaintiff, Gerda DeWeerth, a West German citizen, inherited from her father, a serious collector of art, a Claude Monet painting that remained in her possession until August 1943, at which time she forwarded the painting and other valuables to her sister's house in southern Germany for safekeeping during World War II. At the war's end in 1945, the sister, who had quartered American soldiers, noticed after their departure that the painting was missing and so advised Gerda DeWeerth that fall. DeWeerth exerted the following efforts on behalf of her lost Monet: In 1946, she filed a report with the military government administering the Bonn-Cologne area; in 1948, she queried her lawyer regarding insurance claims on her lost property, including the Monet; in 1955, she requested, to no avail, a former art professor to investigate the painting's whereabouts, sending him a photograph of the lost Monet; in 1957, she sent a list of her artwork lost during the war to the West German federal bureau of investigation. None of her efforts to locate the Monet were fruitful, and she gave up.

Meanwhile, the Monet surfaced on the art market in December 1956, when it was acquired on consignment by the New York gallery of Wildenstein & Co. from an art dealer in Switzerland. The painting remained in Wildenstein's possession until June 1957, when it was sold for $30,900 to defendant Edith Baldinger, a good-faith purchaser. Baldinger retained the Monet in her New York City apartment.

In 1981, DeWeerth's nephew, Peter von der Heydt, learned that his aunt had owned a Monet that had disappeared during the war. Shortly thereafter, von der Heydt identified the painting in a *catalogue raisonné* of Monet's works located in a museum less than twenty miles from where DeWeerth had been living since 1957. Through the *catalogue raisonné*, von der Heydt traced the painting to the Wildenstein gallery and then compelled Wildenstein to identify Baldinger, the current owner. In December 1982, DeWeerth by letter demanded the Monet's return, and in February 1983, Baldinger by letter refused, whereupon DeWeerth immediately initiated an action to recover her painting.

A New York federal district court ruled that DeWeerth owned the painting and ordered Baldinger to return it, finding that the action was timely, since DeWeerth had exercised reasonable diligence in searching for the painting.[91] The Second Circuit court reversed, holding that New York's limitations law includes "an obligation to attempt to locate stolen property"[92] and that DeWeerth failed to meet the diligent-search requirement by neglecting to conduct any search for the twenty-four years from 1957 to 1981. Her "failure to consult the catalogue raisonné," which enabled her nephew to trace the painting to the Wildenstein gallery within three days, was "particularly inexcusable."[93]

Therefore, under *DeWeerth*, which remained the law in New York from 1987 until February 1991, a cause of action for either replevin or conversion against a good-faith purchaser did not accrue until three factors coalesced:[94]

- The plaintiff had to demand the artwork's return, and the defendant had to refuse to comply with the demand.

- Once the plaintiff located the property, the demand had to be made with no unreasonable delay.

- To satisfy the "no unreasonable delay" requirement, the plaintiff had to use reasonable diligence in locating the stolen property.

Then, with the advent of the case of *Guggenheim v. Lubell*,[95] which is currently the law in New York, the due-diligence requirement was abolished; the aggrieved original owner may now make a demand in timely fashion under the limitations statute whenever he happens to discover the whereabouts of the lost property. Nevertheless, as seen in *Guggenheim*, the fact that an aggrieved party is able to bring timely suit forty years, for example, after the loss of his property does not preclude the current possessor of an artwork from asserting other affirmative defenses.

Laches Approach: New York's Current Law

Guggenheim v. Lubell was an action brought by the Solomon R. Guggenheim Foundation, operating the Guggenheim Museum in New York City, to recover a Marc Chagall gouache worth an estimated $200,000 from the defendant, Rachael Lubell. She and her late husband, good-faith purchasers, had bought the painting in 1967 from the art dealer Robert Elkon, and it hung in their apartment in New York City for the subsequent nineteen years, except for two occasions in 1969 and 1973, when it was exhibited publicly at the Robert Elkon Gallery.

The gouache, painted by Chagall in 1912 in preparation for an oil painting and known as both *Menageries* and *Le Marchand de Bestiaux (The Cattle Dealer)*, was acquired by the museum in 1937. It remained in the museum's possession (except for some short-term loans) until sometime after April 1965, when it was reported missing. The reported loss was not confirmed until 1969, when the museum inventoried its paintings.

In August 1985, a transparency of *Menageries* was brought to Sotheby's for an appraisal. The transparency was seen by a former employee of the Guggenheim, who identified the Chagall as the one missing from the museum's collection. After determining the identity of the art dealer's client (Rachael Lubell), the museum in January 1986 requested the return of the gouache. Lubell refused, and the museum subsequently brought an action in the New York State Supreme Court to recover the gouache. The court, relying heavily on the three-pronged rule of *DeWeerth*, dismissed the museum's suit as time-barred.

However, in January 1990, the appellate court dismissed the statute-of-limitations defense. In so doing, the court held that whether the museum was obliged to do more than it did in its quest for the gouache depends on

> whether it was unreasonable *not* to do more, and whether it was unreasonable not to do more is an issue of fact *relevant to the defense of laches* and not the statute of limitations.[96] [all italics ours]

Unlike the statute-of-limitations defense, the defense of laches signifies a delay that warrants a presumption that the aggrieved party has waived its rights; it usually involves knowledge by the aggrieved party of its rights, an unreasonable delay in exercising those rights, and a change of position working to the detriment of the defendant.[97] Laches is an affirmative defense that is based on equitable arguments. That is, to successfully assert the defense of laches, the defendant Rachael Lubell in *Guggenheim* was required to show that she was prejudiced by the museum's delay in demanding the return of the gouache. Moreover, the appellate court noted that the defendant's vigilance was as much at issue here as was the plaintiff's diligence; that is, information on the face of the bill of sale transferring the gouache to Lubell arguably raised "bright red flags" that would have generated suspicions in the mind of a prudent purchaser about the gouache's provenance, leading to further inquiries. That was another reason, according to the appellate court, why the defense should be characterized as laches.[98]

The appellate court, in citing the Uniform Commercial Code (U.C.C.),[99] noted that if Lubell was a good-faith purchaser and the gouache was not stolen, her title was superior to that of the original owner. Here, however, was an issue of fact as to whether the gouache was indeed stolen. Accordingly, the burden of proof should fall on Lubell to establish that the gouache was *not* stolen and that she thereby acquired good title to it. The court recognized that doing so was an onerous burden but concluded that the burden nevertheless

> serves to give effect to the principle that "'[persons] deal with the property in chattels or exercise acts of ownership over them at their peril.'"[100]

In February 1991, the New York Court of Appeals affirmed the holding of the appellate court and concluded that the federal court of appeals in *DeWeerth* should not have imposed a duty of reasonable diligence on the original owners for the purposes of the statute of limitations. As it noted,

> [w]hile the demand and refusal rule is not the only possible method of measuring the accrual of replevin claims, it does appear to be the rule that affords the most protection to the true owners of stolen property.[101]

The court went on to note, however, that New York case law does recognize that the true owner, having discovered the location of the lost property, cannot unreasonably delay making a demand for the return of the property.[102]

The court also noted that its decision was in part influenced by its recognition that New York enjoys a worldwide reputation as a preeminent cultural center. Further,

> [to] place the burden of locating stolen artwork on the true owner and to foreclose the rights of that owner to recover its property if the burden is not met would . . . encourage illicit trafficking in stolen art. Three years after the theft, any purchaser, good faith or not, would be able to hold onto stolen artwork unless the true owner was able to establish that it had undertaken a reasonable search for the missing art.[103]

In affirming the appellate court's order, however, the New York Court of Appeals stressed that its holding should not be viewed as sanctioning the Guggenheim Museum's conduct here and that, indeed, the defendant's contention that the museum did not exercise reasonable diligence in locating the painting should be considered by the trial judge in the context of the laches defense.[104] Accordingly, the Guggenheim Museum won the right to pursue recovery of the Chagall gouache from Lubell.

Postscript to DeWeerth

In the light of the *Guggenheim* decision, holding that for limitations purposes, the plaintiff is under no obligation to use reasonable diligence in locating his stolen property, Gerda DeWeerth, in May 1991, brought a motion before the Second Circuit to vacate the judgment in which the Second Circuit had awarded the Monet painting to the purchaser, Edith Baldinger. The Second Circuit later that month denied DeWeerth's motion without opinion.[105] In September 1991, DeWeerth moved in a New York federal district court for relief from final judgment pursuant to the Rule 60(b) of the Federal Rules of Civil Procedure. In October 1992, her motion was granted, and Baldinger was ordered to surrender the Monet to DeWeerth.[106] Judgment was entered in February 1993, and Baldinger appealed to the Second Circuit. The Second Circuit, in awarding the Monet once again to Baldinger, held in October 1994 that the federal district court abused its discretion in ruling that the

> important interest in the finality of the judgment in this case, which was more than four years old at the time of that ruling, was outweighed by any injustice DeWeerth believes she has suffered by litigating her case in the federal as opposed to state forum.[107]

The next month, DeWeerth petitioned the United States Supreme Court for certiorari, which was denied.[108] And so it appears that the Monet shall remain with Baldinger.

Laches Reinforced in New York

In New York, subsequent to the *Guggenheim* case, the Republic of Turkey sought to recover from the Metropolitan Museum of Art artifacts exported to the United States in contravention of Turkish law.[109] Citing the New York appellate division's decision in *Guggenheim*, a New York federal district court in July 1990 ruled that Turkey was not time-barred from bringing suit and that any claims by the museum of unreasonable delay on the part of Turkey in bringing suit would be relevant to a defense based on laches, not the statute of limitations. The case was settled in September 1993 with the Metropolitan Museum's agreement to return certain gold and silver items to Turkey.

In *Hoelzer v. City of Stamford*,[110] a subsequent suit recalling *Guggenheim*, an art restorer who had for many years been in possession of a massive set of six mural paintings created in the 1930s was ordered by the United States Court of Appeals in May 1991 to return the murals to the city of Stamford, Connecticut. In that case, the six murals, painted by the artist James Daugherty and commissioned by the federal government's Works Progress Administration (WPA) during the Great Depression of the 1930s, had from 1934 to 1970 hung on the walls of a music room in Stamford High School, a public school operated by the defendant city of Stamford. In 1970, the school underwent major renovation and, contrary to the school's instruction to retain the murals, they were removed from the walls by workmen and placed, with construction debris, in a heap near the outside dumpster. A student, recognizing their value, retrieved them from the trash and later turned them over to the General Services Administration (GSA), the federal agency in charge of locating and preserving WPA art. In 1971, the government delivered the murals for restoration to Hiram Hoelzer, an art restorer from Armonk, New York, and the plaintiff in this case.

Hoelzer, understanding that he would eventually be compensated for his efforts and believing the artwork to be the property of the federal government, accepted the murals, commenced preliminary restoration procedures, and kept them in storage for a number of years while awaiting compensation.

In 1980, Hoelzer was visited by an official of the Stamford public school system and also by a Ph.D. candidate at the City University of New York. On each occasion, Hoelzer was told that the murals should be placed again in the city of Stamford. In 1981, Hoelzer complained to the GSA that it was abandoning him with the murals without their being relocated and without any compensation to him.

Sometime during the summer of 1986, the GSA informed Hoelzer, as yet uncompensated for his services, that the murals were the property of Stamford High School. Shortly thereafter, the city of Stamford requested that Hoelzer return the murals. In October 1986, Hoelzer responded that the murals were his, that they had been abandoned by Stamford more than fifteen years before, and that he would be willing to sell them for a fair price. The murals had been appraised by Sotheby's at $1.25 million and by the firm of Connecticut Fine Arts at between $90,000 and $100,000. In 1989, Hoelzer brought an action against the city of Stamford, seeking a declaratory judgment to quiet title in the murals; he claimed, among other points, that Stamford unreasonably delayed its demand for return of the artwork and, accordingly, that the statute of limitations for its claim had expired.

In affirming a New York federal district court's holding[111] that title rested with the city of Stamford, the Second Circuit, citing *Guggenheim*, concluded, among other points:

> [W]e note that this case gives us an opportunity to implement
> what has become the law of the State of New York, namely, that
> there is no due diligence requirement affecting running of stat-
> ute of limitations in actions for repossession of lost or stolen
> art.[112]

The *Guggenheim* approach was upheld yet again by the Second
Circuit in 1991 in the *Golden Buddha*[113] case, in which, in vacating a
judgment by a New York federal district court, the court held that as
some of the defendants could have received some of the disputed
treasure trove honestly, the statute of limitations would not begin to
run until there was a demand for the treasure's return and a refusal on
the part of those defendants—that is, the limitations period was
tolled (stopped temporarily) for the seventeen years that the plaintiff
was unable to make a demand for the return of the treasure, and any
unreasonable delay was pertinent solely to a laches defense. In that
case, the plaintiff was the assignee-in-interest of a party who in 1971
had unearthed a treasure trove that had been hidden in the Philip-
pines by Japanese occupation forces during World War II. The
trove—which consisted of gold bullion, precious stones, jewelry, artwork, coins, and a golden buddha—was allegedly stolen by Ferdinand and Imelda Marcos under color of law. The Marcoses reputedly
entered into a scheme with the defendant-entities to hide the treasure and to convert it and its proceeds into realty and personal property in New York for the Marcoses' own use.

The Trouble with Laches

Under New York law, as expressed in *Guggenheim*, the bona fide
purchaser of an artwork, when sued by an aggrieved original owner,
may assert as a defense the doctrine of laches. To do so, however, the
purchaser must prove (1) the original owner's unreasonable and inexcusable delay in bringing suit *and* (2) prejudice (or harm) to the
purchaser resulting from that delay.[114] Proving those facts places a
heavy evidentiary burden on the purchaser; as the crux of an investigation into delay focuses on its unreasonableness, rather than on its
length, it may be difficult to amass documentary evidence as to a de-

lay's unreasonableness, since over the passage of, say, forty or fifty years, such evidence may well be lost or destroyed. Moreover, a court may be hard-pressed, as in the case of *Guggenheim*, to perceive any harm accruing to a purchaser who, because of the aggrieved original owner's delay, enjoys protracted possession of and pleasure in a work of art. In addition, a laches investigation—involving, as it does, a "multi-factor balancing of all the equities"[115]—precludes any bright-line rules of guidance and virtually ensures protracted (read "expensive") litigation. The *Guggenheim* demand-refusal rule, coupled with a laches defense that stresses the unreasonableness, rather than the length, of the delay, tilts the balance far too unfairly, it seems, in favor of an aggrieved original owner, particularly when such an owner is not diligent and the bona fide purchaser is.[116]

Laches Revisited

When asserted by an innocent purchaser of artwork, the laches defense can bar a replevin or conversion action brought by the artwork's original owner if the court finds the defendant can prove that two events have occurred. The defendant must show, first, that the plaintiff unreasonably and inexcusably delayed commencing the suit and, second, that the defendant was prejudiced as a result of such delay.[117] Determination of whether laches can be used to bar an action is a fact-sensitive inquiry that is made on a case-by-case basis. As a result, an objective standard for making such a determination does not exist, and the few criteria or guidelines that have been set forth are of little assistance in clarifying whether an action should be defeated on the basis of laches.

In determining whether a delay is unreasonable, courts have focused not on the length of plaintiff's delay in filing the claim, but rather on the reasonableness of plaintiff's actions. This inquiry includes measures actually taken by the plaintiff, measures potentially available to the plaintiff, and measures the plaintiff should have taken.[118] A court generally considers the plaintiff's "diligence," or lack thereof, in searching for or attempting to recover his lost or stolen artwork. Since *Guggenheim*,[119] any claim asserting unreasonable delay and questioning the plaintiff's diligence became pertinent solely to a laches defense, as opposed to a statute of limitations defense.

If a defendant is able to prove that a plaintiff unreasonably delayed bringing suit, the court must then consider whether the delay (or in other words, plaintiff's lack of diligence) prejudiced the defendant in some way. There are two general categories of prejudice that will support a defense of laches: (1) loss of evidence that would support the defendant's position, such as lost documents, death of witnesses, or faded memories and (2) a material change in the defendant's position that would not have occurred but for the delay, including changes in the law, a change of title, or other intervening equities or harm caused by plaintiff's delay.[120] In *Robins Island Preservation Fund, Inc. v. Southold Development Corp.*,[121] the Second Circuit expressed itself similarly, stating that

> [a] defendant may suffer prejudice either because it would be inequitable, in light of a change in defendant's position, to allow plaintiff's claim to proceed or because the delay makes it difficult to garner evidence to vindicate his or her rights.

But often cases dealing with the laches defense in the context of stolen or lost artwork do not discuss concretely what constitutes prejudice or unreasonable delay because their fact-specific nature requires they be sent to trial. *Guggenheim*[122] is one such example, where the question of whether the museum exercised reasonable diligence in locating the painting was an issue to be considered solely by the trial judge in the context of the laches defense. A more recent example, discussed below, is that of *Czartoryski-Borbon v. Turcotte*,[123] where the court reserved for trial the question of plaintiff's family's due diligence in locating stolen artwork. Both cases were ultimately settled, leaving it unclear as to how the laches defense would have fared at trial.

Other cases, however, have specified more clearly what constitutes laches. In *Hutchinson v. Horowitz*,[124] also discussed below, the defense of laches successfully defeated an action in replevin. There, the court held that the unreasonable delay of nearly 100 years in commencing the suit prejudiced the defendant because there were no witnesses left with personal knowledge of the events surrounding the original or any subsequent disposition of the painting at issue. Similarly, in *Greek Orthodox Patriarchate of Jerusalem v. Christie's*,[125] the court held that the laches defense barred the plaintiff's claim because plaintiff was not diligent, having failed to search for its missing manuscript for seventy years, and defendant suffered prejudice because the seventy-year delay made it difficult to garner evidence for defendant to prove ownership. Further, the critical witness was deceased, memories had faded, and key documents were missing.

Still, these more recent cases do not give much additional insight into what is necessary to assert a successful laches defense. In particular, it remains somewhat difficult to understand what constitutes prejudice. Aside from the initial two categories of prejudice mentioned above, the cases do not introduce any other examples or facts that would support a finding of prejudice as a result of an unreasonably long delay in bringing suit.

As noted above, *Czartoryski-Borbon v. Turcotte*[126] was ultimately settled, so a decision on the laches defense was not reached. There, the plaintiff, Prince Czartoryski, brought an action in replevin for the return of a painting allegedly stolen from his family when the Nazis invaded Poland during World War II. The painting allegedly belonged to the Czartoryski family for more than 100 years and was part of the Czartoryski Collection, located in a museum of the same name in Krakow, Poland.[127] During the German occupation, the painting was seized and held in the National Museum of Warsaw until the museum was looted by the Germans in April 1942 and the painting subsequently disappeared.[128] The art gallery M. Knoedler and Company sold the painting in 1963 to defendant's mother, who subsequently gave it to her son, the defendant, Turcotte. The plaintiff first learned of the painting's whereabouts in January 1997 when the defendant consigned it to auction at Sotheby's. The plaintiff immediately undertook steps to claim the painting, and Sotheby's notified defendant of the plaintiff's claim. The defendant refused to return the painting.

As *Guggenheim*[129] made clear, under New York law an owner whose property has been stolen has a right to recover that property

through a replevin action even if it is in the possession of a good-faith
purchaser for value. In examining the record, the court concluded
that the painting was in fact stolen from the Czartoryski family.
Guggenheim also stated that the three-year statute of limitations begins to run when the owner demands the return of the property and
the possessor refuses to return it, and that the plaintiff need not exercise "due diligence" in attempting to locate the stolen property to
defeat a statute of limitations defense. Prince Czartoryski clearly satisfied the statute of limitations period, having demanded the return
of the painting, having been refused, and then having commenced
the action in May 1997 after learning of defendant's intention to sell
in January.

However, the court noted, as *Guggenheim* established "due diligence" in an attempt to locate the property must be shown to defeat
the laches defense argued by the defendant. The burden of proof in
establishing laches is on the party raising the defense (the defendant),
and that party must establish that there was an unreasonable delay and
that the delay resulted in prejudice to the defendant. The prince argued that laches should not apply because the various registers and
listings of art stolen by the Nazis were not available to Polish citizens
under Communist rule. But that argument failed because the prince,
a subject of England, had never lived in Poland and evidence showed
that numerous members of his family (including the one from whom
he inherited the painting) may have resided in Western Europe during the fourteen years that elapsed between the end of the war and
defendant's mother's purchase of the painting. The court stated that

> it would appear that plaintiff has not taken steps to research the
> whereabouts of the painting or to put the art world on notice of
> its claim since apparently Sotheby's learned of the claim only
> days before the scheduled auction. It is therefore unclear from
> the record before the court whether the Prince's family exer-
> cised due diligence in pursuing their claim before defendant's
> mother purchased the painting in 1959. At trial, the court will
> have the opportunity to consider whether, under all the cir-
> cumstances, the Czartoryskis were diligent in pursuing their
> claim.[130]

The court denied both parties' motions for summary judgment, and, as noted above, the case was settled on a confidential basis.

The decision in *Czartoryski-Borbon v. Turcotte* can be contrasted with that of *Hutchinson v. Horowitz*,[131] where the New York State Supreme Court dismissed plaintiffs' replevin action on the basis of a laches defense and granted defendant's motion for summary judgment. There, the plaintiffs, descendants of the heirs of painter Theodore Robinson, sought in September 1997 to recover a painting entitled *Low Tide—Riverside Yacht Club*, bought in 1964 by the defendant from Parke-Bernet Galleries (now Sotheby's). They alleged that the painting was actually stolen either from an 1896 auction of Robinson's estate or while on exhibit at about the time of his death.[132]

Four years after acquiring the painting, defendant wrote to Robert Hutchinson, a descendant of Robinson, informing him of his ownership of the painting and another by Robinson, and of his interest in acquiring more of Robinson's work. Robert Hutchinson died in January 1997, before any sales between the two were consummated. His sister Anne, who had researched Robinson's paintings, predeceased her brother by two years. The plaintiffs, children of both Robert and his brother, demanded return of the painting in a letter dated September 22, 1994, to which defendant several days later refused, prompting the filing of this action on September 26, 1997.

The defendant moved for summary judgment, claiming the action was barred by the statute of limitations and the laches defense. With regard to the statute of limitations defense, the defendant contended that Robinson's heirs, having known of defendant's possession since 1968, unreasonably delayed making a demand upon them by waiting until 1994. Plaintiffs, in response, contended that the 1968 letter was sent to the descendants of Robinson's brother, not themselves, and that neither the 1968 letter, nor the two-year delay from discovering the painting missing in 1992[133] until the demand for its return in 1994, can be determined as unreasonable. Under *Guggenheim*, the court noted, a party may not unreasonably delay making demand upon a person in possession of property. This rule applies equally to stolen works of art. In holding that the plaintiffs' delay was unreasonable as a matter of law, the court particularly focused on plaintiffs' failure to discover the painting missing for decades and their involvement in similar litigation with respect to other paintings since 1980. Plaintiffs then argued that since under *Guggenheim* there is no duty of due diligence, the statute of limitations cannot be applied to anyone other than the heirs of Robert Hutchinson, since it was he who received defendant's letter in 1968. The court was unpersuaded by this rationale, finding that "since all plaintiffs purportedly own[ed] the painting jointly . . . the knowledge of one [plaintiff] is imputed to all."

The defendant also contended that even if the action was not barred by the statute of limitations, it should still be barred by the defense of laches because plaintiffs and their predecessors never asserted a claim to the painting until twenty-six years after receiving notice that the defendant owned the painting (via the 1968 letter) and nearly 100 years after the alleged theft. Plaintiffs responded that they did not know of the facts giving rise to their action until 1992 and 1994, so they could not be charged with laches before those dates. Under *Guggenheim*, the court noted, a laches defense takes into consideration not only the actual knowledge of a plaintiff, but also what a plaintiff should know.[134] Here, plaintiffs relied on documents dated from 1926 as evidence of the theft, but offered no explanation as to why no inquiry was pursued for nearly seventy years. As such their delay was unreasonable. The court also found that the lack of witnesses with personal knowledge of the events surrounding the original or subsequent dispositions of the painting would be prejudicial to defendant[135] and agreed that had plaintiffs raised their claim in a timely fashion, the issue of ownership would have been resolved long before defendant's purchase of the painting. In dismissing the action on the basis of laches, the court stated that

> [t]o allow a claim now, a century after the alleged theft, would place an onerous burden on anyone owning old artwork . . . such [that it] could always be subject to claims by descendants of improper transfer.[136]

The rationale for granting defendant summary judgment in *Hutchinson* was followed in *Greek Orthodox Patriarchate of Jerusalem v. Christie's, Inc.*[137] There, the plaintiff sought return of a 174-page palimpsest (a text whose original writing has been washed off so that the paper may be reused) written in the tenth century and believed to be the oldest and most authentic copies of Archimedes' treatises *On Floating Bodies* and *Method of Mechanical Theorems.*[138] Sometime in the twelfth or thirteenth century, the original lettering of the manuscript was partially washed away and written over with Greek liturgical text. The palimpsest was at some point housed in a monastery library in Palestine, whose collection in the nineteenth century was incorporated into the Library of the Patriarchate of Jerusalem. Hundreds of manuscripts, including the palimpsest, were subsequently transferred to the Metochion monastery in what was then Constantinople. Scholarly documentation verified the existence of the palimpsest in the Metochion collection as late as 1909, but it was unclear what happened to it after that point and before it was acquired by a French collector in the 1920s. The circumstances surrounding that acquisition were also unknown.[139] The plaintiff asserted that it must have been stolen by either the French collector or a third party because the Metochion had no authority to sell or remove the manuscript without the Patriarchate's permission, but it has been suggested that a monk from the Patriarchate may have sold the palimpsest to the collector[140] or that it may have been lost in the Turkish civil war that followed the First World War.[141]

After 1947, the collector's daughter, co-defendant Anne Guersan, became the custodian of the palimpsest, and sometime after inheriting it, she showed it in the 1960s to a number of professors to evaluate its condition. Eventually, concern over its deterioration led her in 1970 to have a professor from Hebrew University in Jerusalem and a clergyman from a historical research center in France work to preserve the manuscript. The preservationists also advised Guersan of the palimpsest's provenance, which prompted the Guersan family to consider its sale. In the early 1970s, they printed two hundred copies of a brochure describing the palimpsest in English and French for this purpose, and although several inquiries were made, a sale was not consummated.[142] But in March 1993, the Guersan family consigned the palimpsest to Christie's. After an initial denial of export authorization, the French Ministry of Culture granted an export license in early 1996, and after undergoing further study at Oxford University, the palimpsest was brought to New York in 1998 for auction. On August 13, 1998, Christie's informed the State of Greece of the auction planned for October 28. One week before the auction, the plaintiff notified Christie's that it believed itself to be the rightful owner of the palimpsest, and on the day of the auction it sought a temporary restraining order to prevent the auction. The request was rejected and the palimpsest sold the next day for $2 million. The Patriarchate then filed this action, and defendants moved for summary judgment.[143]

The court concluded that the laches defense asserted by the defendants barred the Patriarchate's claim to the palimpsest after finding that there was unreasonable delay by the plaintiff that resulted in unfair prejudice toward the defendant, citing the previously discussed *Robins Island* and *Czartoryski* cases. The court noted that New York law strongly favors the rights of original owners,[144] but that nevertheless, *Guggenheim* and its progeny "allow a significant role for the laches defense."[145] To defeat a defense of laches in the context of lost or stolen art has meant that a plaintiff must show due diligence in attempting to locate the stolen property.[146] Though ordinarily the fact-specific nature of the inquiry and the weighing of competing interests lend themselves better to application of the defense at trial, here, the court noted, where the record was sufficiently clear to determine whether the plaintiff was or was not diligent for purposes of summary judgment, *Elicofon*[147] allowed the court to make that determination alone.[148] The record suggested that the plaintiff was unaware that the palimpsest had been missing, despite its absence from the Metochion collection since the 1930s. Still, the plaintiff, prior to this action, failed to assert any claim to other Metochion manuscripts or announce that any were missing, despite knowledge that such manuscripts had, since the 1930s and 1940s, been publicly claimed to be owned by and displayed as part of the collections of the Bibliothèque Nationale de France, the University of Chicago, and the

Cleveland Museum of Art. Nor had the plaintiff, before the announcement of the auction, shown any great interest in the palimpsest. These facts, in combination with the plaintiff's lack of effort to inquire into the palimpsest's whereabouts for seventy years, weighed against the plaintiff with regard to diligence.[149]

Again citing *Robins Island*, the court noted that in balancing the equities raised by the laches defense, it must also be determined whether

> "[a] defendant may suffer prejudice either because it would be inequitable, in light of a change in defendant's position, to allow plaintiff's claim to proceed or because the delay makes it difficult to garner evidence to vindicate his or her rights."[150]

Here, the court asserted that there were difficulties in garnering evidence, as well as difficulties resulting from the large distance over which the transfer of title may have occurred (in Constantinople, Paris, or any point in between). Though Guersan provided no evidence to prove her good-faith acquisition of the manuscript—no receipt, bill of sale, or other evidence to support its valid purchase—the court reasoned that the Patriarchate's seventy-year delay in claiming ownership of the palimpsest rendered it virtually impossible for the Guersan family to prove ownership.[151] Specifically, the court noted that the critical witness (Guersan's father) was deceased, memories had faded, and key documents (if they existed at all) were missing. With no opportunity for defendant to obtain witnesses or gather evidence, the court held, the Patriarchate's delay rendered defendant's case much more difficult to prove, an inequity that under the doctrine of laches barred plaintiff's claim.

The factors taken into consideration by the court in balancing the equities accord well with the *DeWeerth*[152] line of reasoning, and as the court correctly pointed out, though there has been disagreement between the New York Court of Appeals and the Second Circuit as to the role of a plaintiff's diligence with regard to a statute of limitations defense, "both courts have explicitly ruled that the claimant's reasonable diligence in locating the lost property is highly relevant to a laches defense."[153] Thus, while the *DeWeerth* court was wrong to analyze the plaintiff's diligence in the context of a statute of limitations defense, its analysis was correct with regard to a defense of laches.[154]

Perhaps more important than awarding defendant summary judgment on the basis of the laches defense was the court's second line of reasoning: that French law, rather than New York law, should apply to award defendant title by prescription.[155] Acquisition of title by prescription is similar to acquiring title by adverse possession (discussed at page 268). To acquire title by prescription under French law, the possession must be continuous and uninterrupted, peaceful, public, unequivocal, and as the owner for thirty years.[156] To determine that French law applied, the court relied upon *Elicofon* and the *Restatement (Second) of Conflict of Laws*, which states in part, "[W]hether there has been a transfer of interest in [artwork]. . . is determined by the local law of the state where the [artwork] was at the time the transfer is claimed to have taken place."[157] In the court's opinion, the relevant transfer of title was not from "Guersan to Christie's, or from Christie's to the Purchaser," but that which occurred, if at all, in France, "from the Patriarchate to [Guersan's father]."[158] After determining that French law applied, the court focused its inquiry on whether defendant "publicly" possessed the palimpsest. Though there was no overwhelming evidence of public possession for the entire thirty-year prescriptive period, the court held that the abundance of evidence of public possession in the early 1970s was essentially close enough without evidence from the plaintiff to suggest that defendant either kept the palimpsest hidden or had motive to do so.[159] Regardless of which law applied, the court noted, the result would be the same simply by virtue of defendant's successful laches defense.[160]

The application of French law in *Greek Orthodox Patriarchate* is in sharp contrast to the decisions of *Menzel v. List*,[161] *DeWeerth*,[162] *Elicofon*,[163] *Greek Orthodox Church of Cyprus*,[164] and *Hutchinson*,[165] all of which involved art whose title was allegedly transferred outside the United States, yet whose opinions either do not even raise the question of foreign law or treat the choice of law issue briefly and choose to apply U.S. law. This approach with regard to choice of law is surprising.[166] Perhaps U.S. courts are not happy with an automatic thirty-year rule and prefer the equitable approach dictated by laches.

In *Wertheimer v. Cirker's Hayes Storage Warehouse*,[167] a still more recent New York State court decision, the choice of law question again arose within the context of a laches defense. The facts that gave rise to *Wertheimer* were not unlike those in *Czartoryski-Borbon* and in *DeWeerth*. The plaintiff, Alain Wertheimer, grandson of the original owner, alleged that a painting, *La Seine—la passerelle de L'Institut, au fond, les quais et le Louvre* by Camille Pissaro, was misappropriated and sold by a person to whom the grandfather's family had entrusted it when the family fled Nazi-occupied France. In a replevin action, the plaintiff sought to recover the painting from the defendant art gallery, which had purchased it for $500,000. The person entrusted with the Wertheimer family's art collection was in 1947 convicted on criminal charges by a French court, and though most of the family's collection was recovered, the painting at issue was not. It was listed on the 1947 "List of Property Removed from France During the War 1939–45," and the grandfather continued to search for its whereabouts throughout the late 1940s and early 1950s, writing letters to a number of European governments charged with recovering lost art.[168]

But after those initial efforts, the family in the 1950s abandoned its attempts to locate the painting and failed to realize that it was advertised for sale between 1951 and 1954 at a New York gallery. The purchaser, a resident of Switzerland, ultimately sold the painting through a series of private transactions to the defendant gallery in 1999.[169] In addition to the family's failure to become aware of the painting during its long period of display, notwithstanding the grandfather's residence in New York at that time, the family failed to take further action to locate the painting, such as contacting the Art Loss Registry or reporting the painting as missing to galleries or museums. The family's lack of diligence, in the court's opinion, substantially prejudiced the defendant by making it virtually impossible for the defendant to prove that any of its predecessors in interest had acquired good title, since none of the parties to the original transaction were alive.[170] Although plaintiff alleged that the defendant had reason to know of the painting's misappropriation, either because it had been obtained by the previous owner during World War II or its immediate aftermath or because of conflicting reports of its provenance and suspicion about its background expressed by another dealer,[171] the court held the action barred by the laches defense.

Regarding the choice of law question, the court cited the *Greek Orthodox Patriarchate* court as authority for deciding that the governing law was that of the jurisdiction in which the property was located at the time of transfer, which in this case was Arizona.[172] But in deciding that Arizona law governed, the *Wertheimer* court did not look to what the *Patriarchate* court would have deemed the "relevant" transaction: the transfer to the Swiss owner. Rather, the court did not even opine that the case may have been governed by Swiss law, which may have warranted the same result of title by prescription to the previous owner as in *Patriarchate*. Furthermore, despite applying Arizona substantive law, the court adhered to the procedural rules of New York, which for plaintiff meant that the action was not time-barred by the statute of limitations or New York's rules governing accrual.[173] Simply put, had the defendant not successfully asserted a defense of laches, plaintiff would have succeeded in his claim and regained possession of his painting, since the claim was not barred by the applicable statute of limitations under New York law. The same result would likely not be true had the court applied Swiss law.

On appeal, the court upheld the decision to dismiss the case, ruling that the doctrine of unclean hands did not bar the defendant art gallery's laches defense despite its alleged knowledge of the painting's questionable provenance and its failure to investigate it further prior to purchase.[174] The court correctly pointed out that the gallery's alleged failure to make reasonable inquiry into the background of the painting before buying it in 1999, and its alleged creation and use of a false provenance to help resell the painting, did not prejudice the plaintiff.

Though the court in *Wertheimer* determined that plaintiff's initial efforts of several years (later abandoned) in trying to relocate his stolen art, which included listing it as stolen with an official registry and contacting officials of numerous European governments, did not constitute "due diligence," what is necessary for due diligence remains unclear.

In *United States v. Fireman's Fund Insurance Co.*,[175] a New York federal district court rejected an argument that due diligence requires giving notice of an artwork's theft to the art community at large, IFAR, or law enforcement officials beyond those of the locality. Instead, the court concluded that the aggrieved owner of a stolen painting responded in an "appropriate and reasonable" fashion by promptly contacting the local (Old Westbury, New York) police upon the painting's theft and then promptly contacting the FBI upon learning of its whereabouts.[176] Nor was the insurer of the painting, who had already paid out its claim, required to do more. Though the period between the work's disappearance and its resurfacing was brief compared to that of *Wertheimer*,[177] the opinion implies no sort of continued post-theft vigilance on the part of the aggrieved owner, in contrast to the *Wertheimer* decision.

The court noted that its decision to grant summary judgment was, in part, influenced by the possessor's failure to provide specific information to support a laches defense and the possessor's own failure to exercise diligence in discovering the painting's theft. The prospective purchaser (not an art dealer) from the possessor easily discovered that the painting was stolen.[178]

The Current Trend

It appears as if the laches defense is becoming stronger against claims of stolen works of art, at least in New York State, where under *Guggenheim*'s demand-and-refusal rule a claim can arise many years after a work of art is lost or stolen. In order to counter the laches defense, the plaintiff must be able to show (as the court in *DeWeerth* thought the law in New York should be with respect to the statute of limitations) that there was a reasonable continuing diligence in trying to locate the stolen property.

Discovery Rule

A number of states, including California,[179] New Jersey,[180] Indiana,[181] Ohio,[182] Pennsylvania,[183] and Oklahoma,[184] have developed a discovery rule for the recovery of stolen art; that is, the court determines when a diligent owner would or should have discovered the stolen property for purposes of commencing the running of the limitations statute. In *O'Keeffe v. Snyder*,[185] for example, the artist Georgia O'Keeffe in 1976 sued a bona fide purchaser for the return of three paintings allegedly stolen in 1946 from an art gallery operated by her husband, the photographer Alfred Stieglitz. Over the years, O'Keeffe made casual and sporadic attempts to locate the missing paintings, which ultimately turned up in a gallery in 1975. The New Jersey Supreme Court, in adopting an equitable discovery rule, noted that

> O'Keeffe's cause of action accrued when she first knew, or reasonably should have known, through the exercise of due diligence, of the cause of action, including the identity of the possessor of the paintings.[186]

Because of open factual issues, including the question of O'Keeffe's diligence, the court remanded for a full trial.

In Indiana, the U.S. Court of Appeals for the Seventh Circuit, in a case popularly known as the *Byzantine Mosaics*,[187] awarded their possession to the Church of Cyprus. Both the Church and the Republic of Cyprus had sought to recover the mosaics, which had been stolen from the Church and ultimately purchased by a gallery owner in Indiana. In making the award, the court dismissed the defendant-gallery's argument that the suit was untimely, noting that Cyprus's cause of action for recovery of the mosaics accrued, within the meaning of Indiana's statute of limitations for replevin actions, when Cyprus learned that the mosaics were in the possession of the defendant and that Cyprus exercised due diligence in searching for the mosaics.

In *Helen Charash v. Oberlin College*,[188] the Sixth Circuit, in applying Ohio law and remanding the case for further proceedings in

1994, noted that in Ohio a cause of action for conversion or replevin must be brought within four years after the cause of action accrues and that such a cause of action does not accrue "until the wrongdoer is discovered" either by actual or constructive knowledge. Plaintiff Helen Charash, the administrator and sole heir of the estate of her sister, the artist Eva Hesse, sued Oberlin College more than twenty years after her sister's death, accusing the college of converting forty-four Eva Hesse drawings that were allegedly misappropriated by a New York art dealer (since deceased), whose brother, in turn, donated the drawings to Oberlin College. Although it was conceded by Oberlin College that Charash lacked actual notice that the drawings in question were in Oberlin's possession, the Sixth Circuit held that there was a genuine issue of fact as to whether Charash had constructive notice of such possession.

In *Gregory Erisoty v. Jacqueline Rizik*,[189] a federal district court applied the discovery rule under Pennsylvania law to determine accrual and in 1995 awarded an aggrieved original owner title to and possession of an eighteenth-century masterpiece by Corrado Giaquinto entitled *Winter*. The masterpiece was stolen from the owner's mother's house in July 1960 and was discovered by a furniture removal company in March 1988 in a plastic trash bag; the artwork had been torn into five pieces. The company consigned the artwork to a Philadelphia auction house to be sold at auction, and it was purchased in 1989 by the plaintiff, a professional conservator. In 1992, the aggrieved original owner, who in 1960 had immediately reported the artwork's theft to the police and the FBI and who over the next thirty years continued to search for the artwork, reported to IFAR (about whose existence he had just learned) the theft of *Winter*. IFAR, working in conjunction with the FBI, tracked the painting to the plaintiff, removed the painting from the plaintiff, and ultimately returned it to the original owner. The plaintiff, after unsuccessfully demanding the return of the artwork, sued for declaratory and injunctive relief. The court, in weighing all the relevant factors to be considered in applying the discovery rule, noted, among many other points, that the original owner was reasonably diligent over the years in searching for the masterpiece and that the plaintiff bought the painting without inquiring into the painting's prior ownership or the consignor's identity or making any inquiry with art or law enforcement agencies and with knowledge that the painting was in five pieces.

As noted earlier, California is the only state where deferred accrual of a claim to recover stolen artwork until the theft victim's discovery of the whereabouts of the property is made explicit in a statute. The statute was adopted in 1983,[190] but two cases dealing with art stolen before 1983 that are still relevant are discussed below.

In *Naftzger v. American Numismatic Society*,[191] gold coins were stolen from the society at some time before 1970. The theft had remained undetected because the thief had substituted similar coins of less value. The society learned that some of the coins were in the possession of a collector, Roy Naftzger, who had purchased them in good faith from the alleged thief. The society immediately notified Naftzger of its claim to the stolen coins and demanded their return. Naftzger refused to return the coins and went into Los Angeles County Superior Court in 1993 to obtain declaratory relief and to quiet title to the coins. The society filed a cross-complaint against Naftzger to recover the coins.

In 1994, the trial court ruled in favor of Naftzger. The court found that the statute of limitations on the filing of an action in replevin had already run against the society. The court ruled that the statute in force at the time of the theft provided for a three-year limit, beginning from the time of the accrual of the cause of action, which was the occurrence of the theft. The court rejected the society's argument that the version of the statute adopted in 1983 should be applied retroactively.

The California Court of Appeal for the Second District reversed the trial court when it held that a discovery rule of accrual requiring the theft victim's actual discovery of the possessor's identity was implicit in the pre-1983 version of the statute of limitations that applied to the recovery of stolen personal property.[192] Accordingly, the society, which filed its action only months after discovering that Naftzger had the coins, had filed its action within the time limit. The court also ruled that whether the society had used due diligence in tracking down the stolen items was of no consequence under the pre-1983 discovery rule.[193]

That holding is restricted to the pre-1983 version of the statute of limitations. *Naftzger* makes it clear that under the current statute of limitations in California only claims to recover articles of "historical, interpretive, scientific or artistic significance" will be delayed by the discovery rule.[194] The court expressed no opinion as to whether, in actions brought in common law or in equity, the plaintiff would be time-barred by laches or placed at a disadvantage by the lack of reasonable diligence in identifying the person in possession of the property. Although the theft victim's diligence is not a component of the *Naftzger* discovery rule, it is still an important factor in the contest for title to stolen art. A theft victim who fails to act reasonably to locate stolen art could be exposed to a laches defense even under *Naftzger.*

The *Naftzger* case should be compared with *Society of California Pioneers v. Baker,*[195] in which a gold cane handle was stolen from the society in 1978 and subsequently passed through a number of hands until Baker, a good-faith buyer, purchased it in 1991. In 1992, the society learned that Baker had the cane handle and filed a replevin action against him. The trial court ruled for Baker, reasoning that the pre-1983, three-year statute of limitations on actions in replevin had run against the society, since the time period began to run when the cause of action accrued—that is, at the time of the theft. The California Court of Appeal reversed and held for the society, finding that the starting time for the pre-1983 statute of limitations was to be reinstated each time the stolen object changed hands. Since the cane handle changed ownership in 1980, the statute was still running when the 1983 amendment became law. Accordingly, the court held that the 1983 statute applied and that the cause of action accrued in 1992, when the society discovered that Baker had the cane handle. Significantly, in a footnote, the court implied that under the amended California statute the discovery standard may be one of constructive notice; therefore, the question of reasonable diligence has some bearing on that issue, since, under the constructive standard, one is sometimes charged with notice of what a reasonable inquiry may disclose.[196]

The court acknowledged that its interpretation of the pre-1983 statute was broader than the rule under the amended statute in that the pre-1983 discovery rule of accrual applies to *any* stolen item, whereas the current rule applies only to objects of historical, interpretive, scientific, or artistic significance.

Drawbacks to the Discovery Rule

The discovery rule is fact-sensitive and fact-intensive. In determining whether to apply the rule, a court must consider and weigh all the relevant factors in a given case. The following list of factors is by no means exhaustive:

(1) the nature of the injury,

(2) the time elapsed since the initial wrongful act,

(3) the availability and the quality of witnesses,

(4) the availability and the quality of physical evidence,

(5) whether an inference can be drawn that the delay was intentional,

(6) whether and to what extent the defendant was prejudiced by the delay,

(7) whether the original owner acted reasonably in searching for the stolen work, and

(8) whether the good-faith purchaser acted reasonably in inquiring about the provenance of the purchased work.

Such information is not generally obtainable without discovery proceedings and a trial, normally a lengthy and costly process. Moreover, such a matrix of factors must be evaluated on a case-by-case basis, which necessarily permits a certain subjective element to influence a given outcome. Moreover, as noted by at least one commentator, under the discovery rule, as with the demand-refusal rule, a bona fide purchaser can never be certain of enjoying repose of title, because there is no definitive date from which the limitations period begins to run.[197]

Bright-Line Rules As a Solution

If the courts adopted uniform bright-line rules to determine title by establishing a hierarchy of preferences, such rules would, it seems to us, be far more equitable for aggrieved original owners and bona fide purchasers alike. A number of commentators have proposed the adoption of bright-line rules.[198] The idea that we find particularly intriguing proposes legislation, ultimately federal legislation but initially state legislation, encouraging aggrieved owners to register stolen artwork with a confidential, computerized international stolen-art registry. Such owners, in the words of the commentators,

> would be protected against a limitations claim by subsequent purchasers. Correspondingly, a purchaser who consulted the registry at the time of purchase would be protected by a three-year limitations period from the date of purchase.[199]

Under that proposal, as the commentators go on to note, so long as a registered owner used reasonable diligence in searching for the art, his time to commence suit would be tolled indefinitely against a subsequent buyer. At the same time, once the purchaser checked the registry and determined that the artwork in question had not been registered, the three-year statute would begin to run in the purchaser's favor. If neither party used the registry, a discovery rule would apply.[200]

We expect New York State to be among the first to introduce a new law addressing title to artworks that balances the rights of innocent owners and innocent buyers based on a policy of computerized registration compliance.

California Holocaust Exception

California enacted a special rule, effective January 1, 2004, allowing any owner, heir, or beneficiary of an owner of "Holocaust-era artwork" to bring an action to recover the artwork from certain entities without regard to any applicable statute of limitations, so long as the action is commenced on or before December 31, 2010.[201] The entities subject to this rule are museums or galleries that display, exhib-it, or sell any article of historical, interpretive, scientific, or artistic significance.[202] Holocaust-era artwork means any article of artistic significance taken as a result of Nazi persecution during the period of 1929 to 1945, inclusive.[203]

International Issues

Discussed in detail in chapter 8 are additional important internation-al cases dealing with the statute of limitations, laches, forfeiture un-der the National Stolen Property Act, recovery of Holocaust-looted art, and similar issues that are relevant to the discussion in this chap-ter.

AUTHENTICITY AND THE STATUTE OF LIMITATIONS

In chapter 2, we discuss the warranty of authenticity under the U.C.C. We now address the representation of authenticity and the statute of limitations. When a buyer of a work of art later discovers that, contrary to the seller's allegations, the artwork is not authentic, the statute of limitations for a suit against the seller is governed by the U.C.C. In most states, the U.C.C. provides that "an action for breach of any contract for sale must be commenced within four years after the cause of action has accrued."[204] That four-year period under the U.C.C. may be reduced by the original contracting parties to a pe-riod of not less than one year, but it may not be extended.[205]

Although the U.C.C. is generally clear as to when such a cause of action has accrued—that is, when tender of delivery is made[206] un-less a warranty explicitly extends to the future performance of the goods—some court decisions have split as to whether a certification of authenticity regarding artwork constitutes an explicit warranty of future performance sufficient to toll the statute of limitations. The conventional and usual position of the federal courts is that a certifi-cation of authenticity does not constitute a warranty of future performance and that, accordingly, the four-year statute of limitations for breach of sale applies, thus causing a plaintiff to be time-barred from bringing suit after that period. Examples of that holding abound in the First, Second, and Third Circuits.

In the case of *Wilson v. Hammer Holdings, Inc.*,[207] for example, the plaintiffs in 1961 purchased for more than $11,000 a painting entitled *Femme Debout* from the Hammer Galleries and received a written guarantee that the painting was an original work of art by the French artist Edouard Vuillard. In 1984, the plaintiffs had the painting examined by an expert in preparation for selling it. When the expert determined that the painting was not by Vuillard and refused to authenticate it, the plaintiffs returned the painting to the Hammer Galleries and filed an action seeking damages for breach of warranty and negligence. The federal district court dismissed the case on the ground that it was time-barred by the applicable statute of limitations. On appeal, the First Circuit affirmed. Citing the applicable provision of the U.C.C. as codified in Massachusetts, the court noted the four-year limitation period from accrual that applies to actions for breach of sale contracts.[208] The court further noted that the breach occurred when tender of delivery of the painting was made. Moreover, the court held that the case did not involve a warranty extending to future performance of the goods, in which the cause of action accrues when the breach is or should have been discovered,[209] nor did it involve a cause of action in negligence under a section of the U.C.C. designed to address breach-of-warranty actions that are in essence product-liability actions.[210]

In the more recent *Firestone*[211] case, the defendant on August 31, 1981, sold a painting to the plaintiffs for $500,000. The painting, *The Bombardment of Fort Sumter*, was believed by both parties to be by a renowned American landscape artist, Albert Bierstadt. In 1985, some art historians began to doubt the accuracy of the attribution. By 1986, the consensus among art experts was that another artist, John Ross Key, not Bierstadt, had done the painting and that it was worth only about $50,000. When the plaintiffs filed suit in October 1986, the Pennsylvania federal court applied the four-year statute, holding that the

[p]laintiffs' claims, if any, accrued at the time of sale. The limitations period is four years. This action is time-barred.[212]

In the still-more-recent *Rosen*[213] case in the Second Circuit, the plaintiffs in 1968 purchased for $15,000 a portrait entitled *The Misses Wertheimer* from the Spanierman Gallery, which had guaranteed that it was an original work by John Singer Sargent. In 1975, 1979, 1980, 1984, and 1986, at the plaintiffs' request, Spanierman provided appraisals of the painting for insurance purposes. In 1987, the plaintiffs decided to sell the painting, then valued at between $175,000 and $250,000. However, when they placed the painting with Christie's for auction in 1987, they were informed that it was a fake, whereupon they immediately filed suit against the gallery. Here again, a federal court in New York applied the four-year statute of limitations and held that the warranty did not extend to future performance and that the plaintiffs could have discovered the breach just as easily immediately after the sale as later.[214]

In New York, subsequent cases have followed the lead of *Rosen*. In *Shaheen v. Hahn*,[215] for example, a New York federal district court in 1994, citing *Rosen*, held that the plaintiff, Shouky Shaheen, a private art collector, was time-barred from suing a New York City art dealer, Stephen Hahn, on a theory of breach of warranty of authenticity. Shaheen had purchased from Hahn in 1978 a pastel entitled *Mother About to Kiss Her Baby*, which, Hahn had represented, was a work by the American impressionist Mary Cassatt. In September 1990, an impressionist specialist in Christie's auction house, in appraising Shaheen's collection for insurance purposes, questioned the authenticity of the Cassatt. In February 1991, Shaheen was advised by letter by the Cassatt Committee, an independent body of experts on Cassatt, that his pastel would not be included in the newly revised *catalogue raisonné* on Cassatt. In May 1992, still another independent expert on the works of Cassatt concluded that the pastel was not authentic, and in November 1992, Shaheen brought suit. In holding Shaheen time-barred, the court noted that

a warranty of authenticity of a painting, unless it explicitly extends to the future condition of the art work, does not fall within the scope of [the] "discovery exception."[216]

In the 1995 case of *Foxley v. Sotheby's*,[217] which also involved a
Cassatt, *Rosen* again was followed. A collector named William Foxley
in December 1987 purchased for $632,500 at a Sotheby's auction a
painting entitled *Lydia Reclining on a Divan*, represented in Sotheby's
auction catalog to be by Mary Cassatt. The authenticity of the painting was guaranteed by Sotheby's in the catalog for a period of five
years after the date of sale. In August 1993, nearly six years after his
purchase, Foxley consigned the painting to Sotheby's for sale at an
auction to be held in December 1993. In November 1993, Sotheby's, informing Foxley that the Cassatt Committee believed that the
painting might be inauthentic, advised him to withdraw it from the
upcoming auction. Foxley did so but left intact with Sotheby's the
remainder of his consignment to preserve the integrity of the auction. In return, Sotheby's allegedly promised to refund Foxley's purchase price for the putative Cassatt. When Sotheby's refused to pay
the refund, Foxley brought suit in September 1994 on an array of
theories, including breach of warranty of authenticity. The federal
district court agreed with Sotheby's that its warranty of authenticity,
as set forth in the auction catalog, did not extend to future performance; rather, it was a limited warranty that expired in December
1992. As to all causes of action in the suit arising from the U.C.C.,
the court held that the statute of limitations expired as of December
1991, four years after the auction. In so holding, the court, citing
Rosen, noted that in that case, the Second Circuit declined to create
an exception to section 2-725 of the U.C.C., in which "the warranty
concerns an immutable quality."[218] The court went on to note that
since subdivision (2) of section 2-725 is itself an exception to the
general statute of limitations on breach of warranty claims, it would
"be inappropriate to expand this exception beyond its plain
terms."[219] Thus, the plaintiff Foxley was held to be time-barred from
asserting his breach of warranty claims.

In contrast to the preceding cases and in direct criticism of the reasoning behind those decisions, a federal court in Hawaii in *Balog v. Center Art Gallery-Hawaii, Inc.*[220] held that in the case of artwork certified as authentic by an expert in the field or by a merchant dealing in goods of that type, the certification of authenticity constitutes an explicit warranty of future performance sufficient to toll—that is, stop temporarily—the statute of limitations under the U.C.C.

In *Balog*, the plaintiffs, residents of the state of Washington on tour in Hawaii, purchased from the defendant art gallery in Hawaii, beginning in 1978 and over a period of four years, a number of pieces, all purportedly by Salvador Dalí. In all, they purchased seven pieces for a total of $36,200. After each sale the defendant mailed to the plaintiffs a "Confidential Appraisal–Certificate of Authenticity" for each of the artworks they had purchased. They received the mailings in 1979, 1980, 1981, 1982, and 1987. In 1988, the plaintiffs first became aware of media reports indicating that representations made by the gallery relative to artwork it sold may be false. The plaintiffs investigated the allegations and ultimately filed a complaint in 1989, alleging, among other claims, breach of warranty. In denying the defendant's motion to dismiss on the grounds that the complaint was not filed within the applicable four-year statute of limitations, the Hawaii federal district court—referring to the preceding cases of *Wilson v. Hammer Holdings, Inc.*, *Firestone*, and *Rosen*—noted the following:

> This court is not bound by decisions coming out of the First, Second or Third Circuits except insofar as decisions emanating from courts within those circuits supply sound reasoning which the court may want to adopt. In the view of this court, far from being based on sound reasoning, these decisions flow from a too-literalistic application of the Code which takes no cognizance of the unique problem presented by the application of the U.C.C. to artwork and other collectibles. . . . [T]his court . . . rejects the defendants' invitation to simply apply the letter of the law with no thought whatsoever about the ramifications of such an application, a practice which, in the view of this court, was engaged in by the courts in *Hammer Holdings*, *Rosen*, and *Firestone*.[221]

The court went on to hold that

> in the case of artwork which is certified authentic by an expert in the field or a merchant dealing in goods of that type, such a certification of authenticity constitutes an *explicit* warranty of future performance sufficient to toll the U.C.C.'s statute of limitations.[222] [italics ours]

The court made clear that its holding applied narrowly to artwork but that it viewed artwork as the "type of thing about which questions as to authenticity normally arise only at some future time, usually the time of resale."[223]

Balog, it seems, is an anomaly. In the ensuing years, it appears that no other court in the United States has followed suit and carved out an exception for artworks, whereby a warranty of authenticity constitutes an explicit warranty of future performance sufficient to toll the statute of limitations. That is, in virtually all other jurisdictions, in the absence of fraud or other conduct intended to deceive or lull inquiry, an aggrieved purchaser of artwork must bring suit for breach of contract within a very few years after purchase.

If, subsequent to the purchase, a buyer learns that a work of art is misattributed, the buyer may revoke acceptance of it if he does so in a timely way when the misattribution substantially impairs the work's value, provided the original acceptance "was reasonably induced either by the difficulty of discovery before acceptance or by the seller's assurances."[224]

In the Sixth Circuit in *Lawson v. London Arts Group*,[225] an action that was time-barred under section 2-725 of the U.C.C. was found to be timely under Michigan's warranty laws relating to artworks. That statute provides that

> in actions for damages based on a breach of warranty of quality or fitness, the claim accrues at the time the breach of the warranty *is discovered or reasonably should be discovered*.[226] [italics ours].

Should a warranty that an artwork is authentic constitute an explicit warranty of future performance? Our answer is no. The general rule set forth in section 2-725 of the U.C.C. is that an action for breach of a sale contract must be commenced within four years after the cause of action has accrued—that is, when tender of delivery is made. The general rule is grounded in sound commercial reasoning: Section 2-725 provides a definite cutoff point in time, after which businesses can destroy their records without being haunted by the fear of subsequent lawsuits for breach of contract or breach of warranty. However, nothing in the general rule prevents a buyer and a seller from negotiating to extend contract liability into the future, thereby activating the exception offered by section 2-725(2).

It has been argued unsuccessfully (in *Rosen*,[227] for example) that because authenticity is an immutable quality, an artwork warranted to be authentic now clearly continues to be authentic; therefore, such a warranty should be viewed as an explicit warranty of future performance. We take issue, however, with the underlying premise. Authenticity in art is not an immutable quality—far from it. Moreover, it is not authenticity but, rather, the *perception* of authenticity that fuels the art market, as shown by the body of work of the seventeenth-century Dutch artist Rembrandt Harmensz van Ryn. In 1900, then-current scholarship held that Rembrandt's oeuvre included no fewer than 700 oil paintings and 1,000 drawings. That body of work shrank by 1995 to include merely 350 oil paintings and seventy drawings, because of the development in the intervening years of sophisticated technologies.[228] And Rembrandt is not an isolated case. Scientific testing, stylistic analysis, and documentation—the three primary methods of authenticating artwork, discussed earlier in this chapter—rely on continually evolving scholarship and technological development. Therefore, what may be considered an authentic Rembrandt or Monet according to the best information available today—information that enables a dealer today to warrant that such a work is, in fact, a Rembrandt or Monet—may well be determined ten years from now to be inauthentic on the basis of newer information. Such circumstances would work too great a hardship on a dealer if the latter's warranty were constrained to apply indefinitely.

Mistake and Fraud

In most states, the U.C.C.'s four-year statute governing the warranty of authenticity should be viewed as controlling, but a lawyer in any jurisdiction should be alert for statutes inconsistent or in conflict with the U.C.C.'s provision. In New York, for example, if the action was based on mistake, rather than breach of warranty of authenticity, the permissible period within which to bring suit for an alleged wrongdoing is six years after the occurrence of the wrongdoing, rather than four years under the U.C.C. provision.[229]

Also in New York, if the action was based on fraud, rather than breach of warranty of authenticity, the permissible period within which to bring suit for an alleged wrongdoing is six years after the occurrence of the wrongdoing, or two years from the date the fraud was or could with reasonable diligence have been discovered.[230] Often, when a collector learns many years after the purchase of an artwork that it is not authentic, fraud is alleged (the dealer knew or should have known the work of art was not authentic) because it is the only way to have a valid claim without being barred by the four-year warranty statute of limitation under section 2-725 of the U.C.C.

In *Rosen*, discussed above, the court noted that it is well settled that to maintain a fraud claim under New York law, a plaintiff must establish that he relied on the defendant's misrepresentations and that this reliance caused him injury.[231] The defendant Spanierman Gallery contended that the fraud claim was asserted only in an attempt to extend the statute of limitations on the Rosen's breach of warranty claim, and that these claims should therefore be dismissed. The court allowed the fraud claim to proceed and the case was thereafter settled.[232] A detailed discussion of the cases and elements of a claim based on fraud or negligent misrepresentation can be found in chapter 7 beginning at page 610. The measure of damages based on a claim of fraud is discussed beginning on page 96.

Notes to Chapter 3

1.   Alan Riding, *Art Theft Is Booming, Bringing an Effort to Respond*, N.Y. TIMES, Nov. 20, 1995 at C-11; Deborah Ball, *A Stash of Stolen Art*, WALL ST. J., Aug. 24, 2004 at B-1; Maryclaire Dale, *Now FBI Task Force to Focus on Art Theft*, Associated Press, Jan. 15, 2005.

2.   Paul Majendie, *Eastern Europe New Art Theft Target*, Reuters World Service, Nov. 15, 1995.

3.   18 IFAR REPS. 5 (Mar. 1997); 11 IFAR REPS. 3 (Apr. 1990).

4.   *See* discussion on the statute of limitations, beginning on page 264.

5.   For an excellent general discussion of artwork title disputes, including a review of some of the resources available for recovering and investigating title to artwork, *see* Petrovich, *The Recovery of Stolen Art: of Paintings, Statues and Statutes of Limitations*, 27 UCLA L. REV. 1122 (1980); Bibas, *The Case Against Statutes of Limitations for Stolen Art*, 103 YALE L. J. 2437 (1994); Hawkins, Rothman & Goldstein, *A Tale of Two Innocents: Creating an Equitable Balance Between the Rights of Former Owners and Good Faith Purchasers of Stolen Art*, 64 FORDHAM L. REV. 49 (1995); Montagu, *Recent Cases on the Recovery of Stolen Art—The Tug of War Between Owners and Good Faith Purchasers Continues*, 18 COLUM.-VLA J. L. & ARTS 75 (1993).

6.   The Art Loss Register is located at 20 East 46th St., Suite 1402, New York, N.Y. 10017; tel.: (212) 297-0941; email: info@ALRny.com. Conversation with Katherine Dugdale, art theft specialist, Mar. 24, 2003.

7.   The Art Dealers Association of America is located at 575 Madison Avenue, New York, N.Y. 10022; tel.: (212) 940-8590. Conversation with Gilbert Edelson, Vice President, Feb. 11, 2003.

8.   The International Foundation for Art Research is located at 500 5th Avenue, Suite 935, New York, N.Y. 10010; tel.: (212) 391-6234.

9.   Art Berman, *Morning Report*, L.A. TIMES, Nov. 28, 1995, at 2-F. The United States maintains its membership in INTERPOL pursuant to 22 U.S.C. § 263a. In 1977, the Justice and Treasury Departments assumed responsibility for representing the interests of the United States in INTERPOL. *See also* www.interpol.int, visited Mar. 20, 2003.

10. *See* www.FBI.gov, visited Mar. 20, 2003. Appendix 8-9 at the end of chapter 8 contains a list of websites that can be searched for missing or stolen works of art.

11. State v. Wright Hepburn Webster Gallery, Ltd., 64 Misc. 2d 423, 314 N.Y.S.2d 661 (Sup. Ct. 1970), *aff'd*, 37 A.D.2d 698, 323 N.Y.S.2d 389 (1971).

12. *Id.*, 64 Misc. 2d at 427, 314 N.Y.S.2d at 667.

13. Wall St. J., July 17, 1987.

14. United States v. Ctr. Art Galleries-Haw., Inc., 991 F.2d 804 (9th Cir. 1993), *reh'g aff'd sub nom.* United States v. Mett, 65 F.3d 1531, 1532 (9th Cir. 1995).

15. Ralph Blumenthal, *Government Sale of Fake Dalís Raises Ire,* Hous. Chron., Nov. 7, 1995, at 4.

16. FTC v. Fed. Sterling Galleries, Inc., No. 87-2072 (D. Ariz. filed Jan. 12, 1989).

17. FTC v. Magui Publishers, Inc., Civ. No. 89-3818, 1991 WL 90895, 1991 U.S. Dist LEXIS 20452 (C.D. Cal. Mar. 15, 1991).

18. *See* United States v. Amiel, 889 F. Supp. 615, 618 (E.D.N.Y. 1995).

19. Artnewsletter, vol. XIX, no. 13 (Feb. 22, 1994), at 3.

20. FTC v. Austin Galleries of Ill., Inc., No. 88 C 3845, 1988 U.S. Dist. LEXIS 12380 (N.D. Ill. Nov. 2, 1988).

21. FTC v. Austin, 138 B.R. 898 (Bankr. N.D. Ill. 1992).

22. United States v. Austin, 54 F.3d 394, 398 (7th Cir. 1995), *later appeal at* 103 F.3d 606 (7th Cir. 1997).

23. *Id.*

24. *Id.* The art world was startled when the United States auctioned the fake art rather than destroying it. *See* Ralph Blumenthal, *12,000 Fake Dalís Under a U.S. Gavel,* N.Y. Times, Nov. 6, 1995, at C-11; Artnewsletter, vol. XXI, no. 5 (Oct. 31, 1995), at 4.

25. Artnewsletter, vol. XIX, no. 20 (May 31, 1994), at 3.

26. *Id.*

27. B. Prisant, *A Surrealist Still Makes a Splash,* Art. Bus. News, May 1, 2004, at 1.

28. Artnewsletter, vol. XIX, no. 21 (June 14, 1994), at 3.

29. *Id.*

30. Art Newspaper (London), Mar. 1994, at 1.

31. *Id.*

32. N.Y. Times, Jan. 4, 1995, at C-9.

33. Aryeh v. Christie's Int'l, Index No. 1030/86 (N.Y. Sup. Ct. 1986).

34. ARTNEWSLETTER, Feb. 2, 1988, at 3.

35. *See Aryeh*, Index No. 1030/86.

36. N.Y. TIMES, June 19, 1996, at C-11.

37. *A Recipe For Art Fraud*, 7 IFAR J. No. 1 (2004); Press Release, Department of Justice, U.S. Attorney, Southern District of New York (Mar. 10, 2004).

38. *See* discussion on the sculpture market, in chapter 5 at 483.

39. N.Y. ARTS & CULT. AFF. LAW §§ 14.05, 14.06, 14.07, 14.08.

40. CAL. CIV. CODE § 1744.

41. IOWA CODE ANN. §§ 715B.1 to 715B.4.

42. *See* L. DUBOFF & S. CAPLAN, DESKBOOK OF ART LAW K-11 (Oceana Publ'ns, 2d ed. 1993).

43. 18 PA. CONS. STAT. § 4101(a).

44. *See, e.g.*, GA. CODE ANN. § 16-9-3; IOWA CODE ANN. § 715A.1; N.H. REV. STAT. ANN. § 638:1; N.J. STAT. ANN. § 2C:21-1; TENN. CODE ANN. § 39-14-114; TEX. PENAL CODE ANN. § 32.21; UTAH CODE § 76-6-501; WYO. STAT. ANN. § 6-3-601.

45. 18 PA. CONS. STAT. § 4101(a).

46. *See, e.g.*, Merryman, *Counterfeit Art*, #1, 1 INT'L J. OF CULTURAL PROP. 27, 49 (1992). This is an excellent journal on the subject of counterfeit art in general.

47. *But see*, as examples of exceptions, MO. REV. STAT. § 570.090; TENN. CODE ANN. § 39-14-114.

48. *See, e.g.*, ALA. CODE §§ 13A-9-2, -3, -4; ALASKA STAT. § 11.46.500 to .510; CONN. GEN. STAT. ANN. § 53a-138, -139, -140; KY. REV. STAT. ANN. § 516.020, .030, .040; N.Y. PENAL LAW § 170.05, .10, .15; TEX. PENAL CODE ANN. § 32.21.

49. N.Y. PENAL LAW § 170.45.

50. *See, e.g.*, ARK. CODE ANN. § 5-37-213; KY. REV. STAT. ANN. § 516.110.

51. *See, e.g.*, ALA. CODE § 13A-9-10; COLO. REV. STAT. ANN. § 18-5-110; CONN. GEN. STAT. ANN. § 53a-141; HAW. REV. STAT. ANN. §§ 708–855; KY. REV. STAT. ANN. § 516.110; N.Y. PENAL LAW § 170.45; OR. REV. STAT. § 165.037; TEX. PENAL CODE ANN. § 32.22. *See* N.Y. ARTS & CULT. AFF. LAW § 13.03 (falsifying certificates of authenticity for work of fine arts is class A misdemeanor).

52. New York v. Wright Hepburn Webster Gallery, Ltd., 64 Misc. 2d 423, 314 N.Y.S.2d 661 (Sup. Ct. 1970), *aff'd*, 37 A.D.2d 698, 323 N.Y.S.2d 389 (1971).

53. H.W. JANSON, HISTORY OF ART 419 (1974).

54. *Id.*

55. *See* Merryman, *supra* note 46, at 32.

56. *Id.* at 43.

57. *See* discussion of expert opinions and liability in chapter 7.

58. Arnold Herstand & Co. v. Gallery: Gertrude Stein, Inc., N.Y.L.J., May 5, 1995, at 25 (N.Y. Sup. Ct. App. Div. Apr. 27, 1995), *rev'd and remanded*, 211 A.D.2d 77, 626 N.Y.S.2d 74 (1995).

59. For a comprehensive and illuminating treatise on the issues involved in authenticating the paintings and drawings of Rembrandt, the seventeenth century Dutch artist, *see* generally, VON SONNENBURG, vol. 1; LIEDTKE, LOGAN, ORENSTEIN & DICKEY, vol. 2, REMBRANDT/NOT REMBRANDT IN THE METROPOLITAN MUSEUM OF ART: ASPECTS OF CONNOISSEURSHIP (Metropolitan Museum of Art 1995).

60. Infrared imaging, along with X-radiography, autoradiography, and other scientific techniques involved in authentication of artworks are surveyed in VON SONNENBURG, *id.* at 11 *et seq.*

61. Autocephalous Greek-Orthodox Church of Cyprus v. Goldberg & Feldman Fine Arts, Inc., 717 F. Supp. 1374 (S.D. Ind. 1989), *aff'd*, 917 F.2d 278 (7th Cir. 1990).

62. Republic of Turkey v. Metro. Museum of Art, 762 F. Supp. 44 (S.D.N.Y. 1990).

63. *See* Republic of Croatia v. Tr. of Marquess of Northampton 1987 Settlement, 203 A.D.2d 167, 610 N.Y.S.2d 263 (1994); Republic of Lebanon v. Sotheby's Tr. of Marquess of Northampton, 167 A.D.2d 142, 561 N.Y.S.2d 566 (1990).

64. ARTNEWSLETTER, Apr. 2, 1991, at 6.

65. ARTNEWSLETTER, June 11, 1991, at 3.

66. *See, e.g.*, K. AKINSHA & G. KOZLOV, BEAUTIFUL LOOT: THE SOVIET PLUNDER OF EUROPE'S ART TREASURES (Random House 1995); L.H. NICHOLAS, THE RAPE OF EUROPA: THE FATE OF EUROPE'S TREASURES IN THE THIRD REICH AND THE SECOND WORLD WAR (Alfred A. Knopf 1994).

67. AKINSHA & KOZLOV, *supra* note 66; NICHOLAS, *supra* note 66.

68. *In the Cellars of the Pushkin*, ECONOMIST, Dec. 24, 1994–Jan. 6, 1995, at 61.

69. Jamey Gambrell, *Displaced Art; Art Seized from Nazi Germany by the Soviet Union after World War II*, 83 ART IN AMERICA, No. 9 (Sept. 1995), at 88.

70. Solomon R. Guggenheim Found. v. Lubell, 77 N.Y.2d 311, 569 N.E.2d 426, 567 N.Y.S.2d 623 (1991), *aff'g* 153 A.D.2d 143, 550 N.Y.S.2d 618 (1990) (modifying an order from the Supreme Court, N.Y.

County, entered February 14, 1989, which denied a motion by plaintiff for discovery and inspection and granted a cross-motion by defendant for summary judgment).

71. RALPH E. LERNER & JUDITH BRESLER, ART LAW: THE GUIDE FOR COLLECTORS, INVESTORS, DEALERS, AND ARTISTS 225 (2d ed. PLI 1998).

72. *Id.* at 82 *et seq.*

73. This proposition under common law, *see* 3 WILLIAM BLACKSTONE COMMENTARIES 145, has been incorporated into the U.C.C. *See* U.C.C. §§ 1-103, 1-201(32), (33) and 2-403(1).

74. *See* D. DOBBS, HANDBOOK ON THE LAW OF REMEDIES 399 (1973).

75. *Id.* at 403.

76. *See* Solomon R. Guggenheim Found. v. Lubell, 153 A.D.2d 143, 550 N.Y.S.2d 618 (1990), *aff'd*, 77 N.Y.2d 311, 569 N.E.2d 426, 567 N.Y.S.2d 623 (1991).

77. CAL. CIV. PROC. CODE § 338(c). (Prior to a 1988 amendment, § 338(c) appeared as § 338(3).)

78. *See* Petrovich, *supra* note 5.

79. *See* Bibas, *supra* note 5.

80. *See* Petrovich, *supra* note 5 at 1128. *See also* Hawkins, Rothman & Goldstein, *supra* note 5; Montagu, *supra* note 5.

81. *See* Petrovich, *supra* note 5, at 1129.

82. *See generally* Petrovich, *supra* note 5; Bibas, *supra* note 5.

83. *See, e.g.*, Redmond v. N.J. Historical Soc'y, 132 N.J. Eq. 464, 28 A.2d 189 (1942). Note: A thief who takes and conceals property cannot get title, however long he holds the property—that is, the statute of limitations does not begin to run. He can, however, take title through adverse possession, since in that case he openly and notoriously holds the property, so the owner could have a reasonable chance of knowing its whereabouts and asserting title. *See* 51 AM. JUR. 2D *Limitation of Actions* § 124, at 694 (1970). *See also* Petrovich, *supra* note 5, at 1141; Bibas, *supra* note 5, at 2441; Thomas, *Adverse Possession: Acquiring Title to Stolen Personal Property*, ABA's PROB. & PROP., Mar./Apr. 1996, at 12, for further discussions of the adverse possession theory of accrual.

84. CAL. CIV. PROC. CODE § 338(c).

85. Menzel v. List, 49 Misc. 2d 300, 267 N.Y.S.2d 804 (Sup. Ct. 1966), *modified as to damages*, 28 A.D.2d 516, 279 N.Y.S.2d 608 (1967), *rev'd as to modifications*, 24 N.Y.2d 91, 246 N.E.2d 742, 298 N.Y.S.2d 979 (1969). *See* discussion related to damages, chapter 2 at 95.

86. *See* Petrovich, *supra* note 5, at 1133.

87.   *See Menzel*, 49 Misc. 2d at 315, 267 N.Y.S.2d at 819.

88.   *See* Petrovich, *supra* note 5, at 1139. *See In re* Spewack, 203 A.D.2d 133, 610 N.Y.S.2d 243 (1994), where the plaintiff's action was time barred against the alleged thief thirty-two years after defendant allegedly stole certain papers relating to the musical production *Kiss Me Kate*. The court noted that "When the stolen object is in the possession of a thief . . . the statute begins to run, anomalously, from the time of the theft, even if the owner was unaware of the theft at the time it occurred" unless the thief is estopped from asserting the statute of limitations under the doctrine of equitable estoppel.

89.   Kunstsammlungen zu Weimar v. Elicofon, 536 F. Supp. 829 (E.D.N.Y. 1981), *aff'd*, 678 F.2d 1150 (2d Cir. 1982).

90.   DeWeerth v. Baldinger, 836 F.2d 103 (2d Cir. 1987) (*rev'g* 658 F. Supp. 688 (S.D.N.Y. 1987)), *cert. denied*, 486 U.S. 1056 (1988), *remanded*, 804 F. Supp. 539 (S.D.N.Y. 1992), *rev'd*, 38 F.3d 1266 (2d Cir.), *cert. denied*, 513 U.S. 1001 (1994).

91.   *Id.*, 836 F.2d 103.

92.   *Id.* at 108.

93.   *Id.* at 111.

94.   *Id.*

95.   *See* Solomon R. Guggenheim Found. v. Lubell, 153 A.D.2d 143, 550 N.Y.S.2d 618 (1990), *aff'd*, 77 N.Y.2d 311, 569 N.E.2d 426, 567 N.Y.S.2d 623 (1991).

96.   *Id.*, 550 N.Y.S.2d at 619. Note that the statute of limitations can bar an action if there is no question of material fact and that the statute of limitations defense is an affirmative defense which means that it attacks the legal right to bring the action as opposed to attacking the truth of the claim.

97.   *Id.* at 620.

98.   *Id.* at 621.

99.   *Id.*; U.C.C. § 2-403(1).

100.   *See Guggenheim Foundation*, 550 N.Y.S.2d at 624 (citing W. KEETON, R. KEETON, D. DOBBS & D. OWEN, PROSSER & KEETON ON TORTS § 15, at 93 (5th ed. 1984 & Supp. 1988), quoting Hollins v. Fowler, L.R. 7 Q.B. 639 (1874)).

101.   *See Guggenheim Foundation*, 567 N.Y.S. at 627.

102.   *Id.*

103.   *Id.* at 628.

104.   *Id.*

105.   *See DeWeerth*, 804 F. Supp. at 545.

106.   *Id.*

107.   *See DeWeerth*, 38 F.3d at 1275.

108. *See DeWeerth*, 513 U.S. 1001.

109. Republic of Turkey v. Metro. Museum of Art, 762 F. Supp. 44 (S.D.N.Y. 1990).

110. Hoelzer v. City of Stamford, 933 F.2d 1131 (2d Cir. 1991).

111. Hoelzer v. City of Stamford, 722 F. Supp. 1106 (S.D.N.Y. 1989).

112. *See* Hoelzer, 933 F.2d at 1138. In a subsequent case, 89 Civ. 641, 1992 WL 18846, 1992 U.S. Dist. LEXIS 783 (S.D.N.Y. Jan. 29, 1992), Hoelzer won a $557,200 judgment from the City of Stamford based on the equitable principle of unjust enrichment. The court imposed a contract where none had existed. On appeal, the Second Circuit affirmed, with modification of the judgment to allow the City of Stamford to elect to satisfy the award by returning the murals to Hoelzer within a reasonable time to be set by the district court. 972 F.2d 495 (2d Cir.), *cert. denied*, 506 U.S. 1035 (1992).

113. Golden Buddha Corp. v. Canadian Land Co. of Am., N.V., 931 F.2d 196 (2d Cir. 1991).

114. *See Guggenheim Foundation*, 153 A.D.2d at 149.

115. *See* Bibas, *supra* note 5, at 2446.

116. *See* Hawkins, Rothman & Goldstein, *supra* note 5, at 59 *et seq.* for an excellent critique of *Guggenheim Foundation*.

117. *See* Hawkins, Rothman & Goldstein, *supra* note 5, at 66–69.

118. *Id.* at 67.

119. Solomon R. Guggenheim Found. v. Lubell, 153 A.D.2d 143, 550 N.Y.S.2d 618 (1990), *aff'd*, 77 N.Y.2d 311, 569 N.E.2d 426, 567 N.Y.S.2d 623 (1991).

120. *See* Hawkins, Rothman & Goldstein, *supra* note 5, at 68.

121. Robins Island Pres. Fund, Inc. v. Southold Dev. Corp., 959 F.2d 409, 424 (2d Cir. 1992).

122. Solomon R. Guggenheim Found. v. Lubell, 153 A.D.2d 143, 550 N.Y.S.2d 618 (1990), *aff'd*, 77 N.Y.2d 311, 569 N.E.2d 426, 567 N.Y.S.2d 623 (1991).

123. Czartoryski-Borbon v. Turcotte, Index No. 107958/97 (N.Y. Sup. Ct. Apr. 15, 1999), N.Y.L.J., Apr. 28, 1999, at 27 col. 2 (Sup. Ct. N.Y. County), *appeal withdrawn*, 264 A.D.2d 545, 697 N.Y.S.2d 228 (1st Dep't 1999).

124. Hutchinson v. Horowitz, No. 604942/47 (N.Y. Sup. Ct. Jan. 8, 1999).

125. Greek Orthodox Patriarchate of Jerusalem v. Christie's, Inc., 1999 WL 673447, 1999 U.S. Dist. LEXIS 13257 (S.D.N.Y. 1999).

126. Czartoryski-Borbon v. Turcotte, Index No. 107958/97 (N.Y. Sup. Ct. Apr. 15, 1999), N.Y.L.J., Apr. 28, 1999, at 27 col. 2 (Sup.

Ct. N.Y. County), *appeal withdrawn*, 264 A.D.2d 545, 697 N.Y.S.2d 228 (1st Dep't 1999).

127.   Since the court's decision, an expert in art history has confirmed the painting is part of the Czartoryski family collection (affidavit of Professor Colin T. Eisler of the Institute of Fine Arts, New York University, stating he has "long been aware of the preeminence of the Czartoryski family collection, [which is] universally regarded as a particularly strong collection of European Paintings among those existing before World War II").

128.   This theft is recorded by THE CATALOGUE OF PAINTINGS REMOVED FROM POLAND BY GERMAN OCCUPATION AUTHORITIES DURING 1939–1945, a book compiled by Professor Wladyslaw Tomkiewicz of Warsaw University and published by the Reparations Section of the Polish Ministry of Culture and Art.

129.   Solomon R. Guggenheim Found. v. Lubell, 153 A.D.2d 143, 550 N.Y.S.2d 618 (1990), *aff'd*, 77 N.Y.2d 311, 569 N.E.2d 426, 567 N.Y.S.2d 623 (1991).

130.   *Czartoryski-Borbon*, N.Y.L.J., Apr. 28, 1999, at 27 col. 2.

131.   Hutchinson v. Horowitz, No. 604942/47 (N.Y. Sup. Ct. Jan. 8, 1999). *See also* Hutchinson v. Spanierman, 190 F.3d 815 (7th Cir. 1999) (holding plaintiff Thomas Hutchinson barred by laches from claiming an interest in certain Thomas Robinson works held by other descendants of the artist); Hutchinson v. Pfeil, 2000 U.S. App. LEXIS 6260 (10th Cir. 2000); Hutchinson v. Pfeil, 2000 U.S. App. LEXIS 6184 (10th Cir. 2000) (denying similar claims of Hutchinson).

132.   Robinson died intestate in 1896, after which many of his paintings were sold at auction in order to pay his debts. The remaining paintings became the property of his two brothers. Robinson exhibited widely during his lifetime.

133.   Plaintiff in an unrelated case in 1992 claimed that the painting at issue in this case had been stolen from Robinson's estate, but in this action they claim the painting had been stolen while on exhibit around the time of Robinson's death.

134.   Hutchinson v. Horowitz, No. 604942/47 (N.Y. Sup. Ct. Jan. 8, 1999) (citing *Guggenheim, supra* note 70, at 628).

135.   In particular, both the acknowledged expert on Robinson and Anne Hutchinson (who allegedly discovered the theft) are deceased.

136.   *Hutchinson*, No. 604942/47.

137.   Greek Orthodox Patriarchate of Jerusalem v. Christie's, Inc., 1999 WL 673447, 1999 U.S. Dist. LEXIS 13257 (S.D.N.Y. 1999). The palimpsest was acquired in the 1920s by Marie Louis Sirieix, a French civil servant, although the circumstances surrounding this acquisition are unknown.

138.   The originals of these texts were believed to be destroyed in the third century by a fire that consumed the library in Alexandria, Egypt. *Id.*, 1999 WL 673447, at *1, 1999 U.S. Dist. LEXIS 13257, at *2.

139.   *Id.*, 1999 WL 673447, at *2, 1999 U.S. Dist. LEXIS 13257, at *3–*6.

140.   William Peakin, *The Sum God*, SUNDAY TIMES MAG., 17 June 2000, at 34.

141.   Köhling, *Greek Orthodox Patriarchate of Jerusalem v. Christie's*, 6 ART ANTIQUITY & L. No. 3 (Sept. 2001).

142.   *Greek Orthodox Patriarchate*, 1999 WL 673447, at *3, 1999 U.S. Dist. LEXIS 13257, at *6–*9.

143.   *Id.*, 1999 WL 673447, at *3, 1999 U.S. Dist. LEXIS 13257, at *8–*9.

144.   *Id.*, 1999 WL 673447, at *7, 1999 U.S. Dist. LEXIS 13257, at *24.

145.   *Id.*, 1999 WL 673447, at *9, 1999 U.S. Dist. LEXIS 13257, at *27.

146.   *Id.*, 1999 WL 673447, at *7, 1999 U.S. Dist. LEXIS 13257, at *24 (citing *Czartoryski-Borbon*, N.Y.L.J., Apr. 28, 1999, at 27 col. 2).

147.   *See* Kunstsammlungen zu Weimar v. Elicofon, 536 F. Supp. 829, 849–52 (E.D.N.Y. 1981).

148.   *Greek Orthodox Patriarchate*, 1999 WL 673447, at *9, 1999 U.S. Dist. LEXIS 13257, at *29–*30.

149.   *Id.*, 1999 WL 673447, at *10, 1999 U.S. Dist. LEXIS 13257, at *30–*32.

150.   *Id.*, 1999 WL 673447, at *10, 1999 U.S. Dist. LEXIS 13257, at *32 (quoting *Robins Island*, 959 F.2d at 424).

151.   *Id.*, 1999 WL 673447, at *10, 1999 U.S. Dist. LEXIS 13257, at *31–*33.

152.   DeWeerth v. Baldinger, 836 F.2d 103 (2d Cir. 1987) (*rev'g* 658 F. Supp. 688 (S.D.N.Y. 1987)), *cert. denied*, 486 U.S. 1056 (1988), *remanded*, 804 F. Supp. 539 (S.D.N.Y. 1992), *rev'd*, 38 F.3d 1266 (2d Cir.), *cert. denied*, 513 U.S. 1001 (1994).

153.   *Greek Orthodox Patriarchate*, 1999 WL 673447, at *7, 1999 U.S. Dist. LEXIS 13257, at *24–*25.

154.   *Id.*, 1999 WL 673447, at *8, 1999 U.S. Dist. LEXIS 13257, at *27. For an excellent discussion of the laches in the context of litigation involving works of art, *see* Epstein, *The Laches Defense in Art Litigation*, N.Y.L.J., Oct. 20, 2000. *See* Warin v. Wildenstein & Co., 297 A.D.2d 214, 746 N.Y.S.2d 282 (2002); Sanchez v. Trs. of Univ. of Pa., No. 04 Civ. 1253 (S.D.N.Y. 2005).

155. Köhling, *supra* note 140.

156. *Greek Orthodox Patriarchate*, 1999 WL 673447, at *6, 1999 U.S. Dist. LEXIS 13257, at *18–*19.

157. *Id.*, 1999 WL 673447, at *4, 1999 U.S. Dist. LEXIS 13257, at *13–*14, citing RESTATEMENT (SECOND) OF CONFLICT OF LAWS § 246 (1971).

158. *Id.*, 1999 WL 673447, at *5, 1999 U.S. Dist. LEXIS 13257, at *14.

159. *Id.*, 1999 WL 673447, at *6–*7, 1999 U.S. Dist. LEXIS 13257, at *19–*23.

160. *Id.*, 1999 WL 673447, at *3, 1999 U.S. Dist. LEXIS 13257, at *10.

161. Menzel v. List, 49 Misc. 2d 300, 267 N.Y.S.2d 804 (Sup. Ct. 1966), *modified as to damages*, 28 A.D.2d 516, 279 N.Y.S.2d 608 (1967), *rev'd as to modifications*, 24 N.Y.2d 91, 246 N.E.2d 742, 298 N.Y.S.2d 979 (1969); *see supra* note 84.

162. DeWeerth v. Baldinger, 836 F.2d 103 (2d Cir. 1987) (*rev'g* 658 F. Supp. 688 (S.D.N.Y. 1987)), *cert. denied*, 486 U.S. 1056 (1988), *remanded*, 804 F. Supp. 539 (S.D.N.Y. 1992), *rev'd*, 38 F.3d 1266 (2d Cir.), *cert. denied*, 513 U.S. 1001 (1994); *see supra* note 89.

163. Kunstsammlungen zu Weimar v. Elicofon, 536 F. Supp. 829 (E.D.N.Y. 1981), *aff'd*, 678 F.2d 1150 (2d Cir. 1982); *see supra* note 88.

164. Autocephalous Greek-Orthodox Church of Cyprus v. Goldberg & Feldman Fine Arts, Inc., 717 F. Supp. 1374 (S.D. Ind. 1989), *aff'd*, 917 F.2d 278 (7th Cir. 1990); *see supra* note 60.

165. Hutchinson v. Horowitz, No. 604942/47 (N.Y. Sup. Ct. Jan. 8, 1999); *see supra* note 123.

166. *See* Köhling, *supra* note 140, at 257, where the author, a German professor, finds the U.S. approach "remarkable."

167. Wertheimer v. Cirker's Hayes Storage Warehouse, 2001 WL 1657237, 2001 U.S. Dist. LEXIS 693 (N.Y. Sup. Ct. 2001), *aff'd*, 300 A.D.2d 117, 752 N.Y.S.2d 295, 2002 N.Y. App. Div. LEXIS 12516 (2002).

168. *Id.*, 2001 U.S. Dist. LEXIS 693, at *2–*6.

169. *Id.* at *6–*7.

170. *Id.* at *18–*19.

171. *Id.* at *8–*10.

172. *Id.* at *12–*13.

173. *Id.* at *13–*17.

174. *Id.*, 300 A.D.2d at 118, 752 N.Y.S.2d at 297. For an argument that *Wertheimer* was wrongly decided, *see* Alexandra Minkovich, *The Successful Use of Laches in World War II-Era Art Theft Disputes: It's Only a*

Matter of Time, 27 COLUM. J. L. & ARTS 349 (2004). *See* Sanchez v. Trs. of Univ. of Pa., No. 04 Civ. 1253 (S.D.N.Y. 2005) (upholding a laches defense against a claim that a collection of pre-Columbian gold art objects in the possession of the University of Pennsylvania had been stolen prior to 1920).

175.   United States v. Fireman's Fund Ins. Co., 2001 WL 88226, 2001 U.S. Dist. LEXIS 804 (S.D.N.Y. 2001).

176.   *Id.*, 2001 WL 88226, at *4, 2001 U.S. Dist. LEXIS 80, at *10–*11.

177.   The painting was stolen on June 10, 1989, and resurfaced in March 1995.

178.   *Fireman's Fund Ins. Co.*, 2001 WL 88226, at *4, 2001 U.S. Dist. LEXIS 804, at *11–*12. *See* United States v. Crawford Tech. Servs., 2004 WL 744670, U.S. Dist. LEXIS 5824 (S.D.N.Y. 2004) (court found it incumbent upon a good-faith purchaser—a dealer—to inquire about the validity of title before completing the transaction).

179.   CAL. CIV. PROC. CODE § 338(c).

180.   O'Keeffe v. Snyder, 83 N.J. 478, 416 A.2d 862 (1980).

181.   Autocephalous Greek-Orthodox Church of Cyprus v. Goldberg & Feldman Fine Arts, Inc., 917 F.2d 278 (7th Cir. 1990), *cert. denied*, 502 U.S. 941 (1991). *See* chapter 8, pages 700–703, where this case is also discussed.

182.   Charash v. Oberlin Coll., 14 F.3d 291 (6th Cir. 1994).

183.   Erisoty v. Rizik, No. 93-6215, 1995 WL 91406, U.S. Dist. LEXIS 2096 (E.D. Pa. Feb. 23, 1995), *aff'd*, No. 95-1807, 1996 U.S. App. LEXIS 14999 (3d Cir. May 7, 1996). *See also* Mucha v. King, 792 F.2d 602, 611–12 (7th Cir. 1986) (discussing applicability of Illinois discovery rule to conversion of bailed work of art); Pickett v. Am. Ordnance Pres. Ass'n, 60 F. Supp. 2d 450 (1999) (discussing application of Pennsylvania discovery rule to fraud claim against a dealer in antique military items).

184.   *In re* 1973 John Deere 4030 Tractor, 816 P.2d 1126 (Okla. 1991).

185.   *See* O'Keeffe v. Snyder, 83 N.J. 478, 416 A.2d 862 (1980).

186.   *Id.*, 83 N.J. at 493, 416 A.2d at 870.

187.   *See* Autocephalous Greek-Orthodox Church of Cyprus v. Goldberg & Feldman Fine Arts, Inc., 917 F.2d 278 (7th Cir. 1990), *cert. denied*, 502 U.S. 941 (1991), *supra* note 180.

188.   *See* Charash v. Oberlin Coll., 14 F.3d 291 (6th Cir. 1994).

189.   *See Erisoty, supra* note 182. In the latest development in the case, No. 93-6215 (E.D. Pa. Oct. 23, 1996), on summary judgment, the court held that the Erisotys were not entitled to compensation for their restoration efforts during the time the painting was in their possession. The

court found that although enriched, the defendants were not unjustly so. First, the court noted that plaintiffs bore the risk that "since the provenance of the painting was unknown, an original owner could appear at any time to reclaim the painting." Additionally, the court reasoned that the benefit which inured to the defendants was incidental to plaintiffs' own interest in restoring the paintings to reap profits from its eventual sale.

190. CAL. CIV. PROC. CODE § 338(c). In 1983, the California legislature implemented an amendment to the statute of limitations, which explicitly deferred commencement of a cause of action to recover stolen cultural property until the date the owner discovered the location of the stolen objects. The statute reads as follows:

> An action for taking, detaining, or injuring any goods or chattels, including actions for the specific recovery of personal property. The cause of action in the case of theft, as defined in section 484 of the Penal Code, of any article of historical, interpretive, scientific, or artistic significance is not deemed to have accrued until the discovery of the whereabouts of the article by the aggrieved party, his or her agent, or the law enforcement agency which originally investigated the theft.

191. Naftzger v. Am. Numismatic Soc'y, 42 Cal. App. 4th 421, 49 Cal. Rptr. 2d 784 (Ct. App. 1996). *See* Shapreau, *Title Bout—The Discovery-Accrual Rule,* DAILY J. (Feb. 29, 1996).

192. *Naftzger,* 42 Cal. App. 4th 421. *See also* Naftzger v. Am. Numismatic Soc'y (Cal. Ct. App. 1999) (Super. Ct. No. BC 075918) (restating much of what was said in the prior *Naftzger* decision but also discussing the "unclean hands" of Roy Naftzger and section 496 of the California Penal Code, which allows treble damages in such cases); *petition for review denied,* 1999 Cal. LEXIS 6134 (Sept. 1, 1999).

193. *Naftzger,* 42 Cal. App. 4th 421. The court in dicta also indicated that the doctrine of adverse possession is not applicable to effect a transfer of title in personalty in stolen property cases.

194. CAL. CIV. PROC. CODE § 338(c).

195. Soc'y of Cal. Pioneers v. Baker, 43 Cal. App. 4th 774, 50 Cal. Rptr. 2d 865 (1996). *See* Adler v. Taylor, CV 04-8472-RGK(FMOx) (C.D. Cal. Feb. 2, 2005) (confirming the holding in *Society of California Pioneers*).

196. *Society of California Pioneers,* 43 Cal. App. 4th 774 at n.10.

197. *See* Hawkins, Rothman & Goldstein, *supra* note 5, at 81. *See also* Springfield Library & Museum Ass'n, Inc. v. Knoedler Archivum, Inc., 341 F. Supp. 2d 32 (D. Mass. 2004) (adopting report and recommendations

of magistrate judge published at 2004 U.S. LEXIS 20437). In the *Springfield Library* case, a museum purchased in 1955 a painting from an art dealer and then returned it in 2001 to the Italian government after a claim that it was stolen during World War II from the Italian Embassy in Poland. The museum sued the art dealer on various contractual claims. The court found that although the statute of limitations would ordinarily bar the claims, there were sufficient facts to infer that the art dealer should be equitably estopped from defeating the museum's claims on statute of limitations grounds. The doctrine of equitable estoppel applies where a defendant lulls a plaintiff into a false belief that it is not necessary to commence suit within the statutory period. Here the court concluded that the art dealer had discouraged the museum from returning the painting and had encouraged the museum to challenge the Italian government in the hope that the painting would never have to be returned.

198.   *See* Hawkins, Rothman & Goldstein, *supra* note 5; Bibas, *supra* note 5; Montagu, *supra* note 5.

199.   Hawkins, Rothman & Goldstein, *supra* note 5, at 54.

200.   *Id.*

201.   CAL. CIV. PROC. CODE § 354.3.

202.   *Id.* The statute does not apply to a claim by an individual. Adler v. Taylor, CV 04-8472-RGK(FMOx) (C.D. Cal. Feb. 2, 2005), *supra* note 195.

203.   *Id.*

204.   U.C.C. § 2-725(1).

205.   *Id.*

206.   U.C.C. § 2-725(2).

207.   Wilson v. Hammer Holdings, Inc., 850 F.2d 3 (1st Cir. 1988).

208.   *Id.* at 4–5.

209.   *Id.* at 6.

210.   *Id.* at 7.

211.   Firestone & Parson, Inc. v. Union League of Phila., 672 F. Supp. 819 (E.D. Pa.), *aff'd*, 833 F.2d 304 (3d Cir. 1987).

212.   *Id.* at 822.

213.   Rosen v. Spanierman, 711 F. Supp. 749 (S.D.N.Y. 1989), *aff'd in part, vacated in part, remanded*, 894 F.2d 28 (2d Cir. 1990).

214.   *Id.*, 894 F.2d at 33.

215.   Shaheen v. Hahn, 92 Civ. 8062, 1994 WL 285439, 1994 U.S. Dist. LEXIS 8571 (S.D.N.Y. June 24, 1994).

216.   *Id.*, 1994 U.S. Dist. LEXIS 2651, at *6 (S.D.N.Y. Mar. 9, 1994) (citing Rosen v. Spanierman, 894 F.2d 28, 31–32 (2d Cir. 1990)).

217.   Foxley v. Sotheby's, Inc., 893 F. Supp. 1224 (S.D.N.Y. 1995).

218.   *Id.* at 1232.

219.   *Id.* However, the court allowed the plaintiff Foxley to proceed on his claim that the appraisals were negligently prepared. The case was subsequently settled on a confidential basis. *See* ARTNEWSLETTER vol. XXI, no. 13 (Feb. 20, 1996), at 2.

220.   Balog v. Ctr. Art Gallery-Haw., Inc., 745 F. Supp. 1556 (D. Haw. 1990). *See* ARTNEWSLETTER vol. XXI, no. 13 (Feb. 20, 1996), at 2.

221.   *Balog*, 745 F. Supp. at 1569.

222.   *Id.* at 1570.

223.   *Id.* at 1570–71.

224.   U.C.C. § 2-725(1).

225.   Lawson v. London Arts Group, 708 F.2d 226 (6th Cir. 1983).

226.   *Id.* at 228.

227.   *See Rosen*, 894 F.2d at 31.

228.   *See* LIEDTKE, LOGAN, ORENSTEIN & DICKEY, *supra* note 59.

229.   N.Y. C.P.L.R. 213(6).

230.   N.Y. C.P.L.R. 213(8), 213(11).

231.   *Rosen*, 894 F.2d at 34.

232.   *Id. See also* Sid Deutsch Gallery, Inc. v. Terry Dintenfass, Inc., N.Y.L.J. Apr. 10, 1997, at 28, in which the plaintiff art dealer alleged fraud against another art merchant regarding a sale of a work of art that took place ten years earlier. In deciding a motion to dismiss, the New York State Supreme Court allowed the fraud claim to proceed.

4

Auctions

Over the past thirty years or so, few aspects of the art market have captured the public imagination (and attracted media attention) with the consistency and intensity of auctions. While art can be sold in a variety of ways, sales by auctions are among the most dramatic. Witness, for example, the headline-dominating sale at Sotheby's in May 2004 of the Picasso painting from his Blue Period *Boy with a Pipe* for $104.2 million—setting a record for a painting sold at auction. Or consider the spectacular, celebrity-studded five-day sale in April 1996 of art, furniture, and other collectibles from the estate of Jacqueline Kennedy Onassis: Sotheby's strategic lowball setting of reserves and estimates on the lots offered for sale, which encouraged numerous potential buyers to bid items up to stratospheric levels (for example, a fake triple-strand pearl necklace with estimates of $500 to $700 that sold to the Franklin Mint for $211,500),[1] became a lesson on the value of celebrity provenance. Or note the record-setting sale of a collection at Christie's when the Victor and Sally Ganz Collection brought $206.5 million in November 1997, or Christie's sale of Picasso's *Femme aux Bras Croisés* in November 2000 for $55 million. There is no question that since the late 1970s, art auctions in the United States have emerged as a thriving, sizable business. One proof of the vitality of auctions as a form of commerce has been the emergence over the past decade of hundreds of online auction services, many of them dealing in art and other collectibles. Preeminent among such services is eBay, which lists millions of items from around the world in thousands of categories and boasts more than 90 million registered users.[2]

Art auction sales are, at times, considered a lagging economic market indicator. In a season that witnessed the Wall Street crash of October 19, 1987, the nation's two largest auction houses—Sotheby's, Inc., and Christie, Manson & Woods International, Inc.—handled a combined national sales volume for 1987–88 of approximately $2.4 billion, up from earlier years. In the face of the flagging economy of the late 1980s and early 1990s, the then-flourishing international art market went on to sustain record sales and peak commercial volume, even while the seeds of significant retrenchment were sown. Witness, for example, the May 1990 sale by Christie's of Vincent van Gogh's *Portrait of Dr. Gachet* for a staggering $82.5 million and by Sotheby's of Pierre-Auguste Renoir's *Au Moulin de la Galette* for $78.1 million.[3]

Although the May 1990 sales of contemporary, impressionist, and modern art at Sotheby's and Christie's, New York, lasting ten days, gave rise to a combined all-time auction record of $890 million[4] (Sotheby's and Christie's, New York, traditionally hold their biggest sales in May and November of each year), the sales surpassed the November 1989 sales result by a mere 3%,[5] causing many market observers at the time to note that the raging speculation fueling the market as recently as 1989 had subsided.

In the late 1980s through 1990, largely as a by-product of their thriving national economy, the Japanese had emerged as a dominant market force in the purchasing of art, particularly impressionist and contemporary art. Indeed, both *Portrait of Dr. Gachet* and *Au Moulin de la Galette* were purchased at auction by Japanese executive Ryoei Saito, the former honorary chairman of Daishowa Paper Manufacturing Co.[6]

In early 1991, in a time marked by internal art-related financial corporate scandals[7] and the effects of the worldwide economic recession, Japan retreated in great measure as a major purchaser in the art market. (Saito, for example, was arrested in 1993 for bribing a government official in 1991 in conjunction with a golf course development project. He was sentenced to a suspended three-year jail term in 1995.)[8] As the 1990s progressed and the world economy began to rebound, the economic recovery began to be reflected in gradual but steadily increasing worldwide art auction sales.

By the early 2000s, the art market's upswing was dramatic. Earnings reports for the first half of 2004 showed gross sales at Sotheby's totaling $1.35 billion (almost twice the 2003 total) and at Christie's totaling $1.235 billion (up from $937 million).[9] In fact, some commentators believed the market was once again overheating.[10]

Of course, Sotheby's and Christie's, although tending to receive the most publicity, are by no means the only way to sell art properties at auction; hundreds of auction houses flourish throughout the nation, and some of them are highly specialized. In December 2000, Bernard Arnault, head of the luxury goods company LVMH Moet Hennessy Louis Vuitton SA, merged his recently acquired auction house, the London-based Phillips, with de Pury & Luxembourg, a high-profile art brokerage and consultancy business, in an effort to make Phillips a true third player in the international art market.[11] The timing seemed auspicious for the entry of a third giant: Sotheby's and Christie's at the time were under investigation by the U.S. Department of Justice for alleged price-fixing of buyers' and sellers' commissions, and it was reasonable to suppose that the public might lose confidence in the auction duopoly. However, Phillips-the-newcomer had generally been obliged to secure the bulk of its important properties either by way of purchase or by offering undisclosed guaranteed minimum prices to its vendors regardless of the auction's outcome—not a financially winning strategy for the long term. Accordingly, Arnaud divested himself of Phillips in 2003.[12] Currently, the scaled-down Phillips is focusing its auction sales on high-end contemporary art, photographs, and a few other categories while remaining active in the impressionist and modern art markets largely through sales by private treaty.

TYPES OF AUCTIONS

Two types of auctions can be found in the American art market: the Dutch auction and, far more commonly, the English auction. Although the objective of each type is to secure the highest possible price for an item from a group of bidders, the procedures governing them are markedly different. In the Dutch auction, rarely seen in the United States, the auctioneer starts with the highest price believed to be remotely obtainable and solicits offers at that level. If none is forthcoming, the auctioneer gradually lowers the price until an offer is made. The Dutch auction, as a rule, generates little drama and suspense.

Operating under different ground rules and often surrounded in mystery, suspense, and excitement is the English auction, typified by auctions at Sotheby's and Christie's. In the English auction, the auctioneer starts the bidding at a low price, and bidders competitively make higher offers until the last responsive offer is made and the hammer falls. A variation of the English auction, found infrequently in the art market, is the silent auction. In the silent auction each bidder may place only one bid, and the seller retains the option of either accepting the highest bid or rejecting it.

An auction sale is one in which property is presented for sale to be bid on by assembled bidders and sold for the highest offer. A bid constitutes an offer by a prospective buyer to pay a specified price for the property being auctioned. Put in traditional contract terms, property for sale is presented by the auctioneer as an invitation to make an offer; bidders make offers for the property, with higher bids canceling lower ones as the bidding progresses; a contract is formed when an offer in the form of the highest bid is accepted by the auctioneer. Bids are usually made orally by those attending the sale, but a raised paddle, for example, as a means of visual communication arranged with the auctioneer, is a common way to convey a bid. On occasion, a more elaborate or secretive bidding signal—such as the wink of an eye, the flick of a finger, or a pat on the chin—is worked out with the auctioneer in advance. A bidder may be so secretive that she arranges to bid by telephone to a bid taker in the auction room.

At the auctioneer's discretion, a bidder need not personally attend the sale; rather, she may make order bids—that is, bids made in writing. Several major auction houses, including Christie's and Sotheby's, permit that practice and place bids on behalf of the order bidder on a particular item or lot (items sold together) up to the maximum figure stated by the customer. Such bids are placed in competition with the bids of those attending the sale; if the order bidder is successful, she acquires the property for a price determined by the next bidding increment above the last bid in the auction room as long as the order bidder's maximum written bid is not exceeded. For example, X places an order bid by mail to Sotheby's of a maximum of $100,000 for a particular work of art up for auction. During the course of the auction, bidding for the work is conducted in increments of $1,000, and the auctioneer has duly submitted bids on X's behalf. If the bidding for the work reaches $75,000 with no further bids offered, X will acquire the work for $76,000.

ONLINE AUCTION SERVICES

The proliferation of online auction services, beginning in the 1990s, brought millions of new participants to the auction process. Online auctions are driving the net worth of the online art and collectibles market to an expected $1.8 billion in 2005.[13] As noted above, eBay, the largest online service, offers more than 10 million items for sale at any one time.[14] In 2005, a single search in eBay's art listing revealed approximately 11,000 artworks for sale, ranging from works by artists who are self-represented to original fine art by legends such as Picasso and Lichtenstein, with bids well into the thousands of dollars.[15] As no two services are identical, what follows is an extremely general description of an online auction service.

Usually, a prospective buyer registers to bid with the service at no cost. The prospective buyer indicates the maximum price she will pay for an item and the auction service makes automatic bids on behalf of that party (up to the designated maximum price) against others who are bidding on that same item. Online auctions may take anywhere from three to ten days. At the conclusion of the auction, the online service notifies the prospective buyer by email as to whether that party is the successful bidder or has been outbid. If the party is the successful bidder, she should email the seller within three business days to claim the item—otherwise, the seller might look to the underbidder for a purchase. The buyer should pay promptly and in accordance with the payment options provided by the seller: often a money order, cashier's check, or personal check. Upon receipt of payment, the seller forwards the item to the buyer. The shipping arrangements are between the buyer and seller: Often, the seller indicates, as part of the property's description, who bears the cost of shipping.

Generally, sellers also register with a service at no cost. Sellers do, however, pay both a listing fee to post their items with the service, and a sale fee at the end of the auction (generally a small percentage of the sale price). The seller furnishes the online service with a description and, often, a photograph of the property. Other information the seller generally provides to the service includes the payment options acceptable to the seller, the shipping arrangements, a reserve price (that is, minimum price at which the item may be sold), a start price (a price to start the bidding), and (ideally) a seller's return policy.

Contrary to much of the current law governing live auctions, online auctions are essentially considered to be seller-to-buyer transactions: Given that auction services never see, let alone examine, the actual physical properties posted for sale, this arrangement is both understandable and appropriate. Nevertheless, in an effort to provide some protection to consumers, online services generally offer the following: a feedback board about sellers from other buyers; removal from their services of sellers generating many negative responses; return policies; requirements that sellers provide return policies; and online dispute resolution services.

APPLICATION OF U.C.C.

The Uniform Commercial Code (U.C.C.) supplements and clarifies some of the contractual laws attendant to auction sales. All the provisions of express warranties,[16] warranty of title,[17] the implied warranties of merchantability[18] and fitness for a particular purpose,[19] and the exclusion or modification of warranties[20] discussed with respect to private sales in chapter 2, as well as the statute of limitations for breach of warranty suits discussed in chapter 3, similarly apply to auctions. In addition, other provisions of the U.C.C. apply uniquely to auctions. If goods are offered for sale in lots, for example, the U.C.C. provides that each lot is the subject of a separate sale.[21] The sale of a lot is completed and the bidder's offer is accepted when the auctioneer so indicates by the fall of a hammer (knocking down) or some other customary manner.[22] However, a bidder may retract her bid at any time before the auctioneer's announcement of the completion of the sale.[23] Moreover, the fall of a hammer need not always complete the sale if the auctioneer fully disclosed the identity of the principals and if the sale is conditioned on the approval of the principals.[24]

When a bid is made during the fall of the auctioneer's hammer in acceptance of a prior bid, the auctioneer, under the U.C.C., may, at her discretion, either reopen the bidding or declare the goods sold for the bid on which the hammer was falling.[25]

Marx v. Sotheby Parke-Bernet, Inc.[26]

In May 1980, the plaintiffs, Leonard and Virginia Marx, both knowledgeable and sophisticated collectors of American antiques, participated in an estate auction conducted by Sotheby's at Pokety Farms in Cambridge, Maryland. The auction was held in a large tent, open at the sides, with between 1,200 and 1,500 people sitting inside the tent and others standing or sitting outside the tent. John Marion, an experienced auctioneer and the chairman of Sotheby's, was conducting the auction. Stationed throughout the tent were other Sotheby's employees known as spotters. The Marxes bid on a federal turned and inlaid mahogany wall sofa, and the hammer came down on their $22,000 bid.

Eight to ten seconds later a spotter drew John Marion's attention to a bidder near the rear of the tent who had bid $22,000 at approximately the same time as the Marx bid. Since there was now confusion as to which of the $22,000 bids the auctioneer had accepted, he reopened the bidding; again the sofa went to the Marx couple but for $34,000. The plaintiffs made no protest at the reopening of the bidding but, rather, purchased the sofa and made arrangements for its shipment. The plaintiffs' first protest to Sotheby's was registered three days after the incident in the form of a letter offering Sotheby's a check in the sum of $22,000 plus the then-standard 10% buyer's premium. Sotheby's rejected the check, insisting on full payment of the $34,000 plus the 10% buyer's premium. The New York State Supreme Court, whose holding was confirmed by the appellate division, found in favor of Sotheby's—that is, the plaintiffs owed the defendant $34,000 plus the buyer's premium, costs, and disbursements. Taking all the circumstances particular to the case into consideration, the court relied on the provision of the U.C.C. (the gist of which was also found in Sotheby's sales contract) that mandates that when a bid is made while the hammer is falling in acceptance of a prior bid, the auctioneer at her election may either reopen the bidding or declare the goods sold for the prior bid.

The Statute of Frauds

The statute of frauds provision of the U.C.C.[27] applies to auctions as well as to private sales. Generally, a contract for the sale of goods costing $500 or more is unenforceable unless there is a written document sufficient to indicate that the contract of sale was made between the parties. The document must be signed by the party against whom enforcement is sought or by her authorized agent or broker. Therefore, in the absence of other statutory provisions, if a work of art costs more than $500, the buyer has to sign a memorandum with respect to an offer to buy the work in order to be bound. A number of states, notably New York and California,[28] have enacted specific legislation permitting the auctioneer to bind the successful bidder by entering a memorandum in a sales book or by a similar procedure. New York's statute provides that, notwithstanding the U.C.C., if goods are sold at public auction and at such time the auctioneer "enters in a sale book, a memorandum specifying the nature and price of the property sold, the terms of the sale, the name of the purchaser, and the name of the person on whose account the sale was made," the memorandum has the same effect as a note of the contract or sale signed by the party against whom enforcement is sought.[29]

In states lacking such specific legislation, a written order bid signed by the purchaser should satisfy the statute of frauds. The typical oral or visual bid, however, requires the auctioneer to memorialize carefully the result of the bidding on each lot offered at auction or incur liability for damages if the consignor suffers loss and can establish negligence on the part of the auctioneer.

The statute of frauds issue may also arise with respect to an agreement between the auction house and a finder or agent seeking a commission for the referral of business. In *Mirisola v. Habsburg Feldman, S.A.*,[30] the court found that a written agreement or memorandum is required to enforce an agreement to pay a finder's fee for the plaintiff's successful efforts to induce prospective sellers to consign objects for sale.

RELATIONSHIPS AMONG THE PARTIES

By its nature, an auction sale often involves the participants in relationships of labyrinthine complexity. A description of the major relationships and some of the attendant issues and responsibilities follows.

The consignor-auctioneer relationship. The consignor relies on the auctioneer for the following:

- A determination of whether the artwork is auctionable
- The decision as to whether the artwork, if auctionable, should be placed in a major or minor auction and in the company of which other artwork
- The suggestion of an estimated price
- The suggested reserve price
- Safekeeping of the artwork delivered for sale
- The collection of sales proceeds
- Standing, as an expert, behind the authenticity of the artwork in the event the authenticity is questioned

The auctioneer, on the other hand, relies on the consignor to support the consignor's ownership of title to the work if its provenance is ever questioned.

The purchaser-auctioneer relationship. The purchaser or successful bidder at auction depends on the auctioneer for a determination that the artwork purchased is authentic and that the estimated purchase price is reasonable. All bidders at an auction are entitled to assume that the auction process has integrity and to base their bids on that assumption. If the auctioneer engages in the practice, unbeknownst to the bidders, of knowingly receiving a bid on the seller's behalf or if the seller makes or procures such a bid, the buyer may choose either to void the sale or to take the goods at the price of the last good-faith bid before the completion of the sale.[31] In addition, the purchaser relies on the auctioneer for some assurance that the auctioneer will grant the purchaser clear title to the artwork.

The purchaser-consignor relationship. Although the buyer is aware that works sold at auction are generally owned by third parties, with the auctioneer serving as agent of a generally undisclosed principal, the following question repeatedly arises: To whom does the buyer look for recourse when either the title to the work or the authenticity of the work is questioned? If the issue is one of authenticity, the buyer may claim against the auctioneer, regardless of whether the identity of the principal (the consignor) is known to the buyer. The purchaser of the work has presumably relied on the credibility and the expertise of the auctioneer and on the representations contained in the auctioneer's catalog. If the issue is one of title, the purchaser looks to the auctioneer when the identity of the principal is undisclosed. If, however, the principal is known, the buyer should be able to seek recourse from both the principal and the auctioneer.

Abrams v. Sotheby Parke Bernet, Inc.[32]

The *Abrams* case illustrates the potential for complexities among the parties in an auction.

In June 1984, Sotheby's sold at auction a number of important Hebrew books and manuscripts that were known to have been in the possession of a German seminary and to have been smuggled out of the country before World War II. At first, Sotheby's refused to disclose the identity of the consignor. The attorney general of the state of New York, on behalf of members of the public who might wish to consult the items for religious or scholarly purposes and on the grounds that it was questionable whether the undisclosed consignor could transfer good title, sought to void the sale and have the books and manuscripts returned to the Jewish people. The case raised a number of provocative issues, including the following:

> Could the seminary under the circumstances have transferred good title to anyone?
>
> How did the consignor receive possession of the documents—that is, was the consignor a smuggler or a good-faith purchaser for value?
>
> Could Sotheby's justify its refusal to disclose the identity of the consignor?
>
> What rights did the buyer have against either the auctioneer or the consignor if title was found to be defective?
>
> What standing did the New York attorney general have to question the proposed sale?
>
> What laws governed each aspect of the transaction?

The attorney general asserted claims under two state laws[33] relating to consumer fraud that enable the attorney general to void consumer transactions when innocent buyers have been misled. Further, the attorney general asserted a claim based on particular restitution laws promulgated by the occupation forces after World War II.[34] Those restitution laws carry a presumption that a transfer of property without consideration, during specific years in parts of Germany, is void as having been performed under duress.

The consignor questioned whether the attorney general was acting properly in pursuing the action in the first place, because the attorney general had failed to take any action in comparable situations. However, the case was settled in July 1985 without any determination of the legal issues involved.

By the reported terms of settlement, Sotheby's was to reclaim approximately thirty of the fifty-nine manuscripts and books sold at auction and to donate them to several institutions for the study of Jewish cultural and religious history. Under the settlement agreement, any buyer who could demonstrate that a copy of the work that the buyer purchased was available in an institution for public use would not have to return it to Sotheby's. Such sales, the parties believed, would generate proceeds in excess of $1 million, which were to be distributed to various institutions to be used to purchase rare, scholarly Jewish materials. The consignor, Professor Alexander Guttmann, a teacher at Hebrew Union College, was to receive approximately $900,000, about half the amount that had been raised by the auction and a separate contemporaneous sale to the Jewish Theological Seminary of two of the most valuable documents.

The court invited public comment on the proposed settlement and met with considerable protest. Hebrew Union College submitted a memorandum urging that Guttmann, the consignor, never owned the collection of books and manuscripts and should not receive the $900,000 due him according to the settlement. The college went on to write that concealment of the materials for forty-four years, never divulging that they survived the Nazi era or that he possessed them, is the fact that dominates any assessment of his credibility.[35]

Guttmann was subsequently dismissed from Hebrew Union College.[36]

THE AUCTION HOUSE AND THE CONSIGNOR

Generally, the relationship between the consignor and the auctioneer is a fiduciary one. To be sure, there is an occasional exception, such as the 2001 Louisiana case of *Neal Auction Co.*,[37] which depicts the auctioneer as a mere conduit between seller and buyer. But in New York—as in most states—the auctioneer stands as an agent on behalf of the consignor with an obligation to "act in the utmost good faith and in the interest of [the consignor] throughout their relationship."[38] Although there are limits to the fiduciary relationship between consignor and auctioneer, as illustrated in the *Koven, Mickle,* and *Nelson* decisions (see pages 348–354), a breach of the fiduciary obligations agreed to gives rise to liability on the part of the agent for damages caused to the consignor-principal, whether the cause of action is based on contract or on negligence.[39] Here we examine some of the specific rights, obligations, and limitations to obligations that flow between auctioneer and consignor.

Standard of Care

The auction house, as the consignor's agent, is considered the bailee of the consigned goods. As such, the auction house is responsible for the safe custody of the works delivered to it for the purpose of sale, and it is liable to the consignor if the works are lost or damaged as a result of the auction house's negligence or that of its agents or employees. It has long been the law[40] that an auction house is bound to take care of a consignor's goods as if they were its own but is not liable for a loss arising from misfortune or an unavoidable accident. That is, auction houses are governed by the common-law rules of bailment law, discussed in some detail in chapter 16. To limit further the potential for exposure, auction houses look to the terms of the consignment agreement and seek insurance coverage.

Negligence

In at least one instance, negligence was found not to lie where an auctioneer sold items at auction that the consignor had requested be withdrawn. In *Clay v. Sotheby's*,[41] which involved the sale of a number of antiques from a private collection, an Ohio federal district court held that despite facts that gave rise to a genuine issue regarding the auctioneer's breach of duty, without a showing of damages for loss of sentimental value or the like, the consignor was made whole by properly remitted payment and negligence could not be found.[42] Nor could negligence be found on the part of the auctioneer for items that allegedly sold below market, because an auction "operate[s] as a true open market."[43]

The court also granted summary judgment to Sotheby's on its counterclaim for breach of contract for post-auction storage costs of items that did not sell. In construing the consignment agreement, the court noted that unlike with commissions and expenses, Sotheby's was under no obligation to collect storage fees prior to releasing the property and that it was illogical to think such fees could be included in plaintiff's settlement check.[44]

Statute of Limitations

Under New York law, if an item consigned to an auction house fails to sell at auction, it is not returned to the consignor, and the consignor subsequently sues for its return, the statue of limitations does not begin to run until the consignor demands the property's return and the auction house refuses to return it, as illustrated in *Pilliard v. Sotheby's*,[45] discussed at length in chapter 7.

Negligence claims against auction houses must be brought within the applicable statute of limitations period, as illustrated in the 2001 case of *Pagliai v. Del Re*.[46] Plaintiff Francesca Pagliai in 1983 stored a painting at defendant Marisa del Re's art gallery. In 1996, del Re, while defending an arbitration suit, gave the painting to art dealer James Goodman, the arbitrator, as collateral to secure the amount that Goodman would determine that del Re owed in the suit. Goodman did not ask for, nor did del Re provide, any record or proof of ownership. Goodman researched both the painting's provenance and its approximate value. Goodman subsequently found against del Re. She defaulted on the arbitration award and instructed Goodman to sell the collateral.[47] Goodman duly consigned the painting to Christies's in November 1996 but did not share with Christie's the identity of del Re, and Christie's did not inquire as to whether Goodman or his "client" had proper title. The painting sold at auction in January 1997. Earlier that month, the plaintiff Pagliai, who had forgotten about the painting after she deposited it with del Re and only now remembered its existence, had sought the painting's return. In 1999, after making several such demands for the painting to no avail, Pagliai sued del Re, alleging conversion and seeking a constructive trust to prevent del Re's unjust enrichment by virtue of her conversion, and in April 2000 joined Goodman and Christie's to the action, alleging conversion and negligence.[48]

In holding the negligence claim time-barred, the court noted that the claim against Goodman accrued upon execution of the consignment agreement, and the claim against Christie's, upon sale of the painting at auction. Both events were more than three years before the defendants were joined in the suit.[49] The court also held that neither Christie's nor Goodman could have converted the painting because there was no evidence indicating that either defendant had intentionally interfered with the plaintiff's rights.[50]

The court concluded, however, that del Re had converted the painting by using it as collateral and representing to Goodman that it was hers. Still, plaintiff's action for conversion was time-barred by the three-year statute of limitations in New York. Moreover, even if del Re could be characterized as a bailee, causing the statute to run from the time plaintiff demanded the return of the painting in January 1997, the court viewed the fourteen-year delay after the painting was left with del Re as unreasonable.[51] Relief was granted, however, in the form of a constructive trust on the amount of debt del Re satisfied through the sale of the painting to prevent her unjust enrichment.[52]

The statute of limitations can bar claims against auction houses for refusal to sell a painting and for damages to that painting while in the auction house's care. In *Leventritt v. Sotheby's*,[53] a New York State court held that where Sotheby's predecessor had refused to sell a painting in 1969 on grounds that it was not authentic, no new cause of action arose when Sotheby's itself refused to sell the painting in 2002. Similarly, plaintiff's claim seeking recovery for damage to the painting was also time-barred. "A bailment," the court reasoned, "was created in 1969 when plaintiff entrusted it to [Sotheby's] predecessor for the purpose of selling it at auction. The bailment ended when [Sotheby's] predecessor refused to sell the painting,"[54] at which point plaintiff could not treat the bailment as continuing, but was required to pursue her remedy within the statutory period. Plaintiff's failure to pursue her remedy for more than thirty years barred any claim she may have.

Duty of Disclosure

An auction house must disclose to the consignor any internal disagreement as to the auctionability of the consigned property. If some persons within the auction house believe that the property, though valuable, is not likely to excite the bidding public and would be better placed with a private dealer, that fact must be brought to the consignor's attention.[55] Further, an auction house may have an obligation not to attempt to auction property if the undertaking reasonably appears to be impossible or impracticable.[56] If an auction house is inclined to accept property on consignment, it must disclose to the consignor the risk of loss of value that may occur if the property is offered for sale at auction and fails to sell.[57]

However, New York courts have held that it is a not a breach of a fiduciary duty if an auction house fails to disclose to the consignor, in estimating prices for the consignor's coins, the involvement of an expert or auctioneer opposed by the consignor purely on grounds of personal animus. In the 2000 case of *Reale v. Sotheby's*,[58] a New York State appellate court also dismissed the plaintiff's claim of negligence for allowing an expert to estimate the price of consigned coins without inspecting them; a claim of breach of good faith and fair dealing by scheduling the auction on the same day as another house's coin auction; a claim of breach of fiduciary duty for failure to disclose to the consignor knowledge of the other auction at the time of consignment; and breach of agreement for failure to disclose that consignor could have a reserve for any lot set at its low presale estimate. Of all of plaintiff's claims, the only one not dismissed on summary judgment was an allegation that Sotheby's unilaterally set a global reserve for the auction, to which plaintiff allegedly did not agree, contrary to the consignment agreement, which provided that reserves were to be set by mutual agreement of the parties prior to the date of sale.

Auction Proceeds Are Tantamount to Trust Funds

This issue was so decided in the New York State Supreme Court case of *Edwards v. Horsemen's Sales Co.*[59] The plaintiff, James Edwards, had consigned five horses to the defendant to be sold at auction at the August 1985 yearling sales at Saratoga Springs, New York. The sale, after the deduction of commissions and expenses, netted $49,002. The proceeds of the sale were never remitted to the plaintiff. In October 1986, the plaintiff was awarded a judgment against the defendant company in the amount of $54,514.73. The plaintiff was never paid. The plaintiff then sought an order holding Steve and Benjamin Ostrer (the directors and officers of the defendant, Horsemen's Sales Co.) liable in that, in violation of their trust and fiduciary responsibilities, they misappropriated and converted the sale proceeds to other uses.

In reply to the defendants' contention that they could not be held personally liable for the defaults of the corporation, the court noted that a corporate officer or director may, indeed, be held personally liable for the conversion or misappropriation of trust funds. The court then went on to note that

[u]nder the consignor's contract, the net proceeds of the auction received were to be remitted within 45 days. . . . The requirement to "remit" was something more than an obligation to pay a debt owed. "Where money or property is entrusted to such an agent for a particular purpose, it is impressed by law with a trust in favor of the principal until it has been devoted to such purpose."[60]

The court further noted that the company was financially troubled and that the defendants decided to divert the sales proceeds to satisfy outstanding corporate debts.

The brothers' reliance on "the (accepted) general practice" of auctioneers not to segregate the funds they take in from the sale of property does not excuse the Ostrer brothers from failing to account for moneys received at auction sales. . . . An auctioneer, as an agent of the seller . . . is in a fiduciary position, and has a duty to turn over the proceeds of the auction sale in full.[61]

Auctioneer's Commission

Because the auctioneer acts as agent of the consignor, the consignor pays the auctioneer's commission. In most auction houses the auctioneer's commission is a percentage of the final bid price for a work of art and is based on a graduated scale, with the commission having an inverse relation to the price: for example, 10% for works having a final bid price of $7,500 or more; 15% for works having a final bid price of $2,000 up to $7,499; 20% for works having a final bid price of less than $2,000.

In recent years, however, Sotheby's and Christie's, whose properties often achieve sale prices of six and seven figures and occasionally eight figures (and once, nine figures), have further refined the percentages of their commission rates for such high-priced properties. At Christie's, for example, a consignor whose properties in a given calendar year achieve an aggregate final bid price of, say, $3 million will be charged a commission at the rate of 2%.[62]

Duty to Obtain Best Price

As fiduciary of the consignor, the auctioneer is under an obligation to obtain the best possible validly offered price for the consignor's offering. That obligation, however, may have been compromised by the development over the past twenty-five years or so of two auction policies: the buyer's premium and the guaranteed price.

Buyer's Premium

With the opening of its New York salesroom in May 1977, Christie's introduced into the United States the concept of the buyer's premium, already in effect in London at both Christie's and Sotheby's. (Christie's had announced the new policy in London in July 1975, and Sotheby's followed suit three days later.) The buyer's premium is an additional charge imposed on the buyer. As of this writing, the buyer's premium at both Sotheby's and Christie's is 20% of the first $200,000 of the final bid price and 12% of any overage.[63] The buyer's premium, which is uniformly imposed and largely non-negotiable,[64] has subsequently been adopted in some form by many smaller and regional auction houses.[65]

The buyer's premium as introduced in this country by Christie's was adopted here by Sotheby's in January 1979 amid a wave of protest. Art dealers complained that the buyer's premium yielded extraordinary advantages to auction houses, their competitors, in that the auctioneers could now reduce or even eliminate the commissions charged to consignors. The buyer's premium may still redound to the ultimate disadvantage of the consignor by depressing the prices that buyers are willing to pay at auction, as the buyer must pay an additional percentage over the bid price. The art dealers questioned the legality of an auctioneer's acceptance of payment from the buyer for whom the auctioneer is rendering no service, since, by law, the auctioneer is the consignor-seller's agent.[66] Dealers' efforts to overturn the buyer's premium, both in the United States and in London, have been unsuccessful.

Guaranteed Price

Under the guaranteed price arrangement, the auction house and the seller agree on a minimum price for an individual work, a lot or group of lots, or an entire consignment. The auction house must pay the seller the minimum price, whether or not the work or lot(s) or consignment is sold. If it is not sold, the auction house becomes the owner. If it is sold for a price in excess of the guarantee, the excess is either paid to the seller or divided between the seller and the auction house, depending on the arrangement between the parties.

As a general rule, the closer the guarantee comes to the low estimate, the greater is the auction house's cut of the hammer price beyond the low estimate.[67] If a consignor is guaranteed, say, 75% of the low estimate, the auction house may receive 25% of the hammer price exceeding the low estimate; if a consignor is guaranteed 85% of the low estimate, the auction house may receive 35% of the hammer price exceeding the low estimate. If the hammer price does not exceed the low estimate, the auction house receives merely its negotiated seller's commission. In all instances it also receives the buyer's premium.

The policy of guaranteed pricing was introduced in New York by Sotheby's in November 1972. In March 1990, Christie's International joined Sotheby's and several smaller auction houses, including Butterfield & Butterfield of San Francisco and Los Angeles and William Doyle Galleries of New York, in offering, selectively, minimum-price guarantees for particular consignments.[68] In reversing its long-standing policy of not issuing guarantees, Christie's acknowledged that on occasion it had to avail itself of that financial device to remain competitive.[69]

Proponents of price guarantees assert that the guarantees are a reasonable way of acquiring business and of removing the burden of risk from such sellers as museums and estates, which may have other financial commitments—for instance, acquiring paintings and paying taxes.[70] Detractors of the policy, such as art dealers, agree that guarantees successfully divert some artwork from galleries to the auction market, and they have been highly vocal in their criticism. They claim that guarantees have inflated prices and, in providing the auction house with a great financial stake in the consignment, have given rise to conflicts of interest.[71]

In November 1989, New York City's Department of Consumer Affairs, after an informal look, found that Sotheby's policies on guarantees were not in violation of the department's auction regulations.[72] Even so, in the wake of continuing sharp criticism, Sotheby's subsequently modified its policies on guarantees. In January 1990, it announced that rather than disclose the existence of guaranteed lots merely in New York sales, Sotheby's would disclose the existence of guarantees anywhere in the world an auction occurs and would do so in explicit language.[73] As of this writing, a Sotheby's catalog, under "Buying at Auction" in its closing pages, does disclose such information as follows:

° Guaranteed Property

The seller of lots with this symbol has been guaranteed a minimum price from one auction or a series of auctions. If every lot in a catalogue is guaranteed, the Conditions of Sale will so state and this symbol will not be used for each lot.[74]

Christie's catalogs, likewise, now clearly indicate when property offered for sale at an auction is subject to a guaranteed minimum price. In a recent catalog, under the section titled "Important Notices and Explanation of Cataloguing Practice," a paragraph entitled "Christie's Interest in Property Consigned for Auction" included the following:

On occasion, Christie's has a direct financial interest in lots consigned for sale which may include guaranteeing a minimum price. . . . Such property is identified in the catalogue by the symbol ° next to the lot number. Where Christie's has . . . [a] financial interest in every lot in the catalogue, Christie's will not designate each lot with a symbol, but will state its interest at the front of the catalogue.[75]

Nonrefundable Advances and Nonrecourse Loans

Since 1992, Sotheby's and Christie's have been implementing, as additional consignor-financing, variations on the traditional guarantee—that is, nonrefundable advances at Sotheby's and Christie's and nonrecourse loans at Christie's.[76] Unlike other advances, those arrangements bar the auction houses from attaching the bank accounts or other financial assets of consignors. Nonrefundable advances require sellers to pledge additional collateral if the initial consignment fails to sell. Nonrecourse loans are secured solely by the consigned artwork; if the property fails to sell at auction, Christie's can recover the advance only by reoffering the work at a later auction or by selling it privately. Unlike the traditional guarantee, in which auction houses become owners of property that fails to sell, the houses at no point take title to the property consigned under a nonrefundable advance or nonrecourse loan.[77]

The regulations of the City of New York require disclosure by auction houses in their catalogs of lots in which they have a financial interest or guarantee,[78] but that requirement does not cover property on which advances are made. Nevertheless, both Sotheby's and Christie's do disclose to the public financial arrangements involving nonrefundable advances and nonrecourse loans. In a recent Sotheby's catalog, under "Buying at Auction," Sotheby's notes the following:

Δ **Property in which Sotheby's has an ownership interest**

Lots with this symbol indicate that Sotheby's owns the lot in whole or in part or has an economic interest in the lot equivalent to an ownership interest.[79]

Similarly, in a recent Christie's catalog, under "Important Notices and Explanation of Cataloguing Practice," Christie's includes the following:

Christie's Interest in Property Consigned for Auction

. . . On occasion, Christie's has a direct financial interest in lots consigned for sale which may include . . . making an advance to the consignor that is secured solely by consigned property. Such property is identified in the catalogue by the symbol ° next to the lot number. . . .[80]

Artwork As Collateral for Loans

The 2002 case of *Christie's v. Davis*[81] addresses the use of artwork as collateral for a loan by an auctioneer. The defendants, an art-collecting couple, had secured multiple loans from Christie's totaling over $15 million with hundreds of pieces of art and antiques as collateral. When the defendants defaulted, Christie's sued in replevin to recover the collateral. The New York federal district court awarded summary judgment to Christie's, stressing the clear language of the loan documents. That is, the loan provided that in the event of default, Christie's, which set the low and high presale estimates of each item of collateral, could foreclose on property whose aggregate value, based on the low presale estimates, was twice the amount of the total outstanding indebtedness. This, with the defendants' concession of default, the court noted, gave Christie's superior right to the collateral and entitlement to possession.[82] The defendants contended that Christie's willingness to dump all the works on the market would be commercially unreasonable. The court, however, noted that defendants could bring a separate suit challenging the commercial reasonableness of such a sale, if eventually warranted, but referred again to the plain language of the loan: that the property, in the event of default, would be disposed of in accordance with Christie's discretion.

Appropriate Estimates and Reserve Prices

The auctioneer, as fiduciary of the consignor, has an obligation to prepare reasonable low and high estimated prices and to set appropriate reserve prices that will properly promote the sale of the consignor's property.[83] Low and high estimated prices provide a range within which, in the auctioneer's opinion, a lot is likely to sell. Estimates are not predictions or guarantees of a lot's actual selling price. The reserve price is the confidential minimum price below which a lot will not be sold. Under the U.C.C., auctions, unless expressly stated to the contrary, are deemed to be using reserve prices.[84] In New York City, under special auction regulations that became effective in April 1987,[85] when property is being sold subject to a reserve price, that fact must be indicated by the auction house in the catalog.[86] The reserve price defends the consignor from involuntarily selling her consigned property at a figure far below the anticipated bids. If the hammer price does not reach the reserve price, then, in the absence of a guaranteed-price agreement or other loan agreement with the auctioneer, the consignor becomes the successful bidder and is said to have "bought in" the work. In return for that security, the consignor pays the auctioneer a commission (generally 5% but often a reduced negotiated rate) based on the reserve price. In all cases in New York City, when the reserve price is not bid, the current auction regulations require the auctioneer to announce that the lot has been "passed," "withdrawn," "returned to owner," or "bought in."[87]

When a principal has consigned several works to a single lot or a series of lots in a given auction, there may be combined reserve prices and floating reserve prices. With combined reserve prices, the consignor and the auctioneer agree that the reserve price on each work will be determined by the price brought or expected to be brought by the other works covered by the combined reserve price. With floating reserve prices, the reserve price may be changed as a particular sale progresses, with the consignor waiting to evaluate the market strength before committing herself to a minimum price.

Historically, one controversial aspect of reserve prices has been their secrecy. Opponents of that secrecy cite the unfairness of inducing prospective buyers to waste their time and, frequently, their traveling expenses to bid on merchandise that they have no hope of acquiring. Such opponents also criticize auctioneers for accepting bids for items at far below the reserve price when the auction, in effect, begins only when the reserve price is reached.

Although those objections are valid, they have failed to hold sway in New York. Under New York City's auction regulations of April 1987, reserve prices may remain secret, although, as noted earlier, if a sale carries a reserve price, that fact, but not the price itself, must be indicated in the auction catalog. Moreover, the response of the auction houses and the professional auctioneers who favor the secrecy of reserve prices is equally valid. They argue that the use of floating and combined reserve prices or even of fixed reserve prices that may be changed at the last minute makes the advance publication of reserve prices impractical. Citing their primary obligation to obtain the best price for the consignor, the auctioneers allege that they can best do so by opening the bidding below the reserve price and allowing the drama and the suspense to build with the rising bids. Besides, most auction houses, major and regional alike, incorporate presale high and low estimates of the expected sale prices of consigned works in their catalogs, providing at least a preliminary idea of whether a prospective purchaser has a chance to bid successfully on a given item. In New York City, the law prohibits the reserve price from exceeding the low estimate.[88] In practice, throughout New York City and New York State and most other jurisdictions, the reserve price is generally below the low estimate.

Liability As Market Expert

Unless the consignment agreement provides otherwise, an auction may be canceled or objects withdrawn from the auction wholly at the discretion of the auctioneer.[89] An auction house, having an obligation to render to its consignor truthful opinions as to the value of the consigned work,[90] may incur liability to the consignor under various theories of tort law for an incorrect appraisal (assessment of the monetary value of a work) or authentication (assessment of the genuineness of a work). Those theories of liability include disparagement, defamation (only rarely), and negligent misrepresentation—all of which are treated at some length in chapter 7. However, as seen in the *Ravenna*[91] case, discussed in chapter 7, an auction house is not liable for providing erroneous information as to value or authenticity where the advice is provided gratuitously and is based on a walk-in inquiry.

What follows here is a brief description of a landmark case arising from an incorrect appraisal (where a duty exists to the requesting party) that illuminates the auction house's all-too-real potential for exposure in the course of its daily business.

Cristallina S.A. v. Christie, Manson & Woods International, Inc.[92]

In February 1981, Dimitry Jodidio—the principal officer of Cristallina, a foreign corporation solely in the business of buying and selling artwork—told David Bathurst, then-president of Christie's, that Cristallina wanted to raise $10 million through the sale of several of its paintings. Bathurst examined some of Cristallina's impressionist paintings and gave Jodidio estimates of their value in three possible contexts: a private sale, a low bid at public auction, and a high bid at public auction. Eight paintings were chosen on Bathurst's advice. Bathurst estimated that the eight could be sold privately for approximately $8 million and that at public auction they could be sold for between $8.5 million (the cumulative low bid) and $12.6 million (the cumulative high bid). Christie's agreed to arrange and pay for the shipment of the paintings to New York and to promote the sale. Christie's further agreed to reduce its seller's commission to 4%, with the understanding that if the total proceeds did not exceed $9.4 million, the auction house would forgo its commission entirely and accept only the buyer's premium.

Christie's was subsequently engaged to sell the eight paintings, and it duly advertised and solicited media coverage for the auction. In February 1981, Bathurst and Jodidio tentatively agreed on a reserve price for each of the paintings; however, the final reserve prices were not established until a day before the auction, which was set for May 19, 1981. In addition to the final reserve prices, Christie's established a floating reserve price of $150,000, which it could add to the established reserve price on any painting if circumstances so dictated. Although all the tickets for the auction were sold, the results of the auction were disappointing; only one painting was sold, bringing a price of $2.2 million. The remaining seven paintings were bought in, since no bid reached the reserve price.

In an apparent effort to avoid embarrassment for all parties, Christie's issued a press release announcing that three of the Cristallina paintings had been sold for a total of $5.6 million. Christie's did inform Jodidio that, in fact, only one painting had been sold, and the unsold paintings were subsequently returned to Cristallina.

Cristallina brought suit against Christie's, alleging that Bathurst and Christie's misrepresented their abilities to accurately assess current market conditions and to accurately estimate the value of the Cristallina paintings. That is, Cristallina alleged that the initial estimates given by Bathurst at the February 1981 meetings were false and were given solely to induce Cristallina to engage Christie's services. Cristallina further alleged that the reserve price for each picture was too high in relation to its actual value, thereby diminishing its chances of being sold at auction. Cristallina also alleged that Christie's failed to warn it of the dangers inherent in an auction— that is, that the failure to sell a painting has an adverse effect on its value in any future sale.

The lower court dismissed the action, but on Cristallina's appeal, the appellate division modified the decision so as to deny, on six of the eight causes of action, the defendant's motion to dismiss the case.[93] In January 1987, after the case had been on trial for a week, the parties reached a settlement, whereby Cristallina dropped all its charges against Christie's in exchange for a cash payment of an undisclosed amount, estimated, in one account, to be possibly more than $1 million. Cristallina had originally sought $5.5 million (including $2.2 million in interest), which it contended was the amount that it lost because of the decrease in value of the paintings after they had failed to sell at auction.[94]

Limitations on Fiduciary Obligations

Contractual Limitations

Although under New York law an auctioneer clearly has a fiduciary duty to its consignor, is it a fiduciary duty of undivided loyalty, or can the fiduciary relationship be, and is it, modified by contract? The *Koven*[95] case made clear that an auctioneer is able to, and generally does, modify its fiduciary relationship with a consignor. The consignor, Jane Koven, an art collector, decided in December 1989 to sell at auction through Christie's a pastel purportedly created by Georges Braque, a noted twentieth-century French painter. Koven and her husband had acquired the pastel from the Rosenberg gallery, a reputable New York art dealer, in 1948 for $1,400. In December 1989, Koven entered into a written consignment agreement with Christie's, a standard-form contract with a number of provisions deleted. Christie's then conducted its standard internal review to assure itself of the Braque's authenticity—an essential procedure, since Christie's guarantees the authenticity of the artwork it sells. Once assured of the pastel's authenticity, Christie's promoted it extensively, and in May 1990 it was offered at auction and purchased for $600,000 by Barbaralee Diamonstein, a person active in the art and cultural world of New York City.

Either shortly before (according to Diamonstein) or after (according to Christie's) the sale,[96] Diamonstein raised questions about the Braque's authenticity. To reassure Diamonstein, Christie's obtained documentation of the pastel's provenance from the Rosenberg gallery and then wrote several letters to Diamonstein averring that Christie's had no doubt about the pastel's authenticity. Diamonstein, unsatisfied, demanded that Christie's provide her with written verification of the pastel's authenticity from a scholar. Christie's duly arranged to have the work authenticated as a Braque by the independent expert Claude Laurens, holder of the *droit moral* for Braque,[97] and in November 1990 had the pastel flown to France, where it could be examined by both Claude Laurens and his son

Quentin, who, by agreement with his father, had recently assumed the authentication of Braque's works.

In January 1991, Quentin Laurens informed Christie's that he did not believe the pastel to be the work of Braque, whereupon Christie's rescinded the sale; it refunded to Diamonstein the $660,000 purchase price (hammer price plus the 10% buyer's premium then in effect) and sought return of the sales proceeds from Koven. Koven refused to return the proceeds, and Christie's filed for reimbursement from its insurance company, which in turn sued Koven in a New York federal district court. Koven claimed that Christie's, as her agent, should not have investigated the authenticity of the pastel. Christie's underwriters won on summary judgment.

In the *Koven* case there were two issues to consider: (1) Did Christie's breach a fiduciary duty owed to Koven simply by undertaking an investigation of Diamonstein's complaints about authenticity? (2) Did Christie's investigatory actions and subsequent rescission breach its duty of care to Koven under the consignment agreement? As to the first issue, the federal district court held that Christie's did not breach any duty to Koven when it undertook to investigate Diamonstein's complaints about authenticity. In reaching that conclusion, the court, although acknowledging that an agent such as Christie's is required under the law to act in a fiduciary capacity on behalf of its consignor-principal, noted that

> the duty of undivided loyalty, however, is not the only pertinent principle. Equally relevant is the principle [citing the Restatement (Second) of Agency, section 387 (1958)] that the terms of an agency relationship may be modified by contract.[98]

The court also cited the *Restatement* for the proposition that an agent, as in the case here with Christie's, can enter into a transaction giving it dual loyalties and that the behavior is permissible if agreed to by the parties.[99] As the court continued:

> Once it is recognized that Christie's fiduciary responsibilities may be modified by agreement, the question becomes whether or not the Consignment Agreement modified Christie's duty of

undivided loyalty in such a way that Christie's investigative actions in response to Diamonstein's complaints were permissible.[100]

The court noted that fiduciary responsibility is a matter of con-
tract interpretation. Turning to the consignment agreement between
Koven and Christie's, the court noted that paragraph 1 made
Christie's obligations to Koven

> explicitly subject to the Conditions of Sale and [the] Limited
> Warranty [guaranteeing the pastel's authenticity] that govern
> the relationship between Diamonstein and Christie's.[101]

In addition, as the court noted, paragraph 9 of the consignment
agreement, which grants Christie's the discretion to seek "the views
of any expert,"[102] presumes that Christie's will do so and that, contrary to Koven's allegations, the discretion is not limited to presale
matters. As also noted, paragraph 15 of the consignment agreement
authorizes Christie's to rescind the sale of any property if Christie's
"in its sole judgment determines"[103] that the sale has subjected or
may subject Christie's to liability under the warranty of authenticity.
In summary, on review of the provisions of the consignment contract
and of agency law in general, the federal district court concluded
that Christie's duty of undivided loyalty to Koven was permissibly
modified by contract in such a way that Christie's investigative actions in response to Diamonstein's complaints were proper.

As to the second issue—whether Christie's exercised the proper
standard of care to Koven in determining to rescind the sale—the
court held in favor of Christie's. Noting again paragraph 15 of the
consignment agreement, which specifically gave Christie's the right
to rescind a sale when it determined in its sole judgment that it might
incur liability as a result of the sale, the court stated that the clause is
highly analogous to the body of law addressing satisfaction clauses
and that in this case the language is clear that a subjective standard of
satisfaction—Christie's satisfaction—rather than a reasonable standard of satisfaction applied.[104] However, since, as the court observed,
Christie's obligations to Koven were grounded in an implied cove-

nant of "good faith and fair dealing," Christie's was required to have an honest belief that it might be subject to litigation prior to rescission. As the court noted, although that

> is undoubtedly not the level of protection Koven would like . . .
> it is significant protection in assuring that Christie's would not
> use its broad power with indifference to Koven's interest.[105]

The court concluded that if Koven sought more protection, she should have bargained for it in the consignment agreement.

The same issues were dealt with in the 1995 case of *Kohler v. Hindman*.[106] Consignors Peter and Walter Kohler sued Chicago auctioneer Leslie Hindman and buyer Richard Thune after the auctioneer agreed to rescind the sale for $90,000 of a painting, *The Plains of Meudon*, allegedly by Theodore Rousseau, when a Rousseau expert confirmed in writing that the painting was not a Rousseau. In reasoning similar to *Koven*, an Illinois federal district court noted that in the consignment agreement

> Hindman reserved a very broad power to rescind a sale if [Hind-
> man] at any time in [its] sole discretion determined that the of-
> fering for sale of any Property . . . subjected [Hindman or the
> Kohlers] to . . . liability."[107]

It should be stressed that the auctioneer's right to rescind a sale, vis-à-vis the consignor, is circumscribed by the consignment agreement, as illustrated by *Nass v. Sotheby's, Inc.*[108] Herbert E. Nass consigned property to Sotheby's that was sold to a telephone bidder. Later that day Sotheby's canceled the sale when the bidder informed Sotheby's that it had made an error by bidding on the wrong lot. In canceling the sale, Sotheby's relied on a clause in the conditions of sale that was incorporated into the consignment agreement. The clause in relevant part stated: "Although in our discretion we will execute order bids or accept telephone bids as a convenience to clients who are not present at auctions, we are not responsible for any errors or omissions in connection therewith." In granting Nass's motion for summary judgment on his cause of action for breach of the consignment contract, the court determined that the property turned over to Sotheby's was offered for sale at public auction by Sotheby's as the consignor's agent. The agent can act only under the authority granted to it by the contract, and in this case the agent had no authority to cancel the sale unless, as provided in the consignment contract, the property was inaccurately described in the catalog or was counterfeit. The exculpatory clause inserted in the conditions of sale is to protect the auction house from any liability to the purchaser, not to the consignor. The court in *Nass* found that Sotheby's may be exculpated from responsibility to the purchaser for an error or an omission made in connection with receipt of a telephone bid, but it is still responsible to the consignor for the rescission of a consummated sale, in violation of the consignment agreement.

In the 2002 decision of *Mickle v. Christie's*,[109] a New York federal district court, following *Koven*, held that where the authenticity of a painting purportedly by the artist Carl Wimar was questioned after its sale at auction, Christie's, in canceling the sale, violated neither any duty of good faith and fair dealing nor any fiduciary duty to the seller. The two relevant provisions of Christie's consignment agreement provided, in pertinent part, as follows:

> Paragraph 8(b). Non-Payment by Buyer. . . . [I]n the event of non-payment by the buyer, Christie's in our sole discretion, as Consignor's agent or on our own behalf, may cancel the sale and return the Property to Consignor. . . .[110]

> Paragraph 8(c). Rescission of Sale. Christie's, as Consignor's agent, is authorized to accept the return and rescind the sale of any lot of Property at any time if Christie's in our sole judgment determines that the offering for sale of any Property has subjected or may subject Christie's and/or Consignor to any liability. . . .[111]

The "Wimar" painting was purchased at a Christie's auction held in May 1999 by the Schwarz Gallery. The Gallery subsequently had doubts about the Wimar attribution and refused to pay for the painting which remained in Christie's custody. After further research by both Christie's and the Gallery during the ensuing two years,

Christie's concluded that it could no longer in good faith sell the painting as a Wimar and notified the consignors by letter of its intention to cancel and rescind the sale. In its letter to the consignors, Christie's noted that it "may be subject to liability under the warranty it provides to [the Gallery] if the sale of [the painting] were enforced.[112] Accordingly, Christie's canceled and rescinded the sale of the painting, and the consignors sought a preliminary injunction and temporary restraining order to prevent Christie's from doing so.

In denying the consignors' motion, the court, after noting that the legal duties of an agent may be defined and circumscribed by agreement between agent and principal, held that the nonpayment provision (paragraph 8(b)) of the consignment agreement unequivocally authorized Christie's to cancel the sale unconditionally, not only at its sole discretion but on its own behalf. The court also found that the rescission-of-sale provision (paragraph 8(c)) provided a second basis upon which Christie's could cancel the sale and rescind the contract. First, the language "at any time" and "sole judgment" compels this conclusion. Second, the language includes present and past events as well as potential liabilities that "may" arise from Christie's sale of the painting. Third, rescission may be triggered by Christie's concern over "any" liability, which includes the issue of authenticity. The court also noted that agreements, like this one, that confer on one party an indefinite right to condition performance upon a determination based on sole discretion may properly be governed by the subjective standard of the acting party—provided the party so empowered exercises honest judgment. In view of the evidence pointing to the questionable authenticity of the painting, the court found that such was the case here.

Other Limitations

Nelson v. Sotheby's[113] further clarifies the limitations to an auctioneer's fiduciary duty. In *Nelson*, the plaintiff, in November 1988, submitted a painting by Italian surrealist Giorgio de Chirico entitled *Piazza de Italia* to Sotheby's for appraisal and possible sale. While in Sotheby's possession, a third party asserted a claim of title, and Sotheby's notified the plaintiff that it would not release the painting until ownership was resolved. The third party sued both Sotheby's and Nelson. Sotheby's filed an answer and counterclaim in that action but did not serve Nelson. That case was dismissed in June 1993.

Throughout the time of that earlier action and until January 2000, Nelson telephoned Sotheby's requesting the painting's return. He claimed he was neither served in nor notified of the earlier action. Sotheby's admitted to holding the painting for an excessive period of time, and when it was returned in March 2000, Nelson sued in an Illinois federal district court claiming breach of fiduciary duty and breach of the consignment agreement.[114]

With regard to plaintiff's claim for breach of fiduciary duty for failure to apprise him of the earlier action, the court observed that there was no indication that Sotheby's was acting as an agent for the sale of the painting; rather, the purpose of the consignment was an appraisal. Citing Illinois law, the court noted that while a fiduciary duty may arise as a matter of law from certain relationships—including that of agent and principal—requiring Sotheby's to apprise plaintiff of the earlier action and its status, in the absence of such a legal relationship or other special circumstances, parties to a contract in general do not owe a fiduciary duty to one another, and plaintiff's claim had to be dismissed.[115]

However, summary judgment was not granted against plaintiff's claim for breach of the consignment agreement. As the court explained, the consignment receipt stating that the painting was "left for evaluation" was a type of bailment, and implied in a contract for bailment is redelivery.[116] Where, as here, the agreement was silent on the subject of redelivery or performance, the bailee's obligation is usually guided by industry custom and usage, or a reasonable time is implied. In the court's opinion, the delay in returning the painting from 1993 until 2000 was a clear failure on Sotheby's part to perform its obligation.[117]

Although a fiduciary duty arises in New York between consignor and auctioneer, the same does not necessarily hold true for other jurisdictions, as seen in the North Carolina case of *Shalford v. Shelley's Jewelry, Inc.*[118] In 1998, the plaintiff, himself an experienced auctioneer, had entered into a consignment contract with Shelley's for the sale of his estate, which included both personal property and the lordship of a land barony in England. Subsequently, the plaintiff grew dissatisfied with various aspects of the pre-auction process, such as the packing, transporting, handling, and pricing of the property. Shelley's, in turn, declined to auction the property, as it believed it was overpriced by the consignor. A short time thereafter, plaintiff, who did in fact sell a fraction of the property through a commercial liquidator for a value well above the total Shelley's thought could be raised at auction, sued Shelley's for breach of fiduciary duty.

In holding against plaintiff, a federal district court applying North Carolina law noted that plaintiff was a licensed auctioneer and that this was not plaintiff's first experience in hiring an auctioneer to sell portions of his estate. But the language of the court evinces a more stringent standard for finding a fiduciary relationship under North Carolina law:

> In North Carolina, "parties to a contract do not thereby become each others' fiduciaries; they generally owe no special duty to one another beyond the terms of the contract". . . . Moreover . . . where mutually interdependent business people, situated in equal bargaining positions and at arms' length, [are not] in a fiduciary relationship. . . . North Carolina law requires a degree of "superiority and influence" [to create] the "special circumstance" of a fiduciary relationship. . . . By all lights, plaintiffs are independent, sophisticated, if small business people.[119]

Though the existence of a fiduciary relationship is ordinarily a question of fact for the jury, the court found, as a matter of law, that plaintiff's experience in and knowledge of the auction business prevented the finding of a fiduciary relationship based on "special circumstances" resulting from one party having "superiority and influence" over the other.[120]

Consignor's Assurances of Good and Clear Title

As noted earlier, the auctioneer relies on the consignor to ensure, usually in the form of a warranty,[121] that the consignor has the right to pass good title to the property consigned, free and clear of all liens, claims, and encumbrances. If that warranty is breached, the auctioneer requires indemnity from the consignor either before or after the auction takes place. If a title dispute arises before the auction, the auctioneer may withdraw the disputed property[122] and, retaining possession, either enter into litigation[123] or seek interpleader, that is, take steps to have the dispute resolved in the courts between the consignor and the person disputing the consignor's title.

A court of law, not the auctioneer, is in a position to decide who, among competing claimants, has title. That being said, however, we know of one relatively recent case in which a major rare-book auctioneer was satisfied with a distinguished university's claim against the consignor that it was the true owner of a disputed volume; the auctioneer withdrew the book from the consignment and returned it to the university. The auctioneer required full indemnification from the university, as well as a release by the university from liability arising from any claims on the volume from the consignor or any other parties.[124]

Consignment Contracts

When artwork is consigned to an auctioneer for the purpose of sale, the relationship that arises between the consignor and the auctioneer is governed by general fiduciary principles. However, the specifics of the consignor-auctioneer relationship are controlled both by the auctioneer's consignment contracts, which frequently modify the fiduciary relationship between consignor and auctioneer, and by other agreements relating to auction sales, such as the buyer's Conditions of Sale and Terms of Guarantee generally found in an auction catalog. The two major auction houses, Sotheby's and Christie's, have over the years developed elaborate consignment documents, the latest versions of which are reproduced at the close of this chapter (Appendixes 4-1 and 4-2). The following is a brief description of some of the major points covered by the documents, along with a notation of any significant differences in the treatment of the points by the two auction houses.

Before exploring some of the areas covered by the consignment documents, we should first state that the doctrine of *contra proferentem* is still viable in New York. Under that rule, ambiguous language in a form contract, such as a consignment agreement between a consignor and an auctioneer, may be construed against the drafter of the contract. New York courts, however, have recognized that the doctrine is to be used as a matter of last resort after other aids of construction have failed to resolve ambiguities.[125] When a consignment agreement is not ambiguous, the courts may enforce its express terms.[126]

Auctioneer's Discretion

The auction house reserves absolute discretion as to the following:

- The place and the date of the sale
- The manner of conducting the sale
- The grouping of property into lots or separate auctions
- Consultations, if any, with experts either before or after the sale
- Providing catalogs and other descriptions of the property
- The marketing and promotion of the sale

Commission

For the auctioneer's services as the seller's agent in organizing, promoting, and holding the auction sale, the auctioneer charges the seller a commission.

As of this writing, the commission structure at Sotheby's (in the absence of other negotiated terms) is as follows:

Hammer Price per Lot

0 USD to 1,999 USD	20% of the hammer price
2,000 USD up to 7,499 USD	15% of the hammer price
7,500 USD or more	10% of the hammer price

As of this writing, the commission structure at Christie's is as follows:

1. If the aggregate final bid price of all property sold by the consignor during the calendar year of the current consignment totals less than $100,000, the commission is 20% of the sale price per lot selling under $2,000, 15% of the sale price per lot selling between $2,000 and $7,499, and 10% of the sale price per lot selling at $7,500 to $99,999.

2. If the aggregate final bid price of all property sold by the consignor during the calendar year of the current consignment totals $100,000 or more, the commission rate per lot is as follows:

Commission Rate per Lot	Total Property Value
8% of final bid price	$100,000 – $249,999
7% of final bid price	$250,000 – $499,999
5% of final bid price	$500,000 – $999,999
4% of final bid price	$1,000,000 – $2,499,999
2% of final bid price	$2,500,000 – $4,999,999
As agreed	$5,000,000 or more

Sotheby's and Christie's charge a minimum commission of $100 per lot sold; Christie's East charges a minimum of $50 per lot sold.

As noted earlier, each auction house further charges a premium to be collected from the buyer. As of this writing, both Sotheby's and Christie's impose a buyer's premium of 20% of the first $200,000 of the final bid price and 12% of any overage.

Settlement of Account

Thirty-five days after the date of the sale, the auction house pays the seller the net sales proceeds minus its commissions, the buyer's premium, and reimbursable expenses.

Seller's Representations and Warranties

The seller must warrant and represent to the auctioneer and the purchaser that the seller has the right and the title to consign the property for sale; that the property is free and clear of all liens, claims, and encumbrances; that the seller has no reason to believe that any lot of property is not authentic or is counterfeit; that there are no restrictions on the auctioneer's right to reproduce photographs of the property; and that where property has been imported into the United States, it has been lawfully imported and any exportation of property from a foreign government is in compliance with that government's laws. In addition, Sotheby's requires a warranty and representation that the seller has provided all information she has concerning the provenance of the consigned property.

Indemnification

Both Sotheby's and Christie's require broad indemnifications from the seller. Under Christie's consignment agreement, the seller's representations and warranties are made for the benefit of the buyer as well as the auction house. Sotheby's consignment agreement requires the seller to provide indemnification to the buyer as well as the auction house.

As indicated, ambiguities in the contract are resolved against the drafter of the contract, which is usually the auction house. An example can be found in *Basmajian v. Christie's*,[127] in which the court ordered Christie's to return funds retained by it to reimburse it for legal fees incurred when a third party, Walt Disney Productions, sued to prevent the sale of Disney celluloids, sketches, and drawings collected by Basmajian. The court found no contractual language entitling Christie's to recover the expense. Christie's attempted to rely on the following provision contained in the consignment contract:

> Seller further agrees to indemnify Christie's and hold it harmless from and against any and all claims, loss, liabilities and expenses (including reasonable attorney's fees) relating to the claims of buyer or person claiming for buyers resulting from Christie's offering for sale or selling any Property consigned hereunder, whether or not it has been returned to Christie's.

The court rejected the argument because Disney was neither a buyer nor a person claiming for a buyer. The contractual provision permitting Christie's to recover payments made on the seller's account was inapplicable because the payments were not made on the seller's behalf. The contractual clause permitting Christie's to deduct any expenses due it, which incorporated the common law of agency, was also unavailable because the fees were not expended to protect Basmajian's interests.

The current Christie's and Sotheby's standard consignment contracts now deal with that problem by expanding the consignor's responsibility to cover claims made by the buyer or any other person.

Expenses

As between the seller and the auction house, generally, the seller bears the expenses for insurance, catalog illustration, packing, shipping and any customs duties, reproduction rights, tests (if any) to verify authenticity, special advertising and promotional efforts, framing and restoration procedures (if any), and storage of property after sale (if applicable). Who will bear specific costs may be negotiable.

Copyright Matters

The auction house reserves an unrestricted right to photograph and to reproduce and distribute photographs of the property consigned for sale. The auction house retains copyright in all blocks, prints, plates, and other illustrations and depictions of the property that it creates.[128]

Buyer's Nonpayment

Each of the two auction houses specifically states that it has no obligation to enforce payment by any purchaser. If a buyer does not pay, each auction house reserves the right to cancel the sale and to return the property to the seller. Christie's contract provides that it may, at its sole election, enforce payment by the buyer. Sotheby's authorizes itself to impose and retain for its account a late charge on the purchaser if payment is not made in accordance with the Conditions of Sale.

Reserve Prices

Both Sotheby's and Christie's agreements provide that the reserve price for a lot will not exceed its low presale estimate. (As noted earlier, the reserve price is the confidential minimum price below which the property will not be sold.) Under Christie's contract the reserve price, unless agreed to by Christie's and the seller and confirmed by the seller in writing, is determined by Christie's in its sole discretion. Under Sotheby's contract the reserve price, unless agreed to by the consignor and the auctioneer and confirmed in writing, is 60% of the lot's latest published low presale estimate. Both Sotheby's and Christie's retain the right to sell any lot below its reserve price, provided the seller receives the net amount to which she would be entitled had the lot been sold at its reserve price.

Rescission

The auction house may rescind the sale of any property if, in its sole judgment, it determines that the sale offering subjects or may subject either the auction house or the seller to any liability.

Private Sales

Sotheby's agreement reserves the right for sixty days after the auction to sell privately as the seller's exclusive agent any bought-in property, provided the seller would realize an amount at least equal to what she would have received had the property sold at auction at the reserve price. Christie's provision is similar except that Christie's limits itself to a thirty-day period.

Withdrawal

Once the consignment agreement is executed, a consignor may not withdraw property from a sale. If Christie's nevertheless *consents* to a withdrawal or if at Sotheby's a consignor in any event withdraws property, the consignor must pay the auction house 20% of the mean of the presale estimates (or, at Christie's, if the reserve price has been set, 20% of the reserve price) plus all out-of-pocket expenses incurred by the auction house related to the sale of the withdrawn property.

The auction house, however, reserves the right to withdraw any property at any time before the sale if, in its sole judgment, there is doubt as to the property's authenticity or attribution; any of the consignor's representations or warranties, such as relating to title, are inaccurate; the consignor has breached any provision of the consignment agreement; or (at Christie's) "other just cause exists."

When the Consignor Is a Dealer

Both Sotheby's and Christie's, as well as a number of other auction houses, offer a special lower commission structure payable to the auction house when the consignor is a dealer in the type of property sold through the auction house. Other than offering dealers a more favorable commission rate, the terms of consignment for dealers and nondealers are virtually identical.

THE AUCTION HOUSE AND THE PURCHASER

Although no fiduciary relationship exists between the auctioneer and the purchaser, the parties are nevertheless bound by certain rights and obligations. The major ones are noted below.

Jurisdiction over Bidders

With out-of-state bidders this question often arises: If a prospective purchaser's bids are taken seriously, do the courts of the state where the auction house is located have jurisdiction over that party if she decides not to go through with the sale? The answer is generally yes. Out-of-state bidders subject themselves to the jurisdiction of the local forum of the auction house. The process of bidding either personally or through an agent serves to bind the successful bidder to a contract enforceable under the substantive and procedural rules of the jurisdiction where the auction house is located.

That issue was decided in New York some years ago.[129] In March 1967, Dr. Robert Franklyn, living in California, received a catalog from Parke-Bernet Galleries describing some paintings to be sold at auction at its New York City galleries on April 6. Franklyn notified Parke-Bernet by letter that he wished to bid up to $71,000 for a particular painting. On the day before the auction, Franklyn called Parke-Bernet and requested that the auction house set up telephone communication during the auction so that Franklyn could participate during the bidding. His desire to participate in that manner was confirmed by telegram, in which he further stated that he might also bid on additional lots.

The auction house accordingly opened a telephone line the evening of the auction and assigned a Parke-Bernet employee to keep Franklyn apprised of the bids being made in the auction room and to relay, in turn, Franklyn's bids. At the close of the auction, Franklyn had acquired two paintings—a Roger de la Fresnaye and a Paul Klee, for $70,000 and $26,000, respectively. After billing Franklyn and receiving no payment, Parke-Bernet sued him for the amount owed. Franklyn moved to dismiss the suit on the ground that the court lacked jurisdiction over his person.

The New York long-arm statute,[130] like long-arm statutes in other states,[131] vests the New York courts with personal jurisdiction over any nondomiciliary who in person or through an agent transacts any business within the state if a cause of action arises from that transaction. The New York courts in the past had concluded that it was the purpose of the long-arm statute to extend the jurisdiction of the state courts to nonresidents who have "engaged in some purposeful activity [here] in connection with the matter in suit . . . [and that] a single transaction in New York would satisfy this statutory requirement."[132] The court in the *Franklyn* case emphasized that physical presence was not required under the long-arm statute and that, indeed, "one can engage in extensive purposeful activity here without ever actually setting foot in the State."[133] The court further noted that the case

> falls between the situation where a defendant was physically
> present at the time the contract was made—the clearest sort of
> case in which our courts would have [long-arm] jurisdiction—
> and the situation where a defendant merely telephones a single
> order from outside the State—a case in which our courts would
> not have such jurisdiction.[134]

The court then noted Franklyn's active participation in the bidding, assisted by the Parke-Bernet employee, and concluded that

> [w]hether we view this case as one in which the defendant had
> personally engaged in purposeful activity here or as one in
> which . . . he had engaged in such activity "through an agent"
> present here, there is ample basis for concluding that the defendant is subject to the jurisdiction of our courts with respect to a
> cause of action arising out of the auction.[135]

It is worth stressing that when a cause of action arises out of a single transaction with a nonresident,

> the appropriate inquiry is whether the [nonresident] purpose-fully avails herself of the privilege of conducting activities in-state, thereby invoking the benefits and protections of the forum state's laws. . . . Jurisdiction is improper if grounded in the uni-lateral activity of the resident.[136]

Accordingly, in a case involving the sale of a stone bust, a Mississippi federal district court granted a defendant New York art gallery's motion to dismiss for lack of personal jurisdiction, finding that a single telephone call and mailing of a check by the defendant to Mississippi was not sufficient to activate Mississippi's long-arm statute. The plaintiff sued the defendant for allegedly auctioning a stone bust through Sotheby's for $22,000 and mailing the plaintiff a mere $5,200 from a private sale, claiming Sotheby's did not accept the stone bust for sale at auction.[137]

Sales Tax

Purchasers of artwork at auction must be aware that they may be liable for sales taxes on their purchases. For example, the sales tax as of June 1, 2005, is 8.375% for property sold in New York City. Many other cities and states also impose sales taxes on property sold within their borders.

The applicable sales taxes are collected by the auction house from the purchasers and are then remitted to the appropriate taxing authorities. If the purchaser is an out-of-state resident and the artwork purchased is delivered by common carrier to the purchaser out-of-state, the sales tax does not apply, but often a use tax in the purchaser's home state is due. If the auction house maintains an office in the out-of-state location of the purchaser, then the auction house will charge that state's sales tax. For example, if a California resident buys something from Christie's in New York, Christie's will bill the California resident for the California sales tax even if the artwork is delivered by common carrier, since Christie's has an office in

California. Purchasers sometimes believe that they can avoid the sales tax by having an art dealer (who has a resale certificate, exempting her from paying the sales tax) buy the artwork on the purchaser's behalf. That belief is not correct, since the art dealer then becomes legally obligated to collect the sales tax from the ultimate purchaser. Sales and use taxes are discussed in detail in chapter 13, beginning at page 1459.

Authenticity

The artwork that a purchaser acquires at auction must be, in terms of authorship, what it is described to be. Some scant case law in the first half of the twentieth century granted aggrieved purchasers alleging fraud on the part of auctioneers relief in the form of rescission of contract,[138] but such cases did little to defeat the public perception of an auction house as a mere (and protected) conduit between seller and buyer. The responsiveness of state and local lawmakers in New York to buyers' concerns, beginning in the 1960s, resulted in legislation that has considerably alleviated purchasers' fears. Before 1966, a New York auction house acted solely as the seller's agent, contending that the buyer must seek any recourse against the seller, a frequently remote figure unidentified to the buyer. In keeping with that assertion, auctioneers, as a rule, disclaimed all warranties and representations and virtually all responsibility with respect to the works offered for sale. Then in 1966 in response to claims of auctioneer unconscionability, New York enacted legislation addressing the creation and the negation of express warranties in the sale of works of fine art.[139] Legislation in 1968 limited the application of the warranties to sales by art merchants to nonmerchants and further curtailed the power to negate such warranties.[140]

In the wake of the legislative diminution of disclaimers arose the 1971 case of *Weisz v. Parke-Bernet Galleries, Inc.*,[141] discussed in more detail in chapter 2. The lower court ruled that the plaintiff-purchasers could recover the purchase prices paid for paintings that Parke-Bernet had incorrectly described as being by Raoul Dufy. As one of its defenses, Parke-Bernet had submitted the traditional plea that it was acting only as an agent and that the purchasers should pursue the responsible party—that is, the consignor. The lower court dismissed that argument, possibly in view of the developing legislation. The lower court was reversed by the appellate court, which noted that at the time of that public auction the law did not recognize the expressed opinion of the seller as giving rise to any implied warranty of authenticity of authorship.[142] However, the case augured a judicial deathblow to the auctioneer's historical stance as a nonculpable agent.

Limited Warranties

In response to the evolving legislative and judicial perception of the auctioneer as a responsible and potentially culpable party, Sotheby's reversed its former position. Beginning in September 1973, on lots sold in its New York salesroom, it guaranteed for five years (1) the authorship of any work executed after 1869 and (2) that the work was not a counterfeit in the case of works executed before 1870. Christie's, on entering the New York market in 1977, offered a similarly limited warranty. The most recent versions of those warranties are included at the close of this chapter (Appendixes 4-3 and 4-4) along with a glossary that clarifies just when the guarantee of authenticity is present (Appendix 4-5). Those warranties extend solely to a work's authorship and do not address either its physical condition or its provenance. While such warranties will not in and of themselves enable a purchaser to prevail against an auction house on, say, a theory of fraud (as seen in the *Zoellner* case[143] discussed in chapter 7), the combined effects, nevertheless, of the legislative, judicial, and trade developments in New York have done much to bolster the protection and the confidence of the purchaser.

Indeed, in a case in the late 1980s involving the authenticity of a Fabergé egg, Christie's was impelled by the purchaser to agree to a settlement. A summary of the dispute, discussed in chapter 3 in the context of modern forgeries, follows.

The Case of the Fabergé Egg[144]

On April 27, 1977, an Iranian-born businessman, Eskandar Aryeh, purchased at auction from Christie's in Geneva a Fabergé Imperial Enameled Easter Egg. The hammer price of $250,000 was, at the time, the highest price paid for a Fabergé Imperial Egg. Shortly after the auction, Aryeh began to doubt the authenticity of the egg because of its slight discoloration and the quality of the workmanship; consequently, he refused to accept delivery or to pay for it unless he was given proof that the egg was genuine. In response, Christie's Geneva issued a letter certifying the egg as an authentic piece from the workshop of Peter Carl Fabergé. After Aryeh refused to accept Christie's certification as adequate proof of authenticity, Christie's brought civil and criminal proceedings against him in Switzerland.

During the course of the proceedings, Christie's delivered to Aryeh, living in New York, a second letter of authentication. That letter, signed by A. Kenneth Snowman, one of the world's foremost experts on Fabergé, persuaded Aryeh to proceed with the purchase. Accordingly, Aryeh paid the $250,000 for the egg, along with $150,000 in legal fees, interest, and other expenses sought by Christie's,[145] and the pending lawsuits against Aryeh were dropped.

Aryeh subsequently placed the egg in a New York City bank vault, where it remained until the fall of 1985, when he decided to sell it at Christie's New York. At a recent sale at Sotheby's, another Fabergé Imperial Easter Egg had sold for $1.6 million.[146] But the sale of Aryeh's egg, scheduled for October 16, 1985, was withdrawn by Christie's on October 3 after Snowman revised his opinion to state that although the egg was by Fabergé, it had been doctored.

Thereupon Aryeh commenced suit against Christie's. He alleged that the 1977 sale to him was fraudulent; that on the eve of the 1977 auction Snowman had examined the egg and had advised Christie's Geneva of his reservations about the egg's authenticity; and that the delivery to him of the alleged Snowman letter of December 1977 was, therefore, part of a fraudulent scheme to induce him to proceed with the purchase of the egg.

Christie's moved to dismiss the complaint, asserting, among other allegations, that the applicable statute of limitations had expired. However, before the proceedings had advanced much further, Christie's reached a settlement of the case with Esther Aryeh; her husband, Eskandar, had died during the course of the action.

Had the case not been settled, however, it is likely that Aryeh would have prevailed on the statute-of-limitations issue, assuming that he could establish a prima facie case of fraudulent conspiracy. That may not have been difficult to establish, since Snowman himself admitted to the London *Times* that on the eve of the 1977 auction he relayed to Christie's Geneva his doubts about the egg's authenticity.[147]

Where fraud has been secretly practiced and a cause of action has not been discovered because of the fraudulent concealment, in most jurisdictions the running of the statute of limitations is suspended until the cause of action either becomes known or should have been discovered.[148] Even if the facts of a case do not indicate a concealed fraud, the running of the limitations statute can still be postponed on evidence of acts or conduct designed to mislead, deceive, or lull inquiry.[149] Surely, in the *Fabergé Egg* case, the December 1977 letter from Snowman, a leading Fabergé expert, authenticating the egg would have served to lull inquiry on the part of Aryeh. In fact, Aryeh apparently relied on the contents of that letter when he ultimately decided to consummate the purchase of the egg. Since the egg was in a bank vault until he sought to sell it in 1985, Aryeh did not discover his cause of action, nor was there any reason for him to do so, until the egg was withdrawn by Christie's from the impending auction. Once Aryeh determined that he had an action, he wasted no time in initiating the suit.

In the *McCloud* case discussed in chapter 2, a New York federal district court (affirmed by the Second Circuit) implied but did not hold that when an auction house knows or should know that the authenticity of an artwork (in that instance, a Picasso drawing) is in dispute, it cannot represent either by omission or by affirmation that the work is authentic.[150]

Another example comes from England, where a person purchased an Egon Schiele painting at auction from Christie's.[151] Shortly after the sale, it was found that the painting was 94% overpainted.
The English court found that the painting was a forgery and that
Christie's did not reasonably rely on the opinions of experts in describing the painting as a Schiele in its catalog.

Purchasers have challenged misrepresentations of authenticity
not only under the U.C.C. and under special fine arts legislation but
also under state consumer statutes. In *Weschler & Son, Inc. v. Klank*,[152]
a District of Columbia appellate court, affirming a trial court's dismissal of a complaint, held that the plaintiff-auctioneer misrepresented in an auction catalog an item as being an authentic antique blanket
chest; the defendant refused to pay for it and, in turn, filed a complaint with the Department of Consumer and Regulatory Affairs alleging an unfair trade practice, which fell within the District of
Columbia Consumer Protection Procedures Act.

Authenticity: An Increased Responsibility to Purchasers?

A decision from England, *Thomson v. Christie's*,[153] is being closely
watched for repercussions about how auctioneers do business. In
1994, the Canadian art collector Taylor Thomson purchased at
Christie's in London for nearly $3.5 million what was described in
the auction catalog as "A pair of Louis XV porphyry and gilt-bronze
two handled vases."[154] The seller, the Marquess of Cholmondeley,
and the provenance, from a collection at Houghton Hall, a British
treasure house dating from the 1730s, appeared to be impeccable.
Thomson, designated a "special client" of Christie's, had access to a
special client advisor whose role was to furnish as much information
as possible to enable the client to be an informed bidder. Thomson
was given the auction catalog, which, in its two-page description of
the urns, depicted them to be from the eighteenth century and included, additionally, a number of unproved attributions. Thomson
was also shown the urns by her special client advisor, who informed
her that they were of museum quality and that a similar pair was in
the Getty Museum in California.

Several years after her purchase, Thomson began to have doubts about the urns and their attribution, believing them to be nineteenth-century works worth approximately $55,000. When Christie's refused to rescind the sale, Thomson brought suit, alleging misrepresentation and negligence. At trial, expert testimony was presented as to the likely dating of the urns. In his opinion, the High Court judge indicated that he was "about 70 percent certain"[155] that the urns actually dated from the eighteenth century, and that Christie's dating of the urns as Louis XV was an opinion that, with its level of expertise, Christie's was entitled to reach. Nevertheless, Christie's cataloging was substandard in that the catalog entry "firmed-up" its description of the urns with stories and attributions that were unsubstantiated. Moreover, a condition report prepared by Christie's experts and available to Thomson and her advisors at Christie's (though not seen by Thomson) was also cited for containing inaccuracies.[156] The court found that the auction house should have warned prospective bidders about the unusual difficulties of dating objects from the Louis XV era because so many imitations were made during the mid 1800s.

However, in finding Christie's to be negligent, the court held Christie's to a higher standard of care in view of Thomson's being a "special client." What is a "special client"? In 1994 (when Thomson was elevated to special-client status), Christie's New York office sought to provide such clients with professional advice, consultations with specialists, private viewings after hours, and enhanced personal service from advisors.[157] Because of Thomson's special-client status at Christie's and her reliance on Christie's advisors and specialists, the court determined that Christie's had not met its duty of care to her. Damages were to be assessed at a later time, and in June 2004 the High Court instructed Christie's to pay one-third of Thomson's court costs.[158] Christie's immediately appealed, and in May 2005, the Court of Appeal reversed, holding that since Christie's had no real doubts that the urns were eighteenth-century works, it was not obliged to tell Thomson that there was a possibility they could be nineteenth-century replicas.[159] The decision was welcomed by professional specialist advisors—including Christie's, which had stopped using the term "special client" in the late 1990s.

Title

Another major concern of the buyer at auction is that the work she purchases carries free and clear title. Under the U.C.C.[160] any sale, whether by auction or otherwise, conveys a warranty of title. The scope of the warranty includes freedom from a security interest "of which the buyer at the time of contracting has no knowledge."[161] In the United States, it has long been held that an auctioneer selling the works of an undisclosed principal stands behind the representations and warranties of title that exist in every contract of sale.[162] It has also been held that one who enters into a contract as an agent without disclosing the name of the principal becomes liable under the contract, even though the agent is known to be acting for another.[163] As to the liability of the auctioneer for warranty of title where the principal is disclosed, under the revised auction regulations in New York City (discussed later in this chapter), the auction house retains its liability and, in any event, cannot disclaim the warranty of title, whether or not the principal is disclosed.[164] Moreover, an auctioneer who sells goods that are stolen or that are subject to a lien is liable to the true owner or the lien holder without regard to the auctioneer's actual or constructive knowledge of the consignor's lack of title or authority to sell.[165] The measure of damages is the value of the item at the time the buyer is required to return it.[166] Moreover, an auctioneer may be liable for conversion of property fraudulently obtained by a consignor when the auctioneer has knowledge of the fraud.[167]

Disclaimers of Warranties

Although, as noted both here and in chapter 2, the law looks dimly on disclaimers of warranties, particularly disclaimers of warranties of title by auctioneers, disclaimers by auctioneers of other warranties are nevertheless sometimes upheld. Disclaimers of authenticity, for example, were upheld in the case of *Kelly v. Brooks*,[168] where in 1993 a New York federal district court dismissed a complaint of breach of warranty, fraud, reckless misrepresentation, and breach of duty of honesty and fair dealing. The plaintiffs, in purchasing a total of seven works of art from the defendant-auctioneer on two separate occasions, signed each time, as required, a bill of sale that included the following disclaimer:

> ALL property is sold "AS IS," and neither [name of auctioneer] nor the consignors make any guarantees, warranties or representations, expressed or implied, with respect to property purchased, and in no event shall the seller nor the consignor be responsible for genuineness, nor deemed to have made any representations of genuineness, authorship, attribution, provenance, period, culture, source, origin, or condition of the purchased property and no verbal statements made regarding this property either before or after the sale of the stated property, or in this bill of sale, or invoice or catalogue or advertisement or elsewhere shall be deemed such a guarantee of genuineness.[169]

On discovering that the paintings were inauthentic, the plaintiffs brought suit, alleging that they purchased the artwork in reliance on the auctioneer's representations that the artwork was authentic.

In dismissing the complaint, the court noted, among other points, that the disclaimer signed by the plaintiffs "in very clear and unequivocal terms absolves defendants from any liability" and that the plaintiffs "present no pertinent law which would make the disclaimer ineffective."[170]

In an earlier example (1982), the New York State Supreme Court, in applying the U.C.C., upheld the disclaimer of an auction house printed in its auction catalog. A brief summary of the case follows.

Giusti v. Sotheby Parke Bernet, Inc.[171]

In April 1974, the plaintiff, Antonio Giusti, purchased at auction at Sotheby's a diamond ring for which he paid $115,000. The auction catalog described the ring as being an emerald-cut diamond of approximately 9.10 carats on a platinum mount, flanked by two baguette diamonds. The description further noted that the central diamond was "certified to be very fine color and flawless."[172] A few days before purchasing the ring, Giusti had examined it at Sotheby's and was advised that the ring was an E color and flawless; he was further advised that before the sale Sotheby's would procure the original certificate from the Gemological Institute of America (GIA). Giusti was the highest bidder for the ring at auction, and he signed, without reading, a "Memorandum of Successful Bid" presented to him by a Sotheby employee immediately after the close of the bidding. On the memorandum was imprinted the following legend: "The Buyer Acknowledges Familiarity With the 'Conditions of Sale' Governing Purchase at Auction As Published In the Catalog." Those conditions of sale contained the following disclaimer:

> Except as so specifically provided in the "Terms of Guarantee" with respect to authenticity of authorship, all property is sold "as is" and neither the Galleries nor the Consignor makes any warranties or representations of any kind or nature with respect to, nor shall they be held responsible or liable for, the correctness of the catalog or other description of the physical condition, size, quality, rarity, importance, provenance, exhibition, literature and historical relevance of the property.[173]

After the auction, Giusti was given a photocopy of the GIA certificate and was advised that the original would be forthcoming. In the ensuing few weeks, Giusti still had not received the original certificate; by then he had learned that the stone bore some slight imperfections.

The ring had been consigned to Sotheby's in February 1974 by Lee Vandervelde of California, who had represented to Sotheby's that the ring weighed 9.09 carats and had been graded E color and either "flawless" or "internally flawless" by GIA. Vandervelde further represented that a certificate stating the foregoing had been issued and would be furnished to Sotheby's; that representation, however, was false. In fact, in 1969 and 1973 Vandervelde procured two GIA certificates as to the diamond. The 1969 certificate assessed the diamond's weight at 9.00 carats, its clarity as "internally flawless," and its color as F (one grade inferior to E). The 1973 certificate assessed the diamond's weight as 9.09 carats, the color grade as E, but the clarity as VVS1—that is, having very slight surface imperfections. What Vandervelde ultimately forwarded to Sotheby's in 1974 for the sale was not a true GIA certificate but, rather, a composite of the 1969 and 1973 certificates. Thus, Vandervelde had willfully misrepresented the characteristics of the ring to Sotheby's.

When Sotheby's received the ring in 1974, pursuant to its consignment agreement, its appraiser made a limited examination of the mounted stone and satisfied himself that it conformed reasonably well to the characteristics Vandervelde had described. After the sale to Giusti and after some extended correspondence among Giusti, Sotheby's, and Vandervelde, the ring was returned to Sotheby's in December 1974 for re-examination by GIA as an unmounted stone. The resultant assessment included a clarity grade of VVS, potentially flawless, and a color grade of F. The examination revealed a small bruise on one facet of the diamond. Giusti accordingly brought suit against Sotheby's and Vandervelde, seeking rescission; damages for breach of warranty, breach of contract, and negligent and reckless misrepresentation against Sotheby's; and damages for breach of warranty and fraudulent misrepresentations against Vandervelde.

The court dismissed the complaint, holding that no recovery was warranted under any theory. The court found that Sotheby's had made neither negligent nor reckless misrepresentations nor any representations that were relied on by Giusti. Moreover, the court found that although Vandervelde misrepresented the certificate he forwarded to Sotheby's, Giusti placed no reliance on either that misrepresentation or the certificate; rather, by his own testimony the principal reason he decided to bid on the ring was because he liked it after having looked at it. Further, the court noted, even if Giusti was found to have relied on Sotheby's or Vandervelde's representations, the question would remain as to whether that reliance was justified in the face of his admitted disregard of the conditions of sale prominently set forth in the catalog and on signs posted throughout the gallery. As the court stated:

> The fact that Giusti neither read this notice in the catalog nor the "as is" disclaimer posted throughout the gallery on the conditions of sale signs, does not in the least diminish the force of the disclaimers nor enhance Giusti's right to recovery. He is bound by the terms of the sale and the limitations clearly imposed thereon and his claimed lack of actual knowledge of them through negligence of inexcusable trustfulness will not relieve him of his contract.[174]

The court noted that Giusti's reliance on the U.C.C. was likewise unavailing and that any express or implied warranties imposed on the transaction by virtue of the U.C.C. provisions were effectively modified or excluded, as provided in the Code,[175] by the conspicuously placed "as is" disclaimers.

When a Buyer Refuses to Pay: Limits to an Auctioneer's Rights

Both the purchaser at auction and the consignor-seller are customarily bound by an auction catalog's conditions of sale that form the basis of the auction agreement. If the successful bidder of an artwork fails to pay for it, the rights assertable by the auctioneer as agent for the consignor-seller are clearly set forth in the conditions of sale. Are those same rights assertable by the auctioneer as *owner* of the artwork? That issue was addressed in 1995 in the New York case of *Christie Manson & Woods International, Inc. v. Brown*.[176] The defendant, a successful bidder at auction in May 1990 of an artwork by Keith Haring, refused to pay for the painting, which then remained in the possession of the auctioneer. Less than two months later, in June 1990, the auctioneer voluntarily paid the consignor-seller the price bid by the defendant at auction and thereafter remained in possession and control of the painting for nearly three years. In February 1993, the auctioneer sold the painting to a third-party buyer for a price significantly less than the defendant's bid and brought the instant suit to recover the deficiency from the defendant.

In dismissing the claim, the New York State Supreme Court noted that the auctioneer's conditions of sale permitted Christie's, among other remedies, to "resell the property" with "the original defaulting buyer [being] liable for the payment of any deficiency in the purchase price and all costs and expenses" but that the remedy was assertable by Christie's *as agent* to mitigate the loss to the original consignor-seller and that the right of resale was:

> extinguished when the painting was "resold" to the auctioneer in June 1990. The February 1993 transaction was merely a sale undertaken by the auctioneer, as the owner of the painting, to an interested party.[177]

Under the conditions of sale, Christie's invoked a right to resell when acting as an agent—not as a buyer. As the court further noted,

> the contract was between the title holder, the seller, and the purchaser, and . . . therefore the damages involved would be those of the seller. The Conditions of Sale do not provide for the auctioneer to reimburse the seller fully and then step into the seller's shoes as title holder and still be able to "resell" when the resale referred to in the Conditions was . . . meant to refer to a single resale by the seller (or the agent on the seller's behalf).[178]

Loans to Buyers

In October 1989, Sotheby's stunned the art world by confirming that it had lent Alan Bond, the Australian financier, approximately half the purchase price of Vincent van Gogh's painting *Irises*, which Bond bought at auction at Sotheby's in November 1987 for the then-record price of $53.9 million. Adding further to the shock was Sotheby's disclosure that in the two years since the painting's purchase the auction house was still in control of *Irises* and was storing the painting at an undisclosed site until Bond completed repayment of the remainder of the purchase price.[179]

The transaction sparked considerable criticism among art deal-ers, rival auction houses, and some art journalists, not only because of the size of the loan but also because of its timing; the purchase of *Irises*, less than one month after the Wall Street crash of October 19, 1987, encouraged a fool's paradise mentality in the art market. The price of that painting—which, many argued, artificially inflated the prices of other artworks—was often cited as proof that art "was a commodity that had weathered the economic crisis."[180]

After four months of severe, ongoing criticism in the press, Sotheby's in January 1990 announced that it would no longer pro-vide buyers at auction with loans secured by the artwork to be pur-chased. Rather, Sotheby's would accept as collateral a work of art only after it was paid for and owned by the purchaser for at least ninety days.[181] Although Sotheby's did modify its policy, it main-tained that it was doing so to correct a mistaken perception that the financial device had inflated the prices of artwork. Moreover, the auction house maintained that such financing was rarely used: only six times on lots sold for more than $1 million and only once on a lot sold for more than $5 million—*Irises*.[182]

As a postscript to *Irises*, immediately after Alan Bond bought the painting, his empire began to fail, and he was unable to pay for the picture. It was eventually sold in March 1990 to the J. Paul Getty Museum in Malibu, California. Although the purchase price was un-disclosed, speculation was that the purchase price was part cash and part securities amounting to a sum slightly below Bond's original purchase price.[183]

Three years later, Bond was accused of fraud by his own publicly held company, Bond Corporation Holdings, Ltd. (BCH), for with-holding information from BCH regarding an opportunity to pur-chase Edouard Manet's 1880 painting *La Promenade* from the leasing company that owned it.[184] Apparently, in 1989, after BCH had laid out $4.5 million in leasing payments for the painting, Bond's family company, Dalhold Investments, was able to buy the painting for a payment of $1.7 million, precluding BCH from buying it. A few months later, the company sold the painting through Sotheby's New York for $14.85 million. Bond used the proceeds to pay off the balance of his $53.9 million debt on *Irises* to Sotheby's. In July 1996, he stood trial in Australia for the fraud, and in the following month, he was convicted of fraud and deception and sentenced to three years in jail.[185]

NEW YORK CITY REGULATION OF AUCTIONEERS

Beginning in December 1984, the New York Department of Consumer Affairs conducted a two-year study of the procedures and the practices of the auction industry. As a result of the study, regulations that had been promulgated in 1974 were updated to address recent market conditions and to monitor courses of conduct that had developed since 1974. A copy of the revised regulations, which became effective April 13, 1987, is included at the end of this chapter (Appendix 4-6). The following is a summary of some of the major provisions of the revised regulations.

Written Contract

There must be a written contract between the consignor and the auctioneer for the auctioning of property.

Disclosure to Consignors

Fees, commissions, and other charges payable by the consignor to the auctioneer must be disclosed.

Consignor Warrants Good Title

Each consignor-auctioneer contract must contain a provision whereby the consignor

(1) warrants that as of the date of the auction she had complete and lawful title in the property auctioned,

(2) indemnifies the auctioneer against any defect of title, and

(3) acknowledges that the intended beneficiary of the warranty is the ultimate purchaser at auction.

Disclosure to Prospective Buyers

Any interest by the auctioneer in the auction property, other than the right to a commission on the sale, must be disclosed. The disclosure must appear in connection with any description of the object in the auction catalog or in any other printed materials published or distributed in connection with the sale.

The auctioneer must disclose in the auction catalog whether the consignor is entitled to a rebate commission or may bid on her own property at the sale.

If there is a reserve price on an article, that fact must be disclosed in the auction catalog. If there is no reserve price, the auctioneer cannot imply that there is one.

If an auctioneer makes loans to consignors or prospective buyers, that fact must be conspicuously disclosed in the auction catalog.

Whenever an estimated value of an item or lot is published in a catalog, a general description of the estimate and its meaning and function must also be included in the publication.

If the reserve price on a lot is not bid, the auctioneer may withdraw a lot from sale by announcing that the withdrawn lot has been "passed," "withdrawn," "returned to owner," or "bought-in." The withdrawal must occur before bidding on another lot begins.

If the auctioneer intends to bid up to the reserve price on behalf of the seller, she must disclose that fact both in the catalog and on signs posted at the entrance to and inside the auction room and it must be announced immediately prior to the commencement of any auction.

Conduct of the Auction

Once the bidding on a lot or an item has reached the reserve price, the auctioneer may not bid or accept bids on behalf of the consignor or of the auction house.

In no event shall the reserve price for any lot exceed its published presale minimum estimated value.

The auctioneer may not disclaim warranty of title of any item sold at auction.

PROPOSED REGULATION IN NEW YORK STATE

In response to the publicity sparked by Sotheby's large loan to financier Alan Bond of the purchase price for van Gogh's *Irises* (discussed earlier), the New York State Assembly's Oversight, Analysis, and Investigation Committee began a systematic inquiry into recent art market practices. The committee was joined in its efforts in December 1990 by the Assembly's Tourism, Arts, and Sports Development Committee. In January 1991, the committees jointly held a daylong public hearing on regulating the New York art market; the hearing received testimony from city and state officials and from art dealers, auction houses, and art-related trade associations addressing a variety of issues.[186]

Among the issues addressed were the desirability of

- Having art sales regulated by the state's Martin Act, which oversees the sale of securities and certain commodities within New York State;

- Disclosing the existence of consignor guarantees to prospective buyers;

- Disclosing the existence of reserve prices and, perhaps, the actual dollar figures of the reserves;

- Eliminating the practice of chandelier or consecutive bids—bids for which there is no bona fide offer or bidder;

- Prohibiting the practice by auction houses or dealers of making loans to prospective buyers; and

- Prohibiting the practice by auction houses or dealers of providing financing for buyers, using the object purchased as collateral.[187]

As a result of testimony received by the committees at the public hearing and additional information received from participants in the art market in further discussions, the committees jointly drafted four bills relating to the statewide regulation of auction practices in New York. As this treatise goes to press some fourteen years later, such bills have yet to be enacted into law.

The latest version of such bills currently pending in the New York State Assembly would amend New York State's General Business Law to provide the following:[188]

- No auction house may solicit or accept any sham bid (that is, a bid made by or on behalf of the seller) unless such bid is identified with the term "for the consignor."

- When an auction house advertises that property will be sold at auction regardless of price, then such property shall be sold to the highest bidder. A bid made by or on behalf of the seller of such property shall not be accepted by the auction house.

- Whenever an auction house accepts a bid that is made for the account of the auction house, the auction house shall announce acceptance of such bid with the term "auction house bid."

ANTITRUST VIOLATIONS AND OTHER FORBIDDEN PRACTICES

The Sotheby's/Christie's Class Action Settlement

In April 2001, a New York federal district court approved a class action settlement of $512 million between the auction houses of Sotheby's and Christie's, on the one hand, and 130,000 buyers and sellers at U.S. auctions, on the other hand, who had alleged they had been defrauded by the two auction houses through price-fixing schemes.[189] In March 2002, the Second Circuit held that buyers and sellers at Sotheby's and Christie's in London and other overseas locations were to be included as well in the settlement, as the foreign transactions sufficiently affected domestic commerce.[190] The plaintiffs had alleged that beginning at least as early as January 1, 1993, the two auction houses conspired to employ a common rate schedule for buyer's premiums and that the conspiracy expanded in 1995 when the houses allegedly agreed to apply similar rates as seller's commissions. In addition, the plaintiffs maintained that the auction houses agreed in 1995 to end their previous practice of negotiating the seller's commission with some customers.

The disclosure of information giving rise to the U.S. Justice Department's antitrust probe of the two houses and the resultant class action settlement stemmed from the release by Christopher M. Davidge, the recently forced-out CEO of Christie's, of hundreds of pages of files to Christie's antitrust counsel. The files included documentation of years of clandestine contacts between Davidge and his Sotheby's counterpart, CEO Diana Brooks, to set commission rates and to fix rates on loans to sellers. The files also included agreements to divvy up the market's high-net-worth clients, rather than competing for them, as well as agreements not to recruit each other's employees.[191]

As a result of Davidge's disclosure, the Justice Department granted both Christie's and Davidge conditional amnesty in exchange for their cooperation in the investigation into, and prosecution of, Sotheby's and its two top executives. Accordingly, in addition to the class action settlement, Sotheby's pleaded guilty in a New York federal district court in October 2000 to Sherman Act violations (colluding with Christie's International to fix seller's commissions) and was sentenced to pay a fine of $45 million.[192] A. Alfred Taubman and Diana Brooks, respectively chairman and CEO of Sotheby's, resigned from their positions. Each was criminally prosecuted. In October 2000, Brooks pleaded guilty in a New York federal district court to fixing commission rates with Christie's.[193] She cooperated in the prosecution of Taubman and in April 2002 was sentenced to three years' probation, including six months of house arrest, a fine of $350,000, and 1,000 hours of community service.[194] In December 2001, Taubman was convicted in a New York federal court for conspiring with his counterpart at Christie's, Sir Anthony Tennant, to fix sellers' commissions over a six-year period. In April 2002, he was sentenced to serve a year and a day in prison and was fined $7.5 million.[195] Tennant was also charged in the case, but he lives in England and has refused to submit to U.S. jurisdiction.

Puffing

Although the legitimacy of various auction practices is frequently dictated by state statutes and by local regulations, such as those enacted in New York City, the prevalent practice of puffing up the sale price by sellers or their agents has historically been declared unlawful. Puffing is also expressly proscribed by the U.C.C.

An auctioneer may not knowingly receive a bid on the seller's behalf, nor may the seller make or procure such a bid, without prior notice to the buyer that the seller has retained the right to do so. Case law has consistently held fictitious bids to be fraudulent and illegal.[196] In the event of such bidding, the U.C.C. provides options for the buyer: The buyer may either rescind the sale or take the goods "at the price of the last good faith bid prior to the completion of the sale."[197] Where a single buyer is making a bid in competition with a fraudulent bid, it has been suggested that the purchase price should be the last good-faith bid before the first fraudulent overbid.[198]

Chill Bidding

Generally illegal under common law[199] was the practice of chill bidding—that is, an agreement between two or more persons to refrain from competitive bidding in order to depress the sales price. The U.C.C. implicitly prohibits chill bidding.[200] As with puffing, the practice is fraudulent, since it prevents a fair price from being determined by fair competition and it distorts, to the detriment of the consignor and the auctioneer, the actual extent of competition among willing buyers. Proof of its existence under common law provided the seller with two options: (1) the right to withdraw her goods from any party involved in the chill, even where the auction was conducted without reserve prices, and (2) the right, predicated on rescission for fraud, to recover the goods sold to a chill bidder.[201] The practice of chill bidding spawned the growth of bidding rings that purchased auctioned goods at artificially low prices, defrauding auctioneers and consignors.

The following is a brief description of a ring in operation. An auction is attended, for example, by a group of six prospective purchasers who know each other, each interested in acquiring the same work of art. The six agree among themselves that—rather than bid against each other, thus raising the purchase price for the consignor's benefit—only one of their number will bid to acquire the artwork. They further agree to later hold a private auction among themselves for the work if their designated bidder is successful. The profit made by the seller in the second auction—the amount over what she bid in the previous auction—is divided among the five unsuccessful bidders at the private auction, thereby benefiting all but the consignor and the auctioneer.

Bidding rings were such a problem in England that Parliament enacted prohibitive legislation. The 1927 Auctions (Bidding Agreements) Act,[202] also known as the Knockout Act, made such arrangements expressly illegal, although it permitted joint-account bidding, provided the agreement was in writing and was deposited with the auctioneer before the purchase. Although there does not appear to be comparable legislation in the United States, an organized ring may be prosecuted under federal or state law as a combination in restraint of trade, provided that proof of the ring's existence is established, which, in the face of informal arrangements, is no mean feat.

One example of chill bidding in New York led to a plea of guilty in August 1991 to a charge of federal conspiracy to restrain trade.[203] In that case, Bernard & S. Dean Levy, Inc., one of New York's major dealers in Early American furniture, and Thomas Schwenke, Inc., a Connecticut antique dealer, had "refrained from bidding against each other" in a 1986 sale at Christie's International PLC's auction house in connection with a Chippendale mahogany late-eighteenth-century chest. Originally identified in the catalog as English in origin and estimated to sell for $1,200 to $1,800, Christie's indicated shortly before the sale that the piece was American-made and had a noted provenance.

Apparently, on the date of the auction, an agent in the employ of the Levys bought the piece at Christie's for $30,800; then, in a parked car outside Christie's, it was auctioned again, this time privately, before a dealer ring and sold for about $38,000 to the Levy firm.[204]

As with the *Levy* case, it has been held in jurisdictions throughout the United States that any agreement or combination intending to stifle fair competition and to chill bidding is unenforceable as being against public policy and will cause a sale to be set aside.[205] However, the courts look to the intention of the parties; if the intention is fair and honest—if the parties' primary purpose is not to suppress competition but, rather, to advance their own interests or protect their rights—the arrangements will be upheld.[206]

Providing Assistance to Bidding Rings

In addition to liability incurred by ring members, an auction house may be liable for restraint of trade violations where it is aware of a ring's activities and provides assistance to the ring. Moreover, as seen in the 2003 decision of *Stolow v. Greg Manning Auctions, Inc.*,[207] the plaintiff in such an action need not be either a seller or an actual bidder. In *Stolow*, an alleged ring of stamp dealers bid among themselves prior to stamp auctions for the right to bid at those auctions without competition from other ring members. After paying off other members of the ring, the "winner" of the pre-auction round would generally submit very high bids at the actual auction. Non-ring-members were then forced to bid at levels where profits were either minimal or resulted in a loss. The auction houses involved would, in turn, extend favorable credit to ring members and reduce the ring's competition by misdescribing stamp collections in their auction catalogs in a manner that discouraged other bidders. The decrease in auction attendance reduced overhead for the auction houses and increased their overall profits. The scheme continued for nearly three decades and significantly reduced both the competition at auctions where a ring member bid and the earnings of the sellers. Plaintiff, a dealer and auctioneer, prohibited ring members from participating in his auctions and was eventually driven out of business. The defendant dealers and auction houses moved to dismiss plaintiff's antitrust claims for lack of standing and for failure to bring suit within the four-year statute of limitations period.

In finding for plaintiff on the issue of standing, the New York federal district court noted that plaintiff fulfilled the two requirements of (1) alleging personal economic injury and (2) alleging an adverse effect on market-wide competition (through assertions of overall decreased bidding when ring members were present, purposeful misdescription of stamp lots, and reduced sellers' profits). The court, however, dismissed the claim as being time-barred by the four-year statute of limitations. An antitrust action accrues, the court stated, when the defendant commits an act that injures the plaintiff's business. Even though the violation was continuous, the plaintiff asserted that he had been driven out of business in August 1997—the last possible date on which he could have suffered a business injury. The suit was filed in April 2002, eight months after the statute of limitations had expired.

The court noted that had plaintiff been able to prove the necessary elements of fraudulent concealment,[208] the statute of limitations could have tolled, but plaintiff's knowledge of the ring's activity prevented such a finding.

Notes to Chapter 4

1. NEWSWEEK, May 6, 1996, at 29.
2. http://pages.ebay.com/education/whatisebay/ (visited Sept. 27, 2004).
3. N.Y. TIMES, May 19, 1990, at A-1, col. 1.
4. ARTNEWSLETTER, May 29, 1990, at 1.
5. *Id.*
6. N.Y. TIMES, *supra* note 3.
7. The most extensive of Japan's numerous art-related scandals (other than the bribery committed by Saito noted in the text), which came to light in 1991, involved the Sumitomo Bank, Japan's most profitable financial institution, and the Itoman Corp., an Osaka trading company. In the face of mounting debt, Itoman purchased at several times their market price more than 7,300 artworks by artists including Picasso, Modigliani, Chagall, and Ryuzaburo Umehara, the noted Japanese artist who studied with Renoir. It was alleged that these artworks were "sweeteners" for real estate deals; that is, real estate sellers would be "sold" a Chagall or a Picasso knowing that for tax purposes it would be "bought back" a few months later for many times what the seller had paid. Leading businessmen and politicians were implicated, Itoman's chairman was forced to resign, and Japanese firms declared bankruptcy. The market for impressionist artwork—of which the Japanese had been the biggest buyers—receded. *See* ARTNEWSLETTER, Feb. 5, 1991, at 1; ARTNEWSLETTER, Mar. 5, 1991, at 2; ARTNEWSLETTER, Oct. 1, 1991, at 3; IRISH TIMES, Jan. 20, 1993, § 3 at 8.

    For details on another major art-related scandal, one involving Mitsubishi Corp., the Saka Gakkai religious organization, and the fraudulent sale of two Renoir paintings, *see* ARTNEWSLETTER, Apr. 16, 1991; ARTNEWSLETTER Oct. 1, 1991.
8. ARTNEWSLETTER, Nov. 28, 1995 at 8.
9. N.Y. SUN, Sept. 2, 2004, at 26.
10. *The Year in Review 2004*, ART NEWSPAPER, Issue 3, at 52.
11. *See, e.g.*, INT'L HERALD TRIBUNE, Jan. 13, 2001, Feature Section, at 7.
12. *See, e.g.*, FINANCIAL TIMES (LONDON), Jan. 28, 2003, at 28.

13.   C. Kucinski, *Artists Find a Market for Their Work Online*, LAN-SING STATE J., Mar. 9, 2005, at 12 TAB.

14.   *Supra* note 2.

15.   *Supra* note 13.

16.   U.C.C. § 2-313.

17.   U.C.C. § 2-312.

18.   U.C.C. § 2-314.

19.   U.C.C. § 2-315.

20.   U.C.C. § 2-316. Mississippi now omits this section of the Code.

21.   U.C.C. § 2-328(1).

22.   U.C.C. § 2-328(2).

23.   U.C.C. § 2-328(3). Note, however, that a bidder's retraction does not revive any previous bid.

24.   Dulman v. Martin Fein & Co., 66 A.D.2d 809, 411 N.Y.S.2d 358 (1978).

25.   U.C.C. § 2-328(2).

26.   Marx v. Sotheby Parke Bernet, Inc., No. 7561/81 (Sup. Ct.), *aff'd*, 102 A.D.2d 729, 476 N.Y.S.2d 482 (1983).

27.   U.C.C. § 2-201.

28.   *See* N.Y. GEN. OBLIG. LAW § 5-701(a)(6); CAL. CIV. CODE § 2363.

29.   *Id.*

30.   Mirisola v. Habsburg Feldman, S.A., 172 A.D.2d 306, 568 N.Y.S.2d 110 (1991). *See also* Chowaiki v. Steinhardt, Index #600250/04 (N.Y. Sup. Ct., N.Y. County, Mar. 28, 2005) (alleged verbal agreement to sell a Chagall painting was void in violation of the statute of frauds).

31.   U.C.C. § 2-328(4). *See also* Nev. Nat'l Leasing Co. v. Hereford, 36 Cal. 3d 146, 680 P.2d 1077, 203 Cal. Rptr. 118 (1984).

32.   Abrams v. Sotheby Parke Bernet, Inc., N.Y.L.J., Sept. 10, 1984, at 6, col. 2 (Sup. Ct. N.Y. County 1984).

33.   N.Y. EXEC. LAW § 63(12); N.Y. GEN. BUS. LAW § 349.

34.   Article 5 of Military Restitution Law No. 59 and Article 4 of the Berlin Restitution Law.

35.   N.Y. TIMES, Aug. 2, 1985, at C-11, col. 1.

36.   N.Y. TIMES, Aug. 7, 1985, at C-15, col. 5.

37.   Succession of Gladys Rhodes Groves v. Neal Auction Co., Inc., 1998-21414 (Dist. Ct. Orleans Parish Div. G., Sec. 11, 3/28/01).

38.   Cristallina S.A. v. Christie, Manson & Woods Int'l, Inc., 117 A.D.2d 284, 292, 502 N.Y.S.2d 165, 171 (1986).

39.   *Id.*

40. Maltby v. Christie, 1 Esp. 340, 179 Eng. Rep. 378 (K.B. 1795).
41. Clay v. Sotheby's, 257 F. Supp. 2d 973 (S.D. Ohio 2003).
42. *Id*. at 982.
43. *Id*. at 981.
44. *Id*. at 985.
45. Pilliard v. Sotheby's, Inc., 1998 WL 126060, 1998 U.S. Dist. LEXIS 3490 (S.D.N.Y. Mar. 19, 1998).
46. Pagliai v. Del Re, 2001 WL 220013, 2001 U.S. Dist. LEXIS 2195 (S.D.N.Y. Mar. 7, 2001).
47. *Id*., 2001 WL 220013, at ★1–★2, 2001 U.S. Dist. LEXIS 2195, at ★3–★6.
48. *Id*., 2001 WL 220013, at ★3, 2001 U.S. Dist. LEXIS 2195, at ★6–★7.
49. *Id*., 2001 WL 220013, at ★7, 2001 U.S. Dist. LEXIS 2195, at ★21.
50. *Id*., 2001 WL 220013, at ★7, 2001 U.S. Dist. LEXIS 2195, at ★20.
51. *Id*., 2001 WL 220013, at ★6, 2001 U.S. Dist. LEXIS 2195, at ★16–18.
52. *Id*., 2001 WL 220013, at ★7, 2001 U.S. Dist. LEXIS 2195, at ★19.
53. Leventritt v. Sotheby's, Inc., 773 N.Y.S.2d 60 (2004).
54. *Id*. at 61.
55. Cristallina S.A. v. Christie, Manson & Woods Int'l, Inc., 117 A.D.2d 284, 502 N.Y.S.2d 165 (1986). *See also* RESTATEMENT (SECOND) OF AGENCY § 381 (1958).
56. *Cristallina*, 117 A.D.2d at n.7 (citing RESTATEMENT (SECOND) OF AGENCY § 384).
57. *Id*., 117 A.D.2d at 293, 502 N.Y.S.2d at 171; *see also* RESTATEMENT (SECOND) OF AGENCY § 381.
58. Reale v. Sotheby's, Inc., 278 A.D.2d 119, 718 N.Y.S.2d 37 (1st Dep't 2000).
59. Edwards v. Horsemen's Sales Co., 148 Misc. 2d 212, 560 N.Y.S.2d 165 (Sup. Ct. 1989).
60. *Id*., 148 Misc. 2d at 212, 560 N.Y.S.2d at 166 (citing Air Traffic Conference v. Downtown Travel Ctr., Inc., 87 Misc. 2d 151, 154, 383 N.Y.S.2d 805 (Sup. Ct. 1976)).
61. *Id*.
62. Based on auctioneer's commission rates at Christie's (New York) in effect in 2004.

63. Christie's (New York) Impressionist and Modern Art (Day Sale) catalog, Wednesday, May 5, 2004, at 224. Before January 1, 2005, Christie's rate was 19.5% on the first $100,000. N.Y. TIMES, Dec. 17, 2004, § E40. Before January 1, 2005, Sotheby's rate was 20% on the first $100,000. Christie's matched Sotheby's increase in rate to 20% on the first $200,000 effective January 17, 2005. N.Y. TIMES, Jan. 14, 2005, at E40.

64. WASH. POST, Mar. 4, 1993, at T-9.

65. Other auction houses that have adopted the buyer's premium rates set by Sotheby's and Christie's in 1993 include Swann Galleries, Inc. (New York), Skinner Inc. (Boston), Grogan and Co. (Boston), and William Doyle Galleries (New York).

66. *See* Sconyers v. Bowers & Ruddy Galleries, Inc., N.Y.L.J., Aug. 7, 1987, at 12, col. 1 (Sup. Ct. N.Y. County 1987).

67. ARTNEWSLETTER, Mar. 21, 1995, at 3.

68. N.Y. TIMES, Mar. 12, 1990, at C-13.

69. *Id.*

70. ARTNEWSLETTER, Jan. 23, 1990, at 1.

71. N.Y. TIMES, Mar. 12, 1990, at C-13.

72. *Id.* at C-16.

73. ARTNEWSLETTER, Jan. 23, 1990, at 1.

74. Sotheby's Impressionist & Modern Art (Part One) catalog, New York, May 6, 2004, at 167.

75. Christie's (New York) Impressionist and Modern Art (Day Sale) catalog, May 5, 2004, at 223.

76. ARTNEWSLETTER, June 8, 1993, at 4.

77. *Id.*

78. Rules of the City of New York (R.C.N.Y.), Title 6, Chapter 2, subchapter M (Auctioneers), § 2-122(d) (2004).

79. Christie's (New York) Impressionist and Modern Art (Day Sale) catalog, May 5, 2004, at 167.

80. ARTNEWSLETTER, June 8, 1993, at 223.

81. Christie's, Inc. v. Davis, 247 F. Supp. 2d 414 (S.D.N.Y. 2002).

82. *Id.* at 419.

83. *See* Cristallina S.A. v. Christie, Manson & Woods Int'l, Inc., 117 A.D.2d 284, 502 N.Y.S.2d 165 (1986). *See also* Kremer v. Janet Fleisher Gallery, Inc., 320 Pa. Super. 384, 467 A.2d 377 (1983).

84. U.C.C. § 2-328(3).

85. *See* Rules of the City of New York, *supra* note 78.

86. *Id.* § 2-122(f)(1).

87. *Id.* § 2-123(a).

88. *Id.* § 2-123(d).

89.   Benjamin v. First Citizens Bank & Trust Co., 248 A.D. 610, 287 N.Y.S. 947 (1936).

90.   *See Cristallina*, 117 A.D.2d at 294, 502 N.Y.S.2d at 172.

91.   Ravenna v. Christie's, Inc., 289 A.D.2d 15, 734 N.Y.S.2d 21 (1st Dep't 2001).

92.   Cristallina S.A. v. Christie, Manson & Woods Int'l, Inc., 117 A.D.2d 284, 292, 502 N.Y.S.2d 165, 171 (1986).

93.   *Id.*

94.   ARTNEWSLETTER, Feb. 3, 1987, at 1.

95.   Greenwood v. Koven, 880 F. Supp. 186 (S.D.N.Y. 1995).

96.   *Id.* at 189.

97.   Under French law, after the death of an artist, an heir or designee by will is empowered to assert the artist's moral rights, including the right to authenticate definitively the works done by the artist. *See* chapter 11 for a full discussion of moral rights.

98.   *Greenwood*, 880 F. Supp. at 194.

99.   *Id.*

100.   *Id.*

101.   *Id.* at 195.

102.   *Id.* at 196.

103.   *Id.*

104.   *Id.* at 199.

105.   *Id.*

106.   Kohler v. Hindman, 93 C 6170, 1995 U.S. Dist. LEXIS 5503 (N.D. Ill. Apr. 26, 1996).

107.   *Id.* at ★14.

108.   Nass v. Sotheby's, Inc., Index No. 11229/91 (Sup. Ct. N.Y. County Aug. 19, 1991).

109.   Mickle v. Christie's, Inc., 207 F. Supp. 2d 237 (S.D.N.Y. 2002).

110.   *Id.* at 244.

111.   *Id.* at 239.

112.   *Id.* at 242.

113.   Nelson v. Sotheby's, 128 F. Supp. 2d 1172 (N.D. Ill. 2001).

114.   *Id.* at 1174–75.

115.   *Id.* at 1178.

116.   *Id.* at 1175.

117.   *Id.* at 1176.

118.   Shalford v. Shelley's Jewelry, Inc., 127 F. Supp. 2d 779 (W.D.N.C. 2000).

119.   *Id.* at 784.

120.   *Id.* at 785.

121.   Ichiyasu v. Christie, Manson & Woods, Int'l, Inc., 630 F. Supp. 340 (N.D. Ill. 1986).

122.   John v. Sotheby's, Inc., 141 F.R.D. 29 (S.D.N.Y. 1992).

123.   Walt Disney Prods. v. Basmajian, 600 F. Supp. 439 (S.D.N.Y. 1984).

124.   The case involved Swann Galleries, New York, and Oxford University, England.

125.   Schering Corp. v. Home Ins. Co., 712 F.2d 4, 10 n.2 (2d Cir. 1983).

126.   DeBruno v. Sotheby Parke Bernet, Inc., Civ. Action No. 84-3021, Bench Opinion (D.N.J. Nov. 8, 1984). The case is reproduced in 2 F. FELDMAN, S. WEIL & S. BIEDERMAN, ART LAW 249 (1986).

127.   Basmajian v. Christie, Manson & Woods Int'l, Inc., 629 F. Supp. 995 (S.D.N.Y. 1986).

128.   Nelson, *The Fine Art of Reproduction: The Doctrine of Fair Use and Auction House Catalogues,* 18 COLUM.-VLA J.L. & ARTS 291 (1994).

129.   Parke-Bernet Galleries, Inc. v. Franklyn, 26 N.Y.2d 13, 256 N.E.2d 506, 308 N.Y.S.2d 337 (1970).

130.   N.Y. C.P.L.R. 302(a), ¶ 1.

131.   *See* Annotation, *Construction and Application of State Statutes or Rules of Court Predicating in Personam Jurisdiction Over Nonresidents or Foreign Corporations on Making or Performing a Contract Within the State,* 23 A.L.R.3D 551 (1969).

132.   *Parke-Bernet Galleries,* 26 N.Y.2d at 16, 256 N.E.2d at 507–08, 308 N.Y.S.2d at 339.

133.   *Id.,* 26 N.Y.2d at 17, 256 N.E.2d at 508, 308 N.Y.S. at 340.

134.   *Id.*

135.   *Id.,* 26 N.Y.2d at 17–18, 256 N.E.2d at 508, 308 N.Y.S.2d at 340.

136.   Zakaria v. Safani, 741 F. Supp. 1263, 1266 (S.D. Miss. 1990).

137.   *Id.* (case generally).

138.   Pasternack v. Esskay Art Galleries, Inc., 90 F. Supp. 849 (W.D. Ark. 1950). *See also* Plimpton v. Friedberg, 166 A. 295 (N.J. 1933). *See also* Voitier v. Antique Art Gallery, 524 So. 2d 80 (La. Ct. App. 3d Cir. 1988) (decided under law of Louisiana, which has not adopted U.C.C. art. 2), *cert. denied,* 531 So. 2d 277 (La. 1988).

139.   N.Y. GEN. BUS. LAW art. 12-D, §§ 219-b to -e, subsequently repealed as of December 31, 1983. These provisions are now covered by N.Y. ARTS & CULT. AFF. LAW art. 13.

140.   N.Y. ARTS & CULT. AFF. LAW art. 13.

141. Weisz v. Parke-Bernet Galleries, Inc., 67 Misc. 2d 1077, 325 N.Y.S.2d 576 (Civ. Ct. 1971), *rev'd*, 77 Misc. 2d 80, 351 N.Y.S.2d 911 (App. Term 1974).

142. *Id.*, 77 Misc. 2d at 80, 351 N.Y.S.2d at 912. For a discussion of holding auction houses responsible for authenticating properties offered at auction, *see* K.B. Singer, *"Sotheby's Sold Me a Fake!"—Holding Auction Houses Accountable for Authenticating and Attributing Works of Fine Art*, 23 COLUM.-VLA J.L. & ARTS 437 (2000).

143. Zoellner v. Christie's, Index #120637/99 (N.Y. Sup. Ct., N.Y. County, Oct. 3, 2003). *See also* Real Prop. Acquisitions v. Christie's, Index #601943/04 (N.Y. Sup. Ct., N.Y. County, Mar. 12, 2005) (in dismissing plaintiff's claim based on repairs to an item of furniture purchased at auction, court pointed out that Christie's, in its Conditions of Sale, made "it clear to all potential bidders, that all lots are sold 'as is'").

144. Aryeh v. Christie's Int'l, Index No. 1030/86 (N.Y. Sup. Ct. 1986).

145. ARTNEWSLETTER, Feb. 2, 1988, at 3.

146. Aryeh v. Christie's Int'l, Index No. 1030/86 (N.Y. Sup. Ct. 1986).

147. TIMES (London), Oct. 1985.

148. *See, e.g.*, Myers v. Canton Nat'l Bank, 109 F.2d 31 (7th Cir. 1940); Rozell v. Kaye, 197 F. Supp. 733 (S.D. Tex. 1961), *modified on other grounds*, 201 F. Supp. 377 (S.D. Tex. 1962); Sylvester v. Bernstein, 283 A.D. 333, 127 N.Y.S.2d 746, *aff'd*, 307 N.Y. 778, 121 N.E.2d 616 (1954).

149. *See, e.g.*, Norris v. Haggin, 136 U.S. 386 (1890); Pratt v. Thompson, 133 Wash. 218, 233 P. 637 (1925); Van Ingin v. Duffin, 158 Ala. 318, 48 So. 507 (1909).

150. McCloud v. Lawrence Gallery, Ltd., 90 Civ. 30, 1991 U.S. Dist. LEXIS 9631 (S.D.N.Y. July 12, 1991), *later proceeding at* 1992 U.S. Dist. LEXIS 170 (S.D.N.Y. Jan. 9, 1992), *aff'd*, 970 F.2d 896 (2d Cir. 1992).

151. DeBalkany v. Christie Manson & Wood Ltd., High Court of Justice Queen's Bench Division, 1993 D. No. 1089.

152. Adam A. Weschler & Son, Inc. v. Klank, 561 A.2d 1003 (D.C. Ct. App. 1989). *But see* Nataros v. Fine Arts Gallery of Scottsdale, Inc., 126 Ariz. 44, 612 P.2d 500 (Ct. App. 1980) (where buyers unsuccessfully challenged sales made at auction under state consumer statutes based on value).

153. Thomson v. Christie Manson & Woods Ltd., High Court of Justice, Queen's Bench Division, 2004 D. No. 267.

154. *Id.*

155. *Id.*

156.   IFAR JOURNAL, Vol.7, No.1, p.8 at 9 (2004).
157.   *Id.* at 10.
158.   Thomson v. Christie Manson & Woods Ltd., High Court of Justice, Queen's Bench Division, 2004 D. No. 265.
159.   N. Tait, *Judges Give Auction Houses Comfort with Ruling on £1.9m Urn Purchase*, FIN. TIMES (London), May 13, 2005, at 6.
160.   U.C.C. § 2-312.
161.   U.C.C. § 2-312(1)(b). *See* Wildenstein & Co. v. Wallis, 756 F. Supp. 158 (S.D.N.Y. 1991), 949 F.2d 632 (2d Cir.), *certified to New York State Court of Appeals*, 79 N.Y.2d 641, 595 N.E.2d 828, 584 N.Y.S.2d 753 (1992), *rev'd without opinion*, 983 F.2d 1047 (2d Cir. 1992). Paintings were on "permanent loan" to the Los Angeles County Museum when the collector-lender's heirs put them up for auction in violation of decedent's instructions and in violation of Wildenstein's rights under a settlement contract with decedent.
162.   *See, e.g.,* Universal C.I.T. Credit Corp. v. State Farm Mut. Auto. Ins. Co., 493 S.W.2d 385 (Mo. Ct. App. 1973). *See also* Itoh v. Kimi Sales, Ltd., 74 Misc. 2d 402, 345 N.Y.S.2d 416 (Civ. Ct. 1973); Meyer v. Redmond, 205 N.Y. 478, 98 N.E. 906 (1912).
163.   *See, e.g.,* De Remer v. Brown, 165 N.Y. 410, 419 (1901); M.N. Bank v. Gallaudet, 120 N.Y. 298, 307 (1890). *See also* H. REUSCHLEIN & W. GREGORY, AGENCY AND PARTNERSHIP § 6 (1979).
164.   Rules of the City of New York, *supra* note 76, § 2-124(a), § 2-122(b)(2), and § 2-122(a).
165.   Levy Bros. & Adler, Rochester, Inc. v. Karp, 124 Misc. 901, 209 N.Y.S. 720 (Sup. Ct. 1924). But note that in a small number of jurisdictions an auctioneer who has neither actual nor constructive knowledge of a claim by a third party is not liable to that third party. *See* Annot., *Auctioneer Liability for Conversion*, 96 A.L.R.2D 208, 214 (1964).
166.   *See* Menzel v. List, 24 N.Y.2d 91, 298 N.Y.S.2d 979, 246 N.E.2d 742 (1969).
167.   Grossman v. Walters, 11 N.Y.S. 471, (Sup. Ct. 1890), *aff'd sub nom.* Grossman v. Kantrowitz, 132 N.Y. 594, 30 N.E. 1151 (1892).
168.   Kelly v. Brooks, 92 Civ. 729, 1993 U.S. Dist. LEXIS 3385 (S.D.N.Y. Mar. 19, 1993).
169.   *Id.* at *2.
170.   *Id.*
171.   Giusti v. Sotheby Parke Bernet, Inc., N.Y.L.J., July 16, 1982, at 5 (Sup. Ct. N.Y. County 1982).
172.   *Id.*
173.   *Id.*

174. *Id.*
175. U.C.C. § 2-316(1), (3).
176. Christie Manson & Woods Int'l, Inc. v. Brown, N.Y.L.J. Aug. 28, 1995, at 29, col. 5 (Sup. Ct. N.Y. County 1995).
177. *Id.*
178. *Id.*
179. N.Y. TIMES, Oct. 18, 1989, at C-15.
180. *Id.*
181. *See, e.g.*, ARTNEWSLETTER, Jan. 23, 1990, at 1; ARTNEWS, Mar. 1990, at 47.
182. ARTNEWSLETTER, Jan. 23, 1990, at 1.
183. *See, e.g.*, N.Y. TIMES, May 27, 1990, Arts & Leisure Section, at 26; ART & AUCTION, May 1990, at 264.
184. ARTNEWSLETTER, July 6, 1993, at 8; ARTNEWSLETTER, Mar. 21, 1995, at 4.
185. ARTNEWSLETTER, Mar. 21, 1995, at 4; Reuters, Limited, Jan. 17, 1996, *Failed Tycoon Alan Bond to Face Trial for Fraud*; ARTNEWSLETTER, Sept. 10, 1996, at 7.
186. *See, e.g.*, ARTNEWSLETTER, Feb. 19, 1991, at 1; ARTS AUCTION, Mar. 1991, at 112.
187. *Id.* Also addressed at the same public hearing were issues related to museum "deaccessioning" and record keeping; the resulting legislation is discussed in the chapter on museums. *See* chapter 16.
188. Assembly Bill 1254, 226th Annual Legislative Session, Jan. 16, 2003.
189. *In re* Auction Houses Antitrust Litig., No. 00 Civ. 0648 (LAK), Apr. 13, 2001.
190. Kruman v. Christie's Int'l PLC, No. 01-7309, Mar. 13, 2002.
191. *See, e.g.*, NAT'L L.J., Vol. 24, No.41, at A-23 (June 24, 2002).
192. *See, e.g.*, N.Y. L.J., Oct. 6, 2000, at 1.
193. *See, e.g.*, N.Y. TIMES, Apr. 30, 2002, at B-3.
194. *Id.*
195. *See, e.g.*, N.Y. TIMES, Apr. 23, 2002, at B-5; N.Y. L.J., Apr. 23, 2002, at 1.
196. *See, e.g.*, Nev. Nat'l Leasing Co. v. Hereford, 36 Cal. 3d 146, 680 P.2d 1077, 203 Cal. Rptr. 118 (1984); Berg v. Hogan, 322 N.W.2d 448 (N.D. 1982); Feaster Trucking Serv., Inc. v. Parks-Davis Auctioneers, Inc., 211 Kan. 78, 505 P.2d 612 (1973).
197. U.C.C. § 2-328(4).
198. 1 W. HAWKLAND, A TRANSACTIONAL GUIDE TO THE UNIFORM COMMERCIAL CODE 54 (1983).

199.   *Id.* at 54–55. *But see* Rawlings v. Gen. Trading Co., 90 K.B. 404 (1921), which, despite a strong dissent indicating that the bidding combination at issue was contrary to public policy as being in restraint of trade, held that an agreement between two prospective purchasers to chill bidding was not illegal.

200.   *But see* W. HAWKLAND, 2 UNIFORM COMMERCIAL CODE SERIES § 2-328:05, at 825 (1991) (suggesting that "chill bidding" may actually be proscribed by the Code). Hawkland argues that the practice, illegal under common law, continues to be illegal under U.C.C. § 1-103. That section provides that unless displaced by specific provisions of the U.C.C., the principles of law and equity—including the law merchant, contract law, and the law of agency—will supplement the Code.

201.   *Id.*

202.   Auctions (Bidding Agreements) Act, 1927, 17 & 18 Geo. 5, ch. 12, 4 Halsbury's Statutes 5 (4th ed. 1987) (Eng).

203.   WALL ST. J., Aug. 20, 1991, at 13.

204.   *Id.*

205.   *See, e.g.*, Preske v. Carroll, 178 Md. 543, 16 A.2d 291 (1940); Konen v. Konen, 165 La. 288, 115 So. 490 (1928); Stewart v. Severance, 43 Mo. 322 (1869).

206.   *See, e.g.*, Jones v. Clary, 194 Va. 804, 75 S.E.2d 504 (1953); Henderson v. Henrie, 61 W. Va. 183, 56 S.E. 369 (1907); Smith v. Ullman, 58 Md. 183 (1882); James v. Fulcrod, 5 Tex. 512 (1851).

207.   Stolow v. Greg Manning Auctions, Inc., 258 F. Supp. 2d 236 (S.D.N.Y. 2003).

208.   As the court observed, fraudulent concealment sufficient to toll the running of the statute of limitations may lie if the plaintiff establishes (1) that the defendant concealed from plaintiff the existence of plaintiff's cause of action, (2) that plaintiff was ignorant of that cause of action until some point within four years of the commencement of her action, and (3) that plaintiff's continuing ignorance was not due to lack of diligence on plaintiff's part. *Id.*, 258 F. Supp. 2d at 251 (citing New York v. Hendrickson Bros., 840 F.2d 1065, 1083 (2d Cir. 1988)).

Appendix 4-1

Sotheby's Standard Agreement

Sotheby's ᴱˢᵀ. ¹⁷⁴⁴ 1334 YORK AVENUE NEW YORK NY 10021
Tel (212) 606-7000 WWW.SOTHEBYS.COM

CONSIGNMENT AGREEMENT

Client Account Number:
Consignment:
Date:
Principal Auctioneer: Tobias Meyer
License No. 0958677

Thank you for consigning property to Sotheby's.

This agreement confirms your and our agreement under which the property listed on the attached Property Schedule ("Property") will be offered for sale at auction, subject to the following terms and our standard Conditions of Sale and Terms of Guarantee to be printed in the catalogue for the sale, by which you hereby agree to be bound.

1. **Selling Commission.** For this consignment of Property, you will pay us a selling commission on each lot as set forth below, except for those items of Property which have specific terms noted on the attached Property Schedule:

Hammer Price Per Lot
0 USD to 1,999 USD........................ 20% of the hammer price
2,000 USD up to 7,499 USD............. 15% of the hammer price
7,500 USD or more........................... 10% of the hammer price

Each item of Property is subject to a minimum commission of 100.00 USD for each sold lot. For any lot of Property which fails to sell at the auction, you will be charged a bought-in commission of 5% of the reserve, subject to a minimum handling charge of 0.00 USD on each unsold lot.

2. **Expenses.** You agree to bear the following expenses:
(a) insurance premium of 1.50% of the Insurance Amount if the Property sells and 0.00% of the Insurance Amount if the Property does not sell for purchasing insurance which will insure you for loss or damage to the Property (please see paragraph 9 below), except for those items of Property which have specific terms noted on the attached Property Schedule;
(b) our standard fees then in effect for catalogue illustration;
(c) packing, shipping and customs duties to our premises;
(d) any agreed-upon advertising;
(e) the cost of any reproduction rights; and
(f) other services, such as framing, restoration and gemological approved by you.
There will be a 20% service charge on the cost of any services performed by others and paid for by us for your account.

3. **Auction.** In connection with any auction, we will have absolute discretion as to (a) consulting any expert either before or after the sale, (b) researching the provenance of the Property either before or after the sale, (c) grouping the Property into lots and providing catalogue and other descriptions as we believe appropriate, (d) the date or dates of an auction, (e) the marketing and promotion of the sale and (f) the manner of conducting the sale.

| 399

Sotheby's EST. 1744 1334 YORK AVENUE NEW YORK NY 10021
Tel (212) 606-7000 WWW.SOTHEBYS.COM

Page 2 of 6

Client Account Number:
Consignment:
Date:
Principal Auctioneer: Tobias Meyer
License No. 0958677

4. Buyer's Premium. You authorize us to charge the buyer and retain for our account a commission on each lot sold (the "buyer's premium"). The Conditions of Sale in the catalogue for the auction will state the rate at which the buyer's premium will be assessed against the buyer, and such rate will be a percentage of the hammer price of each lot sold. We reserve the right, without further notice to you, to pay out of our commissions a fee to any third party introducing property or clients to us.

5. Settlement. On the Settlement Date(s) (as defined below), we will mail to you the sale proceeds we collect and receive, after deducting our selling commission, buyer's premium and reimbursable expenses (the "net sale proceeds"), unless the purchaser has notified us of intention to rescind the sale (as provided in paragraph 11). We may also deduct and retain from the net sale proceeds any other amount you owe us or any of our affiliated entities, whether arising out of the sale of the Property or otherwise. In addition to other remedies available to us by law, we reserve the right to impose a late charge of 1.5% per month on any amount due us or any of our affiliated entities and remaining unpaid for more than fifteen days after we notify you.

If all of the Property is sold in the same auction, the "Settlement Date" will be the date that is thirty-five days after the last session of the auction. If the Property is to be sold in more than one auction, then the "Settlement Dates" will be the dates that are thirty-five days after the last session of each auction.

We have no obligation to enforce payment by any purchaser. If a purchaser does not pay, and you and we do not agree on another course of action, we reserve the right to cancel the sale and return the Property to you.

Notwithstanding the preceding sentence, if we pay you all or part of the net sale proceeds for any lot of the Property and have not collected from the purchaser of such Property payment of the amount we paid to you, simultaneously with, and to the extent of, any such payment by us to you, you assign to us any and all rights you may have againstsuch purchaser, whether at law, in equity or under the Conditions of Sale. You agree to execute any documents we may reasonably request evidencing this assignment, and you agree that all of your representations, warranties and indemnities set forth in this Agreement shall apply to us or the purchaser, as the case may be, with respect to such item. You authorize us, in our discretion, to impose on any purchaser and retain for our account a late charge if payment is not made in accordance with the Conditions of Sale.

6. Reserves. Unless a different reserve has been agreed upon by you and us and confirmed in writing before the auction, the reserve for each lot of the Property will be (a) the reserve specifically noted on the Property Schedule, or (b) if no reserve is noted on the Property Schedule, 60% of our latest announced or published low pre-sale estimate. However, we may sell any lot of the Property at a price below the reserve, provided that we pay you in accordance with paragraph 5 above the net amount which you would have been entitled to receive had such lot of the Property been sold at the reserve (that is, the reserve less our selling commission, reimbursable expenses and any amount you owe us or any of our affiliated entities). No reserve for a lot will exceed its low pre-sale estimate.

You agree not to bid on the Property. Although we shall be entitled to bid on your behalf up to the amount of the reserve, you shall not instruct or permit any other person to bid for the Property on your behalf. If, however, you violate your foregoing commitment and you or your agent become the successful bidder on the Property, you will pay us the selling commission as set forth in paragraph 1 and the buyer's premium on the hammer price, the Property may be sold without any reserve, and you will not be entitled to the benefit of any warranties under the Conditions of Sale of Terms of Guarantee.

In the event any lot is bought-in, we will make an announcement that such lot has been "passed", "returned to owner", "withdrawn" or "bought-in".

7. Sotheby's Arcade Auctions. If we deem it appropriate, we may, in our sole discretion, include in a Sotheby's Arcade Auction any Property with a low pre-sale estimate in our opinion of 5,000 USD or less. In such event, or if you and we agree to include any property in a Sotheby's Arcade Auction, we will offer the

CONSIGNOR COPY

Sotheby's
EST. 1744
1334 YORK AVENUE NEW YORK NY 10021
Tel (212) 606-7000 WWW.SOTHEBYS.COM

Page 3 of 6

Client Account Number:
Consignment:
Date:
Principal Auctioneer: Tobias Meyer
License No. 0958677

Property subject to the provisions of this Agreement and our Conditions of Sale for Sotheby's Arcade Auctions printed in the catalogue.

8. Representations and Warranties; Indemnity. You represent and warrant to us and each purchaser that you have the right to consign the Property for sale; that it is now, and through and including its sale will be kept, free of all liens, claims and encumbrances of others including, but not limited to, claims of governments or governmental agencies; that good title and right to possession will pass to the purchaser free of all liens, claims and encumbrances; that you have provided us with any information you have concerning the provenance of the Property; that you have no reason to believe that any lot of Property is not authentic or is counterfeit; that where the Property has been imported into the United States, the Property has been lawfully imported into the United States and has been lawfully and permanently exported as required by the laws of any country (including any laws or regulations applicable in the European Union) in which it was located; that required declarations upon the export and import of the Property have been properly made and any duties and taxes on the export and import of the Property have been paid; that you have paid or will pay any and all taxes and/or duties that may be due on the net sale proceeds of the Property and you have notified us in writing of any and all taxes and/or duties that are payable by us on your behalf in any country other than the United States; and that there are no restrictions on our right to reproduce photographs of it. We retain the exclusive copyright to all catalogue and other illustrations and descriptions of the Property created by us.

You agree to indemnify and hold us and each purchaser harmless from and against any and all claims, actions, damages, losses, liabilities and expenses (including reasonable attorneys' fees) relating to the breach or alleged breach of any of your agreements, representations or warranties in this Agreement.

Your representations, warranties and indemnity will survive completion of the transactions contemplated by this Agreement.

9. Insurance for loss or Damage. Unless, at the time you deliver the Property to us, you provide us with a certificate of insurance with a waiver of subrogation each in form acceptable to us, by executing this Agreement, you authorize us to purchase insurance to cover the risk of loss or damage to the Property from the time of our receipt of such Property until it ceases to be in our custody or control, in the amount set forth in the paragraph below, Insurance Amount. Such insurance will be arranged by us and you authorize and instruct us, whether or not the Property is sold, to pay insurance premiums on your behalf. The insurer's and our combined liability to you resulting from loss or damage to any lot of Property shall not exceed the Insurance Amount of such Property.

Insurance Amount. The amount of the insurance we are purchasing on your behalf and to which you agree is: (a) for Property which has been sold, the hammer price (excluding buyer's premium), (b) for Property which has failed to sell at the auction, the reserve, or (c) for Property not yet offered for sale, the mean of our latest pre-sale estimates. In the event of a total loss (Property which has been lost, or Property which has been damaged and has depreciated in value, in the insurer's opinion, by more than 50%), the insurer will pay you the foregoing amount, less in any case the selling commission and expenses payable by you under this Agreement, and the Property will belong to the insurer.

In the event of a partial loss (Property which has been partially damaged or lost and has depreciated in value, in the insurer's opinion, by less than 50%), the insurer, in its sole discretion, will either (i) pay you the amount of depreciation and such Property will be offered for sale or returned to you or (ii) pay you the "Insurance Amount" for the Property as set forth in the preceding sentence, and the Property will belong to the insurer. Neither the insurer nor we will be liable for damage to frames or glass covering prints, paintings or other works, or for damage occurring in the course of any process undertaken by independent contractors employed with your consent (including restoration, framing or cleaning), or for damage caused by changes in humidity or temperature, inherent conditions or defects, normal wear and tear, war, acts of terrorism, nuclear fission or

Client Account Number:
Consignment:
Date:
Principal Auctioneer: Tobias Meyer
License No. 0958677

radioactive contamination.

10. Withdrawal. You may not withdraw any Property from sale after the date on which we issue a receipt or you sign this Agreement, whichever is earlier. Regardless of whether we have previously issued a receipt, published a catalogue including the Property or advertised its sale, we may withdraw any Property at any time before sale if in our sole judgment (a) there is doubt as to its authenticity or attribution, (b) there is doubt as to the accuracy of any of your representations or warranties, or (c) you have breached any provision of this Agreement. If we withdraw any Property under (b) or (c) of this paragraph 10, you must within ten days of our notice to you of withdrawal pay us a withdrawal fee equal to 20% of the mean of our latest pre-sale estimates for the withdrawn Property, as well as all out-of-pocket expenses incurred by us up to and including the date of withdrawal (the "Withdrawal Fee"). If any Property is withdrawn by you in breach of this Agreement, you will pay us a Withdrawal Fee as well as any special, incidental or consequential damages incurred as a result of your breach, notwithstanding anything to the contrary in this Agreement. If any Property is withdrawn under (a) above, you will not be charged a Withdrawal Fee and, subject to any liens or claims to the Property, such Property will be returned to you at your expense.

11. Rescission. You authorize us to rescind the sale of any Property in accordance with the Conditions of Sale and Terms of Guarantee, or if we learn that the Property is inaccurately described in the catalogue, or if we learn that the Property is a counterfeit (a modern forgery intended to deceive), or if we determine in our sole judgment that the offering for sale of any lot of Property has subjected or may subject us and/or you to any liability, including liability under the warranty of title or warranty of authenticity included in the Terms of Guarantee. If we receive from a purchaser notice of intention to rescind and we determine that a lot of the Property is subject to rescission under the Terms of Guarantee or as otherwise set forth above, we will credit the purchaser with the purchase price, you will return to us on ten days' notice to you any sale proceeds for such Property paid by us to you or to a third party as directed by you, and we will return the Property to you upon your reimbursing us for expenses incurred in connection with the rescinded sale, and paying us any other amounts you owe us or any of our affiliated entities.

12. Private Sales. If any lot fails to reach its reserve and is bought-in for your account, you authorize us, as your exclusive agent, for a period of 60 days following the auction, to sell the lot privately for a price that will result in a payment to you of not less than the net amount (after our selling commission and expenses) to which you would have been entitled had the lot been sold at a price equal to the agreed reserve. In such event, your obligations to us hereunder with respect to such lot are the same as if it had been sold at auction.

13. Treatment of Unsold Property. If any Property remains unsold for any reason after the auction, we will notify you. If such Property has not been sold privately pursuant to paragraph 12, and if it is not reconsigned to us for sale on mutually agreed-upon terms or picked up within 60 days after such notification, we may (a) return it to you at your expense, (b) sell it at public auction without reserve at a place and date determined by us or (c) transfer it to a third-party warehouse. The proceeds of any sale pursuant to (b) above will be applied to any amount you owe us or any of our affiliated entities, including, but not limited to, our commissions and expenses, and any excess will be remitted to you. In the event of the transfer of any unsold Property to a third-party warehouse, you shall bear all cost and risk thereof and will be liable to such warehouse for the payment of all storage and insurance charges at such warehouse's standard rates.

You shall not be entitled to reclaim any unsold Property until all commissions, expenses and other amounts owed to us or any of our affiliates have been paid in full. Unless and until we reoffer and sell such Property or return it to you, we will hold it without charge for a period of 30 days after the auction in which it is offered but not sold. Thereafter, a handling charge of 1 % per month of the mean of our pre-sale estimates will be payable by you to cover our costs of handling.

Sotheby's

EST.1744

1334 YORK AVENUE NEW YORK NY 10021
Tel (212) 606-7000 WWW.SOTHEBYS.COM

Client Account Number:
Consignment:
Date:
Principal Auctioneer: Tobias Meyer
License No. 0958677

14.   Estimates; Catalogue Descriptions.   Pre-sale estimates, if any, are intended as guides for prospective bidders. We make no representations or warranties of the anticipated selling price of any Property and no estimate anywhere by us of the selling price of any Property may be relied upon as a prediction of the actual selling price. Estimates included in receipts, catalogues or elsewhere are preliminary only and are subject to revision by us from time to time in our sole discretion.

We will not be liable for any errors or omissions with respect to the auction or in the catalogue or other descriptions of the Property and make no guarantees, representations or warranties whatsoever to you with respect to the Property, its authenticity, attribution, legal title, condition, value or otherwise.

15.   Use of Name. We may use your name as owner of the Property as set forth on the first page of this Agreement or we may designate the Property as indicated below (please initial the box next to it), when we offer the Property for sale, advertise or otherwise promote the sale, both before or after the auction. If you do not want us to use your name or otherwise designate the Property, please initial the box below.

You may designate the Property as follows: [ ]
The Property of Libby Alexander
You may not use my name: [ ]

16.   Legal Status. If you are acting as a fiduciary in executing this Agreement and in the transactions contemplated hereunder, please initial "Fiduciary" and sign and return to us our standard "Fiduciary Agreement".

Fiduciary [ ]

If you are acting as an agent for someone who is not signing this Agreement, you and your principal jointly and severally assume your obligations and liabilities hereunder to the same extent as if you were acting as principal.

17.   Reconsignment. We may, at our discretion, reconsign any lot of Property so that it shall be offered for sale at public auction by one of our affiliates, unless you object in writing within ten days of the date of our notice of reconsignment. Any reconsigned lot shall be offered for sale pursuant to the terms of this Agreement, and subject to the Conditions of Business and the Authenticity Guarantee, if any, applicable to the auction where offered. If there is a conflict between the applicable Conditions of Business and the Authenticity Guarantee and the terms of this Agreement, the terms of this Agreement shall control. With respect to any such reconsigned lot, the terms "Conditions of Sale" and "Terms of Guarantee" referred to in this Agreement shall mean the Conditions of Business and the Authenticity Guarantee, if any, applicable to such auction. Any net sale proceeds of the Property in such sale shall be remitted to you in the currency in which the auction is conducted, and all local taxes shall apply.

18.   Amendment. Neither you nor we may amend, supplement or waive any provision of this Agreement other than by means of a writing signed by both parties except that if at any time we propose by written notice to amend or supplement any provision of this Agreement, or provide additional terms or conditions as to your future consignments, you will be deemed to have agreed thereto with respect to any property received by us at any time after such notice, unless you advise us in writing to the contrary before such property is received by us.

19.   Privacy. Sotheby's Holdings, Inc., its subsidiaries and affiliates ("Sotheby's Group") will record any information that you supply to us or that we obtain about you in its data systems shared within Sotheby's Group. Your information will be kept confidential within Sotheby's Group. From time to time Sotheby's Group may send you information about its sales and events, or about products and services of other organizations

Client Account Number:
Consignment:
Date:
Principal Auctioneer: Tobias Meyer
License No. 0958677

with which it has a relationship.

     20. Miscellaneous. This Agreement shall be governed by and construed and enforced in accordance with the laws of the State of New York, except in the case of a reconsignment pursuant to paragraph 17, in which event the Agreement shall be construed and enforced in accordance with the laws of the state or country in which the Property is offered for sale. In the event of a dispute hereunder, you agree to submit to the exclusive jurisdiction of the state courts of and the federal courts sitting in the State of New York and to the exclusive jurisdiction of the courts of the state or country in which the Property is offered for sale. This Agreement shall be binding upon your heirs, executors, beneficiaries, successors and assigns, but you may not assign this Agreement without our prior written consent. Neither party shall be liable to the other for any special, consequential or incidental damages. This Agreement, including the Schedules hereto, and the Conditions of Sale and any Terms of Guarantee, constitute the entire agreement between the parties with respect to the transactions contemplated hereby and supersede all prior or contemporaneous written, oral or implied understandings, representations and agreements of the parties relating to the subject matter of this Agreement. As used in this Agreement, "we" "us" and "ours" mean Sotheby's, Inc. and any affiliated company offering Property for sale under this Agreement, and "you" and "your" mean the individual, corporation or other entity listed above (jointly and severally if there is more than one listed above). You agree that you will not disclose the terms of this Agreement to any third-party without our prior written consent, except to attorneys and accountants on a need-to-know basis, or as a result of valid legal process compelling the disclosure, provided you first give us prompt written notice of such service of process and allow us, if we deem it appropriate, to obtain a protective order. Any notices given hereunder to you or us shall be in writing to the respective address indicated on the first page of this Agreement (or to such other address as you or we may notify the other in writing) and shall be deemed to have been given five calendar days after mailing to such address or within one business day of delivery by hand or telecopier. You agree to provide us, upon our request, verification of identity in an appropriate form. The paragraph headings contained in this Agreement are for convenience of reference only and shall not affect in any way the meaning or interpretation of this Agreement.

     Please confirm your agreement with the foregoing by dating, signing and returning to us the duplicate copy of this Agreement.

Consignor
Accepted and agreed:

                    Sotheby's, Inc.

_____

By: _____

CONSIGNOR COPY

1334 YORK AVENUE NEW YORK NY 10021
Tel (212) 606-7000 WWW.SOTHEBYS.COM

EST. 1744

Page 1 of 1

Property Schedule

Client Account Number:
Consignment:
Date:

Item ID	Description	Low estimate	High estimate	Reserve
32PGQ	Lama, Gilt Copper, Tibet	4,000.00 USD	6,000.00 USD	0.00
	Department: Indian/S.E. Asian			
32PGR	Bust of Buddha Gray Schist Gandhara	80,000.00 USD	120,000.00 USD	0.00
	Department: Indian/S.E. Asian			
32PGS	Molded Yaozhou Conical Bowl	12,000.00 USD	15,000.00 USD	0.00
	Department: Chinese Works Of Art			

Selling commission for this item only: Hammer Price Per Lot
0 USD to 10,000 USD............5.00% of the hammer price
10,001 USD or more..........2.00% of the hammer price

Insurance Premium for this item only: You agree to bear the following expenses:
Insurance premium of 0.00% of the insurance amount if the property sells and 0.00% of the insurance amount if the property does not sell for purchasing insurance which will insure you for loss or damage to the Property (please see paragraph 9 in your Consignment agreement).

CONSIGNOR COPY

This Property Schedule is subject to the terms of your Consignment Agreement.

Appendix 4-2

Christie's Standard Agreement

Date:	Commission Type:
Client No.:	MCC:
Stock No.:	

CHRISTIE'S
CONSIGNMENT AGREEMENT BETWEEN

"CONSIGNOR"   AND   "CHRISTIE'S"

NAME:	CHRISTIE'S INC.
ADDRESS:	20 ROCKEFELLER PLAZA
TELEPHONE:	NEW YORK, NY 10020
	TEL: (212) 636-2000

Thank you for consigning your property to Christie's.
The terms and conditions of the consignment are as follows:

1. CONSIGNMENT

You (the "Consignor") hereby consign to Christie's the property identified on the attached schedule, as amended from time to time, (the "Property") which Christie's, as the exclusive agent for Consignor, will offer for sale at public auction, unless otherwise agreed, subject to the provisions set forth below and Christie's standard Conditions of Sale and Limited Warranty in effect at the time of the auction. In the event of a conflict between the Conditions of Sale and Limited Warranty, on the one hand, and this Agreement, on the other hand, the terms of this Agreement shall control.

2. COMMISSION

(a) In consideration of its services and subject to subparagraph (c), below, Christie's will receive and retain from the proceeds of the sale of the Property a commission from the Seller based upon the aggregate final bid price of all property (including, without limitation, the Property) sold by Seller at Christie's thus far during the calendar year as follows:

TOTAL LOTS SOLD:	COMMISSION RATE:
$5,000,000 or more	As agreed
$2,500,000 - $4,999,999	2% of the final bid price
$1,000,000 - $2,499,999	4% of the final bid price
$500,000 - $999,999	5% of the final bid price
$250,000 - $499,999	7% of the final bid price
$100,000 - $249,999	8% of the final bid price

OR TRADE

TOTAL LOTS SOLD:	COMMISSION RATE:
$5,000,000 or more	As agreed
$2,500,000 - $4,999,999	2% of the final bid price
$1,000,000 - $2,499,999	4% of the final bid price
$100,000 - $999,999	5% of the final bid price

OR INSTITUTIONAL

2

TOTAL LOTS SOLD:	COMMISSION RATE:
$5,000,000 or more	As agreed
$1,000,000 - $4,999,999	2% of the final bid price
$100,000 - $999,999	4% of the final bid price

(b) Subject to subparagraph (c) below, if the sum of the aggregate final bid price of all Property sold by Seller at Christie's thus far during the calendar year is less than $100,000, Christie's will receive and retain from the proceeds of sale a commission based upon the final bid price of each lot sold as follows:

FINAL BID PRICE OF LOT:	COMMISSION RATE:
$7,500 - $99,999	10% of the final bid price
$2,000 - $7,499	15% of the final bid price
less than $2,000	20% of the final bid price

OR TRADE

FINAL BID PRICE OF LOT:	COMMISSION RATE:
$7,500 - $99,999	6% of the final bid price
$2,000 - $7,499	10% of the final bid price
less than $2,000	15% of the final bid price

OR INSTITUTIONAL

FINAL BID PRICE OF LOT:	COMMISSION RATE:
$7,500 - $99,999	10% of the final bid price
$2,000 - $7,499	15% of the final bid price
less than $2,000	20% of the final bid price

(c)   If Consignor has sold property through Christie's during the prior calendar year, the commission rate payable shall be the lesser of (i) the rate to be charged pursuant to subparagraph (a) or (b) above or (ii) the rate that would have been paid by Consignor during the prior calendar year under the commission scale outlined above.

(d)   Christie's shall also receive a premium to be collected from the buyer of 20% of the final bid price up to and including $100,000, plus 12% of the final bid price above $100,000, or such other amounts as shall be published by Christie's from time to time.

(e)   There will be a minimum commission charge of $100 per lot for each lot sold at Christie's main galleries.

3A. EXPENSES
Consignor agrees to pay all costs relating to:
(a) packing and shipping the Property to Christie's;
(b)   packing and shipping the Property from Christie's if any Property is returned to Consignor;
(c)   insurance, as provided in paragraph 4 below;
(d)   transit insurance, as provided in paragraph 4 below;
(e)   all applicable customs duties and customs user fees;
(f)   catalogue illustration up to a maximum of $900 per lot for color illustration and $300 per lot for black and white illustration;
(g)   restoration;
(h)   framing;

3

(i)   tests or procedures that Christie's deems necessary or desirable to verify authenticity, attribution or quality of any Property and any fees in connection therewith;
(j)   any special marketing costs;
(k)   storage of the Property after the sale, including in a third-party warehouse, as provided in paragraph 8(e) below;
(l)   an unsold property charge in the event that any lot fails to sell, as provided in paragraph 8(e) below;
(m)   such additional costs and expenses not set forth above as may be agreed to by Consignor.

Expenses incurred by Christie's for Consignor's account pursuant to this paragraph shall include a 10% service charge.

3B.   Christie's agrees to pay all costs relating to:
(a)   packing and shipping the Property to Christie's;
(b)   packing and shipping the Property from Christie's if any Property is returned to Consignor;
(c)   insurance, as provided in paragraph 4 below;
(d)   transit insurance, as provided in paragraph 4 below;
(e)   all applicable customs duties and customs user fees;
(f)   catalogue illustration of the Property;
(g)   restoration;
(h)   framing;
(i)   tests or procedures that Christie's deems necessary or desirable to verify authenticity, attribution or quality of any Property and any fees in connection therewith;
(j)   any special marketing costs;
(k)   storage of the Property after the sale, including in a third-party warehouse, as provided in paragraph 8(e) below;
(l)   such additional costs and expenses not set forth above as may be agreed to by Consignor.

4.   CHRISTIE'S INSURANCE
(a)   Unless Christie's and Consignor agree otherwise, each lot of Property will be insured at Consignor's expense under and subject to the terms of Christie's insurance policy, as shall be in effect from time to time, from the time of receipt by Christie's until it ceases to be in Christie's custody for an amount equal to (i) the mean of the pre-sale estimates prior to sale, (ii) the amount of the final bid price if sold, or (iii) the amount of the reserve if unsold (in each case, the "Insured Value").

(b)   Insurance for Property received at Christie's auction premises will be charged to Consignor at a rate of 1.5% of the Insured Value for all Property other than breakables, such as porcelain or glass, and 2% of the Insured Value for all breakable property. Insurance for Property received at one of Christie's regional offices or at any location other than its auction premises will be charged to Consignor at an additional rate of 0.5% of the Insured Value to cover transit to Christie's auction premises. Whenever Consignor is responsible for packing and shipping charges, Christie's shall have no liability whatsoever to Consignor in connection therewith, even when Christie's has recommended a carrier.

(c)   Each lot of Property will remain insured until 30 days after the sale. If any such lot has not been sold, there will be an additional charge for insurance after that date.

(d)   Christie's liability to Consignor resulting from loss of or damage to any lot of Property shall not exceed the Insured Value of such Property. While Christie's undertakes to exercise reasonable care in handling the

Property, we shall not be responsible for any damage to any Property caused by climatic or atmospheric conditions or for any damage to picture frames or to glass therein.

4.   CONSIGNOR'S INSURANCE

If Consignor has instructed Christie's not to insure the Property, it will be insured at Consignor's expense under Consignor's insurance policy from the time of receipt by Christie's until it ceases to be in Christie's custody. Christie's shall have no liability to Consignor whatsoever resulting from loss of or damage to any Property. Consignor shall execute and deliver to Christie's an insurance waiver letter in form and substance satisfactory to Christie's or shall deliver to Christie's a certificate of insurance naming Christie's as an additional named insured.

5.   CONSIGNOR'S REPRESENTATIONS AND WARRANTIES, COVENANTS AND INDEMNIFICATION

(a)   Consignor represents and warrants to Christie's that: (i) Consignor has the right and title to consign the Property for sale; (ii) the Property is, and until the completion of sale by Christie's will be, free and clear of all liens, claims and encumbrances of others or restrictions on Christie's right to offer and sell the Property; (iii) upon sale, good and marketable title and right to possession will pass to the buyer free of any such liens, claims, encumbrances or restrictions; (iv) Consignor has no reason to believe that any lot of Property is not authentic or is counterfeit; (v) the Property is not "confiscated Property" within the meaning of any United States federal or state laws; (vi) Consignor's consignment to and authorization of Christie's to sell the Property is in full compliance with all United States federal and state laws; (vii) the exportation, if any, of the Property from any foreign country has been in full conformity with the laws of such country and the importation of the Property into the United States has been or will be in full conformity with the laws of the United States; and (viii) there are not, and until the completion of sale by Christie's there will not be, any restrictions on Christie's right to photograph, reproduce photographs of or exhibit the Property.   ·

(b)   Consignor agrees that such representations and warranties are for the benefit of Christie's and buyers of the Property and that such representations and warranties shall survive the completion of the transactions contemplated hereby. Consignor agrees to notify Christie's promptly in writing of any events or circumstances that may cause the foregoing representations and warranties to be inaccurate or breached in any way.

(c)   If Consignor is acting as an agent for a principal, Consignor and principal, jointly and severally, assume all of Consignor's obligations set forth in this Agreement.

(d)   Consignor grants to Christie's the right to illustrate and photograph the Property and to use such photographs, illustrations or images at any time before or after the sale and for such purposes as Christie's deems appropriate. Consignor agrees that all catalogue and other photographs, illustrations and descriptions of the Property created by or for Christie's are not "works made for hire" on behalf of Consignor under copyright law, and that Christie's shall own the exclusive copyright and all other rights relating to all such photographs, illustrations and descriptions.

(e)   Consignor shall defend, indemnify and hold harmless Christie's from and against any and all losses, damages, liabilities and claims, and all fees, costs and expenses of any kind related thereto (including, without limitation, reasonable attorney's fees), arising out of, based upon or resulting from (i) any act by or omission of Consignor or Consignor's agents (other than Christie's) or representatives relating to or affecting

5

the Property or (ii) any inaccuracy or alleged inaccuracy, asserted by Christie's or any third party in a court action, of any representation or warranty made by Consignor pursuant to this Agreement.

6. SALE ARRANGEMENTS

(a) Christie's shall have complete discretion as to (i) the place and date of sale and the manner in which such sale is conducted, including the Conditions of Sale then in effect, (ii) the illustration, if any, and the description of the Property in our catalogues and other literature, (iii) seeking the views of any expert, either before or after the sale, and (iv) the combination or division of the Property into such lots and/or separate auctions as Christie's in our sole judgement may deem appropriate.

(b) Any written or oral appraisal, estimate or other statement of Christie's or our representatives with respect to the estimated or expected selling price of any lot of Property is a statement of opinion only and shall not be relied upon by Consignor or any third party as a prediction or guarantee of the actual selling price. Christie's makes no representations or warranties to Consignor with respect to the Property, its authenticity, attribution, condition or otherwise. Christie's shall not be liable for any errors or omissions in catalogue or other descriptions of the Property. Printed pre-sale estimates shall not include the buyer's premium or taxes.

(c) No Property may be withdrawn from sale after the date of this Agreement without Christie's consent. If Christie's consents to a withdrawal, a lot of Property may be withdrawn upon payment of 20% of the reserve price or 20% of the mean of the pre-sale estimates if the reserve has not yet been set plus all out-of-pocket expenses incurred by Christie's.

(d) Christie's reserves the right to withdraw any Property at any time before sale if in Christie's sole judgment (i) there is doubt as to its attribution or authenticity, (ii) there is doubt as to the accuracy of any of Consignor's representations or warranties set forth herein, (iii) Consignor has breached any provision of this Agreement or (iv) other just cause exists. There shall be no charge to Consignor, other than Christie's out-of-pocket expenses, for a withdrawal pursuant to clause (i) or (iv). In the event of a withdrawal pursuant to clause (ii) or (iii), Consignor shall be liable for the withdrawal charges and other expenses set forth in subparagraph (c) of this paragraph 6.

7. CONDUCT OF THE SALE

(a) *Reserves.* Unless otherwise agreed, each lot of Property will be sold subject to a reserve (the confidential minimum price below which such Property will not be sold) which shall not exceed the low pre-sale estimate therefor and shall not include the buyer's premium or taxes. Unless the reserve is mutually agreed upon and confirmed by Consignor in writing before the sale, the reserve will be determined by Christie's in our sole discretion. Any reserve set in an amount other than a bidding increment will be rounded down to the next bidding increment.

(b) *Selling Below Reserve.* Christie's may sell any lot below the reserve if Consignor receives the amount, less Consignor's commission and any sale-related expenses, which Consignor would have received had such lot been sold at the reserve.

(c) *Christie's Acting to Protect Reserve.* As Consignor's agent, Christie's shall act to protect the reserve by bidding through the auctioneer.

6

(d) *No Bidding by Consignor.* Under no circumstances shall Consignor (as agent or principal), its representatives, employees or agents, if any (other than Christie's acting as Consignor's agent in accordance with paragraph 7 (c) above), enter or cause to be entered a bid on any lot of Property being offered for sale.

(e) *Limited Liability.* In no event shall Christie's be liable for the failure of any lot of Property to be sold at or within its estimate range or to reach the reserve.

8. AFTER THE SALE
(a) *Settlement of Account.* Provided Christie's has received payment in full from the buyer, and subject to the next sentence hereof, 35 calendar days after the sale (the "Settlement Date"), Christie's will pay Consignor the net proceeds (the final bid price less Consignor's commission payable to Christie's pursuant to paragraph 2 above, any reimbursable expenses and any other amounts due Christie's or any of our affiliates, whether arising out of the sale of the Property or otherwise) received and collected from the sale of the Property. Christie's will not make such payment if Christie's shall have received notice of the buyer's intention to rescind the sale or of any other bona fide claim relating to the Property or its sale prior to the Settlement Date. In the event that Consignor has agreed to arrangements for payment by the buyer which extend beyond the Settlement Date, such date and the amount payable to Consignor thereon shall be adjusted accordingly. Payment will be made in United States dollars unless Consignor instructs Christie's otherwise in writing. If Consignor requires payment other than in United States dollars, Christie's shall charge Consignor for any currency costs incurred, and shall retain such costs from the proceeds of the sale. Sale proceeds due will be calculated at the forward rate of exchange obtained by Christie's on the next working day after the date of the auction or, if applicable, the date of the post-auction sale, for value on the due date for payment.

(b) *Non-Payment by Buyer.* Christie's shall have no obligation to enforce payment by the buyer. However, in the event of non-payment by the buyer, Christie's in our sole discretion, as Consignor's agent or on our own behalf, may cancel the sale and return the Property to Consignor, enforce payment by the buyer or take any other actions permitted by law. Christie's shall not, under any circumstances, be liable for any consequential damages to Consignor as a result of non-payment by the buyer.

(c) *Rescission of Sale.* Christie's, as Consignor's agent, is authorized to accept the return and rescind the sale of any lot of Property at any time if Christie's in our sole judgment determines that the offering for sale of any Property has subjected or may subject Christie's and/or Consignor to any liability, including liability under warranty of authenticity or title. In such event, Christie's is further authorized to refund or credit to the buyer the purchase price of such returned Property. If Christie's has already remitted to Consignor any proceeds of the rescinded sale, Consignor forthwith shall pay Christie's upon request an amount equal to the remitted proceeds.

(d) *Post-Auction Sales.* If any lot is bought-in for failure to reach its reserve, Christie's as Consignor's exclusive agent is authorized for a period of 30 days following the auction to sell the lot privately for a price that will result in payment to Consignor of an amount at least equal to the amount, after deduction of Consignor's commission and Christie's reimbursable expenses, that Consignor would have received if the lot had been sold at the reserve, or for such lesser amount as Christie's and Consignor shall agree. In such event, all other provisions of this Agreement shall remain in full force and effect.

(e) *Unsold Property.* For each lot offered but not sold, Consignor shall pay Christie's a service charge of 5% of the reserve. Property remaining unsold following the auction or the expiration of the 30-day period

7

referred to in paragraph 8 (d) above and not reconsigned to Christie's for sale must be collected by Consignor at Consignor's expense within 35 days following the date on which Christie's offered such Property for sale. Thereafter, Consignor will incur a storage charge of $10 per day per lot. Consignor shall not be entitled to reclaim any unsold Property until all commission, expenses and other amounts owed to Christie's or any of our affiliates have been paid in full. In Christie's sole discretion, any Property not picked up or reconsigned for sale within 60 days following the date on which Christie's offered such Property for sale may be returned to Consignor at Consignor's expense, transferred to a third-party warehouse or sold at public auction by Christie's at Christie's standard commission rates and charges with a reserve, if any, set in Christie's sole discretion. The proceeds of such sale shall first be applied to the expenses of such sale, then to any indebtedness owing to Christie's or any of our affiliates and any excess shall be remitted to Consignor. In the event of transfer of any unsold Property to a third-party warehouse, Consignor shall bear all cost and risk thereof and shall be liable to such warehouse for the payment of storage and insurance charges of at least $10 per day per lot.

9.   ADDITIONAL CONSIGNMENTS

Christie's agrees that prior to December 31 of this calendar year, Christie's may, upon Consignor's request, offer for sale at appropriate auctions to be held during this calendar year any additional property of Consignor that Christie's considers suitable for sale at such auction. Such additional property will be offered for sale by Christie's upon the same terms and conditions as those which govern this Agreement. Christie's will mail to Consignor a property Schedule for such additional property. The return of such Schedule signed by Consignor shall be evidence of, and shall constitute Christie's and Consignor's agreement with respect to, the consignment to Christie's of the property listed on such property Schedule upon such terms and conditions. Such property shall thereupon constitute "Property" under the terms of this Agreement.

10.   OTHER MATTERS

(a)   This Agreement constitutes the entire agreement and understanding between the parties with respect to the transactions contemplated hereby and supersedes all prior agreements relating to the Property.

(b)   This Agreement shall be governed by and construed in accordance with the laws of the State of New York. In the event of any dispute hereunder, (i) the parties hereby consent to the exclusive jurisdiction of the courts of the State of New York and the Federal courts of the United States of America located in the Southern District of New York and (ii) neither party shall be liable to the other for any special, consequential or incidental damages.

(c)   This Agreement shall be binding upon Consignor's heirs, distributees, executors, legal representatives, successors and assigns.

(d)   Consignor may not assign its rights and/or obligations under this Agreement without the prior written consent of Christie's.

The parties agree to the foregoing by signing in the space provided below.

[Company]   CHRISTIE'S INC.

[By]_____   By_____
      [Signee]   Licensed by the New York City
                                                        Department of Consumer Affairs
                                                        Principal Auctioneer: Christopher J. Burge
                                                        License #761543

Appendix 4-3

Sotheby's Warranty and Disclosure in Its Auction Catalogs

CONDITIONS OF SALE

The following Conditions of Sale and Terms of Guarantee are Sotheby's, Inc. and the Consignor's entire agreement with the purchaser relative to the property listed in this catalogue.

The Conditions of Sale, Terms of Guarantee, the glossary, if any, and all other contents of this catalogue are subject to amendment by us by the posting of notices or by oral announcements made during the sale. The property will be offered by us as agent for the Consignor, unless the catalogue indicates otherwise.

By participating in any sale, you acknowledge that you are bound by these terms and conditions.

AS IS

1.   Goods auctioned are often of some age. The authenticity of the Authorship of property listed in the catalogue is guaranteed as stated in the Terms of Guarantee and except for the Limited Warranty contained therein, all property is sold "AS IS" without any representations or warranties by us or the Consignor as to merchantability, fitness for a particular purpose, the correctness of the catalogue or other description of the physical condition, size, quality, rarity, importance, medium, provenance, exhibitions, literature or historical relevance of any property and no statement anywhere, whether oral or written, whether made in the catalogue, an advertisement, a bill of sale, a salesroom posting or announcement, or elsewhere, shall be deemed such a warranty, representation or assumption of liability. We and the Consignor make no representations and

warranties, express or implied, as to whether the purchaser acquires any copyrights, including but not limited to, any reproduction rights in any property. We and the Consignor are not responsible for errors and omissions in the catalogue, glossary, or any supplemental material.

INSPECTION

2.   Prospective bidders should inspect the property before bidding to determine its condition, size, and whether or not it has been repaired or restored.

BUYER'S PREMIUM

3.   A buyer's premium will be added to the successful bid price and is payable by the purchaser as part of the total purchase price. The buyer's premium is 20% of the successful bid price up to and including $200,000; and 12% on any amount in excess of $200,000.

WITHDRAWAL

4.   We reserve the right to withdraw any property before the sale and shall have no liability whatsoever for such withdrawal.

PER LOT

5.   Unless otherwise announced by the auctioneer, all bids are per lot as numbered in the catalogue.

BIDDING

6.   We reserve the right to reject any bid. The highest bidder acknowledged by the auctioneer will be the purchaser. In the event of any dispute between bidders, or in the event of doubt on our part as to the validity of any bid, the auctioneer will have the final discretion to determine the successful bidder, cancel the sale, or to reoffer and resell the article in dispute. If any dispute arises after the sale, our sale record is conclusive. Although in our discretion we will execute order or absentee bids or accept telephone bids as a convenience to clients who are not present at auctions, we are not responsible for any errors or omissions in connection therewith.

BIDS BELOW RESERVE

7.   If the auctioneer decides that any opening bid is below the reserve of the article offered, he may reject the same and withdraw the article from sale, and if, having acknowledged an opening bid, he decides that any advance thereafter is insufficient, he may reject the advance.

PURCHASER'S RESPONSIBILITY

8.   Subject to fulfillment of all of the conditions set forth herein, on the fall of the auctioneer's hammer, title to the offered lot will pass to the highest bidder acknowledged by the auctioneer, and such bidder thereupon (a) assumes full risk and responsibility therefore (including, without limitation, liability for or damage to frames or glass covering prints, paintings or other works), and (b) will immediately pay the full purchase price or such part as we may require. In addition to other remedies available to us by law, we reserve the right to impose from the date of sale a late charge of 1½% per month of the total purchase price if payment is not made in accordance with the conditions set forth herein. All property must be removed from our premises by the purchaser at his expense not later than 10 business days following its sale and, if it is not so removed, (i) a handling charge of 1% of the total purchase price per month from the tenth day after the sale until its removal will be payable to us by the purchaser, with a minimum of 5% of the total purchase price for any property not so removed within 60 days after the sale, and (ii) we may send the purchased property to a public warehouse for the account, at the risk and expense of the purchaser.

If any applicable conditions herein are not complied with by the purchaser, the purchaser will be in default and in addition to any and all other remedies available to us and the Consignor by law, including, without limitation, the right to hold the purchaser liable for the total purchase price, including all fees, charges and expenses more fully set forth herein, we, at our option, may (x) cancel the sale of that, or any other lot or lots sold to the defaulting purchaser at the same or any other auction, retaining as liquidated damages all payments made by the purchaser, or (y) resell the purchased property, whether at public auction or by private sale, or (z) effect any combination thereof. In any case, the purchaser will be liable for any deficiency, any and all costs, handling charges, late charges, expenses of both sales, our commissions on both sales at our regular rates, legal fees and expenses, collection fees and incidental damages. We may, in our sole discretion, apply any proceeds of sale then due or thereafter becoming due to the purchaser from us or any affiliated company, or any payment made by the purchaser to us or any affiliated company, whether or not intended to reduce the purchaser's obligations with respect to the unpaid lot or lots, to the deficiency and any other amounts due to us or any affiliated companies. In addition, a defaulting purchaser will be deemed to have granted and assigned to us and our affiliated companies, a continuing security interest of first priority in any property or money of or owing to such purchaser in our possession or in the possession of any of our affiliated companies, and we may retain and apply such property or money as collateral security for the obligations due to us or to any affiliated company of ours. We shall have all of the rights accorded a secured party under the New York Uniform Commercial Code. Payment will not be deemed to have been made in full until we have collected good funds. In the event the purchaser fails to pay any or all of the total purchase price for any lot and Sotheby's nonetheless elects to pay the Consignor any portion of the sale proceeds, the purchaser acknowledges that Sotheby's shall have all of the rights of the Consignor to pursue the purchaser for any amounts paid to the Consignor, whether at law, in equity, or under these Conditions of Sale.

RESERVE

9.   All lots in this catalogue are offered subject to a reserve, which is the confidential minimum price acceptable to the Consignor. No reserve will exceed the low presale estimate stated in the catalogue, or as amended by oral or posted notices. We may implement such reserve by opening the bidding on behalf of the Consignor and may bid up to the amount of the reserve, by placing successive or consecutive bids for a lot, or bids in response to other bidders. In instances where we have an interest in the lot other than our commission, we may bid up to the reserve to protect such interest. In certain instances, the Consignor may pay us less than the standard commission rate where a lot is "bought-in" to protect its reserve.

TAX

10.   Unless exempted by law, the purchaser will be required to pay the combined New York State and local sales tax, any applicable compensating use tax of another state, and if applicable, any federal luxury or other tax, on the total purchase price. The rate of such combined tax is 8.625% in New York City and ranges from 4.25% to 8.75% elsewhere in New York.

GOVERNING LAW AND JURISDICTION

11.   These Conditions of Sale and Terms of Guarantee, as well as the purchaser's and our respective rights and obligations hereunder, shall be governed by and construed and enforced in accordance with the laws of the State of New York. By bidding at an auction, whether present in person or by agent, order bid, telephone or other means, the purchaser shall be deemed to have consent-

ed to the jurisdiction of the state courts of, and the federal courts sitting in, the State of New York.

PACKING AND SHIPPING

12. We are not responsible for the acts or omissions in our packing or shipping of purchased lots or of other carriers or packers of purchased lots, whether or not recommended by us. Packing and handling of purchased lots is at the entire risk of the purchaser. If we obtain on behalf of the purchaser an export license for an item containing an endangered species, there will be a charge of $150 for each license obtained.

LIMITATION OF LIABILITY

13. In no event will our liability to a purchaser exceed the purchase price actually paid.

DATA PROTECTION

14. Sotheby's will use information provided by its clients or which Sotheby's otherwise obtains relating to its clients for the provision of auction and other art-related services, real estate and insurance services, client administration, marketing and otherwise to manage and operate its business, or as required by law.

Some gathering of information about Sotheby's clients will take place using technical means to identify their preferences and provide a higher quality of service to them, and Sotheby's may gather information about its clients through video images or through the use of monitoring devices used to record telephone conversations.

Sotheby's will generally seek clients' express consent before gathering any sensitive data, unless otherwise permitted by law. Clients agree that Sotheby's may use any sensitive information that they supply to Sotheby's.

By agreeing to these Conditions of Sale, clients agree to the processing of their personal information and also to the disclosure and transfer of such information to any Sotheby's Company and to third parties anywhere in the world for the above purposes, including to countries which may not offer equivalent protection of personal information to that offered in the US. Clients can prevent the use of their personal information for marketing purposes at any time by notifying Sotheby's.

TERMS OF GUARANTEE

Sotheby's warrants the authenticity of Authorship of each lot contained in this catalogue on the terms and conditions set forth below.

DEFINITION OF AUTHORSHIP

1.   "Authorship" is defined as the creator, period, culture, source of origin, as the case may be, as set forth in the CAPITALIZED HEADING (*e.g.*, A PIERRE CHAREAU EBONIZED FRUITWOOD TABLE, CIRCA 1925) of a lot in this catalogue, as amended by any oral or written salesroom notices or announcements. If there is a "Glossary" of terms in this catalogue, please note that any such heading represents a qualified statement or opinion and is not subject to these Terms of Guarantee.

Sotheby's makes no warranties whatsoever, whether express or implied, with respect to any material in the catalogue, other than that appearing in CAPITALIZED HEADING and subject to the exclusions in 5 and 6 below.

GUARANTEE COVERAGE

2.   Subject to the exclusions in 5 and 6 below, Sotheby's warrants the Authorship (as defined above) of a lot for a period of five years from the date of sale of such lot and only to the original purchaser of record at the auction. If it is determined to Sotheby's satisfaction that the CAPITALIZED HEADING is incorrect, the sale will be rescinded as set forth in 3 and 4 below, provided the lot is returned to Sotheby's at the original selling location in the same condition in which it was at the time of sale. It is Sotheby's general policy, and Sotheby's shall have the right to have the purchaser obtain, at the purchaser's expense, the opinion of two recognized experts in the field, mutually acceptable to Sotheby's and the purchaser, before Sotheby's determines whether to rescind a sale under the above warranty. If the purchaser requests, Sotheby's will provide the purchaser with the names of experts acceptable to it.

NON-ASSIGNABILITY

3.   The benefits of this warranty are not assignable and shall be applicable only to the original purchaser of record and not to any subsequent owners (including, without limitation, heirs, successors, beneficiaries or assigns) who have, or may acquire, an interest in any purchased property.

SOLE REMEDY

4.   It is specifically understood and agreed that the rescission of a sale and the refund of the original purchase price paid (the successful bid price, plus the buyer's premium) is exclusive and in lieu of any other remedy which might otherwise be available as a matter of law, or in equity. Sotheby's and the Consignor shall not be liable for any incidental or consequential damages incurred or claimed.

EXCLUSIONS

5.   This warranty does not apply to: (i) Authorship of any paintings, drawings or sculpture created prior to 1870, unless the lot is determined to be a counterfeit (a modern forgery intended to deceive) which has a value at the date of the claim for rescission which is materially less than the purchase price paid for the lot; or (ii) any catalogue description where it was specifically mentioned that there is a conflict of specialist opinion on the Authorship of a lot; or (iii) Authorship which on the date of sale was in accordance with the then generally accepted opinion of scholars and specialists; or (iv) the identification of periods or dates of execution which may be proven inaccurate by means of scientific processes not generally accepted for use until after publication of the catalogue, or which were unreasonably expensive or impractical to use.

LIMITED WARRANTY

As stated in paragraph 1 of the Conditions of Sale, neither Sotheby's nor the Consignor makes any express or implied representations or warranties whatsoever concerning any property in the catalogue, including without limitation, any warranty of merchantability or fitness for a particular purpose, except as specifically provided herein.

Appendix 4-4

Christie's Warranty and Disclosure in Its Auction Catalogs

CONDITIONS OF SALE

These Conditions of Sale and the Important Notices and Explanation of Cataloguing Practice contain all the terms on which Christie's and the seller contract with the buyer. They may be amended by posted notices or oral announcements made during the sale. By bidding at auction you agree to be bound by these terms.

1. CHRISTIE'S AS AGENT

Except as otherwise stated Christie's acts as agent for the seller. The contract for the sale of the property is therefore made between the seller and the buyer.

2. BEFORE THE SALE

(a) Examination of property

Prospective buyers are strongly advised to examine personally any property in which they are interested, before the auction takes place. Condition reports are usually available on request. Neither Christie's nor the seller provides any guarantee in relation to the nature of the property apart from the Limited Warranty in paragraph 6 below. The property is otherwise sold "as is."

Our cataloguing practice is explained in the Important Notices and Explanations of Cataloguing Practice after the catalogue entries. All statements by us in the catalogue entry for the property or in the condition report, or made orally in writing elsewhere, are statements of opinion and are not to be relied on as statements of fact. Such statements do not constitute a representation, warranty or assumption of liability by us of any kind. References in the catalogue entry or the condition report to damage or restoration are for guidance only and should be evaluated by personal inspection by the bidder or a knowledgeable representative. The absence of such a reference does not imply that an item is free from defects or restoration, nor does a reference to particular defects imply the absence of any others. Estimates of the selling price should not be relied on as a statement that this is the price at which the item will sell or its value for any other purpose. Except as set forth in paragraph 6 below, neither Christie's nor the seller is responsible in any way for errors and omission in the catalogue or any supplemental material.

(b) Buyer's responsibility

Except as stated in the Limited Warranty in paragraph 6 below, all property is sold "as is" without any representation or warranty of any kind by Christie's or the seller. Buyers are responsible for satisfying themselves concerning the condition of the property and the matters referred to in the catalogue entry.

3. AT THE SALE

(a) Refusal of admission

Christie's has the right, at our complete discretion, to refuse admission to the premises or participation in any action and to reject any bid.

(b) Registration before bidding

A prospective buyer must complete and sign a registration from and provide identification before bidding. We may require the production of bank or other financial references.

(c) Bidding as principal

When making a bid, a bidder is accepting personal liability to pay the purchase price, including the buyer's premium and all applicable taxes, plus all other applicable charges, unless it has been explicitly agreed in writing with Christie's before the commencement of the sale that the bidder is acting as agent on behalf of an identified third party acceptable to Christie's, and that Christie's will only look to the principal for payment.

(d)   Absentee bids

We will use reasonable efforts to carry out written bids delivered to us prior to the sale for the convenience of clients who are not present at the auction in person, by an agent or by telephone. Bids must be placed in the currency of the place of the sale. Please refer to the catalogue for the Absentee Bids Form. If we receive written bids on a particular lot for identical amounts, and at the auction these are the highest bids on the lot, it will be sold to the person whose written bid was received and accepted first. Execution of written bids is a free service undertaken subject to other commitments at the time of the sale and we do not accept liability for failing to execute a written bid for errors and omissions in connection with it.

(e)   Telephone bids

If a prospective buyer makes arrangements with us prior to the commencement of the sale we will use reasonable efforts to contact them to enable them to participate in the bidding by telephone but we do not accept liability for failure to do so or for errors and omissions in connection with telephone bidding.

(f)   Currency converter

At some auctions a currency converter may be operated. Errors may occur in the operation of the currency converter and we do not accept liability to bidders who follow the currency converter rather than the actual bidding in the saleroom.

(g)   Video or digital images

At some auctions there may be a video or digital screen. Errors may occur in its operation and in the quality of the image and we do not accept liability for such errors.

(h)   Reserves

Unless otherwise indicated, all lots are offered subject to a reserve, which is the confidential minimum price below which the lot will not be sold. The reserve will not exceed the low estimate printed in the catalogue. If any lots are not subject to a reserve, they will be identified with the symbol • next to the lot number. The auctioneer may open the bidding on any lot below the reserve by placing a bid on behalf of the seller. The auctioneer may continue to bid on behalf of the seller up to the amount of the reserve, either by placing consecutive bids or by placing bids in response to other bidders. With respect to lots that are offered without reserve, unless there are already competing bids, the auction-eer, in his or her discretion will generally open the bidding at 50% of the low pre-sale estimate for the lot. In the absence of a bid at that level, the auctioneer will proceed backwards in his or her discretion until a bid is recognized, and then continue up from that amount. Absentee bids will, in the absence of a higher bid, be executed at approximately 50% of the low pre-sale estimate or at the amount of the bid if it is less than 50% of the low pre-sale estimate. In the event that there is no bid on a lot, the auctioneer may deem such lot unsold.

(i)   Auctioneer's discretion

The auctioneer has the right at his absolute and sole discretion to refuse any bid, to advance the bidding in such a manner as he may decide, to withdraw or divide any lot, to combine any two or more lots and, in the case of error or dis-pute, and whether during or after the sale, to determine the successful bidder, to continue the bidding, to cancel the sale or to reoffer and resell the item in dispute. If any dispute arises after the sale, our sale record is conclusive.

(j)   Successful bid and passing of risk

Subject to the auctioneer's discretion, the highest bidder accepted by the auc-tioneer will be the buyer and the striking of his hammer marks the acceptance of the highest bid and the conclusion of a contract for sale between the seller and the buyer. Risk and responsibility for the lot (including frames or glass where relevant) passes to the buyer at the expiration of seven calendar days from the date of the sale or on collection by the buyer if earlier.

4.   AFTER THE SALE

(a)   Buyer's premium

In addition to the hammer price, the buyer agrees to pay to us the buyer's pre-mium together with any applicable value added tax, sales or compensating use tax or equivalent tax in the place of sale. The buyer's premium is 20% of the hammer price on each lot up to and including $200,000 plus 12% of any amount in excess of $200,000.

(b)   Payment and passing of title

Immediately following the sale, the buyer must provide us with his or her name and permanent address and, if so requested, details of the bank from which pay-ment will be made. The buyer must pay the full amount due (comprising the hammer price, buyer's premium and any applicable taxes) not later than 4.30 pm on the seventh calendar day following the sale. This applies even if the buyer wishes to export the lot and an export license is, or may be, required. The buyer will not acquire title to the lot until all amounts due to us from the buyer have been received by us in good cleared funds even in circumstances where we have released the lot to the buyer.

(c)   Collection of purchases

We shall be entitled to retain items sold until all amounts due to us, or to Christie's International plc, or to any of its affiliates, subsidiaries or parent companies worldwide, have been received in full in good cleared funds or until the buyer has satisfied such other terms as we, in our sole discretion, shall require. Subject to this, the buyer shall collect purchased lots within seven calendar days from the date of the sale unless otherwise agreed between us and the buyer.

(d)   Packing, handling and shipping

Although we shall use reasonable efforts to take care when handling, packing and shipping a purchased lot, we are not responsible for the acts or omissions of third parties whom we might retain for these purposes. Similarly, where we may suggest other handlers, packers or carriers if so requested, we do not accept responsibility or liability for their acts or omissions.

(e)   Export license

Unless otherwise agreed by us in writing, the fact that the buyer wishes to apply for an export license does not affect is or her obligation to make payment within seven days nor our right to charge interest or storage charges on late payment. If the buyer requests us to apply for an export license on his or her behalf, we shall be entitled to make a charge for this service. We shall not be obliged to rescind a sale nor to refund any interest or other expenses incurred by the buyer where payment is made by the buyer in circumstances where an export license is required.

(f)   Remedies for non payment

If the buyer fails to make payment in full in good cleared funds within the time required by paragraph 4(b) above, we shall be entitled in our absolute discretion to exercise one or more of the following rights or remedies (in addition to asserting any other rights or remedies available to us by law):

(i)   to charge interest at such rate as we shall reasonably decide;

(ii)   to hold the defaulting buyer liable for the total amount due and to commence legal proceedings for its recovery together with interest, legal fees and costs to the fullest extent permitted under applicable law;

(iii) to cancel the sale;

(iv)   to resell the property publicly or privately on such terms as we shall think fit;

(v)   to pay the seller an amount up to the net proceeds payable in respect of the amount bid by the defaulting buyer;

(vi)   to set off against any amounts which we, or Christie's International plc, or any of its affiliates, subsidiaries or parent companies worldwide, may owe the buyer in any other transactions, the outstanding amount remaining unpaid by the buyer;

(vii) where several amounts are owed by the buyer to us, or to Christie's International plc, or to any of its affiliates, subsidiaries or parent companies worldwide, in respect of different transactions, to apply any amount paid to discharge any amount owed in respect of any particular transaction, whether or not the buyer so directs;

(viii) to reject at any future auction any bids made by or on behalf of the buyer or to obtain a deposit from the buyer before accepting any bids;

(ix)   to exercise all the rights and remedies of a person holding security over any property in our possession owned by the buyer, whether by way of pledge, security interest or in any other way, to the fullest extent permitted by the law of the place where such property is located. The buyer will be deemed to have granted such security to us and we may retain such property as collateral security for such buyer's obligations to us;

(x)   to take such other action as we deem necessary or appropriate.

If we resell the property under paragraph (iv) above, the defaulting buyer shall be liable for payment of any deficiency between the total amount originally due to us and the price obtained upon resale as well as for all costs, expenses, damages, legal fees and commissions and premiums of whatever kind associated with both sales or otherwise arising from the default. If we pay any amount to the seller under paragraph (v) above, the buyer acknowledges that Christie's shall have all of the rights of the seller, however arising, to pursue the buyer for such amount.

(g) Failure to collect purchases

Where purchases are not collected within seven calendar days from the date of the sale, whether or not payment has been made, we shall be permitted to remove the property to a third party warehouse at the buyer's expense, and only release the items after payment in full has been made of removal, storage, handling, insurance and any other costs incurred, together with payment of all other amounts due to us.

(h) Selling Property at Christie's

In addition to expenses such as transport and insurance, all consignors pay a commission according to a fixed scale of charges based upon the value of the property sold by the consignor at Christie's in a calendar year. Commissions are charged on a sale by sale basis.

5. EXTENT OF CHRISTIE'S LIABILITY

We agree to refund the purchase price in the circumstances of the Limited Warranty set out in paragraph 6 below. Apart from that, neither the seller nor we, nor any of our officers, employees or agents, are responsible for the correctness of any statement of whatever kind concerning any lot, whether written or oral, nor for any other errors or omissions in description or for any faults or defects in any lot. Except as stated in paragraph 6 below, neither the seller, ourselves, our officers, employees or agents, give any representation, warranty or guarantee or assume any liability of any kind in respect of any lot with regard to merchantability, fitness for a particular purpose, description, size, quality, condition, attribution, authenticity, rarity, importance, medium, provenance, exhibition history, literature or historical relevance. Except as required by local law any warranty of any kind whatsoever is excluded by this paragraph.

6. LIMITED WARRANTY

Subject to the terms and conditions of this paragraph, Christie's warrants for a period of five years from the date of the sale that any property described in headings printed in UPPER CASE TYPE (*i.e.*, headings having all capital-letter type) in this catalogue (as such description may be amended by any saleroom notice or announcement) which is stated without qualification to be the work of a named author or authorship, is authentic and not a forgery. The term "author" or "authorship" refers to the creator of the property or to the period, culture, source or origin, as the case may be, with which the creation of such property is identified in the UPPER CASE description of the property in this catalogue. Only UPPER CASE TYPE headings of lots in this catalogue indicate what is being warranted by Christie's. Christie's warranty does not apply to supplemental material which appears below the UPPER CASE TYPE headings of each lot and Christie's is not responsible for any errors or omissions in such material. The terms used in the headings are further explained in Important Notices and Explanation of Cataloguing Practice. The warranty does not apply to any heading which is stated to represent a qualified opinion. The warranty is subject to the following:

(i)   It does not apply where (a) the catalogue description or saleroom notice corresponded to the generally accepted opinion of scholars or experts at the date of the sale or fairly indicated that there was a conflict of opinions; or (b) correct identification of a lot can be demonstrated only by means of either a scientific process not generally accepted for use until after publication of the catalogue or a process which at the date of publication of the catalogue was unreasonably expensive or impractical or likely to have caused damage to the property.

(ii) The benefits of the warranty are not assignable and shall apply only to the original buyer of the lot as shown on the invoice originally issued by Christie's when the lot was sold at auction.

(iii) The original buyer must have remained the owner of the lot without disposing of any interest in it to any third party.

(iv) The buyer's sole and exclusive remedy against Christie's and the seller, in place of any other remedy which might be available, is the cancellation of the sale and the refund of the original purchase price paid for the lot. Neither Christie's nor the seller will be liable for any special, incidental or consequential damages including, without limitation, loss of profits nor for interest.

(v)   The buyer must give written notice of claim to us within five years from the date of the auction. It is Christie's general policy, and Christie's shall have the right, to require the buyer to obtain the written opinions of two recognized experts in the field, mutually acceptable to Christie's and the buyer, before Christie's decides whether or not to cancel the sale under the warranty.

(vi) The buyer must return the lot to the Christie's saleroom at which it was purchased in the same condition as at the time of the sale.

7. COPYRIGHT

The copyright in all images, illustrations and written material produced by or for Christie's relating to a lot including the contents of this catalogue, is and shall remain at all times the property of Christie's and shall not be used by the buyer, nor by anyone else, without our prior written consent. Christie's and the seller make no representation or warranty that the buyer of a property will acquire any copyright or other reproduction rights in it.

8. SEVERABILITY

If any part of these Conditions of Sale is found by any court to be invalid, illegal or unenforceable, that part shall be discounted and the rest of the conditions shall continue to be valid to the fullest extent permitted by law.

9. LAW AND JURISDICTION

The rights and obligations of the parties with respect to these Conditions of Sale, the conduct of the auction and any matters connected with any of the foregoing shall be governed and interpreted by the laws of the jurisdiction in which the auction is held. By bidding at auction, whether present in person or by agent, by written bid, telephone or other means, the buyer shall be deemed to have submitted, for the benefit of Christie's, to the exclusive jurisdiction of the courts of that country, state, county or province, and (if applicable) of the federal courts sitting in such state.

Appendix 4-5

Christie's Explanation of Cataloguing Practice for Pictures, Drawings, Prints and Miniatures

1. PABLO PICASSO
In Christie's opinion a work by the artist.

2. Attributed to PABLO PICASSO★
In Christie's qualified opinion a work of the period of the artist which may be in whole or part the work of the artist.

3. After PABLO PICASSO★
In Christie's qualified opinion a copy of the work of the artist.

4. 'signed'
Has a signature which in Christie's qualified opinion is the signature of the artist.

5. 'bears signature'
Has a signature which in Christie's qualified opinion might be the signature of the artist.

6. 'dated'
Is so dated and in Christie's qualified opinion was executed at about that date.

7. 'bears date'
Is so dated and in Christie's qualified opinion may have been executed at about that date.

★ This term and its definition in this Explanation of Cataloguing Practice are a qualified statement as to Authorship. While the use of this term is based upon careful study and represents the opinion of experts, Christie's and the consignor assume no risk, liability and responsibility for the authenticity of authorship of any lot in this catalogue described by this term.

Appendix 4-6

City of New York Auctioneer Rules

ADMINISTRATIVE CODE OF THE CITY OF NEW YORK

TITLE 20: CONSUMER AFFAIRS

CHAPTER 2: LICENSES

SUBCHAPTER 13: AUCTIONEERS

§ 20-278   **License required.** It shall be unlawful for any person to engage in the business of auctioneer without a license therefor.

§ 20-279   **Fee; bond; fingerprinting.**

a.   The annual fee for such license shall be two hundred dollars.

b.   Each applicant for such license shall file with the commissioner, a bond with two good sureties, in the penal sum of two thousand dollars, which bond shall meet with the approval of the commissioner.

c.   The commissioner shall require that applicants for licenses issued pursuant to this subchapter be fingerprinted for the purpose of securing criminal history records from the state division of criminal justice services. The applicant shall pay a processing fee as required by the state division of criminal justice services. Fingerprints shall be taken of the individual owner if the applicant is a sole proprietorship; the general partners if the applicant is a partnership; and the officers, principals, directors, and stockholders owning more than ten percent of the outstanding stock of the corporation if the applicant is a corporation. Any person required to be fingerprinted hereunder shall furnish to the department three current passport-size photographs of such person. Notwithstanding the foregoing, the commissioner need not require applicants for licenses required under this subchapter to be fingerprinted if criminal history records concerning such applicants are not available from the state division of criminal justice services.

§ 20-279.1 Refusal to issue or renew, or suspension or revocation based on criminal conviction.

In addition to any of the powers that may be exercised by the commissioner pursuant to this subchapter or chapter one of this title, the commissioner, after notice and an opportunity to be heard, may refuse to issue or renew, or may suspend or revoke, a license required under this subchapter if the applicant or licensee, or any of its principals, officers or directors, or any of its stockholders owning more than ten percent of the outstanding stock of the corporation has been convicted of a crime which, in the judgment of the commissioner, has a direct relationship to such person's fitness or ability to perform any of the activities for which a license is required under this subchapter or has been convicted of any other crime which, in accordance with article twenty-three-a of the correction law, would provide a justification for the commissioner to refuse to issue or renew, or to suspend or revoke, such license.

§ 20-280 Requirements for auctioneers. Each auctioneer shall cause his or her name and license number to be conspicuously displayed at any place where he or she shall conduct an auction sale during such sale.

§ 20-281 Persons acting as auctioneers. It shall be unlawful for any person not licensed as an auctioneer to represent or circulate or place before the public any announcement, or to insert or cause to be inserted in any city, business or telephone directory, any notice that he or she is conducting the business of auctioneering.

§ 20-282 Advertising. Every auctioneer in his or her own name, shall give notice in one or more of the public newspapers printed in the city, of every auction sale to be conducted by him or her. In the event that such auctioneer shall be connected with any firm or other person his or her name shall in all cases precede the name of such firm or other person.

§ 20-283 Night auctions.

a. The sale by public auction of all goods except as set forth in subdivision b hereof shall be made in the daytime, between eight o'clock in the morning and eight o'clock in the evening.

b. Any sale by auction of the following goods after eight o'clock in the evening shall be conducted pursuant to a special permit issued by the commissioner, in his or her discretion and upon such reasonable conditions as he or she shall prescribe:

1. Books and prints;

2. Goods sold in the original package, as imported, according to a printed catalogue, of which samples shall have been opened and exposed to public inspection at least one day previous to the sale;

3. Horses and live stock;

4. Fruit and other farm products;

5. Paintings, statuary, bronzes and other works of art and specimens of natural history, which shall have been on public exhibition in the city for at least one day immediately preceding the time of sale, provided that public notice of the time and place of such exhibition shall have been given by advertisement for at least one day immediately preceding the day of such exhibition, in one or more of the designated daily newspapers printed in the city.

c. The commissioner from time to time, by a notice to be filed in his or her office and printed for five consecutive days in the City Record, shall designate the newspapers in which such advertisements may be printed, and the commissioner, at any time, by a like notice may revoke the designation of any such newspaper.

§ 20-284 Sale of jewelry.

a. Each auctioneer shall cause to be delivered to the purchaser of diamonds, precious stones or other jewelry, a signed document containing a description of the article sold and the representations made in regard thereto at the time of the sale.

b. Each article of jewelry sold at public auction shall have affixed thereto a tag, on which shall be printed or written a correct description of such article.

§ 20-285 Restrictions.

a. It shall be unlawful for any auctioneer, his or her agent, employee or servant to sell at public auction or expose for such sale:

1. Any dry-goods, clothing, hardware, household furniture, woodenware or tinware by retail or in small parcels or pieces, in any street or public place;

2. Any goods, wares, merchandise or other things to any person who, at the time of bidding for or while examining such articles, shall be on any street;

3. Any goods, wares, merchandise or other things in any street or public place, or place them thereon, unless he or she first shall obtain the consent or permission, in writing, of the occupant of the lot or building before which such articles or any part thereof shall be placed or exposed for sale.

b. It shall be unlawful to employ any means of attracting the attention of purchasers, other than a sign or flag, at or near any place of sale, auction room, residence of any auctioneer, or at or near any auction whatsoever.

c. Every article sold or exposed for sale at public auction, in any street or public place, shall be removed therefrom by sunset on the day of such sale or display.

§ 20-286 Sale of real property; fees.

a. It shall be unlawful for any auctioneer to demand or receive for his or her services, in selling, at public auction, any real estate directed to be sold by any judgment or decree of any court of this state, a greater fee than fifty dollars for each parcel separately sold, except that in all sales of real estate conducted by any auctioneer pursuant to a judgment or decree of any court of this state in any action brought to foreclose a mortgage or other lien on real estate, the fees of such auctioneers shall be as follows:

1. in all cases where the judgment of foreclosure is for an amount not exceeding five thousand dollars, the fee shall be fifteen dollars;

2. in all cases where the judgment of foreclosure is for an amount in excess of five thousand dollars, but not exceeding twenty-five thousand dollars, the fee shall be twenty-five dollars;

3. in all cases where the judgment of foreclosure is for an amount in excess of twenty-five thousand dollars, the fee shall be fifty dollars.

b. Where such sale is made at any public salesroom, such auctioneer may demand and receive such further amount not exceeding ten dollars for each parcel separately sold as he or she may have actually paid for the privilege or right of making the sale in such salesroom.

c. Where one or more lots are so sold at public auction with the option to the purchaser of taking one or more additional lots at the same rates or price, nothing herein contained shall be construed to prevent the auctioneer making such sale from demanding and receiving for his or her services the compensation or fee above allowed, for each additional lot taken by such purchaser under such option.

§ 20-287 **Split fees.** It shall be unlawful for any auctioneer, either directly or indirectly, to allow or pay to the receiver, referee, sheriff, or other officer under whose direction a sale is made, pursuant to section 20-286 of this subchapter or to any of the attorneys in the action or proceeding from which such sale arises, any portion of his or her fee or compensation.

§ 20-288 **False or fraudulent representations.** Any auctioneer who shall have knowledge of any false or fraudulent representations or statements or who makes or causes any such statements to be made in respect to the character of any sale, or the party authorizing the same, or the quality, condition, ownership, situation, or value of any property, real or personal, exposed, put up, or offered by him or her for sale at public auction, shall be deemed guilty of a misdemeanor, and, upon conviction thereof, shall be punished by imprisonment not exceeding one year or by a fine not exceeding one thousand dollars.

§ 20-289 **Complaints.**

a. The commissioner may take testimony, under oath, relating to and upon the complaint of any person who claims he or she has been defrauded by any auctioneer, his or her clerk, agent or assignee, or relating to and upon the complaint of any person who has consigned real or personal property for sale and to whom such auctioneer shall not have accounted fully. The license of each such auctioneer may be revoked and his or her bond declared forfeited if, in the opinion of the commissioner, such charge is sustained. Any such person whose license has been revoked for cause shall not be granted another such license.

b.   The commissioner may take testimony, under oath, relating to and upon the complaint of any person who claims that any auctioneer, his or her clerk, agent or assignee, has been guilty of misconduct relating to the business transacted under such auctioneer's license, and if such charge, in his or her opinion, shall be sustained, the commissioner may suspend such license for a period not to exceed six months.

§ 20-290   **Marshals exempt.** Nothing in this subchapter shall apply to a duly appointed marshal, who, by virtue of his or her office sells real or personal property, levied upon by him or her under legal process.

RULES OF THE CITY OF NEW YORK

TITLE 6: DEPARTMENT OF CONSUMER AFFAIRS

CHAPTER 2: LICENSES

SUBCHAPTER M: AUCTIONEERS

§ 2-121   **Standards, Licenses and Application of Regulations.**

(a)   The auctioneer will be held responsible for the truth of any statement contained in any catalogue, advertisement, announcement, press release or other public statement made by the auctioneer relating to any auction.

(b)   The auctioneer shall be held responsible for full compliance by his employer or principal with all rules and regulations of the Department and pertinent provisions of law.

(c)   Each application for a license shall be accompanied by the affidavits of three citizens who are residents of New York City and who have known the applicant not less than two years.

(d)   The fee for a permit to auction publicly after 8 p.m. the goods or any of them specified in § 20-283 of the Administrative Code shall be ten dollars for the first permit in any license year. Subsequent permits issued during the same license year may be issued without fee.

(e)   Each applicant for a permit to auction publicly after 8 p.m. shall furnish with the application for the permit a catalogue of the articles to be auctioned, and a copy of the advertisement to be published in connection with said auction. In the case of an auction of fruit, vegetables or other farm products, the catalogue shall be filed as soon as it has been printed.

(f)   All licensed auctioneers and auction houses must include their Department of Consumer Affairs license number, or the license number assigned to their auction house or principal auctioneer and identify it as such in all advertisements in any medium, and on all written contracts, catalogues and announcements, relating to auction activity in New York City.

(g)   These rules and regulations do not apply to auction sales of real property.

§ 2-122   **Requirements and Obligations of Licensees.**

(a)   Contracts required. No personal property may be auctioned except pursuant to a written contract between the consignor or his or her agent or authorized representative and the auctioneer, unless auctioned pursuant to an order of a court of competent jurisdiction.

(b)   Every contract required pursuant to § 2-122(a) must contain the following provisions:

   (1)   All fees, commissions and charges to be paid by the consignor to the auctioneer or his or her agents, principals, employees, employers or assigns shall:

      (i)   to the extent practicable, be itemized and specified as to amount (which may be stated as a percentage of the reserve price or any final bid), and

      (ii)   if such itemization and specification as to amount is not practicable, be described with sufficient particularity to inform the consignor of the nature of the services for which such fees, commissions and charges will be imposed.

   (2)   That as of the date of the auction the consignor warrants that he or she has complete and lawful right, title and interest in the property auctioned, and that the consignor shall identify the auctioneer, his or her agents, principals, employees, employers or assigns in the event of any defect in title, and that an intended beneficiary of this warranty is the ultimate purchaser at auction.

(c)   Where articles are referred to by catalogue or advertisement as having been obtained from any specific person, place or source, such articles must be separately enumerated and identified.

(d)   If an auctioneer or public salesroom has any interest, direct or indirect, in an article, including a guaranteed minimum, other than the selling commission, the fact such interest exists must be disclosed in connection with any description of the article or articles in the catalogue or any other printed material published or distributed in relation to the sale. Such notice may be denoted by a symbol or letter which will refer the reader to an explanation of the nature of the interest the symbol or letter denotes. For the purpose of this subdivision (d), advertisements in newspapers or other periodicals shall not constitute printed material. Where no printed material is provided in connection with an auction, the auctioneer shall have available during any advertised inspection period, information as to whether such an interest exists with relation to a particular item and shall announce before he or she commences the auction that such information is available upon request.

(e) Where a consignor is to receive a rebate commission in whole or in part, or where he or she will be permitted to bid upon and to buy back his or her own article at the sale, disclosure of such a condition must be made in connection with any description of the item or items so affected in the catalogue or any other printed material published or distributed in relation to the sale. The existence of such a condition may be denoted by a symbol or letter which will refer the reader to an explanation of the nature of the interest the symbol or letter denotes. For the purpose of this subdivision (e), advertisements in newspapers or other periodicals shall not constitute printed material. Where no printed material is provided in connection with the auction, the auctioneer shall have available during any advertised inspection period information of whether such a condition exists with relation to a particular item and shall announce before he or she commences the auction that such information is available upon request.

(f) (1) If the consignor has fixed a price below which an article will not be sold, the "reserve price," the fact that the lot is being sold subject to reserve must be disclosed in connection with the description of any lot so affected in the catalogue or any other printed material published or distributed in relation to the sale. The existence of a reserve price may be denoted by a symbol or letter which will refer the reader to an explanation of reserve price. For the purpose of this subdivision (f), advertisements in newspapers or other periodicals shall not constitute printed material. Where no printed material is provided in connection with the auction an auctioneer shall have available during any advertised inspection period information as to whether a particular lot is to be sold subject to reserve and shall announce before he or she commences the auction that such information is available upon request.

(2) When a lot is not subject to a reserve price, the auctioneer shall not indicate in any manner that the lot is subject to a reserve price.

(g) The auctioneer shall:

(1) Provide information as to the number of jewels, approximate number of carats, number of points (diamond), principal metal content, and manufacturer's name, if known, for all articles of jewelry, including watches. The information required by this subdivision (g) shall be provided either in the catalogue de-

scriptions of such items or by attaching to each such item a tag or marking containing the information.

(2) Issue or cause to be issued to each purchaser an invoice which shall contain all the following information:

(i) The auctioneer's name, business address and license number;

(ii) The name and address of the auctioneer's employer or principal;

(iii) The date of sale;

(iv) The lot number, description, quantity and selling price of each lot;

(v) The total amount of purchase with a separate statement of sales tax;

(vi) All deposits made against the purchase price.

This does not apply to the auction sale of fruit, vegetables or other farm products.

(3) Notify the department ten days in advance regarding the name and address of a new employer or the new location of activity.

(4) [Reserved]

(5) Advertise each auction sale at least once in the seven day period immediately preceding the auction.

(6) Notify the person whose property is being auctioned (and any other person entitled to be notified according to law) as to the date, place and time of sale.

(7) Permit (prior to the start of the auction) prospective purchasers to inspect each and every article to be offered for sale.

(8) Furnish to any buyer, consignor or owner of an article, upon request, information as to the whereabouts of that article that comes into his or her possession or that is sold or offered for sale by him or her.

(9) Send check for net amount received on all sales to persons entitled to the proceeds thereof within fourteen days of date of sale (except as otherwise agreed in writing or otherwise provided by law) together with a complete detailed statement including lot number, quantity, description and selling price of each lot; total amount received on sale; and disbursements listing commission, cost of advertisement, labor, charges and allowances, and sundry expenses.

(10) Report to the Department of Consumer Affairs the date and place of any sale of merchandise which includes a scale, in time to permit the Department to have an inspector present at the sale.

(11) Notify the department in advance if he or she is unable because of sickness or other valid reason to conduct a duly advertised auction; and then a licensed auctioneer may act as his or her substitute.

(12) When an auctioneer has a number of the same kind of articles to be sold and intends to dispose of each of them at the amount at which the first is sold, he or she shall make an announcement to that effect prior to opening the sale of the first article.

(h) If an auctioneer makes loans or advances money to consignors or prospective purchasers, this fact must be conspicuously disclosed in the auctioneer's catalogue or printed material. If the auctioneer does not provide any such printed material, he or she shall make the disclosure, either by conspicuously posting a sign, or in another similarly conspicuous manner, at the time of any advertised inspection periods prior to the auctions. For the purpose of this subdivision (h) advertisements in newspapers or other periodicals shall not constitute printed material.

(i) Except to implement a reserve price, and subject to § 2-123(b), no auctioneer, his or her consignor, employee, employer, assignee or agent for any of them may bid for his or her own account at any auction if any of them shall have access to information not otherwise available to the public regarding reserves, value or other material facts relating to the articles which are the subject of the auction, unless their "insider" status and intended participation is disclosed in the auctioneer's catalogue and any printed material and on signs posted at the auction.

(j) Wherever an estimate or estimated value of an item or lot is published in a catalogue or any other printed material published or distributed in relation to an auction sale, a general description of the estimate and its meaning and function must be included in such printed material. For the purpose of this subdivision (j), advertisements in newspapers or other periodicals shall not constitute printed material. Where no printed material is provided, and an estimate or estimated value is announced or disseminated in any manner, a general description of the estimate and its meaning and function must be available for distribution and its availability must be announced at the commencement of the auction.

(k) In any advertisement indicating an auction sale due to a business' loss of lease or liquidation, the auctioneer must include the name of the consignor or business authorizing the auction. In any sale advertised as pursuant to a security agreement, the name of the debtor shall be indicated conspicuously.

(l) The following newspapers published in the City of New York are hereby designated as newspapers in which auctioneers shall advertise as required by §§ 20-282 and 20-283 of the Administrative Code:

New York Times
New York Journal of Commerce
New York Post
New York Daily Fruit Reporter
Newsday
Staten Island Advance
New York Daily News
New York Law Journal
American Banker
Action
Il Progresso
China Post
China Times
Chinese Journal
France-Amerique
Aufbau
National Herald
Novoye Russkoye Slovo
El Diario
El Mirador
Svoboda
Jewish Daily Forward
Barbininkas

§ 2-123   Reserves.

(a) If the reserve price is not bid, the auctioneer may withdraw a lot from sale. At the time of such withdrawal, and before bidding on another lot begins, the auctioneer shall announce that the withdrawn lot has been "passed", "withdrawn", "returned to owner" or "bought-in".

(b) *Affirmative disclosure.* Before bidding on any lot has reached its reserve price no auctioneer may make or place consecutive or successive bids, or place bids in response to bids from others, on behalf of the consignor, unless the fact that the auctioneer will or may bid in such a manner is clearly and conspicuously disclosed in any catalogue and any other printed material published or distributed in connection with the sale. For the purposes of this subdivision (b) advertisements in newspapers or other periodicals shall not constitute printed material. This disclosure must also be made on signs prominently displayed in the auction room and at the entrance thereto, and must be announced by the auctioneer immediately prior to the commencement of any auction.

The sign required by this subdivision (b) must be at least 12 inches by 18 inches in dimension with letters at least one inch high, and must read as follows, or convey a substantially similar disclosure:

> The auctioneer may open bidding on any lot by placing a bid on behalf of the seller. The auctioneer may further bid on behalf of the seller, up to the amount of the reserve, by placing successive or consecutive bids for a lot, or by placing bids in response to other bidders.

(c)   After bidding has reached the reserve price of a lot:

   (1)   the auctioneer may not bid on behalf of the consignor or the auction house; and

   (2)   the auctioneer may only accept bids from persons other than the consignor or the auction house except absentee telephone, order or other agent's bids;

   (3)   This subdivision (c) shall not apply to auction sales conducted pursuant to an order of a court of competent jurisdiction, including an order of a bankruptcy judge or trustee, or a sale of secured property pursuant to the Uniform Commercial Code, or the sale of property which is subject to a lien or assignment pursuant to the laws of the State of New York.

(d)   In no event shall the reserve price for any lot exceed the minimum estimated value of the lot as published in any catalogue or other printed material distributed by the auctioneer.

§ 2-124 Prohibited Practices.

(a)   An auctioneer may not disclaim warranty of title of any item sold at auction. The auctioneer shall reimburse any purchaser in an amount equal to the successful bid at auction plus any buyer's commission paid in the event it is determined that the purchaser has not acquired transferable title to the item.

(b) At the auction sale premises only exterior signs may be displayed advertising the auction sale but the same shall not be excessive in size.

(c) An auctioneer may not:

(1) Offer more than one article for sale at any one time unless the combining of articles or lots is so indicated prior to the initial bid.

(2) Represent an article to be guaranteed by the manufacturer or the owner unless a manufacturer's or owner's guarantee accompanies the article.

(3) Offer an article contained in a carton, package or other container commonly known as a blind article unless prior to the offer it is announced that the highest bidder may reject the article if not satisfactory to him or her. This provision does not refer to an auction of articles in bulk where a sample is displayed and balance of articles are represented to conform with the sample.

(4) Use a loudspeaker outlet located within ten feet of any entrance or exit or which is beamed in any direction except away from said entrance or exit. In any event loud-speaker apparatus must not attract attention from outside auction premises.

(5) Accept as payment or exchange any article previously knocked down or sold to a successful bidder. The article knocked down or sold must be delivered to the bidder or, if the auctioneer is willing and at the bidder's election, the purchase price refunded in full. No other article may be offered to said bidder as a substitute or replacement. Such refund shall take place within a reasonable time or may be applied as part payment or payment for any other article purchased at auction by the same bidder.

§ 2-125   Records; Miscellaneous.

(a) An auctioneer must keep a written record of all details of each sale including copies of advertisements; lot number, quantity, description and selling price of each lot; record of disbursements; and net amount sent to persons entitled to proceeds of sale for a period of six years from the date of the auction.

(b) *Exceptions.* § 2-122(c) through (e) inclusive above shall not apply to:

(1) Any auction sale involving a printed catalogue when all of the following conditions are met:

(i)   the printed catalogue is distributed and available for a reasonable period of time prior to the auction being held;

(ii) said catalogue contains a precise, detailed description of the items to be auctioned and the terms used to describe the items have a widely accepted, standardized usage in the field;

(iii) the value of the items described in said catalogue can be verified by reference to standard recognized reference sources commonly known of and utilized in the field; and

(iv) the sale of the item at the auction is not final until the purchaser has had a reasonable opportunity to verify independently that the item purchased was accurately described in said catalogue.

(2)   Any auction sales conducted for primarily commercial purposes where all of the bidders at such auction can reasonably be anticipated to be purchasing for use in a commercial endeavor and not for use by the purchaser, or the purchaser's family, as consumer goods as that term is defined in the Consumer Protection Law of 1969 of The City of New York (Administrative Code of The City of New York, § 20-700 et seq.).

HISTORICAL NOTE: Regulations were amended as the result of a two-year study of the auction industry conducted by the Department. These regulations were amended to update those existing in order to conform to current conditions and to regulate new practices that had developed in the period since the previous regulations had been enacted. Regulations were published twice for comments in the City Record, they were published for adoption on March 13, 1987, and became effective April 13, 1987.

5

Prints and
Sculpture Multiples

Few art forms spawn abuse more readily than fine art multiples. Striking technological advances beckon the forger. As products of a multistage process, both the print and the sculpture multiple tempt the printer, publisher, colorist, foundry worker, artist, and anyone else involved. A public uninformed as to factors determining a multiple's value lures the dishonest dealer and the profferer of tax shelter scams. Art multiples invite commercial abuse for a number of reasons: lack of uniform, industry-wide controls in the production process; lack of art-market consensus about such fundamentals as what constitutes an original print; and lack of state consumer legislation or, in the few states having such legislation, lack of enforcement.

Headlines—and court calendars—continue to be rife with counterfeit art multiple scandals. In 2002, for instance, an art dealer was convicted by an Indiana federal district court on counts of both mail fraud and wire fraud[1] in connection with the offering for sale of Walt Disney movie "cels," that is, painted drawings of popular cartoon characters on clear plastic or acetates. Some of the cels sold were counterfeit; others, which were limited-edition cels, were misrepresented as being the more valuable one-of-a-kind production cels.

Another example involved multitudes of Salvador Dalí counterfeit prints. The sensational case of *Center Art Galleries-Hawaii, Inc. v. United States*,[2] which in 1989 uncovered thousands of fake Dalís and which "broke a major link in the international ring of Dalí forgeries,"[3] was in the news again six years later. In October 1995, some 12,000 of those fake Dalí prints were auctioned off to the public in Belmont, California, by the United States Postal Inspection Service for $250,000 to the outrage of the art market and federal law enforcement agents.[4] The auction boasted 400 registered bidders, including many dealers. The purpose of the court-ordered auction was to recoup more than $2 million in fines not paid by Center Art Galleries, but the result was again to put thousands of fake Dalís on the market. That time, records of the multiples were forwarded to the International Association of Appraisers and to the International Foundation for Art Research (IFAR); the works on paper were identified on the back as being counterfeit, and the sculpture multiples bore stickers declaring their resale as original Dalís illegal. Nevertheless, the Postal Inspection Service reaped substantial and justifiable criticism for placing fake art on the market. After all, stamps can be eradicated and stickers detached.

In contrast, the Federal Trade Commission customarily shreds any fake prints subject to its seizure.[5] Such timely and appropriate destructions in the multiples market can help to eliminate art fraud.

PRINTS

Prints may be either (1) reproductions of original works in another medium produced in limited editions and signed by the artist or (2) art-making in primary form, with the artist working directly on a stone, plate, or block. One way of categorizing prints is by the printmaking process itself; a brief sketch of some of the major processes follows.

Printmaking Techniques

Among the major processes of printmaking are relief prints, intaglio prints, collagraphs, screen prints, lithographs, and photomechanical reproductions.[6] Computer technology adds new techniques, such as giclee prints. All of these processes are discussed below.

Relief Prints

Relief printmaking dates back to at least 4000 B.C., when the Sumerians created impressions in moist clay from carved reliefs of such materials as lapis lazuli and alabaster. Multiple printing became a theoretical possibility more than 2000 years ago with the invention of paper in China in approximately 100 B.C. Multiple printing became a reality there some 700 years later, when examples of printing on paper and on textiles began to appear. At about the same time in Egypt, wood began to surpass clay and stone as a stamping device.[7]

In a relief print, the image is derived from the surface of the block or plate; the areas of the surface that are not part of the image are cut away, creating the white or nonprinting areas. Usually, the artist works from a block of wood, but other materials, such as linoleum and cardboard, can be used. For a collage print, the relief surface is often created from an adhesive—such as plastic, wood, liquid steel, or liquid aluminum—that is applied to a support plate and dries to a firm consistency. In all relief prints, the raised surface is covered with ink, and paper is applied to that surface. Then, either the back of the paper is rubbed by hand or the paper is run through a press to produce an image. One of the best-known and most popular forms of relief-printmaking is the woodcut.[8]

Intaglio Prints

Unlike the relief processes, intaglio techniques evolved relatively recently. The earliest intaglio print bearing a date is entitled *Flagellation*, done in 1446, from the series *The Passion of Christ* by an anonymous German engraver.[9]

The term "intaglio" (from the Italian *intagliare*, meaning to carve or cut into)[10] encompasses an array of print techniques that are the inverse of relief processes. That is, an image is produced by inking the incised lines and depressions in a plate and then wiping the plate's surface clean, leaving ink solely in the recessed areas. When damp paper is placed over such a plate and the plate and paper are rolled with substantial pressure through an etching press, the ink remaining in the recessed areas is transferred to the paper, producing a richly inked impression. Intaglio processes can be divided into two broad categories: those that use acid to create an image on a plate and those that use sharp tools, needles, or power tools to produce the image. Among the best-known techniques involving acid are etching, aquatint, and embossing. The most common processes using tools include engraving, drypoint, and mezzotint.[11] Each is described briefly below.

Etching

In etching, an acid-proof hard ground of asphalt, beeswax, rosin, and a solvent covers a metal plate of zinc, copper, or brass. The artist then scratches lines or textures on the ground, allowing the acid to bite into the plate with sharp definition. The longer the plate remains in the acid, the deeper the lines and the textures in the metal plate become, causing them to print a darker, heavier image. The process of etching originated in the sixteenth century but began to flourish in the seventeenth century with the introduction of copper plate and improvements in its chemical processes. Among the most gifted etchers of all time was the seventeenth-century Dutch artist Rembrandt van Rijn.[12]

Aquatint

Aquatint, often combined with line etching and other methods, achieves tonal areas in an intaglio plate. First, the surface of the plate is partially covered with tiny particles of rosin that, when heated, adhere. The acid then bites the open areas around those particles, creating pits in the plate. The longer the plate remains in the acid, the deeper the pits and, therefore, the darker the printed tone. Splendid examples of aquatint prints are found in the works of the late-eighteenth-early-nineteenth-century Spanish artist Francisco de Goya, whose *Caprichos* were a devastating series of satirical prints on the corrupt court life of Charles IV and the Inquisition.[13]

Embossing

In embossing, a plate achieves deeply bitten areas through traditional line etching and long immersion in acid. The plate is then run through the press uninked. The recessed areas of the plate form raised areas on the print.[14]

Engraving

As noted above, engraving does not use acid. Rather, a hard steel tool called a burin is pushed into a copper or brass plate to create sharply defined lines. The wider the burin and the deeper it is pushed into the metal, the thicker the line. Tonal areas on the print are developed by engraving parallel and crosshatched lines on the plate. The gifted fifteenth-century German artist Martin Schongauer, the first engraver on metal known by name, was a significant influence on another German artist, Albrecht Dürer, who some forty years later—as a master of woodcut, engraving, drypoint, and etching—was to become one of the most illustrious printmakers of all time.[15]

Drypoint

Unlike the sharply defined line of etching or engraving, drypoint yields a rich, rough line with soft edges. The procedure is to scratch into the plate with a sharp needle, which yields a metal burr that catches and holds the ink when the plate is wiped. Rembrandt created a number of splendid prints by using drypoint in combination with etching to enhance the drama of the interplay of black, white, and gray.[16]

Mezzotint

Mezzotint is a nonacid technique that achieves tonality in a print by repeatedly pressing a curved, serrated tool over the surface of a copper plate to create thousands of tiny indentations. Once the entire plate surface is roughened, the artist uses scrapers and burnishers to shave down the raised areas to a variety of heights, which, when inked and wiped, achieve tones through gray to white. Ludwig van Siegen, a seventeenth-century amateur Dutch artist, is credited with inventing this process in 1646.[17]

Collagraphs

A collagraph is a print created from a collage—that is, a compilation—of an array of materials glued together on a plate that can be metal, cardboard, hardboard, or plastic. A collagraph plate can be printed either as an intaglio plate, a relief plate, or a mixture of the two processes. Collagraphs can be combined with such other techniques as etching and with totally different media, such as screen printing, to produce a mixed media print. Collagraphy most likely originated in the nineteenth century. The assemblage efforts of such artists as Pablo Picasso, Georges Braque, and Juan Gris in the early twentieth century inspired subsequent novelties in printmaking that placed real objects—such as bits of cloth, silk, burlap, sand, and pieces of tin—on a plate. Printmakers who developed the innovation in the 1930s and 1940s include Rolf Nesch, a Norwegian artist, and the American artists Boris Margo and Edmond Casarella.[18]

Screen Prints

One of the simplest procedures for achieving multicolor images, a screen print is produced by stretching fabric (such as silk, nylon, polyester, or organdy) over a rectangular frame, blocking out the fabric where unprinted areas will be, and then squeegeeing or brushing water- or oil-based color through the open mesh of the remainder of the stretched fabric to produce an image on the surface underneath. Generally, a squeegee is used to push and guide the color through the fabric's mesh; the instrument is a plastic or rubber blade, created in various sizes and shapes, that is inserted into a wood or metal handle. Screen printing has its origins in stenciling, which dates back to prehistoric times; the walls of caves in the French Pyrenées are covered with many dozens of decorative hand prints, both positive and negative. For negative prints, blacks, reds, and ochres from the earth were probably daubed around the hands to create a colored background; for positive prints, the hands were simply dipped into colors and pressed on the walls.[19]

Stenciling on silk was cultivated for many centuries in both China and Japan, but such experimentation did not occur in Western Europe until the late nineteenth century; indeed, only as recently as 1907 was a recorded patent for a silkscreen process first awarded to an Englishman. In the United States, the screen print developed in the context of commercial printing, with a commercial artist receiving a patent for a multicolor screen process in 1914, thus encouraging the production of posters, billboards, and signs. Soon, other commercial applications were developed, along with printing on a variety of objects and surfaces, such as furniture, glassware, toys, and textiles. Some artists and printmakers in the United States began to view the screen print as a vehicle for personal expression as early as the 1930s, but it was not until the 1960s, with the advent of pop art, that the screen print as an art form hit its stride. Popularizers of the medium include Andy Warhol with his soup-can images of 1962, James Rosenquist with his experience as a billboard artist, and Roy Lichtenstein with his knowledge of commercial printing processes.[20]

Lithographs

Lithography is unique among the aforementioned processes in that it does not rely on the physical separation of inked and uninked areas to produce an image; rather, it is the repellency of grease to water and water to grease that is the basis for the lithographic image. The process was developed in 1798–99 by a German, Alois Senefelder, in the course of—as the apocryphal story goes—writing a laundry list with homemade ink on limestone in the absence of paper. The basic lithographic process is as follows: On a piece of limestone or fine-grained metal moistened with water, an image drawn with a greasy crayon or stick is then etched with a dilute acidic mixture to fix the drawing to the stone and keep the undrawn areas from receiving the ink; a print is made when a sheet of paper is placed on the inked stone and pressed against it. Masters of the technique in the nineteenth century include the Spanish artist Francisco de Goya and the French satirist Honoré Daumier, in whose hands lithography evolved into a fine art. Subsequently, the lithographic medium was adopted by numerous great artists, including Edouard Manet, Edgar Degas, Paul Cézanne, and such twentieth-century masters as Pablo Picasso, Henri Matisse, and Joan Miró.[21]

Photomechanical Reproductions

In photomechanical processes[22] the artist uses neither a plate nor a screen to produce the image. The reproductions are printed images, usually on paper, of a preexisting two-dimensional artwork—for example, an oil painting, a watercolor, a collage, or a drawing. The basic procedure is to have a professional photographer photograph the preexisting image on large-size color transparency film, which is then removed to a color-separation laboratory and mounted by skilled technicians into an electronic machine called a laser-scanner. The scanner reads the transparency through its color filters and reproduces on big films the original image, which the scanner has now broken down into perhaps millions of dots of color that are arranged in rows but that, to the naked eye, blend into "smooth tonal transitions of photographic clarity of image."[23] The films are then sent to the printer's preparation shop, where they are carefully pressed facedown against a printing plate that has been coated with a light-sensitive emulsion. Then a powerful light containing ultraviolet radiation is directed over the film, causing the image of the film to be transposed onto the master plate. The master plate is then sponged off and brought to a printing press, which, under the printer's control, produces the photomechanical reproduction on paper that is automatically fed to the press.

Giclee Prints

Giclee prints are not actually original prints, "giclee" being simply another term for the ink jet printer. To make a giclee print, the artwork or a photograph of the artwork is scanned into a computer and printed out. It is then signed and numbered on the margin. Perhaps the artist may alter some colors on the image before pushing the print button.[24]

Print Terminology

Edition Size

Once a master plate is produced to the artist's satisfaction, the size of the edition must be determined. Edition size depends on an array of factors, including the demand for the artist's work, the durability of the block or plate, and the time it takes to print. When an artist is relatively unknown, it is common to pull only a small number of prints; editions of twenty-five to fifty may well be practicable. When an edition of any size is handled by a dealer, the price generally goes up as the edition sells out.[25]

Edition Signing and Numbering

The artist's practice of signing a print is relatively recent. The nineteenth-century American artist James McNeill Whistler was among the first to do so. The practice of numbering prints is even newer, having only become the custom in the twentieth century. Since many contracts between artists and print publishers permit a maximum of 10% to 15% of an edition to be labeled "artist's proof," the custom of numbering prints devolves primarily to the art dealer's benefit; after all, when an edition is numbered, a dealer is better able to control the number of proofs in each edition and to keep track of how many prints are left to sell.

When signing an edition of prints, the artist must first examine the prints carefully to make sure that they are satisfactory: Any print accepted for signature by the artist must be free of all defects. The printer usually produces prints that exceed the agreed-on edition size by 10% to 15% on the reasonable assumption that not all the prints presented to the artist will be found flawless.

The artist customarily signs and numbers a print in pencil. The inscription is generally placed under the image, with the signature on the right, the title in the middle, and the number on the left. The number usually appears as a fraction, with the denominator giving the edition size and the numerator giving the sequential number of the print in hand. However, if all the prints in an edition are produced at the same time, it is virtually impossible for the numerator to reflect the actual printing sequence; once the prints are dried, whether under blotters or under newsprint, they are stacked and shuffled many times before they are signed and numbered. Therefore, the numerator merely indicates a satisfactory impression in the edition.[26]

When an artist signs and numbers a limited-edition print, the artist is affirming to the buyer that there are and can only be as many signed and numbered copies in the edition as is indicated by the denominator. Moreover, the buyer can rely on the fact that additional copies will never enter the market and dilute the fair market value of that buyer's print.[27] Unfortunately, the process of signing and numbering prints has spawned an array of abusive practices that have made newspaper headlines and sensational court cases, discussed later in this chapter.

Proofs

Prints are pulled at various stages of the production process. Those pulled in the course of preparing the print are termed working proofs; a predesignated number of flawless prints pulled simultaneously with the edition prints are either artist's proofs, presentation proofs, or printer's proofs. Any additional prints, flawless or otherwise, pulled simultaneously with the edition prints are called "overs" and should be destroyed. Proofs can be sold but should be labeled as proofs. It is important to be able to distinguish among the different designations of proofs. Most publishers, printers, and artists would not care to have working proofs surface for sale on the open market and should, accordingly, destroy such proofs when no longer needed. Below is an explanation of some of the more common terms.

Trial Proof

A trial proof is an early working print with experimental changes in, for example, color or wiping to enable the artist or the printmaker to visualize certain effects. It is usually labeled "T/P."[28]

***Bon à Tirer* Proof**

French for "good to pull," a *bon à tirer* (BAT) proof is a print that satisfies the artist's aesthetic and technical demands and is used by the printer as a guide during the printing of the edition.[29]

Artist's Proof

A number of prints, usually equivalent to 10% to 15% of an edition size, are reserved to the artist. An artist's proof or print is pulled simultaneously with the edition but is not part of the edition. Such a print is ordinarily labeled "A/P."[30]

Presentation Proof

A presentation proof is identical to those in the edition, but it is reserved as a gift for a person or an institution and is ordinarily not sold.[31]

Printer's Proof

The artist presents a printer's proof to the printer after the edition is completed.[32]

Cancellation Proof

To preserve the integrity of the limited edition (although this method of doing so may be questionable), a plate or a block may be defaced with a scratch, hole, or chip once the edition is completed to make sure that any further prints pulled will bear the cancellation mark. Occasionally, such prints are pulled and sold on the open market. When a plate or a block by a famous artist is selected for such a restrike, the resultant prints can bring substantial prices.[33]

Hors de Commerce

Marked "H/C" or "H.C." (*hors de commerce*, French for "outside of commerce"), these prints may well be overs and should not be sold. In fact, they should be destroyed or permanently defaced. However, some publishers and distributors do sell such prints. A skilled print curator can easily erase the penciled "H/C" notation (written where the edition number is usually placed) and write in a salable mark, such as "A/P."[34]

Restrike

A restrike is a proof resulting from the reprinting of a plate that is not in the artist's possession or control. Unfortunately, such proofs can be of superb quality if the plates are not worn or damaged, resulting in the possible sale of illicit copies for a great deal of money.[35]

Chop Mark

Commonly embossed on the lower right margin of a print, near the artist's signature, a chop mark is a printer's, publisher's, or workshop's identification symbol. On occasion, when an artist is deceased, the artist's estate may be authorized to apply a posthumous chop mark to those prints permitted by the artist to be pulled after the artist's death.[36]

Posthumous Prints

An artist can authorize his estate to print an edition of the artist's work after the artist's death. In such a case, the estate may apply a posthumous chop mark to each such print but should never affix the artist's signature without a qualifier, as such a work would then be considered a forgery.[37]

What Constitutes an Original Print?

Largely as a result of the scope of abuse in the print market, the International Fine Print Dealers Association (IFPDA) was established in 1987 to promulgate professional standards in the fine-print market and to protect collectors and buyers from print abuse. In *David Tunick, Inc. v. Kornfeld*, discussed in chapter 2 with respect to express warranties, a New York federal district court determined that two prints by the same artist and from the same plates are not interchangeable.[38] To inform the public about prints, the IFPDA has published an essay entitled "What Is a Print?" The essay assesses prints "without using the term 'originality,'"[39] since, according to the IFPDA, that term is "bankrupt and imprecise"[40] in the evaluation of prints. Instead, the IFPDA divides prints into seven categories depending on the extent of artist involvement "in the creation of the print."[41] These are the categories:[42]

1. The artist alone prepares and creates the matrix.[43]

2. The artist and the collaborator(s) prepare and create the matrix. The collaborator usually contributes technical expertise or performs laborious, time-consuming tasks.

3. The artist does not work on the matrix. The physical labor is performed by a collaborator. The artist provides a design to be copied and is critically involved in directing the work, suggesting modifications, and approving the results.

4. The artist has no meaningful involvement in the matrix production. The artist or the artist's agent supplies a printmaker with a design to be reproduced as faithful to the original as the chosen print medium will allow.

5. The artist or the artist's agent authorizes the reproduction of one of the artist's existing works.

6. A reproduction is made without the permission of the artist or the artist's agent.

7. A print is made from the primary matrix without the artist's authorization.

At least one fine-print commentator[44] has objected to the foregoing categorization, noting, for example, that it does not address

(1) the nature of the print (woodblock, etching, engraving, etc.),

(2) whether the artist participated in the actual printing of the image, and

(3) whether the image is a reproduction of the artist's work in another medium or was created solely for the edition of prints.

Such information seems to be significant to the prospective buyer of a fine *contemporary* print and should appropriately be supplied by the dealer. However, much of the information is unobtainable for old prints; it is questionable, for example, whether the sixteenth-century German artist Albrecht Dürer, a master of the woodcut, actually prepared his own woodblock or whether the fifteenth-century German engraver Martin Schongauer participated in the actual printing of the impressions in each series. Moreover, such questions were not necessarily an issue a few centuries ago; the concept of what constitutes an original print has been ever-changing. In the light of widespread print abuse in the latter half of the twentieth century, however, there seems to be some merit in preserving and refining the concept of an original fine print.

The following are criteria that have been proposed for living artists wishing to create an original fine print. If all the criteria are satisfied, the fine print should undoubtedly be deemed original.[45]

1. The artist, working alone or with only incidental assistance on mechanical chores of the preparatory process, has created

and prepared the image components needed to produce the completed print image. The print image was conceived by the artist for solely one print edition or was adapted by the artist from a preexisting version of any image of the artist's own art.

2. The artist, working alone or with only incidental assistance on routine chores of the master-making process, has personally made the master from which the prints will be pulled *or* has delivered the component images to a specialized craftsman who performs the actual required processing under the artist's direct supervision.

3. The artist, working alone or with only incidental assistance on routine chores of the printing process, has personally printed the master *or* has delivered the master (or component masters) to a craftsman-printer to do the actual printing under the artist's direct supervision. In the latter case, the artist remains with the printer at least until a completed proof of the entire image is obtained that is satisfactory to the artist, who then signs and dates the approval proof or *bon à tirer*.

4. The artist personally signs his name on every copy of the print edition.

5. The artist prepares and issues a print-documentation sheet for the print edition, attesting to the truth and the accuracy of the four criteria noted above. The sheet is signed by the artist and notarized, and the artist provides copies of it to anyone on request.

What makes an original fine print so desirable to the public? In chapter 3, we discuss the concept of an original work of art in the context of art forgery and note that a forged work may be as aesthetically pleasing as an original but that, unlike the original, it is not a piece of history, and that difference, once known, is consistently reflected in the art market in economic terms. With fine prints the issue is less art forgery, as has been suggested,[46] than art by committee—that is, an artist working hand in hand with a publisher (who may suggest a salable image), a printer (who may make creative decisions involving, for example, inking pressures), and a colorist (who may make creative choices involving, for instance, shades of color). Such joint creation dilutes an artist's unalloyed vision unless it is closely supervised by the artist at every stage.

Print Abuse

The past thirty-five to forty years have witnessed an explosion of fine prints as collectibles to be mass-marketed, a development that spawned an array of fraudulent commercial practices. The works of such modern artists as Salvador Dalí, Pablo Picasso, and Joan Miró seem to lend themselves particularly to acts of forgery and other fraudulent practices, at times with the apparent collusion of the artist. Dalí, for one, signed blank sheets of paper on which reproductions of his work were subsequently printed, with the sheets then being numbered and issued as original prints.

Many abusive practices in the limited edition original fine print market fall into two broad categories—(1) forgeries and (2) perversions of the edition size. The case of *Magui Publishers*,[47] discussed below, provides an example of both. But other abusive practices abound and are also discussed below.

Forgeries

Magui Publishers

In 1991, the Federal Trade Commission (FTC) brought suit in a California federal district court against Magui Publishers, Inc., a California publisher and marketer of fine-art prints to retailers throughout the United States, and its principal, Pierre Marcand. The FTC alleged that the defendants' fraudulent marketing and sale of etchings and lithographs, purportedly by Salvador Dalí, violated section 5(a) of the FTC Act.[48]

On various occasions Dalí signed quantities of blank sheets of paper suitable for use in editions of his works at the request of publishers who were producing specific editions of his work. Beginning in 1979, Dalí's health suffered serious deterioration, rendering him no longer capable of creating or participating in the production of print editions or even of signing blank sheets of paper for a print edition of his work.

The defendant Magui between 1982 and 1989 published and marketed at least thirty-two separate editions of 1,000 prints each of works by Salvador Dalí; twenty-eight of the editions were allegedly etchings, and the remaining four editions were supposedly lithographs. The Dalí prints were sold to retailers and other third parties throughout the United States. Magui made oral representations by the sales staff, wrote representations on the advertisements and promotional materials, and issued a certificate of authenticity and *tirage* signed by Marcand that accompanied each Magui Dalí work. That certificate purportedly guaranteed that, among other points, the artist producing the title was Salvador Dalí, the print was an etching or lithograph, the artwork was printed on a particular type of paper signed or presigned by Dalí, the edition was produced at a particular location, and the printing plate was canceled after the completion of the edition. The certificate also noted the size of any Magui editions of the print and the total number of prints produced. The average price of a Magui Dalí print was $457, and Magui's gross sales of prints attributed to Dalí was at least $3.96 million.

The FTC charged and the court found that the evidence supported the charges that the defendants made five misrepresentations with respect to the sale of Dalí artworks to the retail purchasers. The misrepresentations were the following:

1. The defendants alleged that Dalí was involved in the creation or the production of the Magui editions or authorized them. The evidence indicated that Magui and its principal Marcand marketed the art as being closely linked to Salvador Dalí. However, the evidence also indicated that not only did Salvador Dalí have no involvement or connection with the Magui works but the works were produced entirely by Magui personnel.

2.   The defendants alleged that the Magui Dalí prints were pro-
     duced on paper that was signed or presigned by Dalí. Al-
     though each Magui print contained a signature purportedly
     by Salvador Dalí and a designation indicating that the work
     was part of a limited edition, the evidence indicated that the
     signature on the Magui prints was a forgery. First, most of
     the Magui Dalí prints used Arches or B.F.K. Rives brand pa-
     per, both of which bear watermarks enabling an observer to
     establish when the paper was milled. An examination of the
     watermarks revealed that the vast majority, if not all, of
     those papers could not have been distributed by the manu-
     facturers to purchasers of the paper before 1980. Moreover,
     in many instances the presence of a secondary watermark,
     changed each year, that was added to the Rives and Arches
     paper from 1982 on indicated that much of the presigned
     paper had been milled in 1982, 1983, 1984, 1985, and 1986.
     The evidence indicated that Dalí had stopped presigning pa-
     per in 1979 at the latest. Second, Dalí's signature was nota-
     bly erratic and inconsistent, unlike the signatures on the
     Magui prints. Third, had the paper actually been presigned
     by Dalí, the etching process would have rendered the pen-
     ciled signatures smudge-proof. On the Magui prints the sig-
     nature could be smudged with ease. Therefore, if the prints
     were produced by the etching process, they could not have
     been presigned by Dalí.

3.   The defendants alleged that the editions of certain titles
     were limited editions of smaller size. In fact, the editions
     were larger than Magui alleged. And, according to the evi-
     dence, with at least three titles—*Last Supper*, *Lincoln in
     Dalívision*, and *Persistence of Memory*—Magui had, at differ-
     ent times and using separate plates, published different edi-
     tions of the same Dalí image, unbeknownst to its purchasers.

4.   The defendants alleged in its promotional materials that all
     the etchings were produced entirely by hand. The evidence
     showed that, with respect to at least nine titles, analyses of
     the prints indicated that most, if not all, of the plates and

prints were produced by a mixture of photographic technology and hand labor.

5. The defendants alleged in its promotional materials that the Magui Dalís were valuable collectibles with significant opportunity for appreciation and were, therefore, excellent investments. In fact, because the Magui prints were interpretations of Dalí images and were produced without Dalí's involvement, the prints had no value in the art resale market and, therefore, no worth as investments. Rather, they were comparable to products sold in museum gift shops.

The federal district court went on to note that Marcand, convicted and imprisoned in Italy in 1984 for the sale of fake Dalí lithographs, was aware of his deceptive practices.[49] On August 21, 1986, acting on behalf of himself and Magui publishers, Marcand had entered into a consent judgment settling charges brought by the New York State attorney general concerning the sale of counterfeit Dalí works from October 1984 to August 1986. Pursuant to the judgment, Marcand and Magui were permanently enjoined from selling counterfeit Dalí artworks in New York State. On August 7, 1986, two weeks before the entry of judgment in the New York case, Marcand was fully deposed regarding all the issues in that case. Therefore, Marcand had knowledge before his actions in the California case about the deceptive nature of his Dalí marketing practices.[50]

Between 1984 and 1987, Magui sold numerous Dalí prints to Federal Sterling Galleries, Austin Galleries, and Shelby Fine Art. Federal Sterling Galleries and Austin Galleries were found liable in separate civil proceedings brought by the FTC for fraudulent misrepresentations about their Dalí art.[51] In a state criminal proceeding in New Mexico, Shelby Fine Art pleaded guilty to fraud charges involving the sale of its Dalí art.[52] Magui was aware of those proceedings.[53]

In the 1991 FTC case, the California federal district court found that Magui was unjustly enriched by $1.96 million. That is, Magui profited from violations of the FTC Act in an amount equal to

Magui's gross revenues from the sale of the Dalí prints (at least $3.96 million) less the cost of producing each print (determined to be roughly $2.0 million). The court also held that Magui and Marcand engaged in "unfair or deceptive acts or practices in or affecting commerce"[54] in violation of section 5(a) of the FTC Act[55] by making the five misrepresentations discussed above.

Further, the court held that Magui and Marcand violated section 5(a) of the FTC Act by providing retailers with a means or an instrumentality—in this case, the "Dalí" prints, accompanying certificates of authenticity, and promotional brochures—to deceive the public.

The court also held that Magui and Marcand violated section 5(a) of the FTC Act by aiding and abetting their retail customers in misleading consumers in that (1) certain of the defendants' retail customers made misrepresentations to their consumers in violation of state and federal law about the Dalí prints and (2) the defendants supplied the deceptive artwork and materials to their retail customers with full knowledge that those customers would use the materials to deceive consumers. Accordingly, the court, under section 13(b) of the FTC Act,[56] issued a permanent injunction under section 5(a) of the FTC Act, prohibiting the defendants' misrepresentations.

The court also issued, in consonance with section 13(b), an order for consumer redress in the amount of $1.96 million, as the FTC was able to establish that the deceptive acts as practices were

> the type of misrepresentations on which a reasonably prudent person would rely, that they were widely disseminated, and that the injured consumers purchased [the product].[57]

In addition and in keeping with section 13(b), the court ordered a disgorgement of profits by the defendants in the amount equivalent to the defendants' unjust enrichment, $1.96 million. To obtain disgorgement, the court, as it did here, must also conclude, aside from the requirements permitting it to order consumer redress, that

(1)   the defendants profited from violations of the FTC Act,

(2)   the profits are causally related to the violations, and

(3) the disgorgement figure reasonably approximates the amount of the unjust enrichment.

Galerie Furstenberg[58]

Numerous cases of fraud in the print market involving other theories of liability abound. In *Galerie Furstenberg v. Coffaro*, for example, the plaintiff, a French art dealer and longtime specialist in Dalí's early prints and purportedly holding exclusive rights to sell certain early prints, successfully alleged under section 1962(c) of the Racketeer Influenced and Corrupt Organizations (RICO) Act that the defendant-art merchants and retailers advertised, distributed, and sold fake Dalí reproductions since December 1980. Section 1962(c) of the RICO Act, in pertinent part, makes it unlawful for anyone employed by or associated with any enterprise engaged in activities affecting interstate or foreign commerce to participate in the conduct of such enterprise's affairs through a pattern of racketeering activity. To plead such a violation, a plaintiff must allege "(1) conduct (2) of an enterprise (3) through a pattern (4) of racketeering activity."[59] The New York federal district court noted that anyone injured in his business or property by reason of a violation of section 1962 of the RICO Act may sue in an appropriate United States district court and recover treble damages and court costs, including a reasonable attorney's fee.

Galerie Furstenberg, as defendants' direct competitor, successfully alleged that the

> defendants' sale of counterfeit Dalís "deprived plaintiff of its rightful ownership of, and interest in, its property rights and/or the exclusive rights granted to plaintiff by Dalí, and of the opportunity to earn profits from the exercise of those rights" as well as "injured . . . plaintiff's professional reputation in the art community."[60]

As to the defendants' claim that the plaintiff failed to plead properly a RICO enterprise, the court noted that the RICO enterprise is a "group of persons associated together for a common purpose of engaging in a course of conduct"[61] and is proved by evidence of an ongoing organization, formal or informal, and by evidence that the various associates function as a continuing unit.[62]

Furstenberg alleged that the defendants purchased for distribution and sale on a continuing basis forged Dalís and listed three examples of defendants' distribution arrangements, specifying dates, money amounts, and individual defendants. Furstenberg's complaint also listed examples of fraudulent authentications, including the specifics; explained defendants' methods of producing counterfeit works; identified the counterfeit works; and listed the sale particulars. The federal district court noted that those allegations sufficiently portrayed a "group associated for a common purpose."[63]

As to the pattern of racketeering activity itself—in this case, mail and wire fraud arising from the distribution, advertising, and sale of counterfeit artwork—the court noted that to allege mail and wire fraud, a plaintiff must claim "(1) a scheme to defraud, and (2) the use of the mails or interstate wires in furtherance of the fraudulent scheme."[64] As the court noted, the plaintiff alleged in the complaint that the defendants conspired together to perpetuate misrepresentations as to

(1) Dalí's involvement in the forged artwork,

(2) the artwork's origin,

(3) the investment value of the artwork,

(4) the existence of a resale market,

(5) the authenticity of the artwork, and

(6) the willingness of the defendants to provide refunds.[65]

The plaintiff further alleged that those misrepresentations were made on the artwork itself, the certificates of authenticity, in 250,000 direct mailings each month, and on other sales materials. Accordingly, the court found that the plaintiff had successfully alleged a violation by the defendants of section 1962(c) of the RICO Act.

Perversions of the Edition Size

As noted earlier in this chapter, the phrase "limited edition" means that the artist who signs a print of that edition affirms to the buyer that (1) there are and can only be a certain number of signed and numbered copies in the edition—that is, the denominator of the fraction indicated on the print, and (2) the buyer may assume that there will never be more than that number of copies entering the stream of commerce to dilute the fair market value of the buyer's print.

Unfortunately, the phrase "limited edition" has been abused almost as often as it has been used. Common examples of edition abuse include the following:

- The stretching of an edition so that additional proofs, such as printer's proofs or artist's proofs, are signed and numbered by the artist

- The issuance of different-numbered editions (for example, an Arabic-numbered edition of 200 and a Roman-numbered edition of 100 or an American edition of 100 and a European edition of 100)

- The publishing of subsequent editions

- The forging of an artist's signature to commercial reproductions

- The wholesaling of signed blank sheets of paper on which reproductions of a painting or drawing are subsequently printed and which are then numbered and issued as original prints

Print-edition abuse has been the subject of litigation for more than twenty years.[66] For example, in *Wildlife Internationale, Inc. v. Clements*,[67] a well-known wildlife artist, John Ruthven, produced and sold lithographs of his own artwork through his own company, Wildlife Internationale, Inc. The defendant, Russell Clements, was the former president and owner of a fine-prints distributorship, DeSales Ltd. In 1967–68, Ruthven and DeSales entered into a total of three contracts whereby DeSales was granted certain rights to reproduce and sell prints of Ruthven paintings for a number of years. In

1969, Ruthven sought to end his relationship with DeSales, and, after a series of lawsuits, the parties' disputes were resolved in 1970 by a restraining order and an entry of judgment.

In 1971, DeSales was adjudicated bankrupt. In December of that year, Wildlife acquired the Ruthven-related assets of the bankrupt DeSales. In 1972, Clements became associated with Old Square Gallery, which was technically a partnership owned by his wife and his daughter. In 1982, Clements informed Ruthven that he was planning to offer certain Ruthven prints for sale to the public unless the two parties could make a "potentially profitable business deal."[68] Later that year, Clements began mailing to potential buyers promotional materials about the Ruthven prints. The artwork included proofs and limited-edition and unlimited-edition prints. The promotional materials indicated that the Ruthven artwork was being offered by Clements through Old Square. The plaintiffs brought suit in an Ohio federal district court on a number of theories, including copyright and trademark infringement and unfair competition under federal and state laws.

As to copyright infringement, the court held, among other findings, that Clements infringed Ruthven's copyright by selling or offering to sell proofs and overruns of the twenty-two copyrighted works listed in the complaint that were acquired by Clements as president of DeSales. In so holding, the court rejected Clements's argument that he acquired those proofs and overruns in keeping with an established DeSales policy whereby he retained approximately fifty prints each of certain subjects for his own use. As the court noted, that policy was never embodied in the contracts between Ruthven and DeSales, nor did the plaintiff ever grant such distribution rights.[69] According to the court, therefore, the distribution through sale or offer of sale to the public or otherwise of copies of any of the above-noted twenty-two artworks constituted an infringement of Ruthven's copyrights in those works—that is, the exclusive right of Ruthven, the copyright holder, to distribute his work. In addition, the court held that Clements's duplication and distribution to the public of advertising brochures containing reproductions of the twenty-two artworks constituted a further infringement of Ruthven's copyright.

As to the plaintiffs' allegations of trademark infringement and unfair competition under section 43(a) of the Lanham Act and under Ohio common law, the court, in its analysis, treated those claims as one. As the court noted, section 43(a) of the Lanham Act provides in pertinent part:

> Any person who shall . . . use in connection with any goods or services . . . a false designation of origin, or any false description or representation . . . and shall cause such goods to enter into commerce . . . shall be liable to a civil action . . . by any person who believes he is or is likely to be damaged by the use of any such false description or representation.[70]

The court noted that section 43(a) extends to false or misleading advertising and that, therefore, Clements's distribution of "random old brochure[s]"[71] of Ruthven prints, portraying his likeness and signature, created a "false impression, likely to cause confusion"[72] that such prints exemplify in style and quality those offered for sale by Clements and that the offering had Ruthven's approval.

Accordingly, Clements was permanently enjoined from reproducing or distributing to the public proofs, overruns, or other copies of the twenty-two copyrighted works and of the brochures.

Other Abusive Practices

Aside from forgeries and perversion of edition size, the print market, as with many other markets, has been subjected to allegations of price-fixing. In *Winn v. Edna Hibel Corp.*,[73] for example, the defendant Edna Hibel, a manufacturer of fine prints, terminated a dealership arrangement with the plaintiff, who was selling Hibel's prints for less than the manufacturer's suggested retail prices. Winn sued Hibel in a federal court for money damages under section 1 of the Sherman Antitrust Act, which provides that concerted action by a manufacturer and its retailers to set or maintain retail prices is per se illegal. Winn claimed that the manufacturer terminated him pursuant to a conspiracy between the manufacturer and a competing dealer. After the trial the court granted the defendant-manufacturer a directed verdict on two grounds: (1) the plaintiff did not establish that the manufacturer was not acting independently, and (2) the dealer failed to prove any economic loss.

Fine prints have also been the subject of tax-shelter schemes,[74] which are treated in detail in chapter 14.

Print-Disclosure Statutes

In an effort to protect the consumer from the abusive practices that are prevalent in the print market, a number of states over the past thirty to thirty-five years have enacted print-disclosure statutes requiring the prospective purchaser to be furnished with detailed information covering the sale of fine prints. The following is a discussion of the state statutes currently in effect.

California

California was the first state to pass a law designed to protect the purchasers of fine art in multiples. Known as the Farr Act for its sponsor, Samuel Farr, and enacted in 1971, the law applies to "any fine print, photograph (positive or negative), sculpture cast, collage or similar art object produced in more than one copy. Pages or sheets taken from books and magazines and offered for sale or sold as art objects shall be included, but books and magazines shall be excluded."[75] The law applies only to multiples sold for more than $100 exclusive of the frame.

The core of the law is a certificate of authenticity containing a body of information about the work that must accompany every fine-art multiple offered for sale, exchange, or consignment.[76] In addition, each time a multiple is offered for sale through a catalog, prospectus, or publication, the seller must include a disclosure paragraph dictated by the statute.[77] Any place of business that offers art multiples for sale must post a notice dictated by the statute notifying potential buyers of their rights under the law.[78]

The Farr Act contains a detailed list of information to be disclosed on the certificate of authenticity, including the name of the artist, whether the signature is on the multiple, whether the artist is alive or dead, the medium, the process of reproduction, the size of the limited edition, and the status of the master plate.[79] The specific information required varies with the kind of multiple involved and the date of its completion. The law provides for four periods and requires the most information for the most recent work: after 1983, from 1982 to 1950, from 1949 to 1900, and before 1900. The Farr Act has been criticized for the complexity of the information required, making compliance with the law a difficult task.

An art dealer who offers or sells a multiple in or from California is responsible, under a standard of strict liability, for certifying the accuracy of all the disclosed information.[80] Whenever an artist offers or sells a multiple of his own creation in or from California, the artist is required to disclose all of the information required under the Farr Act but is not otherwise regarded as an art dealer.[81]

For a purchaser to seek relief under the Farr Act, the work must first be returned to the seller. Then the act offers civil remedies but no criminal punishment. The injured buyer can seek rescission with interest, reasonable attorney's fees, treble damages for willful noncompliance, and any other damages or other remedies otherwise available in the particular situation.[82]

New York

Passed in 1982 and amended in 1991 to extend protection to purchasers of sculpture in multiples (discussed later in this chapter), New York's act[83] was modeled on the California statute and retains most of its features: written disclosure of similar information with all sales and consignments, a notification paragraph to be included in all catalog selling of multiples,[84] a posted notice in the place of business,[85] and a similar range of civil remedies.[86] In New York, however, injunctions are reserved for the attorney general, and civil penalties are limited to $500.[87]

The greatest difference between the California law and the New York law is that New York does not hold the merchant-dealer to a standard of strict liability.[88] Furthermore, if the selling art dealer "can establish that his liability results from incorrect information which was provided by the consignor, artist or merchant to him in writing" and on which the dealer relied, then the dealer, along with the purchaser, may look to the selling artist-merchant for remedies.[89]

Other States

Arkansas, Georgia, Hawaii, Illinois, Iowa, Maryland, Massachusetts, Michigan, Minnesota, North Carolina, Oregon, Rhode Island and South Carolina have laws protecting consumers in the purchase of art multiples.[90] Statutes in those states are less rigorous and less inclusive than in California and New York, although each statute is based on the concept of written disclosure and most statutes[91] require the name of the artist, the year of the printing, the size and the specifications of limited editions, the demise of the plate, whether the work is posthumous, and the name of the workshop where the edition was printed.

In most states, the plaintiff's recovery is limited to the purchase price of the print plus interest, unless willful violation is found; in such an event, damages of treble the purchase price may be awarded.

Are Print-Disclosure Statutes Effective?

Although the intention of print-disclosure statutes—to eradicate print fraud by informing the purchaser of exactly what he is buying—is admirable, the statutes lack bite. First, with the exception of New York and California, the statutes create a purely private right of action; if the aggrieved buyer does not pursue the action, the state cannot intervene. Moreover, an aggrieved buyer often fails to bring such an action; the buyer may be unaware that the purchased print is a forgery or, as a connoisseur, may not wish his ignorance to be brought to light. Second, although New York's and California's laws do empower each state's attorney general to bring suit when a private party does not, the imposition by a court of merely civil penalties—such as rescission, court costs, interest, expert witness fees, treble damages for willful noncompliance, and injunctive relief—will not deter the determined forger. Significantly, as of this writing, only two cases exist, one in California[92] and one in Hawaii,[93] that refer to the print-disclosure legislation.

In addition to lacking the necessary force to discourage fraud, the statutes' complexity—particularly in California, New York, and Michigan—actually discourages compliance. Dealers are required to provide to the purchasers considerable detailed information as to each fine print to be sold and, in California, New York, and Michigan, to determine the date of the print's production and then decipher the date codes in order to determine what information to provide to the purchaser.

All that is not to say that print-disclosure state statutes are without merit; far from it. However, they could be made more effective. It has been suggested,[94] first, that the language and the organization of the statutes be simplified, thereby encouraging compliance by the dealers. Second, the statutes might include the criminal penalties of fines and imprisonment to discourage forgery and other fraudulent practices. Third, the artist must bear the burden of furnishing to the dealer (who, in turn, discloses to the public) the accurate information required by statute regarding the artist's prints. If the artist sells directly to the public, the artist under the disclosure legislation should be considered a dealer, subject to the same strict liability and the same penalties as a merchant-dealer.

Other Proposals to Curb Fraudulent Practices

Aside from print-disclosure legislation, a number of other solutions have been proposed for eradicating fraud in the print market. For example, to ensure authenticity, an art registry, organized by the names of the artists or the sellers, might be established to record all transactions regarding art multiples.[95] When a buyer purchases a print, the artist or the seller would file with a central administrative agency certified material, including a photograph of the print and information identifying the buyer. If the print is resold, the seller would record the transaction, listing the new owner. Collector, artist, dealer, and law enforcement officers alike would have access to the registry information. In theory that may be a good idea, but its effectiveness depends on the cooperation of each artist or seller, as the case may be, in filing the requisite information with the art registry. To the extent that the party obligated to file finds the requirements burdensome and fails to fulfill them, the registry's effectiveness is diminished.

A second idea proposed to assure authenticity involves the creation of an identification system whereby the artist would affix each artwork with

> a fingerprint preserved by a chemical treatment or a special design and code impressed in a color of the spectrum with a high atomic weight that is discernible via x-rays or ultraviolet light."[96]

Of course, the system could only apply to artworks created after its formation and, as with the earlier suggestion, its efficacy would depend on the cooperation of each artist.

More promising, it seems, is still another idea addressing authenticity disputes, a new idea that has already been implemented by the San Francisco-based firm of Verification Technologies, Inc. On the basis of the premise that all objects contain unique microscopic anomalies that cannot be duplicated, the firm has developed a digital registration process known as Intrinsic Signature Identification System (ISIS) that, by using a high-powered video-microscope, magnifies and photographs details of an artwork.[97] The photograph is then formatted and encrypted onto a registration record that is stored in the company's computer archive, along with descriptive text. How extensively the system will be used remains to be seen, but the enterprise seems to be off to a propitious start.

Suggestions have also been made with a view to curbing perversions of edition size. For example, one commentator who is also a professional print artist has proposed that throughout the print-making process each party responsible for a particular stage of the process should, in addition, verify the controls applied to make sure that the print edition is truly limited in accordance with its description.[98] To ensure a properly limited graphic-print edition, the commentator proposes that the artist either remain in attendance for the full printing or require that the master printer (that is, the technical director) formally accept the responsibility, in the artist's place, to count "the number of blank sheets in the pile of edition paper which begins the printing, and count the sheets [having] signature-grade images on them at the completion of printing"[99] and to attest legally to that number. From the period of completion of printing to the day the artist signs and numbers the prints, the masters and the unsigned images must be safely locked away by the master printer. The moment the artist has completed signing and numbering the images, whether in the master printer's facility or in another location, the master printer must be notified and directed immediately to destroy all printing masters and intermediate images, to forward the fragments promptly to the artist, and to attest formally that those actions have been completed. The commentator suggests that metal plates be cut into pieces and that lithographic stones, which cannot reasonably be required to be destroyed, be permanently defaced with a sharp blade. Close-up photographs of the stones should be furnished to the artist.[100] The artist, too, has responsibilities in controlling a limited-edition size. For example, when an artist has finished signing and numbering (or otherwise identifying, as in the case of proofs) signature-grade images, some "overs" usually remain—excess, signature-grade images that are pulled in case the artist makes a few mistakes in signing and numbering. The artist must destroy or preside over the destruction of all such "overs" if the limited edition is to have integrity. Destruction can be effected, among other ways, by removing a triangular corner of the print that includes a portion of the image: Such a copy, along with other types of defaced copies, may be used by salespeople as a show print for dealers.[101]

Artist Versus Printer: A Copyright Issue

Besides preserving the integrity of the size of the limited edition, an artist must retain control of the print image for purposes of copyright. In 1993, a private ruling by the United States Copyright Office awarded the copyright in and to the reproductions of an image created by an artist to the unsuspecting printer, rather than to the artist.[102] In that case, the artist had for a decade been registering her underlying artworks and the resultant prints on a single application, in accordance with instructions from the Copyright Office. To comply with state print-disclosure laws, she included in small print, at the bottom of each reproduction, the edition size, the method of reproduction, and the printer's name. In reviewing some of her recent applications, the Copyright Office noticed the printer's name and, after contacting the artist and ascertaining that the artist did not herself print the reproductions, awarded the copyright in the reproductions to the printer. Its reasoning (disputed by the artist) was that the printer added enough originality to the process to make the reproductions derivative works. The artist subsequently had the printer assign any and all rights it may have had in the prints back to her, thereby avoiding the necessity of suing the Copyright Office in federal court in an attempt to effect a change in the ruling. Although the artist landed on her feet, the ruling stands, carrying the potential to throw into question copyright ownership of untold thousands of limited-edition prints, posters, and photographs.

What is an artist (or a publisher, if the publisher is to hold copyright) to do? For all future artworks, the artist (or the publisher), as a matter of course, should obtain from the printer a written assignment of any and all rights in and to the reproductions of the artwork before any work is performed. Such an assignment should be included in any agreement with the printer, and a separate assignment of copyright should be drawn up, executed, and filed with the Copyright Office. As to preexisting works, the artist or the publisher, on a case-by-case basis, may need to obtain such a written assignment from the printer of all rights held by the printer in the reproductions—that is, derivative work.

SCULPTURE MULTIPLES

The multiple—that is, a three-dimensional artwork made in quantity—carries a historic tradition rooted in the Renaissance; as early as the fifteenth century, workshops and, later, factories produced bronze and porcelain statuary in limited amounts or editions.[103] Those multiples were sold at a lower price than were unique artworks, yet the multiples still retained their desirability as original works of art.[104] In 1959, the artist Daniel Spoerri established the Parisian firm Editions M.A.T. (Multiplication Arts Transformable), which produced multiples in editions of one hundred at reasonable prices by such modern artists as Man Ray, Victor Vasarely, Marcel Duchamp, and Alexander Calder.[105] The popularity of multiples among collectors who recognized investment potential in the art form soared with the rise in the 1960s of pop art, a movement that incorporated into its art mass-produced objects from daily life.[106]

Multiples Abuse

As in the print market, reproduction of sculpture has seen widespread abuse. Among the all-too-common practices here and abroad are the following:[107]

- Surmoulage, which is casting bronzes not from the artist's approved master waxes or plasters but from other bronzes made either by the artist in life or by the artist's estate

- Enlargement of a sculptor's work by someone other than the artist

- Casting a sculptor's work in a medium other than that clearly intended by the sculptor for the final version of his work without authorization

- The sale of inexpensive copies as valuable sculpture

- The representation of limited editions as being more limited than, in fact, they are

- The failure to disclose the existence of multiple copies of a sculpture

Those practices are inimical to the interests of both the artist and the public. The abuses denigrate the artist's right of control over his own castings; they violate the quality of the original sculptures, since the making of a second edition from a bronze, rather than a master wax or plaster, is of diminished definition; they cause the owners of the original work to see their piece devalued; and they cause confusion in the public mind as to the origins of a particular work.

A number of factors account for those abusive practices. One factor is the public's lack of understanding of the determinants that make a sculpture valuable. Other factors include technological advances in the production of sculpture multiples and a proliferation of deliberately exploitative marketing techniques.

Multiples Legislation

In an effort to curb abuse in the sculpture multiples market, New York on January 1, 1991, became the first and only state to implement a disclosure law exclusively aimed at transactions involving sculpture.[108] (California addresses sculpture multiples and fine prints in a single disclosure statute; that state's Farr Act is discussed earlier in this chapter. Rhode Island's multiples legislation, more limited in scope and also referred to earlier, addresses fine prints and sculpture multiples together.)

New York's enactment of sculpture multiples legislation was the culmination of more than twenty years of vigorous lobbying by collectors and dealers alike who sought to be spared the time and expenses involved in litigating accusations of fraud. Modeled after New York's disclosure statute for fine prints, New York's sculpture multiples legislation makes it illegal to produce, consign, or sell a sculpture valued at $1,500 or more that is produced on or after January 1, 1991, without disclosing in writing before or at the time of the transaction certain information, including the following:

- The name of the artist
- The title of the sculpture

- The name, if known, of the foundry or the person who produced, fabricated, or carved the sculpture
- The medium or the process used in producing the sculpture
- The dimensions of the sculpture
- The year the sculpture was produced
- The number of sculpture casts, according to the best information available, that were produced, fabricated, or carved as of the date of the sale
- Whether the artist was deceased when the sculpture was produced
- Whether the sculpture is authorized by the artist or, if the sculpture was produced after the artist's death, whether it was authorized in writing by the artist or by the estate, heirs, or other legal representatives of the artist

Additional information must be disclosed for works produced as limited editions on or after January 1, 1991. Among such additional information is the following:

- Whether and how the sculpture and the edition are numbered
- The size of the proposed or previous editions of the same sculpture
- Whether the artist intends to produce additional casts

The information required to be disclosed under the statute is deemed to be an express warranty by the seller, consignor, or party required to furnish such information. Record keeping regarding the production and the sale of sculptures created on or after January 1, 1991, is required of both foundries and dealers. Civil penalties of up to $5,000 a work can be imposed on foundries that mislabel or fail to identify their works with both the foundry's mark and the year the sculpture was made. In addition, anyone defacing or tampering with foundry marks is subject to criminal prosecution and a civil fine of up to $5,000. It is also illegal to produce or sell a counterfeit sculpture, multiple, or cast unless the phrase "This is a reproduction" is imprinted on each work in a clear, legible manner. The one medium specifically excluded by the law is glass.[109]

To date, no reported cases have tested New York's sculpture multiples legislation (or California's, for that matter), and the effectiveness of the legislation in combating abuses has yet to be determined.

Notes to Chapter 5

1. United States v. Schaefer, 2002 U.S. Dist. LEXIS 23082 (S.D. Ind. Nov. 25, 2002), *rev'd and remanded on an issue of sentencing*, 384 F.3d 326 (7th Cir. 2004).
2. Ctr. Art Galleries-Haw., Inc. v. United States, 875 F.2d 747 (9th Cir. 1989). *See* comments on case in chapter 3, pages 250–251.
3. ARTNEWSLETTER, Oct. 31, 1995, at 4.
4. N.Y. TIMES, Nov. 6, 1995, at C-11.
5. ARTNEWSLETTER, Oct. 31, 1995, at 4.
6. JOHN ROSS, CLARE ROMANO, & TIM ROSS, THE COMPLETE PRINTMAKER (1990). This is an excellent and comprehensive treatise on both the art and business of printmaking.
7. *Id.* at 2.
8. *Id.* at 1, 9–56.
9. *Id.* at 66.
10. *Id.* at 75.
11. *Id.*
12. *Id.* at 69, 76.
13. *Id.* at 71, 76.
14. *Id.* at 76.
15. *Id.* at 66–68, 75.
16. *Id.* at 68–70, 75.
17. *Id.* at 70–71, 75.
18. *Id.* at 76, 131–32.
19. *Id.* at 143–44.
20. *Id.* at 144–45.
21. *Id.* at 191–96.
22. *See generally* MEL HUNTER, THE CURRENT SAD STATE OF THE PRINT MARKET (1993), a compilation of three thought-provoking essays on the curbing of abusive practices in the print market.
23. *Id.* at 65.
24. S. Natzmer, *Art Prints: The Michigan Art Multiples Sales Act*, 83 MICH. B. J. 30 (Feb. 2004).

25. ROSS, *supra* note 6, at 306.

26. *Id.* at 307.

27. HUNTER, *supra* note 22, at 67.

28. ROSS, *supra* note 6, at 306.

29. *Id.*

30. *Id.*

31. *Id.*

32. *Id.*

33. *Id.*

34. HUNTER, *supra* note 22, at 35.

35. ROSS, *supra* note 6, at 307.

36. *Id.*

37. INTERNATIONAL FINE PRINT DEALERS ASSOCIATION, WHAT IS A PRINT? 17 (1995).

38. David Tunick, Inc. v. Kornfeld, 838 F. Supp. 848, 851 (S.D.N.Y. 1993). *But see* W.C. Lowengrub, *Unique or Ubiquitous: Art Prints and the Uniform Commercial Code*, 72 IND. L.J. 595 (Spring 1997).

39. INTERNATIONAL FINE PRINT DEALERS ASSOCIATION, *supra* note 37, at 11.

40. *Id.*

41. *Id.* at 12.

42. *Id.* at 13.

43. The term "matrix" in the categories refers to the material on which the image to be printed is prepared. A matrix, for example, may be a metal plate, a wood block, a linoleum block, or a smooth stone.

44. HUNTER, *supra* note 22, at 14.

45. *Id.* at 21–25.

46. *Id.* at 19.

47. FTC v. Magui Publishers, Inc., Civ. No. 89-3818, 1991 U.S. Dist. LEXIS 20452 (C.D. Cal. Mar. 15, 1991). *See* chapter 3, pages 251–252.

48. 15 U.S.C. § 45(a).

49. *See Magui Publishers*, 1991 U.S. Dist. LEXIS 20452, at *31.

50. *Id.* at *34.

51. FTC v. Fed. Sterling Galleries, Inc., No. 87-2072 (D. Ariz. Jan. 12, 1989); FTC v. Austin Galleries of Ill., Inc., No. 88 C 3845, 1988 U.S. Dist. LEXIS 12380 (N.D. Ill. Nov. 2, 1988).

52. New Mexico v. Caven, Dist. Ct., 2d Jud. Dist., #44201.

53. *Magui Publishers*, 1991 U.S. Dist. LEXIS 20452, at *35.

54. *Id.* at *39.

55. 15 U.S.C. § 45(a).

56. 15 U.S.C. § 53(b).

57. *Magui Publishers*, 1991 U.S. Dist. LEXIS 20452, at *45.

58. Galerie Furstenberg v. Coffaro, 697 F. Supp. 1282 (S.D.N.Y. 1988). *See also* FTC v. Hang-Ups Art Enters., Inc., CV95-0027, 1995 U.S. Dist. LEXIS 21444 (C.D. Cal. Sept. 26, 1995). In this case the defendant, a California auctioneer of art, violated FTC regulations by falsely representing that a quantity of Miró, Dalí, Chagall, and Picasso prints being auctioned were authentic. (In conducting charity auctions, the auctioneer would split resultant sales proceeds with the sponsoring organization.) To settle charges, the defendant auctioneer agreed to a proposed consent judgment whereby it would pay $150,000 into a fund to be distributed to consumers. The defendant was also prohibited from making any false claims with respect to the nature of any art it auctioned in the future. *See also* Balog v. Ctr. Art Gallery-Haw., Inc., 745 F. Supp. 1556 (D. Haw. 1990), discussed in chapter 3, pages 302–303.

59. *See Galerie Furstenberg*, 697 F. Supp. at 1286.

60. *Id.*

61. *Id.* at 1287.

62. *Id.*

63. *Id.*

64. *Id.* at 1288.

65. *Id.*

66. *See, e.g.*, Perkins v. Hartford Ins. Group, 932 F.2d 1392 (11th Cir. 1991) (regarding the disposal in a dumpster of extra prints which were then distributed). *See also* Walt Disney Prods. v. Basmajian, 600 F. Supp. 439 (S.D.N.Y. 1984) (former Disney employee amassed valuable collection of discarded animated Disney cels; when, years later, he sought to auction the collection through Christie's, Disney sought to enjoin the sale, claiming title to cels; employee was awarded title and sold the collection for $496,110—nearly twice the presale estimate).

67. Wildlife Internationale, Inc. v. Clements, 591 F. Supp. 1542 (S.D. Ohio 1984).

68. *Id.* at 1544.

69. *Id.* at 1546.

70. *Id.* at 1548.

71. *Id.*

72. *Id.*

73. Winn v. Edna Hibel Corp., 858 F.2d 1517 (11th Cir. 1988).

74. *See, e.g.*, Shuman v. United States, 891 F.2d 557 (9th Cir. 1990), *cert. denied*, 495 U.S. 933 (1990); Hunter v. Comm'r, 51 T.C.M. (CCH) 1533, T.C. Memo 1986-308 (1986).

75.　CAL. CIV. CODE § 1740 et seq.

76.　Id. § 1740(j).

77.　Id. § 1742(b).

78.　Id. § 1742(c).

79.　Id. § 1744.

80.　Id. § 1745(a).

81.　Id. § 1742(e).

82.　Id. § 1745(a), (b), (d), (e).

83.　N.Y. ARTS & CULT. AFF. LAW § 11.01, § 13.05, and § 15.01 et seq.

84.　Id. § 15.01(2).

85.　Id. § 15.01(3).

86.　Id. § 15.15.

87.　Id. § 15.17.

88.　Id. § 15.15(2).

89.　Id. § 15.13(5). See Wesselmann v. Int'l Images, Inc., N.Y.L.J., May 2, 1996, at 30, col. 3 (Sup. Ct. N.Y. County 1996), discussed in detail in chapter 1. In a case of first impression, *Wesselmann* makes clear that a publisher and seller of prints is an art merchant within the meaning of the N.Y. Arts and Cultural Affairs Law. By implication, a publisher also bears liability for misrepresentation, error, or omission.

90.　ARK. CODE ANN. § 4-73-301 et seq.; GA. CODE ANN. § 10-1-430 et seq.; HAW. REV. STAT. ANN. § 481F et seq.; 815 ILL. COMP. STAT. ANN. 345/1 et seq.; IOWA CODE ANN. § 715B.1 et seq.; MD. CODE ANN., COM. LAW § 14-501 et seq.; MASS. ANN. LAWS, ch. 94, § 277C; MICH. COMP. LAWS § 442.351a et seq.; MINN. STAT. ANN. § 324.06 et seq.; N.C. GEN. STAT. § 25C-10 et seq.; OR. REV. STAT. § 359.300 et seq.; R.I. GEN. LAWS § 5-62-11 et seq.; S.C. CODE § 39-16-10 et seq.

91.　The disclosure statutes in Massachusetts and Rhode Island are far less stringent.

92.　Grogan-Beall v. Ferdinand Roten Galleries, Inc., 133 Cal. App. 3d 969, 184 Cal. Rptr. 411 (1982).

93.　Vazquez v. Ctr. Art Gallery, 485 F. Supp. 1015 (D.C. 1980).

94.　For an excellent discussion of fine print state legislation throughout the United States, and its shortcomings, see Katherine Marik Thompson, *Regulation of Fine Art Multiples*, 10 ENT. & SPORTS LAW. 8 (Summer 1992).

95.　Id. at 13.

96.　Id.

97.　*Art; Have Forgers Finally Met Their Match?*, L.A. TIMES, July 2, 1995, at 50.

98. HUNTER, *supra* note 22, at 25.

99. *Id.* at 31.

100. *Id.* at 32.

101. *Id.* at 35.

102. Joshua J. Kaufman, *So Whose Prints Are They, Anyway?* ART BUS. NEWS, Jan. 1993, at 1. *Cf. Wesselmann, supra* note 89.

103. ROBERT ATKINS, ARTSPEAK 106 (1990).

104. *Id.*

105. *Id.*

106. *Id.*

107. For an excellent discussion of sculpture abuse and available means of protection, *see* DuBoff, *Bronze Sculptures: Casting Around for Protection*, 3 CARDOZO ARTS & ENT. L.J. 235 (1984).

108. N.Y. ARTS & CULT. AFF. LAW §§ 11.01, 14.05, 14.06, 14.07, 14.08, 15.01, 15.03, 15.05, 15.07, 15.09, 15.10, 15.11, 15.13, 15.15, 15.17, 15.19.

109. *Id.* § 11.01.11.

6

Commissioned Works

Commissioning an artist to create a work of art is fraught with problems. What must the artist do, and who is to determine if the agreement has been fulfilled? Having a clear and understandable agreement is important to both the artist and the purchaser.

PRIVATE COMMISSIONS

There should always be a written agreement between the artist and the person who commissions the artist to create a work of art. Any agreement should include the following terms and conditions:

- Brief description of what is to be created
- Medium to be used
- Size of the work

- Time when the work of art is to be completed
- Agreement as to sketches and models
- Location of delivery and installation and who pays for any shipping charges and the cost of installation
- Price and a payment schedule for the work
- Agreement as to who owns the copyright
- What happens if the artist becomes ill or dies before completion and what happens if the artist simply does not complete the work
- Inspection of the work in progress
- Insurance coverage during creation
- Satisfaction of the purchaser

Purchaser Satisfaction

When an artist agrees to perform to the satisfaction of the commissioning party (that is, the purchaser), misunderstandings abound. The artist may think she has created a masterpiece, but the purchaser may be completely dissatisfied. The general rule is that if the agreement provides that the commissioning party must be satisfied, the fact that her dissatisfaction is completely unreasonable is not relevant. That rule is illustrated by several cases on point, both old and recent.

In *Zaleski v. Clark*,[1] an action was brought in 1876 by the artist, Zaleski, against Mrs. Clark, for whom the artist had made a bust of her deceased husband. The artist never dealt directly with Mrs. Clark; he was represented by another person acting as his agent. The agent, without the artist's knowledge, represented to Mrs. Clark that there was no risk, since "she need not take it [the bust] unless she was satisfied with it." The court found that the artist's agent had general authority to make the contract and that under the contract Mrs. Clark had to be satisfied; therefore, the artist had not completed the contract. The court stated:

It is not enough to say that she [Mrs. Clark] ought to be satisfied with it, and that her dissatisfaction is unreasonable. She, and not the court, is entitled to be the judge of that. The contract was not to make one that she ought to be satisfied with, but to make one that she would be satisfied with.[2]

In *Pennington v. Howland*,[3] an action was brought in 1898 by the artist, Pennington, against Howland, for whom the artist had painted a portrait of his wife. Howland testified that, over his objections, the artist began to paint the portrait of Mrs. Howland in street dress and hat. Howland said that the artist stated that "it was an artistic idea which he wished to carry out and that if it was not satisfactory he would paint the defendant one 'until satisfied.'" The artist testified that the defendant accepted the portrait. The court held the following:

When the subject of the contract is one which involves personal taste or feeling, an agreement that it shall be satisfactory to the buyer necessarily makes him the sole judge whether it answers that condition. He cannot be required to take it because other people might be satisfied with it; for that is not what he agreed to do. Personal tastes differ widely, and if one has agreed to submit his work to such a test he must abide by the result.[4]

The court distinguished the line of cases that require work to be performed in "a satisfactory manner" from the case at hand, in which the work had to be performed to the satisfaction of Howland.

The 1940 case of *Wolff v. Smith*[5] involved a disagreement between an artist and the commissioning party about a portrait of the commissioning party's deceased father. The court, in finding against the artist, cited the well-established applicable principles of law: In contracts involving matters of fancy, taste, or judgment, where one party agrees to perform to the satisfaction of the other, the first party renders the other party the sole judge of what is satisfaction without regard to the justice or the reasonableness of the decision, and a court or a jury cannot say that the second party should have been satisfied. Where the subject of a contract is one that involves personal taste or feeling, an agreement that it be satisfactory to the promisor necessar-

ily makes that person the sole judge of whether it answers that condition. The person cannot be required to take it because other
people ought to be satisfied with it, for that is not what the person
agreed to do.[6]

There is no substitute for a clear written contract that defines the
understanding between the artist and the commissioning party (that
is, the purchaser). Such an agreement should specify at what points
during the process of creation payments will be made and what portion of those payments are refundable if the work of art is not satisfactory. The artist needs an agreement that defines the acceptance of
the work of art when a model or sketches are approved by the purchaser. And the purchaser needs an agreement that reserves the decision on acceptance until the work is complete and the purchaser is
completely satisfied. (See the private commission agreements at the
end of this chapter, Appendixes 6-1 and 6-2.)

Copyright Ownership

When a commissioning party engages an artist to create a particular
work, who owns the copyright in that work—the artist or the commissioning party? That question is addressed in considerable detail in
chapter 10, but a brief treatment of the issues involved is appropriate
here. Case law under the 1909 Copyright Act—which applies to
works created before January 1, 1978, that are still under copyright
protection—looked to the parties' intent, where cognizable,[7] in determining whether the copyright to a work was initially vested in the
independent contractor–artist or in the commissioning party. Where
that intention was not expressly stated, most case law generally held
that the copyright in the work was initially vested in the commissioning party.[8]

Unlike the 1909 Act, the 1976 Copyright Act—which applies to
works created on or after January 1, 1978—codified the conditions
under which a specially commissioned work causes the copyright to
be vested initially in the commissioning party. To wit:[9] both parties
must expressly agree in a mutually signed written instrument that the

work shall be considered "a work made for hire," and the work must fall into one of the following nine categories:

(1) contributions to collective works;

(2) parts of motion pictures or other audiovisual works;

(3) translations;

(4) supplementary works;

(5) compilations;

(6) instructional texts;

(7) tests;

(8) answer materials for tests;

(9) atlases.

If a commissioned work under the 1976 Act does not satisfy both requirements, the copyright is initially vested in the commissioned artist.[10]

Although the statute is clear enough on that point, there are situations in which the commissioning party, as well as the artist, contributes to the preparation and the creation of the work. Such a situation raises the question of joint copyright ownership—that is, if a court finds that the commissioning party and the artist prepared the work "with the intention that their contributions be merged into inseparable or interdependent parts of a unitary whole,"[11] copyright is initially vested in both parties. Not surprisingly, the issue of joint copyright has been raised in a significant amount of litigation involving commissioned works.[12] *Community for Creative Non-Violence (CCNV) v. Reid*,[13] treated in detail in chapter 10, is one such example.

Community for Creative Non-Violence (CCNV), a nonprofit association devoted to the welfare of homeless people, retained the artist James Earl Reid in the fall of 1985 to create a sculptured Nativity scene dramatizing the plight of the homeless to be exhibited in the annual Christmastime Pageant of Peace in Washington, D.C. The agreement was made orally with little more than a handshake, and copyright in the sculpture was not discussed. CCNV had conceived the idea for the nature of the sculpture: A modern Nativity scene in which two life-sized black adult figures and their infant would appear as contemporary homeless people huddled on a streetside steam grate. The grate would be atop a platform base, within which equipment would produce simulated steam that would rise through the grid to swirl about the figures. CCNV also created a title for the work, *Third World America*, and a legend for the base: "and still there is no room at the inn." The artist Reid was engaged to sculpt the three human figures. CCNV made the steam grate and the base for the statue.

A few months after Reid delivered the statue to CCNV, a dispute arose between the two parties, and Reid and CCNV subsequently filed competing certificates of copyright registration. The United States Supreme Court affirmed the District of Columbia circuit court's holding that although CCNV was not the author of *Third World America*, it could, by virtue of the 1976 Act's work-for-hire provisions, on remand to the federal district court, be held by that court to be a joint author with Reid.[14]

In January 1991, the District of Columbia federal district court entered a consent judgment, confirming exclusive ownership of the original sculpture in CCNV, conferring exclusive ownership of the copyright for three-dimensional reproductions on Reid, and acknowledging joint ownership of the copyright for two-dimensional reproductions, thereby presumably ending the protracted litigation.[15]

So vituperative, however, were the parties that later that year the case came yet again before the federal district court.[16] Apparently, Reid wished to make a mold of the sculpture to capitalize on his exclusive three-dimensional reproduction rights. CCNV, in possession of the sculpture, refused to grant Reid access. Accordingly, it required a court order to direct CCNV to deliver *Third World America* to a craftsman of Reid's choice for the sole purpose of making a master mold. Reid, in turn, was required to insure the sculpture adequately while it was in his possession and to return it to CCNV within a month.

PUBLIC COMMISSIONS

An unprecedented boom in the public commission of works of art has resulted from the laws passed by various states that require commercial buildings to allocate a percentage of total construction costs for the purchase of artwork for display in public areas of the building, the efforts of the General Services Administration (GSA) and the National Endowment for the Arts, and the efforts of countless municipalities that want their own artwork. Although many public commissions are for paintings, most seem to be for sculptures, which demand more time, materials, and expense for the artist. A public commission always entails a formal contract, and an artist should always have legal representation before signing any commission agreement for a public work of art.[17]

Checklist for a Commission Agreement

At the end of this chapter is the model form of the General Services Administration contract for fine-art services (see Appendix 6-3). The contract is the result of the federal government's art-in-architecture program, under which major works of art are commissioned for incorporation into federal buildings. Also attached to this chapter is a copy of a public-commission contract that was used by Battery Park City Authority in New York City (see Appendix 6-4). Public-commission contracts for municipalities and other public agencies vary but cover the same general issues discussed below. Each issue must be discussed with the artist before she becomes involved in a public commission. If basic terms are not complied with or not understood, a public commission can turn into an unpleasant experience for the artist.

Manner of Selection

Generally, a public commission is awarded after a competition or a review by a selection committee. The artist should fully understand how the process works, who is on the selection committee, and what happens to any models or sketches submitted.

Terms Defined

As in any good contract, a section should define as many terms peculiar to the contract as possible, including design, fabrication, transportation, completion, acceptance, permanent installation, access, site, artist's illness, materials, and labor.

Artist's Services

What is the artist to do, and how is it to be done? The contract should be specific when it comes to the artist's responsibility for fabrication, transportation, and installation. The contract should accurately describe the materials, size, color, and purpose of the artwork. Most public commissions require a model and detailed specifications of the costs of full-scale construction. If the artist is to have artistic freedom to vary the design, even if only slightly, that flexibility must be written into the contract. The artist must be able to price her costs, since public commissions are generally fixed-price contracts, not cost-plus contracts. The artist must understand that the costs of materials and labor may increase over the period during which the work of art is made, and some flexibility for that increase should be built into the contract.

Completion Time

The artist must be given a reasonable amount of time to complete the work of art. The artist may not be able to meet the deadline for the opening of the building if enough time is not allowed. The artist, particularly one who has not previously worked on a public commission, must be made to understand that she has the responsibility to complete the work in a timely fashion. If possible, some leeway should be in the contract to cover illness, other unusual personal circumstances of the artist, and unusual fabrication or installation problems that were unforeseen at the inception. Obviously, strikes, material shortages, fires, and the like are beyond the control of the artist.

The commission may call for periodic progress reports and inspections. The artist who believes that such reports and inspections may interfere with her creative abilities should not accept a public commission. The artist is dealing with a bureaucracy, and its rules demand compliance.

Structural Requirements

The public commission may require the artist to obtain a structural engineer's report, and the artist must include that report in her costs. Even if such a report is not required, the artist is well advised to obtain as complete an engineering report as possible for her own protection in case the work of art falls or breaks and injures someone.

Installation and Maintenance

The contract should be specific as to exactly where the work of art is to be installed. Although the contract may call for the installation to be permanent, circumstances may require its removal. The artist should attempt to obtain a provision that requires the artist to be consulted if the work of art is to be removed to another site. (See the discussion of the *Tilted Arc* case below.)

The contract should specify who is to prepare the site for installation, the cost of the preparation, and the timing of the preparation.

The contract must cover the responsibility for the work of art during its on-site installation. Often, an artist resides hundreds of miles from the installation site, and the work must be protected during the time the artist is not present.

Payment

The artist must obtain a schedule of payments, so that she does not face large bills for fabrication costs with no funds to pay the bills. Ideally, the artist should have the entity that commissioned the work of art pay the engineering, materials, fabrication, and other costs directly, based on specific estimates. The contract should also provide a fee schedule for payment to the artist and the method and the timing of final acceptance of the work and final payment.

Nonperformance Clause

A nonperformance clause should cover both the artist and the commissioning entity. The artist must be protected for costs and expenses if full funding for the commission is not forthcoming. The entity that commissioned the work of art must also be protected in case the artist does not complete the artwork in a timely manner or does not complete it in accordance with agreed-on specifications.

Insurance Coverage

The artist may be required to take out a comprehensive liability insurance policy and to pay the full premium. If the contract is not examined carefully, the artist may not realize until too late that the cost of the insurance wipes out the entire profit on the commission. The artist or the artist's representative must examine the indemnification provisions and understand just what the artist is responsible for. Generally, the artist bears the risk of loss until the work of art is finally accepted, and any risk should be covered by insurance.

Warranties

The public commission may require the artist to warrant the work of art against defective materials and workmanship. The artist's attorney should argue that any such warranty be only for a limited period of time. If the work of art is a painted sculpture that is to be located outdoors, provision should be made for repainting it, and the contract should specify who pays for the repainting. The language pertaining to the sculpture's not presently being a danger to any person should be modified so that once the work of art is accepted, the responsibility for the safety of the public shifts to the entity that commissioned the work. Any warranty clause must be examined and reviewed with the artist in detail.

Models and Sketches

Ownership of models and sketches must be addressed in the commission contract.

Copyright

If the public commission is from the federal government, the copyright cannot be retained by the artist. In other public commissions, the artist may retain the copyright, and that fact can be covered in the contract. The artist may want to protect the work of art from being used on posters, stationery, T-shirts, and the like. Further, the contract may require the artist to warrant that the work of art being created is unique and that no future work will be the same or similar. The word "similar" is too broad; the contract must define just what future works may be prohibited, so as not to restrict unduly the artist's creative abilities. The commissioning entity needs protection against the artist's creating identical works of art for someone else that would detract from the value and the uniqueness of the commissioned work of art.

Repair and Restoration

The contract should provide how and when any repairs or restoration should be done and, if the artist is alive, that the artist be consulted and paid for her time on any repair or restoration that may change the work of art.

Acceptance of the Artwork

Acceptance should not be subjective and dependent on final satisfaction of the entity that ordered the public commission. The work should be deemed approved on the basis of the model or sketches. And if it is built, made, constructed, or painted to specifications, it should be deemed accepted. That is an objective test, as opposed to the subjective test of satisfaction that the artist may encounter when dealing with a private commission.

An artist commissioned by a public entity cannot compel that entity to accept the resultant artwork—certainly not by way of the First Amendment. In *Silvette v. Art Commission of Virginia*,[18] a portrait painter, David Silvette, was commissioned late in 1973 or early 1974 to paint a portrait of Dr. Richard Lee Morton to be placed in Morton Hall at the College of William and Mary, a state institution. On February 8, 1974, Silvette delivered the finished portrait to the Art Commission of Virginia for approval as a gift to the state. On February 9, the commission called a special meeting to review the portrait and recommended to the governor of Virginia that on various aesthetic grounds the portrait not be accepted. To wit: The left hand was poorly painted, part of the necktie and some books in the painting were too prominent and therefore distracting, the subject appears not to be seated on the chair, and the shadows were poorly executed.[19]

The governor rejected the portrait on February 25, and Silvette, rather than making the suggested modifications, sued the Art Commission of Virginia on, among other theories, the grounds that sections 9-11 and 9-12 of the Code of Virginia violated his First Amendment right of free expression.

Section 9-11 provided in pertinent part the following:

> [No] work of art shall become the property of the State by purchase, gift or otherwise unless such work of art . . . shall have been submitted to and approved by the Governor acting with the advice and counsel of the Art Commission . . . ; nor shall [the provisions of this section] apply to any portrait, tablet or work of art acquired by museums operated in conjunction with art or architectural departments at State colleges or universities.[20]

Section 9-12 provided in pertinent part the following:

> [No] work of art shall be so accepted until submitted to the Art Commission or otherwise brought to its attention for its advice and counsel to the Governor.[21]

In rejecting Silvette's claim, the federal district court noted that

> the authority to accept gifts tendered the State of Virginia was delegated by the General Assembly to the Governor of Virginia with the advice and counsel of the Art Commission—[which is] compatible with Virginia law.[22]

As the court further noted, that does not mean that administrative officers cannot have discretion in administering the law. Sections 9-11 and 9-12, far from abridging an artist's First Amendment rights, merely delineate the means by which the Commonwealth of Virginia may acquire artwork. The court compared the advisory function of the art commission to that of a law review's editorial board in that each involves "an assessment of judgment."[23] The commission's duty to counsel and advise includes the right to state the underlying reasons. As the court noted, the artist is free to accept or reject suggested changes posed by the commission, but she cannot compel the commonwealth to accept and display her painting any more than an author can compel the publication of her article.[24]

Sales Taxes

If any sales taxes are due and have to be collected by the artist, the contract should provide that the entity that ordered the public commission pay those taxes.

Local Laws

Sometimes local zoning laws or other local laws or ordinances can cause delays or other problems with the installation. The contract should make the entity that ordered the public commission responsible for obtaining all permits and for dealing with any local problems of a legal nature.

Removal of the Artwork

Serra *Case*

The late 1980s case of *Serra v. United States General Services Administration*[25] illustrates the problems that can be encountered with a public commission. The case, which received enormous publicity, involved a commission awarded to the artist Richard Serra under the United States government's art-in-architecture program, which is administered by the General Services Administration (GSA). The GSA had a contract with Serra for an outdoor sculpture to be located in Federal Plaza in lower Manhattan. The sculpture was a 120-foot-long piece of steel, twelve feet tall, weighing seventy-three tons, entitled *Tilted Arc*. The sculpture cost $175,000. The GSA contract that Serra signed provided the following: "All designs, sketches, models and the work produced under this agreement . . . shall be the property of the United States of America."[26] The work was completed in December 1981, and Serra signed a general release in favor of the United States.

As soon as *Tilted Arc* was installed, the GSA began receiving complaints. Eventually, the complaints grew into an avalanche, and petitions with thousands of signatures called for the sculpture's removal. The GSA held public hearings, which generated great passion on both sides. Serra contended that his sculpture was site-specific and that its removal would effect a destruction of the work and would violate both the GSA contract and his constitutional rights. On the other side, some said that a once-beautiful plaza was rendered useless by an ugly rusted steel wall. After the hearing, the GSA decided to relocate the sculpture.

Serra brought suit in federal court, casting his complaint in multiple claims: breach of contract, copyright violation, trademark violation, violation of New York statutory law, and violation of his First and Fifth Amendment rights.

A New York federal district court held that it lacked jurisdiction to adjudicate Serra's contract, copyright, trademark, and state-law claims, because the United States had not waived its sovereign immunity. Under the doctrine of sovereign immunity, the United States government may not be sued without its consent, and the existence of consent is a prerequisite for jurisdiction.[27] The court so held even though Serra had not sued the United States directly but, instead, had sued the GSA and its three senior officials.

Serra argued that sovereign immunity was inapplicable, since the government had consented to district court jurisdiction to resolve the GSA contract claim under either the Tucker Act or the Administrative Procedure Act.[28] The court held that the government had not so consented under either act.

The court held that the Administrative Procedure Act expressly denies jurisdiction in the district court for Serra's copyright claim[29] and that no statute of the United States contains a consent from the United States that it may be sued for trademark infringement.[30] The court further noted that the trademark of *Tilted Arc* was not even at issue in the case, which was about the location of the sculpture. The court further dismissed any state-law claim, since no state had jurisdiction.[31]

Serra's constitutional claims were also dismissed. Serra contended that *Tilted Arc* was a constitutionally protected expression of free speech and that the government's actions to remove it violated his First Amendment rights. He further argued that the actions to remove the sculpture were in violation of the procedural due-process requirement of the Fifth Amendment.

The court outlined the extensive administrative procedures followed by the GSA and found no procedural due-process violation.

The court finally addressed the First Amendment question as to whether *Tilted Arc* was constitutionally protected expression and whether the GSA's decision to relocate the sculpture violated Serra's freedom of speech.[32] Without deciding whether *Tilted Arc* was speech entitled to First Amendment protection, the court assumed for the purpose of its decision that the sculpture was indeed expression protected to some extent by the First Amendment. But even so, Serra's First Amendment rights must be balanced against the authority and the mission of the GSA stemming from the Constitution itself and against the fact that Serra conveyed title in the work to the GSA.[33]

The court weighed Serra's First Amendment rights against the legitimate government interest, as determined by the GSA. The court found no evidence in the record that the GSA's decision to relocate the sculpture was based on the content of its message. The court concluded:

> GSA's decision to relocate Tilted Arc is a valid content-neutral determination. It furthers an important governmental interest unrelated to the suppression of speech and the incidental restriction on alleged First Amendment freedoms and is no greater than is essential to the furtherance of that interest.[34]

The government had not attempted to ban Serra's sculpture generally, and the argument that the sculpture was site-specific was not sufficient to paralyze the GSA's ability to reasonably manage government buildings. Therefore, the decision of the GSA to relocate *Tilted Arc* did not violate Serra's First Amendment rights.[35]

Serra appealed the decision to the Second Circuit, which affirmed the judgment of the district court.[36] The appeal was heard on the basis of the alleged violation of Serra's First Amendment right of freedom of speech and his Fifth Amendment right of due process.

The court once again reviewed the facts in the case, specifically recognizing that the contract that Serra signed, provided that "All designs, sketches, models and the work produced under this agreement . . . shall be the property of the United States of America."[37]

The court noted that the purpose of the First Amendment is to protect private expression, and nothing in the guarantee precludes the government from controlling its own expression or that of its agents.[38] The court found that the artistic expression belongs to the government, rather than to Serra, since under the contract he transferred all ownership rights to the government. Serra had the opportunity to bargain for the right to control the duration of the exhibition of his work when he made the contract for its sale. The court concluded that

[t]he Government's action in this case is limited to an exercise of discretion with respect to the display of its own property. . . . [N]othing GSA has done here encroaches in any way on Serra's or any other individual's right to communicate.[39]

The court went on to observe that even assuming that Serra retained some First Amendment interest in the continued display of *Tilted Arc*, the removal of the sculpture was a permissible time, place, and manner restriction. (First Amendment rights may be restricted, provided that the restrictions are justified without reference to the content of the regulated speech, that they are narrowly tailored to serve a significant governmental interest, and that they leave open ample alternative channels for communication of the information.)[40]

The court found that the GSA had a significant interest in keeping the plaza where the sculpture was installed unobstructed, an interest that may be furthered only by removing the sculpture. Further, the relocation of *Tilted Arc* would not preclude Serra from communicating his ideas in other ways. The court observed that the First Amendment protects the freedom to express one's views, not the freedom to continue speaking forever. The court went on to affirm the view of the district court that

[t]here is no evidence in the record that GSA's decision to relocate the sculpture was based on the content of its message. . . . GSA's decision to relocate the structure was undertaken for functional purposes—in order to regain the openness of the plaza.[41]

Serra also argued that under the holding of *Board of Education v. Pico*[42] he was entitled to a jury trial to determine whether, in fact, the removal of the sculpture was impermissibly content-based. The court recognized that the *Serra* case posed at least the potential for a *Pico*-type First Amendment violation. However, the court concluded that

[e]ven if we assume, without deciding, that Serra has standing to assert a *Pico*-type claim, it is clear that under any reading of the record in this case, the removal of "Tilted Arc" did not violate

the principles of *Pico*. . . . Serra has failed to present any facts to support a claim that Government officials acted in a narrowly partisan or political manner.[43]

In fact, the court went further when it stated that to the extent that the GSA's decision may have been motivated by the sculpture's lack of aesthetic appeal, the decision to remove it was still entirely permissible.

The court concluded that Serra's due-process claim failed as a matter of law, even if his factual allegations were accepted as true. The lengthy and comprehensive hearing that was provided was more process than what was due.[44]

In March 1989, *Tilted Arc* was removed from its location in Federal Plaza. The decision of the General Services Administration was that, if possible, it should remain in place until another suitable site was located. However, finding another suitable site proved to be more difficult than originally anticipated, so the sculpture was dismantled and carted away to a warehouse in Brooklyn where it remains today in pieces.[45]

Any artist contemplating a commissioned work would do well to review the *Serra* case carefully, so that she will be aware of the scope of the government's rights in connection with a commissioned work of art.

Comite Pro-Celebracion *Case*

Serra can be distinguished on First Amendment grounds from a more recent case, *Comite Pro-Celebracion v. Claypool.*[46] In *Serra*, the United States Government owned the sculpture itself and all designs, sketches, and models of it, thereby rendering slight any First Amendment rights the plaintiff may have had in the sculpture. Such was not the situation in *Comite Pro-Celebracion*, in which the plaintiff undertook to pay for both the erection and the continued maintenance of the sculpture.

The plaintiff was El Comite Pro-Celebracion, a committee largely of Puerto Rican residents of Chicago established to celebrate the centennial of the birth of Dr. Pedro Campos, a prominent figure in Puerto Rican politics and an advocate of Puerto Rican independence. The group sought in 1992 to erect and place a six-foot bronze statue of Dr. Campos in Humboldt Park, located in a predominantly Puerto Rican neighborhood of Chicago. As part of its proposal, El Comite Pro-Celebracion agreed to pay the expenses of maintaining the statue. Around November 1992, it received the requisite approval from the Chicago Public Art Advisory Committee, which in turn was to recommend to the board of the Chicago Park District that they accept the statue. Believing that board acceptance was virtually a foregone conclusion, El Comite raised $35,000 and proceeded to have the statue cast. However, in August 1993, the board officially refused to accept the statue; the new park superintendent opposed the plan because he disagreed with Dr. Campos's political beliefs and actions.

No statues of Puerto Ricans were located in the Chicago Park District parks or anywhere else in Chicago; however, the Chicago Park District had accepted and erected approximately sixteen monuments donated by Italian, German, Danish, Polish, Norwegian, Swedish, Bohemian, and Czechoslovakian organizations. El Comite sued the board of the Chicago Park District in the Illinois federal district court, asserting, among other claims, that the board violated its First Amendment rights when it refused to erect the statue. The defendant filed a motion to dismiss. In denying the board's motion to dismiss that claim, the court noted that in a First Amendment case involving an alleged abridgment of free speech a three-part inquiry is in order:[47]

(1) Is the proposed speech protected under the Constitution?

(2) Is the forum nonpublic (thereby giving the state greater than usual leeway to limit speech) or public?

(3) Are the state's proffered justifications for restricting speech sufficient to satisfy the standards applicable in that particular forum?

The federal district court found that the statue was an expressive structure entitled to at least some constitutional protection. The

court further found that Humboldt Park is a "quintessential traditional public forum,"[48] thereby limiting the board's ability to restrict
expression. As the court noted, a traditional public forum is a place
"whose use is 'inextricably linked with expressive activities.'"[49] Citing the United States Supreme Court, the court found the following:

> Wherever the title of streets and parks may rest, they have im-
> memorially been held in trust for the use of the public and time
> out of mind, have been used for purposes of assembly, commu-
> nicating between citizens and discussing public questions. Such
> use of the streets and public places has, from ancient times, been
> part of the privileges, immunities, rights and liberties of citi-
> zens.[50]

If, on the contrary, Humboldt Park was not a public forum, the state,
according to the court,[51] would have a great deal of discretion in determining how citizens may use the property or whether they may
use it at all.

The court then noted that the plaintiff alleged sufficient facts
from which the court could decide that the board's decision was content-based.[52] As the court observed, a content-based restriction of
speech in a public forum is invalid unless it is necessary to serve a
compelling state interest and is narrowly tailored to achieve that
end.[53] The court noted that although it was denying the defendant's
motion to dismiss the plaintiff's First Amendment claim, the defendant was certainly not precluded from giving evidence at a later date
that its rejection of the plaintiff's statue was narrowly drawn to serve
a significant governmental interest.[54]

In *Serra*, as seen, the government's restriction was not content-
based. Moreover, even if it had been, the government was able to
show that its restrictions were based on compelling state interests.

Temporary Artwork

Not all art is created to be permanent. An artist sometimes creates an installation piece—that is, a work of art designed for a particular space, often in conjunction with a show of the artist's work. The

artwork may have no practical sale value and is meant to be destroyed at the end of the show. At other times an artist creates a work under a public or private commission, and in either case the work has an effect on public space, even though the artwork is intended to be only temporary.

For example, the artists Christo and Jeanne-Claude have hung a curtain across a deep valley in Colorado, have made a fence of white nylon fabric running across twenty-four miles of Marin County, have wrapped in cloth the Pont Neuf in Paris, have installed in a simultaneous display a total of 3,100 unfurled umbrellas in Los Angeles and Japan, and have wrapped Berlin's Reichstag in silver fabric. From February 12 through February 27, 2005, Central Park in New York City was home to the *Gates*, approximately 7,500 gates festooned with saffron-colored fabric panels along twenty-three miles of Central Park's pedestrian walkways. Christo and Jeanne-Claude worked on the concept for the project (and raised the $20 million cost) for more than twenty years—although *Gates* would only be on display for fifteen days. Those public-space works of art were intended to be only temporary.[55]

The creation of an installation work or other temporary work should be covered by a written agreement. In addition to the terms noted earlier, the agreement should specify the duration of the work's existence, who has the authority to remove the work, how it should be removed, who will pay for its removal, whether it can be sold, what is to be done with any left-over materials, who owns any sketches or photographs, who owns the copyright, and whether the work can be removed before the end of its agreed-on existence if it is perceived as pornographic, defamatory, or otherwise offensive to the general public. A written agreement with respect to those terms is particularly important in light of the adoption in the United States of moral rights for artists under the Visual Artists Rights Act (discussed in chapter 11). If the work is on public property, as is Christo's work, permission from the appropriate authority must be obtained, and the agreement should specify whose responsibility it is to obtain that permission.

Notes to Chapter 6

1. Zaleski v. Clark, 44 Conn. 218 (1876). *See also* Zaleski v. Clark, 45 Conn. 397 (1877).

2. *Zaleski*, 44 Conn. at 219.

3. Pennington v. Howland, 21 R.I. 65, 41 A. 891 (1898).

4. *Id.*, 21 R.I. at 66.

5. Wolff v. Smith, 25 N.E.2d 399, 303 Ill. App. 413 (1940).

6. 17A AM. JUR. 2D *Contracts* § 648 (1991); *see* Erikson v. Ward, 107 N.E. 593, 266 Ill. 259 (1914); Kendall v. West, 63 N.E. 683, 196 Ill. 221 (1902).

7. *See* 1 MELVILLE B. NIMMER & DAVID NIMMER, NIMMER ON COPYRIGHT § 5.03[B][a][i] (2004).

8. *Id.*

9. 17 U.S.C. § 101.

10. Vane v. Fair, Inc., 676 F. Supp. 133 (E.D. Tex. 1987), *aff'd*, 849 F.2d 186 (5th Cir. 1988), *cert. denied*, 488 U.S. 1008 (1989).

11. 17 U.S.C. § 101.

12. *See, e.g.,* Johannsen v. Brown, 797 F. Supp. 835 (D. Or. 1992); Morita v. Omni Publ'ns Int'l, Ltd., 741 F. Supp. 1107 (S.D.N.Y. 1990), *vacated*, 760 F. Supp. 45 (S.D.N.Y. 1991); Strauss v. Hearst Corp., 8 U.S.P.Q.2d (BNA) 1832 (S.D.N.Y. 1988); Olan Mills, Inc. v. Eckard Drug of Tex., CA3-88-0333-D, 1989 U.S. Dist. LEXIS 13768 (N.D. Tex. Apr. 21, 1989).

13. Cmty. for Creative Non-Violence (CCNV) v. Reid, 652 F. Supp. 1453 (D.D.C. 1987), *rev'd*, 846 F.2d 1485 (Ct. App. D.C. 1988), *aff'd*, 490 U.S. 730 (1989).

14. *Id.*, 490 U.S. 730.

15. Cmty. for Creative Non-Violence (CCNV) v. Reid, No. 86-1507, 1991 U.S. Dist. LEXIS 21020 (D.D.C. Jan. 7, 1991).

16. Cmty. for Creative Non-Violence (CCNV) v. Reid, No. 86-1507, 1991 U.S. Dist. LEXIS 20227 (D.D.C. Oct. 16, 1991).

17. *See generally* J. MERRYMAN & A. ELSEN, LAW, ETHICS, AND THE VISUAL ARTS ch. 5 (2d ed. 1987); 1 F. FELDMAN, S. WEIL & S. BIEDERMAN, ART LAW ch. 4 (1986); Committee on Art Law of the Association of the Bar the City of New York, *Commissioning a Work of Public Art: An*

Annotated Model Agreement, 10 COLUM. J.L. & ARTS 1 (1985); Balfe & Wyszominski, *Public Art and Public Policy*, 15 J. ARTS MGMT. & L. 5 (Winter 1986); Martin & Smith, *Commissioning Public Works of Sculpture: An Examination of the Contract*, 12 COLUM. J.L. & ARTS 505 (1988).

18.   Silvette v. Art Comm'n of Va., 413 F. Supp. 1342 (E.D. Va. 1976).

19.   *Id.* at 1343.

20.   *Id.* at 1344.

21.   *Id.*

22.   *Id.* at 1345.

23.   *Id.* at 1346.

24.   *Id.*

25.   Serra v. United States Gen. Servs. Admin., 667 F. Supp. 1042 (S.D.N.Y. 1987), *aff'd*, 847 F.2d 1045 (2d Cir. 1988). *See also* Serra v. United States Gen. Servs. Admin., 664 F. Supp. 798 (S.D.N.Y. 1987).

26.   *Id.*, 667 F. Supp. at 1044. *See* chapter 11 for a discussion of the moral rights issues raised by this case despite the U.S. government's ownership of the physical chattel.

27.   *Id.* at 1046; United States v. Mitchell, 463 U.S. 206 (1983).

28.   Tucker Act, 28 U.S.C. § 1346(a)(2), grants jurisdiction in the district court in certain limited situations covering claims against the United States in amounts not exceeding $10,000. The limited jurisdiction over contract claims was withdrawn by the Contract Disputes Act, 41 U.S.C. §§ 601–13. *See also* Administrative Procedure Act, 5 U.S.C. § 702.

29.   *Serra*, 667 F. Supp. at 1051; 5 U.S.C. § 702; 28 U.S.C. § 1498(b).

30.   *Serra*, 667 F. Supp. at 1051.

31.   *Id.* at 1052. Serra's state law claim was based on N.Y. ARTS & CULT. AFF. LAW § 14.03, which prohibits the public display of an artwork in an altered, defaced, mutilated, or modified form without the artist's consent.

32.   *See* chapter 9 for a detailed discussion of the First Amendment rights of artists.

33.   *Serra*, 667 F. Supp. at 1055.

34.   *Id.* at 1056.

35.   *Id.* at 1057.

36.   *Id.* at 1045.

37.   *Id.* at 1047.

38.   *Id.* at 1048.

39.   *Id.* at 1049.

40.   Clark v. Cmty. for Creative Non-Violence, 468 U.S. 288, 293 (1984). *See* chapter 9 of the text where the case is discussed.

41.   *Serra*, 847 F.2d at 1050.
42.   Bd. of Educ. v. Pico, 457 U.S. 853 (1982), where the Supreme Court held, in a case involving the removal of books from a school library by the local school board, that such discretion may not be exercised in a narrowly partisan or political manner.
43.   *Serra*, 847 F.2d at 1050–51.
44.   *Id*. at 1052.
45.   R.J. Sherman, *The Visual Artists Rights Act of 1990: American Artists Burned Again*, 17 CARDOZO L. REV. 373 (1995). As an example of the difficulty in situations like this, Richard Serra was a defendant in a lawsuit in the early 1970s involving a worker helping to install a two-piece sculpture by Serra; the worker was killed when one of the steel plates fell over. The jury found that the fault was with the steel fabricator, for using a poor technique in making the piece, and the rigger, for failing to follow instructions. Serra was absolved of any blame in the accident. In October 1988, two workers were injured when a sixteen-ton steel sculpture by Serra toppled over when the workers were removing the sculpture from the Leo Castelli gallery. *See* N.Y. TIMES, Oct. 27, 1988, at B6.
46.   Comite Pro-Celebracion v. Claypool, 863 F. Supp. 682 (N.D. Ill. 1994).
47.   *Id*. at 686.
48.   *Id*. at 687.
49.   *Id*.
50.   *Id*.
51.   *Id*.
52.   *Id*. at 688.
53.   *Id*.
54.   *Id*. at 689.
55.   Carol Vogel, *Work Begins on Colossal Artwork-in-the-Park*, N.Y. TIMES, Jan. 4, 2005 at E1.

Appendix 6-1

Private Commission Agreement—Sculpture
(Without Waiver of Moral Rights)

THIS AGREEMENT, made and entered into this ___ day of _____, 20__, by and between _____, _____, (hereinafter referred to as the "Artist"), and _____, (hereinafter referred to as the "Patron").

W I T N E S S E T H

WHEREAS, the Artist is engaged in the creation of works of art; and

WHEREAS, the Patron is desirous of commissioning the Artist to create a work of art for him (hereinafter referred to as the "Sculpture").

NOW THEREFORE, in consideration of the mutual promises contained herein, each party agrees as follows:

1. The Artist agrees to create a Sculpture to be entitled "_____". The Sculpture is described as *[brief description]*.

2. The Sculpture will be constructed as follows:

    a. Size—all dimensions:

    b. Materials to be used:

    c. Manner of construction:

  d. Location of construction:

  e. Final location of Sculpture:

  3. The Artist agrees to prepare two drawings and a scale model for the Patron's approval. Under all circumstances, other than that specified in Paragraph 12 of this Agreement, the drawings and model shall be the property of the Patron.

  4. The Sculpture will be completed by [Completion Date], PROVIDED, HOWEVER, under extenuating circumstances that prevent the Artist from working, the Artist may extend the time _____ months.

  5. The Patron shall pay all costs of removing the Sculpture from the Artist's studio, transporting it to the final location, and installing it at the final location. The Artist agrees to submit a site plan and to supervise the installation at the final location. The cost of preparing the site shall be paid by the Patron. The Patron agrees to pay the Artist's transportation and living costs during the installation at the final location.

  6. The Artist shall arrange for and pay for all fabricating and construction costs.

  7. The Artist agrees to transfer in writing the copyright to the Sculpture to the Patron.

  8. The Patron agrees to pay the Artist as follows:

  a. $_____ upon the signing of this Agreement.

  b. $_____ upon the approval by the Patron of the sketches and model.

  c. $_____ upon the completion of one-half of the Sculpture.

  d. $_____ upon the completion of the Sculpture, its final approval and acceptance by the Patron, and prior to its removal from the Artist's studio.

  e. The amount paid under (a) and (b) above shall not be refundable.

9.   The Artist at his expense agrees to keep the Sculpture fully insured until final approval and delivery at the Artist's studio. The Patron agrees at his expense to insure the Sculpture from the time it leaves the Artist's studio until it is installed at the final location.

10.   If the Artist becomes ill, dies, or is otherwise unable to complete the Sculpture by the Completion Date, the Artist agrees to refund to the Patron all amounts paid to the Artist other than the amounts paid in Paragraphs (a) and (b) of Clause 8 of this Agreement. Under such circumstances the sketches, model, and Sculpture (to the extent completed) shall be the property of the Patron.

11.   The Artist represents that the Sculpture is unique and that no identical or greatly similar sculpture will be created by him.

12.   Final approval and acceptance of the Sculpture shall be solely within the discretion of the Patron. The Patron agrees to accept or reject the Sculpture by . If the Sculpture is rejected, the amounts paid under Paragraphs (a), (b), and (c) of Clause 8 of this Agreement shall be retained by the Artist, and the Patron shall not be required to pay the amount specified in Paragraph (d) of Clause 8 of this Agreement. If the Sculpture is rejected by the Patron, it, the sketches, the model, and the copyright shall be the property of the Artist.

13.   The Artist shall furnish the Patron with written recommendations concerning the maintenance of the Work and the Patron shall use reasonable efforts to maintain the Work in accordance with such recommendations.

14.   This Agreement represents the entire understanding of the Parties hereto, supersedes any and all other and prior agreements between the Parties, and declares all such prior agreements between the Parties null and void. The terms of this Agreement may not be modified or amended, except in writing. This Agreement and all matters relating to it shall be governed by the Uniform Commercial Code and the laws of the State of _____.

IN WITNESS WHEREOF, the Parties hereto have hereunto signed their hands and seals the day and year first above written.

_____

Artist

_____

Patron

Appendix 6-2

Private Commission Agreement—Painting (With Waiver of Moral Rights)

This Agreement, made and entered into this _____ day of _____, 20__ by and between _____, residing at _____, _____ _____ (hereinafter referred to as the "Artist"), and _____, having an office at _____, _____, _____ (hereinafter referred to as "Builder").

W I T N E S S E T H:

WHEREAS, the Artist is engaged in the creation of works of art: and

WHEREAS, _____ is constructing a building at _____; and

WHEREAS, Builder is desirous of commissioning the Artist to create a work of art (the "Work") on the scale of _____ by _____ for the site wall in the lobby of the building to be constructed at _____ (the "Building").

NOW, THEREFORE, in consideration of the mutual promises and agreements contained herein, each party agrees as follows:

1. ARTIST'S SERVICES.

    A.   The Artist agrees to create the Work, as yet untitled, to be entitled by the Artist. The Work is to be in the style of the Artist's recent works, incorporating _____ images, appropriate for a public installation. The artistic expression, design, and color of the Work shall be determined by the Artist. The Work will be designed to consist of three panels which taken together shall be the Work referred to in this Agreement.

B.   The Work will be created as follows:

i.   The Artist agrees to prepare sketches of three (3) proposals of the Work to be submitted to Builder no later than _____, 20__. The proposals shall indicate size, materials and colors to be used and shall be in accordance with the written instructions delivered to the Artist dated _____ 20__, a copy of which is attached hereto.

ii.   Upon notification from Builder in accordance with Paragraph 2A below as to the selection of the proposal to be used, the Artist agrees to create the Work. The Artist agrees to consult with Builder and its architects in order to receive approval of materials to be used, exact dimensions, installation requirements, and all other details as may be required by the architects for the Building. If and when requested by the architects, the Artist agrees to have shipped to Builder a blank stretched canvas of exact size to be used for the Work for the purpose of measurement or testing.

iii.   The Artist agrees to prepare written documentation of the Work's creation indicating materials used.

iv.   The Artist agrees to allow Builder to visit the Artist's studio from time to time to review the progress made in the creation of the Work and to photograph and videotape the Work as it is being created.

v.   The Artist agrees to finish the Work by _____ __, 20__ and to allow Builder to photograph and videotape the finished Work. Prior to the final inspection of the finished Work by Builder, the Artist agrees to notify Builder that the Work is finished and to furnish Builder with a photograph of the finished Work.

vi.   The Artist agrees to pay all expenses in the making and creation of the Work.

vii.   The Artist agrees to arrange for the delivery of the Work to Builder via common carrier at Builder's expense.

viii.   The Artist agrees to supervise the installation of the Work in the Building; provided, however, that Builder shall pay the Artist's transportation and hotel expenses during the installation.

2.   BUILDER'S DUTIES.

A.   Builder agrees to notify the Artist as to the selection of the proposal for the Work no later than _____ __, 20__. The two proposals not selected will be returned to the Artist. If Builder notifies the Artist that all three proposals have been rejected, then the Artist agrees to prepare sketches of two (2) new proposals of the Work and deliver them to Builder by _____ __, 20__. Builder agrees to notify the Artist as to the selection of the new proposal for the Work no later than _____ __, 20__. If Builder notifies the Artist that the two new proposals have been rejected, then Builder agrees to immediately pay the sum of $_____ to the Artist and this Agreement shall be considered terminated.

B.   After a proposal sketch has been selected, Builder agrees to make the following payments to the Artist by making payments to the Artist's bank account:

i. $_____ by _____ __, 20__ with notification that a proposed sketch has been selected.

ii. $_____ by _____ __, 20__ on visit by Builder or its representative to the Artist's studio and Builder's determination and judgment that the Work is progressing in accordance with the selected sketch.

iii. $_____ by _____ __, 20__ after the visit by Builder or its representative to the Artist's studio and Builder's determination and judgment that the Work is finished, is in accordance with the selected sketch, and is approved by Builder.

iv. $_____ by _____ __, 20__ after final installation of the completed Work at the Building.

C.   Builder agrees to pay all costs of crating, packing and shipping the Work to the Building and installing it in the Building.

3.   TITLE TO THE WORK.

Simultaneously with receiving the final payment for the Work, the Artist agrees to transfer in writing the title to the Work to Builder or its designee.

4.   COPYRIGHT TO THE WORK.

A.   Simultaneously with receiving the final payment for the Work, the Artist agrees to transfer in writing the copyright to the Work to Builder or its designee.

B.   Any and all sketches, drawings, details, models and other materials prepared by the Artist in connection with the creation of the Work shall be the property of Builder or its designee and delivered to it on completion of the Work. The Artist shall be permitted to retain copies of such items for information and reference. Builder or its designee agree that such items will be kept for information and reference and not used for any other purpose without the permission of the Artist.

C.   Builder or its designee agree that if reproductions are made of the Work for commercial purposes and are sold by any person, then ten percent (10%) of any revenue received on any such sale shall be paid to the Artist.

5.   ARTIST'S REPRESENTATIONS AND WARRANTIES.

A.   The Artist represents and warrants that (i) the Work is an original design of his own creative efforts, (ii) the Work is unique and an edition of one, (iii) the Work will not be offered for sale elsewhere, (iv) no identical or greatly similar Work will be created by him, and (v) the Work will not infringe the patent or copyright of any person.

B.   The Artist agrees to indemnify and hold Builder, its officers, and directors harmless from any and all demands, claims, suits, judgments, or other liability (including all legal fees and other expenses incurred by Builder in connection therewith) asserted or awarded to any person or entity arising by reason of the Artist's breach or alleged breach of any representation or warranty contained in this Agreement.

6.   INSURANCE.

A.   Prior to the completion of the Work and its shipment to the Building, the Artist agrees to insure at the cost of the Artist the Work from damage due to fire, water, theft or similar casualties in an amount at least equal to the amount of cumulative total payments paid to the Artist by Builder. The insurance policy shall name the Artist and Builder as insured parties as their interests may appear.

B.   Builder shall insure at its cost the Work for all risks upon completion of the Work and its packing, crating and being picked up for shipment to the Building.

7.   EXTENUATING CIRCUMSTANCES.

If the Artist dies, becomes ill so that he cannot work, or is otherwise unable to complete the Work by _____ __, 20__, then Builder shall owe no additional payments to the Artist other than the amounts already made by Builder. Under such circumstances, the Work (to the extent completed) shall be delivered to and be the property of Builder. Builder shall have the right to have the Work completed by the Artist's studio, or if that is not possible, another artist.

If the Artist does not complete the Work by _____ __, 20__, for any reason other than illness or death, then Builder shall have the right to cancel this Agreement and the Artist shall refund to Builder all amounts paid to him under this Agreement.

Builder, at its sole option, may elect to postpone the completion date of the Work and continue with this Agreement to have the Work finished by the Artist and the balance of the payments due made.

If the Work cannot be timely installed at the site due to an error of the Artist in preparing the canvases for the Work, then the Artist shall at his expense correct any such error and reimburse Builder for any penalty it is required to pay as a result of the delay in installing the Work.

8.   MAINTENANCE, REPAIR AND RESTORATION.

Builder shall consider written recommendations provided by the Artist concerning the maintenance of the Work and shall use reasonable effort to maintain the Work in accordance with such recommendations.

9.   WAIVER OF MORAL RIGHTS

The Artist agrees and acknowledges that, notwithstanding any statute or provision of United States, _____ State or foreign law, Builder or its designee shall have the following rights: (i) the right to destroy the Work, (ii) the right to remove and store the Work, even if such removal for the purpose of storage might result in the destruction, mutilation, distortion or modification of the Work, and (iii) the right to relocate the Work to some other location. So long as the integrity of the Work is preserved, it can continue to be described as created by the Artist.

10.   DEALER'S COMMISSION.

The Artist represents that he has employed no dealer or other person in connection with this Agreement other than _____ _____. The

Artist indemnifies and agrees to hold Builder free and harmless from the claims of any broker or other person (other than _____) claiming a fee against Builder by reason of this Agreement. Builder agrees to pay any fee due _____ by reason of this Agreement pursuant to a separate agreement.

11. <u>MISCELLANEOUS</u>.

This Agreement represents the entire understanding of the Parties hereto, supersedes any and all other and prior agreements between the Parties, and declares all such prior agreements between the Parties null and void. The terms of this Agreement may not be modified or amended, except in writing. This Agreement and all matters relating to it shall be governed by the Uniform Commercial Code and the laws of the State of _____.

IN WITNESS WHEREOF, the Parties hereto have hereunder signed their hands and seals the day and year first-above written.

_____

_____

Artist

_____

_____

Corporation (Builder)

By:

_____

Appendix 6-3

General Services Administration
Public Buildings Service Contract for Fine Arts
Services

On this _____ day of _____, 20__, the United States of America (hereinafter referred to as the Government), acting by and through the General Services Administration, and _____ (hereinafter referred to as the Artist), an individual whose address is _____, do hereby mutually agree as follows:

ARTICLE 1. Definitions

(a) The term "head of the agency" as used herein means the Administrator of General Services, and the term "his duly authorized representative" means any person or persons or board (other than the Contracting Officer) authorized to act for the head of the agency.

(b) The term "Contracting Officer" as used herein means the person executing this contract on behalf of the Government and includes a duly appointed successor or authorized representative.

ARTICLE 2. Scope of Services

(a) The Artist shall perform all services and furnish all supplies, material and equipment as necessary for the design, execution and installation of _____ (hereinafter referred to as "the work") to be placed in _____ at the location shown on Contract Drawing No. _____ attached hereto. The Artist shall execute the work in an artistic, professional manner and in strict compliance with all terms and conditions of this contract.

(b)   The Artist shall determine the artistic expression, subject to its being acceptable to the Government. The Artist shall submit to the Government a sketch or other document which conveys a meaningful presentation of the work which he/she proposes to furnish in fulfillment of this contract; he/she shall allow _____ calendar days for the Government to determine acceptability of the proposed artistic expression.

(c)   The work shall be of a material and size mutually acceptable to the Government and to the Artist.

(d)   The Artist shall install the work, in the location shown on the attached drawings.

(e)   The Artist shall be responsible for prepayment of all mailing or shipping charges on sketches, models or other submissions to the Government.

(f)   Upon installation the artist is to provide written instructions to the contracting officer for appropriate maintenance and preservation of the artwork. The Government is responsible for the proper care and maintenance of the work.

(g)   The Artist shall furnish the Government with the following photographs of the finished work as installed:

1.   One black and white negative 4" × 5"

2.   One color negative 4" × 5"

3.   Two black and white prints 8" × 10"

4.   Two color prints 8" × 10"

5.   One color transparency 4" × 5"

6.   Five representative 35mm color slides

ARTICLE 3. Changes

(a)   The Artist shall make any revision necessary to comply with such recommendations as the Contracting Officer may make for practical (non-aesthetic) reasons.

(b)   If the Contracting Officer makes any recommendations within the scope of paragraph (a) above, after approval of any submission by the Artist, the Artist's fee shall be equitably adjusted for any increase or decrease in the Artist's cost of, or time required for, performance of any services under this contract; the contract shall be modified in writing to reflect any such adjustment. Any claim of the Artist for adjustment under this clause must be asserted in writing within 30 days from the date of receipt by the Artist of the recommendation, unless the Contracting Officer grants a further period of time before the date of final payment under the contract.

(c) If the Contracting Officer makes any recommendations within the scope of paragraph (a) above, prior to the approval of any submission by the Artist, the Artist shall make the revisions necessary to comply with these recommendations, at no additional cost to the Government.

(d) No services for which an additional cost or fee will be charged by the Artist shall be furnished without the prior written authorization of the Contracting Officer.

ARTICLE 4. Inspection and Care

(a) The Artist shall furnish facilities for inspection of the work in progress by authorized representatives of the Contracting Officer. The Government will contact the Artist in advance of any inspection to arrange a mutually convenient time.

(b) The Artist shall be responsible for the care and protection of all work performed by him/her until completion of the installed work and acceptance by the Contracting Officer and shall repair or restore any damaged work; provided, however, that the Artist shall not be responsible for any damage which occurs after installation is complete and before acceptance by the Contracting Officer which is not caused by any acts or omissions of the Artist or any of his/her agents or employees.

(c) The Artist shall give the Contracting Officer at least 10 days advance written notice of the date the work will be fully completed and ready for final inspection. Final inspection will be started within 10 days from the date specified in the aforesaid notice unless the Contracting Officer determines that the work is not ready for final inspection and so informs the Artist.

ARTICLE 5. Time for Completion

The Artist shall complete all work as follows:

(a) The preliminary submittal as required by Article 2.(b): _____ calendar days after the receipt of notice to proceed.

(b) The completed work in place: _____ calendar days after receipt of notice to proceed.

ARTICLE 6. Ownership

All designs, sketches, models, and the work produced under this Agreement for which payment is made under the provisions of this contract shall be the property of the UNITED STATES OF AMERICA. All such items may be conveyed by the Contracting Officer to the National Collection of Fine Arts-Smithsonian Institution for exhibiting purposes and permanent safekeeping.

The Artist shall neither publicly exhibit the final work, nor shall he/she make exact reproductions or reductions of the finished work except by written permission of the Contracting Officer.

ARTICLE 7. Fee and Payment

In consideration of the Artist's performance of the services required by this contract, the Government shall pay the Artist a fixed fee not to exceed $_____. The fee shall be paid in installments as follows:

(a) $_____ upon approval of the proposed artistic expression as required by Article 2.(b).

(b) $_____ when the work is completed, approved and ready for installation.

(c) $_____ upon completion, and acceptance by the Government, of all services required under this contract. The Contracting Officer shall advise the Artist in writing of the approval or reasons for disapproval within 30 days after (i) receipt of the document(s) showing the artistic expression, (ii) receipt of the notice that the work is completed and ready for installation, or (iii) after inspection of the installed work.

Upon approval and/or acceptance (whichever is applicable) of the work performed under this contract, the amount due the Artist shall be paid as soon as practicable after receipt of a correct billing from the Artist. Prior to the final payment, the Artist shall furnish the Government with a release of all claims against the Government under this Agreement, other than such claims as the Artist may except. The Artist shall describe and state the amount of each excepted claim.

ARTICLE 8. Travel

All travel by the Artist and his/her agents or employees as may be necessary for proper performance of the services required under this contract is included in the fee amount set out in Article 7, above, and shall be at no additional cost to the Government.

ARTICLE 9. Responsibility of the Artist

(a)   Neither the Government's review, approval or acceptance of, nor payment for, any of the services required under this contract shall be construed to operate as a waiver of any rights under this contract or of any cause of action arising out of the performance of this contract, and the Artist shall be and remain liable to the Government in accordance with applicable law for all damages to the Government caused by the Artist's negligent performance of any of the services furnished under this contract.

(b)   The rights and remedies of the Government provided for under this contract are in addition to any other rights and remedies provided by law.

(c)   The Artist guarantees all work to be free from defective or inferior materials and workmanship for one year after the date of final acceptance by the Government. If within one year the Contracting Officer finds the work in need of repair because of defective materials or workmanship, the Artist shall, without additional expense to the Government, promptly and satisfactorily make the necessary repairs.

ARTICLE 10. Suspension of Work

(a)   The Contracting Officer may order the Artist in writing to suspend all or any part of the work for such period of time as he may determine to be appropriate for the convenience of the Government.

(b)   If the performance of all or any part of the work is for an unreasonable period of time, suspended or delayed by an act of the Contracting Officer in the administration of this contract, or by his failure to act within the time specified in this contract (or if no time is specified, within a reasonable time), an adjustment shall be made for any increase in cost of performance of this contract (excluding profit) necessarily caused by such unreasonable suspension or delay, and the contract modified in writing accordingly. However, no adjustment shall be made under this clause for any suspension or delay to the extent (1) that performance would have been suspended or delayed by any other cause, including the fault or negligence of the Artist or (2) for which an equitable adjustment is provided for or excluded under any other provision of this contract.

(c)   No claim under this clause shall be allowed (1) or any costs incurred more than 20 days before the Artist shall have notified the Contracting Officer in writing of the act or failure to act involved (but this requirement shall not apply as to a claim resulting from a suspension order), and (2) unless the claim, in an amount stated, is asserted in writing as soon as practicable after the termination of such suspension or delay, but not later than the date of final payment. No part of any claim based on the provisions of this clause shall be allowed if not supported by adequate evidence showing that the cost would not have been incurred but for a delay within the provisions of this clause.

ARTICLE 11. Termination

(a) The Contracting Officer may, by written notice to the Artist, terminate this contract in whole or in part at any time, either for the Government's convenience or because of the failure of the Artist to fulfill his/ her contractual obligations. Upon receipt of such notice, the Artist shall immediately discontinue all services affected (unless the notice directs otherwise).

(b) If the termination is for the convenience of the Government, the Artist shall at his/her option have the right to either:

(1) An equitable adjustment in the price (without allowance for anticipated profit on unperformed services) in which event the Government shall have the right to possession and transfer of title to all sketches, designs, models, the work (whether completed or uncompleted) and all other items produced by the Artist in the course of performing the contract prior to the date of termination, which right may be exercised or not at the sole discretion of the Contracting Officer; or

(2) The possession of all sketches, designs, models or other documents or materials produced and submitted to the Government in the course of the Artist's performance of the work prior to termination, in which case the Artist shall remit to the Government a sum equal to all payments (if any) made pursuant to this contract prior to the termination.

(c) If the termination is due to the failure of the Artist to fulfill his contract obligations, the Government shall return to the Artist all sketches, designs, models or other documents or materials produced and submitted to the Government in the course of the Artist's performance of the work prior to termination, in which case the Artist shall remit to the Government a sum equal to all payments (if any) made pursuant to this contract prior to the termination.

(d) If, after notice of termination for failure to fulfill contract obligations, it is determined that the Artist had not so failed, the termination shall be deemed to have been effected for the convenience of the Government. In such event, the provisions of paragraph (b) of this Article shall be deemed applicable.

Appendix 6-4

Public Commission Agreement Used by Battery Park City Authority

AGREEMENT

between

BATTERY PARK CITY AUTHORITY

and

Dated as of _____ 199_
Contract No.

(Public Art -

AGREEMENT

THIS AGREEMENT is made as of the   day of   ___
199   between the BATTERY PARK CITY AUTHORITY, a public benefit corporation, having an office at 1 World Financial Center, New York, New York 10281 ("BPCA") and   , having a studio at   , New York, NY 10012 ("Artist").

WHEREAS, BPCA is developing a new facility for   (the "Project") for the New York City Board of Education (the "Board") at Battery Park City pursuant to an agreement between BPCA, the City of New York (the "City"), and the Board (the "City Agreement"); and

WHEREAS, the City Agreement provides that the City will supply all funds for the design and construction of the Project but that the City shall pay such funds directly to BPCA, who shall be responsible for and retain entities for the purpose of providing all design, construction, construction management, furniture and equipment purchasing and any other services or goods including works of art required to complete the Project; and

WHEREAS, pursuant to the City Agreement BPCA has, leased the   site to the Board for a term of years which will commence at the earlier of substantial completion of the Project or the date of first occupancy by the Board at which time BPCA will convey to the Board a deed of the improvements to the   site; and

WHEREAS, the Artist has been selected to create a unique and original work of art to be located in the interior of the Project (the "Site") as part of the New York City Department of Cultural Affairs Percent for Art Program ("Percent for Art") and while this agreement is between BPCA and Artist, the process of supervision and approval of the work of art developed will be a joint, coordinated effort of BPCA, the Project Architect, the Board, Percent for Art, and the   Coalition (the "Coalition"), collectively, the "Supervisory Group", and the Artwork, when completed, will be submitted to the Municipal Art Commission (the "Art Commission") for its approval.

NOW, THEREFORE, for good and valuable consideration the receipt of which is acknowledged, the parties agree as follows:

ARTICLE 1 - COMMISSION

Subject to the terms and conditions of this Agreement, BPCA commissions Artist to design, construct and install a single work of art consisting of separate stone components, which shall, in the entirety, constitute a single work of art (the "Artwork") similar to the Artist's proposed design (the "Design") created and submitted by Artist pursuant to the Initial Design Agreement dated 11/3/89 between BPCA and Artist (the "Design Agreement"), which Design has been accepted and approved by the Supervisory Group, the Art Commission and BPCA pursuant to such agreement. The Artwork is to be located at sites selected by BPCA within the Building at Battery Park City. The site preparation for the Artwork (the "Site Preparation"), shall be completed by BPCA, in accordance with data and details furnished by Artist.

ARTICLE 2

2.1. STRUCTURAL DESIGN REVIEW

a. After consultation and collaboration with BPCA, the Artist shall prepare and submit to BPCA detailed working drawings of the Artwork including drawings for etching and fabrication, and its placement at the Site, together with such other graphic material as may reasonably be requested by BPCA and the Supervisory Group as necessary to portray the Artwork and Site Preparation. Upon the Artist's request, BPCA shall furnish to, or obtain for, the Artist all information, materials and assistance required by the Artist in connection with said submission.

b. The Artist agrees to make such revisions to the Artwork as are necessary to comply with applicable statutes, ordinances and/or regulations of any governmental regulatory agency having jurisdiction over the project.

c. The Supervisory Group shall promptly review the working drawings and shall notify the Artist of its approval of the working drawings, prior to fabrication.

d. The Supervisory Group shall have the right to review the Artwork at reasonable times during fabrication, and Artist shall submit progress reports to BPCA in accordance with and as provided for in the schedule annexed hereto as Schedule A.

e. A prototype of the Artwork of fabricated etched stone (the "Prototype") shall be presented to the Supervisory Group for its approval.

-2-

f. The Artist shall complete the fabrication and installation of the Artwork in substantial conformity with the approved Design. During fabrication, the Artist shall immediately present to the Supervisory Group, in writing, any proposed significant changes to the Artwork not in substantial conformity with the Design for further review and approval. For the purpose of this agreement, a significant change is any change in the scope, design, color, size or material of the Artwork which affects cost, installation, Site Preparation, maintenance and concept as represented in the Design.

2.2. INSTALLATION

a. The Artist shall notify BPCA in writing when the Artwork is completed and ready for delivery and installation. BPCA shall thereupon notify the Commission that the Artwork is completed and may be inspected. Representatives of the Supervisory Group shall inspect the Artwork for conformity with the Design and structural requirements and shall within ten (10) days after receipt of notice by BPCA from Artist approve the Artwork if it is in conformity with the Design, including workmanship of a like quality as the Design, and in conformity with the Working Drawings. The Supervisory Group shall give written approval of the Artwork to Artist.

b. Upon the Artist's receipt of the Supervisory Group's approval pursuant to paragraph 2.2.a, the Artist will deliver and cause the completed Artwork to be delivered to the Site for installation so as to permit installation as provided for in the approved schedule or at such other date as may be mutually agreed upon. In order that the Artwork created hereunder be integrated into the underlying construction Project, the Artist agrees that it will utilize the services of the stone setting contractor retained by BPCA at the Project, for the purpose of setting the components of the Artwork into the Project. BPCA shall be responsible for coordination of setting stonework into the Project.

c. BPCA shall be responsible for all expenses, labor and equipment necessary to prepare the Site for the installation of the Artwork. BPCA shall also be responsible to pay the stone setting contractor up to   for its costs attributable to installation of the Artwork, which payment shall be deemed part of the Percent for Art allocation to this Project.

2.3 POST-INSTALLATION AND FINAL ACCEPTANCE

a. Within sixty (60) days after the installation of the Artwork, the Artist shall furnish BPCA with the following:

-3-

(i)   Three sets of 35mm. color slides of the
      completed work, taken from each of three
      different viewpoints;

(ii) Three sets of three different 8" x 10"
      glossy black and white prints of the Work
      and negatives;

        b.   Upon installation of the Artwork, the Artist
shall provide the Supervisory Group with written recommendations
for appropriate maintenance and preservation of the Artwork.

        c.   Within sixty (60) days following the next
regularly scheduled Art Commission meeting after receipt of
notice that the Artwork has been installed, the Supervisory
Group shall notify the Artist of the Art Commission's decision
as to whether the final Artwork is accepted or rejected. The
Supervisory Group and the Artist shall be available to meet with
the Art Commission to discuss the final Artwork.

        d.   If the Art Commission rejects the final Artwork,
the Supervisory Group shall provide the Artist with a copy of
the Art Commissions Certificate of Resolution rejecting the
final Artwork and the Artist shall have the opportunity either
to revise the Artwork, at the Artist's expense, within a
reasonable period of time specified by the Art Commission, or to
terminate this Agreement. If the Artist revises the Artwork,
the final Artwork shall be reinspected by the Art Commission.
If the resubmitted Artwork is again rejected, BPCA shall provide
the Artist with a copy of the Art Commission's Certificate of
Resolution rejecting the resubmission, final payment shall be
withheld, and the Artwork shall be subject to the terms and
conditions of Article 5.

        e.   If the Art Commission approves the final Artwork,
the Supervisory Group shall notify the Artist in writing of the
City's acceptance of the Artwork.

        f.   Final acceptance shall be effective as of the
date of the Supervisory Group letter notifying the Artist of the
City's acceptance of the Artwork.

        g.   The Artist shall be available at such time or
times as may be agreed between the Supervisory Group and the
Artist to attend any inauguration or presentation ceremonies
relating to the Artwork.

        2.4. RISK OF LOSS.

        The risk of loss or damage to the Artwork shall be
borne by the Artist until final acceptance and the Artist shall

-4-

take appropriate measures to protect the Artwork from loss or damage until such acceptance. Notwithstanding the foregoing, the risk of loss or damage shall be borne by BPCA prior to final acceptance for such periods of time as the practically or wholly completed Artwork is in the custody, control or supervision of BPCA or its agents for the purposes of storing, installing or performing any other ancillary services to the Artwork, provided, however, that any loss or damage to the Artwork is not the result of the Artist's negligence.

2.5. TITLE AND OWNERSHIP

a. Subject to the rights outlined in Article 9 and 10, all rights and interest in, title to, and ownership of, the Artwork, Design and copies of the working drawings, where applicable, as approved by the Art Commission, shall pass to the Board upon final acceptance.

b. All studies, drawings and designs prepared and submitted under this Agreement shall, at the Board's option, become its property. Should the Board elect not to retain such materials, the Artist agrees to use her best efforts to make available to the Board at its option the use of said materials for exhibition, repair or other related purpose, on reasonable notice.

c. The Artist agrees that she shall not sell, exhibit or reproduce the Design prior to final acceptance of the Artwork without the express written authorization of the Percent for Art Program.

ARTICLE 3 - COMPENSATION AND PAYMENT SCHEDULE

3.1. Fee Schedule

BPCA shall pay the Artist a fee of _____ which shall constitute full compensation for all services to be performed, and materials to be furnished, by the Artist under this Agreement. The fee shall be paid in accordance with the schedule annexed as Schedule B hereto, each installment contained therein to represent full and final payment for all services and materials provided prior to the payment thereof. Payment shall be made after requisition therefor has been processed by the City and the Board and funds for such payment are received from the City by BPCA. BPCA will take all steps to assure prompt processing of payment requests. The said sum of _____ is part of the total Percent for Art allocation of _____ for the creation, construction and installation of the Artwork commissioned hereunder. The parties acknowledge that _____ out of the total allocation has been paid to Artist

pursuant to the Design Agreement and that up to ·   will be
paid to the stone setting contractor pursuant to Section
2.2.(b).

3.2. Artist Incurred Costs

The Artist shall be responsible for the payment of all
mailings or shipping charges on submissions required under this
Agreement, and the cost of transporting the Artwork to the Site.

3.3. Acceptance of Final Payment

Receipt and negotiation by the Artist, or by any
person claiming under this Agreement, of the Final Payment
hereunder, notwithstanding whether such payment be made pursuant
to any judgement or order of any court, shall constitute a
general release of BPCA and the Board from any and all claims
and liability for anything done, furnished, or relating to the
labor, materials, or services provided, or for any act of
omission or commission of BPCA, the Board or their agent and
employees. Said release shall be effective against the Artist
and the Artist's representatives, heirs, executors,
administrators, successors, and assigns.

4. SECURITY: FAILURE TO COMPLETE ARTWORK

4.1. Grant of Security. As security for the
performance by the Artist of her obligations under this
Agreement, the Artist hereby grants to BPCA a security interest
in (i) the Design; and (ii) work in progress and all materials
purchased in connection with the fabrication of the Artwork;
(collectively, the "Collateral").

4.2. Financing Statements; Consent of Fabricator. In
furtherance of the foregoing, the Artist agrees (i) to execute
for filing, such financing statements or other instruments as
may be required by the laws of any applicable jurisdiction in
order to perfect BPCA's security interest in the Collateral; and
(ii) to deliver to BPCA, on or prior to the date of Artist's
Agreement with a fabricator other than Artist, the consent and
agreement of the fabricator(s), if any, to the conditional
assignment of the contract between the Artist and such
fabricator.

4.3. Release of Security Interest BPCA shall release
its security interest in the Collateral at the same time that
final payment for the Artwork is due, or at such time as this
Agreement is terminated under circumstances whereby BPCA shall
not be entitled to possession and title to the Collateral.

4.4. <u>Additional Rights of BPCA</u>. In addition to
BPCA's rights at law, in the event the Artist fails for any
reason to complete, deliver and install the Artwork pursuant to
this Agreement, BPCA shall have the right:

> (i)   To exercise its rights as a secured party
> under applicable law to seize the collateral
> however, BPCA agrees that it will not sell the
> Collateral at either a public or private sale;

> (ii)   In the event of the seizure of the
> collateral pursuant to (i), or the death or
> incapacity of the Artist prior to completion and
> installation of the Artwork, BPCA reserves the
> right subject, to the provisions set forth in
> (iii) below, to have the Artwork completed; and

> (iii) If the Artwork is completed by a person
> designated by Artist for that purpose, the
> Artwork when completed shall be known as "Work of
> Art by _____, completed by (name of
> person completing)". If the Artwork is completed
> by a person not so designated, Artist, or his
> representative, reserves the right to disclaim
> authorship or to permit it to be known as a "Work
> of Art by _____, completed by (name of
> person completing same)". Artist will furnish
> the name of a person or persons designated to
> complete the Work of Art in her behalf, and
> reserves the right at any time, upon notice to
> BPCA, to cancel or change the name of the person
> or persons so designated.

ARTICLE 5 - TERMINATION

5.1. The services to be performed under this
Agreement may be terminated by BPCA for convenience,
subject to written notice submitted thirty (30) days before
termination. The notice shall specify that the termination is
for convenience. Upon such termination for the convenience of
BPCA, the Artist shall have the right to an equitable adjustment
in the fee (without allowance for anticipated profit on
unperformed services, but including an allowance for reasonable
attorney fees incurred by Artist, if any, in arriving at an
equitable adjustment), in which event BPCA shall have the right,
at its discretion, to possession and transfer of title to the
drawings, materials being fabricated and Design already prepared
and submitted or prepared for submission to BPCA by the Artist
under this Agreement prior to the date of termination, provided
however, that no right to sell, fabricate or execute the Work

shall pass to BPCA, nor shall BPCA or the Board have the right
to exhibit or display the Work or any part thereof. In the
event BPCA exercises its right to possession and title pursuant
to this section, Artist, for a period of ninety days after the
effective date of such termination, shall have the absolute
right to purchase BPCA's right to possession and title to the
Work, by remitting to BPCA a sum of money equal to all payments
made to Artist pursuant to the Agreement and the Initial Design
Agreement between BPCA and Artist.

5.2. If either party to this Agreement shall
willfully or negligently fail to fulfill in a timely and proper
manner, or otherwise violate, any of the covenants, agreements
or stipulations material to this Agreement, the other party
shall thereupon have the right to terminate this Agreement by
giving written notice to the defaulting party of its intent to
terminate specifying the grounds for termination. The
defaulting party shall have thirty (30) days after receipt of
the notice to cure the default. If it is not cured, then this
Agreement shall terminate. In the event of default by BPCA,
BPCA shall promptly compensate the Artist for all services
performed by the Artist prior to termination. In the event of
default by the Artist then at BPCA's option, (1) all finished
and unfinished drawings, sketches, preliminary plans and working
drawings, photographs, and other work products prepared and
submitted or prepared for submission by the Artist under this
Agreement, including the Artwork or any of its component parts
in whatever stage of fabrication at the time of termination,
shall at BPCA's option become its property and BPCA shall have
the right to fabricate, execute and install the Work but not as
a work of Artist, and BPCA shall compensate the Artist pursuant
to Article 3 for all services performed by the Artist prior to
termination less the cost of transportation to the Site, or (2)
the Artist shall remit to BPCA a sum equal to all payments (if
any) made to the Artist pursuant to the Agreement and the
Initial Design Agreement between BPCA and Artist.
Notwithstanding the previous sentence, the Artist shall not be
relieved of liability to BPCA for damages sustained by BPCA by
virtue of any breach of the Agreement by the Artist, and BPCA
may reasonably withhold payments to the Artist until such time
as the exact amount of such damages due BPCA from the Artist is
determined.

ARTICLE 6 - TIME OF PERFORMANCE

6.1. Duration

The services required of the Artist shall be in
accordance with the schedule for completion of the Artwork, as

-8-

set forth in Schedule A, provided that such time limits may be
extended by written agreement between the Artist and the BPCA.
Said schedule shall coincide, as closely as possible, to the
Project, construction schedule.

6.2. Construction Delays

In the event that the Artist completes fabrication of
the Artwork in accordance with the above Schedule and is delayed
from installing it on or before the time specified in the
Schedule as a result of the construction of the Project not
being sufficiently completed to reasonably permit installation
of the Artwork, BPCA agrees to store the Artwork at a secure
place on its premises until such time as construction is
sufficiently completed to reasonably permit installation of the
Artwork.

6.3. Early Completion of the Artwork

The Artist shall bear the cost of transporting and
storing the Artwork should it be completed prior to the
project's schedule.

6.4. Time Extensions

A reasonable extension of time will be granted in the
event there is a delay on the part of BPCA in providing the
reviews or acceptance necessary under this Agreement or in
completing the underlying Project or should conditions beyond
BPCA's or Artist's control or acts of God render performance of
services impossible. Failure to fulfill contract obligations
due to conditions beyond either party's reasonable control shall
not be considered a breach of contract. Notwithstanding the
above, the time for the performance of the parties' obligations
shall only be extended for a period equal to the duration of the
contingency that occasioned the interruption or delay.

ARTICLE 7 - WARRANTIES

7.1. Warranties of Title

The Artist represents and warrants that: (a) the
Artwork is the original creation of the Artist and is solely the
result of the Artistic effort of the Artist; (b) the Artwork
does not infringe upon any copyright, trademark or any other
property or personal right; (c) the Artwork or a duplicate
thereof, has not been offered or accepted for sale, display or
exhibition elsewhere; (d) the Artwork is free and clear of liens
or encumbrances from any source whatsoever; and (e) Artist knows

-9-

of no adverse claims to the Artwork and that neither the Artwork nor any portion thereof is in the public domain.

7.2. Warranties of Quality and Condition of the Artwork

a. The Artist represents and warrants, except as otherwise previously disclosed to the BPCA that: (a) the execution and fabrication of the Artwork will be performed in a workmanlike manner; (b) the Artwork, as fabricated and installed, will be free of defects in material and workmanship, including any defects consisting of inherent vice, defined as qualities which cause or accelerate deterioration of the Artwork; and (c) reasonable maintenance of the Artwork will not require procedures substantially in excess of those described in the maintenance recommendation submitted by the Artist pursuant to paragraph 2.3.b.

b. The warranties described in this paragraph shall survive for a period of one year after the final acceptance of the Artwork. In the event of any breach of a warranty which is curable by the Artist and which cure is consistent with generally accepted professional conservation standards (including, for example, cure by means of repair or fabrication of the Artwork), the Artist shall, at the request of the BPCA or the Board, cure such breach at no cost to the BPCA or the Board. BPCA or the Board shall give notice to the Artist of any such observed breach with reasonable promptness, and, if required hereunder, the Artist shall cure such breach with reasonable promptness.

7.3. Hold Harmless.

Artist shall be solely responsible for all injuries to persons, including death, or damage to property, sustained during her performance of this Agreement and resulting from any negligence, fault, or default of the Artist or any of her employees, authorized agents, servants or independent contractors hired by Artist, or any subcontractor hired by any of the foregoing. Artist agrees to indemnify and hold BPCA, the Board and the City harmless from any liability upon any and all claims for damages on account of the negligence, fault or default of the Artist, her employees, authorized agents, servants or independent contractors hired by Artist, or any subcontractor hired by any of the foregoing until final acceptance. Anything to the contrary notwithstanding, Artist indemnification will not include claims for damages on account of the negligence, fault or default of the stone setting contractor.

-10-

ARTICLE 8 - REPRODUCTION RIGHTS

8.1. Copyright

The Artist and the City shall have a joint copyright in the Artwork and shall retain any and all rights provided under the Copyright Act of 1976, 17 U.S.C. Sections 101 <u>et. seq.</u> Since it is the intention of the parties that the Artwork shall be unique, the City and the Artist hereby agree not to make a duplicate or reproduction of the final Artwork or permit others to do so except by written permission of each. The Artist and BPCA hereby grant to each other and their assigns, including the Board and the City an irrevocable license to make photographs, drawings, videotapes and other reproductions of the Artwork for noncommercial purposes, including but not limited to reproductions used in advertising, brochures, media publicity, noncommercial reproductions, catalogues or other similar publications, provided that these rights are exercised in a reasonable manner.

8.2. Artwork Credit

The Artist and BPCA for itself and its assigns agree to include a credit on any reproductions of the Artwork or Design exhibited to the public which reads substantially "(c) Artist's name, year of completion, an original work commissioned by the Board of Education of the City of New York, Percent for Art Program and the BPCA".

ARTICLE 9 - ARTIST'S RIGHTS

9.1. Signage

The Artist shall prepare and install at the Site, pursuant to the approval and written instructions of BPCA or the Board, a plaque identifying the Artist, the title of the Artwork, the copyright symbol c and the date of completion.

9.2. Maintenance, Repair and Restoration

a. The BPCA or its assignee, the Board, will use reasonable efforts to maintain the Artwork in accordance with written recommendations provided by the Artist pursuant to paragraph 2.3.b herein. Notwithstanding the above, the BPCA or the Board as its assignee shall have the exclusive right to determine whether repairs to, or restoration of the Artwork will be made. The Board, through the Percent for Art Program shall use reasonable efforts to consult with the Artist, during the

-11-

first (5) years after acceptance of the Artwork on all questions involving repairs or restoration and the BPCA shall use reasonable efforts to obtain the Artist's services for the actual repair or restoration or supervision of such work by any other party retained by the provided, however, that the Board shall not be obligated to communicate with the Artist except at her last known address, notice of which must be given to the BPCA pursuant to Paragraph 12.d, herein.

b. Any repairs on, and restorations to, the Artwork shall be made in accordance with generally recognized principles of conservation, subject to the prior approval of the Commission.

9.3. Alteration of the Work or of the Site.

If alterations to the Site are made by the Board, and said alterations will affect the character and appearance of the Artwork, the Board as the assignee of BPCA shall notify Artist of such proposed alteration and shall make reasonable efforts to consult with the Artist in the planning of such alterations. Notwithstanding the foregoing, the Board may at its discretion relocate, remove from public display, sell or otherwise dispose of the Artwork with notification to the Artist provided, however, that the Board shall not be obligated to communicate with the Artist except at her last known address, notice of which must be given to the BPCA pursuant to Paragraph 12.d herein.

9.4. Moral Right

The Board will not use the Artwork in any manner which would reflect discredit on the Artist's name or reputation as an Artist or which would violate the spirit of the Work. Artist's sole remedy for breach of the provision shall be limited to the Artist's right to disclaim authorship of the Work and to require that her name be removed from the Work.

ARTICLE 10 - ADDITIONAL RIGHTS & REMEDIES,
LIMITATIONS OF ACTIONS

The rights and remedies of the parties herein specified shall be cumulative, and not exclusive of any other rights and remedies herein provided or allowed by law. Notwithstanding any other provision of this Agreement, no action or special proceeding shall lie or be maintained by the Artist or Artist's successors in interest against BPCA, the Board or the City upon any claim arising out of or based upon this

Agreement or out of anything in connection with this contract, unless such action or special proceeding is commenced within one year after the date of final payment to the Artist, or if this contract is breached or terminated prior to final payment, unless such action or special proceeding is commenced within one (1) year of such breach or termination.

ARTICLE 11 - RELATIONSHIP OF THE PARTIES

The Artist is entering into this agreement as an independent contractor and shall not hold herself out as otherwise. Nothing herein contained shall be deemed to constitute the Artist and BPCA, the Board or the City as partners, co-venturers, or employer-employee. Neither shall the Artist be considered an agent or employee of BPCA nor shall she hold herself out as such.

(a)   This Agreement shall be construed and enforced in accordance with the laws of the State of New York.

(b)   This Agreement may not be changed, waived, discharged or terminated orally, nor may it be assigned by Artist. It will be binding against assignees or successors in interest of BPCA and against successors in interest or heirs of Artist.

(c)   This Agreement may be executed in several counterparts, each of which shall be an original, but all of which, together shall constitute one and the same instrument.

(d)   Any notice given under this Agreement shall be in writing and shall be hand delivered or mailed, certified mail, postage prepaid, to the addressee at its address set forth or to such other address as the party to whom notice is to be given shall designate in writing.

If to BPCA: One World Financial Center
                     18th Floor
                     New York, NY 10281
                     Attn: Project Director,

                     cc: General Counsel

If to Board:

-13-

If to Artist:

(e) Nothing in this agreement shall create or shall give to third parties any claim or right of action against BPCA its assignees, agents or licensees, the Board, the City or the State of New York beyond such as may legally exist irrespective of this agreement.

(f) BPCA's "Prompt Payment Policy" dated July 12, 1988, a copy of which is annexed hereto, is incorporated into and made a part of this Agreement.

ARTICLE 12 - NO PERSONAL LIABILITY

Neither the Members of BPCA nor the Board, nor any officer, employee, agent or representative of BPCA the Board or of the City shall be personally liable, based upon any theory of law or equity, to the Artist or to any party claiming on behalf of or through the Artist, under this Agreement, or by reason of any individual's actions or failure to act in any way connected with this Agreement, whether or not the action shall have been within or without an individual's scope of authority. The scope of this provision includes personal injury to any personal interest (commercial or otherwise), physical injury (including death), property damages, and any pecuniary damages where such injuries or damages result from or arise out of negligence. The Artist further waivers any and all rights to make a claim or commence an action or special proceeding, in law or equity, against any of the aforementioned individuals, and the Artist hereby assigns its complete right, title, and interest in any such claim, action, or special proceeding to the Board.

IN WITNESS WHEREOF, the parties hereto have caused this Agreement to be duly executed as of the day and year first written above.

BATTERY PARK CITY AUTHORITY

By:_____

_____
ARTIST

-14-

SCHEDULE A

Progress Schedule

July 15, 1990   Completion of drawings for fabrication and etching.

August 15, 1990   Completion of etched Prototype.

November 15, 1990   Completion of etched stonework.

December 15, 1990   Completed stone work ready for delivery to site.

December 30, 1990   Installation of Artwork.

SCHEDULE B

Fee Schedule

        This schedule totals   . and does not include
the   already paid to the Artist for the preliminary
design and the   for the installation to be reserved for
the stone installer.

(a)   upon execution of this Agreement and the
        Commission's approval of the Design for the
        Artwork.

(b)   after the Supervisory Group's approval of
        the preparatory drawings for etching and
        fabrication as required under Section 2.1.

(c)   after etched Prototype has been approved
        by the Supervisory Group and Artist has entered
        into an agreement with fabricator for fabrication
        of stone.

(d)   after Supervisory Group has approved the
        Artwork but prior to its delivery to the Site.

(e)   after delivery of the Artwork to the
        Site.

(f)   after final acceptance of the Artwork
        pursuant to the provisions of this Agreement.

        For each payment, the Artist shall provide BPCA with a
notice indicating the completion of each phase of the Artwork
and the status of the relevant approval.

7

Expert Opinions and Liabilities

As the United States art market continues to be plagued with fakes, forgeries, and works of dubious provenance—including some highly publicized plunder from World War II, and some works that have been repatriated in the glare of the media and the law—expert opinions have become ever more crucial in serving to rid the market of unwanted material. Accordingly, the appraisal of art by art appraisers and the authentication of art by art historians, *droit moral* holders[1] for a given artist, and art specialists have become big business. Appraisers of fine art, who perform appraisals in the traditional manner, may become affiliated with one or more of three major trade associations, each with its own code of ethics and accreditation procedures. In addition, the development of online appraisals (discussed below) has given rise to a trade association devoted exclusively to such appraisals.

As to the traditional trade associations, the Appraisers Association of America, Inc. (AAA),[2] founded in 1949, is the oldest professional association of personal-property appraisers in the United States and numbers more than 1,000 members throughout the United States, Canada, Europe, and Asia. Members specialize in more than fifty major categories of personal property, such as European and American paintings, and more than 600 subspecialties of personal property, including such arcane categories as animation art, dolls, and baseball memorabilia. The American Society of Appraisers (ASA),[3] which has chapters in the United States and thirty-four other countries, represents all categories of property valuation including realty, personal property, business valuation, machinery and technical specialties, gems and jewelry, and appraisal-review management. The International Society of Appraisers (ISA),[4] established in 1979, now numbers more than 1,400 members dedicated to personal property appraising and is affiliated with the University of Maryland. The university provides academic guidance to the ISA Certified Appraiser of Personal Property (CAPP) professional education program, which recognizes the professional status of personal property appraisers.

The Appraisal Foundation was founded in 1987 as a nonprofit corporation by eight leading appraisal organizations to develop national professional appraisal standards. As a result, the Appraisal Standards Board of the Appraisal Foundation was established to develop, publish, interpret, and amend the Uniform Standards of Professional Appraisal Practice (USPAP) on behalf of appraisers.[5] Although USPAP was originally developed to apply to real-estate appraisals, Standards 7 and 8 (copies of which are reproduced at the end of this chapter along with other USPAP materials in Appendix 7-1) are specifically applicable to personal property appraisals. Although the standards are not legally applicable to personal property appraisals, the standards offer an excellent guide for the well-prepared appraisal of personal property.

The advent of the Internet has spawned the performance of online appraisals. To ensure that both the public and the appraisal profession are well served by the use of electronic technologies, the Association of Online Appraisers (AOA) was established. The AOA,[6] whose stated mission is to promote and encourage professionalism and ethical conduct among online personal property appraisers, has adopted the applicable standards of USPAP, along with its core code of ethics for the providers of online appraisal reports. The AOA has three categories of membership:

(1) candidate members, that is, individuals with fewer than three years of appraisal experience,

(2) regular members, that is, individuals having at least three years of appraisal experience within an area of specialization, and

(3) sponsoring members, that is, individuals or organizations that support the AOA precepts but do not do appraisals.

In addition to the above-noted appraisal organizations, the authentication service of the International Foundation for Art Research (IFAR)[7] (described in chapter 3) works with art historians and other scholars, as a service to owners of artwork, in helping to resolve questions of authenticity and attribution of artworks. As an authenticator, unlike an appraisal service, IFAR's service does not appraise the monetary value of works of art.

Art criticism has also emerged as an established and influential force in the art market. One organization, the International Association of Art Critics (IAAC),[8] was established in 1948 and currently has national associations in seventy-two countries; it has approximately 4,000 worldwide members, of which 400 are in the United States. The association, whose membership is by invitation only, includes critics who work freelance, scholarly commentators, and newspaper critics.

Although art critics are a potent force in the formation of reputation in the art world, the opinion of the art expert, not the art critic, has the most direct effect on art transactions. The prospective purchaser or seller of an artwork, for example, often consults an appraiser, never an art critic, for an assessment of the artwork's fair market value. When such a prospective buyer or seller commissions the services of an appraiser, a legal relationship is established between the two parties that gives rise to an affirmative duty of care on the part of the appraiser to the commissioning party. The services of an art critic, who usually publishes an opinion about an artwork in a magazine or a newspaper to an audience at large, are not generally commissioned; therefore, the art critic lacks a parallel affirmative duty of care to a specific party. Those contrasting circumstances, along with the protective shield accorded the art critic under current defamation law, are reflected in existing judicial decisions. Case law is rife with examples of tort liabilities incurred by art experts and virtually devoid of suits involving art critics. This chapter, therefore, focuses primarily on the tort liability that can be incurred by the art expert in the rendering of opinions about artwork, and on how the expert can limit such liability.

In the course of appraising or authenticating an artwork, an art expert can incur liability under a variety of tort theories: most notably, disparagement, defamation, negligence, negligent misrepresentation, and fraud. Each is examined in this chapter.

ONLINE APPRAISALS

Unquestionably, the most far-reaching development affecting the rendering of expert opinions on works of art and other collectibles over the past few years has been the proliferation of online appraisals (OLAs). The growth, however, was short-lived since many OLA companies, along with the dotcoms, folded in the economic downturn in the first years of the new millennium.

OLAs generally operate as follows: The party seeking an appraisal, that is, the OLA client, submits to the OLA company digital images of the item of property to be appraised along with a detailed description of the property, including facts about its condition, provenance, and title and whether the item is subject to any restrictions or conditions. This information is submitted in a detailed questionnaire prepared by the OLA company and signed by the client. The OLA company then arranges for the images and description to be forwarded to an appraiser affiliated with the OLA company. The appraiser performs an appraisal of the property and prepares a written appraisal report, relying solely on the information and digital images provided: No physical examination of the property is conducted. Generally, the appraiser cannot request additional information about the property. Other than not physically examining the property, the appraiser acts follows standard appraisal procedure and methodology. Generally, the appraisal report is not signed by the appraiser, and the appraiser's name is not disclosed.

Do OLAs Satisfy the Substantiation Requirements for Charitable Deductions Set Forth in the Internal Revenue Code Regulations?

One who donates tangible personal property valued at $250 or more must substantiate the donation with a contemporaneous written acknowledgment from the donee charity.[9]

The amount of income tax deduction that is being claimed by the donor determines the substantiation requirements for the donation. There are three levels of substantiation requirements:

(1) those for a deduction of $500 or less;

(2) those for a deduction of $501 to $5,000; and

(3) those for a deduction of more than $5,000.[10]

Deduction of $500 or Less

The substantiation requirements for a deduction of $500 or less require the donor either (1) to receive a receipt from the charity or (2) to maintain reliable written records regarding the donation.

Charitable Receipt

A receipt from the donee charity may be either a formal receipt or a written statement acknowledging the donation.[11] The receipt must contain the name of the donee charity, the date and location of the contribution, and a description of the property in reasonably sufficient detail. "Reasonably sufficient detail" depends on the fair market value of the donated property: An item of property worth $500, for example, requires more detail than an item worth $50.

Reliable Written Records

A donor required to maintain reliable written records has the burden proving their reliability. The written records must contain the following information:[12]

(a) The name and address of the donee;

(b) The date and location of the contribution;

(c) A description of the property in reasonably sufficient detail, including its value;

(d) The fair market value of the property contributed, the method used to determine the fair market value, and if an appraisal was used, a copy of the appraiser's signed report;

(e) In the case of ordinary income property or capital gain property for which a reduction is required under section 170(e), the adjusted basis of the property, the amount of the required reduction, and the manner in which the reduction was computed;

(f) When less than the donor's entire interest in the property is contributed during the taxable year, the amount claimed as a deduction for the taxable year for the gift of the property, the amount claimed as a deduction in any prior years for gifts of other interests in the same property, the name and address of each donee to which such gifts were made, the place where any such property which is tangible is physically located and the name of any person other than the donee who has actual possession of the property; and

(g) The terms of any agreement or understanding which places conditions or restrictions on the use, sale or other disposition of the property by the donee.

The information required to be maintained in the donor's written records must be furnished with the income tax return if required by the return or its instructions. The Internal Revenue Service (IRS) does not require such information to be furnished with the return if the deduction for all tangible personal property gifts is $500 or less.[13]

Assuming that the donor also has a written record of the charity's name and address and the date and place of donation, an OLA should be sufficient to meet the reliable written records requirement, since an OLA will provide a description of the property and a statement of its fair market value. If a donor has a digital image and the other facts readily available that were provided when the OLA was prepared, there should be a sufficient basis for dealing with any questions raised by the IRS.[14]

Limited in scope as it is, an OLA most likely will not be sufficient to establish the fair market value of the property in an audit. For example, assume a donor contributes tangible personal property to a charity and bases an income tax deduction on the value determined in an OLA. The IRS audits the taxpayer's return, challenging the amount of the deduction. While an OLA should be sufficient to satisfy the substantiation requirement that the taxpayer retain reliable records, an OLA will not be sufficient evidence of the property's fair market value: The party who prepared the OLA did not conduct a physical examination of the property and did not sign the OLA. Moreover, the OLA would lack comparable sales data and a market analysis, both of which are included in an appraisal following proper appraisal methodology. In this situation, the donor will need to obtain a formal appraisal of the property in order to substantiate the amount of the claimed deduction.

As a practical matter, the IRS does not spend much time auditing donations of $500 or less and with appropriate disclaimers, the OLA should be sufficient in the vast majority of cases. If consumers are advised of this use of the OLA, they would be encouraged to "seek the advice of their tax advisor" before proceeding.

Deduction of $501 to $5,000

The donor must retain the same reliable written records required for a deduction of $500 or less.[15] In addition, the donor must identify the manner of acquisition of the property and the adjusted basis of the property. The donor must also complete Form 8283 and submit it to the IRS along with the income tax return.[16] On Form 8283, the donor must state (among other things) the fair market value of the property donated and the method used to determine the fair market value. Therefore, the main difference between the substantiation requirements for a deduction of less than $500 and a deduction of $501 to $5,000 is that for the latter, the donor must submit information about the property to the IRS, rather than merely retaining the information in his records.

Similar to the first category of deductions, a formal appraisal is not required for a deduction of $501 to $5,000, although the taxpayer would need to obtain a formal appraisal if the return is audited. Again, an OLA should be sufficient to satisfy the reliable written records requirement, but in an audit an OLA will not be sufficient to support the taxpayer's contention as to the property's fair market value. Although the donor would require a formal appraisal if the return were audited, the OLA with the digital image would be an excellent starting place for the formal preparation of an appraisal. Perhaps with the network of appraisers associated with the OLA company, the OLA company could offer to arrange an appraisal in the case of an IRS audit at some fixed cost. A more cautious approach is to obtain the appraisal at the time of the donation so there is no problem at a later date.

Deduction of More Than $5,000

To substantiate a deduction in excess of $5,000, the donor must:

(1) maintain reliable written records of the donation;

(2) obtain a qualified appraisal; and

(3) attach an appraisal summary to his income tax return.[17]

Reliable Written Records

The donor must retain the same reliable written records required for a deduction of $500 or less.[18] As with the first two categories of substantiation requirements, the donor has the burden of proving the reliability of the records. They should therefore be prepared contemporaneously with (or as close as possible to) the donation.

Qualified Appraisal

For claimed deductions between $5,001 and $19,999, the qualified appraisal need not be submitted with the donor's income tax return. It must, however, be retained with the donor's other records of the donation in case the deduction is challenged by the IRS. For claimed deductions of $20,000 or more, the donor must submit a copy of the qualified appraisal with the income tax return.

A qualified appraisal is a written appraisal document that

(1) refers to an appraisal made not earlier than sixty days prior to the date of donation of the property and not later than the due date of the donor's income tax return on which the charitable contribution deduction is claimed;

(2) contains certain specific information (described below);

(3) is prepared, signed, and dated by a qualified appraiser (described below); and

(4) states that no part of the fee arrangement for the appraisal is based, in effect, on a percentage (or set of percentages) of the appraised value of the property.[19]

The following information must be included in a qualified appraisal:

(a) A description of the property in detail sufficient for a person not generally familiar with that type of property to ascertain that the property appraised is the property contributed;

(b) In the case of tangible property, the physical condition of the property;

(c) The date of the contribution to the donee;

(d) The terms of any agreement or understanding entered (or expected to be entered) into by or on behalf of the donor or donee relating to the use, sale, or other disposition of the property donated, including, for example, the terms of any agreement or understanding that—

(1) restricts temporarily or permanently a donee's right to use or dispose of the donated property,

(2) reserves to, or confers upon, anyone (other than a donee organization or an organization participating with a donee organization in cooperative fundraising) any right to the income from the contributed property or to the possession of the property, including the right to vote donated securities, to acquire the property by purchase or otherwise, or to designate the person having such income, possession or right to acquire, or

(3) earmarks donated property for a particular use;

(e) The name, address, and identifying number[20] of the qualified appraiser; and, if the qualified appraiser is so acting as a partner in a partnership, an employee of any party, or an independent contractor engaged by a person other than the donor, the name, address and taxpayer identification number[21] of the partnership or the person who employs or engages the qualified appraiser;

(f) The qualifications of the qualified appraiser who signs the appraisal, including the appraiser's background, experience, education, and membership, if any, in professional appraisal associations;

(g) A statement that the appraisal was prepared for income tax purposes;

(h) The date(s) on which the property was appraised;

(i) The appraised fair market value[22] of the property on the date (or expected date) of contribution;

(j) The method of valuation used to determine the fair market value, such as the income approach, the market-data approach, and the replacement-cost-less-depreciation approach; and

(k) The specific basis for the valuation, such as specific comparable sales transactions or statistical sampling, including a justification for using sampling and an explanation of the sampling procedure employed.[23]

In addition, for works of art,[24] the IRS states that a qualified appraisal should include the following information:

(a) A complete description of the object, including the:

   (1) Size,

   (2) Subject matter,

   (3) Medium,

   (4) Name of the artist (or culture), and

   (5) Approximate date created;

(b) The cost, date, and manner of acquisition;

(c) A history of the item, including proof of authenticity;

(d) A photograph of a size and quality fully showing the object, preferably a ten-by-twelve-inch print;

(e) The facts on which the appraisal was based, such as:

   (1) Sales or analyses of similar works by the artist, particularly on or around the valuation date,

   (2) Quoted prices in dealer's catalogs of the artist's works or works of other artists of comparable statute,

   (3) A record of any exhibitions at which the specific art object had been displayed,

   (4) The economic state of the art market at the time of valuation, particularly with respect to the specific property,

   (5) The artist's professional standing in general and in the context of the artist's school or time period, in particular.

In order for an appraisal to be a qualified appraisal, it must be prepared by a qualified appraiser. A qualified appraiser is an individual who includes on the appraisal summary a declaration that:

(a) The individual either holds himself out to the public as an appraiser or performs appraisals on a regular basis;

(b) Because of the appraiser's qualifications as described in the appraisal, the appraiser is qualified to make appraisals of the type of property being valued;

(c) The appraiser is not (i) the donor; (ii) the person who sold, exchanged, or gave the property to the donor, unless the property is donated within two months of the date of acquisition and its appraised value does not exceed its acquisition price; (iii) the donee; (iv) any person employed by any of the foregoing; (v) any person related to any of the foregoing; and (vi) an appraiser who is regularly used by any of the foregoing and who does not perform a majority of appraisals made during his taxable year for other persons;[25] and

(d) The appraiser understands that an intentionally false or fraudulent overstatement of the value of the property described in the qualified appraisal or appraisal summary may subject the appraiser to a civil penalty for aiding and abetting an understatement of tax liability, and the appraisal may be disregarded pursuant to 31 U.S.C. § 330(c).[26]

Appraisal Summary

The donor must attach an appraisal summary to his income tax return. An appraisal summary is made on IRS Form 8283, and must be signed and dated by the donor, the donee, and the qualified appraiser. The appraisal summary must include the following information:

(a) The name and taxpayer identification number of the donor;

(b) A description of the property in detail sufficient for a person not generally familiar with that type of property to ascertain that the property appraised is the property contributed;

(c) In the case of tangible property, the physical condition of the property at the time of the contribution;

(d) The manner of acquisition (for example, purchase, exchange, gift, or bequest) and the date of acquisition of the property by the donor, or, if the property was created, by or for the donor, a statement to that effect and the approximate date the property was substantially completed;

(e)   The cost or other basis of the property;[27]

(f)   The name, address, and taxpayer identification number of the donee;

(g)   The date the donee received the property;

(h)   A statement explaining whether or not the charitable donation was made by means of a bargain sale and the amount of any consideration received from the donee for the donation;

(i)   The name, address, and identifying number[28] of the qualified appraiser who signs the appraisal summary;

(j)   The appraised fair market value of the property on the date of the contribution; and

(k)   A declaration by the appraiser stating that—

   (1)   No part of the fee arrangement for the appraisal is based, in effect, on a percentage (or set of percentages) of the appraised value of the property, and

   (2)   Appraisals prepared by the appraiser are not being disregarded pursuant to 31 U.S.C. § 330(c) on the date the appraisal summary is signed by the appraiser.[29]

Photographs: Compliance with Substantiation Requirements and Weight Given Appraisal

An OLA provided by an OLA company might conceivably meet the bare minimum standards to satisfy the requirements in the Regulations for a qualified appraisal. However, a taxpayer would be foolish to rely on an OLA as a qualified appraisal since it would be given very little, if any, credibility by the IRS. The appraiser might be able to provide the information required for a qualified appraisal through the use of the digital images of the property, the factual information provided by the taxpayer, and the appraiser's independent research and analysis. However, the OLA procedure would have to be changed so it includes the name, address, and taxpayer identification number of the appraiser, and a resume of the appraiser's qualifications. In addition, the OLA would have to be signed by the appraiser.

Could the appraiser's signature be in electronic form? President Clinton signed the Electronic Signatures in Global and National Commerce ("E-Sign") Act on June 30, 2000.[30] The law, most of which took effect on October 1, 2000, creates important new rules for e-commerce. It covers the validity of electronic signatures and electronic records, as well as new approaches for obtaining required consumer consents and providing required consumer disclosures. At its heart, the E-Sign Act provides that signatures, contracts, and other records may not be denied effect because they exist only in electronic form. It also addresses the interplay between state and federal laws on electronic transactions. While the scope of the E-Sign Act is broad, it does not apply to wills, trusts, adoptions or divorces, and, other than sales and leases, does not apply to transactions governed by the Uniform Commercial Code. Moreover, it does not apply to consumer notices of product recalls, cancellations of utility services, cancellations of health or life insurance benefits, or foreclosures on primary residences. The E-Sign Act does not require written signatures for contracts or notices of these types: It simply does not validate electronic ones.

It still must be confirmed with the IRS whether or not an OLA can be signed electronically. Since the IRS now allows electronic filing of income tax returns prepared by accountants and the accountant and the taxpayer must sign the return, it may be possible to obtain this approval. Additionally, a qualified appraisal for a work of art must include a photograph of the art.[31] It is an open question as to whether a digital image of the art would be an acceptable substitute.

A different and more problematic issue arises if the taxpayer's deduction is challenged by the IRS. The IRS does not accept appraisals without question.[32] It is the taxpayer's responsibility to provide support for the fair market value of property for which a deduction is claimed on an income tax return. Moreover, the weight given to an appraisal depends on the completeness of the report, the qualifications of the appraiser, and the appraiser's demonstrated knowledge of the donated property.[33] An appraisal will not be given much weight if

(1) all the factors that apply are not considered,

(2) the opinion is not supported with facts, such as purchase price and comparable sales, or

(3) the opinion is not consistent with known facts.

Finally, the IRS states that the appraiser's opinion is never more valid than the facts on which it is based; without these facts it is simply a guess.

One crucial factor which must be fully considered in an appraisal determining the fair market value of personal property such as a piece of furniture or a painting is the object's physical condition—including, with art and antiques, the extent of any restoration.[34] For example, the IRS notes that "an antique in damaged condition, or lacking the 'original brasses,' may be worth much less than a similar piece in excellent condition."[35]

Appraisals offered by an OLA company are based on an examination of digital images of the property, rather than on an examination of the property itself. One can imagine a situation where extensive restoration of a painting would not be noticeable in a digital image, but would be apparent if a physical inspection of the painting were conducted. It is therefore questionable whether reliance by an appraiser on digital images of art is can provide the appraiser with sufficient accurate evidence about the art to render the appraisal credible. The specific concern for a taxpayer relying on an OLA is that the appraisal, based on digital images, will be accorded substantially less weight by the IRS and the courts than an appraisal based on a physical examination of the property.

The courts have addressed this issue in the context of appraisers' reliance on photographs of works of art. As the Tax Court noted in *Johnson v. Commissioner*,[36] "[r]eliance on photographs is not unusual in the appraisal of art. Indeed, photographs generally serve as the basis for appraisals by the Art Advisory Panel to the Internal Revenue Service." Case law indicates that whether an appraisal of an artwork based on an examination of photographs of the artwork will be given much weight by the courts depends on the nature of the artwork, the purpose of the examination, and the quality of the photographs.

Some works of art, by their nature, are harder than others to appraise without a physical inspection. For example, the appearance of statues and other three-dimensional objects may vary with the angle and the lighting of the photograph. Two-dimensional objects, on the other hand, are generally better subjects for photographic examination. Even with two-dimensional objects, however, an appraisal based on the examination of photographs may be accorded little weight by the IRS and the courts if the object is, for example, a painting with extensive retouching where the retouching is not apparent in the photographs.

The purpose of the examination may also affect whether an expert opinion based on photographs will be accorded much weight by the IRS and the courts. In *Sammons v. Commissioner*,[37] the Ninth Circuit held that an examination of photographs was insufficient where the purpose of the appraisal was to determine the fair market value of the property for charitable contribution purposes. The taxpayers donated to a museum their collection of North American Indian artifacts which included items such as "painted buffalo hides, buckskin clothing, medicine pipes, war bonnets, human scalps, medicine rattles made from buffalo scrotums and many other items."[38]

The Tax Court held (and the appellate court affirmed) that the taxpayer's appraisal was not entitled to any weight in determining fair market value. The taxpayer's experts testified at trial that basing their appraisal on photographs alone made it "difficult, if not impossible, to determine the condition, authenticity, or age of artifacts.[39] The Ninth Circuit specifically noted that the taxpayer's appraisal was not rejected solely because it was based on photographs, but because the photographs so limited the appraisers' ability to evaluate the property that they were *"forced to assume* that the donated artifacts were genuine and of average to good condition."[40]

Still another factor to consider is the quality of the photographs. The photographs must clearly and accurately depict the property to be appraised, and must be of sufficient size, sharpness, and color quality to provide a basis for the appraiser to render an opinion. For example, for charitable contribution deductions for art valued at $20,000 or more, the IRS requires an eight-by-ten-inch color photograph or a color transparency no smaller than four by five inches.[41]

The poor quality of photographic evidence had a direct effect on the court's holding in *Johnson v. Commissioner*.[42] In *Johnson*, the taxpayers donated a number of Indian artifacts and etchings to a museum. The taxpayers' appraiser did not view the artifact collection to make his appraisal, but instead relied on photographs of the objects and descriptions supplied by petitioners. In his testimony, the appraiser "indicated that the photographs were not particularly helpful due to poor photocopying quality. Therefore, he relied primarily on the descriptions [provided by the taxpayers]."[43] The court refused to accept the values determined by the taxpayer's expert because his values "were based primarily on the descriptions drafted by [the taxpayers] without the benefit of independent and reliable visual examination."[44] Therefore, poor quality images will decrease the weight the courts give to an appraisal.

The cases cited above indicate that the nature of the property appraised, the purpose of the appraisal, and the quality of the images relied on by the appraiser will all affect the weight given to the appraisal. The best course of action for an OLA company is to advise potential appraisal clients (through statements in the appraisal agreement) that these factors may substantially lower the weight accorded the appraisal by the IRS or the courts. Even safer and probably more accurately, the OLA company should advise the taxpayer that an OLA is an estimate of value and is not a formal appraisal or a "qualified" appraisal for tax purposes.

For purposes of this discussion, we are assuming that the digital images provided to the OLA company will be of average quality for digital images. The goal for the digital images is to make them comparable to a high-quality photograph, of sufficient size as to render the image accurately and with good color quality and clarity. Again, however, taxpayers should be put on notice that an appraisal provided through an OLA company will be given substantially less weight by the IRS and the courts than an appraisal which includes a physical inspection of the property.

Even more problematic than the issue of appraisals based on digital images is the OLA's discussion of appraisal methodology. Generally, the party preparing the OLA renders a valuation without providing any underlying basis for it; similarly, if comparable sales data is provided, it is devoid of any accompanying rationale as to *why* such sales are comparable. The preparer of the OLA can rely only on the information furnished by the taxpayer and therefore may be unable to accurately determine comparable sales transactions as required by the IRS. A mere listing of the item of tangible personal property with a valuation figure next to it is not a "qualified appraisal" as required by the IRS even if the valuation is based on computer data.

Conclusion

An OLA should satisfy the reliable written records substantiation requirements for a charitable income tax deduction of $5,000 or less. However, if a deduction of $5,000 or less is challenged by the IRS, the taxpayer will need to obtain a formal appraisal to support the taxpayer's position with regard to the fair market value of the donated property.

Although it may be possible to have an OLA that could satisfy the substantiation requirements in the Regulations for charitable deductions in excess of $5,000, it is unlikely that it would be of much use. An OLA relies on digital images of the appraised property so the question of condition remains uncertain; there will not be a list of comparable sales or an analysis of the appraisal methodology used, and the OLA may not have the signature and taxpayer identification number of the preparer of the OLA. Each of these factors will cause the IRS and the courts to accord less weight to an OLA than to an appraisal based upon a physical examination of the property.

In short, an OLA is an estimate of value. It is not—and should not purport to be—a formal appraisal or a qualified appraisal prepared for tax purposes under precise appraisal methodology.

Do OLAs Comply with the Guidelines for Appraisers Set Forth in the Uniform Standards of Professional Appraisal Practice (USPAP)?

The USPAP publication, promulgated by the Appraisal Standards Board of the Appraisal Foundation, contains guidelines for professional appraisal practice. While these guidelines are nonbinding in the sense that neither the Appraisal Standards Board nor the Appraisal Foundation is a government entity with the ability to enforce the guidelines, they are widely recognized as the standard for professional appraisal activity.

USPAP Standards 7 and 8 address the appraisal of personal property. Standard 7 applies to the development of the appraisal, and Standard 8 applies to the written appraisal report. Standards Rule 7-2 provides in part:

> In developing a personal property appraisal, an appraiser must:
> (e)   identify the characteristics of the property that are relevant to the purpose and intended use of the appraisal, including:
>   (i)   sufficient characteristics to establish the identity of the item including the method of identification;
>   (ii) sufficient characteristics to establish the relative quality of the item (and its component parts, where applicable) within its type;
>   (iii) all other physical and economic attributes with a material effect on value; . . .

This means that the appraiser must take into consideration in determining value the condition, style, quality, manufacturer, author, materials, origin, age, provenance, alterations, and restorations of the property.

The question raised by Standard 7 is whether an appraisal during which the appraiser studies digital images of the property, rather than conducting a physical examination, is sufficient to meet the standard. As noted above, Standards Rule 7-2 requires the appraiser to consider the condition and quality of, and alterations and restorations to, the property in order to determine its value. The problem with an appraisal that relies on digital images is that some or all of these factors may not be apparent in the digital images, although they would be apparent if the property were viewed by the naked eye. Thus it appears that an appraisal conducted by examination of digital images would not satisfy Standards Rule 7-2, which requires the appraiser to identify the physical attributes that have a material effect on value.

However, the official comments to Standards Rule 7-2 state that if the necessary subject property information is not available because of conditions limiting the appraiser's ability to inspect or research the subject property, the appraiser can (i) obtain the necessary information before proceeding (an available condition report or similar description), or (ii) use an extraordinary assumption about such information. An appraiser may use any combination of a property inspection and documents or other resources to identify the relevant characteristics of the subject property so long as the information used is from sources the appraiser reasonably believes are reliable. An extraordinary assumption as to the condition of the property (a verbal opinion from someone who has examined the property) may be used in the appraisal only if: the appraiser has a reasonable basis for the extraordinary assumption; it is required to properly develop the appraiser's opinion and conclusion; and the appraiser fully discloses in the appraisal that he has made an extraordinary assumption—that is, only digital images have been examined, so the property is assumed to be in good condition.

Therefore, the appraiser who relies on digital images of the property will be in compliance with USPAP so long as the appraiser feels that he is giving an appraisal with "credible" results, despite the limitations inherent in the analysis of digital images. An OLA entity should include language in its contract or guidelines for appraisals addressing the fact that the property was not physically inspected by the appraiser, and should require the client to sign a statement indicating that the client understands that reliance on digital images or third-party information may impact the conclusions reached in the appraisal and the weight it is given by the IRS.

Standards Rule 8-1 provides: "Each written or oral personal property appraisal report must: . . . (c) clearly and accurately disclose any extraordinary assumption, hypothetical condition, or limiting condition that directly affects the appraisal, and indicate its impact on value." Standards Rule 8-3 requires the appraiser to include in the appraisal report a signed statement indicating whether the appraiser has or has not made a personal inspection of the property appraised. To satisfy these standards, OLA entities should ensure that its appraisers include a statement in their appraisal reports indicating that the appraisal has been prepared in reliance on digital images and that the appraiser has not made a personal inspection of the property appraised.

Conclusion

By properly invoking the Departure Rule and by disclosing the appraiser's reliance on digital images to the taxpayer, appraisals provided by OLAs will be in compliance with USPAP. It should be noted that the Association of Online Appraisers (AOA), a not-for-profit international association for personal property appraisers who are involved in offering online written appraisal reports through the use of digital images and Internet online reporting, takes the position that online appraisal reports will be "complete" appraisals as defined by USPAP: that is, that the Departure Rule need not be invoked. However, we believe that this is a precipitous conclusion that will not find support in case law.

DISPARAGEMENT

The seminal case in art disparagement law is *Hahn v. Duveen*,[45] a 1920s episode that rocked the worlds of art, journalism, and connoisseurship.

On June 17, 1920,[46] the *New York World* newspaper made history by publishing a comment by Sir Joseph Duveen (later Baron Duveen of Millbank), one of the most spectacular art dealers of all time. Andrée Hahn, a stunning French war bride, had received as a gift from her godmother upon her marriage to Harry Hahn, an American serviceman, a painting supposedly by Leonardo da Vinci, *La Belle Ferronière*. The Hahns moved to the United States and in 1920 brought the painting here, billing it as "the first Leonardo to arrive in America" and announcing its prospective sale to the Kansas City Art Gallery for $250,000. The *New York World* sent a reporter to solicit Duveen's opinion, advising him that the painting had been authenticated by a well-known French art expert, Georges Sortais. Duveen, having seen no more than a photograph of the work, replied that the Hahn painting was a

> copy, hundreds of which have been made of this and other Leonardo subjects, and offered in the market as genuine. . . . [Leonardo's] original *La Belle Ferroniere* is in the Louvre. Georges Sortais' certificate is worthless, if it really relates to the Kansas City picture. He is not an expert in the works of Leonardo.[47]

The Kansas City sale fell through, and Andrée Hahn sued Duveen for $500,000, alleging that his disparagement of her painting made it virtually worthless anywhere in the world. Duveen responded that the sacred right of free speech would be destroyed if he could not render a statement of opinion in good faith.

The case was ultimately tried in New York in 1929, resulting in a court decision that was not satisfactory to either party. After a long jury trial in which a parade of experts gave conflicting testimony as to the authenticity of both the Hahn painting and the Louvre painting, the jury was unable to reach the required unanimous verdict, and the judge ordered a retrial.[48] One month before the retrial, a settlement was reached, no doubt casting a chilling effect on the volubility of the art expert; Duveen paid the Hahns court costs plus $60,000 in damages.

In 1985, after many years in storage and a few odd years in various museums, mainly as a subject of study or special exhibition, the Hahn painting once again surfaced on the market in Nebraska. Its current owner, in an attempt to sell the painting, billed it as an original Leonardo.[49] However, in March 1993, the painting, which was under negotiation for sale in Nebraska for $80 million, was branded a copy by the British authority on Leonardo, Professor Martin Kemp of St. Andrew's University.[50] Kemp's assessment reportedly knocked $75 million off the painting's value.[51]

Elements of Disparagement

An action for disparagement may be against a person whose false statement about an artwork has reduced the market value of the work.[52] When the issue is properly raised, a plaintiff in a disparagement case must prove the following:[53]

1. A legally protected interest was affected by the comment.

2. The comment had an injurious character.

3. The comment was false.

4. The comment was published.

5. The circumstances of publication were such that reliance on the comment by a third party was reasonably foreseeable.

6. The third-party recipient understood the comment in its injurious sense.

7. The third-party recipient understood the comment as applicable to the plaintiff's interests.

8. Pecuniary loss resulted from the publication of the comment.

9. The defendant knew his statement was false or acted with reckless disregard of its truth or falsity.

Example 1: Suppose that at a cocktail party an art appraiser sees a painting by Jan Doe, a famous living artist, hanging on the wall. A fellow guest informs the art appraiser that their host is trying to decide whether or not to buy the painting from a dealer. The art appraiser approaches the host, who is surrounded by people, and, knowing that his statement is false, announces that there is a diminishing secondary market for Jan Does and that the painting is not a good investment. The host of the party heeds the appraiser's remark and does not buy the painting. The result? The art appraiser would be subject to liability to the dealer for disparagement.

Example 2: The facts are the same except that this time the appraiser merely has a high degree of awareness of the probable falseness of his statement. The result is the same: The appraiser would be subject to liability to the dealer for disparagement. Reckless disregard of the truth or falsity of one's statement renders the speaker liable as surely as does knowledge of a statement's falsity.

Example 3: Again, the facts are the same except that this time the party host approaches the art appraiser, draws him into a private room, tells him that he is trying to decide whether or not to buy the Jan Doe, and asks for his advice. The appraiser, believing in good faith that his statement is true and that he has a sufficient knowledge of the market to justify it—although, in fact, his statement is false and would be shown to be false by a reasonably diligent investigation—advises his host not to buy the Jan Doe. The host heeds the appraiser's remark and does not buy the painting. The result: The appraiser would not be liable to the dealer because, when communicating a statement to a prospective buyer at the buyer's request, the art appraiser may avail himself of the conditional privilege of protection of interests of third persons.[54] That the prospective buyer—that is, someone with an interest to protect—has made the request for information indicates that he regards the matter as sufficiently important to justify the publication of any defamatory material that may be involved in response to his request for information. Therefore, the art appraiser who publishes that information or causes it to be published—in the example, a verbal or written statement about the Jan Doe work to anyone other than the dealer or Jan Doe—is not required to microscopically evaluate the interest the prospective buyer seeks to protect, nor is he required to compare (as he otherwise would be required, had he volunteered his opinion) the harm likely to be done to the dealer if his statement is false with the harm likely to be done to his friend if his statement is true. In this example, of course, the statement is false. Nevertheless, here the appraiser is protected by the conditional privilege as long as he does not make the statement with either knowledge of its falsity or reckless disregard as to its truth or falsity.[55]

In addition to the conditional privilege described above, the appraiser in the example may be able to avail himself of the absolute privilege of consent.[56] Indeed, had the party host already purchased the Jan Doe when he came to the appraiser for an opinion, he would be held to have consented to whatever the appraiser told him about it, disparaging or not, so long as the statement did not exceed the scope of his consent. Of course, if the appraiser were relaying his opinion solely to the host as owner of the Jan Doe, there would be no action for disparagement in any event, as publication would not have occurred. However, in relaying the information to his host, the prospective buyer, the appraiser could argue that the dealer, in letting his painting out on approval, assumed the risk of negative opinions.[57]

Although not seen in court every day, product disparagement remains a viable, if difficult, theory of liability on which to bring suit, as illustrated in the case of *Kirby v. Wildenstein*.[58] A New York federal district court dismissed the lawsuit, which was based on disparagement arising under the following circumstances:

In March 1988, the plaintiff, owner of a painting entitled *La Rue de la Paix* by the nineteenth-century French artist Jean Beraud, consigned it to Christie's auction house for sale at auction in May 1988. A reserve price for the painting was set at approximately $160,000. Under the terms of the consignment agreement, the painting would be included in the forthcoming Beraud *catalogue raisonné*[59] being prepared by Patrick Offenstadt, the recognized expert on Beraud, and the Offenstadt reference would be included in Christie's sales catalog; indeed, the painting could not be sold without the reference.

Christie's sought confirmation from Offenstadt—who was working at Foundation Wildenstein, a nonprofit French corporation engaged in art historical research and the publishing of art catalogs—that the painting would appear in the *catalogue raisonné*. In reply, Offenstadt had Daniel Wildenstein, the director of the foundation and a renowned expert on nineteenth-century art, travel to New York to examine the painting, which Wildenstein did at his New York gallery in April 1988. After giving the painting a careful examination,

Wildenstein concluded that it was either a fake or suffered from the removal of paint through overcleaning.

In early May 1988, Offenstadt informed Christie's that the painting would not be included in the forthcoming *catalogue raisonné*; also, Joseph Baillio, an employee of Wildenstein's New York gallery, informed Christie's that Wildenstein did not like the painting and did not believe that it was authentic. Christie's then withdrew the painting from the May 1988 auction.

However, still believing in the painting's genuineness, Christie's was able to secure documents in June 1988 conclusively establishing its authenticity, whereupon Christie's forwarded the documents to the foundation. Later that month, the foundation informed Christie's by letter that it had revised its opinion as to the genuineness of the painting and that it would be listed in the forthcoming *catalogue raisonné* as an authentic Beraud but would bear a notation that the painting had been damaged by "an abusive restoration and cleaning."

Christie's subsequently included the painting in an auction scheduled for late October 1988. The Christie's sales catalog for that auction noted that the painting would be listed in the forthcoming Beraud *catalogue raisonné* but did not mention its condition.

No one bid on the painting at the October 1988 auction, and it remained unsold. The plaintiff made no further efforts at resale after the auction and in March 1989 brought suit against Wildenstein and the foundation, alleging product disparagement and seeking damages of $250,000, later amended to $200,000.

In dismissing the suit, the New York federal district court noted that the plaintiff failed to demonstrate a triable issue of fact with respect to special damages, one of the requisite elements of disparagement. As the court observed,

> [s]pecial damages are limited to losses having pecuniary or economic value, and must be "fully and accurately stated . . . with sufficient particularity to identify actual losses." . . . In addition . . . [they] must be the "natural and immediate consequence of the disparaging statements" to be recoverable.[60]

In the suit the plaintiff failed to specify the losses underlying, first, the $250,000 figure and then the $200,000 figure, nor did the plaintiff at any time identify any particular person who would have bid on the painting but for the alleged disparagement. As the court noted:

> The rule . . . that lost customers must be named where the special damages claimed are lost sales—is well-entrenched and has been consistently followed.[61]

Moreover, as the court observed, the plaintiff failed to demonstrate a requisite causal connection between Wildenstein's statements and any losses sustained by the plaintiff. Wildenstein asserted that he disclosed the statements only to Christie's, Offenstadt, Baillio, and one other foundation employee working on the *catalogue raisonné*. Although the disclosures to the last three parties technically constitute publication, none of those parties was a potential buyer of the painting, and there was no evidence that they disseminated the statements to outside parties. Accordingly, the case was dismissed.

DEFAMATION

At first glance, disparagement and defamation are similar: Under each theory, liability is incurred for injuries sustained through false statements about the plaintiff published to third parties. Nevertheless, differences abound, and the differences are fundamental. A disparagement suit centers on the economic interests of the aggrieved party, whether that party is an artist, an art dealer, or an art collector. A defamation suit, on the other hand, is to protect the personal reputation and good name of that aggrieved party. To bring an action in defamation, an artist, an art dealer, or an art collector must establish the following elements:[62]

1. The statement in question was defamatory.
2. The statement was of purported fact.
3. The statement was false.

4. The statement was about the plaintiff.

5. The statement was published by the defendant to a third party.

6. The statement was made with the requisite element of fault, where applicable.[63]

The Defamatory Statement

A statement is defamatory if it tends to harm the reputation of another, lowering the party in the estimation of the community or deterring third persons from associating or dealing with that party.[64] The recipient need not believe the statement to be true; it is enough that the recipient understands the statement in its defamatory sense.[65] Moreover, in most jurisdictions, statements that are ambiguous or capable of carrying a defamatory meaning may be deemed actionable. Further, a statement need not be explicit in order for it to be deemed defamatory; mere insinuation will suffice.[66] For example, in the 1991 case of *Weller v. American Broadcasting Company*,[67] a California state appellate court affirmed an award of $2.3 million to the plaintiff, an art dealer whose sale of two rare silver candelabra for $65,000 to the de Young Museum was attacked in a series of television broadcasts. As to the defamatory statements about the plaintiff, the court noted the following:

> There is no question that the news reports in this case could have been understood as implying that [plaintiff] had, at worst, knowingly sold stolen property to the de Young Museum and, at best, had lied about the Texas origin and sold them at a "grossly inflated price." This implication is conveyed by the persistent efforts to tie . . . a convicted felon [of insurance fraud involving silver] to the transaction or at least to [plaintiff].[68]

However, when an artist or another plaintiff is controversial or in the vanguard of an emerging artistic movement or the artist's work has become a cultural icon, humorous commentary targeting the artist or the artist's work is not ordinarily viewed as defamatory and, consequently, is nonactionable. And on rare occasions an aggrieved art dealer, collector, or artist has a questionable reputation that, under defamation law, is not capable of being injured.[69]

Of Purported Fact

In June 1990, the United States Supreme Court in *Milkovich v. Lorain Journal Co.*[70] determined that there is no special federal First Amendment protection for statements of opinion by media defendants[71] on matters of public concern. In eschewing "an artificial dichotomy between 'opinion' and fact," the Court determined that only the following statements *cannot* be subject to liability in defamation:[72]

- Those statements containing no provably false factual connotations

- Those statements that cannot be reasonably interpreted as stating actual facts about a person

The Court also noted that "loose, figurative or hyperbolic language . . . would negate the impression"[73] that a person was making a serious accusation based on fact.

The following two examples illuminate the holding in the *Milkovich* case.

Example 1: *X* is a society reporter for a local newspaper. In the course of attending, both as a guest and as a reporter, a local dinner party hosted by a major local figure, *X* observes Jane Doe, another guest, quietly slip a magnificent diamond necklace into her purse and later leave with it. *X* is aware that the particular piece of jewelry belongs to the host. The next day, without investigating any of the circumstances relating to Doe's acquisition of the necklace, *X* files a story with the local newspaper describing the dinner party, including an incomplete description of Doe's acquisition. The story, which is published, includes the statement, "In my opinion Jane Doe is a thief." The result? Both *X* and the newspaper would be subject to liability to Jane Doe for defamation; *X*'s statement, made with deliberate absence of investigation into the circumstances of the acquisition, contained a provably false factual connotation, since Jane

Doe could establish that she was not a thief and, in fact, had secured permission to borrow the necklace from the host.

Example 2: The facts are the same except that this time the story filed by X and published in the local paper includes the statement, "In my opinion Jane Doe exhibited elephantine avarice in walking out with the diamond necklace." The result? Most likely, neither X nor the newspaper would be subject to liability to Jane Doe for defamation; X's statement not only contained no provably false factual connotation but also contained hyperbolic language that tends to negate the impression that she was making a serious accusation based on fact.

The guidelines set forth in *Milkovich* are evolving into settled law. In the previously noted *Weller* case, the California appellate court cited *Milkovich* in holding that the defendant-broadcaster's statement that the de Young Museum bought the candelabra at a "grossly inflated price" was an allegedly defamatory fact that could be "objectively verified."[74]

Another art case in 1991, *McNally v. Yarnall*,[75] which involved an aggrieved art collector, was also analyzed in light of *Milkovich*. The facts in the case provide an object lesson in the treacherous power of words when they are misused.

Sean and Janet McNally, New Jersey residents, were for fourteen years engaged in the purchase and sale of the works of the artist John La Farge. La Farge was a turn-of-the-century American artist who worked in a variety of media and who achieved, in particular, world renown for his stained-glass work. The McNallys offered some of their La Farge works for sale through the Graham Gallery in New York City and at a La Farge exhibition sponsored by the William Vareika Fine Arts Gallery in Newport, Rhode Island. Sean McNally, an acknowledged expert on the works of La Farge, was in the process of writing a book on La Farge and the history of his works. James Yarnall, a resident of the District of Columbia, was both an art historian specializing in the works of La Farge and a computer expert heading a company that provides computer database services to museums.

In 1985, Yale University Press selected Yarnall to direct the publication of *The Catalogue Raisonné of the Works of John La Farge*. And in

1985 through 1989, the Metropolitan Museum of Art in New York City retained Yarnall as an independent contractor to assist the departments of American art in coordinating the computerization of information concerning the American Wing collections.

In early 1988, Richard J. Schwartz, a collector of art and a benefactor of the museum, advised the museum that he wished to acquire a stained-glass window by La Farge. Through museum intermediaries Yarnall advised Schwartz that *Moon Window*, a window by La Farge depicting a moon, was for sale. At a subsequent viewing of the window at the museum—a viewing that involved, among others, Schwartz, Yarnall, and Lewis Sharp, the curator and administrator of the American Wing—Yarnall stated his belief that on the basis of a drawing of the window with which he was familiar, La Farge designed it in the 1880s. Schwartz subsequently bought the window for his personal collection for $165,000. Sometime earlier McNally had had an opportunity to view the window. Believing that La Farge may have designed the window but did not execute it, McNally valued the window at a mere $20,000. Shortly after Schwartz's purchase, a supposed companion window to Schwartz's window sold at auction at Christie's for $14,200.

In December 1988, at the Graham Gallery in New York City, the Schwartzes viewed for possible purchase another La Farge window known as *Garland of Fruit and Flowers*. The asking price for that window was $150,000. Present at the viewing at the Schwartzes' request were the same people who participated in the viewing of *Moon Window*. On their arrival at the gallery, the Schwartzes and their party learned that *Garland of Fruit and Flowers* belonged to the McNallys. In the course of the viewing, Yarnall pointed out some areas of fracture and noted that the window appeared to have been restored with some sort of epoxy or glue. The Schwartzes did not purchase the window.

Subsequently, McNally arranged for several stained-glass restorers to provide Graham Gallery with an explanation for the presence of epoxy on *Garland of Fruit and Flowers*. The restorers sent the gallery several letters detailing the process of crizzling, the structural decomposition of glass that occurs with the diminution of the quantity of limestone in the glass over time. The letters noted that it was customary to apply epoxy to seal the glass once crizzling had set in.

In January 1989, the art historian Yarnall entered into a second contract with the museum, this one as a research associate, for the purpose of continuing his work on the La Farge *catalogue raisonné*. The benefactors of the research grant were the Schwartzes.

At approximately the same time, Sean McNally and the Vareika gallery began planning an exhibition of La Farge works to be held in July 1989 in Newport, Rhode Island. Of the approximately 117 works consigned to be sold through the exhibition, seventy belonged to the McNallys. In the months preceding the exhibition, Vareika on several occasions sent to Yarnall for review some photographs of many of the works to be included in the exhibition. Each time, Yarnall rendered an opinion, usually over the telephone. The result of the exchange was that the works he told Vareika were not in his opinion the works of La Farge were not included in either the exhibition or the exhibition catalog. At some point, McNally asked the Vareika gallery to cease forwarding photographs of his items to Yarnall; some of the works consigned by McNally had been heretofore undiscovered, and McNally apparently wanted to introduce them in his upcoming book.

At some time early in 1989, the Vareika gallery invited Yarnall to participate in a La Farge symposium to be held in conjunction with the exhibition. In April 1989, Yarnall declined, citing time constraints and adding that holding a symposium, as opposed to a lecture series, involving people with a "history of disagreeing with each other" was not a good way to promote the exhibition.

In June 1989, Vareika placed an advertisement for the upcoming exhibition in *Art & Antiques Magazine*. The advertisement included a photo of a stained-glass window owned by the McNallys and depicting a rooster. In response to Vareika's request for an opinion, Yarnall replied that the window was not recognized as a La Farge either by himself or by the *catalogue raisonné*, that the rooster motif was unknown in La Farge's work, and that the window was probably by Thomas Wright, La Farge's studio assistant and himself a prolific artist.

The advertisement was discontinued, and the window was removed from the exhibition.

The invitation to the exhibition depicted a stained-glass window owned by the McNallys and known as *Morgan Hollyhocks*. The picture of the window in the invitation was captioned "Window originally from the J. Pierpont Morgan House, New York, New York." Although it is disputed whether the Vareika gallery actually solicited Yarnall's opinion, Yarnall informed Vareika that in the opinion of the *catalogue raisonné* and in his opinion there was no certainty that the window featured in the invitation was originally from the Morgan House. He stated that his opinion was based in part on the fact that La Farge's grandson had made a similar determination in 1984; at that time, the grandson wrote to McNally, giving his opinion and his knowledge of the window's provenance.

On August 4, 1989, Yarnall wrote to McNally on *catalogue raisonné* stationery discussing the rooster window. The letter, published solely to McNally and to Mary La Farge, the widow of La Farge's grandson, stated:

> Mary . . . [would] write for elucidation on the works you own that are in Vareika's show. . . . [M]any of these are not known to the catalogue raisonné, and not all of them seem to be by La Farge.[76]

On August 19, 1989, Yarnall wrote to the Vareika gallery on museum stationery, assessing the exhibition catalog. The assessment was negative. Yarnall indicated, among other things, that the catalog was filled with misinformation and misattributions and that a fair number of the works in the exhibition would eventually be identified as the works of Thomas Wright or other La Farge assistants. Included in Yarnall's letter to Vareika was the following statement: "It appears that [McNally] has the history of many works that he owns muddled, rendering anything he says about them suspect."[77]

In bringing suit against Yarnall on a theory of defamation, McNally alleged that Yarnall's statements in the two letters and about the various windows diminished the value of the McNallys' collection and called into question Sean McNally's professional reputation as a collector of the works of John La Farge and as an expert on them. The New York federal district court refused to grant a summary judgment, because at least one of the statements made by Yarnall might be actionable. Citing *Milkovitch*, the court noted that statements on matters of public concern are not actionable as long as they (1) do not contain a provably false factual connotation and (2) cannot reasonably be interpreted as stating actual facts about a person. Accordingly, the court systematically assessed all the comments made by Yarnall that were included in McNally's allegations in keeping with the standards of *Milkovitch*. For example:

1. The garland window. Although the court acknowledged that Yarnall's statements regarding the condition of the window and its restoration were capable of being proved false, McNally, to recover damages for defamation, must also show that Yarnall made the statements with the requisite degree of fault (see discussion below), which in New York is gross irresponsibility.[78] When Yarnall provided Schwartz, at the latter's request, with his opinion at the informal viewing, Yarnall did not, in the court's opinion, act with gross irresponsibility.[79]

2. The rooster window. The court noted that Yarnall's statement that the rooster window was not recognized as a La-Farge by Yarnall or by the *catalogue raisonné* is a proposition that cannot be disproved.[80] The alleged statement refers to Yarnall's personal belief and to the incontrovertible fact that the rooster window is not currently included in the *catalogue raisonné*.

3. The hollyhocks window. According to the court, Yarnall's statement—that in his and the *catalogue raisonné*'s opinion there is no certainty that the window featured in the invitation was originally from the Morgan House—is not capable of being proved false, given the lack of signature on the window and the existence of other windows featuring a hollyhocks motif.[81] Moreover, as the court noted, Yarnall

supported his statement with disclosed facts: Henry La-Farge's earlier determination and the work's provenance.

4. August 4, 1989, letter. The court determined that the letter's statements were incapable of being proved false; rather, they describe a set of facts relating to the *catalogue raisonné* at a particular time that no one would dispute.[82]

5. August 19, 1989, letter. The court found that in Yarnall's letter to Vareika, the statement that McNally "has the history of many works that he owns muddled, rendering anything he says about them suspect" could well be actionable. That statement addressed McNally's reliability as a dealer; targeted his competence, character, or performance; and was capable of being proved false.[83]

In the more recent case of *Daniel Goldreyer Ltd. v. Van de Wetering*,[84] a New York State appellate court found that an aggrieved art restorer had a triable case in defamation against a media defendant. Daniel Goldreyer, a noted art restorer, had been paid more than $270,000 by the Stedelijk Museum in Amsterdam to restore a $3.1 million painting by Barnett Newman, *Who's Afraid of Red, Yellow and Blue III*, which had been slashed in 1986 by an enraged museumgoer. The resultant restoration proved controversial; an art critic accused Goldreyer of completing his repairs with a paint roller. In reporting on the controversy, the *Wall Street Journal* in its December 24, 1991, issue ran an article entitled, "For That Price, Why Not Have the Whole Museum Repainted?" The article asserted that Goldreyer had performed a restoration on a masterpiece by using a roller brush and house paint and "implied that the results warranted possible criminal charges after an official investigation."[85] The article referred to an official report of a laboratory analysis made of the restoration and the analysis's conclusion that "Mr. Newman's canvas was completely painted over using an inappropriate type of paint."[86] The article, however, did not publish the details of the method and the findings of the analysis. Accordingly, the appellate court affirmed a lower court holding that the statements in the *Wall Street Journal* were "opinion based upon fact, and therefore actionable since there were implications of additional undisclosed facts."[87]

False Statement

A defamatory statement must be false in order to be actionable. If the defendant's statement addresses a matter of public interest or public concern, the First Amendment freedom of expression is implicated, and the plaintiff must prove the falsity of the statement.[88] If the defendant's statement addresses a purely private matter, the statement is presumed false, and the defendant must prove its truth as an affirmative defense.[89] Art-related issues may be either public or private matters. If the statement in question is embodied in a work of art, the chances are that the matter is one of public concern, and First Amendment issues come into play; if, however, the defendant's statement is made in a business dispute between, say, two art dealers, the matter is likely to be deemed a purely private one.

Boule v. Hutton

The case of *Boule v. Hutton*[90] illuminates the viability of defamation as a source of legal exposure for experts while at the same time highlighting for a potential plaintiff the burdens inherent in establishing a prima facie case in disparagement and some other theories of liability.

The plaintiffs Claude and Rene Boule are Parisian art collectors who, at the time of trial, owned 161 works on paper as well as one oil painting, all attributed to the artist Lazar Khidekel. Khidekel, born early in the twentieth century, was, in his younger years, associated with the Suprematist movement in Russian art, and was a student of the movement's leader and most celebrated artist, Kazimir Malevich. From 1930 until the mid 1980s when he died, however, Khidekel taught architecture at the Leningrad Institute of Civil Engineering. The Boules acquired the works of art on paper over a four-year period beginning in 1984. They acquired the art from one Vladmir Tsarenkov, a private dealer who provided no provenance for any of the art and who requested that the Boules conceal his identity. The Boules paid him a total purchase price of 1.5 million French francs,[91] cash, and did not consult with any third parties to confirm the works' authenticity at the time of the purchases. In 1991, the Boules acquired the oil painting at a Sotheby's auction in London for £2,800.[92]

In the summer of 1988, Jean-Claude Marcade, a French art historian, brought Mark Khidekel, son of the artist and a Russian citizen, to the Boules' home in Paris to examine some of his late father's art. Mark Khidekel, who also had a collection of his father's art, expressed no skepticism at that time about the authenticity of the Boules' collection. In 1989, Helene Larroche, owner of a Paris bookstore and art gallery, proposed a joint exhibition of the two Khidekel collections, the Boules' and Mark's. In July 1989, the Boules and Mark signed an agreement for this joint exhibition. The exhibition, however, was ultimately canceled because Mark failed to furnish his father's works by the date specified in the contract.

Throughout 1989, 1990, and 1991, Mark visited the Boule family, brought his wife Regina to visit the Boules, showed them some slides of his collection of his father's work, and brought several gifts. During this time, Mark and Regina learned that the Boules were planning to lend their works to an exhibition at the Joliette Museum of Art in Montreal, Canada. Mark and Regina expressed no reservations regarding the authenticity of the Boules' collection; rather, they expressed their desire to attend the exhibition in order both to lecture there and to show slides of their own collection of Khidekels. During a visit by Mark and Regina to the Boule home in June 1991, Mark signed sixteen certificates of authenticity for the Boules. The number of certificates he signed was limited only by the amount of cash the Boules had on hand: For their 40,000 French francs, he signed sixteen certificates at 2,500 francs per certificate. Before signing the certificates, Mark chose among the forty-four original Khidekel works then at the Boule residence, the other works being in transit to the Joliette exhibition. In selecting the works in the presence of Regina, Mark examined them with a magnifying glass and signed certificates of authenticity on the backs of photographs corresponding to the selected works. Throughout 1991 and the spring of 1992, Mark and Regina sought to participate in the Joliette exhibition. Ultimately, however, their participation did not come to pass.

The Boules' collection was exhibited in galleries throughout Canada from August 1992 to August 1993, after which time a few of their Khidekel works were exhibited in a show in France. At the International Fair of Contemporary Art (FIAC) in Paris in October 1994, Yvette Moch, a retired art gallery manager still involved in the art world, approached defendant Ingrid Hutton of the New York-based Leonard Hutton Galleries—reputedly a major gallery for Russian avant-garde art—to show her a catalog of an exhibition for which Moch had been the curator. Apparently, Hutton saw a Khidekel from the Boules' collection while flipping through the catalog and said, "that is no good." Moch understood her to be referring to the authenticity of the work. In late 1995, when Hutton was solicited for her opinion of the Boules' Khidekels by Slava Kogan, another art dealer who traded in artworks from the Soviet Union, Hutton again indicated—this time in no uncertain terms—that the Boules' collection of Khidekels consisted of fakes. Additionally, she told Kogan that the Boules' certificates of authenticity signed by Mark Khidekel were also fakes.

Meanwhile, after learning that the Hutton Galleries exhibited and offered for sale some of Mark and Regina's Khidekel collection at FIAC in Paris in 1994, the Boules decided to try to sell some of their collection. They consigned four of their Khidekel works to Edith and Roland Flak, owners of a Parisian gallery specializing in twentieth-century art. These works were displayed at the April 1995 Art Messe in Frankfurt, but none sold. In December 1995, the Flaks orally agreed to purchase, at 40,000 French francs per work, a group of the Boules' Khidekel works over a two-to-three-year period, but did not work out any details of payment. In February and March of 1995, the Hutton Galleries exhibited and offered for sale several dozen Khidekels from Mark and Regina's collection, at prices averaging over $18,000 each.[93] Only four works sold.

From October 1994 through February 1996, Mark and Regina Khidekel and Ingrid Hutton made a number of statements impugning the authenticity of the Boules' Khidekels:

1. *Statement by Mark and Regina Khidekel and Ingrid Hutton.* In January 1996, the three defendants issued a letter on Hutton Galleries letterhead to at least twenty-five museums throughout the world. The letter completely repudiated the catalog of the Khidekel exhibition published by the Musée d'Art de Joliette, Quebec, Canada in 1992. It went on to note that

> [w]e will not permit this catalogue to be cited in connection with any works by Lazar Markovich Khidekel coming from the Khidekel Family or from the Leonard Hutton Galleries nor should this catalogue be cited by any other person or institution as reference material or in any other way in connection with works by Khidekel coming from the Khidekel Family or Leonard Hutton Galleries.[94]

2. *Statements by the Hutton Defendants.* The Hutton Galleries' catalog for its February and March 1995 show of Mark and Regina's Khidekels noted that

> [w]e present for the first time anywhere the work of Lazar Markovich Khidekel. . . . In his lifetime [Lazar Khidekel] never had a solo show, nor did he or his family ever sell or part with any of his works.[95]

3. *Statements by Mark and Regina.* The Khidekels told Patricia Railing, an art historian who lived in England and visited the Khidekels at their New York apartment, that the Boules' collection was "not by my father, they're fakes."[96] The magazine *ARTnews*, in its February 1996 issue, published an article entitled "The Betrayal of the Russian Avant Garde," addressing the prevalence of misattributed and forged works in Russian avant-garde art. The article included the following quote from Regina:

> When [Mark and Regina] finally saw the works, which belong to Paris collectors Claude and Rene Boule, they were . . . puzzled. "I don't know whether they're fakes or works of some-

body else," says Regina. "I only know and we are absolutely sure, that they have nothing to do with Khidekel."[97]

In the same article, Mark and Regina are quoted as saying that upon initially seeing the Boules' collection at the Boules' Paris home, "they told the Boules the works were not Khidekels."[98]

The Montreal publication *Le Devoir*, in its February 23, 1996, issue, quotes Regina as saying: "I am categorical: these works are not by Khidekel."[99] She is also quoted in the article as saying that "neither she nor her husband ever 'authenticated' anything and that fake certificates were forged."[100] In the February 22–28, 1996, issue of the Montreal periodical *Voir*, Mark and Regina are quoted as saying that the works in the Boules' collection are "not those of Khidekel."[101]

After *ARTnews* published Mark and Regina's statements challenging the authenticity of the Boules' collection, the Flaks withdrew their arrangement with the Boules and the Boules brought suit on a variety of theories: The federal Lanham Act, and various New York state law claims including violations of the New York General Business Law, product disparagement, defamation, tortuous interference with business relationships, common law unfair competition, unjust enrichment, breach of contract, common law fraud, prima facie tort, and the tort of "false light." The Lanham Act claim was against the Hutton defendants for statements in their 1995 exhibition catalog (see statement #2 above). The thrust of this claim was that certain statements attributed to the Huttons falsely disparaged the authenticity of the Boules' collection in order to promote the sale of Regina and Mark's Khidekel paintings at the Hutton galleries.

The New York federal district court noted at the outset that to prevail on their claims under the Lanham Act, the New York General Business Law, product disparagement, and unfair competition, the Boules had the burden of proving by a preponderance of the credible evidence that the defendants' statements were false.[102] That is, the Boules were required to prove that their works were, in fact, created by Lazar Khidekel. However, the court subsequently determined that the evidence submitted concerning authenticity was insufficient, and therefore the Boules did not sustain their burden of proving the essential element of falsity of the statements by a preponderance of the evidence.

As the court observed with respect to the defamation claim (citing a recent Second Circuit case),[103] if a statement involves a matter of "public concern," a plaintiff suing for defamation must prove the falsity of the defamatory statement. The Boules' collection, which was displayed throughout the world at public exhibitions, museums, and art shows, and portions of which collection were offered for sale to the public, was, according to the court, a matter of public concern. Therefore, as the Boules were unable to prove the authenticity of their collection by a preponderance of the evidence, they were unable, as the court noted, to prove the falsity of each statement impugning the authenticity of the Boules' collection.

However, the court concluded that the Boules had proved, by a preponderance of the credible evidence, the falsity of the statements in *ARTnews* by Mark and Regina that they initially informed the Boules that the works were not authentic. The court found that the Boules had likewise met their burden with respect to the statement in *Le Devoir* in which Regina denied that Mark ever wrote certificates of authenticity.

The requisite degree of fault was another element of defamation that required consideration by the court.[104] A public figure suing for defamation must show that the allegedly defamatory material was published with "actual malice"—that is, knowledge of falsity or reckless disregard of its truth or falsity.[105] A defamation plaintiff who is not a public figure bears a lighter burden: If the allegedly defamatory statement involved a matter of public concern, a private plaintiff must prove that the defendant made the statement with "gross irresponsibility"; and if the statement did not involve a matter of public concern, a private plaintiff need only prove that the defendant acted negligently in making the false statement.[106] In the instant case, the parties disputed whether the Boules should be treated as limited public figures for the purpose of the litigation. As the court noted,

[a] plaintiff may be considered a limited public figure for a specific litigation if the defendant has shown that the plaintiff has (1) successfully invited public attention to his views in an effort to influence other[s] prior to the incident that is the subject of litigation; (2) voluntarily injected himself into a public controversy related to the subject of litigation; (3) assumed a position of prominence in the public controversy; and (4) maintained regular and continuing access to the media.[107]

However, as the court concluded, the Boules satisfied their burden of proving fault regardless of which standard of fault would obtain.

Still another element of defamation the court was required to consider was whether there existed special damages or per se actionability. As the court observed, in applying New York law, one who sues for defamation must prove special damages unless the defamatory statement is deemed to be defamatory per se.[108] As to special damages, described by the court as "consist[ing] of the loss of something having economic or pecuniary value which must flow directly from the injury to reputation caused by the defamation,"[109] the Boules were not found to have proven special damages resulting from the statements in *ARTnews* and *Le Devoir*. If a statement is defamatory per se, injury to the plaintiff is assumed—even where the plaintiff can show no actual damages at all. In determining the presence of per se actionability, the court applied the general rule that a writing that tends to disparage a person in the way of his profession, trade, or office is defamatory per se.[110] Applying this rule to the Boules, the court found that as they are not professional art dealers, and as Rene Boule, though having a master's degree in art history, was a dental surgeon by profession, the statements were not defamatory per se as to the Boules as a couple or to Rene personally. However, the court found that as to Claude Boule, an art historian and lecturer and writer in the field of Russian avant-garde art, the statements would be presumed to injure her professional reputation for integrity—provided that readers of the statements knew that Claude was a respected art historian.[111] The court determined that readers of the *ARTnews* piece addressing fake and misattributed Russian avant-garde works would reasonably have known of Claude's profession, whereas readers of *Le Devoir*, a general daily newspaper, would not reasonably have known of her expertise. The court therefore found that only Claude Boule proved libel per se—and only with respect to the false and defamatory statement in the *ARTnews* article.

Finally, the court considered the issue of damages resulting from the defamatory statement. The court ruled out punitive damages: As it observed, "[p]laintiffs must prove by a preponderance of the evidence that the libelous statements were made out of hatred, ill will, or spite,"[112] and the Boules produced no evidence to that effect. As to actual damages, the court noted that although there was a presumption of injury to Claude's professional reputation as a result of the *ARTnews* statements, the Boules produced very little evidence that the statements caused Claude to suffer actual harm. Accordingly, the court found that she was entitled to nominal damages only.[113]

Concerning the Plaintiff

A recipient other than the plaintiff must understand that the defamatory communication applies to the plaintiff for the statement to be actionable. The plaintiff must be living but need not be named; therefore, an artist may be identifiable by his artwork or by being visually depicted through the work of another.[114] Mere membership in a large group, such as the Art Dealers Association of America, that is being defamed provides too flimsy a connection for any one person to bring suit unless that person is singled out.[115]

Published by the Defendant to a Third Party

To be actionable, a defamatory statement must be published—that is, communicated to at least one person other than the plaintiff. That third party must understand that the statement is defamatory and that it relates to the plaintiff.[116]

Requisite Element of Fault

If the plaintiff is a public official or a public figure, he must prove by clear and convincing evidence that the defamatory statement was published "with knowledge of falsity or reckless disregard of truth or falsity."[117] By placing themselves or their work in the public eye, artists may be considered public figures for determining the requisite standard of fault.[118] In *Yarnall v. McNally*, the New York federal district court, in denying a motion to dismiss, noted that "assuming, arguendo, that McNally is a limited purpose public figure, he has still raised a factual issue as to . . . malice."[119] For purposes of defamation, "malice" under New York law has been defined as "personal spite or ill will, or culpable recklessness or negligence."[120] As the court further noted in *Yarnall v. McNally*,

> [t]he evidence concerning the valuation of the Moon Window, taken in the light most favorable to the plaintiff, established a professional rivalry between McNally and Yarnall from which ill will might be inferred. . . . Moreover . . . [t]he evidence shows that Yarnall did not look at many of the works owned by McNally that he rejected as being true La Farges. The fact that it was McNally who withheld the photographs does not erase completely this evidence of recklessness or negligence.[121]

If, however, the plaintiff is a private person, the protection of his reputation assumes greater priority than for a public figure. In that case, the plaintiff need only prove the standard of fault required by the applicable state law. Generally, that standard is negligence,[122] although some states, such as New York, require a higher standard of gross negligence or even, as in Colorado and Indiana, constitutional malice.[123] Matters of public interest or public concern are quite broadly defined, as seen, for example, in *Yarnall v. McNally*. In finding that Yarnall's alleged statements about La Farge's works are clearly a matter of public concern, the New York federal district court made the following observation:[124]

> Granted, the topic of La Farge may not be of interest to the population as a whole. Where, however, as here, the statements

of Yarnall on the authenticity and value of works attributed to La Farge affect the market for and the tax implications of donating La Farge's works among the segment of the population that trades such works as well as the community of scholars with an interest in La Farge, such statements are of public import.

As seen from existing case law, an aggrieved plaintiff—such as an artist, a dealer, or a collector—can clearly bring suit for damages on a theory of defamation arising from an art expert's statements. (The artist as the defendant in a defamation suit is addressed in chapter 9.) If, however, the art expert's statements address a matter of public interest or public concern, he has at least some First Amendment protections. That protection renders defamation, for an aggrieved plaintiff seeking redress, a difficult if viable avenue to take. An aggrieved plaintiff can obtain redress far more successfully, when appropriate, on a theory of negligence. Case law indicates that art experts publish statements bespeaking negligence far more frequently than statements riddled with malice.

In *Daniel Goldreyer Ltd. v. Dow Jones & Co.*,[125] a case related to the earlier *Goldreyer v. Van de Wetering*[126] case, referred to on page 587, the appellate court, in reversing a lower court opinion, granted summary judgment to Dow Jones and dismissed Goldreyer's suit in defamation. As the appellate court noted, Goldreyer, an art restorer well-known and controversial within the profession but not well-known outside of it, was engaged by the Stedelijk Museum in Amsterdam to restore a $3.1 million painting by Barnett Newman, *Who's Afraid of Red, Yellow and Blue III*, which had been slashed horizontally and vertically eight times in 1986 by an enraged museumgoer. During the three years it took Goldreyer to restore the painting, he was paid $270,000 plus expenses. The resultant restoration job was criticized by various segments in the art community, and a number of publications, including *Time International* and the *Wall Street Journal*, reported on the controversy. *Time International*, in a December 30, 1991, issue, ran an article entitled "Was a Masterpiece Murdered?" At about the same time, the *Wall Street Journal* (owned by Dow Jones & Company) published an article with the headline, "For That Price, Why Not Have the Whole Museum Repainted?"

The *Time* article reported that a laboratory analysis made of the restoration concluded among other points that the restorer used "a synthetic paint commonly used on window frames." The *Journal* article, among other points, referred to the laboratory analysis and the analysis's conclusion that "Mr. Newman's canvas was completely painted over using an inappropriate type of paint."[127]

In dismissing Goldreyer's complaint, the court concluded that Goldreyer, in those circumstances, was "cast as an involuntary limited purpose public figure" and, as such, was required to prove "that a reasonable jury might find that actual malice has been shown with convincing clarity."[128] The court determined that there was a clear absence of evidence suggesting that either the *Time* or Dow Jones defendants were aware that (1) any statements in the respective articles were false or (2) were published with reckless disregard for the truth (the two elements comprising actual malice). Therefore, as the court reasoned, no actual malice on the part of the defendants could be established with clear and convincing proof.[129]

A contrary determination was made by a New York federal district court in the case of *Sepenuk v. Marshall.*[130] The plaintiff Rochelle Sepenuk and the defendants Joseph and Annette Marshall each were art dealers of nineteenth-century French antiques and were rival art gallery owners. Although competitors, the parties had frequent contact with each other in the course of their business. In the 1980s, Sepenuk purchased from the Marshalls two items: (1) a nineteenth-century Italian onyx, bronze, and marble sculpture by Caradossi of an Egyptian woman for $23,000 ("Cleopatra sculpture") and (2) a J.E. Zweiner nineteenth-century French roll-top Bureauplat desk for $76,000. In August 1997, Frank Hudson, a past client of both parties, sought to acquire from Sepenuk, among other items, the Cleopatra sculpture and the Zweiner desk. Sepenuk offered a combined purchase price of $660,000 for all of the items.

Before proceeding with the purchase, Hudson consulted with the Marshalls by telephone. In that conversation, Annette Marshall told Hudson that the Marshalls had once sold the Cleopatra sculpture to the entertainer Kenny Rogers who, in turn, consigned it to Sotheby's for auction. While in Sotheby's custody, the sculpture broke into pieces; it was reacquired by the Marshalls, who had it glued together and then resold it to Sepenuk. Annette Marshall claimed that the sculpture had "more glue than marble" and that Hudson "would be a fool to buy it."[131] Joseph Marshall confirmed the story, asserted that Hudson would not be able to sell the Cleopatra sculpture because of past breakage, estimated the value of the Zweiner desk and other items at well below Sepenuk's asking price and added that Sepenuk was "looking for suckers." Hudson recorded the telephone discussion with the Marshalls without their consent.

Sepenuk asserted that the Marshalls' remarks were false and were intended to dissuade Hudson from doing business with her. She claimed that the Cleopatra sculpture was not damaged while in Sotheby's custody and that when the Marshalls sold it to her, it was valued, for insurance purposes, at $30,000. Sepenuk further asserted—as did Hudson—that the Marshalls spoke highly of the sculpture at various times both before and after Hudson's proposal to buy it. The Marshalls countered that Hudson, a customer as well as a friend, sought their professional opinion on important works of art. They maintained that the Cleopatra sculpture had indeed been broken in the past and that glue lines were visible on the piece. They further asserted that even if the statements imputed to them were accurate, they were entitled to dismissal of the claim on summary judgment as a matter of law.

The parties agreed that New York law was applicable. As the court noted,[132] under New York law, the plaintiff must establish four elements in order to prevail on a defamation claim:

(1) a false and defamatory statement of fact;

(2) about the plaintiff;

(3) published by the defendant to a third party; and

(4) resulting injury to the plaintiff.

The defendants argued that their alleged statements were statements of opinion protected by the United States Constitution. The New York federal district court observed that as both the federal Constitution and the New York State Constitution provide protections for free speech, with the state's Constitution affording broader protection than the federal, the court need only determine if the Marshalls' statements qualify as opinion under the protection of the state Constitution. In applying New York State's constitutional law, the court noted[133] that a statement is protected opinion, as opposed to unprotected fact, if

(1) the language lacks a readily understood meaning,

(2) it is incapable of being proven false, and

(3) the specific text or the social context signals to the reader that the statement is opinion rather than fact.

The court determined that many of the Marshalls' statements had a factual connotation and were capable of being proven false, and may therefore be understood by the reasonable listener as being statements of fact. Accordingly, the court determined that the Marshalls could not avail themselves of either the federal Constitution or the New York Constitution.

Next, the Marshalls argued that their statements about the antiques were made on a matter of public concern, thereby requiring an additional showing that they acted with "gross irresponsibility."[134] As the court observed, however, the Marshalls' statements not only focused on the quality of the art—arguably a matter of public concern[135]—but also focused on Sepenuk's reputation, indisputably not a matter of public concern. In fact, in comparing the case with *McNally v. Yarnall*,[136] on which the Marshalls apparently relied, the court noted that in *McNally*, the court distinguished between statements addressing the art at issue and statements targeting McNally's "character and performance," finding the latter actionable.[137]

The Marshalls then asserted that their remarks were protected by a qualified privilege that applies to good faith communications based upon common interests. While the court acknowledged that Hudson, from time to time, sought the Marshalls' advice and guidance with respect to his art collection, the court observed that a plaintiff may overcome the privilege by a showing that the defendant's statement was false or was made with a reckless disregard as to its veracity.[138] Here, as the court noted, Sepenuk's evidence, if credited by a jury, raised doubts about the Marshalls' good faith. In addition, the court found that the "general tenor" of the Marshalls' comments "could be construed as spiteful or ill-willed."[139]

Finally, the Marshalls claimed that their recitation of the provenance and condition of the Cleopatra sculpture was true and unchallenged. The court, however, found that Sepenuk challenged the extent of prior damage, if any, to the sculpture and disputed the accuracy of the Marshalls' statements to Hudson. Accordingly, the court denied the Marshalls' motion for dismissal of Sepenuk's defamation claim on summary judgment.

NEGLIGENCE

As a theory of liability based on the failure to provide a reasonable level of care when a duty exists to do so, negligence is well-illustrated by the case of the *Estate of Querbach*.[140] The decedent, Eleanor Querbach, in February 1985 left an estate chockablock full of a variety of antiques. The Sturbridge Village Museum in Massachusetts, a residuary legatee, sought to have some of Querbach's antiques credited at the appraised fair market value against its interest in the estate. Accordingly, the executor of the estate, after conducting a lengthy search for an appraiser, hired the A&B Appraisal Service, which asserted that it had been in business for fifty years and came well-recommended. The estate advised the appraisal service that the appraisal was for purposes of federal estate tax and New Jersey inheritance tax and to affix individual values on the property. The appraisal service accordingly conducted a room-by-room, item-by-item appraisal of the tangible personal property at the decedent's residence. One of the items listed in the living room was "Three (3) Small Unframed Oil Paintings, $50 ea. $150."

A female acquaintance of the executor was interested in buying one of those three small unframed oils; after the executor received the appraisal, he sold it to her for $50. The acquaintance took the painting to be framed and then, on the suggestion of the framer, had the painting appraised for insurance purposes. That appraiser, far from valuing it at $50, determined that the painting was by J.F. Cropsey, a noted nineteenth-century American artist of the Hudson River school, and was worth $14,800. The acquaintance promptly informed the executor of the estate, who, in turn, sued the A&B Appraisal Service for negligence, alleging that the defendant failed to exercise the requisite degree of care for a professional appraiser and failed to follow proper appraiser methods.

The New Jersey Superior Court found no cases setting forth proper appraisal methods. However, it did note that the A&B Appraisal Service represented that it was a member of the International Society of Appraisers, which has adopted a code of ethics and standards of professional conduct for its members, and further noted that the defendant was advised that the appraisal was intended for use in connection with the IRS, which has adopted criteria for fine-art appraisals for federal tax purposes. In sum, the court found that the painting in question was an authentic J. F. Cropsey on the basis of the following evidence:

1. The signature on the painting was "J. F. Cropsey, 1882."

2. The technique and pigments were typical of the Hudson River school in the late nineteenth century.

3. The painting's stretch frame was typical of the artist.

4. The back of the painting bore a remnant of a paper label reading "St. Lawrence J. F. Cropsey, 57 West . . . ," which was a partial address of a location where the artist was known to have a studio.

5. The subject matter of the painting was typical of the artist.

Accordingly, the court held that the A&B Appraisal Service failed in its professional responsibilities in that the defendant:

1. Failed to recognize J.F. Cropsey as being a noted American painter of the Hudson River school;

2. Having failed to recognize the name, also failed to determine whether the artist's name had any significance in the art world;

3. Failed to recognize the painting as being a fine example of the Hudson River school of art; and

4. Failed, obviously, to closely examine either the front or the back of the painting.

In holding the A&B Appraisal Service liable for negligence in the amount of $14,700, the court noted that the public is entitled to expect that persons holding themselves out as fine-art appraisers are able to recognize or to use professional methods to identify and evaluate fine art.

As noted earlier, certification programs for appraisers have been instituted by the Appraisers Association of America, the American Society of Appraisers, and the International Society of Appraisers. Those organizations have guidelines on proper appraisal methods to be followed by appraisers. Following proper appraisal methods goes a long way in avoiding liability for negligence.

Who Can Sue for Negligence?

Generally, anyone with an interest to protect who engages an art expert to render an opinion is a potential plaintiff. The expert's duty is readily ascertained from the contractual relationship.

Duty of Care

To avoid liability for negligence, the art expert must have knowledge of the subject and must apply that knowledge properly. Liability for an opinion that turns out to be erroneous may be found if one or more of the following are shown:

1. The expert lacks the minimal necessary knowledge, whether or not he is aware of it.

2. The expert's information is distorted or outdated to such an extent that his knowledge really amounts to mere belief. Again, the expert may or may not be aware of the shortcoming.

3. The expert either intentionally or inadvertently neglects to apply his knowledge; for example, a stylistic expert may fail to consider one or more major stylistic conventions of a historical period when authenticating a work.

4. The expert has the proper knowledge but applies it badly; for example, an expert may fail to draw the proper conclusions from comparative analyses.[141]

The proper standard of care, however, is not an absolute; rather, it depends in part on the extent of the expert's responsibilities in a given situation. Those responsibilities are largely determined by the express and implied understandings about the scope of the expert's opinion.[142] Moreover, an expert's qualifications also play a major role in determining his responsibilities.[143] An expert specializing in scientific methods, for example, may not be held responsible for stylistic considerations.

Once the extent of the responsibilities assumed is determined, the appropriate standard of care can be addressed. For example, an expert who asserts that he has special skills and knowledge is held to apply and exercise those special skills and knowledge.[144] An expert who claims to have less skill or knowledge than that normally possessed by other experts in the community is bound to exercise only that lesser level of skill or knowledge.[145] An expert who makes no representations about skills or knowledge is required to exercise the skill and knowledge normally possessed by other experts in the community.[146] For example, an expert on the paintings of Auguste Renoir who offers an opinion on the authenticity of one of his outdoor café scenes must use care that is reasonable in the light of his special knowledge and may be found negligent, in view of such special knowledge, if he furnishes an erroneous opinion. However, an expert who does not specialize in Renoir per se but who does possess general knowledge of the art produced in Renoir's historical period may not, under the same circumstances, be found negligent if he furnishes an erroneous opinion about the café scene, as long as the expert's skill and knowledge were not misrepresented. An expert with little knowledge of the works of Renoir or of his historical period who nonetheless furnishes an opinion on the painting's authenticity may be found negligent if he gives an erroneous opinion based on inadequate knowledge.

The case of *Travis v. Sotheby Parke Bernet, Inc.*[147] illustrates the proper standard of care that must be rendered by an art expert expressing an opinion. The plaintiff, Stuart Travis, wanted to contribute a painting he owned to the Metropolitan Museum of Art in order to obtain an income tax charitable deduction. There was a question whether that painting, purchased by him at a Plaza Art Galleries auction in New York for $17,000, was by Joshua Reynolds or by Tilly Kettle. If the painting was by Reynolds, it would be worth considerably more than $17,000.

In 1978, within a year after purchasing the painting, Travis asked Sotheby's for an opinion as to its value. Sotheby's expert, Brenda Auslander, determined that the painting was by Tilly Kettle and not by Joshua Reynolds. However, on two previous occasions unrelated to Travis, Sotheby's or its predecessor firm had described the painting as a Reynolds. Therefore, Travis claimed in his lawsuit that Sotheby's must have been negligent on at least one of those occasions. If the painting was really by Reynolds, he was losing a valuable tax deduction; if it was by Tilly Kettle, then Sotheby's prior opinions led him astray in purchasing the painting when he did so at auction.

The court found that the expert, Brenda Auslander, was not negligent, reasoning that she had examined the painting; she had looked the painting up in an authoritative book on Reynolds by Ellis Waterhouse; and, when she did not find the painting in that book, she got in touch with Waterhouse, who was the prime authority on Joshua Reynolds. Waterhouse advised her that he considered the painting to be a Tilly Kettle. Auslander was found to have gone beyond the call of duty by seeking out the prime authority on Reynolds.

As to Sotheby's, the court held that even if its earlier pronouncements that the painting was by Reynolds had been negligent, Sotheby's had no duty of care to Travis at the time those pronouncements were made. Moreover, Travis suffered no damages, for he had acquired a painting that according to his own experts was worth anywhere from $5,000 to $450,000.

The more recent Arizona case of *Estate of Nelson v. Rice*[148] is also consistent with the settled law on the proper standard of care to which an expert is held in the rendering of an opinion. Here, Edward Franz and Kenneth Newman, personal representatives of the estate of Martha Nelson, a woman who died in February 1996, engaged two appraisers, McKenzie-Larson and an Indian art expert, to evaluate the estate's collection of Indian art and artifacts in preparation for an estate sale. McKenzie-Larson specifically told Newman that she was not a fine art appraiser and that if she saw any, the representatives would have to hire an additional appraiser. The representatives were not concerned about McKenzie-Larson's lack of expertise in fine art, as they believed that the only property of value in the estate was the house and the Indian art collection. McKenzie-Larson did not advise the estate that it needed to engage a fine art appraiser, and so, relying on McKenzie-Larson's silence, the estate's representatives priced and sold the personal property in the estate. Responding to a newspaper advertisement, the defendant Carl Rice, an ambulance service employee, attended the public estate sale and paid the estate's asking price of $60 for two oil paintings of flowers. Although Rice had bought and sold some art in the past, he was not an educated art purchaser. At home, consulting a book of artists' signatures, he noticed that the signatures on his two paintings appeared to be similar to that of the artist Martin Johnson Heade. Rice and his wife Annette sent pictures of the paintings to Christie's in New York, hoping they might be by Heade. Christie's authenticated the paintings and subsequently sold them at auction for $1,072,000. After commissions were deducted, the Rices realized $911,780 from the sale.

In January 1998, the Nelson estate sued the Rices, alleging the sale contract should be rescinded on grounds of mutual mistake and unconscionability. The estate argued that the parties were not aware the transaction had involved fine art, believing instead that the items were mere wall decorations. The Rices argued that the estate bore the risk of mistake and that unconscionability was not a basis for rescission. The trial court found that although the parties had been mistaken about the value of the paintings, the estate bore the risk of the mistake. The court also ruled that the contract was not unconscionable, as the parties had not negotiated anything and Rice merely paid the prices the estate had set. On appeal, Arizona's appellate court affirmed the grant of summary judgment to the Rices. The court held that the estate must bear the risk of the mutual mistake on the grounds of conscious ignorance. In so holding, the court quoted the *Restatement of Contracts*:

> Even though the mistaken party did not agree to bear the risk, he may have been aware when he made the contract that his knowledge with respect to the facts to which the mistake relates was limited. If he was not only so aware that his knowledge was limited but undertook to perform in the face of that awareness, he bears the risk of the mistake. . . .[149]

As the appellate court observed, by relying on the opinion of McKenzie-Larson—who admitted she was unqualified to appraise fine art—in order to determine the existence of fine art, the estate's representatives consciously ignored the possibility that the estate's assets might include fine art, thereby assuming such a risk.[150] Neither the trial court nor the appellate court indicated that McKenzie-Larson was held to any standard of care beyond her level of expertise.

The expert's duty of care extends beyond the rendering of an opinion about the value or authorship of a work of art. As illustrated in *Pilliard v. Sotheby's*,[151] an expert can incur liability in negligence for losing or damaging property taken into custody for study or evaluation. Here, the plaintiff, Martha Pilliard, living in Honolulu, Hawaii, agreed, in a discussion with Sotheby's in March 1989, to consign for sale at auction her wooden jar purportedly sculpted by the artist Paul Gauguin. The jar was listed in a 1963 catalog by an expert, Christopher Gray, entitled *Sculptures and Ceramics of Paul Gauguin*. That same month, Pilliard duly shipped the jar to Sotheby's in New York and Sotheby's issued Pilliard a consignment receipt for it. The receipt included, among other information, Sotheby's preliminary estimates of the jar's sale value: $80,000 to $100,000. Sotheby's also forwarded to Pilliard for her signature a consignment agreement, which included the following provisions, among others:

- Sotheby's would bear the risk of any loss or damage to the jar;

- Sotheby's liability would not exceed the mean of its latest presale estimates;

- Sotheby's could revise its presale estimates at its sole discretion; and

- Sotheby's could withdraw the jar from sale if doubt arose as to its authenticity.[152]

Pilliard agreed to these points and signed Sotheby's consignment agreement. She did, however, add a provision: If the jar was not sold at auction, Pilliard wanted its immediate return. She did not permit Sotheby's its standard sixty-day period to attempt a sale by private treaty in the event the jar failed to sell at auction. The following month—April 1989—Sotheby's decided not to sell the jar. Its experts had apparently decided that the jar was not authentic and this opinion was confirmed by experts at New York's Metropolitan Museum of Art. Accordingly, Sotheby's notified Pilliard by telephone and she requested that the auction house return the jar to her by air freight.

A few years passed and Martha Pilliard had yet to receive her jar from Sotheby's. In November 1993, Pilliard wrote to Sotheby's demanding the jar's return. In January 1994, Sotheby's wrote back to Pilliard, noting that "after an enormous amount of time and effort"[153] it was unable to locate the jar and because it could not find the jar, Sotheby's would process the insurance claim in light of the "aggravation this situation has caused"[154] Pilliard in the amount of $1,000.

In January 1995, Pilliard sued Sotheby's in a New York federal district court for

(1) $200,000, seeking the return of her jar,

(2) an additional $90,000 on her breach of contract claim ($90,000 being the mean of the presale estimates), and

(3) additional damages on her negligence claim, calculated on the highest value of the jar from the time she consigned it to Sotheby's to the time she learned that Sotheby's could not locate it.

Sotheby's moved to dismiss the case, claiming that all of Pilliard's claims were barred by the statute of limitations. The court considered each claim in turn.

As to the breach of contract claim, the court noted that the consignment agreement was an agency agreement for services, with Sotheby's acting as Pilliard's agent to sell the jar at auction. As it was an agency agreement, Pilliard was entitled to the benefit of a six-year statute of limitations. Therefore, her claim for breach of contract was timely.

As to Pilliard's claim seeking the return of the jar, the court, in applying New York law, observed that a plaintiff must bring suit within three years after the cause of action accrues. However, as the court noted, where a party lawfully acquires possession of property (as was the case here, since the jar was willingly consigned to Sotheby's), then the original owner must demand the property's return and the possessor must refuse to return it before the three-year time period starts to run. Here, Pilliard demanded the return of her jar both in her April 1989 telephone discussion with Sotheby's and in her November 1993 letter. Sotheby's January 1994 letter to Pilliard constituted Sotheby's refusal. Only then did the three-year time period start to run. Since Pilliard brought suit in 1995, her action was certainly timely.

As to Pilliard's negligence claim, the court noted that under New York law, negligence, too, has a three-year statute of limitations period in which to sue for injury to property. However, the three-year period does not begin to run until an injury is sustained. That is, Pilliard's negligence claim did not become complete until Sotheby's breached its duty by refusing to return the jar upon demand. Since, again, Sotheby's refusal was its January 1994 letter to Pilliard, her negligence claim was also timely.

NEGLIGENT MISREPRESENTATION

Negligent misrepresentation is the making of a false material representation to another person without a reasonable belief that the representation is true, and the other person reasonably relies on the representation and is induced to act to his detriment.[155] The misrepresentation may be one of fact or, under certain circumstances, one of opinion.[156] Misrepresentations of opinion may be a basis for relief when the parties stand in a relation of trust and confidence, as do partners, attorneys and their clients, and close friends. If it is a misrepresentation of opinion given by an expert, it may be relied on as if it were a statement of fact.[157]

As a theory of liability, negligent misrepresentation is far less accessible to a potential plaintiff than is simple negligence; mere breach of an agreement between the parties does not confer standing to sue. In *Amsterdam v. Goldreyer*,[158] for example, the defendant art restorer stated that in restoring a knife-slashed masterpiece by the artist Barnett Newman, he did not engage in overpainting; but a New York federal district court denied the art restorer's motion to dismiss a claim by the city of Amsterdam for negligent misrepresentation. In so doing, the court acknowledged the restoration agreement between the parties but noted that "there . . . must be some relationship of trust from which the defendant's duty to plaintiff arises."[159] It follows that an absence of such a relationship proves fatal to a potential plaintiff's standing to sue, as illustrated in the case below.

Struna v. Wolf[160]

In February 1982, Lewis Sharp, the then-curator of the American Wing of the Metropolitan Museum of Art, examined a work by the sculptor Elie Nadelman entitled *La Femme Assise* at the request of an art dealer who thought that the museum might want to acquire the sculpture and who was showing it on behalf of the plaintiff, William Struna. Sharp subsequently advised the dealer that the museum would not buy the work, but he afterward contacted Erving and Daniel Wolf, private collectors, who were interested and who agreed to purchase the sculpture for $120,000. On February 11, 1982, the Wolfs paid Struna $15,000 and executed a promissory note for the balance of $105,000, payable February 16, 1982. In addition, the Wolfs issued Struna a check for $105,000, postdated February 16, 1982.

The balance was never paid, the postdated check bounced when it was deposited, and Struna sued the Wolfs and the museum for breach of contract and for payment of the note and the check. Struna contended that although neither the note nor the check was signed by anyone at the Metropolitan Museum of Art, the museum was liable as a party to the contract because Struna understood that the purchase was being conducted as a joint venture between the Wolfs, as benefactors, and the museum, as the party that would ultimately acquire the sculpture. As an alternative cause of action against the museum, Struna asserted negligent misrepresentation. He claimed that the museum examined the sculpture and advised him that it was genuine, whereupon, relying on that authentication, Struna purchased the sculpture; if the sculpture was not, in fact, authentic, the museum acted negligently in its authentication, causing Struna to sustain damages of at least $100,000.

The court granted the museum's motion to dismiss the case with the following reasoning: Neither Struna nor the dealer ever advised the museum that at the time the authentication was allegedly requested and rendered Struna was not the owner of the sculpture but, rather, a mere consignee. Neither the museum nor its curator knew or should have known that Struna planned to rely on the authentication. (The court did not reach any finding on the question of whether the work was or was not authentic.) Further, the museum could in no way have realized that its rendering of an erroneous authentication could have served to the detriment of Struna. As the court noted:

> [C]ases [alleging negligent misrepresentation] routinely require the existence of a "special relationship" between the parties creating a duty of care owed to the plaintiff thus entitling the plaintiff to rely upon the defendant's representations. Whether or not a "special relationship" exists depends on many considerations

. . . more often than not . . . it arises out of a contract where the defendant was specifically employed for the purpose of rendering an appraisal to the plaintiff knowing that the plaintiff intended to rely on it. Here, on the other hand, by the plaintiff's own admission . . . [he] was acting at arm's length in attempting to achieve a sale of the sculpture to the museum. This relationship . . . appears to be the very antithesis of the "special relationship" ordinarily required. . . .[161]

Under New York law a "special relationship" is no less than a fiduciary duty owed the plaintiff by the defendant.[162]

The *Ravenna* Case

A more recent case illustrating the contrast in accessibility as a cause of action between negligence and negligent misrepresentation, as well as highlighting the risks in evaluating a work of art based on photographs—let alone digital images—is *Ravenna v. Christie's*.[163] Here, the plaintiff, Guido Ravenna, then the owner of an oil painting of the crucified Christ known as *Pietà*, sought to recover the loss he sustained by relying on the allegedly false, negligent, and incompetent evaluation by Christie's auction house of the authorship and value of *Pietà*.

In July 1999, Ravenna, a resident of Buenos Aires, was visited by a French art dealer named Stromboni, who offered to pay him $50,000 for *Pietà*. Stromboni insisted on a prompt acceptance or rejection of his offer. Ravenna, who even before Stromboni's visit had decided to sell *Pietà*, but had no idea of its authorship or value, telephoned his wife Ana, who was visiting in New York and had in her possession color photographs of the painting. Ravenna instructed her to consult Christie's in order to determine if he should accept Stromboni's offer or consign, instead, the painting for sale at auction. Ana duly consulted at Christie's with a specialist in Old Master paintings, James Bruce-Gardyne. Gardyne studied the photographs and informed her that *Pietà* was the work of the studio of a relatively minor seventeenth-century Italian artist named Nuvolone; he estimated its value to be $10,000 to $15,000. Ana Ravenna reported

Christie's evaluation of *Pietà* to her husband who, in reliance upon it, accepted Stromboni's $50,000 offer.

In fact, *Pietà* was the work of Ludovico Carracci, a great master of the Italian Baroque of the late sixteenth and early seventeenth century. In January 2000—six months after Ana Ravenna visited Christie's—it was sold at auction by Christie's to the Metropolitan Museum of Art in New York City for $5,227,500. Christie's catalog for that auction describes *Pietà* as

> a highly important rediscovery of a work by one of the great masters of the Italian Baroque, Ludovico Carracci. . . . There are a number of touches that reveal the hand of a master: the superb still life quality of the crown of thorns, the richly impasted topmost corner of the shroud that is pulled back under the weight of Christ's body. . . . The artist has boldly foreshortened the Madonna's left arm, the crisp folds of her sleeve contrasting with the soft flesh of her hand. Hanging limply her index finger and thumb rest lightly on the hand of Jesus. However, it is not the lifeless hand of a dead man that she touches but the dislocated wrist of the crucified Christ, rendered with great naturalism. . . .[164]

Clearly, such an intimate and detailed description of the painting could arise only from a physical examination of the work, not from examining mere photographs. And *Pietà* was surely so examined by Christie's as part of its standard procedure for accepting and cataloging consigned works to be offered at auction. In view of *Pietà*'s ultimate purchase price, Ravenna subsequently sued Christie's for damages in a New York federal district court in the amount of $5,187,500—the difference between the price obtained at auction and the price Ravenna received for the painting from Stromboni.

Unfortunately, plaintiff's sole cause of action was for negligent misrepresentation. The court noted that where words are negligently imparted to another with knowledge or notice that they will be acted upon, such negligently imparted information may be the basis for recovering damages. Here, the court concluded that Gardyne was indisputably aware that the plaintiff would use the information he provided in deciding whether or not to sell the painting to a dealer or to consign the work with Christie's. However, as the court also noted, to sustain a cause of action in negligent misrepresentation, "there must be a fiduciary or special relationship between the parties suggesting a closer degree of trust than that of the ordinary buyer and seller."[165] Observing that no such relationship existed between Ravenna and Christie's, the court granted the defendants' motion to dismiss the complaint.

In *Christie's v. Croce*,[166] where defendant was awarded damages by a jury on a counterclaim against Christie's for negligent misrepresentation, a New York federal court held defendant could recover costs and prejudgment interest but not attorneys' fees. To recover attorneys' fees under New York law in a breach of contract action against a debtor, defendant's consignment agreement would have had to have been a "consumer contract," which as the court noted requires a transaction that is primarily for personal, family, and household purposes.[167] Here, defendant did not qualify. The purpose of the $3.1 million advance, secured by paintings and drawings which Christie's had appraised at a value of $4.6 to $6.6 million, was to make a speculative stock investment and refinance a prior loan from Sotheby's also used for investment in stock.[168]

FRAUD

Since the mid 1980s, the courts appear to have become receptive to claims of fraud against art experts who render knowingly false opinions on works of art. One such case, *Goldman v. Barnett*,[169] has possible far-reaching implications for consignors of artwork.

The *Goldman* Case

The plaintiff, David Goldman, a business executive in Massachusetts who sought to acquire an art collection, was introduced by a mutual acquaintance to David Barnett, a Wisconsin art dealer who both owned and held on consignment many works, including a collection from the Milton Avery Trust. In May 1988, Goldman bought two paintings by the artist Milton Avery from Barnett and received, aside from the paintings, an insurance appraisal for the Averys written on Barnett's business stationery and signed by Barnett. The stationery revealed that Barnett was a member of the Appraisers Association of America. Subsequently, Goldman and Barnett visited each other a number of times. Throughout the spring and summer of 1988, Goldman bought more than sixty additional paintings from Barnett, including ten other Milton Averys. Those ten Averys had been consigned to Barnett by the Milton Avery Trust, and Goldman was aware that Barnett received a commission for sales of consigned works. Before the sale of each of those additional artworks, Barnett supplied Goldman with an oral appraisal and then a written appraisal essentially similar to those given for the two Averys purchased in May. The purchase price for the entire collection of sixty-odd paintings slightly exceeded $1 million, a figure substantially below the appraised total value of the collection. Most of the purchase price was attributed to the Avery paintings. Because the Milton Avery Trust set the lowest figures for which the Averys could be sold, Barnett, who was the sole negotiator and contact for the trust, obtained the trustees' consent for the prices Goldman paid for the Avery art.

Goldman, in a payment plan approved by the Milton Avery Trust, made a substantial down payment for the collection and agreed to pay slightly more than $100,000 monthly until his debt was paid in full. After making several monthly payments, however, Goldman came to believe that his paintings were worth substantially less than their purchase price and far less than their appraised value. Accordingly, he stopped making payments and eventually sued Barnett and the Milton Avery Trust on a variety of theories, including fraud.

In claiming fraud, Goldman alleged, among other points, that Barnett, as agent for the Milton Avery Trust, claimed that the Avery art was appraised at the fair market value. In denying the defendant's motion for summary judgment as to fraud, the Massachusetts federal district court noted that the trust may be liable on Goldman's fraud theory only if Barnett committed actionable fraud and Barnett's fraud is imputable to the trust.

Actionable Fraud

The court found that there was sufficient evidence on the record to allow a jury to find that Barnett committed fraud—that is, that Barnett made a false representation of material fact with knowledge of its falsity for the purpose of inducing Goldman to act on it—and that Goldman relied on the representation as true and acted on it to his detriment. As indicated by the evidence,

(1) at least one other expert placed Barnett's appraisals 400% higher than the fair market value;

(2) the commissions Barnett received on the sale of the consigned art (which included the ten Averys) could induce him to inflate the purchase price; and

(3) a jury could find that Barnett held himself out as an expert appraiser, enabling the jury reasonably to infer that Barnett did know the artworks' true market values.[170]

Imputable to the Trust

The court found there was sufficient evidence in the record for a jury to find that Barnett's alleged fraud was attributable to the Milton Avery Trust. According to the evidence, on July 26, 1988, Barnett wrote to Goldman:

> I spoke with Mrs. Avery [a trustee] . . . and did the best I could for you re: price and payment schedule. I am pleased to be able to offer . . . a 14% discount off of the appraised value of $1,028,035.00 or $886,185.00."[171]

As the court noted, a jury could find that the defendant-trustee was aware of Barnett's alleged misrepresentation and ratified it. Moreover, as the court observed, a jury could find that the trust's vesting Barnett with authority to negotiate the purchase price and to consummate the sale on its behalf constituted an affirmative act sufficient to cloak Barnett with apparent authority to make the allegedly fraudulent misrepresentations as to fair market value. As to the defendants' argument that Barnett's statement of the paintings' value constituted his opinion and not a misrepresentation of a material fact, the court noted that a jury could find that Barnett held himself out as an expert art appraiser, particularly of Avery's paintings. Barnett's representations that the paintings had a given fixed market value may be found by a jury to have been a representation by one possessing knowledge, rather than mere opinion.

Implications

The *Goldman* case should be read as a caveat to the consignor, whether artist or collector: An art dealer's fraudulent actions vis-à-vis a potential buyer may be imputable to the consignor. In view of *Goldman*, a consignor of art, in negotiating a consignment agreement with a dealer, should insist on retaining as much control as possible over the pricing of his artwork. As part and parcel of that control, when appraisals are requested by a buyer before a purchase, the consignor should insist that the dealer secure an appraisal from a third party whose independence will not affect (that is, whose commissions or fees do not depend on) the value affixed to the artwork.

Goldman should also reinforce to the art dealer the hazards of self-appraising the art he sells either before or after a buyer's purchase. If the dealer owns the art sold, a court may find that he has a vested interest in inflating the value to secure a higher purchase price; if the art sold was consigned, the dealer may be tempted to inflate the artwork's value to secure a higher commission.

The *Amsterdam* Case

Art restorers are also experts, and their comments, too, render them vulnerable to charges of fraud, as demonstrated in *Amsterdam v. Goldreyer*.[172] The eminent New York art restorer Daniel Goldreyer was retained by the City of Amsterdam in 1988 to restore a valuable Barnett Newman painting, *Who's Afraid of Red, Yellow and Blue III*, owned by the City of Amsterdam and slashed in 1986 by a vandal while it was hanging in Amsterdam's Stedelijk Museum. The restoration agreement signed by the parties called for Goldreyer to restore the painting to its best possible condition. In the course of the restoration process, Goldreyer repeatedly reassured representatives from Amsterdam and the Stedelijk that he was using the pinpointing method of restoration and that he did not engage in overpainting.

Once the painting was returned to the Stedelijk and publicly displayed, the international art community, including *Time* magazine and the *Wall Street Journal*, claimed that the damaged and undamaged areas of the painting had been overpainted and described the work as "ruined." The City of Amsterdam subsequently submitted the painting to a forensic laboratory in the Netherlands for analysis. The analysis revealed that the damaged areas of the artwork had been painted over and that an alkyd varnish had been applied as a sealer, allegedly destroying the painting's original translucency. According to the City of Amsterdam, Goldreyer's overpainting and his application of the sealer—techniques he allegedly did not disclose—were inconsistent with industry restoration standards because the new paint and the sealer were not removable without causing damage to the artwork.

The City of Amsterdam sued on several theories, including fraud, to recover damages for breach of contract. Goldreyer made a motion to dismiss the suit for failure to state a cause of action on which relief can be granted. The New York federal district court, in denying Goldreyer's motion in its entirety, found that the City of Amsterdam, in its allegations, established a *prima facie* case of fraud against Goldreyer. These were the City of Amsterdam's allegations before the matter was settled:

1. Goldreyer falsely told a museum representative that the pinpointing technique would be used to restore the painting.

2. Goldreyer, with intent to deceive, failed to advise Amsterdam of his intent to overpaint the artwork.

3. Goldreyer and his attorney represented, with intent to deceive, that the pinpointing restoration method had been used and that the artwork had not been overpainted.

4. Amsterdam detrimentally relied on those alleged misrepresentations.

5. That reliance resulted in an injury to the City of Amsterdam in the amount of $3.5 million.

The *Pickett* Case

A still more recent case sounding in fraud is *Pickett v. American Ordnance Preservation Association*,[173] involving the Civil War artifacts of Confederate Major General George E. Pickett. On July 3, 1863, at Gettysburg, Pickett and more than 10,000 soldiers under his command were decisively defeated in what has come to be known as "Pickett's Charge." Marking the turning point in the Civil War, Pickett's Charge created a market among collectors for Pickett memorabilia.

The defendant American Ordnance Preservation Association (AOPA) was co-owned by Enos Pritchard III, a dealer, museum consultant, and appraiser of eighteenth- and nineteenth-century military items. Using a letter signed by the mayor of the City of Harrisburg, Pritchard introduced himself by telephone and mailed communication to the plaintiff, George E. Pickett V, a direct descendant of the general, who lived in North Carolina. Pritchard explained that he was acting on behalf of the city of Harrisburg to secure items for display in a Civil War museum the City was constructing. Pickett testified that without the Mayor's letter of introduction, he would neither have met with nor sold to Pritchard. Pritchard convincingly dissuaded Pickett from approaching an auction house with his collection, suggesting that "dealers would collude . . . and get together and cheat about holding the prices down. . . ."

Over a series of three trips to North Carolina in the fall of 1995, Pritchard was able to secure from Pickett an assortment of his ancestor's artifacts. Among the memorabilia Pritchard acquired were the general's kepi (cap) and sash, a lock of his hair, some of his photographs, and a uniform. For these items he paid Pickett $62,000 ($5,000 in cash and $57,000 in check) and promised to deliver a computer to Pickett in the future. The third trip secured letters and other documents for $16,000 in cash. In November 1995, mere weeks after his final trip to North Carolina, Pritchard sold the artifacts to the City of Harrisburg for $880,000—a 1,000% markup from his purchase price.

Pickett learned of the city's purchase in June 1998. At that time he was visiting in Gettysburg and attending a dinner hosted by the Friends of the National Park of Gettysburg. During the dinner, Pickett inquired of Earl Coates, the organization's president, as to the value of the general's kepi. Coates named a price that exceeded the amount Pickett had been paid for all of the items together. Coates's response prompted a joint visit by Coates and Pickett to a local Civil War dealer. The visit revealed that Pritchard had "restored and framed" photographic laser copies of portraits of the late general under the guise of having framed restored originals. Using his art contacts, Coates was able to ascertain the City of Harrisburg's purchase price for the Pickett collection, thus triggering a lawsuit in fraud.

The jury verdict was in Pickett's favor, awarding him damages of $806,140, and the Pennsylvania federal district court upheld the verdict. Particularly damaging to the AOPA was the "abundance of evidence that Pickett trusted and relied on Pritchard." Ruling against the defendant, the court noted that Pickett did not have a duty to obtain a second opinion on the value of what he owned before any sale to Pritchard. The court also said it was for the jury to decide whether Pickett had failed to exercise due diligence in relying on Pritchard's representations as a Civil War expert and in not confirming the purchase price with the City of Harrisburg. The court refused to grant defendant a judgment as a matter of law or a new trial because "the jury's verdict did not result in a miscarriage of justice, does not cry out to be overturned, and does not shock the conscience of the court."[174] The court held that

> [t]here was more than enough evidence for the jury to find by the clear and convincing standard "(1) a misrepresentation, (2) a fraudulent utterance thereof, (3) an intention by the maker that the recipient will thereby be induced to act, (4) justifiable reliance by the recipient upon the misrepresentation, and (5) damage to the recipient as a proximate result."[175]

In August 2002, Pritchard, his son Russell Pritchard Jr., long-time director of the Civil War Library and Museum in Philadelphia, and his partner and veteran dealer George Juno were convicted for staging fake appraisals on the PBS series *Antiques Roadshow*.[176] Their fake appraisals helped Pritchard and Juno defraud families by gaining access to treasures that would have otherwise remained in family collections.

Guilty Knowledge: The *Cohen* and *Zoellner* Cases

Key to establishing a prima facie case in fraud is scienter: that is, previous knowledge of a state of facts—guilty knowledge. Such knowledge is often difficult to establish. It was found to be adequately alleged in the 2004 case of *Cohen v. Mazoh* and was found not to be established in the 2003 case of *Zoellner v. Christie's*.

Cohen v. Mazoh

In *Cohen v. Mazoh*,[177] the plaintiff Joseph Cohen, a collector of fine art, contacted the defendant, art dealer Steven Mazoh, in 1990, to discuss Cohen's interest in buying a Baroque painting entitled *Joseph and Potiphar's Wife*, purportedly by Orazio Gentileschi. Mazoh represented that the painting was authentic. Based on Mazoh's representation, Cohen bought the painting by exchanging it for four other works in his collection that, allegedly, were collectively worth $1.2 million. A few years later, in 1995, Cohen insured his painting, which was appraised at $1 million.

In the fall of 2000, Cohen engaged the services of Diane Kunkel, an art research consultant, to catalog his art collection. Shortly after she was retained, Kunkel, on behalf of Cohen, contacted Keith Christiansen, a curator of the Metropolitan Museum of Art in New York, offering to lend Cohen's painting for an upcoming Gentileschi exhibit to be held at the museum. Much to Kunkel's surprise, Christiansen declined the offer: He indicated that the painting was irrelevant to the Met's Gentileschi exhibit and that in any event, it was the wrong size for the exhibition. When Kunkel asked Christiansen if he had any doubts about the authenticity of Cohen's Gentileschi, Christiansen advised Kunkel to consult the Ward Bissell *catalogue raisonné* on Gentileschi. Kunkel did so and found that the *catalogue raisonné* indicated that the "Gentileschi painting was genuine and within 'the ranks of Gentileschi's autograph works.'"[178] Subsequently, Christiansen declined Kunkel's invitation to examine Cohen's painting, advising her that he had already seen it on several occasions including at Mazoh's gallery before he sold it to Cohen.

In September 2001, Christie's appraised Cohen's painting for estate tax purposes in the amount of $1 million. In January 2002, Mazoh provided Kunkel with a fact sheet about the Gentileschi painting. The fact sheet revealed that the painting had once been owned by a Hans Wetzlar of Amsterdam. Wetzlar, as it happens, though it was not indicated on the fact sheet, was a Nazi collaborator during World War II. In the next month, Kunkel again contacted Christiansen to inquire about the painting. During a telephone discussion with Kunkel, Christiansen allegedly (according to Kunkel) indicated to her for the first time that he did not believe the painting was an authentic Gentileschi.

Upon learning of the exchange between Christiansen and Kunkel, Cohen sued Mazoh for, among other claims, fraud. In his suit, Cohen alleged (1) that Mazoh represented that the Gentileschi was authentic and (2) that in order to induce Cohen to buy the painting, Mazoh failed to inform him that the painting had been owned by a Nazi collaborator. In moving to dismiss the claim regarding authenticity, Mazoh argued that he did not falsely represent that the Gentileschi painting was authentic, because the definitive scholarly view—both at the time of its sale to Cohen and at the time of the lawsuit—was that the painting is authentic. To support his argument, Mazoh cited the Ward Bissell *catalogue raisonné* and Bissell's reference to the German art historian Hermann Voss, who, in 1954, also determined that *Joseph and Potiphar's Wife* was an authentic work by Gentileschi. Moreover, as Mazoh noted, during each of the two times Cohen had the painting appraised—1995 and 2001—the painting was valued at $1 million, and neither appraisal questioned its authenticity. The New York State Supreme Court agreed, finding that Cohen's vague allegations about Christiansen's doubts as to the painting's authenticity were insufficient to sustain a cause of action in fraud against Mazoh.

In moving to dismiss Cohen's claim regarding provenance, Mazoh argued that Cohen's allegation that Mazoh knew that Wetzlar was a Nazi collaborator during World War II was irrelevant and nevertheless belied by the fact sheet summarizing the Gentileschi's provenance: a document simply stating, without supplying dates or any other details about Wetzlar's ownership, that the painting was part of the collection of Dr. Hans Wetzlar of Amsterdam. That is, Mazoh asserted that Cohen did not explain how, in 1990, Mazoh either could or should have known that Wetzlar had been a Nazi collaborator. Once again, the court agreed. It noted that Cohen's bare allegation was insufficient to sustain a claim for fraudulent omission because the allegation was unsupported by a single fact detailing the basis for Mazoh's alleged "knowledge" in 1990 of Wetzlar's collaboration. The court therefore dismissed the case for lack of scienter.

Upon appeal by Cohen, the Appellate Division of the New York State Supreme Court reinstated Cohen's claim for fraud[179] solely insofar as it related to the authenticity of the Gentileschi, holding that the elements of fraud were alleged with the requisite particularity, establishing an issue of fact for a jury but not finding that there was fraud.[180] The case has been settled without a trial.

Zoellner v. Christie's

In *Zoellner v. Christie's*,[181] the defendant auction house held a stamp auction in March 1987 of "The Louis Grunin Collection of U.S. Stamps, 1851–1857." The plaintiff, Robert Zoellner, a stamp collector, was the successful bidder for lot 51 of the collection, entitled "The Consul Klep Cover," which he purchased for $121,000, including the buyer's premium.

Christie's sales catalog provided, in pertinent part, that

[a]ll lots are sold as authentic and correctly described (unless the catalogue descriptions or sale room notices or announcements provide otherwise, in which case lots are sold "as is").[182]

Zoellner claimed that the Consul Klep Cover was not sold "as is," nor were there any indications in catalog descriptions, sale room notices, or announcements that the lot was not authentic. Accordingly, he reasonably relied on Christie's representation that the Consul Klep Cover was authentic.

Eleven years later—in October 1998—Zoellner offered his stamp collection for sale at auction through another gallery. He was, however, forced to withdraw it, pending further investigation, when the gallery questioned the authenticity of the Consul Klep Cover. In January 1999, the Philatelic Foundation issued a final opinion that the Consul Klep Cover was counterfeit. Zoellner subsequently asked Christie's to rescind the 1987 sale and to return his purchase price.

When Christie's refused (its limited warranty ran for five years following the date of sale), Zoellner sued for fraud, claiming that Christie's either knew or should have known that the authenticity of the Consul Klep Cover was questionable. Christie's moved to dismiss the case on the ground that Zoellner's claims were time-barred in that he failed to show that he could not have discovered the alleged fraud earlier by using reasonable diligence. However, as the New York State Supreme Court noted, even assuming that Zoellner's claims were timely brought, on the ground that he had no reason to suspect the authenticity of the stamp collection until he tried to sell it in 1998, Zoellner failed to submit any evidence demonstrating that Christie's had any knowledge or any reason to believe that the Consul Klep Cover was anything but genuine. That is, once again, the plaintiff was unable to demonstrate scienter, or guilty knowledge of an earlier state of facts.

ANTITRUST CLAIMS AND AUTHENTICATION

The United States has no formal *droit moral* as it exists in European countries, by which the authority to authenticate a work of art is inherited from the artist by his heirs. However, after the death of an American artist, a *catalogue raisonné* may be prepared by a scholar or group of scholars. Often, the *catalogue raisonné* is prepared in conjunction with a foundation or other entity established by the artist's heirs to maintain the integrity of the deceased artist's work and to serve as a board of review to authenticate works of art from time to time. As discussed earlier in this chapter, whenever an opinion is expressed about the authenticity of a work of art, those giving their opinion must follow proper authentication methodology in order to avoid liability. Any alleged liability is usually expressed as a tort. A different allegation took place in the lawsuit involving the Pollock-Krasner Foundation, the Pollock-Krasner Authentication Board, Sotheby's, and Christie's.[183]

David Kramer, an art dealer, bought a painting privately for $15,000 that he alleges could be worth $10 million if it were authenticated as a Jackson Pollock and sold at auction. Both Christie's and Sotheby's told Kramer that they would auction the painting if it were authenticated by the Pollock-Krasner Authentication Board. After a careful review the board refused to authenticate the painting. Kramer sued, alleging, among other causes of action, antitrust violations pursuant to sections 1 and 2 of the Sherman Antitrust Act. Kramer also alleged that an antitrust conspiracy began at Pollock's death and that the goal of the conspiracy was to exclude certain authentic Pollock pieces from the accepted canon of his work and thereby from the market in an attempt to increase the value of Pollock paintings owned by the foundation and auctioned by Christie's and Sotheby's.

The court dismissed all of Kramer's allegations for failure to state a cause of action.[184] In order to survive a motion to dismiss, a claim under the Sherman Antitrust Act must allege a relevant geographic and product market in which trade was unreasonably restrained or monopolized. The court noted that

> the problem in Kramer's product market theory is that he has not, and cannot, allege that his painting and others like it are saleable only at the two defendant auction houses in Manhattan.[185]

Kramer has a reasonable alternative to selling his painting at auction (he could sell it through a private dealer), so no market restraint existed.

The court also found that the complaint failed to support the existence of a conspiracy because it presented no coherent theory of participation by Sotheby's or Christie's in the alleged conspiracy. Sotheby's and Christie's had an independent interest in not selling forgeries because of potential damage to their reputations, not to mention legal liability.[186] As for the board, the court found that the board was not the only group of experts that could provide opinions of authenticity for Pollocks.[187] Kramer admitted that he could obtain and had obtained authentication opinions from other art experts and that the board's refusal to authenticate did not prevent him from selling privately. Accordingly, there was no conspiracy.

Although all Kramer's complaints were dismissed, the opinion is interesting in that it examines an area unique to the art world with respect to an authentication committee and possible antitrust violations. Even though such a committee may be self-appointed, if its members follow correct and consistent authentication methods, the members of such a committee should not have any liability under any antitrust or monopoly theory.

LIMITATIONS ON LIABILITY

As seen in the preceding pages, ill-chosen words on art-related matters uttered by an art expert can be treacherous and costly. Accordingly, the following two sections are devoted to the curtailing of the art expert's liability. The first section, on limitations by contract, addresses art appraisers. Nevertheless, many other art experts whose livelihoods involve the rendering of expert opinion, such as authenticators, art advisors, and possibly art restorers, may find this section of value. A model art advisory agreement is found at the end of this chapter (Appendix 7-3). The second section, a brief discussion of limitations by insurance, should be useful to virtually all art experts.

Limitations by Contract

As a matter of course, an art appraiser, when commissioned by another person to examine and affix a dollar value to an artwork or group of artworks, should precede the appraisal with an appraisal *contract*. The appraisal contract serves to memorialize in writing the understanding between the appraiser and the client as to the purpose of the appraisal and the parameters of the appraiser's responsibilities. A model of a short appraisal contract (a document separate and apart from the appraisal itself) is found at the close of this chapter (Appendix 7-2). Below is a checklist of the issues that should be included in such a document:

- The date on which the appraisal shall be done.
- A broad general description of the property.
- The address where the property to be appraised is located. The address is the geographic location of the valuation. If the property is to be valued according to a different location, that fact, along with the actual location of the valuation, should be clearly stated in the appraisal. That distinction may apply where, say, a Renoir painting located in Des Moines, Iowa, is being appraised. Since there are more Renoirs and more of a market for Renoirs in New York City than in Des Moines, the Renoir would be appraised according to New York City fair market value.
- The commissioning party to furnish the appraiser with information. On the appraiser's request the commissioning party should furnish any factual information he has about the property to be appraised. If the information so furnished is false or incorrect and materially contributes to the appraiser's erroneous opinion, the appraiser, if subsequently sued for negligence, may successfully assert a defense of contributory negligence.
- Appraisal preparation. The appraiser should state what he will do in preparing the appraisal—that is, physically inspect the property, prepare a detailed description of it, evaluate it,

and submit a written signed report to the commissioning party.

• Methods of evaluation to be used and those not to be used. The appraiser should indicate the methods of evaluation— for example, stylistic analysis and comparable sales—that will be used in rendering an opinion. Equally important, the appraiser should identify the methods—for example—scientific testing—that will not be used because they are beyond the appraiser's area of expertise. Stating the methods that will not be used in an evaluation serves to limit an appraiser's potential exposure in a negligence suit by holding the appraiser to an appropriate, rather than unreasonably high, standard of care. (See the discussion on duty of care on pages 603–607.)

• Sole purpose of the appraisal. Is the appraisal, for example, for insurance purposes? For charitable donation purposes? Since the type of valuation and other elements in a correctly prepared appraisal depend on the purpose of the appraisal, an appraisal for insurance purposes (which uses a replacement valuation) should not be used in connection with a charitable donation (which demands a fair market valuation). (See the discussion in chapter 14 dealing with the preparation of appraisals for tax purposes.)

• No dissemination to third parties unrelated to the immediate purpose of the appraisal. The contract should indicate that the appraisal is to be used solely by the commissioning party. That restriction precludes unrelated third parties—all potential plaintiffs—from relying on the appraisal.

• Rate of payment. An appraiser can properly be paid by the hour, by the day, or by the piece. The appraiser's fee should *not* be based on a percentage of the appraised value of the property. An appraisal for charitable-donation purposes with such a fee structure is disqualified by the IRS, and appraisals for other purposes with such a fee structure are given little credence by the IRS. (See the discussion in chapter 14.)

• Additional fee for future related services. If an appraiser must subsequently defend the appraisal to the IRS or in court, he should charge an additional fee. Those additional services should not be included in the original appraisal fee.

- Disclaimer language. The appraisal contract should clearly state that the appraisal will in no event constitute a representation or warranty as to value, authenticity, provenance, or the like. The appraiser is thereby protected from suit for breach of warranty.

- Defense by commissioning party. The commissioning party should be required to defend the appraiser against any actions or claims involving the appraisal brought by third parties unrelated to the immediate purpose of the appraisal. That requirement helps make sure that the commissioning party does not disseminate the appraisal to those potential plaintiffs who are not entitled to rely on it.

- Manner of resolving controversies. The appraisal contract should indicate the process by which any future controversies will be settled. One example is by judicial process, in which case there should be an acknowledgment that the parties, by signing the contract, are thereby submitting themselves to the jurisdiction of a specified state; another example, used in the model agreement, is by means of arbitration in accordance with the requirements of the American Arbitration Association.

Use of Exculpatory Language

A properly drafted appraisal or authentication contract can provide the art expert with an effective shield against liabilities, as seen in *Lariviere v. Thaw*.[188]

In 1994, Kenneth Lariviere, owner of an alleged Jackson Pollock piece entitled *Vertical Infinity*, asked the Pollock-Krasner Authentication Board to examine his painting. At that time, Lariviere signed an agreement specifically acknowledging that he was requesting "an informal opinion" and that he agreed to hold the board harmless from any liability to him or others arising from its rendition of, or refusal to render, an opinion. The agreement also contained a broad arbitration clause. In seeking an opinion from the board, Lariviere indicated that he had acquired the work through the estate sale of the late Mrs. Frederick Schwankovsky. The late Frederick Schwankovsky had been Pollock's high school teacher in Los Angeles in the late 1920s.

In 1995, the board notified Lariviere of its determination that the work was not by Jackson Pollock. The board had declined to authenticate the very same painting when it was submitted two years earlier by a different owner. In its second evaluation of the work, the board noted that in the interim, the misspelled name "Pollack" as the work's author, as well as the misspelled name "Schwankasky" as the alleged recipient, had been added to the back of the canvas. In his complaint, Lariviere alleged that although the board refused to authenticate the painting for the prior owner, it should have authenticated the painting for him (Lariviere) because he provided both a provenance for the painting and a handwriting analysis of Jackson Pollock's signature.

Provenance. The provenance consisted of an affidavit purportedly signed by the daughter of Frederick Schwankovsky (Pollock's high school teacher), alleging that the painting was a gift in 1953 from Pollock to her father and that the inscription on the back of the painting was true, accurate, and correct. The daughter failed to explain, however, the misspellings of both Pollock's and her father's name. The New York State Supreme Court found that the inscription was added in the interim between the board's two reviews of the painting (that is, in the 1990s).

Handwriting Analysis. The court noted that the plaintiff's examiner was not certified by any professional association and that his experience as a handwriting examiner was apparently limited to sports memorabilia. Moreover, the court observed that the examiner worked solely from photographs of Jackson Pollock's signature—photographs generally not being the best method when the original is available—and that apparently the examiner initially was not asked to examine a photograph of the back of the painting where Pollock's name was misspelled.

Granting the board's motion for summary judgment, the court held that the parties' written agreement "by its terms, clearly bars this action."[189] The court also went on to note that

> [i]n the absence of a contravening public policy, exculpatory provisions in a contract, purporting to insulate one of the parties from liability resulting from that party's own negligence, although disfavored by the law and closely scrutinized by the courts, generally are enforced. . . . Where the language of the exculpatory agreement expresses in unequivocal terms the intention of the parties to relieve a defendant's negligence, the agreement will be enforced.[190]

Limitations of Contractual Exculpatory Language: The Foxley Case

The effective shield of exculpatory language has proven to be semipermeable: It does not necessarily render the appraiser invulnerable to acts of possible bad faith or possible gross negligence, as was made clear in the case of *Foxley v. Sotheby's*.[191]

William C. Foxley, a Dallas art collector and cattle rancher, bought at auction at Sotheby's in December 1987 a painting entitled *Lydia Reclining on a Divan*, represented to be by the American artist Mary Cassatt, for $632,500. Sotheby's auction catalog guaranteed the authenticity of the painting for a period of five years after the date of sale. The catalog also stated that the painting would be accompanied by a copy of a letter discussing the work from Adelyn Breeskin, once considered an authority on Cassatt.

In 1989, two years after Foxley's purchase, Sotheby's reappraised the painting for him at $650,000. Foxley asserted that in 1992 he realized that he had never received the Breeskin letter and notified Sotheby's to that effect. He finally received a copy of the letter from Sotheby's in 1993, when he learned for the first time that Breeskin's comments about the Cassatt painting were based on her review of a mere color transparency, rather than of the original painting. Foxley claimed that had he known that before the auction, he would never have bid on the painting.

In 1993, Sotheby's again reappraised the Cassatt for Foxley at $650,000. Then in August 1993, nearly six years after his purchase, Foxley consigned the painting to Sotheby's for sale at an auction to take place in December 1993. On November 30, two days before the auction, Sotheby's informed Foxley that the Cassatt Committee (the definitive authenticating group for Cassatt's works) determined that the painting might be inauthentic and advised him to withdraw it from the auction. Foxley did so and allowed the rest of his sizable consignment to remain in the auction so as not to damage the integrity of the sale; Foxley alleged that, in return, Sotheby's had promised to give him a refund of his purchase price for the Cassatt. In September 1994, after Sotheby's refused to make the refund, Foxley brought suit against Sotheby's on a variety of theories, including fraud, negligent misrepresentation, breach of contract, and negligent appraisals.

The New York federal district court dismissed virtually all Foxley's claims except for two claims of negligent appraisal on the basis of Sotheby's 1989 and 1993 appraisals. Although Foxley also claimed that Sotheby's, in its two appraisals, breached its contract, the court held that Sotheby's correctly argued that appraisals estimate fair market value and do not, unlike authentications, purport to confirm authorship. The court noted that Sotheby's position was clearly supported by the disclaimer language in the appraisal contracts:

> [O]ur appraisal . . . is not to be deemed a representation or warranty with respect to the authenticity of authorship . . . genuineness . . . [or] attribution.[192]

As to each of the two surviving claims of negligent appraisal, the court again looked to the exculpatory language in the appraisal contract, which provided the following:

> In consideration of our furnishing the appraisal, you hereby release Sotheby's . . . from any liability or damages whatsoever arising out of or related to the appraisal . . . unless . . . due to Sotheby's gross negligence or bad faith.[193]

The court noted that—since Sotheby's twice appraised the Cassatt at $650,000, when, in fact, it may have been worthless—there was sufficient evidence to support the two claims of negligent appraisal. Foxley, moreover, alleged that the 1993 appraisal suggested bad faith. As the court observed, Sotheby's alleged knowledge of the painting's inauthenticity at the time of the appraisals, if proven at trial, would "clearly constitute—not merely gross negligence but also—*mala fides*."[194]

In June 2001, in *E.S.T., Inc. v. Christie's*, Christie's became awash in litigation over negligence and breach of fiduciary duties claims that its appraisal of a seventeenth-century Old Master painting cost its former owner, E.S.T., Inc., more than $280,000.[195] The case arose from the auction house's handling of an oil painting allegedly created by a pupil of the seventeenth-century master Annibale Caracci, entitled *The Entombment of Christ*. In March 1998, E.S.T. had delivered the painting to Christie's for consignment. Upon delivery, the painting was identified by Anthony Crichton-Stuart, at that time a Christie's specialist and a leading authority on Old Master paintings. Stuart attributed the work to Sisto Badalocchio, a student of Caracci.

On the basis of Stuart's attribution, E.S.T. executed a consignment agreement in April 1998 for the painting to be sold at auction. Listed in Christie's auction catalog as *The Entombment of Christ*, and attributed to Sisto Badalocchio, the painting sold on May 22, 1998, for $12,000. Subsequent to the auction, however, E.S.T. learned that the painting was, in fact, created by Caracci himself, increasing its value to $300,000 rather than the $12,000 initially pegged by Stuart. E.S.T. claimed that Christie's was negligent and breached its fiduciary duty by failing to recognize the painting's true authorship and dramatically higher value.

In its defense, Christie's argued that under its consignment agreement with E.S.T., its duty was to offer the painting for sale at auction—period. Christie's referred to language in the consignment agreement which stated that Christie's made "no representation or warranties to Consignor with respect to the Property, its authenticity, condition or otherwise." The relevant contract provision stated in its entirety:

6. SALE ARRANGEMENTS

(b) "Any written or oral appraisal, estimate or other statement of Christie's or our representatives with respect to the estimated or expected selling price of any lot of Property is a statement of opinion only and shall not be relied upon by Consignor or any third party as a prediction or guarantee of the actual selling price. Christie's makes no representations or warranties to Consignor with respect to the Property, its authenticity, condition or otherwise. Christie's shall not be liable for errors or omissions in catalogue or other descriptions of the Property. Printed pre-sale estimates shall not include the buyer's premium or taxes."

A critical component in the dispute was whether "authenticity" encompasses the word "attribution" or whether, instead, the provision itself was too vague. While the New York Supreme Court did not rule on these issues, it did find the clause too ambiguous to grant Christie's motion to dismiss. In its opinion, the court held that it "[could] not determine as a matter of law that misattribution of the painting is included in the matters listed in paragraph 6(b) of the Consignment Agreement."[196] Although the case was settled before further arguments could be heard, it appears to us that the court was wrong in its attempt to distinguish between the words "authenticity" and "attribution." In any event, the auction houses have changed their consignment agreements to make it clear that the auction house makes "no representations or warranties to the Consignor with respect to the Property, its authenticity, attribution, condition or otherwise."

Limitations by Insurance

In recent years, specialty insurance organizations, such as Fine Arts Risk Management, Inc. (FARM), have begun to develop professional-liability programs to service various segments of the fine-arts communities. For example, the FARM insurance program available to members of the Appraisers Association of America is basically an errors and omissions policy that reinforces the importance of adhering to proper appraisal methods. The policy covers errors, omissions, and acts of negligence committed by an appraiser in the course of rendering an appraisal. The insurer will defend the appraiser even if the suit is groundless or fraudulent. The policy will not, however, cover acts of dishonesty—such as fraud, intentional omissions, acts of bad faith, defamatory acts, and acts of product disparagement—nor will it cover appraisals on a contingent-fee basis.

Notes to Chapter 7

1. When an artist is deceased, the holder of the decedent-artist's *droit moral* (in nations recognizing the *droit moral* and a postmortem application of such rights) generally asserts the right to authenticate works attributed to the artist. (*See* chapter 11 for an examination of the *droit moral*.)

2. *See* www.appraisersassoc.org/index.htm (last visited on July 15, 2004). The Appraisers Association of America is located at 386 Park Avenue South, Suite 2000, New York, NY 10016.

3. *See* www.appraisers.org/about/chapters (last visited on July 15, 2004). The American Society of Appraisers is located at 555 Herndon Parkway, Suite 125, Herndon, VA 20170-5226.

4. *See* www.isa-appraisers.org/index.html (last visited on July 15, 2004). The International Society of Appraisers is located at 1131 SW 7th St. STE 105, Renton, WA 98055.

5. The Appraisal Foundation is located in Washington, D.C. Copies of the annual edition of the Uniform Standards of Professional Appraisal Practice may be ordered from: The Appraisal Foundation, 1029 Vermont Ave., NW, Suite 900, Washington, D.C. 20005-3517.

6. For further information about the AOA, see www.aoaonline.org (last visited on July 15, 2004).

7. For further information about IFAR, see www.ifar.org (last visited on July 15, 2004).

8. *See* www.aicausa.org/whoweare.html (last visited on July 15, 2004).

9. I.R.C. § 170(f)(8); Treas. Reg. § 1.170A-13(f). In addition, such donors must comply with Treas. Reg. § 1.170A-13(b) and (c).   .

10. In determining which of the substantiation requirements applies, the deduction is based on either a single item or a group of similar items. A group of similar items refers to property in the same generic category or type (whether or not donated to the same charity), such as stamps, coins, books, jewelry, and furniture. Treas. Reg. § 1.170A-13(c)(7)(iii). For example, if a donor contributes books to Charities *A, B*, and *C* and deducts $2,000, $5,000, and $900, respectively, he must meet the substantiation requirements for a deduction of more than $5,000.

11. Treas. Reg. § 1.170A-13(f)(3).

12.   Treas. Reg. § 1.170A-13(b)(2)(ii).

13.   In such cases, the total claimed as a deduction for gifts of tangible personal property is stated on the return and Form 8283 is not required to be attached.

14.   If the donated property is property that has appreciated in value, the donor will be responsible for any issues regarding the "related use" rule. I.R.C. § 170(e)(1)(B)(i). A deduction for the full fair market value of appreciated tangible personal property is allowable only if the donated property is related to the tax-exempt purpose of the donee charity.

15.   Treas. Reg. § 1.170A-13(b)(2)(ii).

16.   Treas. Reg. § 1.170A-13(b) and (c).

17.   Treas. Reg. § 1.170A-13(c)(2)(i).

18.   Treas. Reg. § 1.170A-13(b)(2)(ii).

19.   Treas. Reg. §§ 1.170A-13(c)(3)(i); 1.170A-13(c)(6)(i).

20.   If a taxpayer identification number is otherwise required by I.R.C. § 6109 and the Regulations thereunder.

21.   If a taxpayer identification number is otherwise required by I.R.C. § 6109 and the Regulations thereunder.

22.   Within the meaning of Treas. Reg. § 1.170A-1(c)(2).

23.   Treas. Reg. § 1.170A-13(v)(3)(ii).

24.   I.R.S. Publication 561, Determining the Value of Donated Property.

25.   Treas. Reg. § 1.170A-13(c)(5)(iv).

26.   Treas. Reg. § 1.170A-13(c)(5)(i). Even if the appraiser meets these requirements, the appraiser will not be a qualified appraiser if the donor had knowledge of facts that would cause a reasonable person to expect the appraiser falsely to overstate the value of the donated property (that is, the donor and the appraiser make an agreement concerning the amount at which the property will be valued and the donor knows that such amount exceeds the fair market value of the property). Treas. Reg. § 1.170A-13(c)(5)(ii).

27.   Adjusted as provided by I.R.C. § 1016.

28.   If a taxpayer identification number is otherwise required by I.R.C. § 6109 and the Regulations thereunder.

29.   Treas. Reg. § 1.170A-13(c)(4)(ii).

30.   Pub. L. No. 106-229, 114 Stat. 464 (2000).

31.   I.R.S. Publication 561, *supra* note 24.

32.   *Id.*

33.   *Id.*

34.   *Id.*

35.   *Id.*

36. Johnson v. Comm'r, 85 T.C. 469, 477 (1985).

37. Sammons v. Comm'r, 838 F.2d 330 (9th Cir. 1988).

38. *Id.* at 332.

39. *Id.* at 334.

40. *Id.* (emphasis added).

41. I.R.S. Publication 561, *supra* note 24.

42. *Johnson*, 85 T.C. 469.

43. *Id.* at 473.

44. *Id.* at 478.

45. Hahn v. Duveen, 133 Misc. 871, 234 N.Y.S. 185 (Sup. Ct. 1929).

46. For an excellent summary of the history of the problem-ridden painting discussed here, *La Belle Ferroniere, see* Decker, *The Multimillion Dollar Belle*, ARTNEWS, Summer 1985, at 86.

47. *Id.* at 89.

48. *See Hahn*, 234 N.Y.S. 185.

49. For additional background information concerning *La Belle Ferroniere, see* SIMPSON, ARTFUL PARTNERS: BERNARD BERENSON AND JO-SEPH DUVEEN 241–43 (1986). *See also* SECREST, DUVEEN: A LIFE IN ART (Knopf 2004).

50. DAILY TELEGRAPH, Apr. 5, 1993, at 16. *See also* DAILY TELE-GRAPH, Jul. 8, 1991, at 1.

51. DAILY TELEGRAPH, Apr. 5, 1993, at 16.

52. The action in disparagement protects economic interests of an injured party. The similar, but distinct, action in defamation protects the personal reputation of an injured party.

53. *See* RESTATEMENT (SECOND) OF TORTS § 651 (2001).

54. *Id.* §§ 646A, 595 cmt. j.

55. *Id.* § 595 comment a, discusses other ways, not pertinent to the example discussed in the text, in which this privilege can be abused, thus causing a loss of its protection.

56. *Id.* § 635 cmts. a, b.

57. *See* Stebbins, *Possible Tort Liability for Opinions Given by Art Experts, in* F. FELDMAN & S. WEIL, ART WORKS: LAW, POLICY, PRACTICE 988 (1974).

58. Kirby v. Wildenstein, 784 F. Supp. 1112 (S.D.N.Y. 1992).

59. A *catalogue raisonné* is perceived as the definitive catalog of the works of a particular artist. Inclusion of a painting in such a catalog serves to authenticate the work, while noninclusion may indicate that the work is not genuine.

60. *See Kirby*, 784 F. Supp. at 1116.

61. *Id.* at 1117.

62. For an excellent analysis of defamation as it relates to the artist, *see* Robert C. Lind, *The Visual Artist and the Law of Defamation*, 2 UCLA ENT. L. REV. 63 (1995).

63. If the statement involves a purely private dispute—that is, does not deal with a matter of public interest or public concern—the issue of fault is not critical.

64. *See* RESTATEMENT (SECOND) OF TORTS § 559; *see also* W. KEETON ET AL., PROSSER & KEETON ON TORTS, § 107, at 774 (5th ed. 1984).

65. *See* Lind, *supra* note 62, at 70.

66. *Id.* at 68.

67. Weller v. Am. Broad. Co., 232 Cal. App. 3d 991, 283 Cal. Rptr. 644 (1991).

68. *Id.*, 232 Cal. App. 3d at 1002, 283 Cal. Rptr. at 651.

69. *See* Lind, *supra* note 62, at 71.

70. Milkovich v. Lorain Journal Co., 497 U.S. 1 (1990).

71. At least one knowledgeable commentator notes that speech made by *non*-media defendants on matters of public concern is afforded virtually identical protections. *See* Robert D. Sack, *Protection of Opinion under the First Amendment: Reflections on Defamation and Privacy Under the First Amendment*, 100 COLUM. L. REV. 294 (Jan. 2000).

72. *Milkovich*, 497 U.S. at 2.

73. *Id. See also* Steven M. Levy, *Liability of the Art Expert for Professional Malpractice*, 1991 WIS. L. REV. 595 (1991) (a comprehensive general discussion of expert opinions and liability of the art expert).

74. *See Weller*, 232 Cal. App. 3d at 1005.

75. McNally v. Yarnall, 764 F. Supp. 838 (S.D.N.Y. 1991).

76. *Id.* at 844.

77. *Id.* at 845.

78. *Id.* at 847.

79. *Id.* at 848.

80. *Id.*

81. *Id.* at 849.

82. *Id.*

83. *Id.* at 850.

84. Daniel Goldreyer Ltd. v. Van de Wetering, 217 A.D.2d 434, 630 N.Y.S.2d 18 (1st Dep't 1995).

85. *Id.*, 217 A.D.2d at 436, 630 N.Y.S.2d at 23.

86. WALL ST. J., Dec. 24, 1991, at B1.

87. *See Goldreyer*, 217 A.D.2d at 436, 630 N.Y.S.2d at 22. The part of the defamation suit against *Time* magazine and Suzanne Schnitzer,

an art critic quoted by *Time* in an article about the restoration, was ordered dismissed by the appellate division decision. The dismissal was in part because the allegedly defamatory statements were ruled to be privileged "opinion." The *Time* article referred to Goldreyer's restoration of the painting with the statement that if it is rehung, it "should be accompanied by a warning sign, Newman according to Goldreyer." The court concluded that the statement does not have a precise meaning; cannot be objectively characterized as true or false; appeared in an immediate context, the "Art" section of *Time* magazine, where the average person would understand it as, or expect to find, expression of opinion or personal taste; and appeared in a broader context of the public debate over the artistic merit of the restoration. Accordingly, the statement was entitled to constitutional protection as privileged opinion in the form of "imaginative expression" or "rhetoric hyperbole."

The *Time* article also referred to a report done by the Dutch Ministry of Justice; and while those statements were not protected as privileged or pure opinion, but were instead opinion based on fact, they were held to be entitled to protection as the "absolute privilege as to fair and true reportage of an official proceeding"—a privilege that is codified at section 74 of the New York Civil Rights Law. This provision requires only that a statement be "substantially accurate" for the privilege to attach.

The defamation case against the Dow Jones Company (owner of the *Wall Street Journal*) was eventually found to be without merit. *See supra* page 597 and notes 125 and 158, *infra*.

88.   *See* Lind, *supra* note 62, at 85.

89.   *Id.*

90.   Boule v. Hutton, 70 F. Supp. 2d 378 (S.D.N.Y. 1999) (granting in part and denying in part defendants' motion for summary judgment); 138 F. Supp. 2d 491 (post-trial decision) (S.D.N.Y. 2001); 170 F. Supp. 2d 441 (S.D.N.Y. 2001) (denying Rule 60(b) motion).

91.   According to the court, this sum was equivalent to approximately $201,000 at the exchange rate in effect at the time of trial.

92.   According to the court, this sum was equivalent to approximately $4,200 at the exchange rate in effect at the time of trial.

93.   *Boule*, 138 F. Supp. 2d at 499.

94.   *Id.*

95.   *Id.*

96.   *Id.* at 500.

97.   *Id.*

98.   *Id.*

99.   *Id.*

100. *Id.*

101. *Id.*

102. *Id.* at 501.

103. *Id.* at 505 (citing Flamm v. Am. Ass'n of Univ. Women, 201 F.3d 144, 149–50 (2d Cir. 2000)).

104. *Id.* at 506. As the court observed, to recover on a claim of libel or slander, a plaintiff must prove by a preponderance of the evidence the following elements: (1) a defamatory statement of fact made by the defendant concerning the plaintiff; (2) written (or oral, in the case of slander) publication to a third party; (3) fault; and (4) per se actionability or special damages. *Id.* at 506.

105. *Id.*

106. *Id.*

107. *Id.* (citing Lerman v. Flynt Distrib. Co., Inc., 745 F.2d 123, 136–37 (2d Cir. 1984)).

108. *Id.*

109. *Id.*

110. *Id.* at 507.

111. *Id.*

112. *Id.* at 508.

113. The court also found that Mark's statements to *ARTnews* constituted breach of contract in that he entered into a contract to write sixteen certificates of authenticity in exchange for 40,000 FF in 1991—and that implicit in the contract was a covenant not to repudiate his opinion in bad faith without reimbursing the Boules. However, as the Boules could neither show that they incurred any damages as a result of relying on Mark's certifications, nor show "benefit of the bargain" damages, that is, the difference between the value of the certified works before the certificates were signed and the amount by which the certificates of authenticity enhanced the value of those works, the court found that the Boules were entitled to recover only the $7,089.56 that they paid to Mark Khidekel for the certificates, plus prejudgment interest. *Id.* at 509–10. The court found that the remaining claims—unjust enrichment, common law fraud, tortuous interference with business relations, prima facie tort, and false light—were without merit.

114. *See* Lind, *supra* note 62, at 85.

115. *Id.* at 87.

116. PROSSER & KEETON, *supra* note 64, § 113 at 797–98.

117. N.Y. Times Co. v. Sullivan, 376 U.S. 254, 279–80 (1964); *see also* Gertz v. Robert Welch, Inc., 418 U.S. 323, 342–43 (1974).

118. Brown v. Kelly Broad. Co., 48 Cal. 3d 711, 732, 771 P.2d 406, 418, 257 Cal. Rptr. 708, 720 (1989).

119.   *See* McNally v. Yarnall, 764 F. Supp. 838, 851 (S.D.N.Y. 1991).

120.   *Id.*

121.   *Id.*

122.   *See* Lind, *supra* note 62, at 105.

123.   *Id.* at note 155.

124.   *See McNally,* 764 F. Supp. at 847.

125.   Daniel Goldreyer Ltd. v. Dow Jones & Co., 259 A.D.2d 353, 687 N.Y.S.2d 64 (1st Dep't 1999).

126.   Daniel Goldreyer Ltd. v. Van de Wetering, 217 A.D.2d 434, 630 N.Y.S.2d 18 (1st Dep't 1995), *supra* note 84.

127.   WALL ST. J., Dec. 24, 1991, at B1.

128.   *Daniel Goldreyer, Ltd.,* 259 A.D.2d at 353.

129.   Daniel Goldreyer filed an appeal, which was granted by Daniel Goldreyer Ltd. v. Dow Jones & Co., 93 N.Y.2d 811, 717 N.E.2d 699, 695 N.Y.S.2d 540 (1999). The appeal was subsequently withdrawn and discontinued in Daniel Goldreyer Ltd. v. Dow Jones & Co., 93 N.Y.2d 1013, 697 N.Y.S.2d 567 (1999).

130.   Sepenuk v. Marshall, 2000 U.S. Dist. LEXIS 17823 (S.D.N.Y. 2000).

131.   *Id.* at *4.

132.   *Id.* at *6.

133.   *Id.* (citing Protic v. Dengler, 46 F. Supp. 2d 277, 281 (S.D.N.Y. 1999), which in turn cited Gross v. N.Y. Times Co., 82 N.Y.2d 146, 603 N.Y.S.2d 813, 623 N.E.2d 1163 (1993)).

134.   "Gross irresponsibility" is defined in Chapadeau v. Utica Observer-Dispatch, 38 N.Y.2d 196, 199, 379 N.Y.S.2d 61, 64 (1975) as lack of "due consideration for the standards of information gathering and dissemination ordinarily followed by responsible parties."

135.   *See* McNally v. Yarnall, 764 F. Supp. 838 (S.D.N.Y. 1991), *supra* note 75, discussed on page 582.

136.   *Id.*

137.   *Sepenuk,* 2000 U.S. Dist. LEXIS 17823, at *9.

138.   *Id.* at *10.

139.   *Id.* at *11.

140.   Estate of Querbach v. A&B Appraisal Serv., No. L-089362-85 (N.J. Super. Ct., Bergen County 1987). The case is reproduced in 1 F. FELDMAN, S. WEIL & S. BIEDERMAN, ART LAW 282 (1988 Supp.).

141.   Karlen, *Fakes, Forgeries and Expert Opinions,* 16 J. ARTS MGMT. & L. 5 at 9 (1986); Levy, *supra* note 73.

142. Karlen, *supra* note 141, at 10.

143. *Id.*

144. *See* RESTATEMENT (SECOND) OF TORTS § 299A.

145. *Id.*

146. *Id.*

147. Travis v. Sotheby Parke Bernet, Inc., Index No. 4290/79 (N.Y. Sup. Ct. Nov. 11, 1982).

148. Estate of Nelson v. Rice, 198 Ariz. 563, 12 P.3d 238, 333 Ariz. Adv. Rep. 25 (2000).

149. RESTATEMENT (SECOND) OF CONTRACTS § 154(b) cmt. c (1979).

150. *Estate of Nelson*, 198 Ariz. at 567.

151. Pilliard v. Sotheby's, Inc., 1998 WL 126060 (S.D.N.Y. Mar. 19, 1998).

152. *Id.* at *1.

153. *Id.* at *2.

154. *Id.*

155. *See* RESTATEMENT (SECOND) OF TORTS §§ 528, 522; *See* PROSSER & KEETON, *supra* note 64, §§ 105, 107.

156. *See* PROSSER & KEETON, *supra* note 64, § 109.

157. *Id.*

158. Amsterdam v. Daniel Goldreyer, Ltd., 882 F. Supp. 1273 (E.D.N.Y. 1995). It was announced by the spokeswoman for the City of Amsterdam on January 11, 1997, that the city agreed to pay Daniel Goldreyer $100,000 to settle the dispute over his restoration of the Barnett Newman painting. As reported by the Associated Press, all legal proceedings between the two parties has come to an end and both sides have agreed to no longer comment on the restoration.

159. *Id.* at 1283.

160. Struna v. Wolf, 126 Misc. 2d 1031, 484 N.Y.S.2d 392 (Sup. Ct. 1985).

161. *Id.* at 1036, 484 N.Y.S.2d at 397. The *Struna* case was subsequently settled out of court; Struna recovered the sculpture and accepted payment of an undisclosed sum of money from the Wolfs. *See also* Rosen v. Spanierman, 711 F. Supp. 749 (S.D.N.Y. 1989), which held that the relationship between the plaintiffs and the gallery, which both sold the painting to the plaintiffs and subsequently appraised the painting for the plaintiffs, was a mere "contractual relationship, insufficient to sustain a cause of action for negligent misrepresentation . . ." and that the appraisals in this case could not create the special relationship necessary to give rise to a cause of action for negligent misrepresentation as the appraisals were conducted after the sale of the painting and "were not part of the sale at issue."

162.   Stewart v. Jackson & Nash, 976 F.2d 86, 90 (2d Cir. 1992). For an interesting discussion of negligent misrepresentation and fraud which suggests the circle of potential plaintiffs to which an appraiser owes a fiduciary duty, *see* Guildhall Ins. Co. v. Silberman, 688 F. Supp. 910 (S.D.N.Y. 1988), where a British insurance company brought suit against a Virginia appraiser of artifacts following the company's payment of $1.8 million for a theft policy and its discovery that the appraisal was almost ten times more than subsequent appraisals. Here, the court had to decide whether to apply New Jersey law which does not require privity in actions for negligent misrepresentation, or New York law which does, in order to protect accountants and by analogy, appraisers, against unlimited liability to unforeseen parties who rely to their detriment on negligently prepared statements. The court applied the stricter New York standard; however, despite the lack of contract between the two parties (the insurance company's client had hired defendant to conduct the appraisal), the court found a fiduciary duty to the insurance company because defendant-appraiser knew the purpose for which he was retained, he was aware that some insurance company would rely on his appraisal, and he certified that his appraisal was made in compliance with the standards of the American Society of Appraisers whose ethical code sets forth an appraiser's duty to third parties. The court therefore denied defendant-appraiser's motion for summary judgment for the fraud and negligence causes asserted against him.

163.   Ravenna v. Christie's, Inc., Index No. 121367-00 (N.Y. Sup. Ct., N.Y. County, Mar. 22, 2001), *aff'd*, 289 A.D.2d 15, 734 N.Y.S.2d 21 (1st Dep't 2001).

164.   Complaint, Ravenna v. Christie's, U.S.D.C. S.D.N.Y., #00Civ. 6316, Aug. 23, 2000.

165.   *Ravenna*, Index No. 121367-00, *supra* note 163, at page 2 of the unpublished state supreme court decision. *See also* N.Y.L.J., Mar. 30, 2001, at 20.

166.   Christie's, Inc. v. Croce, 5 F. Supp. 2d 206 (S.D.N.Y. 1998).

167.   *Id.* at 207 (discussing N.Y. GEN. OBLIG. LAW § 5-327).

168.   *Id.* at 208.

169.   Goldman v. Barnett, 793 F. Supp. 28 (D. Mass. 1992).

170.   A tremendous discrepancy in pricing over a short period of time can also be indicative of fraud. In Arteurial, S.A. v. Lowenthal, 763 F. Supp. 768 (S.D.N.Y. 1991), a New York federal district court found that a painting allegedly by Manglo Millares was fraudulently authenticated based, in part, on the fact that the defendant paid $2,200 for it and resold it two months later for $180,000.

171.   *Id.* at 31.

172. *See Amsterdam*, 882 F. Supp. 1273, *supra* note 158.

173. Pickett v. Am. Ordnance Pres. Ass'n, 60 F. Supp. 2d 450 (E.D. Pa. 1999).

174. *Id.* at 456 (citing Williamson v Consol. Rail Corp., 926 F.2d 1344, 1353 (3d Cir. 1991)).

175. *Id.* (citing Mellon Bank Corp. v. First Union, 951 F.2d 1399, 1409 (3d Cir. 1991)).

176. Francis X. Clines, *Civil War Relics Draw Visitors, and Con Artists*, N.Y. TIMES, Aug. 4, 2002, sec. 1, at 16.

177. Cohen v. Mazoh, Index No. 604029/02 (N.Y. Sup. Ct., N.Y. County, May 21, 2003).

178. *Id.*

179. Cohen v. Mazoh, 12 A.D.3d 296, 784 N.Y.S.2d 857 (1st Dep't 2004). Cohen's other claims, which were also reinstated solely in connection with the painting's authenticity, included negligent misrepresentation, unjust enrichment, and promissory estoppel.

180. The Appellate Division noted, however, that the allegations do not amount to wanton or willful fraud sufficient to warrant punitive damages. *Id.*

181. Zoellner v. Christie's, Index No. 120637/99 (N.Y. Sup. Ct., N.Y. County, Oct. 3, 2003). *See also* Real Prop. Acquisitions v. Christie's, Index No. 601943/04 (N.Y. Sup. Ct., N.Y. County, Mar. 12, 2005) (in dismissing plaintiff's claim based on allegedly undisclosed repairs to an item of furniture purchased at auction, court pointed out that Christie's, in its Conditions of Sale, made "it clear to all potential bidders, that all lots are sold 'as is'").

182. *Id.*

183. Kramer v. Pollock-Krasner Found., 890 F. Supp. 250 (S.D.N.Y. 1995).

184. *Id.* at 253.

185. *Id.* at 255. *See* Vitale v. Marlborough Gallery, 32 U.S.P.Q.2d (BNA) 1283 (S.D.N.Y. 1994), where Kramer's counsel brought a similar case for a different plaintiff alleging a similar conspiracy against the Board, the Foundation and Marlborough Gallery, but not against Sotheby's or Christie's. The court granted summary judgment to the defendants but did note that "Pollock paintings may constitute a submarket, the monopolization of which may be unlawful" under 15 U.S.C. §§ 1 or 2 (Sherman Act).

186. *Kramer*, 890 F. Supp. at 256 (citing Greenwood v. Koven, 880 F. Supp. 186 (S.D.N.Y. 1995)).

187. *Id.* The Pollock-Krasner Authentication Board has been disbanded. *See* Goldberg, *A Pollock Possibility*, 18 IFAR REP. 3 (Mar. 1997).

188.   Lariviere v. Thaw, Index No. 100627/99 (N.Y. Civ. Sup. Ct., New York County, Part 17, June 26, 2000).

189.   *Id*. at 6.

190.   *Id*. at 5 (citations omitted).

191.   Foxley v. Sotheby's, Inc., 893 F. Supp. 1224 (S.D.N.Y. 1995). The case was settled amicably in February 1996, under confidential terms.

192.   *Id*. at 1235.

193.   *Id*. at 1236.

194.   *Id*. at 1237.

195.   E.S.T., Inc. v. Christie's, Inc., N.Y.L.J., June 28, 2001, at 17, col. 1 (Sup. Ct. N.Y. County June 2001).

196.   *Id*. at 4.

Appendix 7-1

Excerpt from Uniform Standards of Professional Appraisal Practice and Advisory Opinions (USPAP) 2004*

ETHICS RULE

To promote and preserve the public trust inherent in professional appraisal practice, an appraiser must observe the highest standards of professional ethics. This ETHICS RULE is divided into four sections: Conduct, Management, Confidentiality, and Record Keeping. The first three sections apply to all appraisal practice, and all four sections apply to appraisal practice performed under Standards 1 through 10.

> Comment: This Rule specifies the personal obligations and responsibilities of the individual appraiser. However, it should also be noted that groups and organizations engaged in appraisal practice share the same ethical obligations.

---

*NOTICE: Pursuant to the passage of the Gramm-Leach-Bliley Act in 1999, numerous agencies have adopted new privacy regulations. Such regulations are focused on the protection of information provided by consumers to those involved in financial activities "found to be closely related to banking or usual in connection with the transaction of banking". These activities have been deemed to include "appraising real or personal property." (Quotations are from the Federal Trade Commission, Privacy of Consumer Financial Information; Final Rule, 16 C.F.R. Part 313.)

Compliance with these Standards is required when either the service or the appraiser is obligated by law or regulation, or by agreement with the client or intended users, to comply. In addition to these requirements, an individual should comply any time that individual represents that he or she is performing the service as an appraiser.

An appraiser must not misrepresent his or her role when providing valuation services that are outside of appraisal practice.

> Comment: Honesty, impartiality, and professional competency are required of all appraisers under these *Uniform Standards of Professional Appraisal Practice* (USPAP). To document recognition and acceptance of his or her USPAP-related responsibilities in communicating an appraisal, appraisal review, or appraisal consulting assignment completed under USPAP, an appraiser is required to certify compliance with these Standards. (See Standards Rules 2-3, 3-3, 5-3, 6-8, 8-3, and 10-3.)

Conduct:

An appraiser must perform assignments ethically and competently, in accordance with USPAP and any supplemental standards agreed to by the appraiser in accepting the assignment. An appraiser must not engage in criminal conduct. An appraiser must perform assignments with impartiality, objectivity, and independence, and without accommodation of personal interests.

In appraisal practice, an appraiser must not perform as an advocate for any party or issue.

> Comment: An appraiser may be an advocate only in support of his or her assignment results. Advocacy in any other form in appraisal practice is a violation of the ETHICS RULE.

An appraiser must not accept an assignment that includes the reporting of predetermined opinions and conclusions.

An appraiser must not communicate assignment results in a misleading or fraudulent manner. An appraiser must not use or communicate a misleading or fraudulent report or knowingly permit an employee or other person to communicate a misleading or fraudulent report.

An appraiser must not use or rely on unsupported conclusions relating to characteristics such as race, color, religion, national origin, gender, marital status, familial status, age, receipt of public assistance income, handicap, or an unsupported conclusion that homogeneity of such characteristics is necessary to maximize value.

> Comment: An individual appraiser employed by a group or organization that conducts itself in a manner that does not conform to these Standards should take steps that are appropriate under the circumstances to ensure compliance with the Standards.

Management:

The payment of undisclosed fees, commissions, or things of value in connection with the procurement of an assignment is unethical.

> Comment: Disclosure of fees, commissions, or things of value connected to the procurement of an assignment must appear in the certification and in any transmittal letter in which conclusions are stated. In groups or organizations engaged in appraisal practice, intra-company payments to employees for business development are not considered to be unethical. Competency, rather than financial incentives, should be the primary basis for awarding an assignment.

It is unethical for an appraiser to accept an assignment, or to have a compensation arrangement for an assignment, that is contingent on any of the following:

1. the reporting of a predetermined result (*e.g.*, opinion of value);

2. a direction in assignment results that favors the cause of the client;

3. the amount of a value opinion;

4. the attainment of a stipulated result; or

5. the occurrence of a subsequent event directly related to the appraiser's opinions and specific to the assignment's purpose.

Advertising for or soliciting assignments in a manner that is false, misleading, or exaggerated is unethical.

Comment: In groups or organizations engaged in appraisal practice, decisions concerning finder or referral fees, contingent compensation, and advertising may not be the responsibility of an individual appraiser, but for a particular assignment, it is the responsibility of the individual appraiser to ascertain that there has been no breach of ethics, that the assignment is prepared in accordance with these Standards, and that the report can be properly certified when required by Standards Rules 2-3, 3-3, 5-3, 6-8, 8-3, or 10-3.

Confidentiality:

An appraiser must protect the confidential nature of the appraiser-client relationship.

An appraiser must act in good faith with regard to the legitimate interests of the client in the use of confidential information and in the communication of assignment results.

An appraiser must be aware of, and comply with, all confidentiality and privacy laws and regulations applicable in an assignment.

An appraiser must not disclose confidential information or assignment results prepared for a client to anyone other than the client and persons specifically authorized by the client; state enforcement agencies and such third parties as may be authorized by due process of law; and a duly authorized professional peer review committee except when such disclosure to a committee would violate applicable law or regulation. It is unethical for a member of a duly authorized professional peer review committee to disclose confidential information presented to the committee.

Comment: When all confidential elements of confidential information are removed through redaction or the process of aggregation, client authorization is not required for the disclosure of the remaining information, as modified.

Record Keeping:

An appraiser must prepare a workfile for each appraisal, appraisal review, or appraisal consulting assignment. The workfile must include:

- the name of the client and the identity, by name or type, of any other intended users;

- true copies of any written reports, documented on any type of media;

- summaries of any oral reports or testimony, or a transcript of testimony, including the appraiser's signed and dated certification; and

- all other data, information, and documentation necessary to support the appraiser's opinions and conclusions and to show compliance with this Rule and all other applicable Standards, or references to the location(s) of such other documentation.

An appraiser must retain the workfile for a period of at least five (5) years after preparation or at least two (2) years after final disposition of any judicial proceeding in which the appraiser provided testimony related to the assignment, whichever period expires last.

An appraiser must have custody of his or her workfile, or make appropriate workfile retention, access, and retrieval arrangements with the party having custody of the workfile.

> Comment: A workfile preserves evidence of the appraiser's consideration of all applicable data and statements required by USPAP and other information as may be required to support the appraiser's opinions, conclusions, and recommendations. For example, the content of a workfile for a Complete Appraisal must reflect consideration of all USPAP requirements applicable to the specific Complete Appraisal assignment. However, the content of a workfile for a Limited Appraisal need only reflect consideration of the USPAP requirements from which there have been no departure and that are required by the specific Limited Appraisal assignment.
>
> A photocopy or an electronic copy of the entire actual written appraisal, appraisal review, or appraisal consulting report sent or delivered to a client satisfies the requirement of a true copy. As an example, a photocopy or electronic copy of the Self-Contained Appraisal Report, Summary Appraisal Report, or Restricted Use Appraisal Report actually issued by an appraiser for a real property appraisal assignment satisfies the true copy requirement for that assignment.
>
> Care should be exercised in the selection of the form, style, and type of medium for written records, which may be handwritten

and informal, to ensure that they are retrievable by the appraiser throughout the prescribed record retention period.

A workfile must be in existence prior to and contemporaneous with the issuance of a written or oral report. A written summary of an oral report must be added to the workfile within a reasonable time after the issuance of the oral report.

A workfile must be made available by the appraiser when required by state enforcement agencies or due process of law. In addition, a workfile in support of a Restricted Use Appraisal Report must be sufficient for the appraiser to produce a Summary Appraisal Report (for assignments under STANDARDS 2 and 8) or an Appraisal Report (for assignments under STANDARD 10), and must be available for inspection by the client in accordance with the Comment to Standards Rules 2-2(c)(ix), 8-2(c)(ix), and 10-2(b)(ix).

COMPETENCY RULE

Prior to accepting an assignment or entering into an agreement to perform any assignment, an appraiser must properly identify the problem to be addressed and have the knowledge and experience to complete the assignment competently; or alternatively, must:

1. **disclose the lack of knowledge and/or experience to the client before accepting the assignment;**

2. **take all steps necessary or appropriate to complete the assignment competently; and**

3. **describe the lack of knowledge and/or experience and the steps taken to complete the assignment competently in the report.**

Comment: Competency applies to factors such as, but not limited to, an appraiser's familiarity with a specific type of property, a market, a geographic area, or an analytical method. If such a factor is necessary for an appraiser to develop credible assignment results, the appraiser is responsible for having the competency to address that factor or for following the steps outlined above to satisfy this COMPETENCY RULE.

The background and experience of appraisers varies widely, and a lack of knowledge or experience can lead to inaccurate or inappropriate appraisal practice. The COMPETENCY RULE requires an appraiser to have both the knowledge and the experience required to perform a specific appraisal service competently.

If an appraiser is offered the opportunity to perform an appraisal service but lacks the necessary knowledge or experience to complete it competently, the appraiser must disclose his or her lack of knowledge or experience to the client before accepting the assignment and then take the necessary or appropriate steps to complete the appraisal service competently. This may be accomplished in various ways, including, but not limited to, personal study by the appraiser, association with an appraiser reasonably believed to have the necessary knowledge or experience, or retention of others who possess the required knowledge or experience.

In an assignment where geographic competency is necessary, an appraiser preparing an appraisal in an unfamiliar location must spend sufficient time to understand the nuances of the local market and the supply and demand factors relating to the specific property type and the location involved. Such understanding will not be imparted solely from a consideration of specific data such as demographics, costs, sales, and rentals. The necessary understanding of local market conditions provides the bridge between a sale and a comparable sale or a rental and a comparable rental. If an appraiser is not in a position to spend the necessary amount of time in a market area to obtain this understanding, affiliation with a qualified local appraiser may be the appropriate response to ensure development of credible assignment results.

Although this Rule requires an appraiser to identify the problem and disclose any deficiency in competence prior to accepting an assignment, facts or conditions uncovered during the course of an assignment could cause an appraiser to discover that he or she lacks the required knowledge or experience to complete the assignment competently. At the point of such discovery, the appraiser is obligated to notify the client and comply with items 2 and 3 of this Rule.

DEPARTURE RULE

This Rule permits exceptions from sections of the Uniform Standards that are classified as specific requirements rather than binding requirements. The burden of proof is on the appraiser to decide before accepting an assignment and invoking this Rule that the scope of work applied will result in opinions or conclusions that are credible. The burden of disclosure is also on the appraiser to report any departures from specific requirements.

An appraiser may enter into an agreement to perform an assignment in which the scope of work is less than, or different from, the work that would otherwise be required by the specific requirements, provided that prior to entering into such an agreement:

1. the appraiser has determined that the appraisal process to be performed is not so limited that the results of the assignment are no longer credible;

2. the appraiser has advised the client that the assignment calls for something less than, or different from, the work required by the specific requirements and that the report will clearly identify and explain the departure(s); and

3. the client has agreed that the performance of a limited appraisal service would be appropriate, given the intended use.

Comment: Not all specific requirements are *applicable* to every assignment. When a specific requirement is *not applicable* to a given assignment, the specific requirement is irrelevant and therefore no departure is needed.

A specific requirement is *applicable* when:

- it addresses factors or conditions that are present in the given assignment, or

- it addresses analysis that is typical practice in such an assignment.

- A specific requirement is *not applicable* when:

- it addresses factors or conditions that are not present in the given assignment,

- it addresses analysis that is not typical practice in such an assignment, or

- it addresses analysis that would not provide meaningful results in the given assignment.

Of those specific requirements that are *applicable* to a given assignment, some may be *necessary* in order to result in opinions or conclusions that are credible. When a specific requirement is *necessary* to a given assignment, departure is not permitted.

Departure is permitted from those specific requirements that are *applicable* to a given assignment but *not necessary* in order to result in opinions or conclusions that are credible.

A specific requirement is considered to be both *applicable* and *necessary* when:

- it addresses factors or conditions that are present in the given assignment, or it addresses analysis that is typical practice in such an assignment, and

- lack of consideration for those factors, conditions, or analyses would significantly affect the credibility of the results.

Typical practice for a given assignment is measured by:

- the expectations of the participants in the market for appraisal services, and

- what an appraiser's peers' actions would be in performing the same or a similar assignment.

If an appraiser enters into an agreement to perform an appraisal service that calls for something less than, or different from, the work that would otherwise be required by the specific requirements, Standards Rules 2-2(a)(xi), 2-2(b)(xi), 2-2(c)(xi), 6-7(p), 8-2(a)(xi), 8-2(b)(xi), 8-2(c)(xi), 10-2(a)(x), and 10-2(b)(x) require that the report clearly identify and explain departure(s) from the specific requirements.

Departure from the following development and reporting Rules is not permitted: Standards Rules 1-1, 1-2, 1-5, 1-6, 2-1, 2-2, 2-3, 3-1, 3-2, 3-3, 4-1, 4-2, 5-1, 5-2, 5-3, 6-1, 6-3, 6-6, 6-7, 6-8, 7-1, 7-2, 7-5, 7-6, 8-1, 8-2, 8-3, 9-1, 9-2, 9-3, 9-5, 10-1, 10-2, and 10-3. This restriction on departure is reiterated throughout the document with the reminder: "This Standards Rule contains binding requirements from which departure is not permitted."

The DEPARTURE RULE does not apply to the DEFINI-
TIONS, PREAMBLE, ETHICS RULE, COMPETENCY
RULE, JURISDICTIONAL EXCEPTION RULE or SUP-
PLEMENTAL STANDARDS RULE.

STANDARD 7: PERSONAL PROPERTY APPRAISAL, DEVELOPMENT

In developing a personal property appraisal, an appraiser must identify the problem to be solved and the scope of work necessary to solve
the problem and correctly complete research and analysis necessary
to produce a credible appraisal.

> Comment: STANDARD 7 is directed toward the substantive
> aspects of developing a competent appraisal of personal proper-
> ty. The requirements set forth in STANDARD 7 follow the ap-
> praisal development process in the order of topics addressed and
> can be used by appraisers and the users of appraisal services as a
> convenient checklist.

Standards Rule 7-1 (This Standards Rule contains binding requirements from which departure is not permitted.)

In developing a personal property appraisal, an appraiser must:

(a) be aware of, understand, and correctly employ those
recognized methods and techniques that are necessary to
produce a credible appraisal;

> Comment: This Standards Rule recognizes that the principle of
> change continues to affect the manner in which appraisers per-
> form appraisal services. Changes and developments in personal
> property practice have a substantial impact on the appraisal pro-
> fession. Important changes in the cost and manner of acquiring,
> producing, and marketing personal property and changes in the
> legal framework in which property rights and interests are cre-
> ated, marketed, conveyed, and financed have resulted in corre-
> sponding changes in appraisal theory and practice. Social change
> has also had an effect on appraisal theory and practice. To keep
> abreast of these changes and developments, the appraisal profes-
> sion reviews and revises appraisal methods and techniques and
> develops methods and techniques to meet new circumstances.
> For this reason, it is not sufficient for appraisers to simply main-
> tain the skills and the knowledge they possess when they be-

come appraisers. Each appraiser must continuously improve his or her skills to remain proficient in personal property appraisal.

(b) not commit a substantial error of omission or commission that significantly affects an appraisal; and

Comment: In performing appraisal services, an appraiser must be certain that the gathering of factual information is conducted in a manner that is sufficiently diligent, given the scope of work as identified according to Standards Rule 7-2(f), to ensure that the data that would have a material or significant effect on the resulting opinions or conclusions are identified and, when necessary, analyzed. Further, an appraiser must use sufficient care in analyzing such data to avoid errors that would significantly affect his or her opinions and conclusions.

(c) not render appraisal services in a careless or negligent manner, such as by making a series of errors that, although individually might not significantly affect the results of an appraisal, in the aggregate affect the credibility of those results.

Comment: Perfection is impossible to attain, and competence does not require perfection. However, an appraiser must not render appraisal services in a careless or negligent manner. This Rule requires an appraiser to use due diligence and due care.

Standards Rule 7-2 (This Standards Rule contains binding requirements from which departure is not permitted.)

In developing a personal property appraisal, an appraiser must:

(a) identify the client and other intended users;

(b) identify the intended use of the appraiser's opinions and conclusions;

Comment: Identification of the intended use is necessary for the appraiser and the client to decide:

- the appropriate scope of work to be completed, and

- the level of information to be provided in communicating the appraisal.

An appraiser must not allow a client's objectives or intended use to cause an analysis to be biased.

(c) **identify the purpose of the assignment (the type and definition of the value to be developed); and, if the value opinion to be developed is market value, ascertain whether the value is to be the most probable price:**

   (i) **in terms of cash; or**

   (ii) **in terms of financial arrangements equivalent to cash; or**

   (iii) **in other precisely defined terms; and**

   (iv) **if the opinion of value is to be based on non-market financing or financing with unusual conditions or incentives, the terms of such financing must be clearly identified and the appraiser's opinion of their contributions to or negative influence on value must be developed by analysis of relevant market data;**

   Comment: When the purpose of an assignment is to develop an opinion of value in a specified market or at a specified market level based on the potential sale of the property, the appraiser must also develop an opinion of reasonable exposure time linked to the value opinion.

(d) **identify the effective date of the appraiser's opinions and conclusions;**

(e) **identify the characteristics of the property that are relevant to the purpose and intended use of the appraisal, including:**

   (i) **sufficient characteristics to establish the identity of the item including the method of identification;**

   (ii) **sufficient characteristics to establish the relative quality of the item (and its component parts, where applicable) within its type;**

   (iii) **all other physical and economic attributes with a material effect on value;**

   Comment: Some examples of physical and economic characteristics include condition, style, size, quality, manufacturer, author, materials, origin, age, provenance, alterations, restorations, and obsolescence. The type of property and the purpose and intended use of the appraisal determine which characteristics have a material effect on value.

(iv) the ownership interest to be valued;

(v) any known restrictions, encumbrances, leases, covenants, contracts, declarations, special assessments, ordinances, or other items of a similar nature; and

(vi) any real property or intangible items that are not personal property but which are included in the appraisal.

Comment on (i)–(vi): If the necessary subject property information is not available because of conditions limiting the appraiser's ability to inspect or research the subject property (such as lighting conditions at an onsite inspection, time constraints, lack of attainable information from reliable third-party sources), an appraiser must:

- obtain the necessary information before proceeding, or

- where possible, in compliance with Standards Rule 7-2(g), use an extraordinary assumption about such information.

An appraiser may use any combination of a property inspection and documents or other resources to identify the relevant characteristics of the subject property. The information used by an appraiser to identify the property characteristics must be from sources the appraiser reasonably believes are reliable.

An appraiser may not be required to value the whole when the subject of the appraisal is a fractional interest, a physical segment, or a partial holding.

(f) identify the scope of work necessary to complete the assignment;

Comment: The scope of work is acceptable when it is consistent with:

- the expectations of participants in the market for the same or similar appraisal services; and

- what the appraiser's peers' actions would be in performing the same or a similar assignment in compliance with US-PAP.

An appraiser must have sound reasons in support of the scope of work decision and must be prepared to support the decision to exclude any information or procedure that would appear to be relevant to the client, intended users, or the appraiser's peers in the same or a similar assignment.

An appraiser must not allow assignment conditions or other factors to limit the extent of research or analysis to such a degree that the resulting opinions and conclusions developed in an assignment are not credible in the context of the purpose and intended use of the appraisal.

(g) identify any extraordinary assumptions necessary in the assignment; and

Comment: An extraordinary assumption may be used in an assignment only if:

- it is required to properly develop credible opinions and conclusions;

- the appraiser has a reasonable basis for the extraordinary assumption;

- use of the extraordinary assumption results in a credible analysis; and

- the appraiser complies with the disclosure requirements set forth in USPAP for extraordinary assumptions.

(h) identify any hypothetical conditions necessary in the assignment.

Comment: A hypothetical condition may be used in an assignment only if:

- use of the hypothetical condition is clearly required for legal purposes, for purposes of reasonable analysis, or for purposes of comparison;

- use of the hypothetical condition results in a credible analysis; and

- the appraiser complies with the disclosure requirements set forth in USPAP for hypothetical conditions.

Standards Rule 7-3 (This Standards Rule contains specific requirements from which departure is permitted. See DEPARTURE RULE.)

In developing a personal property appraisal, an appraiser must collect, verify, analyze, and reconcile all information pertinent to the appraisal problem, given the scope of work identified in accordance with Standards Rule 7-2(f).

(a) Where applicable, identify the effect of highest and best use by measuring and analyzing the current use and alternative uses to encompass what is profitable, legal, and physically possible, as relevant to the purpose and intended use of the appraisal;

(b) Personal property has several measurable marketplaces; therefore, the appraiser must define and analyze the appropriate market consistent with the purpose of the appraisal; and

Comment: The appraiser must recognize that there are distinct levels of trade and each may generate its own data. For example, a property may have a different value at a wholesale level of trade, a retail level of trade, or under various auction conditions. Therefore, the appraiser must analyze the subject property within the correct market context.

(c) Analyze the relevant economic conditions at the time of the valuation, including market acceptability of the property and supply, demand, scarcity, or rarity.

Standards Rule 7-4 (This Standards Rule contains specific requirements from which departure is permitted. See DEPARTURE RULE.)

In developing a personal property appraisal, an appraiser must collect, verify, and analyze all information applicable to the appraisal problem and the type of property, given the scope of work identified in accordance with Standards Rule 7-2(f).

(a) When a sales comparison approach is applicable, an appraiser must analyze such comparable sales data as are available to indicate a value conclusion.

(b) When a cost approach is applicable, an appraiser must:

  (i) analyze such comparable cost data as are available to estimate the cost new of the property; and

  (ii) analyze such comparable data as are available to estimate the difference between cost new and the present worth of the property (accrued depreciation).

(c) When an income approach is applicable, an appraiser must:

  (i) analyze such comparable data as are available to estimate the market income of the property;

  (ii) analyze such comparable operating expense data as are available to estimate the operating expenses of the property;

  (iii) analyze such comparable data as are available to estimate rates of capitalization and/or rates of discount; and

  (iv) base projections of future income and expenses on reasonably clear and appropriate evidence.

Comment: An appraiser must, in developing income and expense statements and cash flow projections, weigh historical information and trends, current supply and demand factors affecting such trends, and competition.

(d) When developing an opinion of the value of a lease or leased property, an appraiser must analyze the effect on value, if any, of the terms and conditions of the lease(s).

(e) An appraiser must analyze the effect on value, if any, of the assemblage of the various component parts of a property and refrain from valuing the whole solely by adding together the individual values of the various component parts.

Comment: Although the value of the whole may be equal to the sum of the separate parts, it also may be greater than or less than the sum of such parts. Therefore, the value of the whole must be tested by reference to appropriate data and supported by an -appropriate analysis of such data.

A similar procedure must be followed when the value of the whole has been established and the appraiser seeks to value a part. The value of any such part must be tested by reference to appropriate data and supported by an appropriate analysis of such data.

(f) An appraiser must analyze the effect on value, if any, of anticipated modifications to the subject property, to the extent that market actions reflect such anticipated modifications as of the effective appraisal date.

(g) An appraiser must analyze the effect on value of any real property or intangible items that are not personal property but are included in the appraisal.

<u>Comment</u>: Competency in real property appraisal (see STANDARD 1) or business appraisal (see STANDARD 9) may be required when it is necessary to allocate the overall value to the property components. In addition, competency in other types of personal property outside of the appraiser's specialty area may be necessary (see STANDARD 7 and the COMPETENCY RULE). A separate valuation, developed in compliance with the STANDARD pertinent to the type of property involved, is required when the value of an item or combination of items is significant to the overall value.

(h) When appraising proposed modifications, an appraiser must examine and have available for future examination:

(i) plans, specifications, or other documentation sufficient to identify the scope and character of the proposed modifications;

(ii) evidence indicating the probable time of completion of the proposed modifications; and

(iii) reasonably clear and appropriate evidence supporting implementation costs, anticipated earnings, and output, as applicable.

<u>Comment</u>: Development of a value opinion for a subject property with proposed modifications as of a current date involves the use of the hypothetical condition that the described modifications have been completed as of the date of value when, in fact, they have not.

The evidence required to be examined and maintained may include such items as vendors' or contractors' estimates relating to cost and the time required to complete the proposed modifications; market and feasibility studies; operating cost data; and the history of recently completed similar developments. The appraisal may require a complete feasibility analysis.

Standards Rule 7-5 (This Standards Rule contains binding requirements from which departure is not permitted.)

In developing a personal property appraisal, when the value opinion to be developed is market value, an appraiser must, if such information is available to the appraiser in the normal course of business:

(a) analyze all agreements of sale, validated offers or third-party offers to sell, options, or listings of the subject property current as of the effective date of the appraisal; and

(b) analyze all prior sales of the subject property that occurred within a reasonable and applicable time period, given the purpose of the assignment and the type of property involved.

Comment: The data needed for the required analyses in SR 7-5(a) and 7-5(b) may not be available or relevant in all assignments. See the Comments to Standards Rules 8-2(a)(ix), 8-2(b)(ix), and 8-2(c)(ix) for corresponding reporting requirements.

Standards Rule 7-6 (This Standards Rule contains binding requirements from which departure is not permitted.)

In developing a personal property appraisal, an appraiser must:

(a) reconcile the quality and quantity of data available and analyzed within the approaches used; and

(b) reconcile the applicability or suitability of the approaches used to arrive at the value conclusion(s).

Comment: See the Comments to Standards Rules 8-2(a)(ix), 8-2(b)(ix), and 8-2(c)(ix) for corresponding reporting requirements.

STANDARD 8: PERSONAL PROPERTY APPRAISAL, REPORTING

In reporting the results of a personal property appraisal, an appraiser must communicate each analysis, opinion, and conclusion in a manner that is not misleading.

Comment: STANDARD 8 addresses the content and level of information required in a report that communicates the results of a personal property appraisal.

STANDARD 8 does not dictate the form, format, or style of personal property appraisal reports, which are functions of the needs of users and appraisers. The substantive content of a report determines its compliance.

Standards Rule 8-1 (This Standards Rule contains binding requirements from which departure is not permitted.)

Each written or oral personal property appraisal report must:

(a) clearly and accurately set forth the appraisal in a manner that will not be misleading;

Comment: Since many reports are used and relied upon by third parties, communications considered adequate by the appraiser's client may not be sufficient. An appraiser must take extreme care to make certain that his or her reports will not be misleading to the intended users of the appraisal report.

(b) contain sufficient information to enable the intended users of the appraisal to understand the report properly; and

Comment: The person(s) expected to receive or rely on a Self-Contained or Summary Appraisal Report are the client and intended users. Only the client is expected to receive or rely on the Restricted Use Appraisal Report.

(c) clearly and accurately disclose any extraordinary assumption, hypothetical condition, or limiting condition that directly affects the appraisal and indicate its impact on value.

Comment: In a written report the disclosure is required in conjunction with each statement of opinion or conclusion that is affected.

Standards Rule 8-2 (This Standards Rule contains binding requirements from which departure is not permitted.)

Each written personal property appraisal report must be prepared under one of the following three options and prominently state which option is used: Self-Contained Appraisal Report, Summary Appraisal Report, or Restricted Use Appraisal Report.

> Comment: When the intended users include parties other than the client, either a Self-Contained Appraisal Report or a Summary Appraisal Report must be provided. When the intended users do not include parties other than the client, a Restricted Use Appraisal Report may be provided. The essential difference among these three options is in the content and level of information provided.
>
> An appraiser must use care when characterizing the type of report and level of information communicated upon completion of an assignment. An appraiser may use any other label in addition to, but not in place of, the label set forth in this Standard for the type of report provided.
>
> The report content and level of information requirements set forth in this Standard are minimums for each type of report. An appraiser must supplement a report form, when necessary, to ensure that any intended user of the appraisal is not misled and that the report complies with the applicable content requirements set forth in this Standards Rule.
>
> A party receiving a copy of a Self-Contained Appraisal Report, Summary Appraisal Report, or Restricted Use Appraisal Report in order to satisfy disclosure requirements does not become an intended user of the appraisal unless the appraiser identifies such party as an intended user as part of the assignment.

(a) **The content of a Self-Contained Appraisal Report must be consistent with the intended use of the appraisal and, at a minimum:**

   (i) **state the identity of the client and any intended users, by name or type;**

> Comment: An appraiser must use care when identifying the client to ensure a clear understanding and to avoid violations of the Confidentiality section of the ETHICS RULE. In those rare instances where the client wishes to remain anonymous, an ap-

praiser must still document the identity of the client in the workfile but may omit the client's identity in the report.

(ii) state the intended use of the appraisal;

(iii) describe information sufficient to identify the property involved in the appraisal, including the physical and economic property characteristics relevant to the assignment;

(iv) state the property interest appraised;

(v) state the purpose of the appraisal; including the type and definition of value and its source;

Comment: Stating the definition of value requires the definition itself, an appropriate reference to the source of the definition, and any comments needed to clearly indicate to the reader how the definition is being applied.

When the purpose of the assignment is to develop an opinion of market value, state whether the opinion of value is:

• in terms of cash or of financing terms equivalent to cash, or

• based on non-market financing or financing with unusual conditions or incentives.

When an opinion of market value is not in terms of cash or based on financing terms equivalent to cash, summarize the terms of such financing and explain their contributions to or negative influence on value.

(vi) state the effective date of the appraisal and the date of the report;

Comment: The effective date of the appraisal establishes the context for the value opinion, while the date of the report indicates whether the perspective of the appraiser on the market or property use conditions as of the effective date of the appraisal was prospective, current, or retrospective.

Reiteration of the date of the report and the effective date of the appraisal at various stages of the report in tandem is important for the clear understanding of the reader whenever market or property use conditions on the date of the report are different from such conditions on the effective date of the appraisal.

(vii) describe sufficient information to disclose to the client and any intended users of the appraisal the scope of work used to develop the appraisal;

Comment: This requirement is to ensure that the client and intended users whose expected reliance on an appraisal may be affected by the extent of the appraiser's investigation are properly informed and are not misled as to the scope of work. The appraiser has the burden of proof to support the scope of work decision and the level of information included in a report.

When any portion of the work involves significant personal property appraisal assistance, the appraiser must describe the extent of that assistance. The signing appraiser must also state the name(s) of those providing the significant personal property appraisal assistance in the certification, in accordance with SR 8-3.

(viii) state all assumptions, hypothetical conditions, and limiting conditions that affected the analyses, opinions, and conclusions;

Comment: Typical or ordinary assumptions and limiting conditions may be grouped together in an identified section of the report. An extraordinary assumption or hypothetical condition must be disclosed in conjunction with statements of each opinion or conclusion that was affected.

(ix) describe the information analyzed, the appraisal procedures followed, and the reasoning that supports the analyses, opinions, and conclusions;

Comment: The appraiser must be certain the information provided is sufficient for the client and intended users to adequately understand the rationale for the opinion and conclusions.

When the purpose of an assignment is to develop an opinion of market value, a summary of the results of analyzing the information required in Standards Rules 7-5 and 7-6 is required. If such information was unobtainable, a statement on the efforts undertaken by the appraiser to obtain the information is required. If such information is irrelevant, a statement acknowledging the existence of the information and citing its lack of relevance is required.

(x) state, as appropriate to the class of personal property involved, the use of the property existing as of the date of value and the use of the property reflected in the appraisal; and, when the purpose of the assignment is market value, describe the support and rationale for the appraiser's opinion of the highest and best use of the property;

Comment: The report must contain the appraiser's opinion as to the highest and best use of the property, unless an opinion as to highest and best use is unnecessary such as in insurance valuation or "value in use" appraisals. If the purpose of the assignment is market value, a summary of the appraiser's support and rationale for the opinion of highest and best use is required. The appraiser's reasoning in support of the opinion must be provided in the depth and detail required by its significance to the appraisal. In the context of personal property, highest and best use may equate to the choice of the appropriate market or market level for the type of item and the purpose and intended use of the report.

(xi) state and explain any permitted departures from specific requirements of STANDARD 7 and the reason for excluding any of the usual valuation approaches; and

Comment: A Self-Contained Appraisal Report must include sufficient information to indicate that the appraiser complied with the requirements of STANDARD 7, including any permitted departures from the specific requirements. The amount of detail required will vary with the significance of the information to the appraisal.

When the DEPARTURE RULE is invoked, the assignment is deemed to be a Limited Appraisal. Use of the term "Limited Appraisal" makes clear that the assignment involved something less than or different from the work that could have and would have been completed if departure had not been invoked. The report of a Limited Appraisal must contain a prominent section that clearly identifies the extent of the appraisal process performed and the departures taken.

The reliability of the results of a Complete Appraisal or a Limited Appraisal developed under STANDARD 7 is not affected by the type of report prepared under STANDARD 8. The extent of the appraisal process performed under STANDARD 7 is the basis for the reliability of the value conclusion.

(xii) include a signed certification in accordance with Standards Rule 8-3.

(b) The content of a Summary Appraisal Report must be consistent with the intended use of the appraisal and, at a minimum:

Comment: The essential difference between the Self-Contained Appraisal Report and the Summary Appraisal Report is the level of detail of presentation.

(i)   state the identity of the client and any intended users, by name or type;

Comment: An appraiser must use care when identifying the client to ensure a clear understanding and to avoid violations of the Confidentiality section of the ETHICS RULE. In those rare instances where the client wishes to remain anonymous, an appraiser must still document the identity of the client in the workfile but may omit the client's identity in the report.

(ii)   state the intended use of the appraisal;

(iii) summarize information sufficient to identify the property involved in the appraisal, including the physical and economic property characteristics relevant to the assignment;

(iv)   state the property interest appraised;

(v)   state the purpose of the appraisal, including the type and definition of value and its source;

Comment: Stating the definition of value requires the definition itself, an appropriate reference to the source of the definition, and any comments needed to clearly indicate to the reader how the definition is being applied.

When the purpose of the assignment is to develop an opinion of market value, state whether the opinion of value is:

•   in terms of cash or of financing terms equivalent to cash, or

- based on non-market financing or financing with unusual conditions or incentives.

When an opinion of market value is not in terms of cash or based on financing terms equivalent to cash, summarize the terms of such financing and explain their contributions to or negative influence on value.

(vi) state the effective date of the appraisal and the date of the report;

Comment: The effective date of the appraisal establishes the context for the value opinion, while the date of the report indicates whether the perspective of the appraiser on the market or property use conditions as of the effective date of the appraisal was prospective, current, or retrospective.

Reiteration of the date of the report and the effective date of the appraisal at various stages of the report in tandem is important for the clear understanding of the reader whenever market or property use conditions on the date of the report are different from such conditions on the effective date of the appraisal.

(vii) summarize sufficient information to disclose to the client and any intended users of the appraisal the scope of work used to develop the appraisal;

Comment: This requirement is to ensure that the client and intended users whose expected reliance on an appraisal may be affected by the extent of the appraiser's investigation are properly informed and are not misled as to the scope of work. The appraiser has the burden of proof to support the scope of work decision and the level of information included in a report.

When any portion of the work involves significant personal property appraisal assistance, the appraiser must summarize the extent of that assistance. The signing appraiser must also state the name(s) of those providing the significant personal property appraisal assistance in the certification, in accordance with SR 8-3.

(viii) state all assumptions, hypothetical conditions, and limiting conditions that affected the analyses, opinions, and conclusions;

Comment: Typical or ordinary assumptions and limiting conditions may be grouped together in an identified section of the report. An extraordinary assumption or hypothetical condition must be disclosed in conjunction with statements of each opinion or conclusion that was affected.

(ix) **summarize the information analyzed, the appraisal procedures followed, and the reasoning that supports the analyses, opinions, and conclusions;**

Comment: The appraiser must be certain that the information provided is sufficient for the client and intended users to adequately understand the rationale for the opinion and conclusions.

When the purpose of an assignment is to develop an opinion of market value, a summary of the results of the analysis of the information required in Standards Rules 7-5 and 7-6 is necessary. If such information was unobtainable, a statement on the efforts undertaken by the appraiser to obtain the information is required. If such information is irrelevant, a statement acknowledging the existence of the information and citing its lack of relevance is required.

(x) **state, as appropriate to the class of personal property involved, the use of the property existing as of the date of value and the use of the property reflected in the appraisal; and, when the purpose of the assignment is a market value, summarize the support and rationale for the appraiser's opinion of the highest and best use of the property;**

Comment: The report must contain the appraiser's opinion as to the highest and best use of the property, unless an opinion as to highest and best use is unnecessary such as in insurance valuation or "value in use" appraisals. If the purpose of the assignment is market value, a summary of the appraiser's support and rationale for the opinion of highest and best use is required. The appraiser's reasoning in support of the opinion must be provided in the depth and detail required by its significance to the appraisal. In the context of personal property, highest and best use may equate to the choice of the appropriate market or market level for the type of item and the purpose and intended use of the report.

(xi) **state and explain any permitted departures from specific requirements of STANDARD 7, and the reason for excluding any of the usual valuation approaches; and**

Comment: A Summary Appraisal Report must include sufficient information to indicate that the appraiser complied with the requirements of STANDARD 7, including any permitted departures from the specific requirements. The amount of detail required will vary with the significance of the information to the appraisal.

When the DEPARTURE RULE is invoked, the assignment is deemed to be a Limited Appraisal. Use of the term "Limited Appraisal" makes clear that the assignment involved something less than or different from the work that could have and would have been completed if departure had not been invoked. The report of a Limited Appraisal must contain a prominent section that clearly identifies the extent of the appraisal process performed and the departures taken.

The reliability of the results of a Complete Appraisal or a Limited Appraisal developed under STANDARD 7 is not affected by the type of report prepared under STANDARD 8. The extent of the appraisal process performed under STANDARD 7 is the basis for the reliability of the value conclusion.

(xii) **include a signed certification in accordance with Standards Rule 8-3.**

(c) **The content of a Restricted Use Appraisal Report must be consistent with the intended use of the appraisal and, at a minimum:**

(i) **state the identity of the client, by name or type;**

Comment: An appraiser must use care when identifying the client to ensure a clear understanding and to avoid violations of the Confidentiality section of the ETHICS RULE. In those rare instances when the client wishes to remain anonymous, an appraiser must still document the identity of the client in the workfile but may omit the client's identity in the report.

(ii)   **state the intended use of the appraisal;**

Comment: The intended use of the appraisal must be consistent with the limitation on use of the Restricted Use Appraisal Report option in this Standards Rule (i.e., client use only).

(iii) **state information sufficient to identify the property involved in the appraisal;**

(iv)   **state the ownership interest appraised;**

(v)   **state the purpose of the appraisal, including the type of value, and refer to the definition of value pertinent to the purpose of the assignment;**

(vi)   **state the effective date of the appraisal and the date of the report;**

Comment: The effective date of the appraisal establishes the context for the value opinion, while the date of the report indicates whether the perspective of the appraiser on the market or property use conditions as of the effective date of the appraisal was prospective, current, or retrospective.

(vii) **state the extent of the process of collecting, confirming, and reporting data or refer to an assignment agreement retained in the appraiser's workfile, which describes the scope of work to be performed;**

Comment: When any portion of the work involves significant personal property appraisal assistance, the appraiser must state the extent of that assistance. The signing appraiser must also state the name(s) of those providing the significant personal property appraisal assistance in the certification, in accordance with SR 8-3.

(viii) **state all assumptions, hypothetical conditions, and limiting conditions that affect the analyses, opinions, and conclusions;**

Comment: Typical or ordinary assumptions and limiting conditions may be grouped together in an identified section of the report. An extraordinary assumption or hypothetical condition must be disclosed in conjunction with statements of each opinion or conclusion that was affected.

(ix) **state the appraisal procedures followed, state the value opinion(s) and conclusion(s) reached, and reference the workfile;**

Comment: An appraiser must maintain a specific, coherent workfile in support of a Restricted Use Appraisal Report. The contents of the workfile must be sufficient for the appraiser to produce a Summary Appraisal Report. The file must be available for inspection by the client (or the client's representatives, such as those engaged to complete an appraisal review), state enforcement agencies, such third parties as may be authorized by due process of law, and a duly authorized professional peer review committee except when such disclosure to a committee would violate applicable law or regulation.

When the purpose of the assignment is to develop an opinion of market value, information analyzed in compliance with Standards Rules 7-5 and 7-6 is significant information that must be disclosed in a Restricted Use Appraisal Report. If such information was unobtainable, a statement on the efforts undertaken by the appraiser to obtain the information is required. If such information is irrelevant, a statement acknowledging the existence of the information and citing its lack of relevance is required.

(x) **state, as appropriate to the class of personal property involved, the use of the property existing as of the date of value and the use of the property reflected in the appraisal; and, when the purpose of the assignment is market value, state the appraiser's opinion of the highest and best use of the property;**

Comment: If an opinion of highest and best use is required, the appraiser's reasoning in support of the opinion must be stated in the depth and detail required by its significance to the appraisal or documented in the workfile and referenced in the report. In the context of personal property, highest and best use may equate to the choice of the appropriate market or market level for the type of item and the purpose and intended use of the report.

(xi) **state and explain any permitted departures from applicable specific requirements of STANDARD 7; state the exclusion of any of the usual valuation approaches;**

and state a prominent use restriction that limits use of the report to the client and warns that the appraiser's opinions and conclusions set forth in the report cannot be understood properly without additional information in the appraiser's workfile; and

Comment: When the DEPARTURE RULE is invoked the. assignment is deemed to be a Limited Appraisal. Use of the term "Limited Appraisal" makes it clear that the assignment involved something less than or different from the work that could have and would have been completed if departure had not been invoked. The report of a Limited Appraisal must contain a prominent section that clearly identifies the extent of the appraisal process performed and the departures taken.

The Restricted Use Appraisal Report is for client use only. Before entering into an agreement, the appraiser should establish with the client the situations where this type of report is to be used and should ensure that the client understands the restricted utility of the Restricted Use Appraisal Report.

(xii) include a signed certification in accordance with Standards Rule 8-3.

Standards Rule 8-3 (This Standards Rule contains binding requirements from which departure is not permitted.)

Each written personal property appraisal report must contain a signed certification that is similar in content to the following form:

I certify that, to the best of my knowledge and belief:

— the statements of fact contained in this report are true and correct.

— the reported analyses, opinions, and conclusions are limited only by the reported assumptions and limiting conditions and are my personal, impartial, and unbiased professional analyses, opinions, and conclusions.

— I have no (or the specified) present or prospective interest in the property that is the subject of this report and no (or the specified) personal interest with respect to the parties involved.

— I have no bias with respect to the property that is the subject of this report or to the parties involved with this assignment.

— my engagement in this assignment was not contingent upon developing or reporting predetermined results.

— my compensation for completing this assignment is not contingent upon the development or reporting of a predetermined value or direction in value that favors the cause of the client, the amount of the value opinion, the attainment of a stipulated result, or the occurrence of a subsequent event directly related to the intended use of this appraisal.

— my analyses, opinions, and conclusions were developed, and this report has been prepared, in conformity with the *Uniform Standards of Professional Appraisal Practice*.

— I have (or have not) made a personal inspection of the property that is the subject of this report. (If more than one person signs this certification, the certification must clearly specify which individuals did and which individuals did not make a personal inspection of the appraised property.)

— no one provided significant personal property appraisal assistance to the person signing this certification. (If there are exceptions, the name of each individual providing significant personal property appraisal assistance must be stated.)

Comment: A signed certification is an integral part of the appraisal report. An appraiser who signs any part of the appraisal report, including a letter of transmittal, must also sign this certification.

Any appraiser(s) who signs a certification accepts full responsibility for all elements of the certification, for the assignment results, and for the contents of the appraisal report.

When a signing appraiser(s) has relied on work done by others who do not sign the certification, the signing appraiser is responsible for the decision to rely on their work. The signing appraiser(s) is required to have a reasonable basis for believing that those individuals performing the work are competent and that their work is credible.

The names of individuals providing significant personal property appraisal assistance who do not sign a certification must be stated in the certification. It is not required that the description of their assistance be contained in the certification, but disclosure of their assistance is required in accordance with SR 8-2(a), (b), or (c)(vii), as applicable.

Standards Rule 8-4 (This Standards Rule contains specific requirements from which departure is permitted. See DEPARTURE RULE.)

An oral personal property appraisal report must, at a minimum, address the substantive matters set forth in Standards Rule 8-2(b).

> Comment: Testimony of an appraiser concerning his or her analyses, opinions, and conclusions is an oral report in which the appraiser must comply with the requirements of this Standards Rule.

See the Record Keeping section of the ETHICS RULE for corresponding requirements.

Appendix 7-2

Appraisal Contract

[To Be Typed on Appraiser's Letterhead]

Dear _____:

This letter will confirm our agreement as to the preparation of the appraisal to be done on _____.

The property to be appraised is broadly described as follows:

The property is located at _____ where you will arrange for us to inspect physically the property and at which time you will supply us with any factual information within your knowledge we may request from you. In preparing the appraisal, _____ will inspect the property, prepare a detailed description of the property, evaluate it and submit a written and signed report to you. In so inspecting and evaluating the property, _____ will principally rely on standard appraisal methodology including stylistic analysis and sale prices of comparable property in the appropriate market place, it being understood that methods of scientific testing are outside his/her particular area of expertise. Scientific testing will be performed only pursuant to your specific written authorization under separate agreement.

The appraisal will be prepared <u>solely</u> for the purpose of _____, and will be used by you, <u>and only you</u>, solely for such purpose. Said appraisal shall not be disseminated to, nor relied upon nor used by, any third party unrelated to the immediate purpose of this appraisal.

The fee for said appraisal shall be _____ per hour/day. In addition, expenses for travelling and other out-of-pocket expenses shall be charged to you. The fee and expenses shall be due and payable upon delivery of the written report. An advance of ___% of the estimated fee and/or expenses is due (upon signing this letter of agreement) (upon commencement of the appraisal inspection). An additional fee will be charged for any required future services pertaining to this appraisal.

Our appraisal will represent our best judgment and opinion as to the current (fair market value/replacement value/etc.) and other factors stated in the appraisal of the appraised property. However, the appraisal will not be a statement or representation of fact nor is it a representation or warranty with respect to authenticity, genuineness or provenance. You shall indemnify, defend and hold us harmless from and against any actions, claims, liabilities or expenses incurred as a result of claims based on or arising from the appraisal, by third parties unrelated to the immediate purpose of this appraisal.

Any controversy or claim arising out of or relating to this contract, or the breach thereof, shall be settled by arbitration in accordance with the Commercial Arbitration Rules of the American Arbitration Association, and judgment upon the award rendered by the Arbitrator(s) may be entered in any Court having jurisdiction thereof.

If you are in agreement with these terms, please sign and return one copy of this letter to us at your earliest convenience.

_____   _____
Appraiser   Client

_____   _____
Date   Date

Appendix 7-3

Art Advisory Agreement

THIS AGREEMENT (the "Agreement"), made effective as of the
_____ day of _____, 200__, between _____
_____, INC., a _____ corporation, having an office
at _____, _____, _____ _____ (hereinafter
referred to as "Advisor") and _____, having an
address at _____ (hereinafter referred to as "Investor").

W I T N E S S E T H :

WHEREAS, Investor from time to time is engaged in the purchase and sale
of items of tangible personal property ("Art Property"); and

WHEREAS, Advisor is engaged in the art consultation business, and
possesses professional skills, expertise, experience and information with respect
to Art Property and investments therein; and

WHEREAS, Investor wishes to retain Advisor to advise it with respect to
the purchase and sale of Art Property; and

WHEREAS, Advisor desires to render such services.

★ Reprinted with permission of the Appraisal Foundation.

NOW THEREFORE, in consideration of the mutual promises contained herein, the parties hereto agree as follows:

1. **Advisory Services.** Advisor agrees to make recommendations to Investor for the purchase and sale of Art Property. Advisor agrees to make itself available from time to time to advise Investor on the appropriateness of the purchase of Art Property.

2. **Authority for Purchase or Sale.** Advisor agrees not to make any purchase or sale of Art Property on behalf of Investor without the prior written authorization of Investor. Any written authorization provided by Investor to Advisor to purchase any Art Property on behalf of Investor shall only be valid for the Art Property specified therein and shall not be authorization to purchase any other or like Art Property or on any other terms. Such authorization shall also only be valid for the duration specified therein.

3. **Warranties.** Advisor warrants that it maintains and has access to certain expertise in the purchase, value, and authenticity of Art Property and further warrants that it will maintain this expertise throughout the term of this Agreement.

4. **Title, Payment and Possession.** Title to any Art Property purchased by Advisor for which specific written authorization has been granted will be purchased and held in the name of Investor. On occasion, when requested and authorized in writing by Investor to do so and only on such occasions, Advisor may acquire title to Art Property in its name as nominee for Investor. In either case, Investor shall be solely responsible for payment of the purchase price for any Art Property purchased, and Investor agrees to make payment of the agreed purchase price either directly to seller thereof or to Advisor as the parties hereto shall agree upon in order to complete any purchase in a timely manner. Investor hereby indemnifies Advisor for any loss or expense (including attorneys' fees) resulting from Investor's failure to make payment for the purchase of any Art Property purchased by Investor pursuant to this Agreement. Advisor shall be responsible for making sure that the Art Property will be delivered to Investor or to such place as Investor designates and will be responsible for the proper safekeeping, storage, and insurance of said Art Property at Investor's expense until such delivery. Investor will thereafter be responsible for safekeeping, including insurance coverage, unless the parties hereto agree otherwise.

5. **Advice.** Advisor does not warrant the authenticity, description, condition or value of any Art Property purchased or sold by Investor on advice received from Advisor but Advisor shall use its best efforts to assure the authenticity of Art Property purchased for Investor, as well as the accuracy of their description, their provenance, their condition and their value. Investor

understands and agrees that there is substantial risk involved in the purchase and sale of Art Property and that Advisor is not responsible for losses in the value of any Art Property or for Investor's failure to resell such Art Property as long as Advisor acts in good faith and in a manner which is not negligent and which is in accordance with its warranted expertise.

Investor understands and agrees that other persons may participate in the services rendered by Advisor and, since Art Property is unique, it may not be possible for Advisor to allocate such Art Property equally among its customers but Advisor agrees to apprise and keep Investor fully informed of any conflicts of interest it may have with regard to these other customers and Advisor agrees that it will never seek the purchase of any Art Property on its own behalf in conflict with Investor, nor will it sell to Investor any Art Property for a price higher than that paid by Advisor unless Advisor informs Investor of any such difference. Investor is also aware that Art Property is not income producing and that Investor can profit only if the Art Property can be resold at a price higher than its cost. From time to time Investor agrees to provide Advisor with its Art Property goals and inform Advisor of any changes in its objectives.

6. **Special Services.** Investor agrees that if it requests Advisor (and such request must be in writing) to arrange for services that will necessitate retaining an expert or other specialist (such as a conservator), Advisor will select such person(s) or firm which it believes to be well qualified to perform such services and Investor agrees to pay the reasonable fee of the expert or specialist for such services. However, Investor understands that Advisor does not warrant or guarantee the work product or results of such expert or specialist and that Advisor is not responsible for any loss or damage to the Art Property which may occur while these services are being performed or which results from such services.

7. **Fees.** Investor agrees to pay Advisor the sum of $_____ per year, such amount to be paid in arrears in equal monthly installments. If this Agreement is terminated during a year then the fee for such year will be $_____ times the number of months during such year for which the Agreement was in effect.

In addition, Investor agrees to pay Advisor an amount equal to between three percent (3%) and ten percent (10%) of the purchase price of any Art Property purchased or sold by Investor on the prior specific written advice of Advisor. Such percentage amount shall be paid to Advisor at the time Investor pays for the Art Property. Notwithstanding the foregoing, the percentage amount for each transaction as well as payment thereof will be conditioned upon the execution of a written agreement between the parties and will depend upon the extent of Advisor's involvement in the transaction.

In addition, Investor will pay Advisor's reasonable travel expenses based on business class travel provided that those expenses are directly related to Investor's Art Property purchases or sales and that Investor has approved such travel in advance. Investor will only pay its correlating portion of travel expenses if Advisor's travel expenses were also incurred on behalf of any of Advisor's other customers.

8. **Termination.** Either Investor or Advisor may terminate this Agreement by 30 day written notice but this Agreement shall expire at the conclusion of one calendar year from its effective date unless both parties manifest their intentions to renew this Agreement, in which case the Agreement shall continue in effect for one additional year and may continue to renew for subsequent years by a similar means. Upon termination any fees due Advisor from Investor shall immediately become due and payable and Advisor shall immediately return all sums due, or held on behalf of, Investor. If any auction bids or other pending transactions are outstanding for the account of Investor at the time of termination and these bids or other transactions cannot be reasonably withdrawn, then the termination shall be deferred until any successful bids have been executed and such transactions completed but Investor shall not be required to pay Advisor any additional fees beyond Advisor's earned commission, if any, pursuant to this Agreement, during this deferral period.

9. **Governing Law and Arbitration.** This Agreement shall be construed under and governed by the laws of the State of _____. Should any dispute arise as to the performance of any party under this Agreement or as to the interpretation of any of its terms, each party agrees that if such dispute can not be informally resolved, in lieu of submitting the matter to formal judicial resolution, the parties shall submit the dispute to be resolved by arbitration before a panel of three arbitrators to be mutually agreed upon by both parties. Such arbitration is to take place in New York pursuant to the rules of arbitration of the American Arbitration Association. Each party agrees that the result of any arbitration taking place pursuant to this provision shall be final and binding on each other party. Judgments upon any award and/or decision of such arbitration may be entered in any court having jurisdiction thereof.

10. **Assignment.** Neither this Agreement nor any right or obligation hereunder shall be assigned, delegated or otherwise transferred in whole or in part, by either party (whether by operation of law or otherwise) without the prior written consent of the other. Any assignment or transfer contrary to the terms hereof shall be null and void and of no force or effect.

11. **Relation of the Parties**. Neither party is the agent, representative, partner, joint venturer or employee of the other party. Each party is an independent contractor.

12. **Notices**. All notices and other communications permitted or required by the provisions of this Agreement shall be in writing and shall be personally delivered or sent by registered or certified mail, return receipt requested, bearing adequate first class airmail postage and addressed as hereinafter provided. Notices delivered in person shall be effective upon the date of delivery. Notices by mail shall be effective upon the receipt thereof by the addressee. Rejection or the refusal to accept notice, or the inability to deliver because of a change in the address of which no notice was given as provided herein shall be deemed to be receipt of the notice. By giving to the other party hereto at least thirty (30) days notice thereof, any party hereto shall have the right from time to time and at any time while this Agreement is in effect to change the respective address thereof and each shall have the right to specify as the address thereof any other address. Each notice to Investor and Advisor shall be addressed until notice of change as aforesaid is made, as follows:

(a)   If intended for Advisor to:

_____

_____

_____

with a copy to:

_____, Esq.

_____

_____

_____

(b)   If intended for Investor to:

_____

_____

_____

with a copy to:

_____, Esq.

_____

_____

_____

13. **Binding Effect**. Subject to Section 9 hereof, this Agreement and the rights of the parties hereto shall inure to the benefit of and be binding upon the parties hereto and their respective successors and assigns.

14. **Headings**. The headings contained in this Agreement are for reference purposes only and shall not in any way affect the meaning or interpretation hereof. Each party agrees that it has sought the advice of competent counsel prior to executing this Agreement, and that both parties actively participated in the preparation and selection of terms herein and that no portion of this Agreement shall be interpreted more or less favorably to the party more actively preparing it.

15. **Pronouns**. All personal pronouns in this Agreement, whether used in the masculine, feminine or neuter gender shall include all other genders and the singular shall include the plural and the plural shall include the singular.

16. **Counterparts**. This Agreement may be executed in multiple counterparts and is effective when each of the parties has executed a copy hereof. Each of the counterparts shall be deemed an original, all counterparts taken together shall comprise one and the same instrument.

17. **Waiver**. No waiver by either party of any right hereunder or of any default hereunder by the other shall be binding upon either party unless granted in a signed writing. No failure by either party to exercise any right hereunder shall operate as a waiver of any other or further exercise of such right. No waiver by either party of any default hereunder shall operate as a waiver of any other or further default. Any indulgence or departure from or disregard of the provisions of this Agreement, at any time, by either party shall not be deemed to modify the same or relate to the future or waive future compliance therewith by the other.

18. **Severability**. In the event that any one or more of the provisions, or parts of any provisions, contained in this Agreement shall for any reason be held to be invalid, illegal, or unenforceable in any respect by a court of competent jurisdiction or by arbitration as specified herein, except in those instances where removal or elimination of such invalid, illegal or unenforceable provision or provisions would result in a failure of consideration under this Agreement, such invalidity, illegality or unenforceability shall not affect any other provision hereof, and this Agreement shall be construed as if such invalid, illegal or unenforceable provision had never been contained herein.

19. **Entire Agreement**. Except as specifically provided in or contemplated by this Agreement to the contrary, this Agreement constitutes the entire agreement between the parties hereto and no modification hereof

shall be effective unless made by a supplemental agreement in writing, executed by both of the parties hereto, and this Agreement completely supersedes any previous agreement by and between the parties hereto with respect to the matters dealt with herein.

IN WITNESS WHEREOF, the parties have signed this Agreement as of the date first above written.

ADVISOR

By:_____
President

INVESTOR

_____